3

WITHDRAWN

AFTER
HOURS

STORY AND ART BY
YUHTA NISHIO

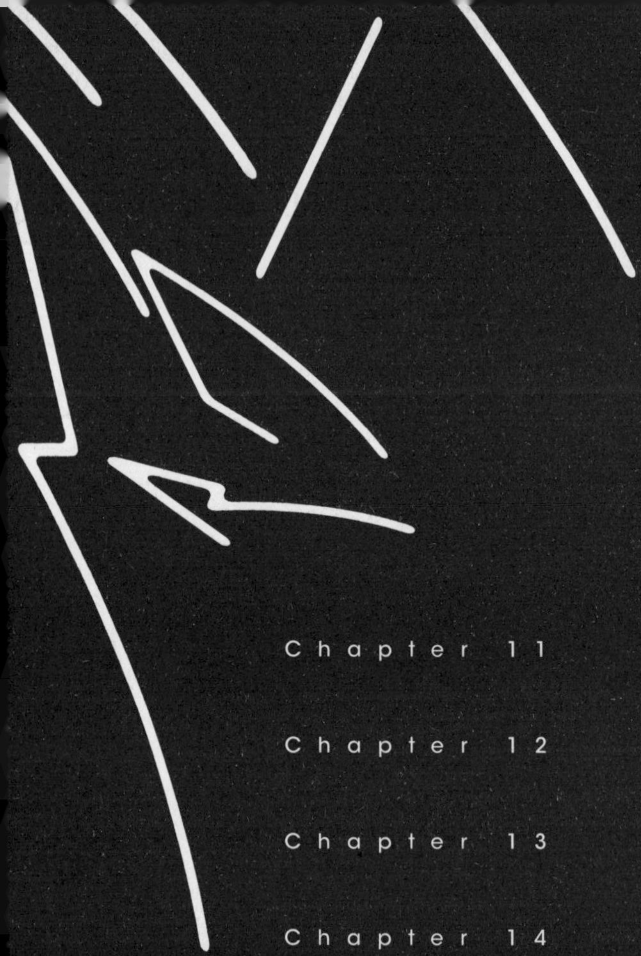

#11

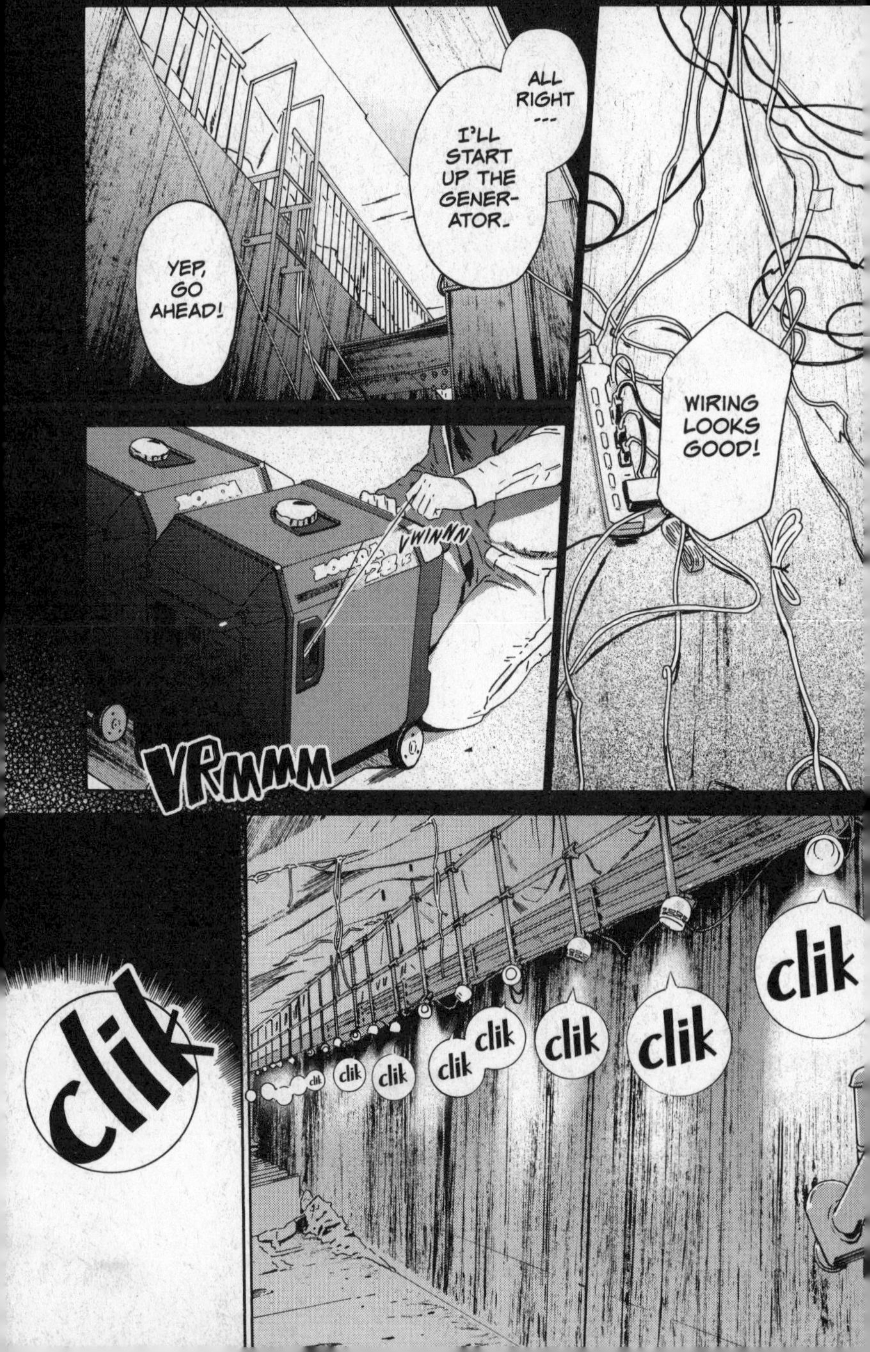
WIRING LOOKS GOOD!
ALL RIGHT ---
I'LL START UP THE GENER-ATOR.
YEP, GO AHEAD!
VWINNN
VRMMM
clik
clik
clik
clik
clik
clik
clik
clik
clik
clik

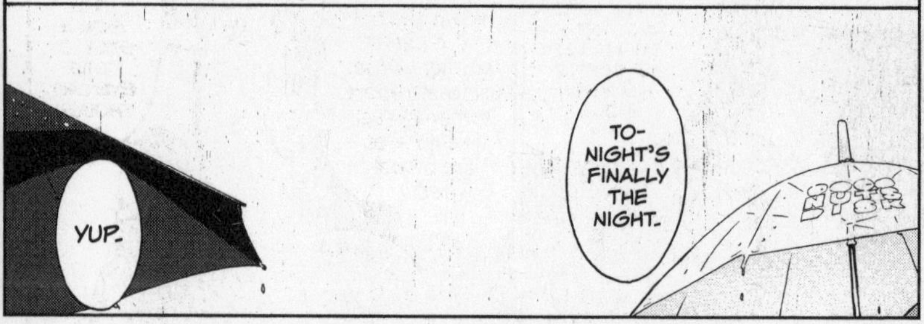
TO-NIGHT'S FINALLY THE NIGHT.
YUP.

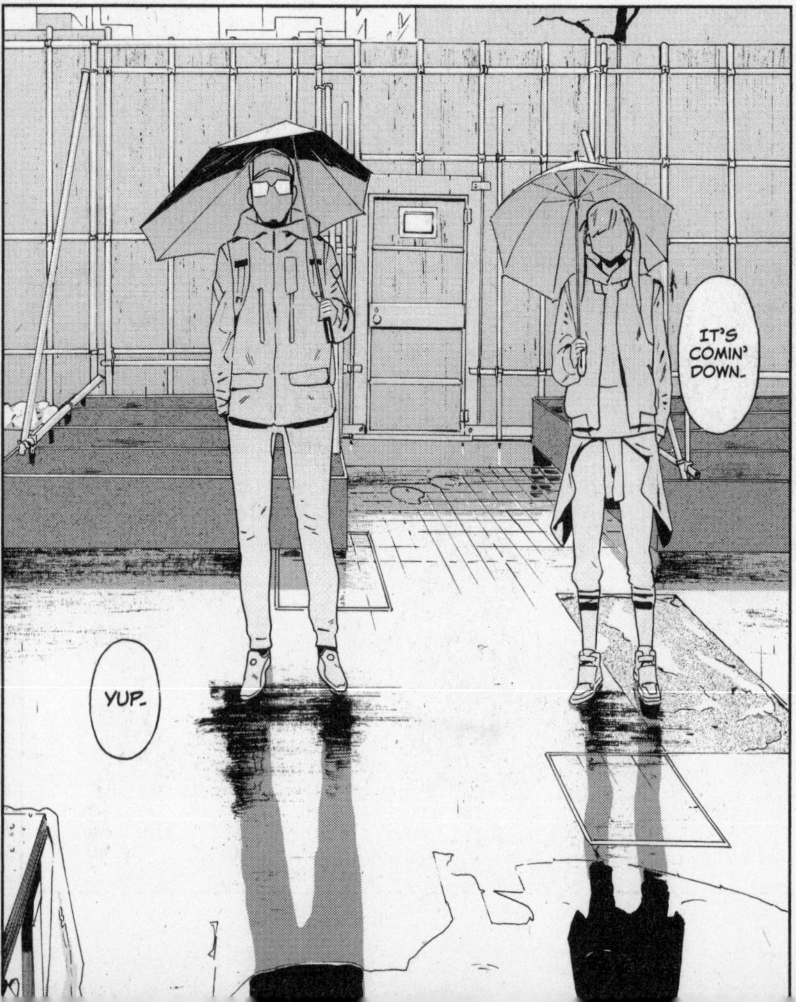
IT'S COMIN' DOWN.
YUP.

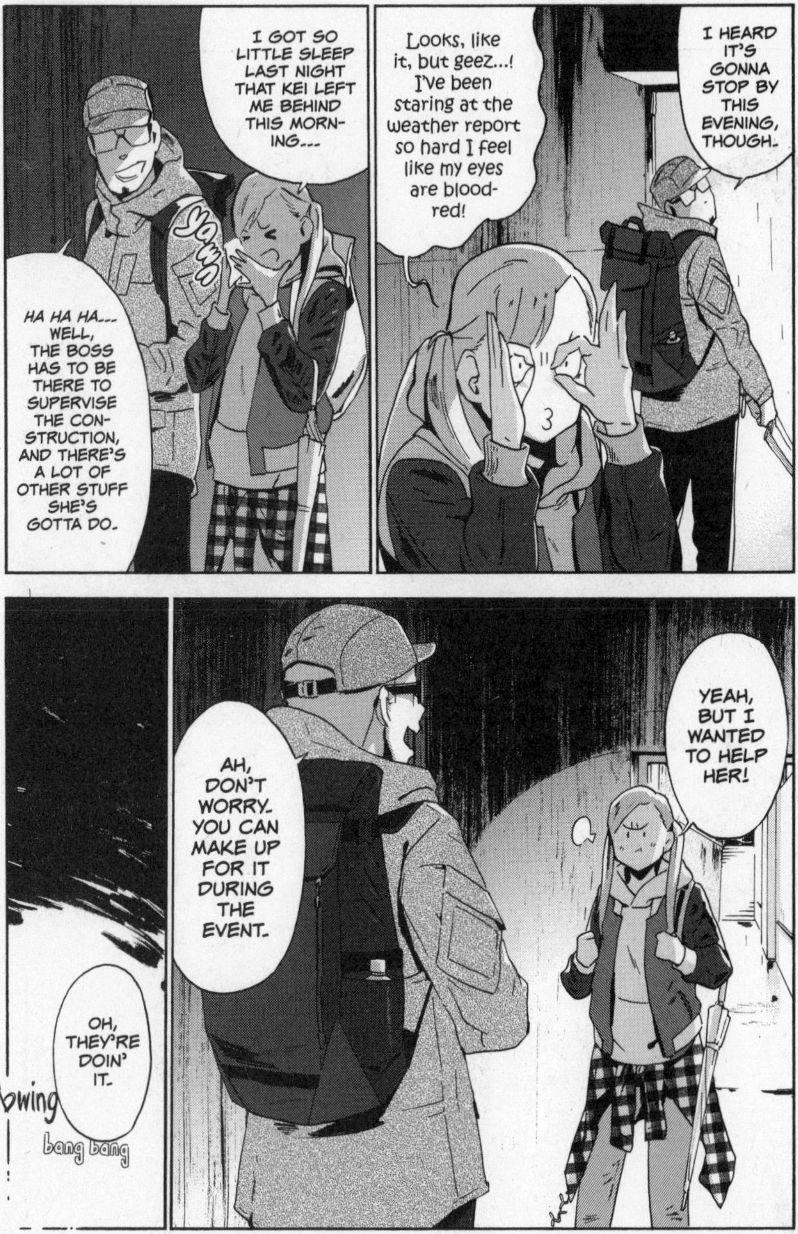
I HEARD IT'S GONNA STOP BY THIS EVENING, THOUGH.
Looks, like it, but geez...! I've been staring at the weather report so hard I feel like my eyes are blood-red!
I GOT SO LITTLE SLEEP LAST NIGHT THAT KEI LEFT ME BEHIND THIS MORNING...
HA HA HA... WELL, THE BOSS HAS TO BE THERE TO SUPERVISE THE CONSTRUCTION, AND THERE'S A LOT OF OTHER STUFF SHE'S GOTTA DO.
YEAH, BUT I WANTED TO HELP HER!
AH, DON'T WORRY. YOU CAN MAKE UP FOR IT DURING THE EVENT.
OH, THEY'RE DOIN' IT.
bwing
bang bang

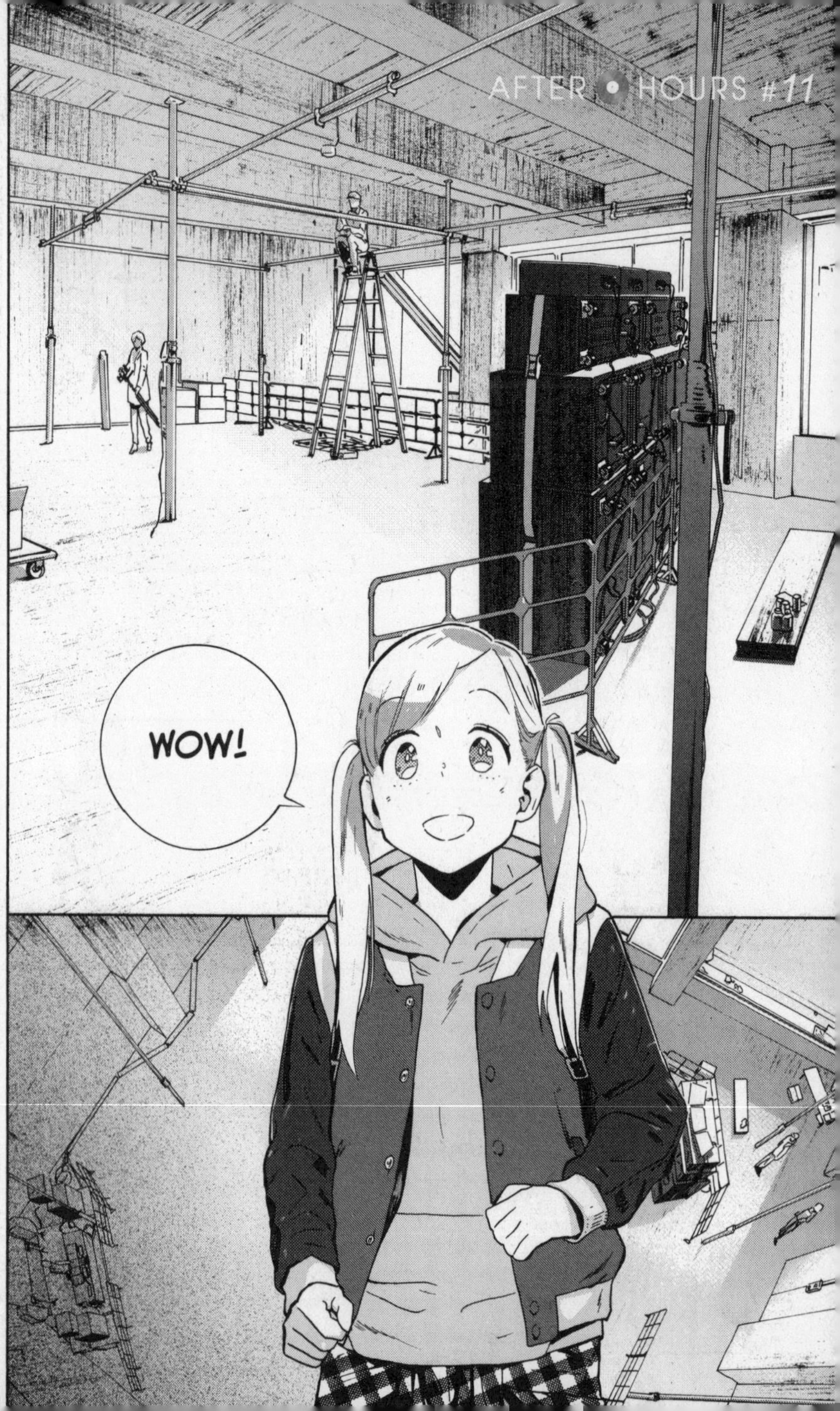
AFTER HOURS #11
WOW!

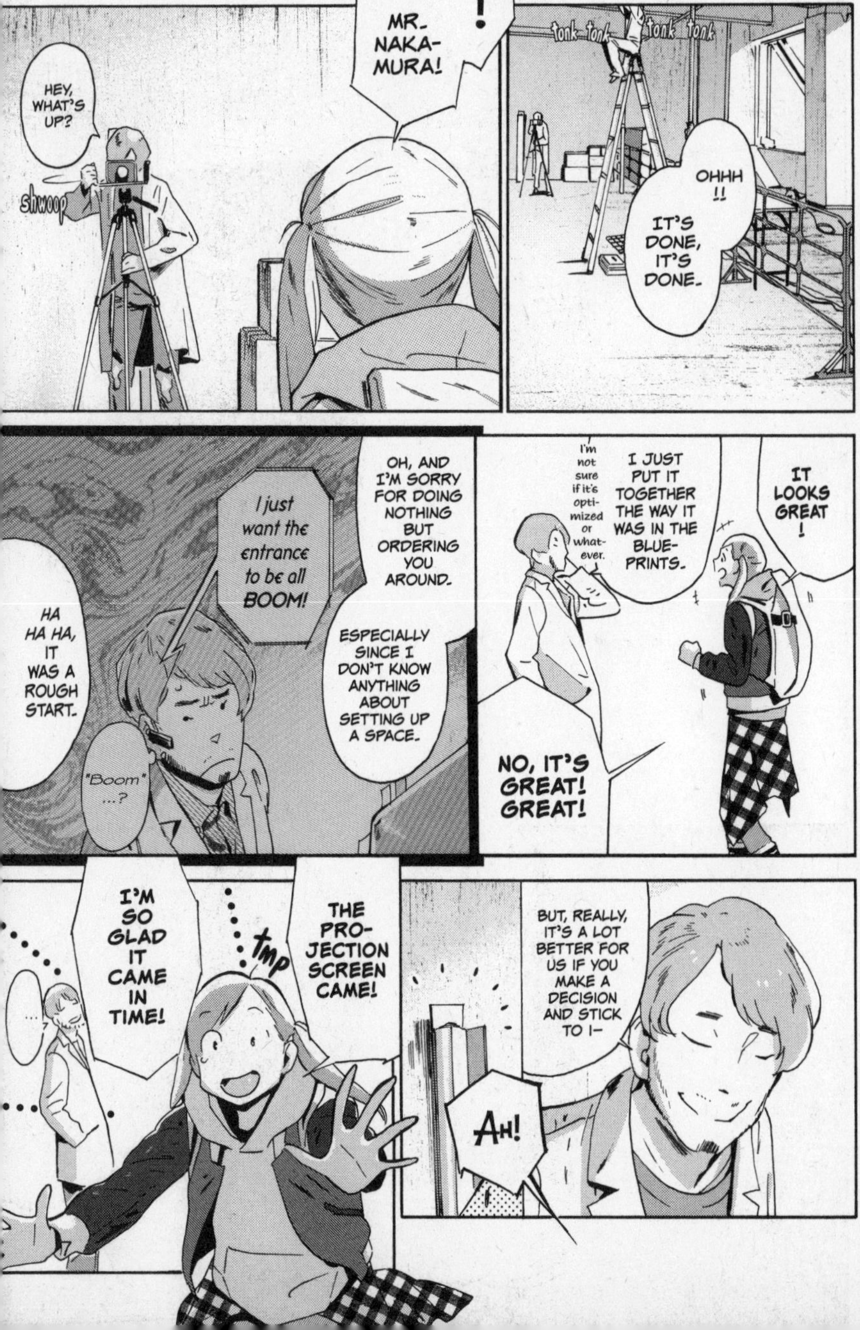
tonk tonk tonk tonk
OHHH!!
IT'S DONE, IT'S DONE.
!
MR. NAKAMURA!
HEY, WHAT'S UP?
shwoop
IT LOOKS GREAT!
I JUST PUT IT TOGETHER THE WAY IT WAS IN THE BLUEPRINTS.
I'm not sure if it's optimized or whatever.
NO, IT'S GREAT! GREAT!
OH, AND I'M SORRY FOR DOING NOTHING BUT ORDERING YOU AROUND.
ESPECIALLY SINCE I DON'T KNOW ANYTHING ABOUT SETTING UP A SPACE.
I just want the entrance to be all BOOM!
HA HA HA, IT WAS A ROUGH START.
"Boom" ...?
BUT, REALLY, IT'S A LOT BETTER FOR US IF YOU MAKE A DECISION AND STICK TO I—
AH!
THE PROJECTION SCREEN CAME!
tmp
I'M SO GLAD IT CAME IN TIME!
...

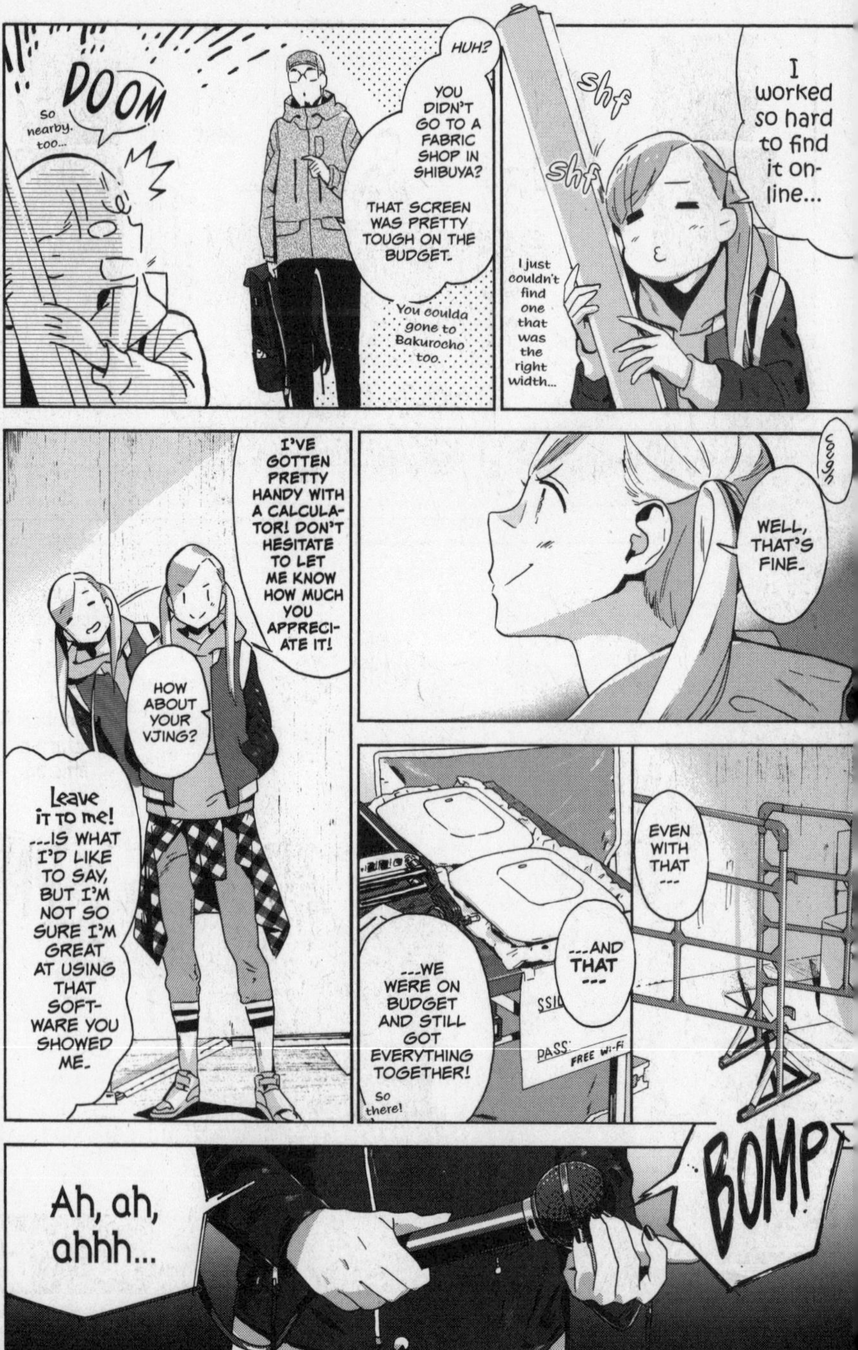
I worked so hard to find it on-line...
shf
shf
I just couldn't find one that was the right width...
HUH?
YOU DIDN'T GO TO A FABRIC SHOP IN SHIBUYA?
THAT SCREEN WAS PRETTY TOUGH ON THE BUDGET.
You coulda gone to Bakurocho too.
DOOM
So nearby, too...
cough
WELL, THAT'S FINE.
EVEN WITH THAT---
---AND THAT---
---WE WERE ON BUDGET AND STILL GOT EVERYTHING TOGETHER!
So there!
PASS:
FREE Wi-Fi
I'VE GOTTEN PRETTY HANDY WITH A CALCULA-TOR! DON'T HESITATE TO LET ME KNOW HOW MUCH YOU APPRECI-ATE IT!
HOW ABOUT YOUR VJING?
Leave it to me! ...IS WHAT I'D LIKE TO SAY, BUT I'M NOT SO SURE I'M GREAT AT USING THAT SOFT-WARE YOU SHOWED ME.
BOMP
Ah, ah, ahhh...

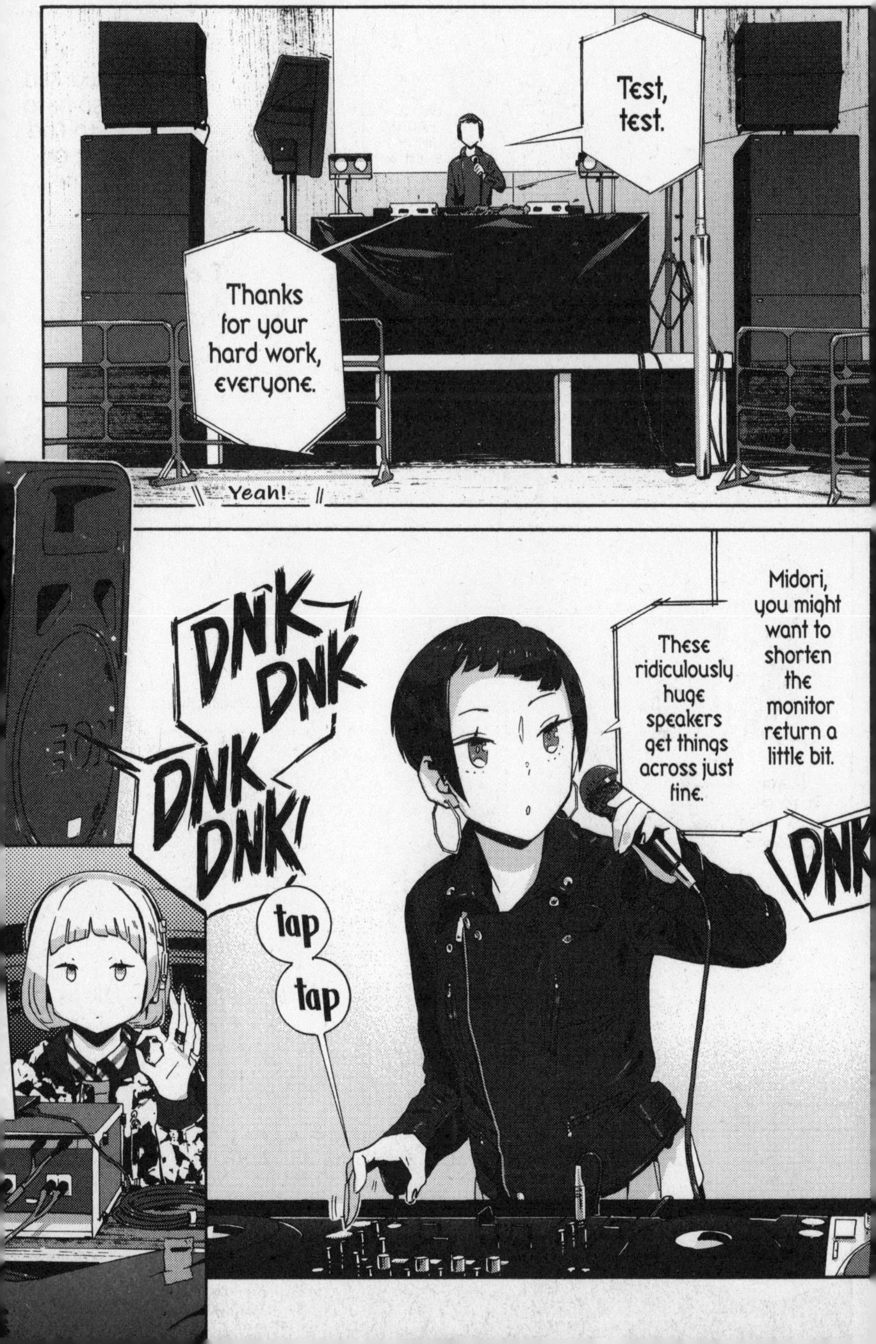
Test, test.
Thanks for your hard work, everyone.
Yeah!
Midori, you might want to shorten the monitor return a little bit.
These ridiculously huge speakers get things across just fine.
DNK
DNK DNK DNK DNK
tap tap

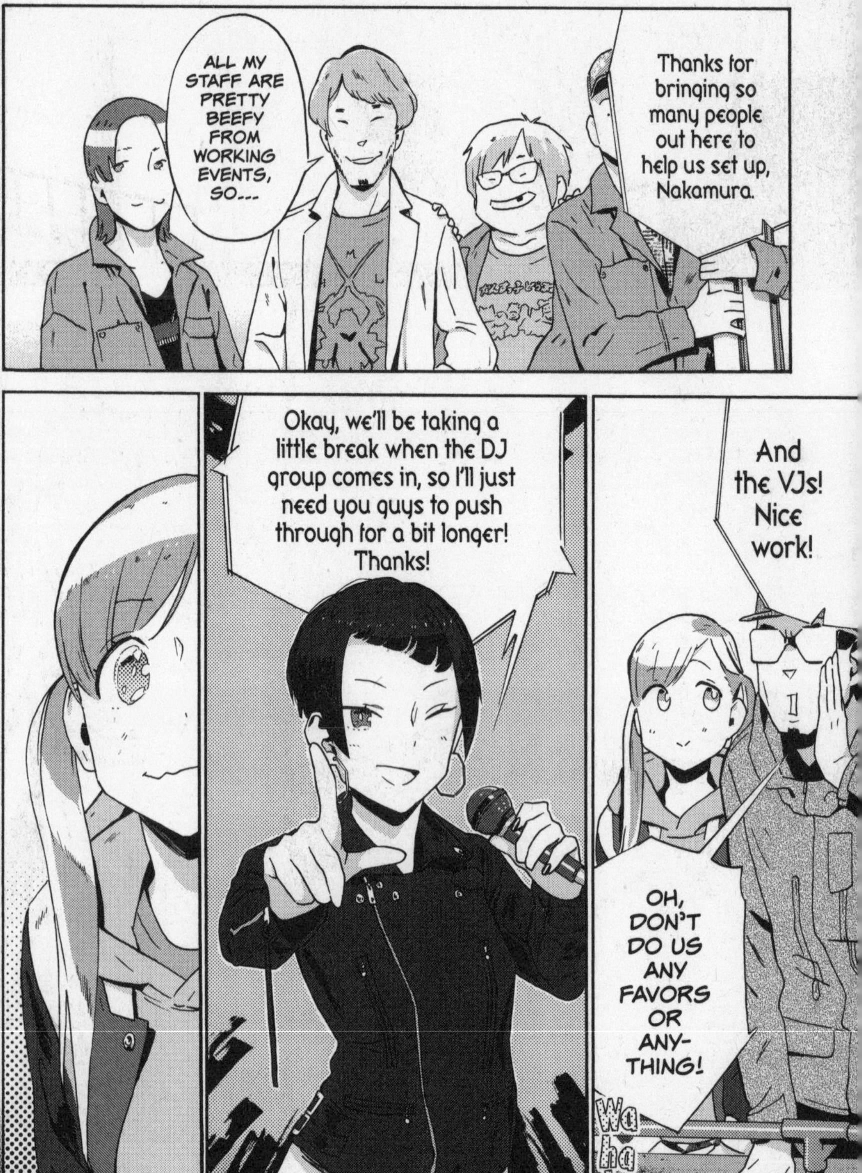
Thanks for bringing so many people out here to help us set up, Nakamura.
ALL MY STAFF ARE PRETTY BEEFY FROM WORKING EVENTS, SO...
And the VJs! Nice work!
OH, DON'T DO US ANY FAVORS OR ANY-THING!
Wahahaha
Okay, we'll be taking a little break when the DJ group comes in, so I'll just need you guys to push through for a bit longer! Thanks!

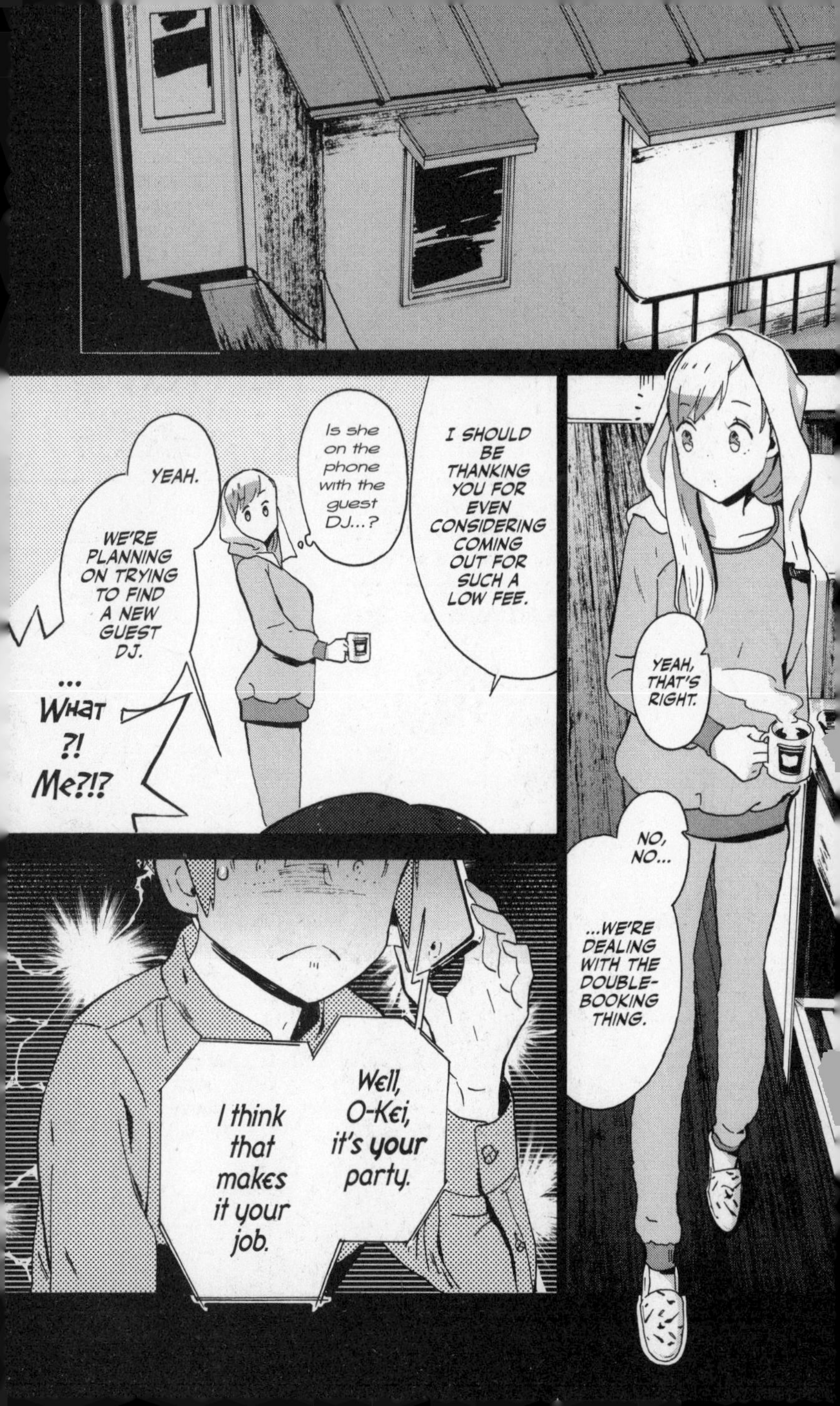
YEAH, THAT'S RIGHT.
NO, NO...
...WE'RE DEALING WITH THE DOUBLE-BOOKING THING.
I SHOULD BE THANKING YOU FOR EVEN CONSIDERING COMING OUT FOR SUCH A LOW FEE.
Is she on the phone with the guest DJ...?
YEAH.
WE'RE PLANNING ON TRYING TO FIND A NEW GUEST DJ.
...WHAT?! Me?!?
Well, O-Kei, it's your party.
I think that makes it your job.

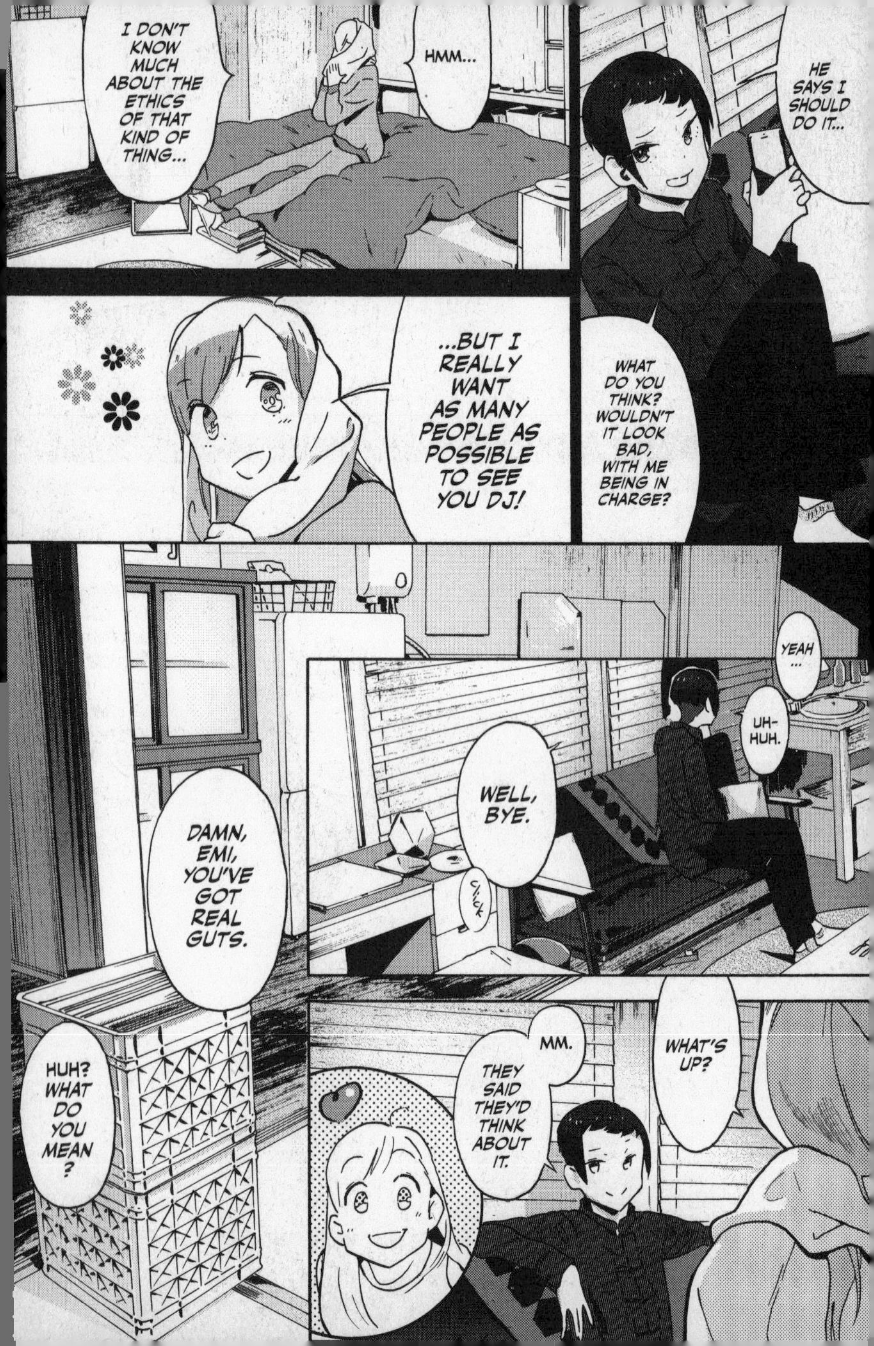
HE SAYS I SHOULD DO IT...
WHAT DO YOU THINK? WOULDN'T IT LOOK BAD, WITH ME BEING IN CHARGE?
HMM...
I DON'T KNOW MUCH ABOUT THE ETHICS OF THAT KIND OF THING...
...BUT I REALLY WANT AS MANY PEOPLE AS POSSIBLE TO SEE YOU DJ!
YEAH...
UH-HUH.
WELL, BYE.
Click
WHAT'S UP?
MM.
THEY SAID THEY'D THINK ABOUT IT.
DAMN, EMI, YOU'VE GOT REAL GUTS.
HUH? WHAT DO YOU MEAN?

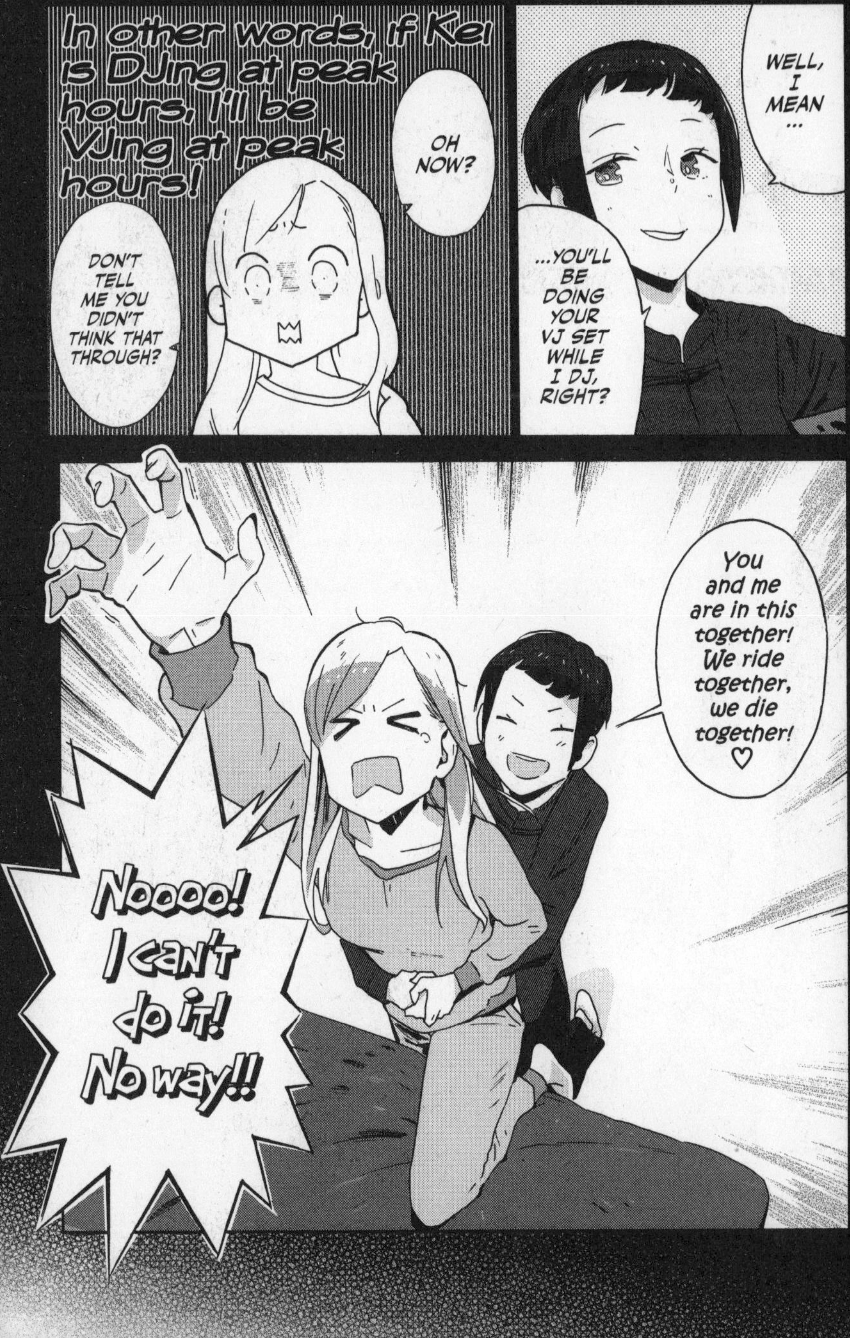
WELL, I MEAN ...
...YOU'LL BE DOING YOUR VJ SET WHILE I DJ, RIGHT?
In other words, if Kei is DJing at peak hours, I'll be VJing at peak hours!
OH NOW?
DON'T TELL ME YOU DIDN'T THINK THAT THROUGH?
You and me are in this together! We ride together, we die together! ♡
Noooo! I can't do it! No way!!

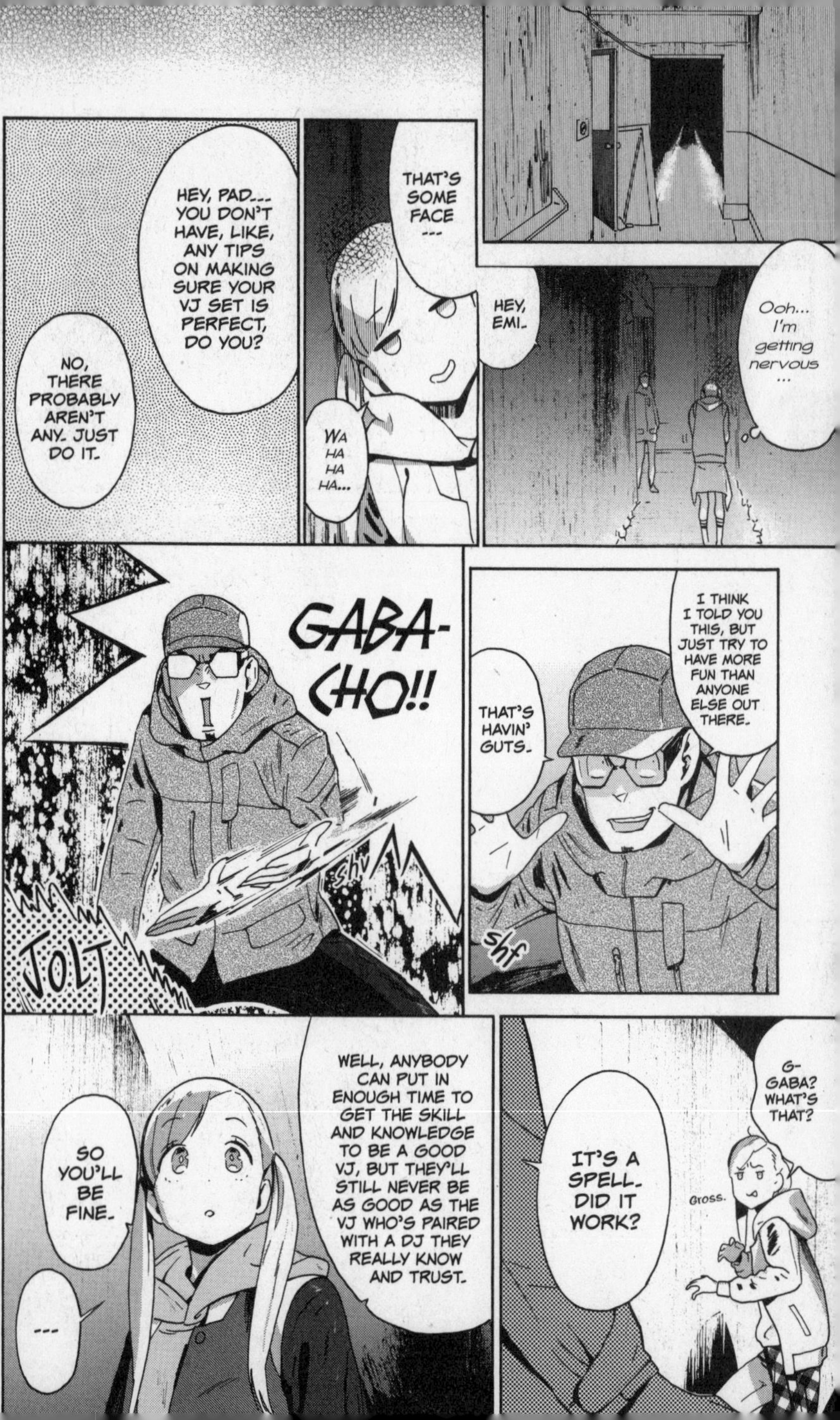
Ooh... I'm getting nervous...
HEY, EMI.
THAT'S SOME FACE...
WA HA HA HA...
HEY, DAD... YOU DON'T HAVE, LIKE, ANY TIPS ON MAKING SURE YOUR VJ SET IS PERFECT, DO YOU?
NO, THERE PROBABLY AREN'T ANY. JUST DO IT.
I THINK I TOLD YOU THIS, BUT JUST TRY TO HAVE MORE FUN THAN ANYONE ELSE OUT THERE.
THAT'S HAVIN' GUTS.
shf
GABA-CHO!!
shv
JOLT
G-GABA? WHAT'S THAT?
IT'S A SPELL. DID IT WORK?
Gross.
WELL, ANYBODY CAN PUT IN ENOUGH TIME TO GET THE SKILL AND KNOWLEDGE TO BE A GOOD VJ, BUT THEY'LL STILL NEVER BE AS GOOD AS THE VJ WHO'S PAIRED WITH A DJ THEY REALLY KNOW AND TRUST.
SO YOU'LL BE FINE.
...

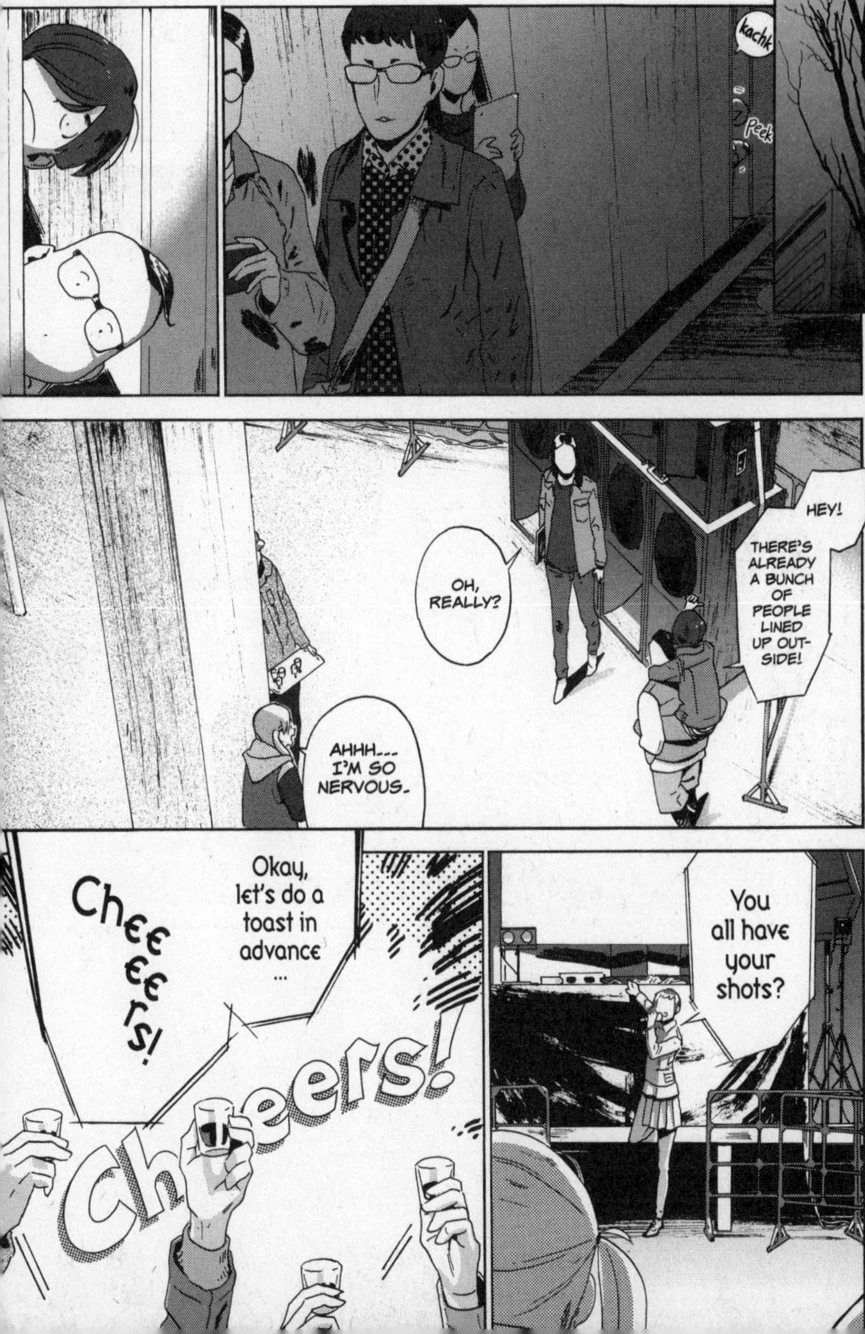
kachk
Peek
HEY!
THERE'S ALREADY A BUNCH OF PEOPLE LINED UP OUT-SIDE!
OH, REALLY?
AHHH... I'M SO NERVOUS.
You all have your shots?
Okay, let's do a toast in advance ...
Cheeeeeers!
Cheers!

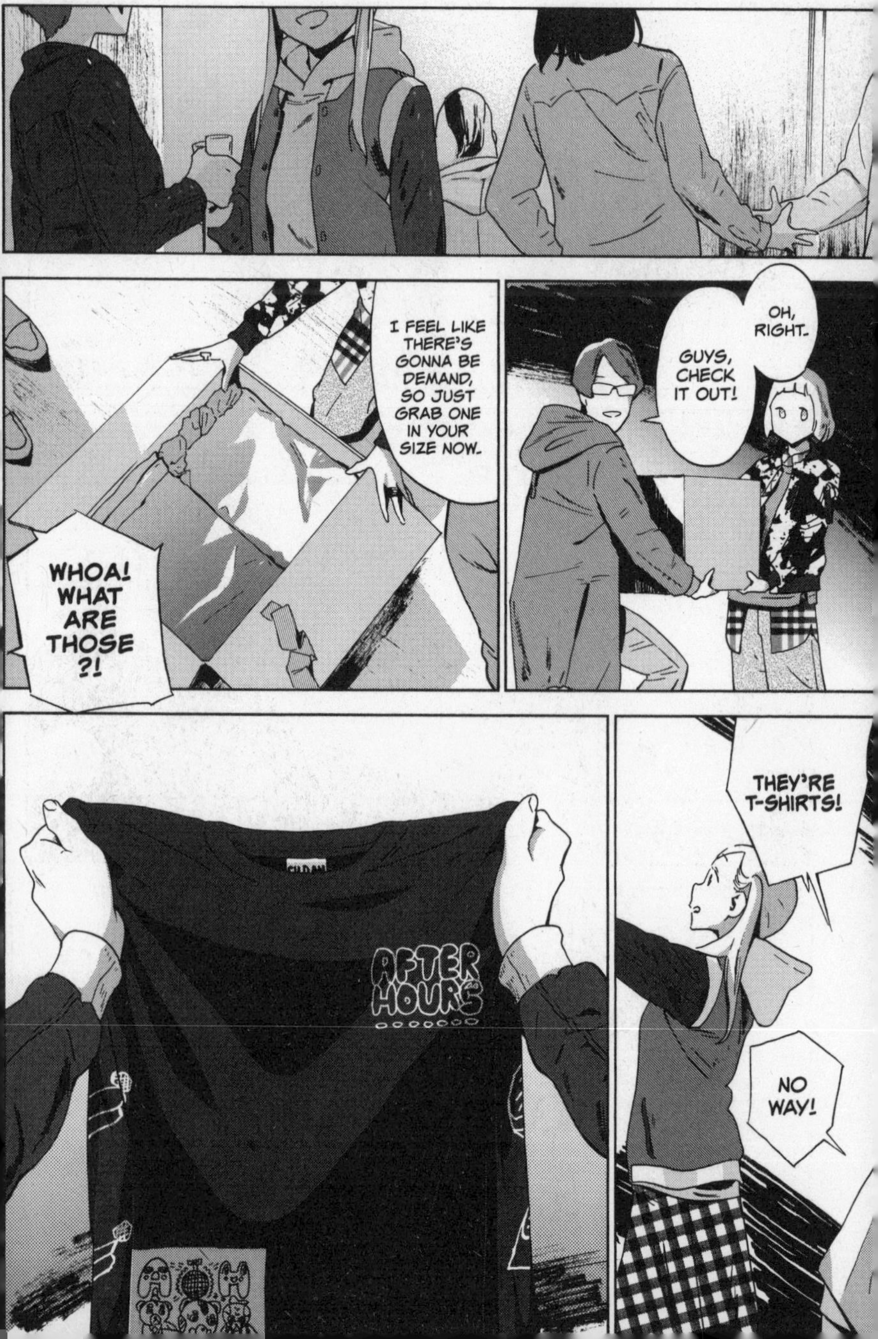
OH, RIGHT.
GUYS, CHECK IT OUT!
I FEEL LIKE THERE'S GONNA BE DEMAND, SO JUST GRAB ONE IN YOUR SIZE NOW.
WHOA! WHAT ARE THOSE ?!
THEY'RE T-SHIRTS!
NO WAY!
AFTER HOURS

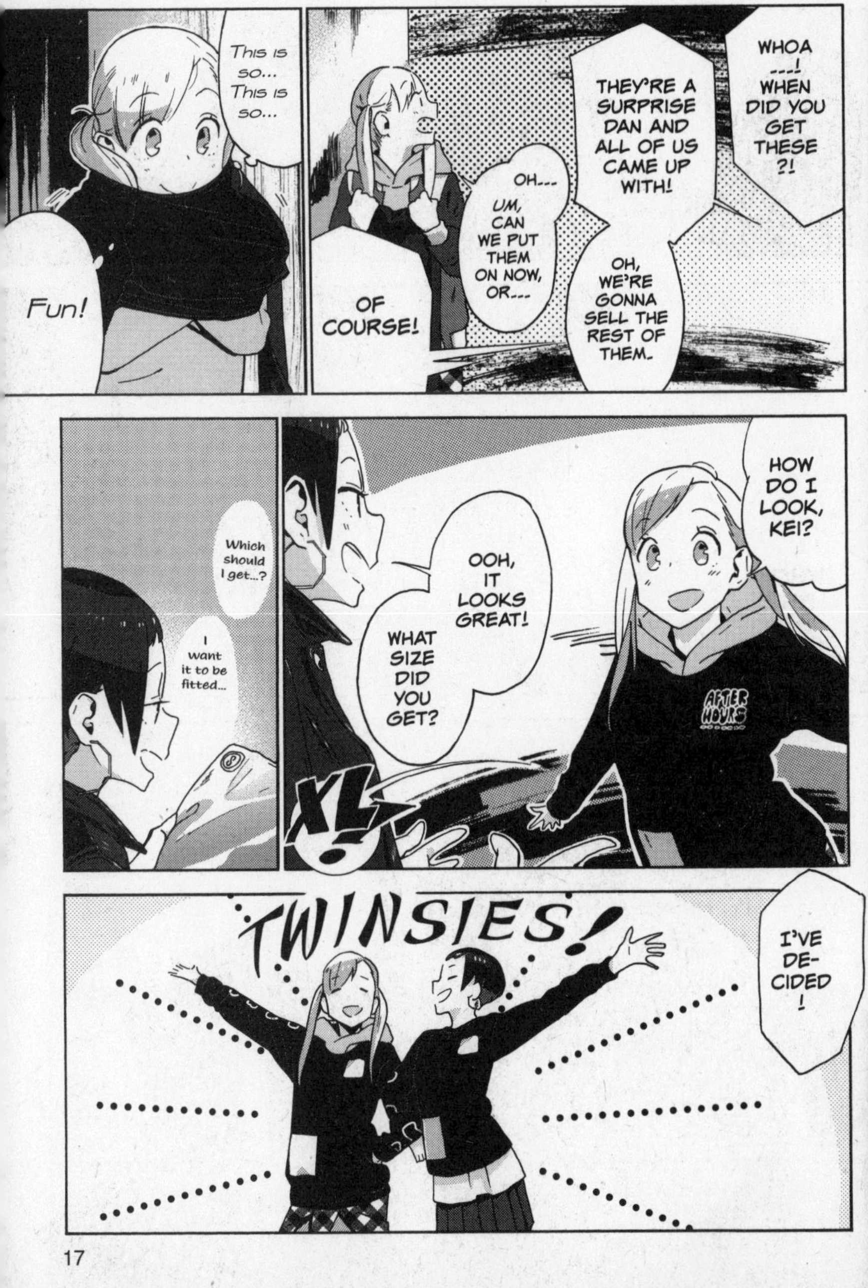
WHOA...! WHEN DID YOU GET THESE?!
THEY'RE A SURPRISE DAN AND ALL OF US CAME UP WITH!
OH... UM, CAN WE PUT THEM ON NOW, OR...
OH, WE'RE GONNA SELL THE REST OF THEM.
OF COURSE!
This is so... This is so...
Fun!
HOW DO I LOOK, KEI?
OOH, IT LOOKS GREAT!
WHAT SIZE DID YOU GET?
AFTER HOURS
XL!
Which should I get...?
I want it to be fitted...
I'VE DE-CIDED!
TWINSIES!

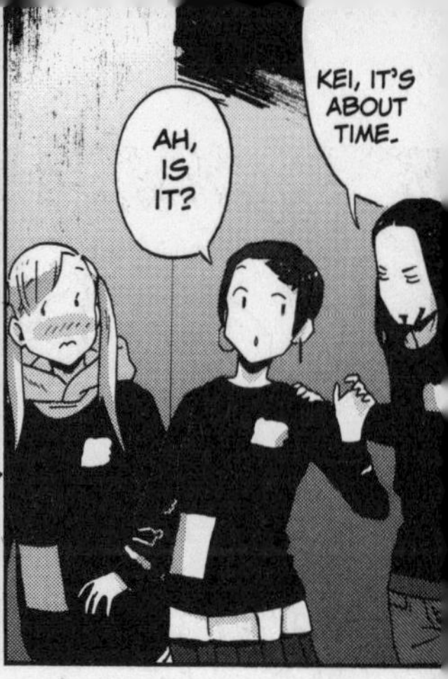
KEI, IT'S ABOUT TIME.
AH, IS IT?

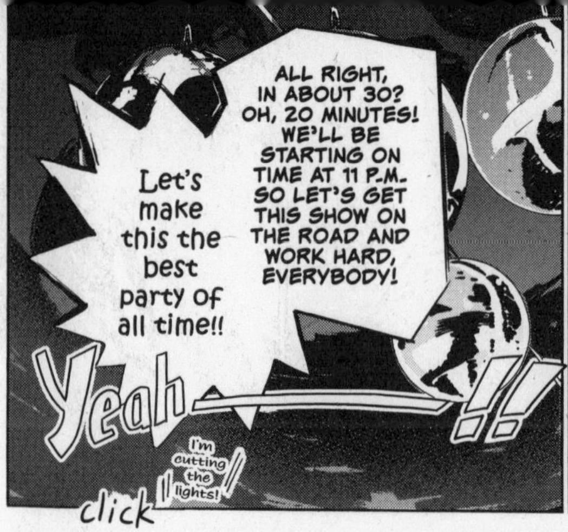
ALL RIGHT, IN ABOUT 30? OH, 20 MINUTES! WE'LL BE STARTING ON TIME AT 11 P.M. SO LET'S GET THIS SHOW ON THE ROAD AND WORK HARD, EVERYBODY!
Let's make this the best party of all time!!
Yeah!!
I'm cutting the lights!
click

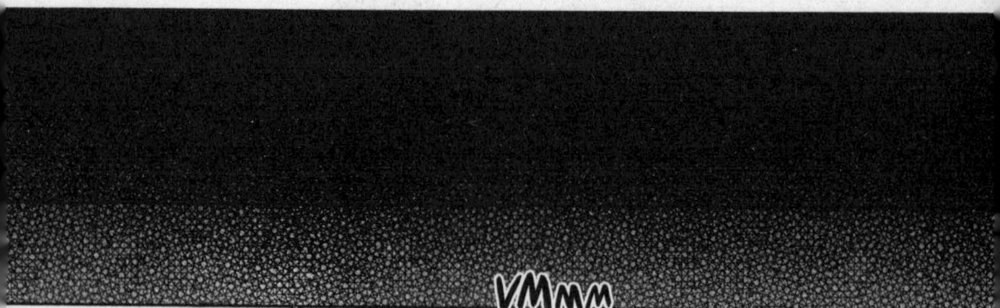

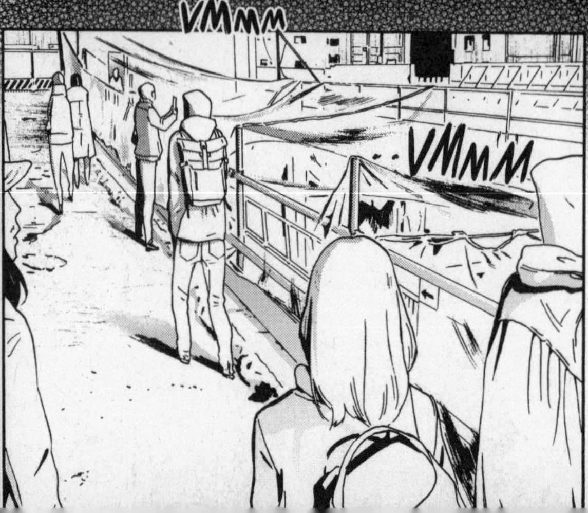
VMMM
VMMM

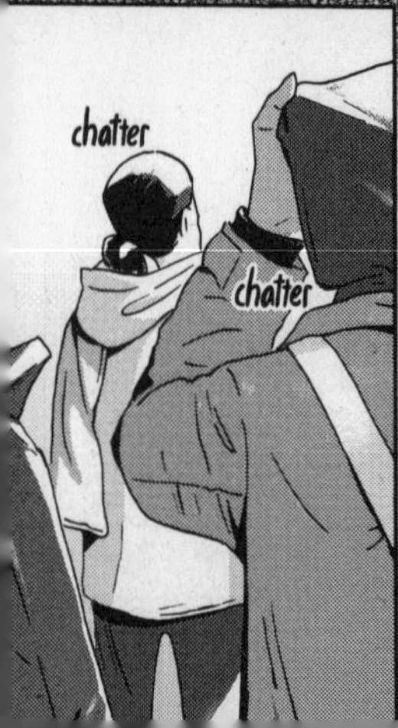
chatter
chatter

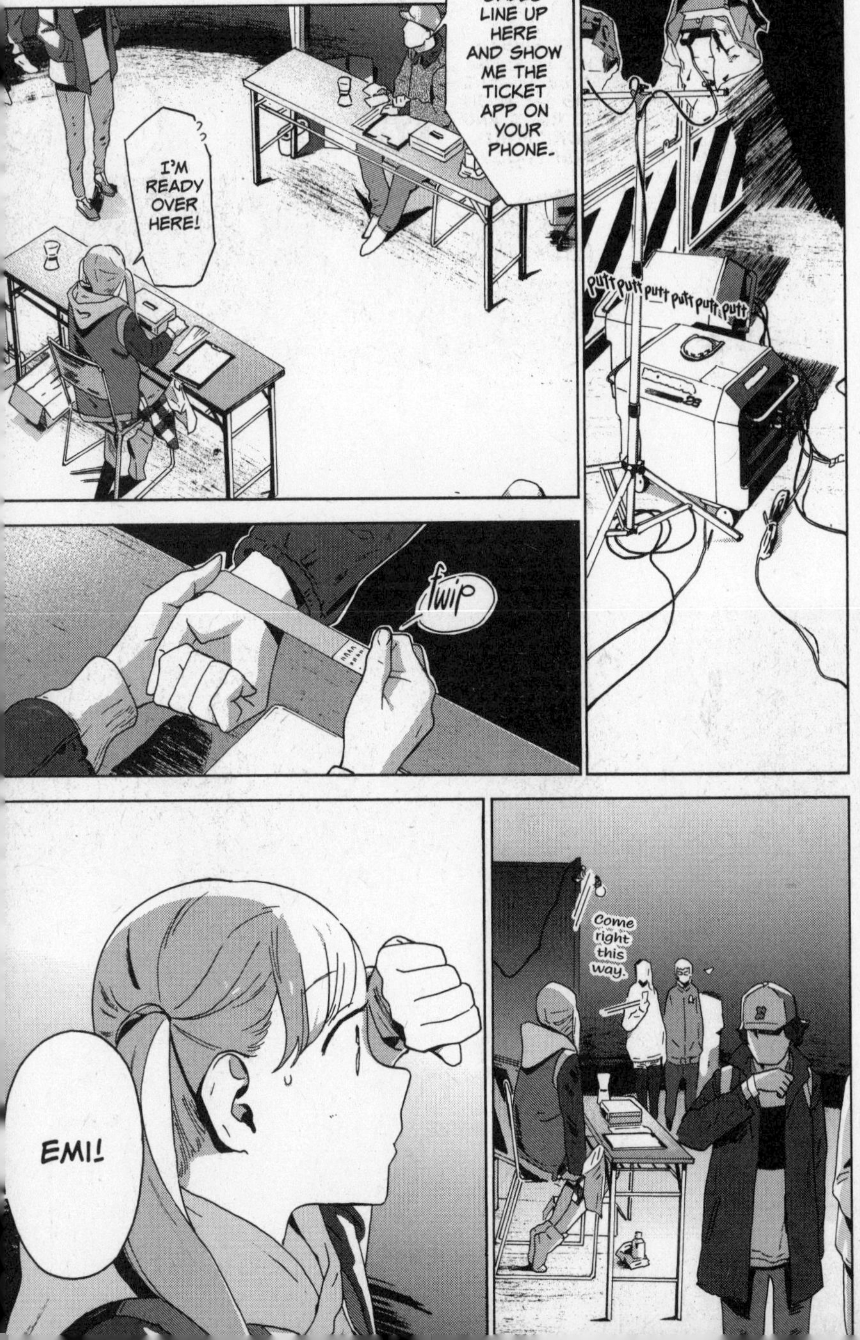
putt putt putt putt putt putt
PRE-SALES LINE UP HERE AND SHOW ME THE TICKET APP ON YOUR PHONE.
I'M READY OVER HERE!
fwip
Come right this way.
EMI!

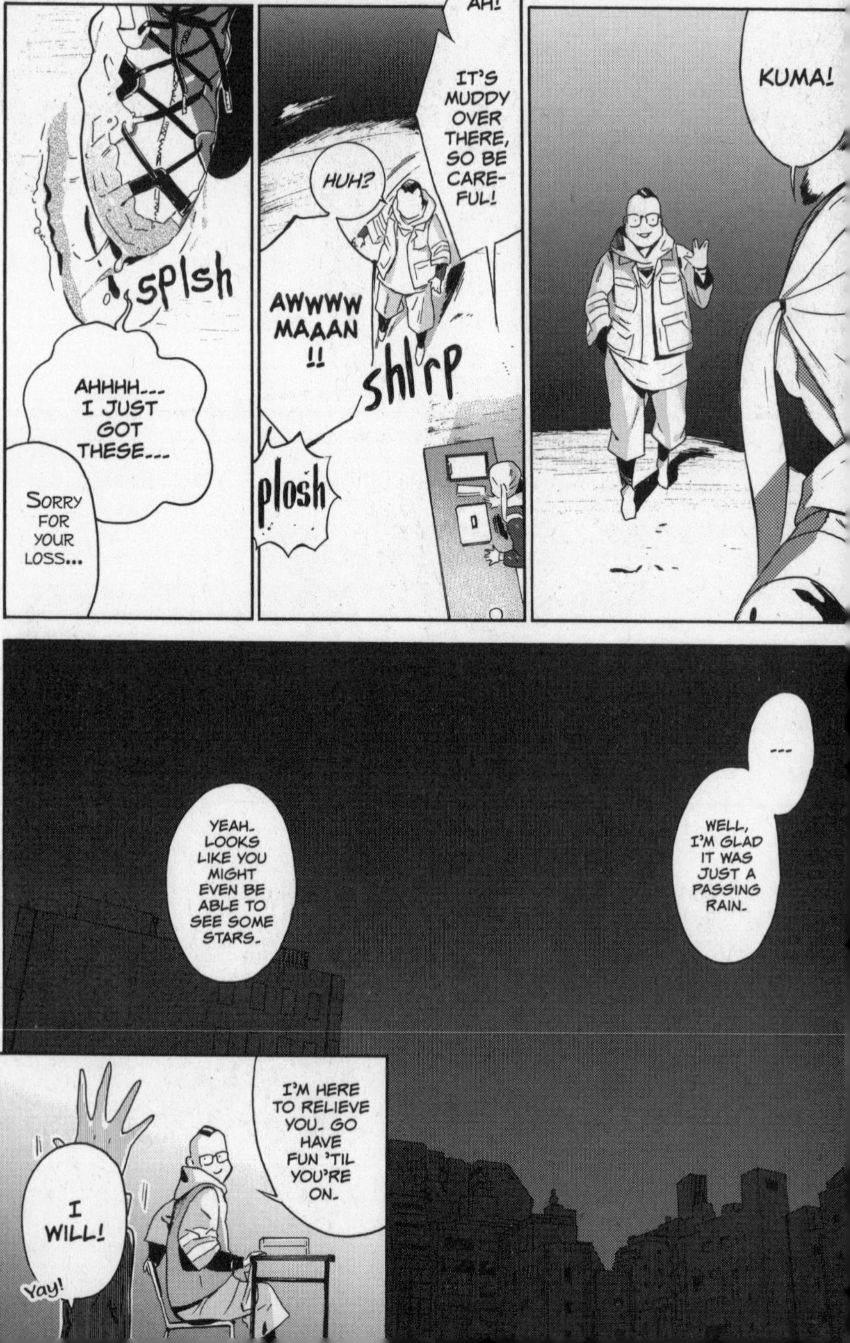
KUMA!
AH!
IT'S MUDDY OVER THERE, SO BE CARE-FUL!
HUH?
AWWWW MAAAN!!
shlrp
plosh
splsh
AHHHH... I JUST GOT THESE...
SORRY FOR YOUR LOSS...
...
WELL, I'M GLAD IT WAS JUST A PASSING RAIN.
YEAH. LOOKS LIKE YOU MIGHT EVEN BE ABLE TO SEE SOME STARS.
I'M HERE TO RELIEVE YOU. GO HAVE FUN 'TIL YOU'RE ON.
I WILL!
Yay!

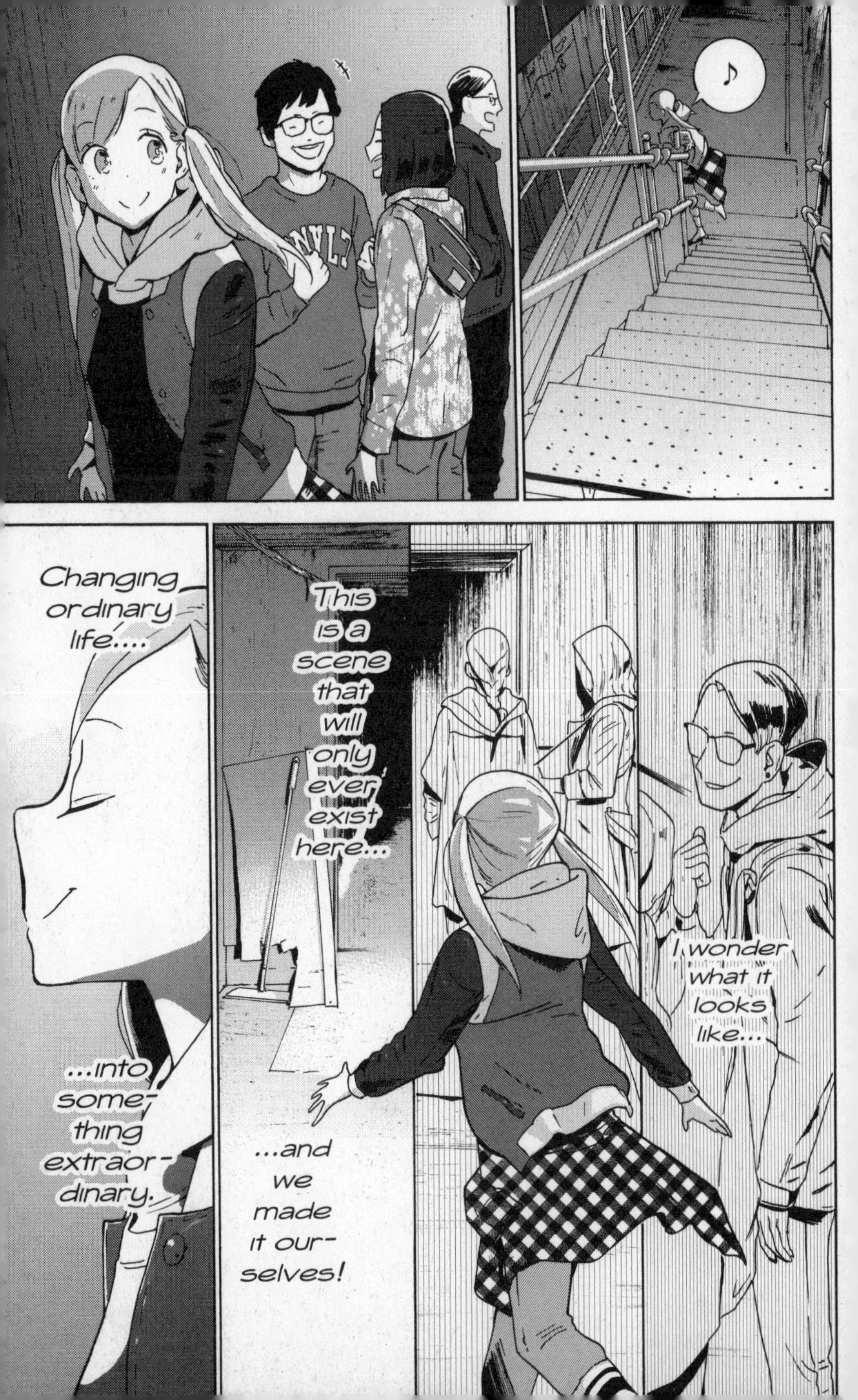
♪
I wonder what it looks like...
This is a scene that will only ever exist here...
...and we made it ourselves!
Changing ordinary life....
...into something extraordinary.

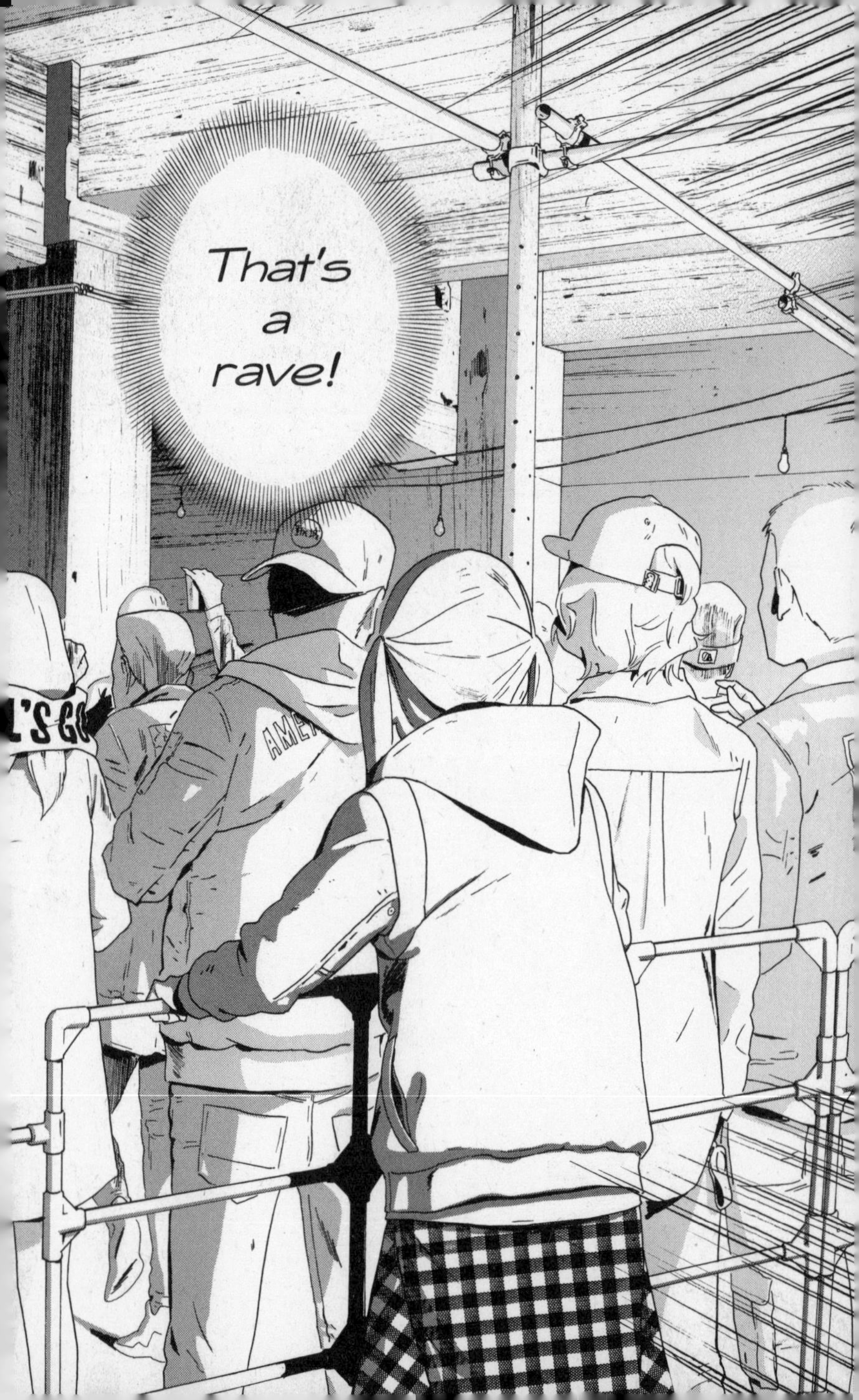
That's a rave!

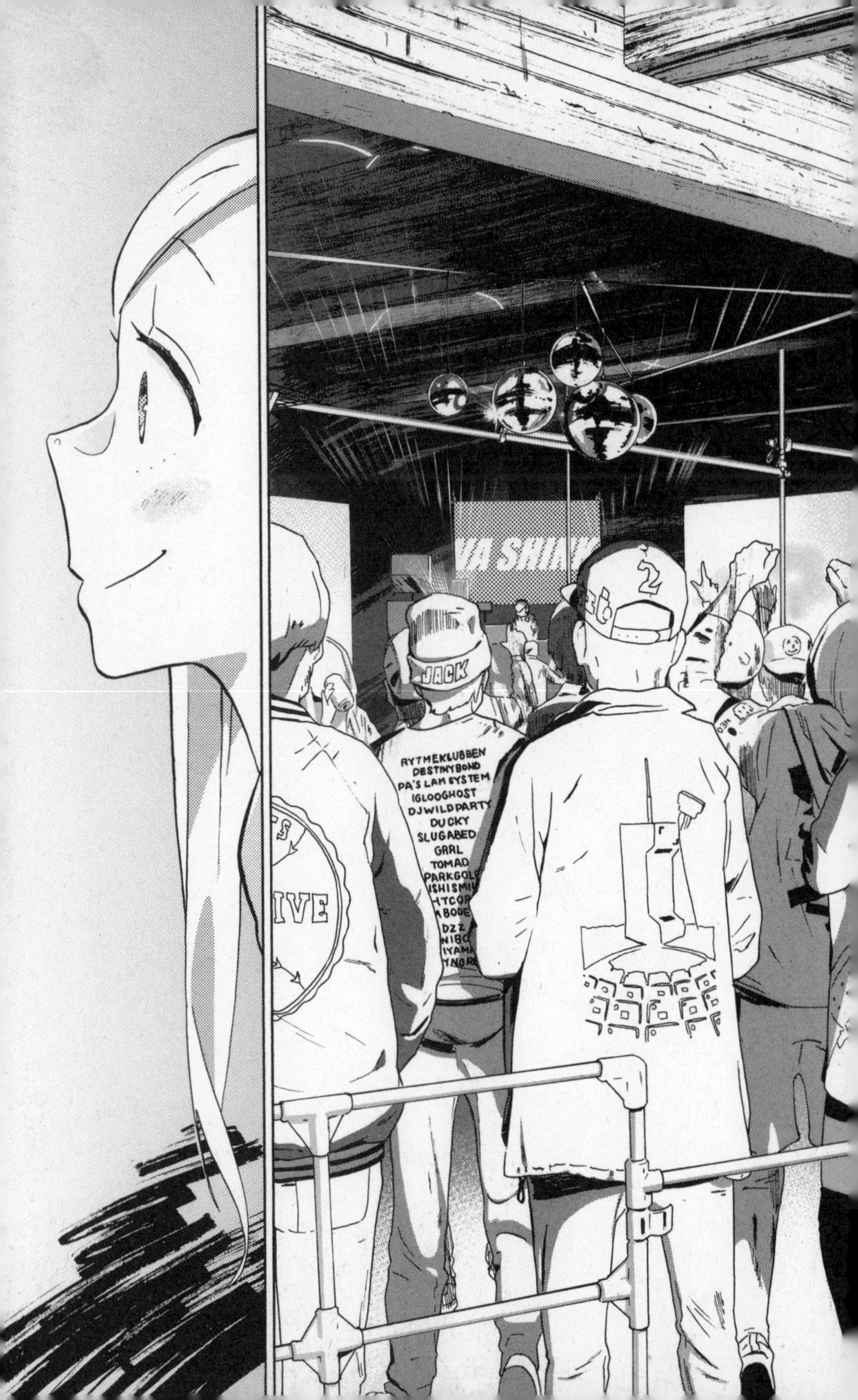
JACK
RY7MEKLUBBEN
DESTINYBOND
PA'S LAM SYSTEM
IGLOOGHOST
DJWILDPARTY
DUCKY
SLUGABED
GRRL
TOMAD

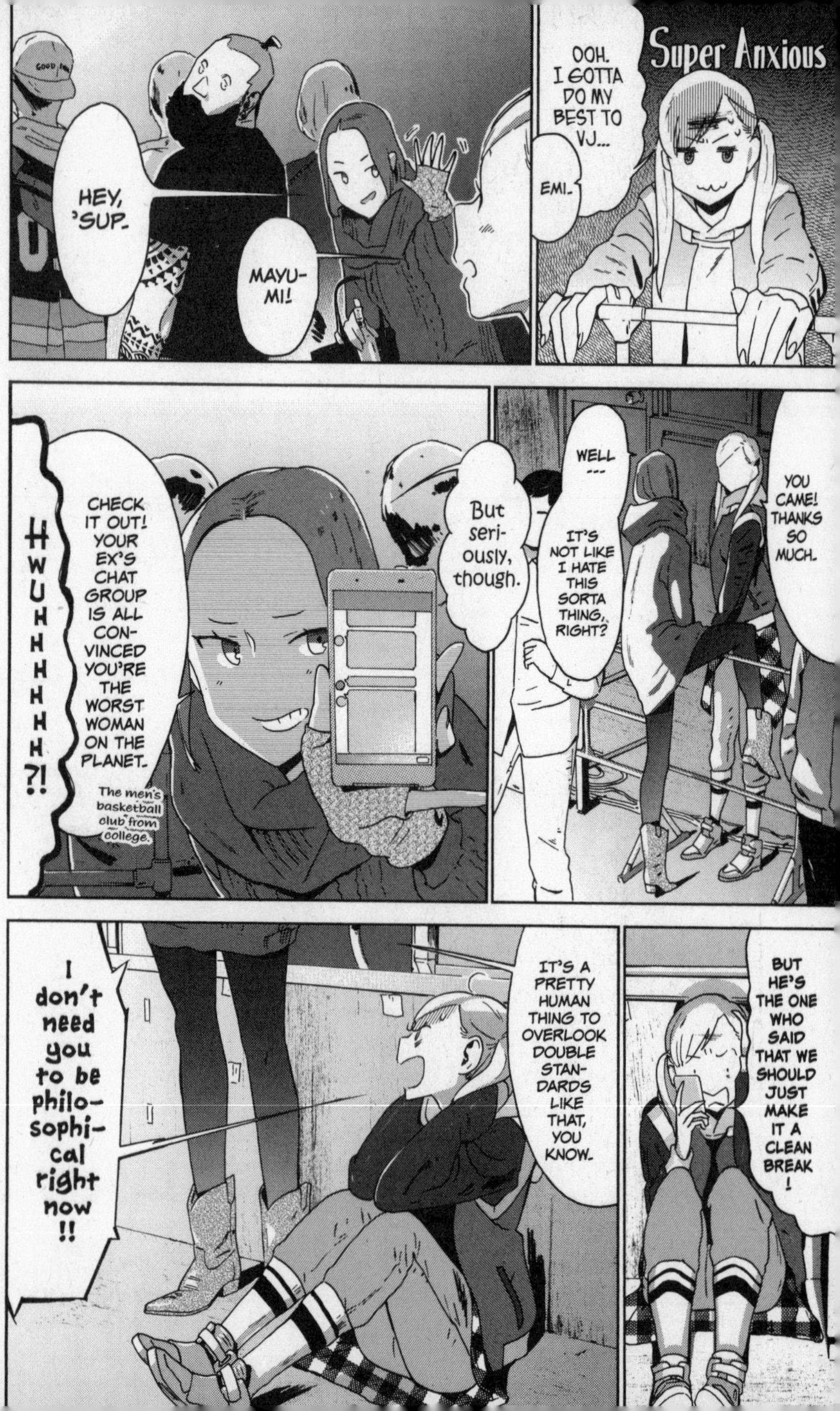
Super Anxious
OOH. I GOTTA DO MY BEST TO VJ...
EMI...
MAYU-MI!
HEY, 'SUP...
YOU CAME! THANKS SO MUCH...
WELL...
IT'S NOT LIKE I HATE THIS SORTA THING, RIGHT?
But seriously, though.
CHECK IT OUT! YOUR EX'S CHAT GROUP IS ALL CONVINCED YOU'RE THE WORST WOMAN ON THE PLANET...
HWUHHHHHHH?!
The men's basketball club from college.
BUT HE'S THE ONE WHO SAID THAT WE SHOULD JUST MAKE IT A CLEAN BREAK!
IT'S A PRETTY HUMAN THING TO OVERLOOK DOUBLE STANDARDS LIKE THAT, YOU KNOW...
I don't need you to be philosophical right now!!

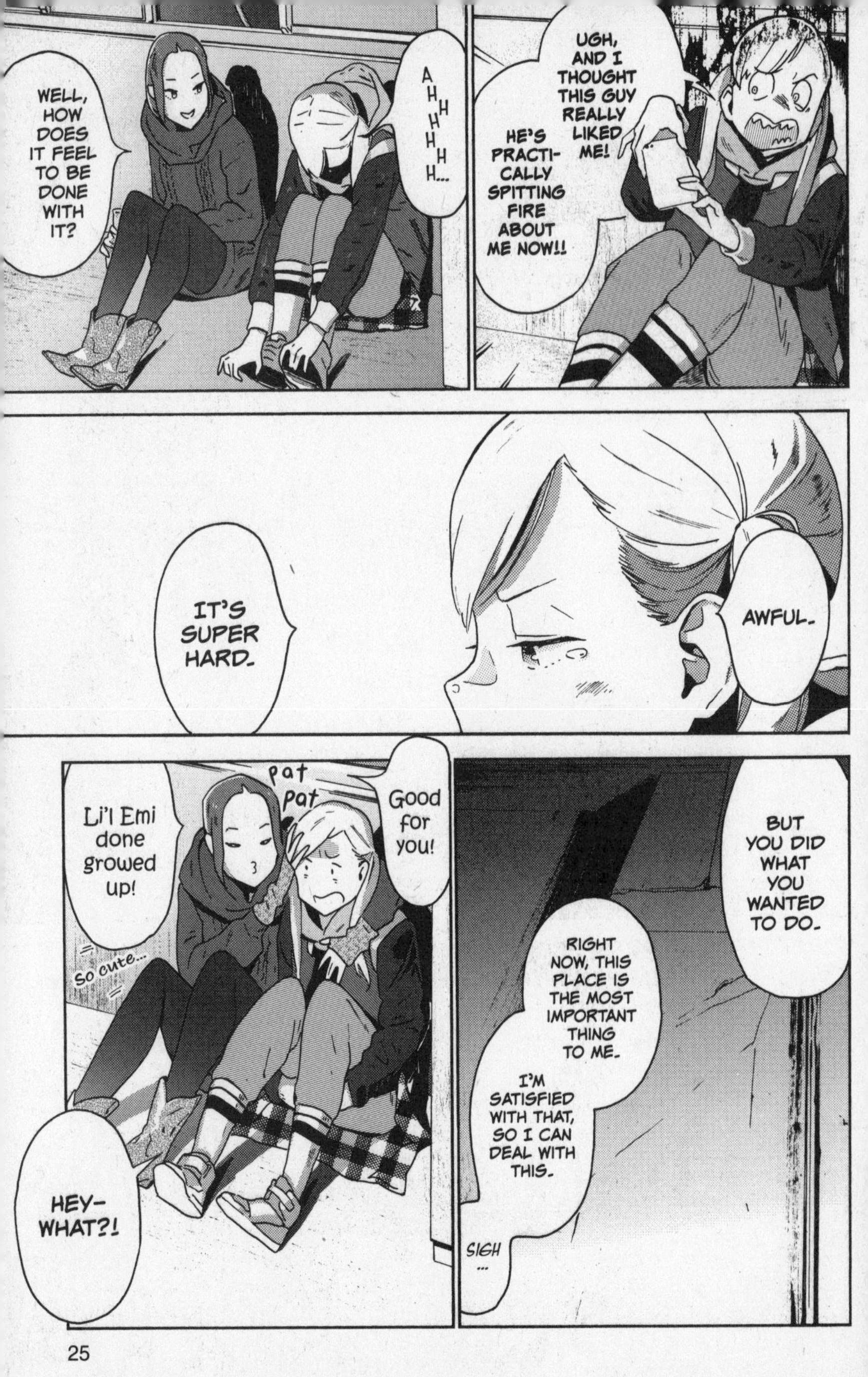
UGH, AND I THOUGHT THIS GUY REALLY LIKED ME!
HE'S PRACTI-CALLY SPITTING FIRE ABOUT ME NOW!!
WELL, HOW DOES IT FEEL TO BE DONE WITH IT?
AHHHHHH...
AWFUL.
IT'S SUPER HARD.
BUT YOU DID WHAT YOU WANTED TO DO.
RIGHT NOW, THIS PLACE IS THE MOST IMPORTANT THING TO ME.
I'M SATISFIED WITH THAT, SO I CAN DEAL WITH THIS.
SIGH...
Good for you!
pat pat
Li'l Emi done growed up!
so cute...
HEY-WHAT?!

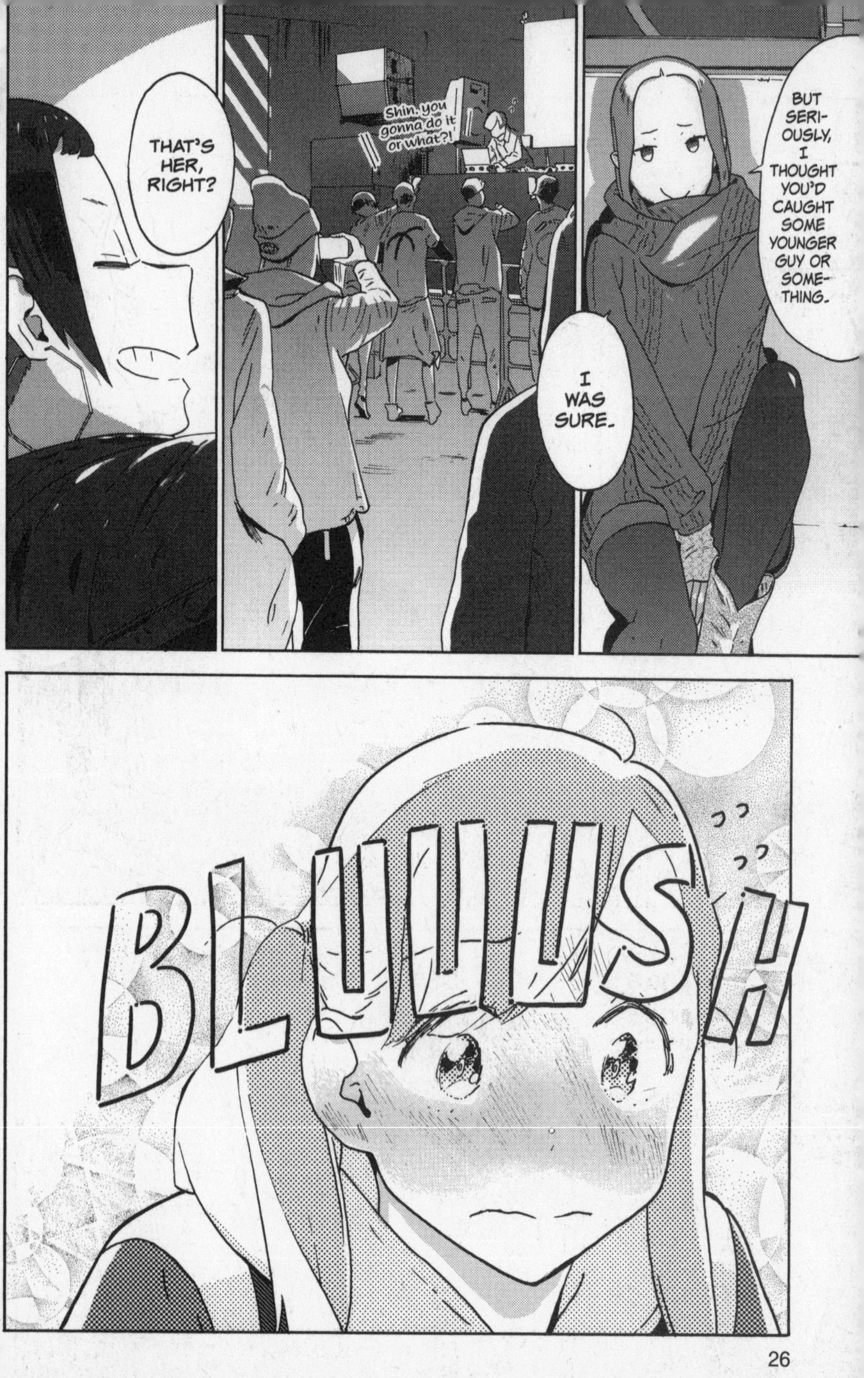
BUT SERIOUSLY, I THOUGHT YOU'D CAUGHT SOME YOUNGER GUY OR SOMETHING.
I WAS SURE.
Shin, you gonna do it or what?!
THAT'S HER, RIGHT?
BLUUUSH

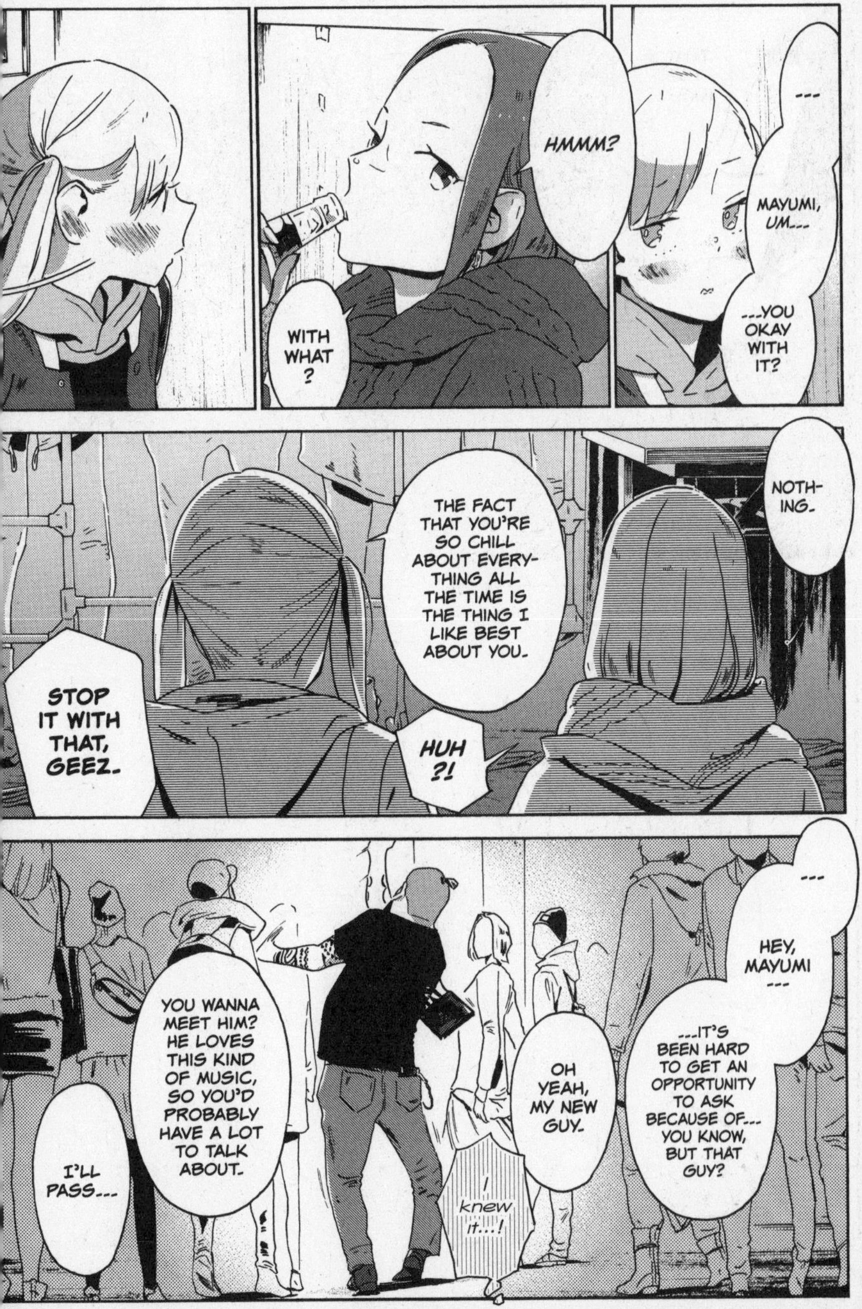
...
MAYUMI, UM...
...YOU OKAY WITH IT?
HMMM?
WITH WHAT?
NOTHING.
THE FACT THAT YOU'RE SO CHILL ABOUT EVERYTHING ALL THE TIME IS THE THING I LIKE BEST ABOUT YOU.
HUH?!
STOP IT WITH THAT, GEEZ.
...
HEY, MAYUMI...
...IT'S BEEN HARD TO GET AN OPPORTUNITY TO ASK BECAUSE OF... YOU KNOW, BUT THAT GUY?
OH YEAH, MY NEW GUY.
I knew it...!
YOU WANNA MEET HIM? HE LOVES THIS KIND OF MUSIC, SO YOU'D PROBABLY HAVE A LOT TO TALK ABOUT.
I'LL PASS...

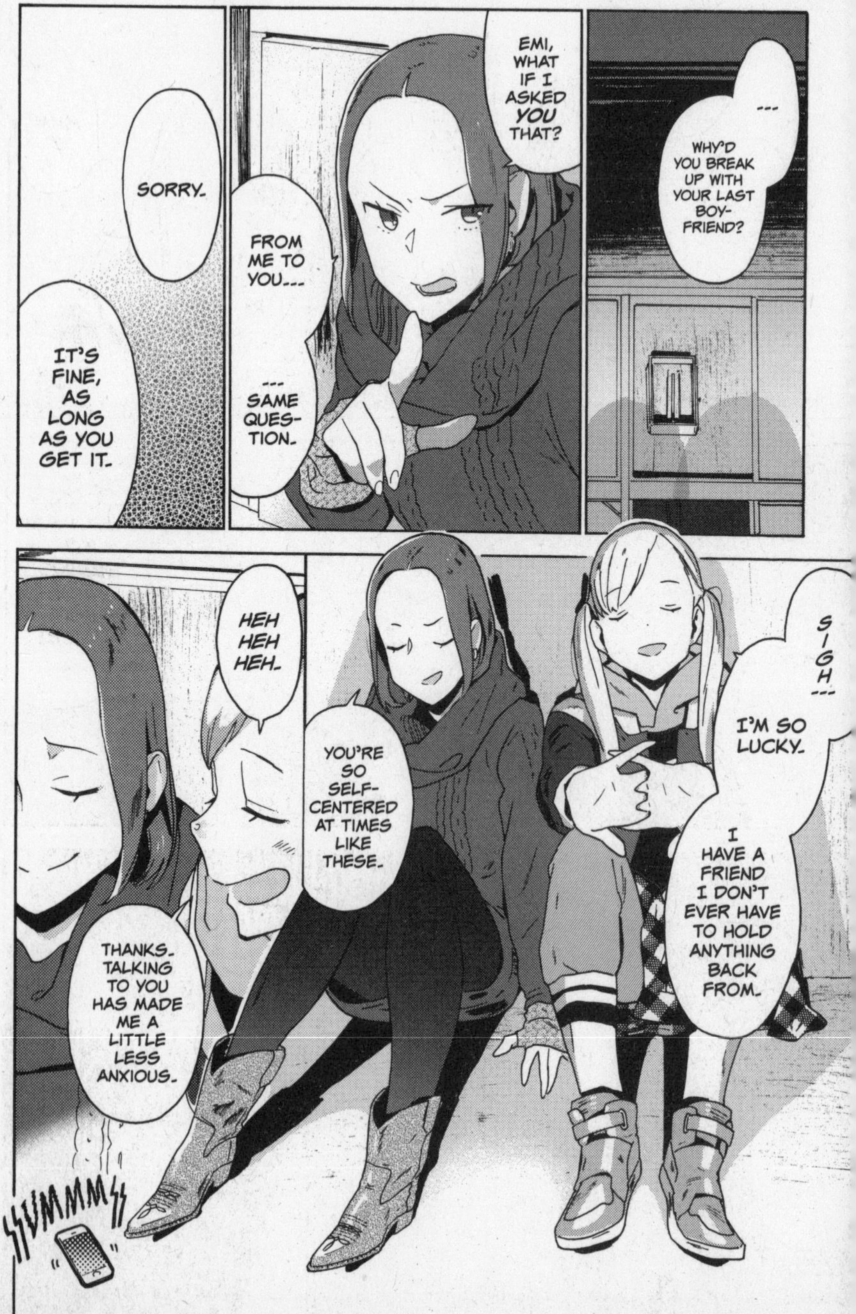
...
WHY'D YOU BREAK UP WITH YOUR LAST BOY-FRIEND?
EMI, WHAT IF I ASKED *YOU* THAT?
FROM ME TO YOU...
...SAME QUES-TION.
SORRY.
IT'S FINE, AS LONG AS YOU GET IT.
SIGH...
I'M SO LUCKY.
I HAVE A FRIEND I DON'T EVER HAVE TO HOLD ANYTHING BACK FROM.
YOU'RE SO SELF-CENTERED AT TIMES LIKE THESE.
HEH HEH HEH.
THANKS. TALKING TO YOU HAS MADE ME A LITTLE LESS ANXIOUS.
VMMM

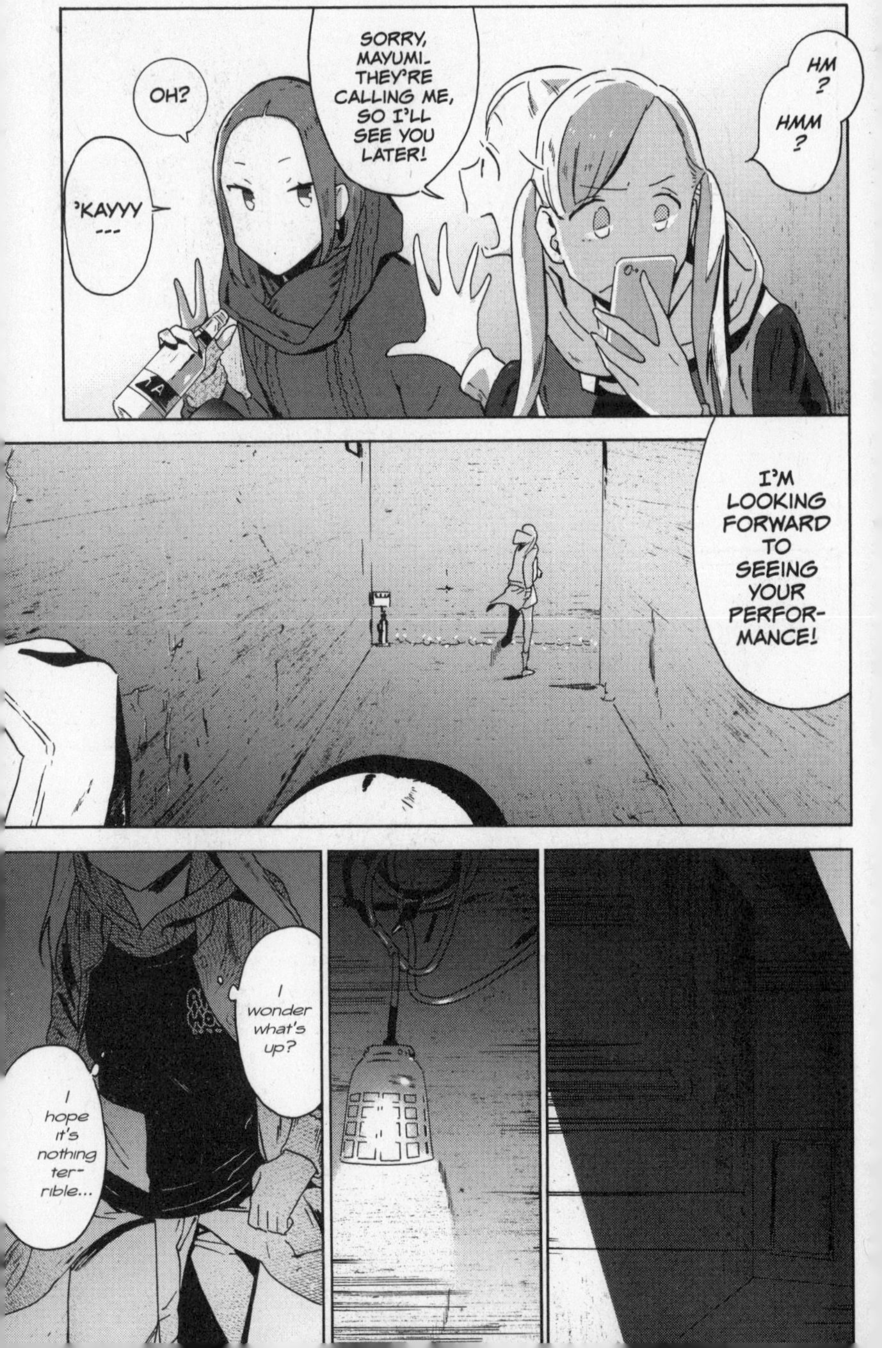
HM? HMM?
SORRY, MAYUMI. THEY'RE CALLING ME, SO I'LL SEE YOU LATER!
OH?
'KAYYY---
I'M LOOKING FORWARD TO SEEING YOUR PERFORMANCE!
I wonder what's up?
I hope it's nothing terrible...

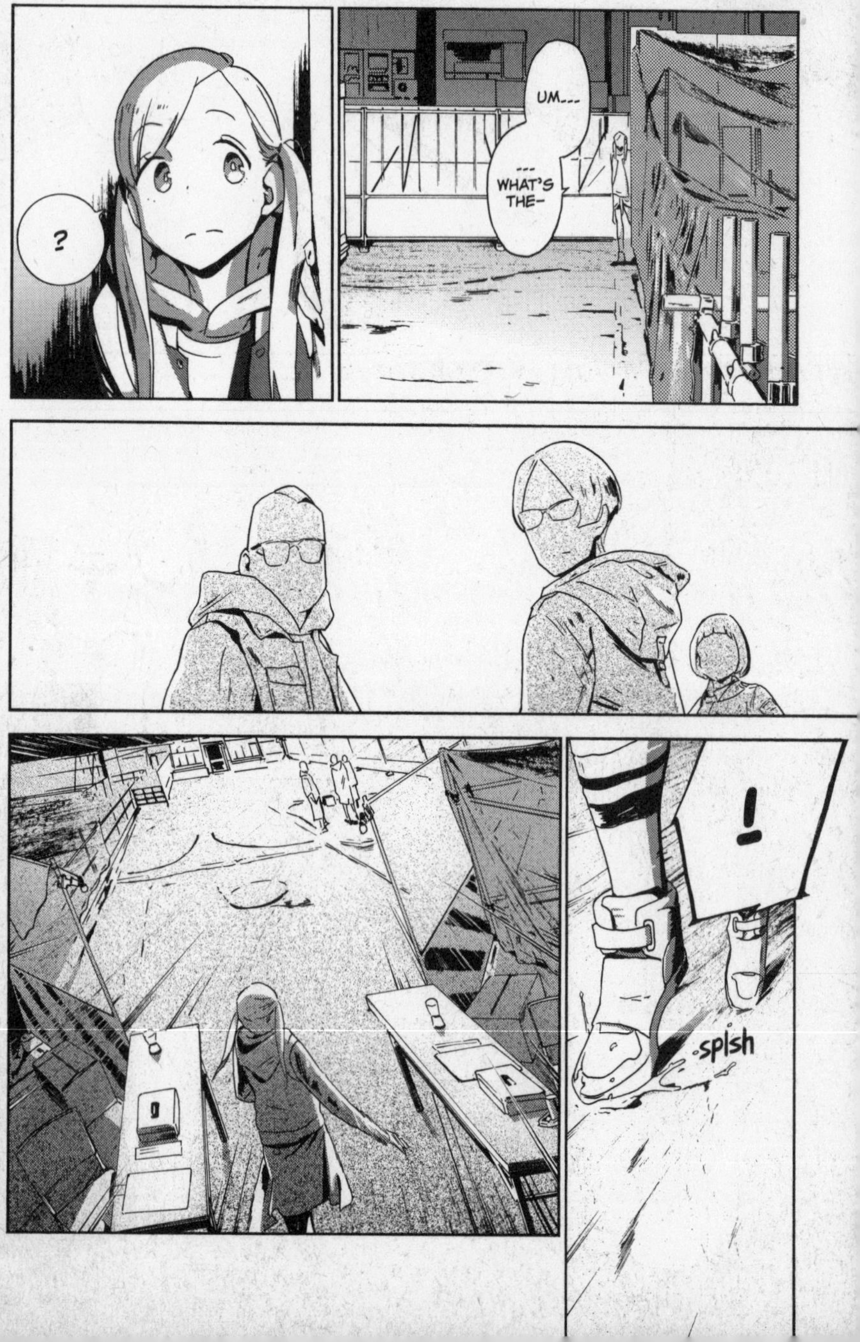
UM... ...WHAT'S THE-
?
!
splsh

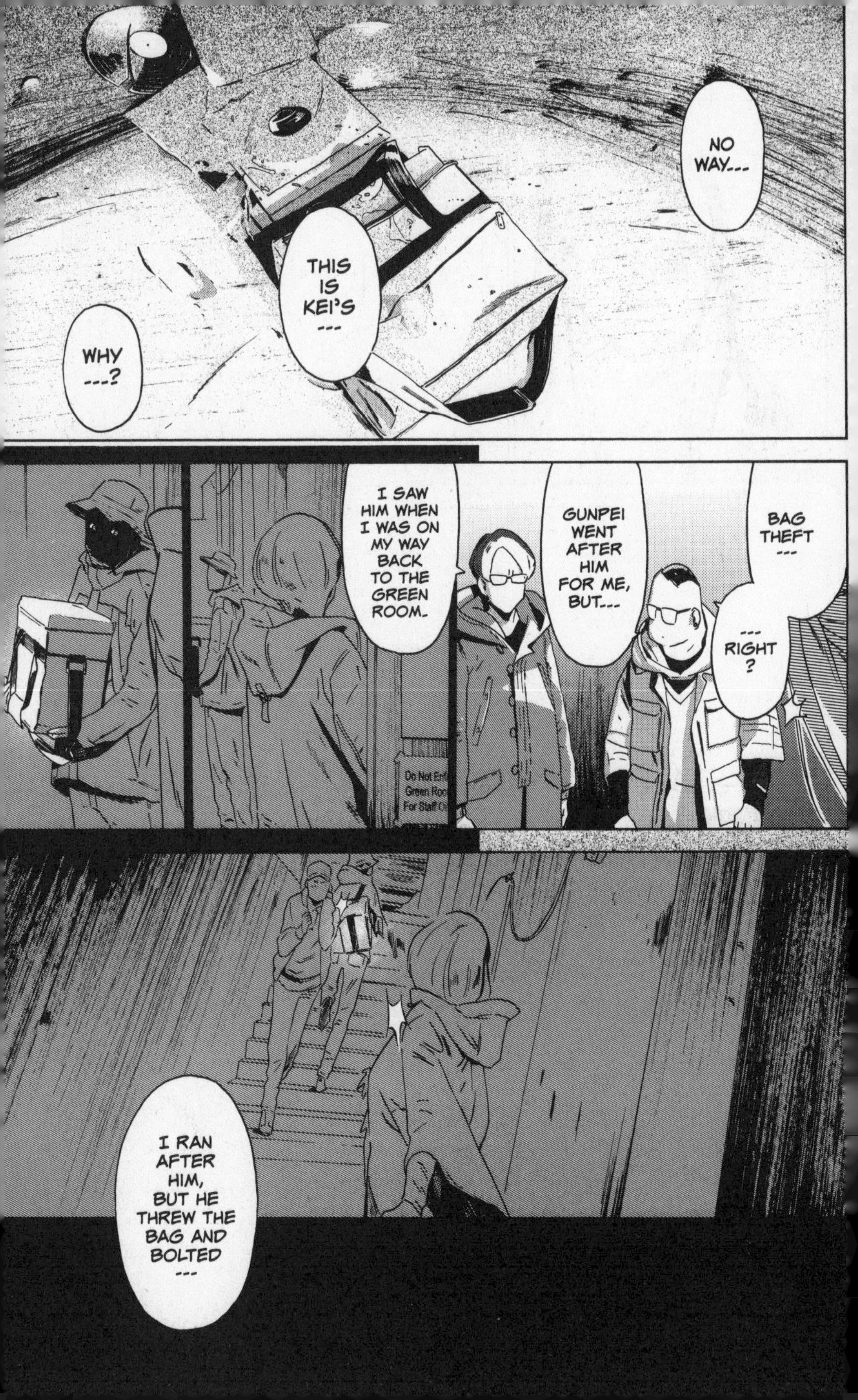
NO WAY...
THIS IS KEI'S ---
WHY ---?
BAG THEFT ---
--- RIGHT ?
GUNPEI WENT AFTER HIM FOR ME, BUT...
I SAW HIM WHEN I WAS ON MY WAY BACK TO THE GREEN ROOM.
I RAN AFTER HIM, BUT HE THREW THE BAG AND BOLTED ---

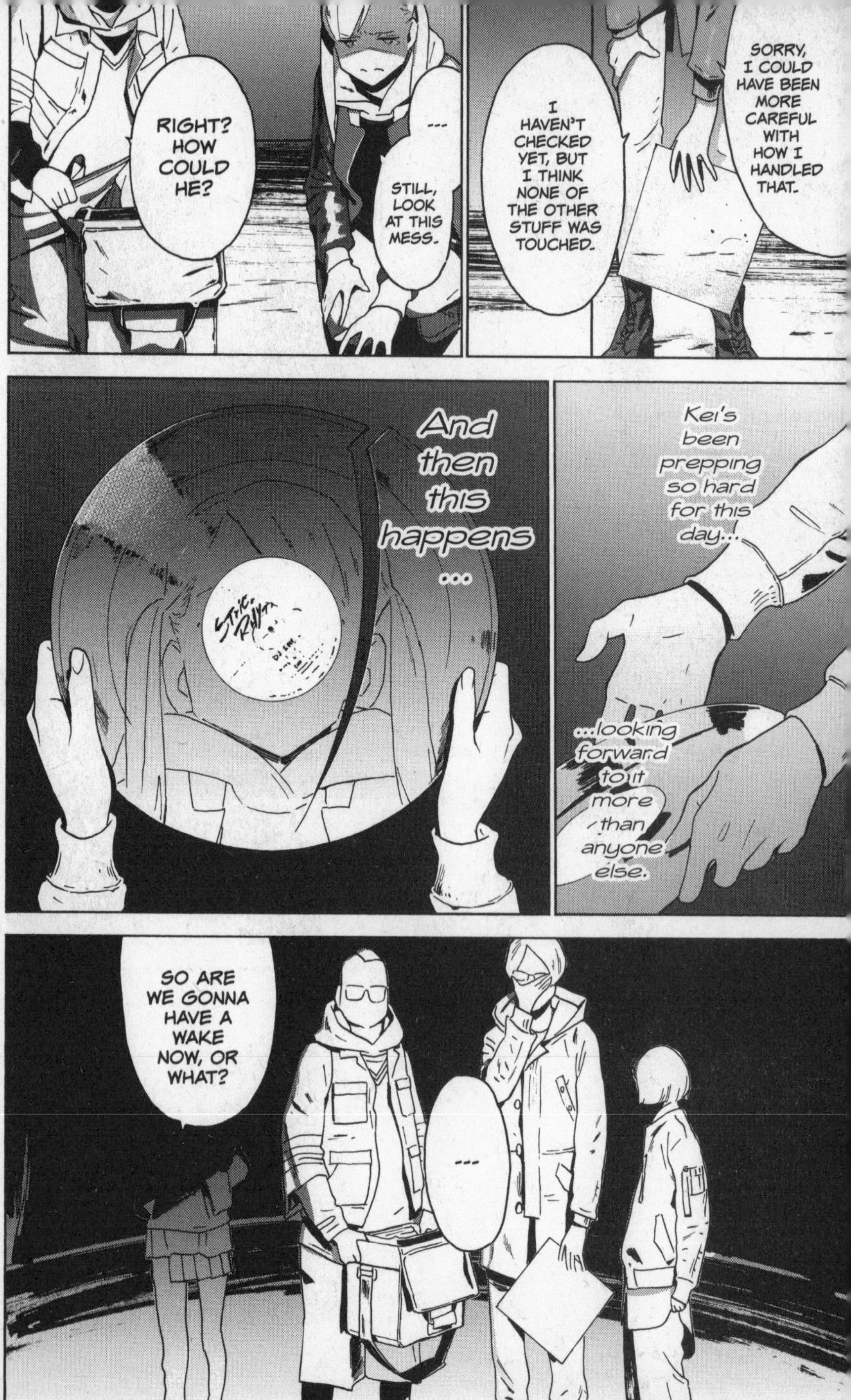
SORRY, I COULD HAVE BEEN MORE CAREFUL WITH HOW I HANDLED THAT.
I HAVEN'T CHECKED YET, BUT I THINK NONE OF THE OTHER STUFF WAS TOUCHED.
...
STILL, LOOK AT THIS MESS.
RIGHT? HOW COULD HE?
Kei's been prepping so hard for this day...
...looking forward to it more than anyone else.
And then this happens...
SO ARE WE GONNA HAVE A WAKE NOW, OR WHAT?
...

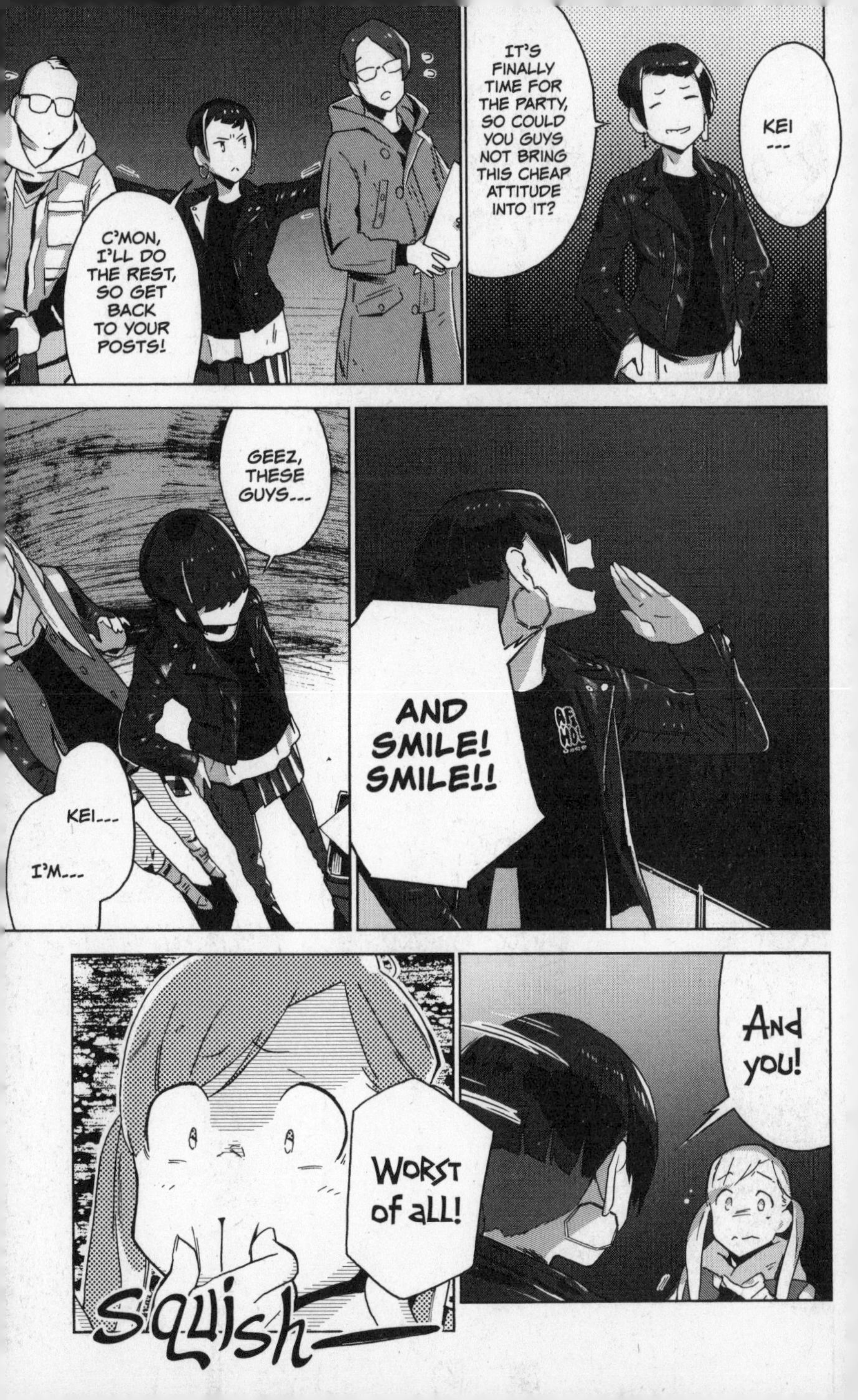
KEI---
IT'S FINALLY TIME FOR THE PARTY, SO COULD YOU GUYS NOT BRING THIS CHEAP ATTITUDE INTO IT?
C'MON, I'LL DO THE REST, SO GET BACK TO YOUR POSTS!
AND SMILE! SMILE!!
GEEZ, THESE GUYS---
KEI---
I'M---
And you!
WORST of all!
Squish—

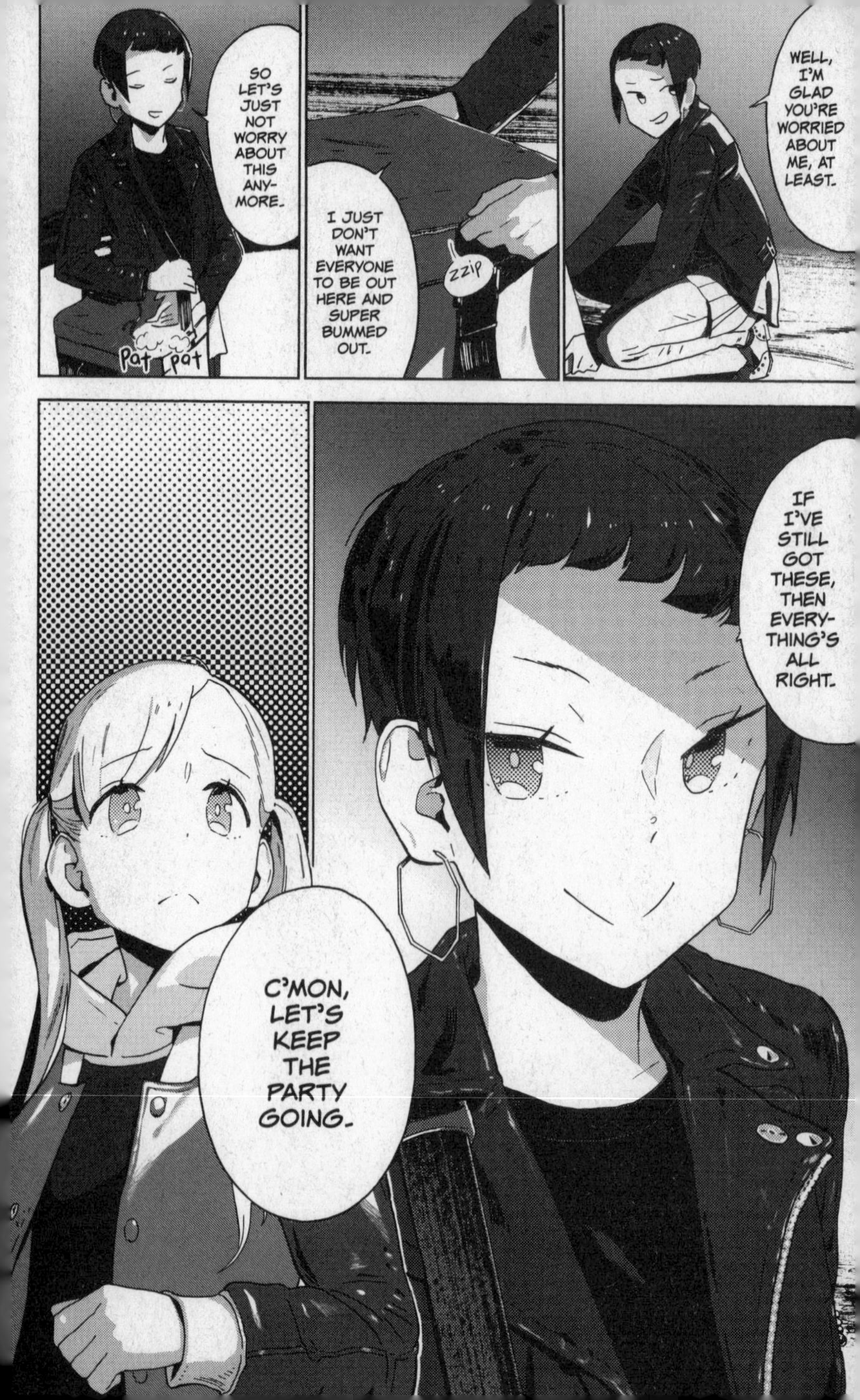
WELL, I'M GLAD YOU'RE WORRIED ABOUT ME, AT LEAST.
I JUST DON'T WANT EVERYONE TO BE OUT HERE AND SUPER BUMMED OUT.
zzip
SO LET'S JUST NOT WORRY ABOUT THIS ANYMORE.
pat pat
IF I'VE STILL GOT THESE, THEN EVERYTHING'S ALL RIGHT.
C'MON, LET'S KEEP THE PARTY GOING.

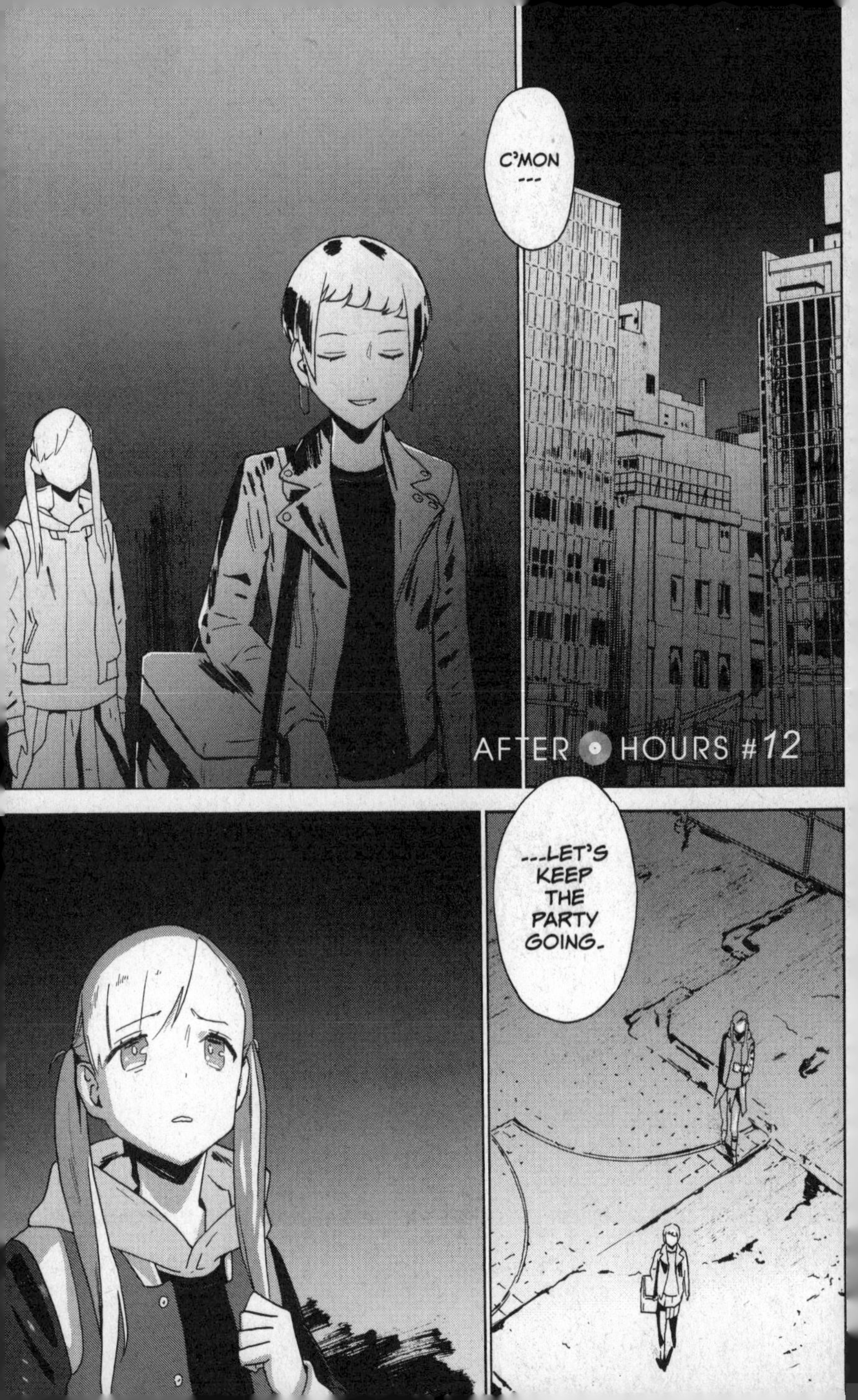
C'MON

AFTER HOURS #12
---LET'S KEEP THE PARTY GOING.

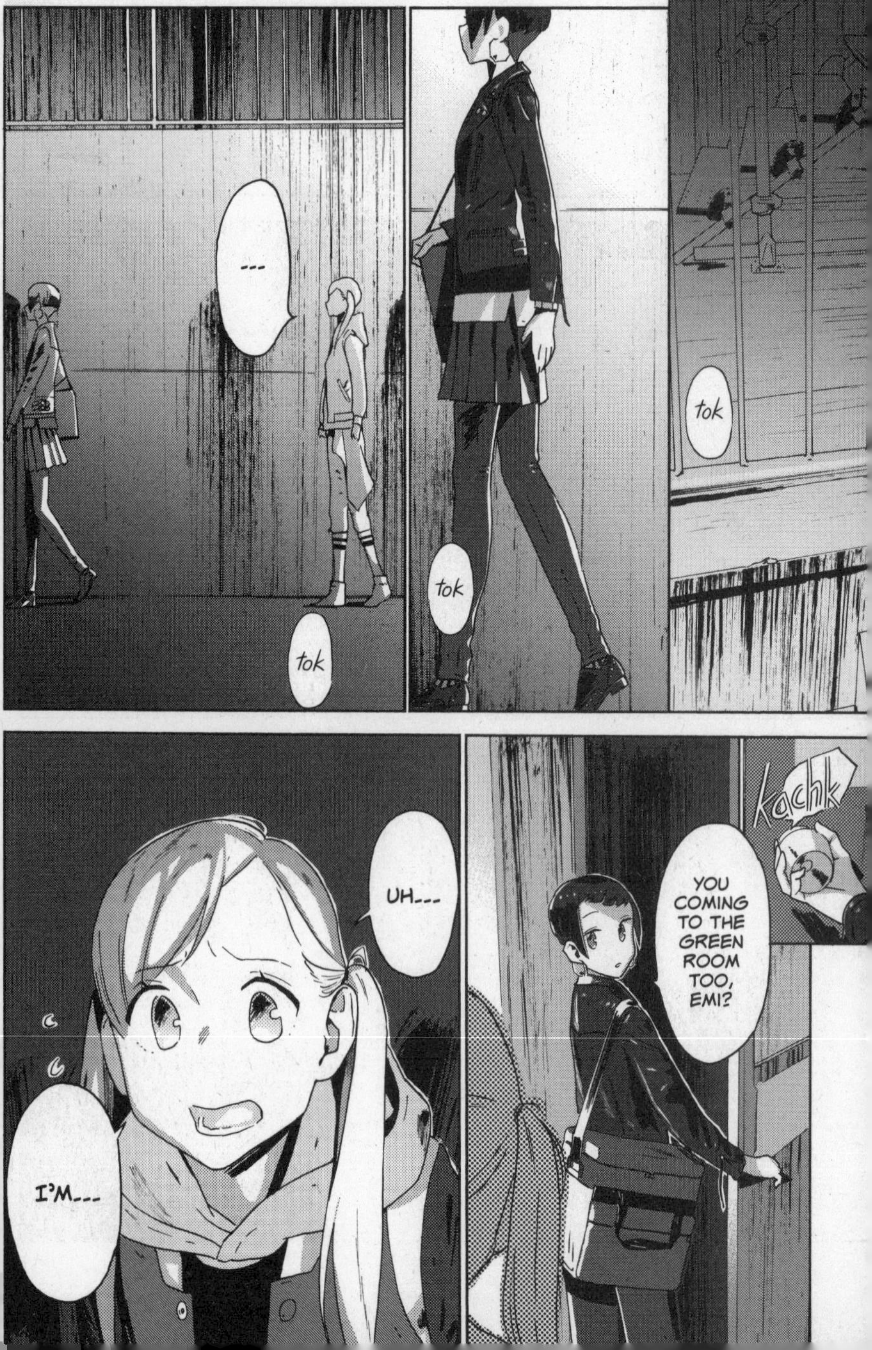
tok
tok
...
tok
kachk
YOU COMING TO THE GREEN ROOM TOO, EMI?
UH...
I'M...

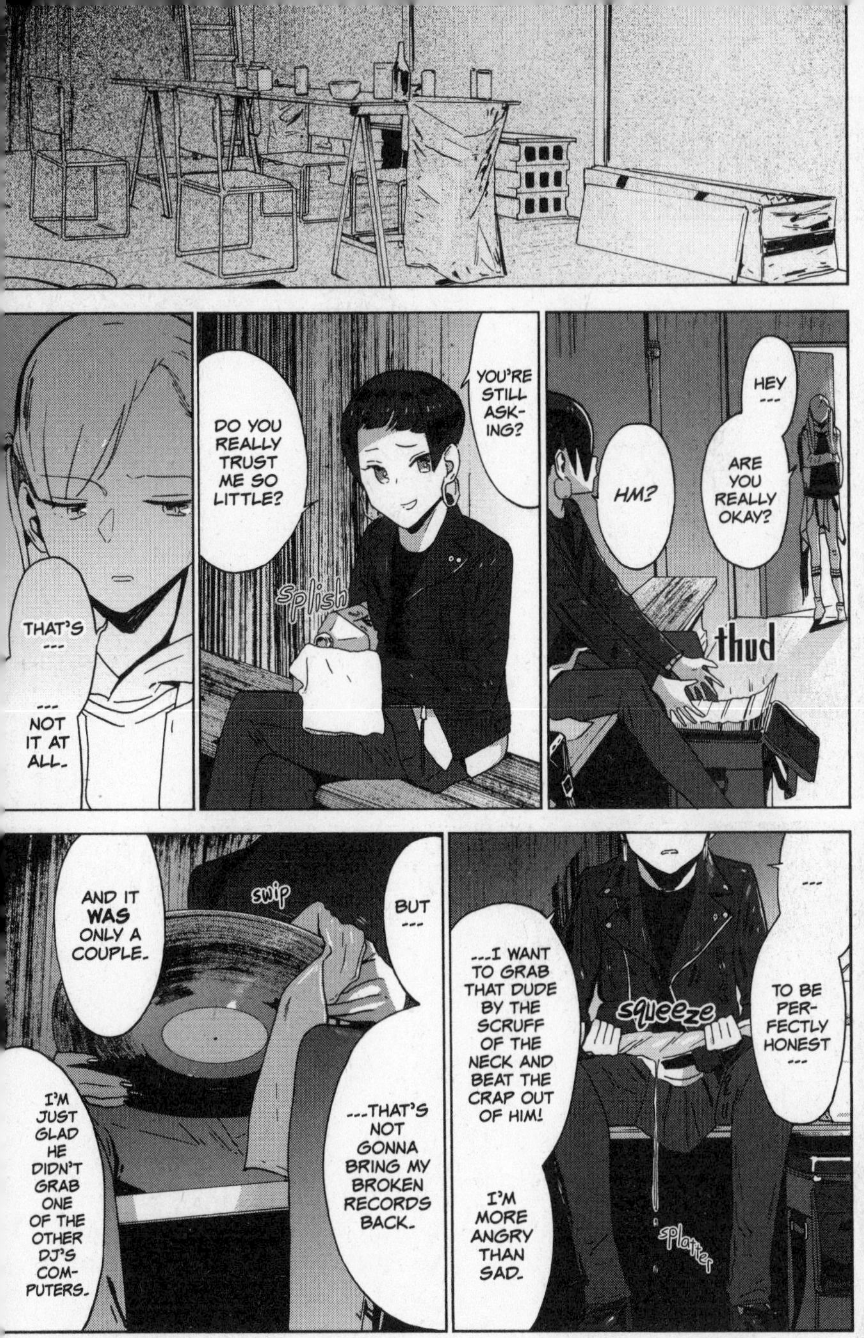
HEY---
ARE YOU REALLY OKAY?
thud
HM?
YOU'RE STILL ASK-ING?
DO YOU REALLY TRUST ME SO LITTLE?
splish
THAT'S---
---NOT IT AT ALL.

TO BE PER-FECTLY HONEST---
---I WANT TO GRAB THAT DUDE BY THE SCRUFF OF THE NECK AND BEAT THE CRAP OUT OF HIM!
squeeze
I'M MORE ANGRY THAN SAD.
splatter
BUT---
---THAT'S NOT GONNA BRING MY BROKEN RECORDS BACK.
AND IT **WAS** ONLY A COUPLE.
swip
I'M JUST GLAD HE DIDN'T GRAB ONE OF THE OTHER DJ'S COM-PUTERS.

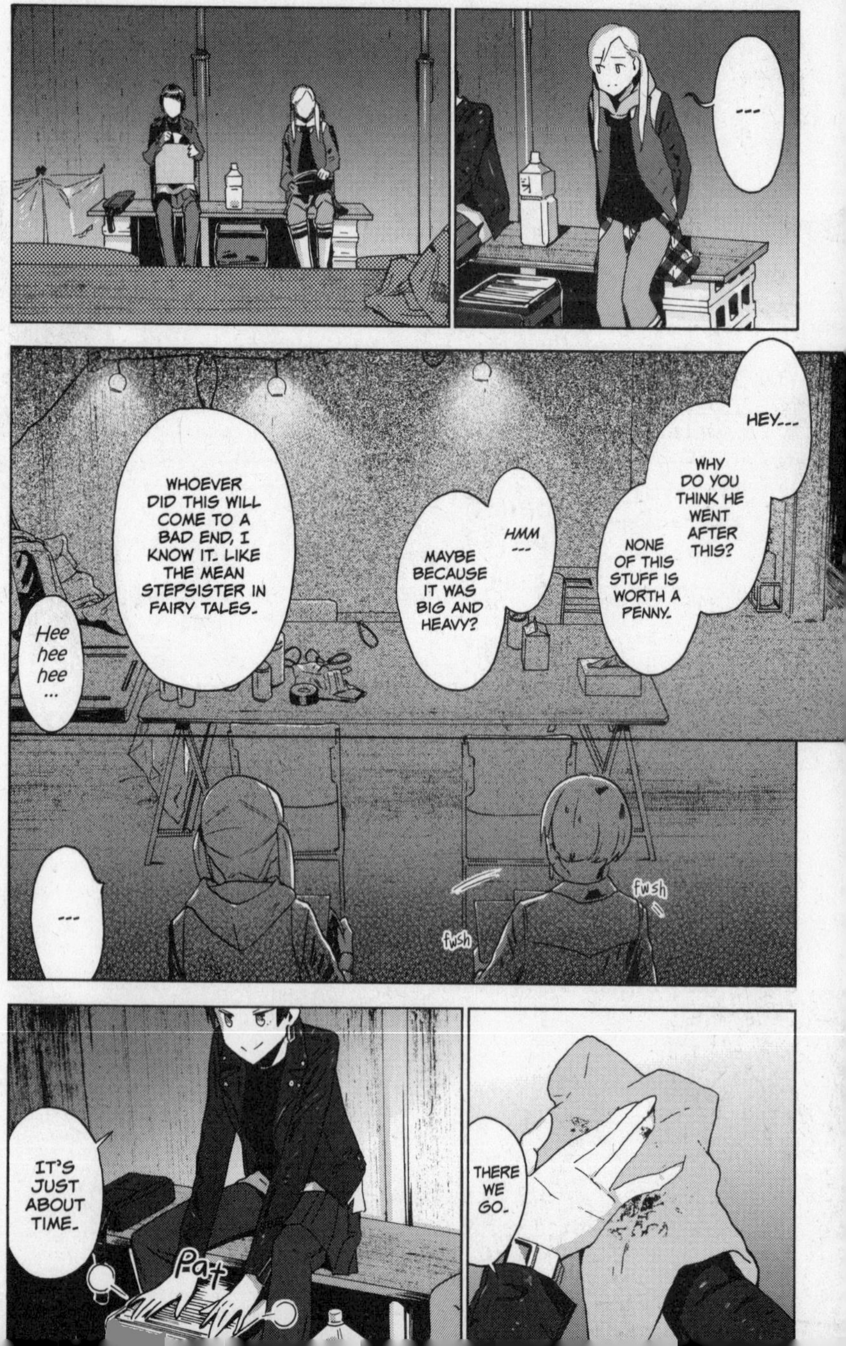

HEY--- WHY DO YOU THINK HE WENT AFTER THIS?
NONE OF THIS STUFF IS WORTH A PENNY.
HMM ---
MAYBE BECAUSE IT WAS BIG AND HEAVY?
WHOEVER DID THIS WILL COME TO A BAD END, I KNOW IT. LIKE THE MEAN STEPSISTER IN FAIRY TALES.
Hee hee hee ...
fwsh
fwsh

THERE WE GO.
IT'S JUST ABOUT TIME.
Pat

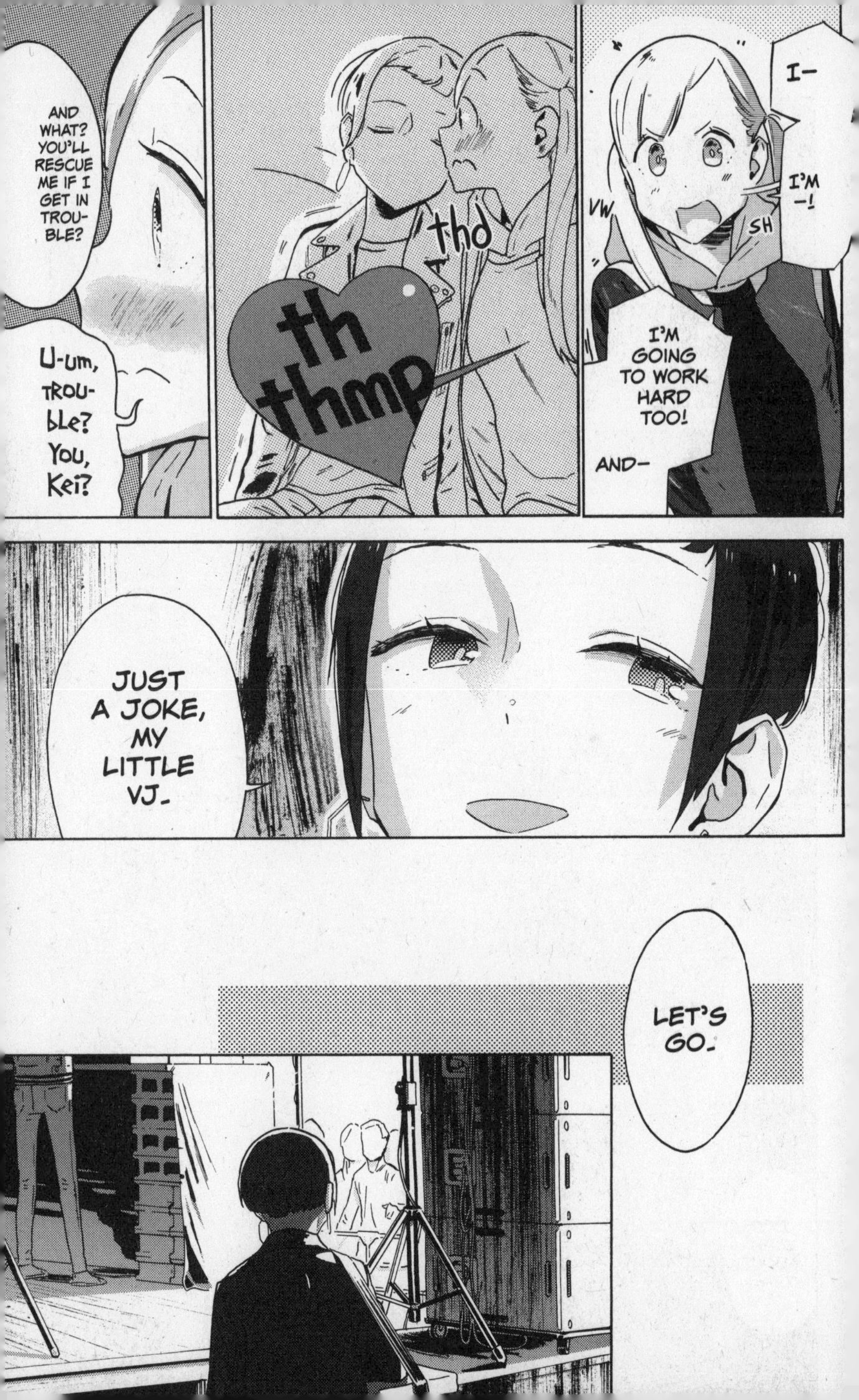
I—
I'M —!
SH
VW
I'M GOING TO WORK HARD TOO!
AND—
thd
th thmp
AND WHAT? YOU'LL RESCUE ME IF I GET IN TROU-BLE?
U-um, trou-ble? You, Kei?
JUST A JOKE, MY LITTLE VJ.
LET'S GO.

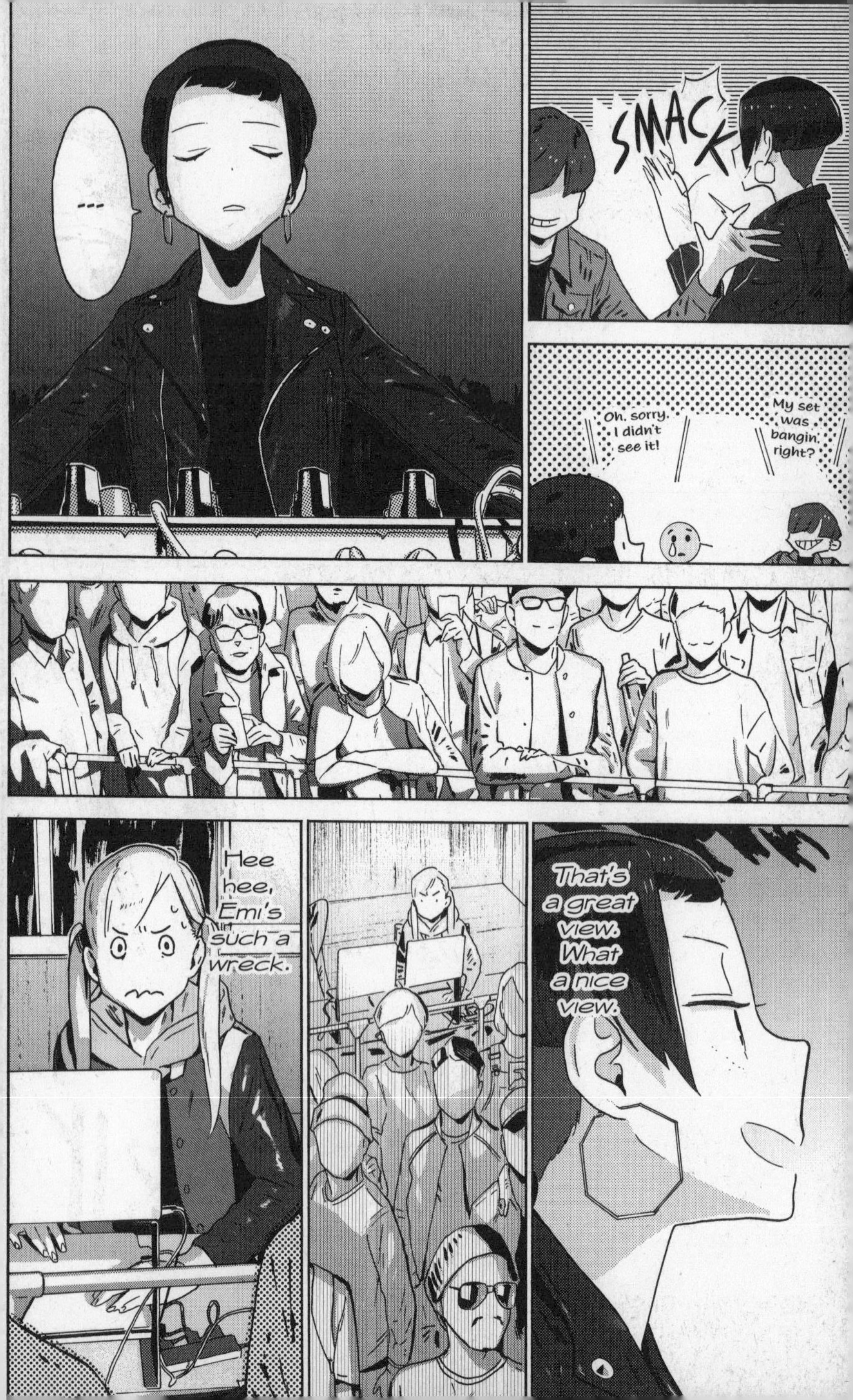
SMACK
My set was bangin. right?
Oh. sorry. I didn't see it!

That's a great view. What a nice view.
Hee hee, Emi's such a wreck.

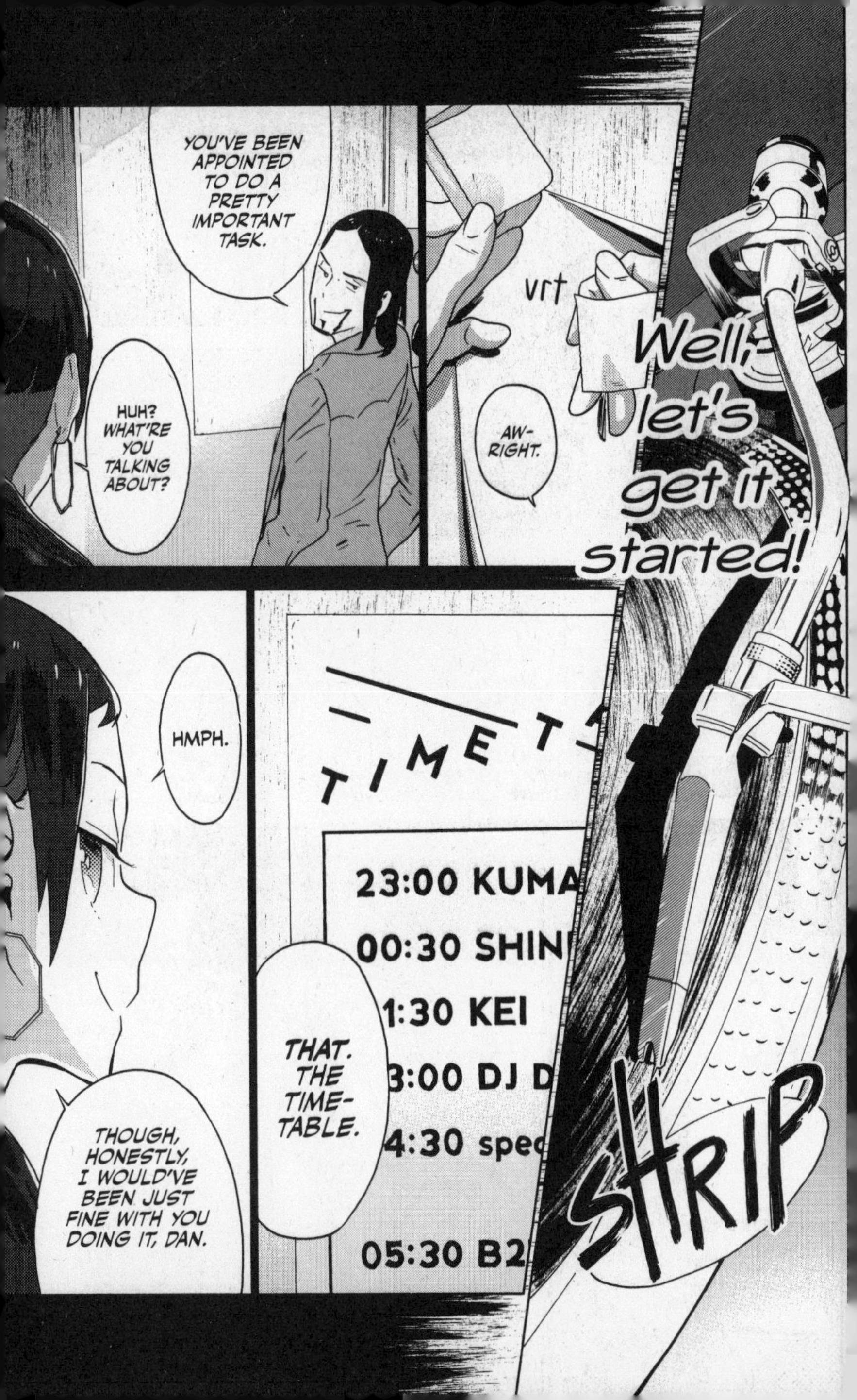
vrt
AW-RIGHT.
YOU'VE BEEN APPOINTED TO DO A PRETTY IMPORTANT TASK.
HUH? WHAT'RE YOU TALKING ABOUT?
THAT. THE TIME-TABLE.
TIMET
23:00 KUMA
00:30 SHIN
1:30 KEI
3:00 DJ D
4:30 spec
05:30 B2
HMPH.
THOUGH, HONESTLY, I WOULD'VE BEEN JUST FINE WITH YOU DOING IT, DAN.
Well, let's get it started!
SHRIP

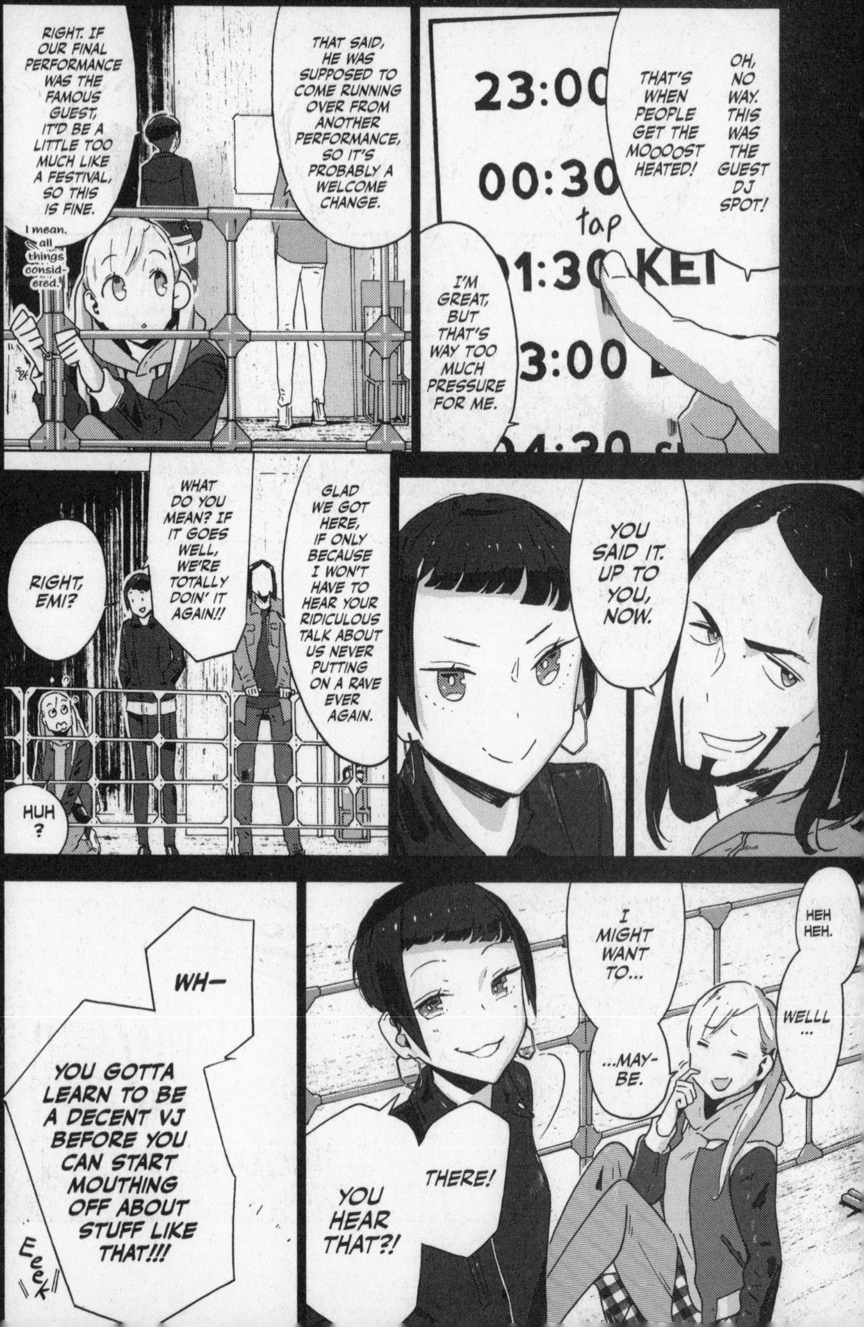
OH, NO WAY. THIS WAS THE GUEST DJ SPOT!
THAT'S WHEN PEOPLE GET THE MOOOOST HEATED!
23:00
00:30
tap
I'M GREAT, BUT THAT'S WAY TOO MUCH PRESSURE FOR ME.
THAT SAID, HE WAS SUPPOSED TO COME RUNNING OVER FROM ANOTHER PERFORMANCE, SO IT'S PROBABLY A WELCOME CHANGE.
RIGHT. IF OUR FINAL PERFORMANCE WAS THE FAMOUS GUEST, IT'D BE A LITTLE TOO MUCH LIKE A FESTIVAL, SO THIS IS FINE.
I mean, all things consid-ered.
YOU SAID IT. UP TO YOU, NOW.
GLAD WE GOT HERE, IF ONLY BECAUSE I WON'T HAVE TO HEAR YOUR RIDICULOUS TALK ABOUT US NEVER PUTTING ON A RAVE EVER AGAIN.
WHAT DO YOU MEAN? IF IT GOES WELL, WE'RE TOTALLY DOIN' IT AGAIN!!
RIGHT, EMI?
HUH?
HEH HEH.
WELLL...
I MIGHT WANT TO...
...MAY-BE.
THERE!
YOU HEAR THAT?!
WH—
YOU GOTTA LEARN TO BE A DECENT VJ BEFORE YOU CAN START MOUTHING OFF ABOUT STUFF LIKE THAT!!!
Eeek

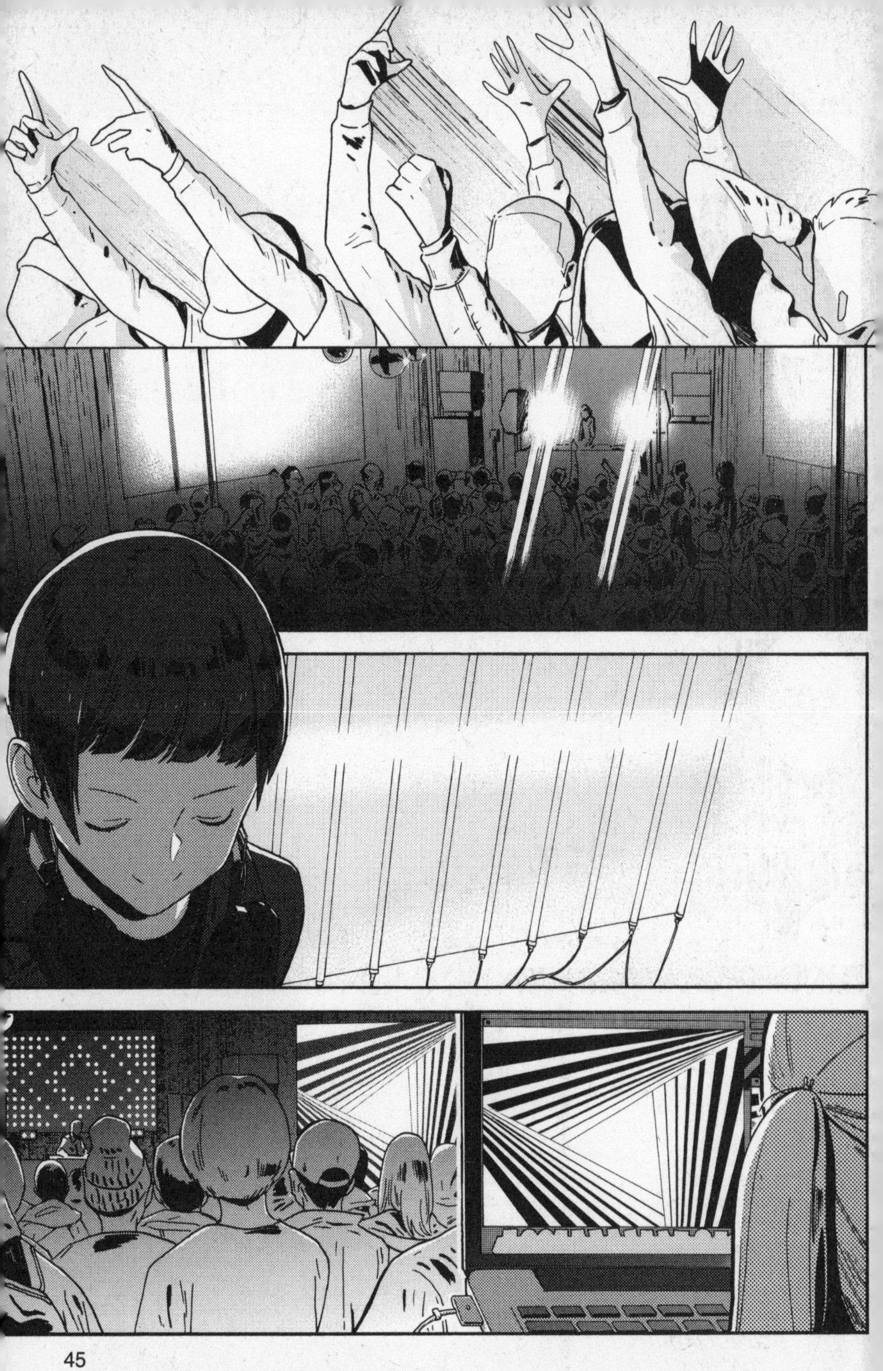

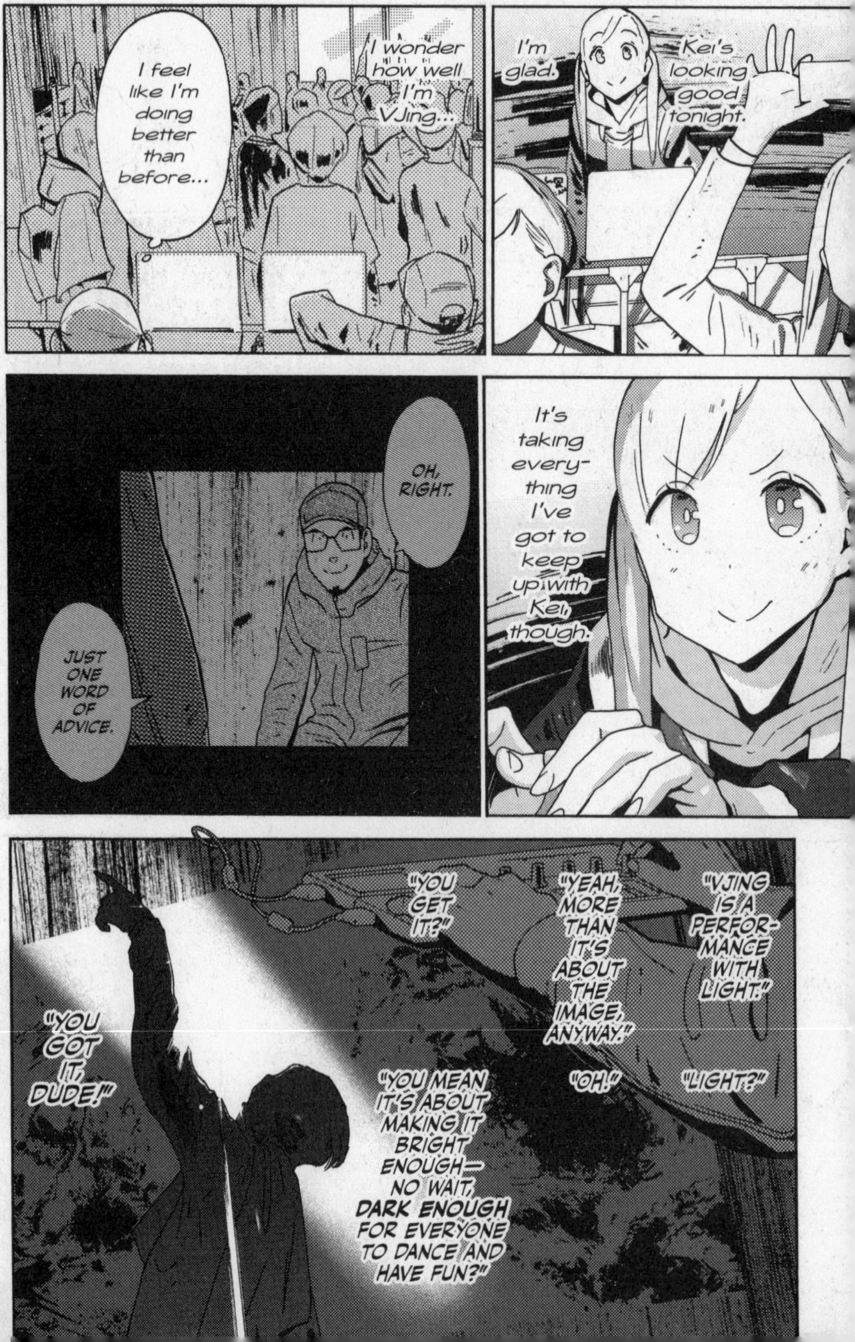
Kei's looking good tonight.
I'm glad.
I wonder how well I'm VJing...
I feel like I'm doing better than before...
It's taking every-thing I've got to keep up with Kei, though.
OH, RIGHT.
JUST ONE WORD OF ADVICE.
"VJING IS A PERFOR-MANCE WITH LIGHT."
"YEAH, MORE THAN IT'S ABOUT THE IMAGE, ANYWAY."
"YOU GET IT?"
"LIGHT?"
"OH."
"YOU MEAN IT'S ABOUT MAKING IT BRIGHT ENOUGH— NO WAIT, DARK ENOUGH FOR EVERYONE TO DANCE AND HAVE FUN?"
"YOU GOT IT, DUDE!"

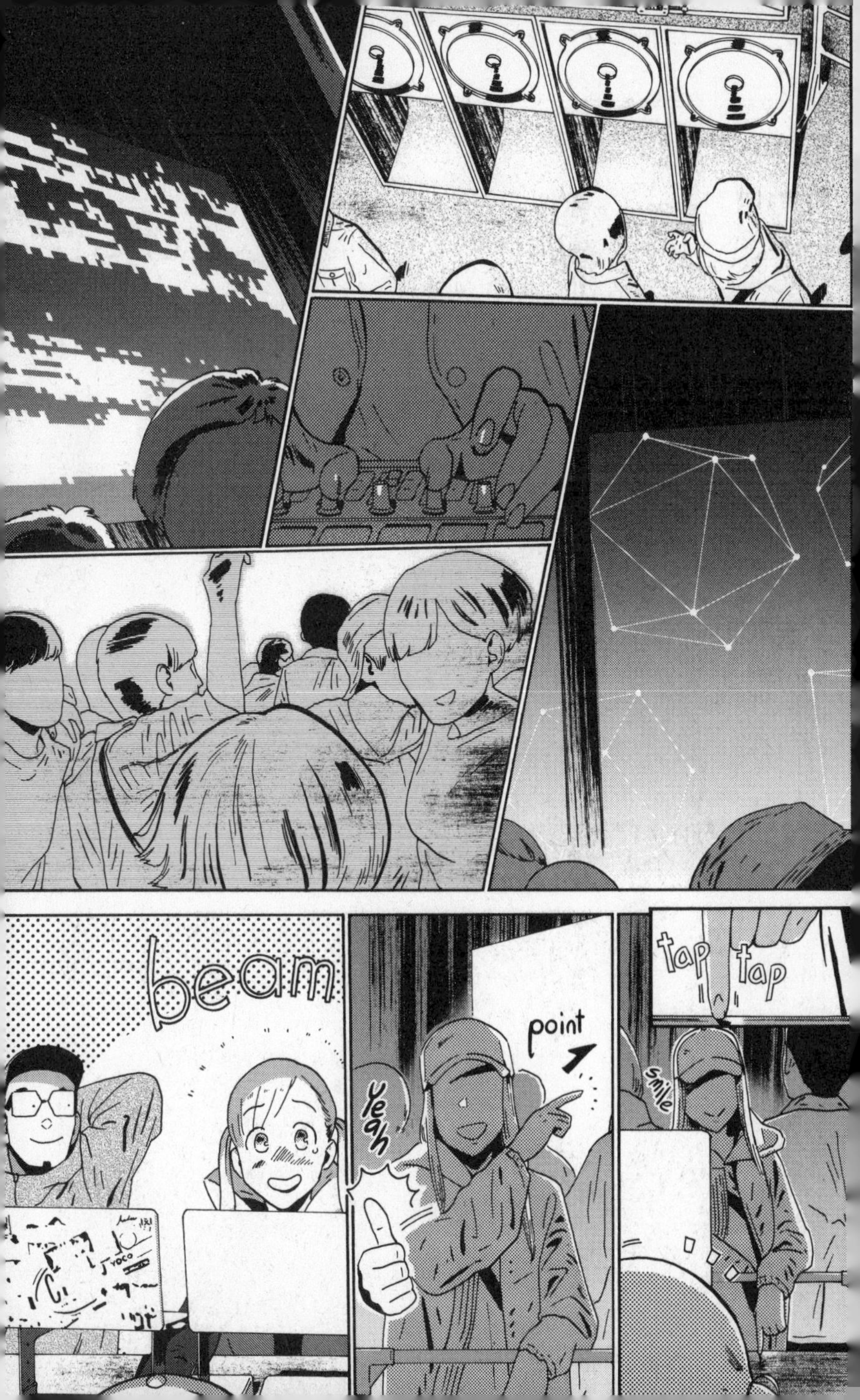
tap
tap
smile
point
Yeah
beam

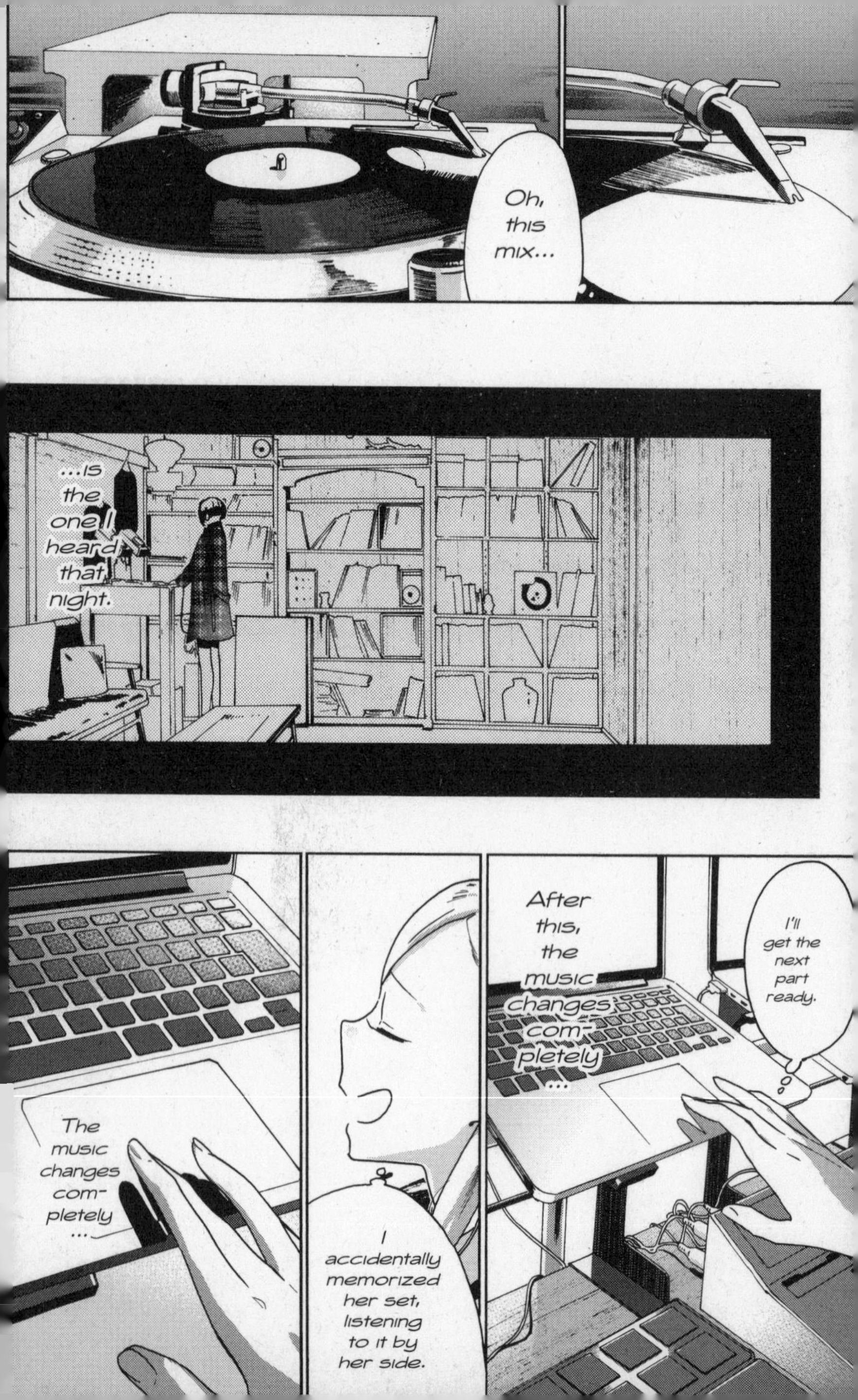
Oh, this mix...
...is the one I heard that night.
I'll get the next part ready.
After this, the music changes com-pletely...
I accidentally memorized her set, listening to it by her side.
The music changes com-pletely...

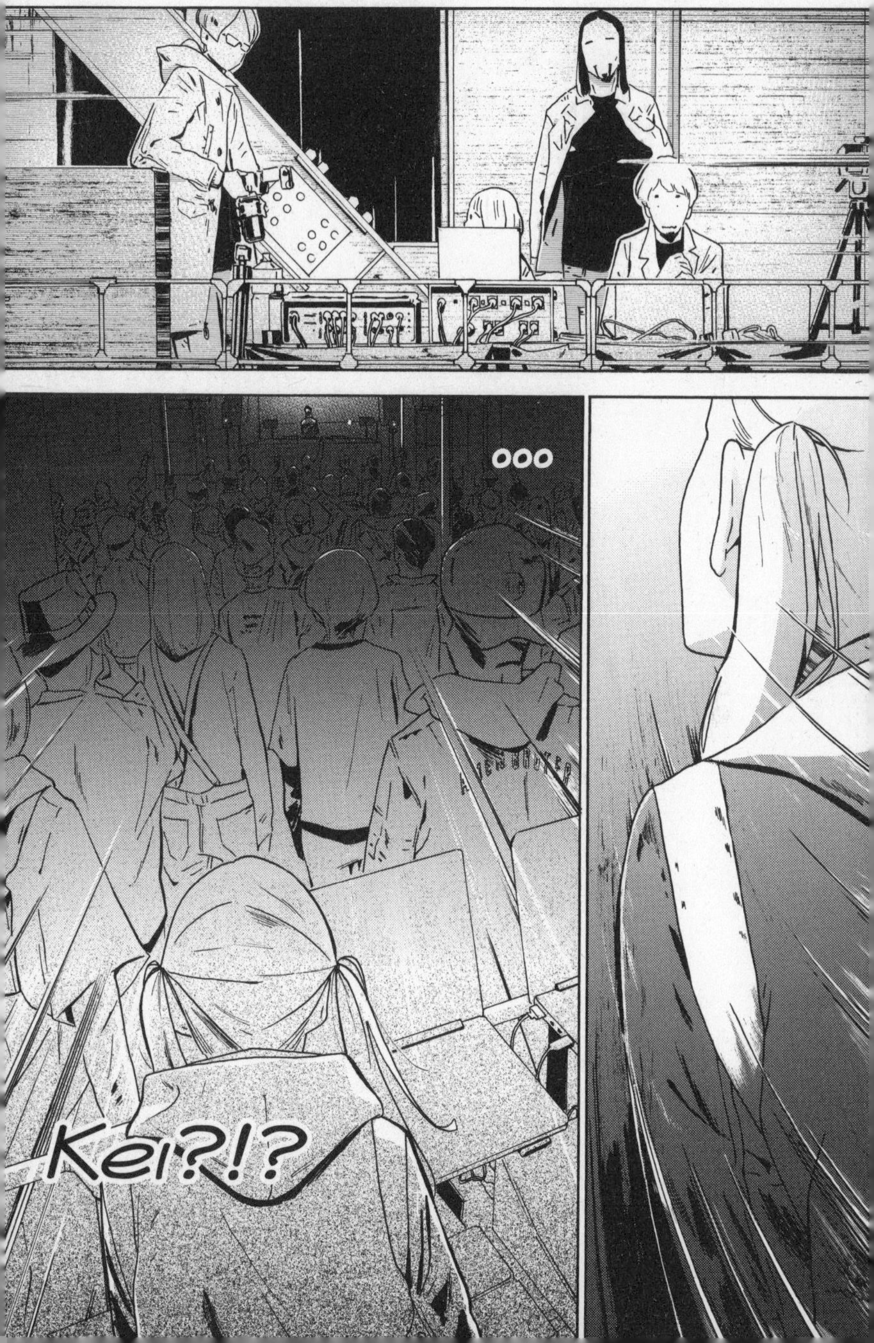
ooo
Kei?!?

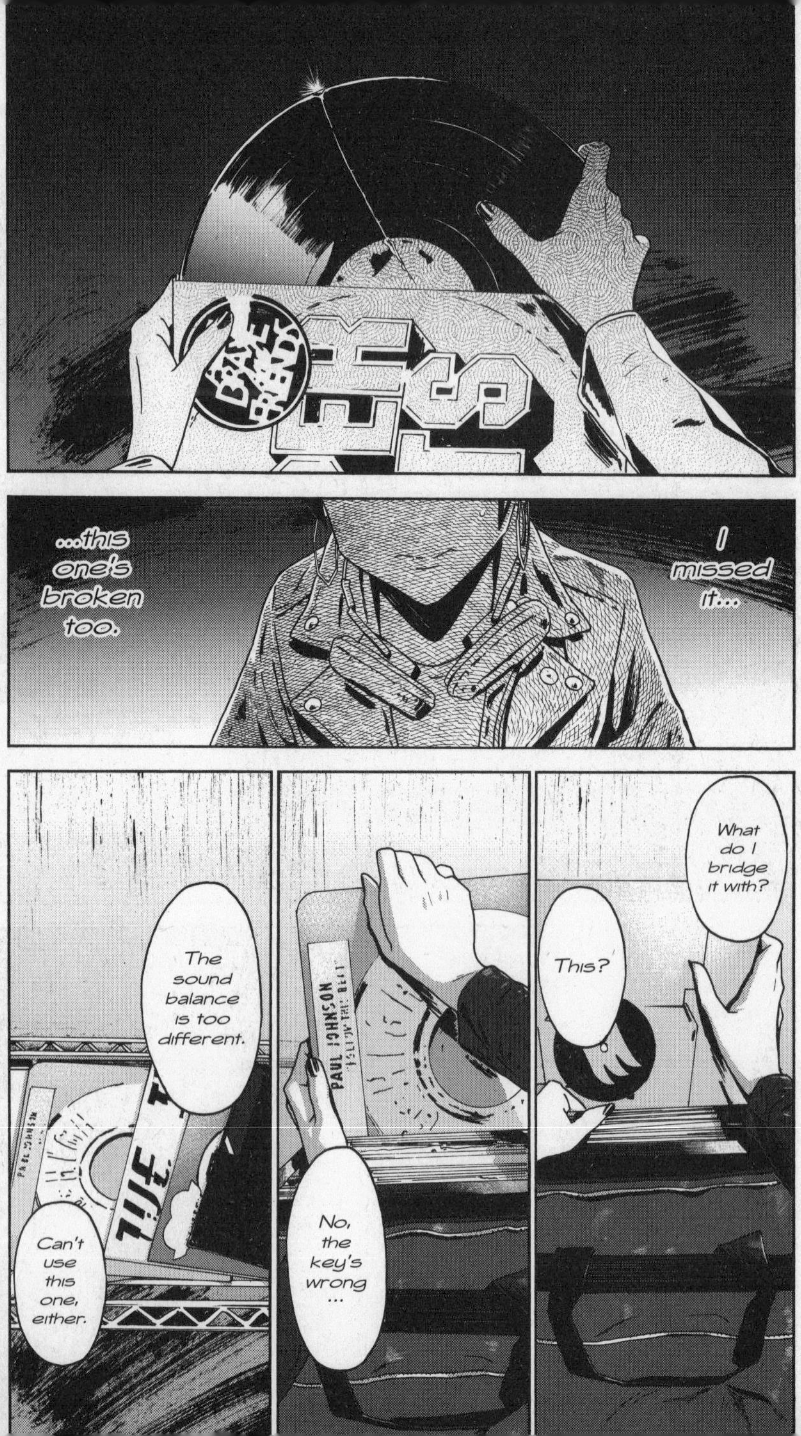
I missed it...
...this one's broken too.
What do I bridge it with?
This?
PAUL JOHNSON
No, the key's wrong ...
The sound balance is too different.
Can't use this one, either.

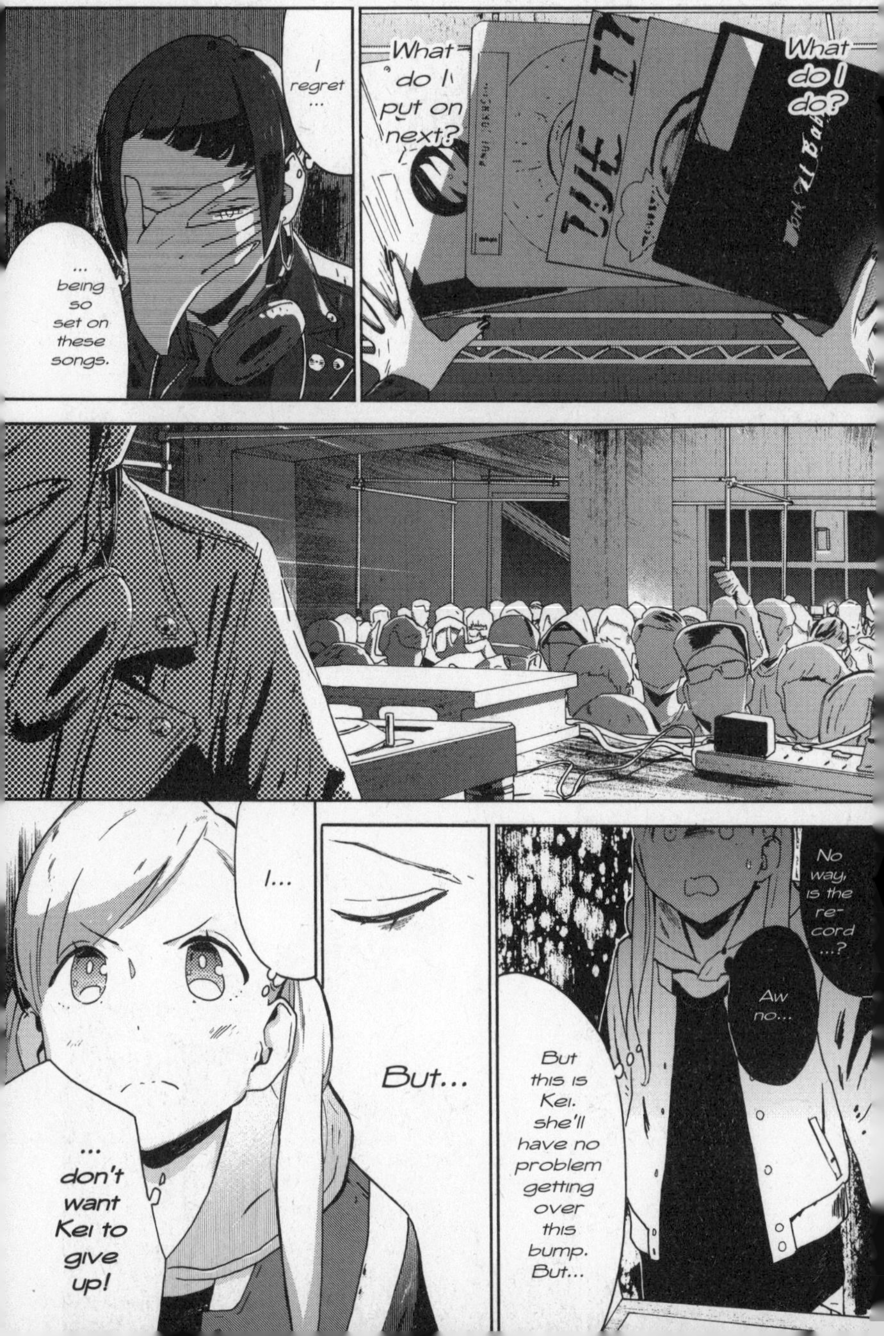
What do I do?
What do I put on next?
I regret ...
... being so set on these songs.
No way, is the re-cord ...?
Aw no...
But this is Kei. she'll have no problem getting over this bump. But...
But...
I...
... don't want Kei to give up!

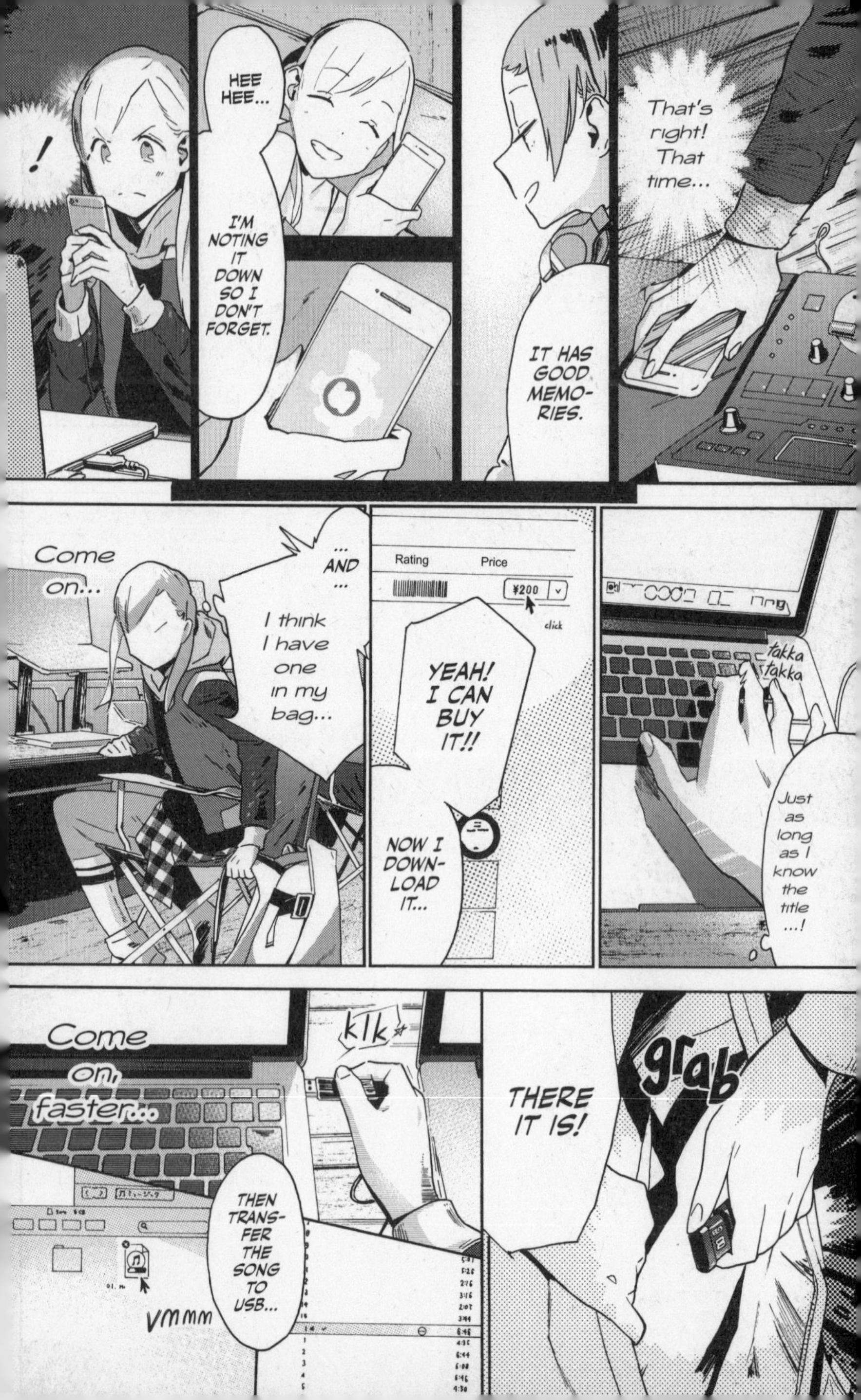
That's right! That time...
IT HAS GOOD MEMORIES.
HEE HEE...
I'M NOTING IT DOWN SO I DON'T FORGET.
!
takka takka
Just as long as I know the title ...!
Rating
Price
¥200
click
YEAH! I CAN BUY IT!!
NOW I DOWNLOAD IT...
... AND ...
I think I have one in my bag...
Come on...
grab
THERE IT IS!
klk
Come on, faster...
THEN TRANSFER THE SONG TO USB...
vmmm

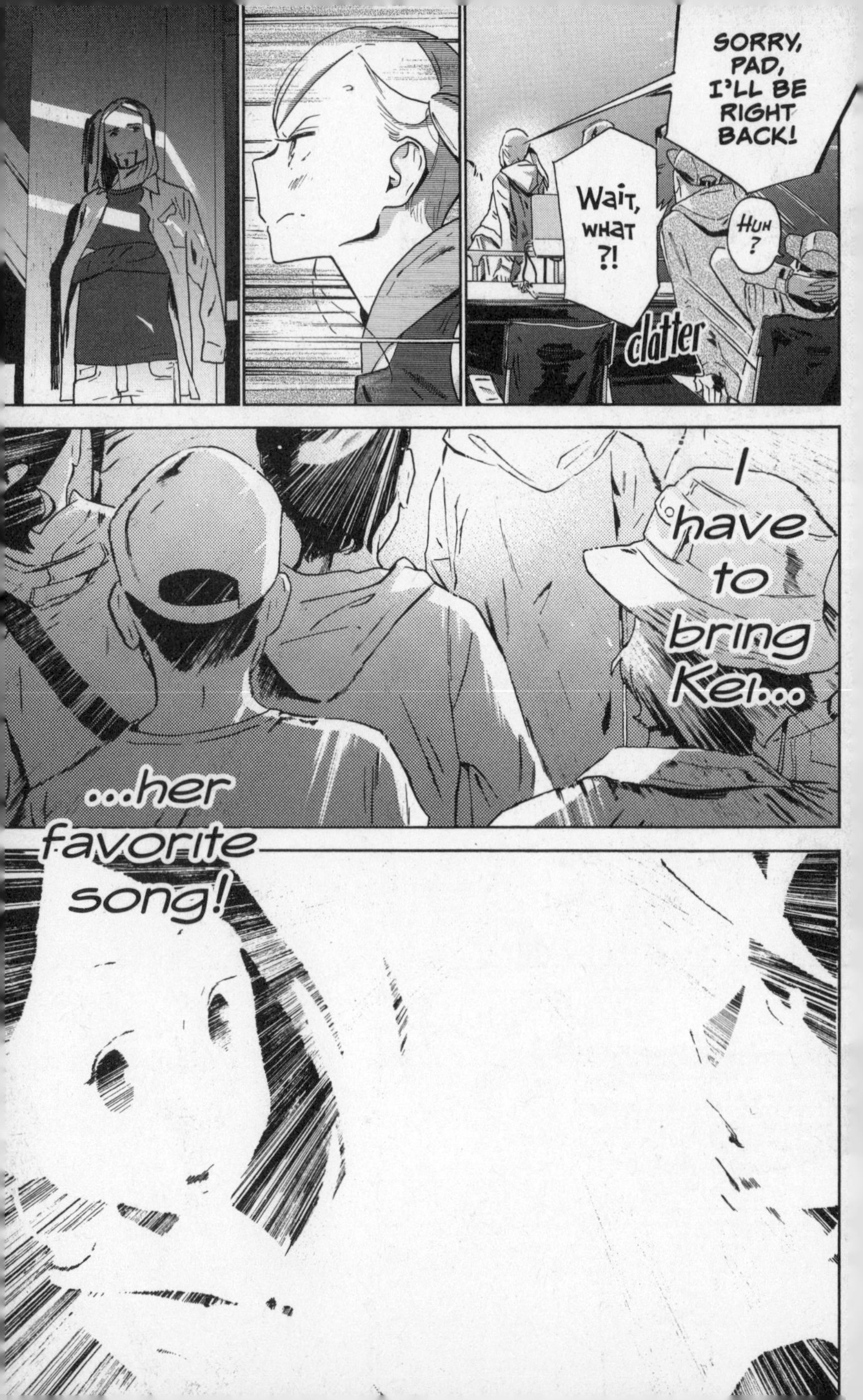
SORRY, PAD, I'LL BE RIGHT BACK!
HUH?
Wait, what?!
clatter
I have to bring Kei...
...her favorite song!

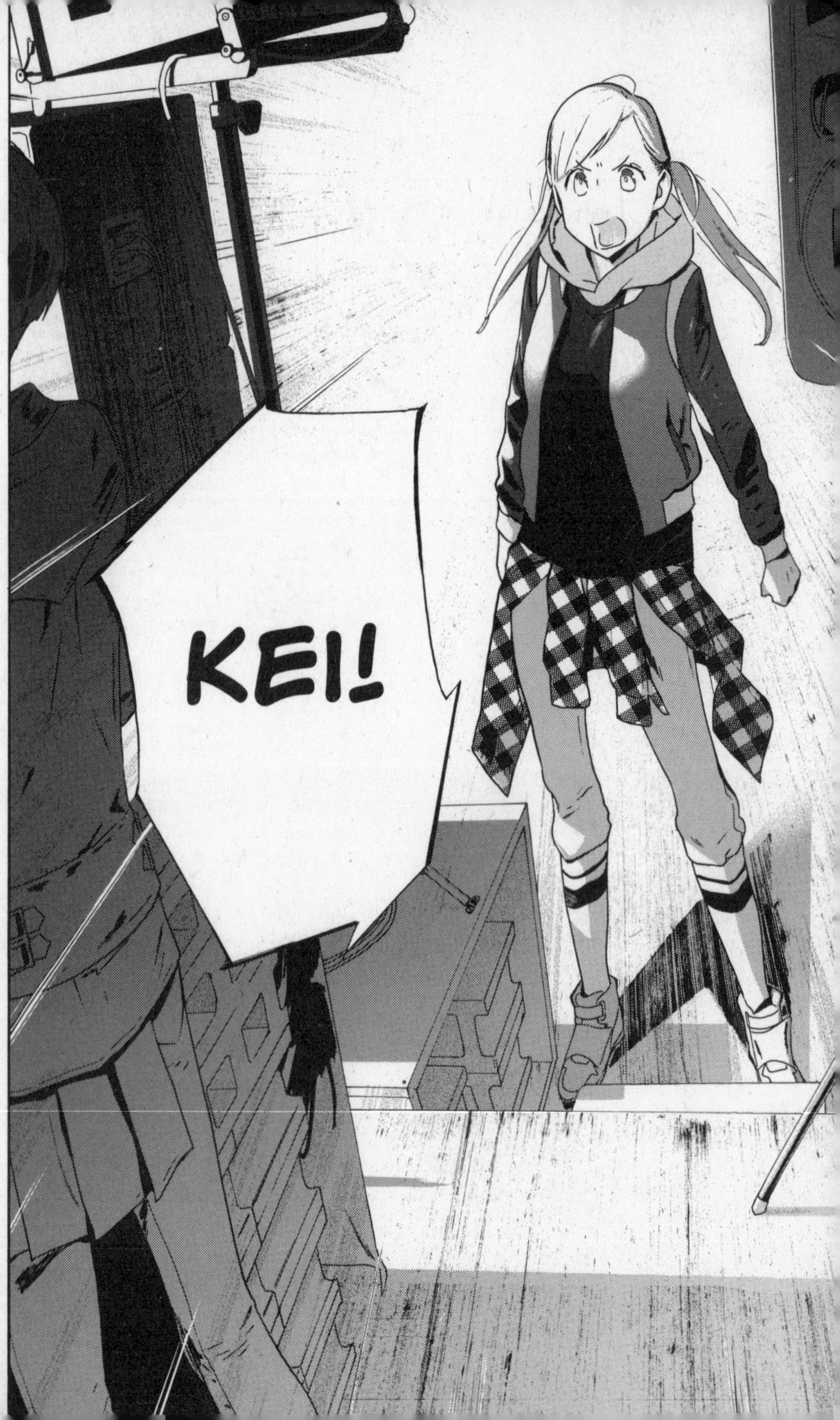
KEI!

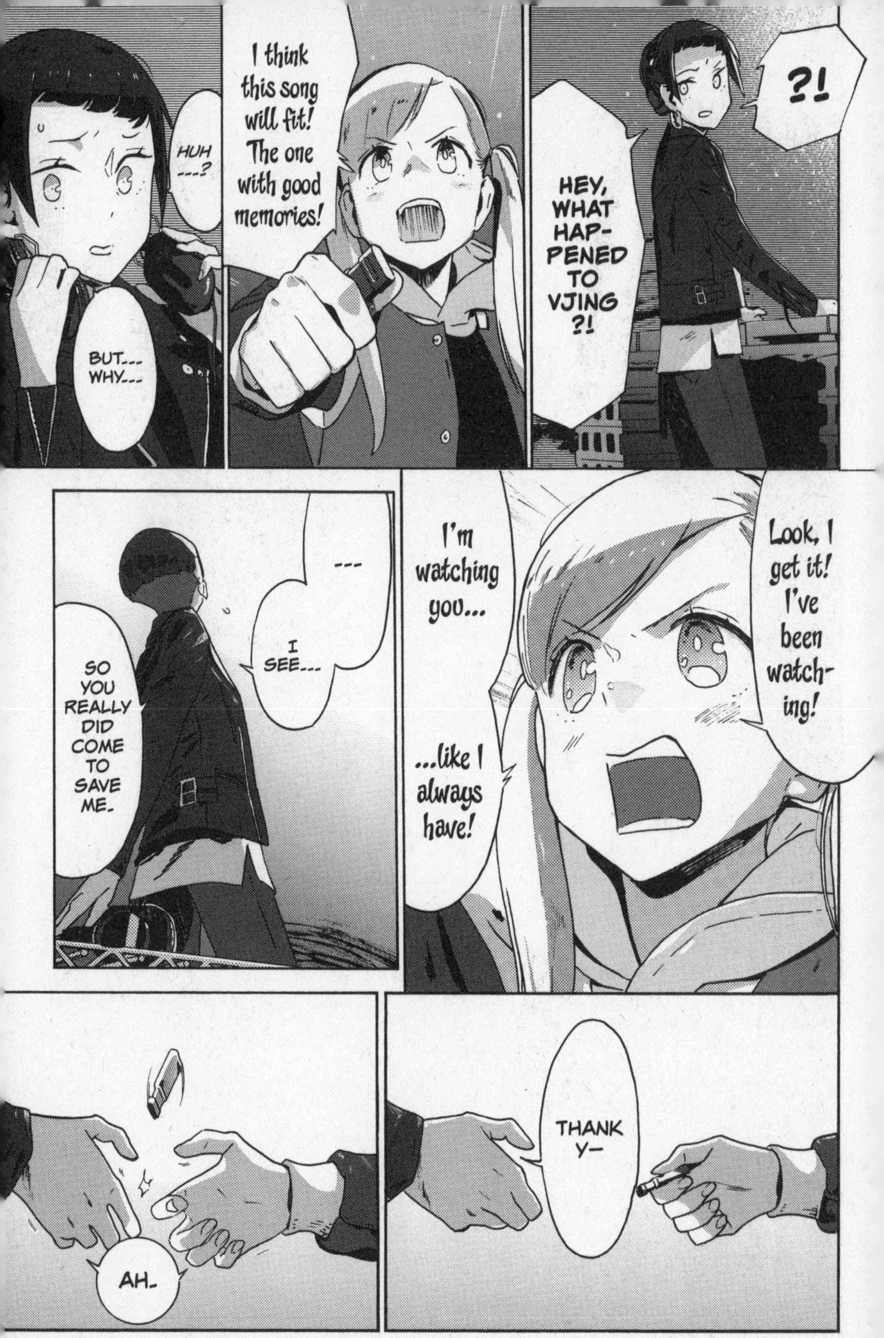
?!
HEY, WHAT HAP-PENED TO VJING ?!
I think this song will fit! The one with good memories!
HUH ---?
BUT--- WHY---
Look, I get it! I've been watch-ing!
I'm watching you...
...like I always have!
--- I SEE---
SO YOU REALLY DID COME TO SAVE ME.
THANK Y-
AH.

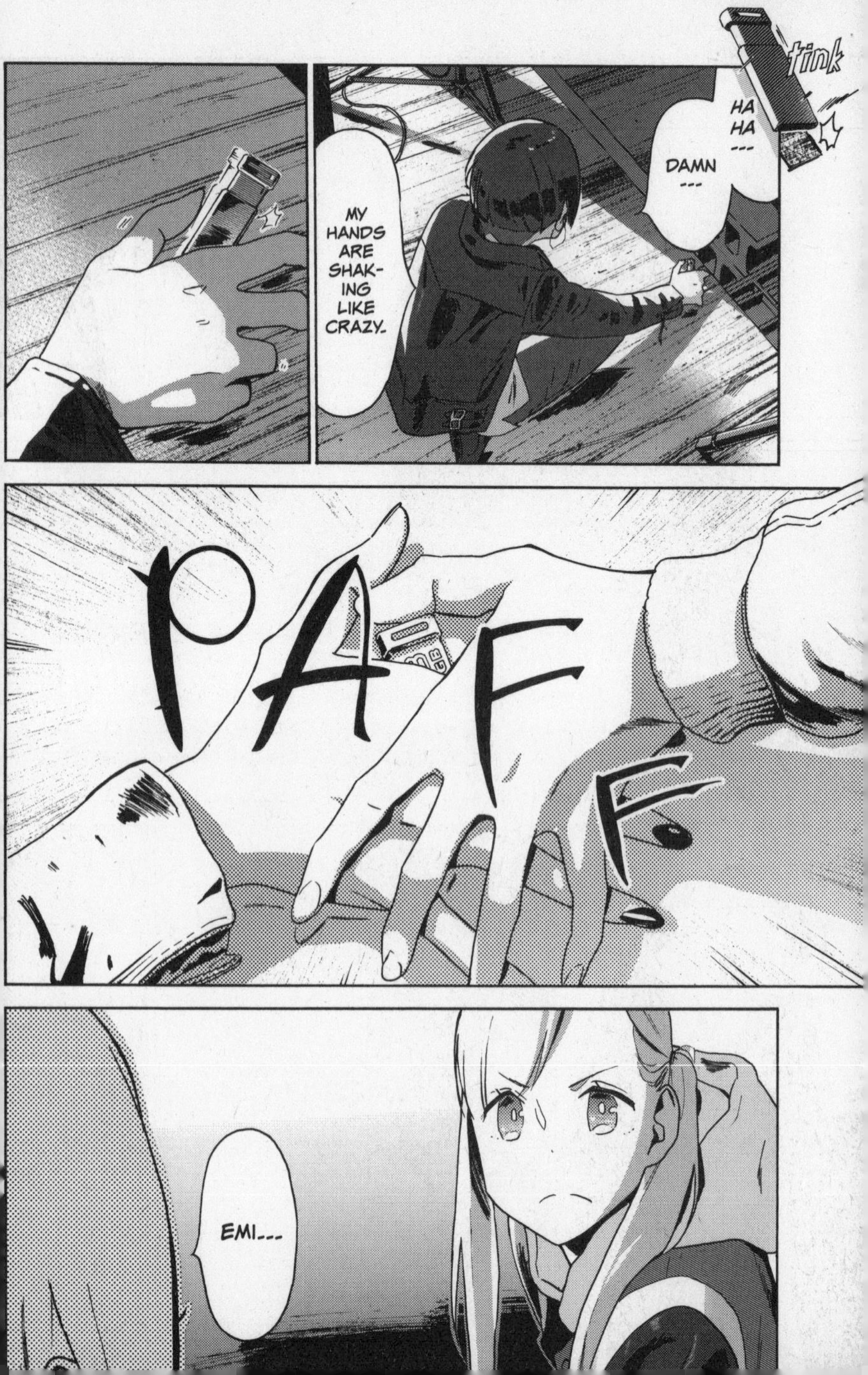
tink
HA HA --- DAMN ---
MY HANDS ARE SHAK-ING LIKE CRAZY.
PAFFF
EMI...

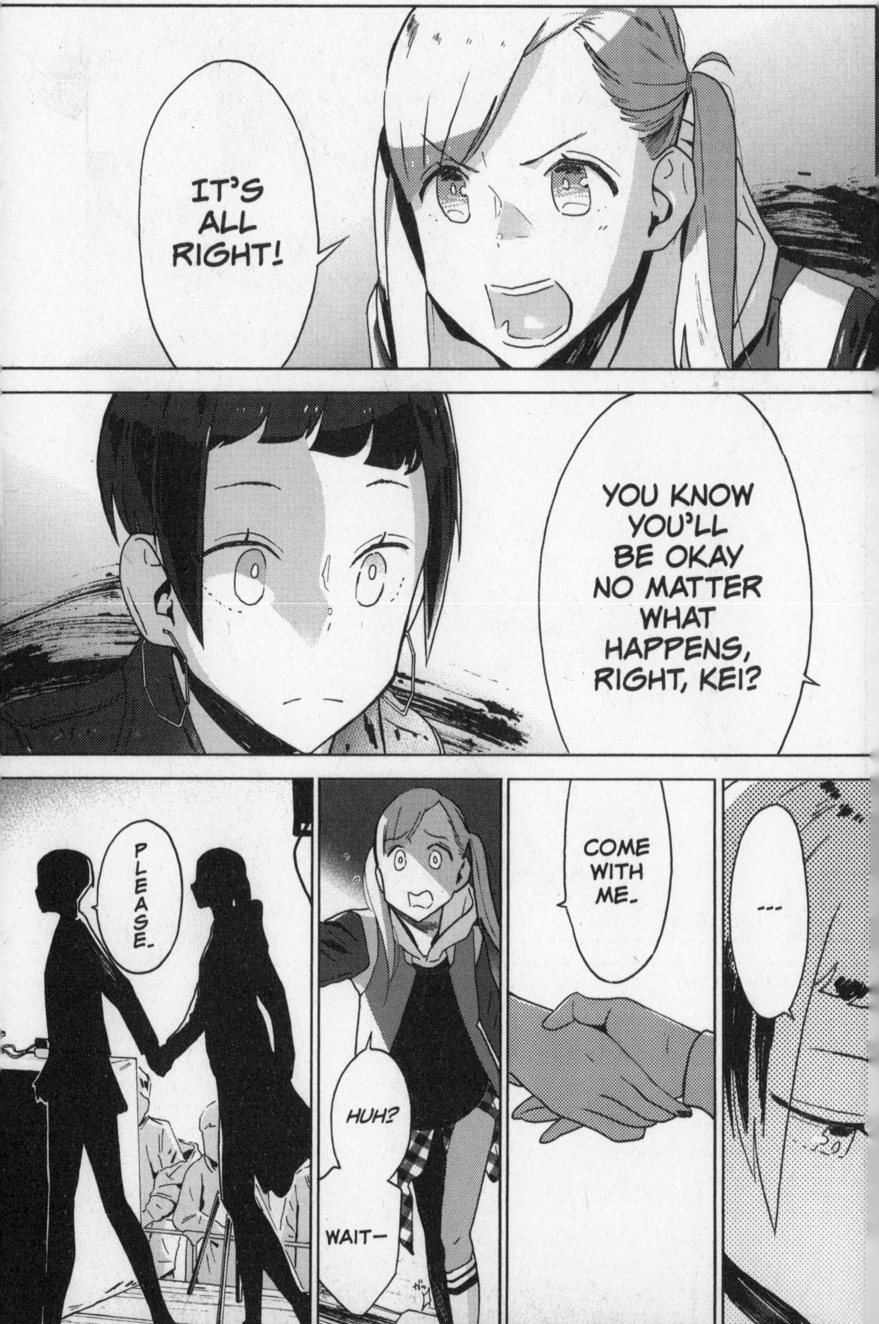
IT'S ALL RIGHT!
YOU KNOW YOU'LL BE OKAY NO MATTER WHAT HAPPENS, RIGHT, KEI?

COME WITH ME.
HUH?
WAIT—
PLEASE.

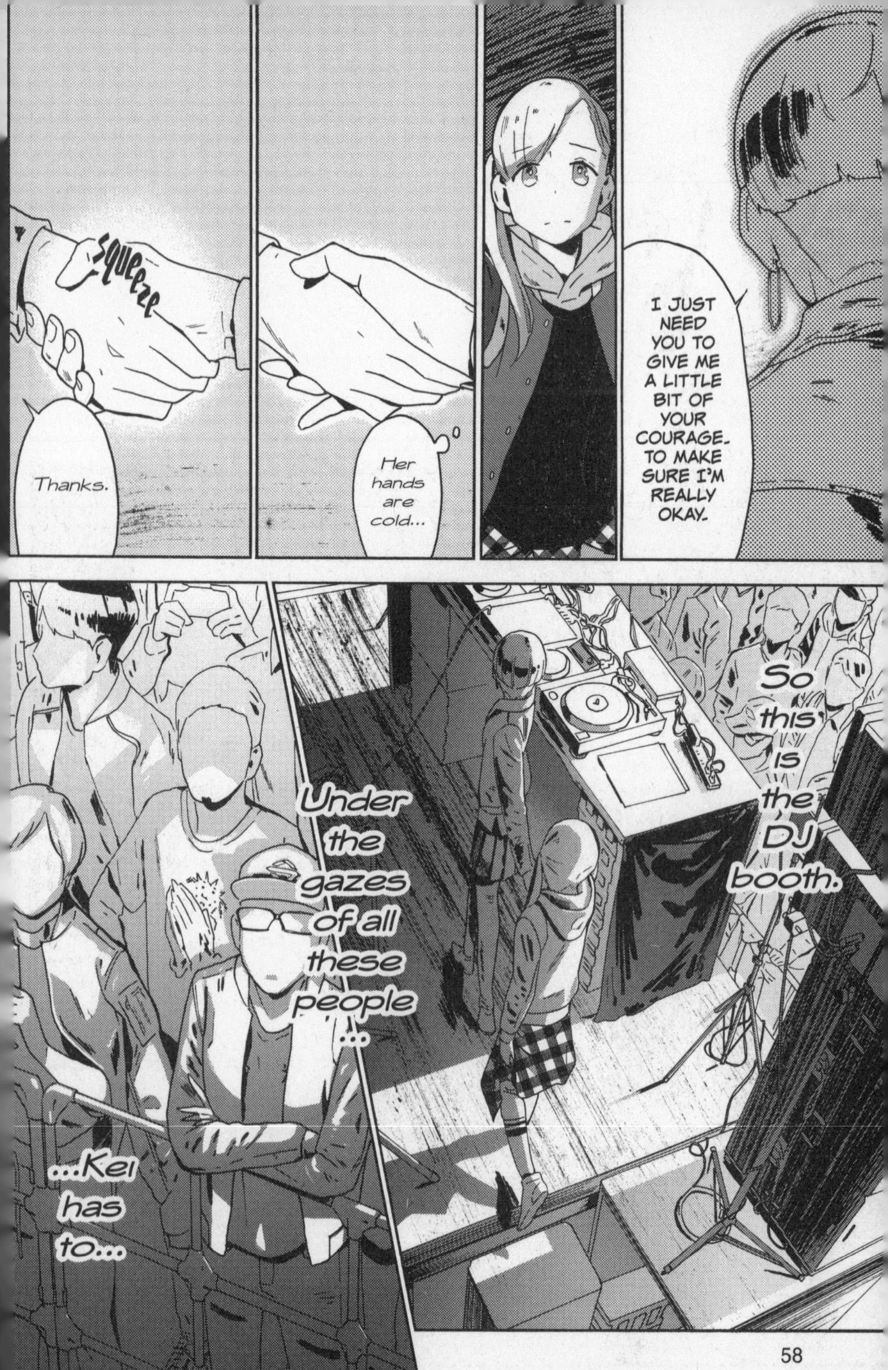
I JUST NEED YOU TO GIVE ME A LITTLE BIT OF YOUR COURAGE. TO MAKE SURE I'M REALLY OKAY.
Her hands are cold...
squeeze
Thanks.
So this is the DJ booth.
Under the gazes of all these people...
...Kei has to...

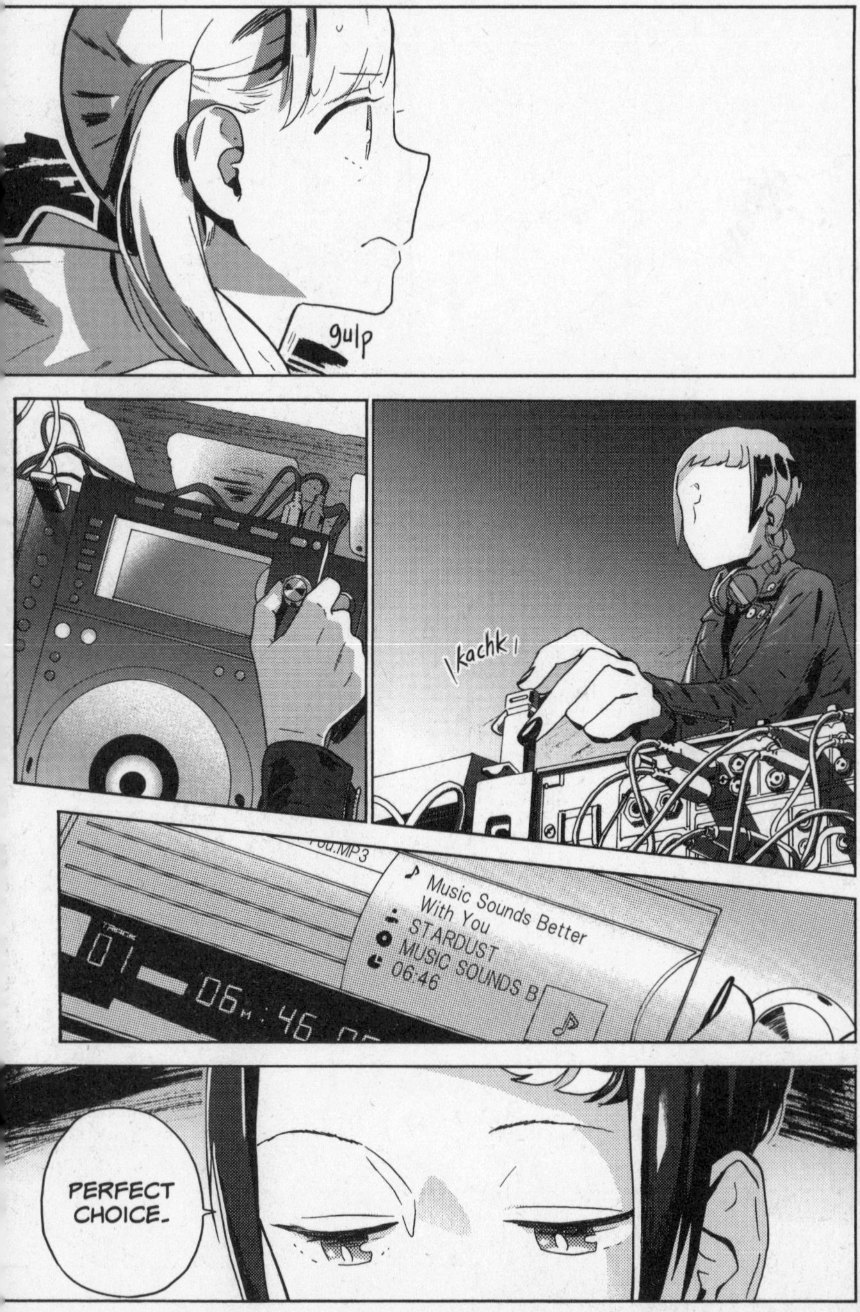
gulp
kachk
...ou.MP3
Music Sounds Better
With You
STARDUST
MUSIC SOUNDS B
06:46
01
06M:46
PERFECT CHOICE.

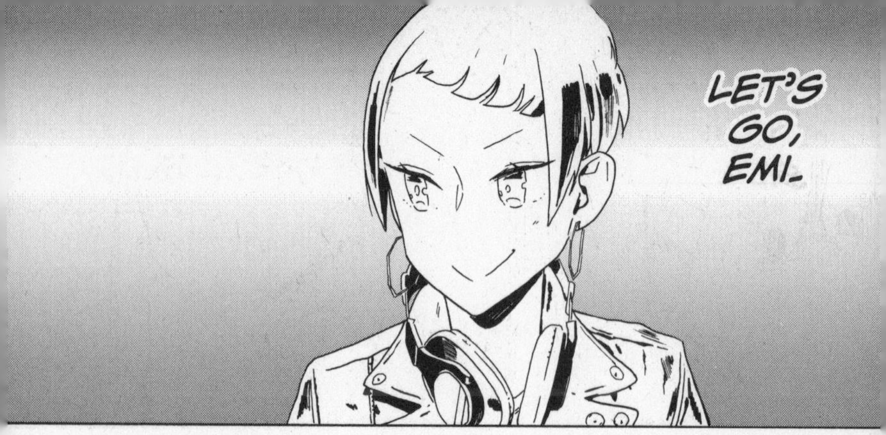
LET'S GO, EMI...

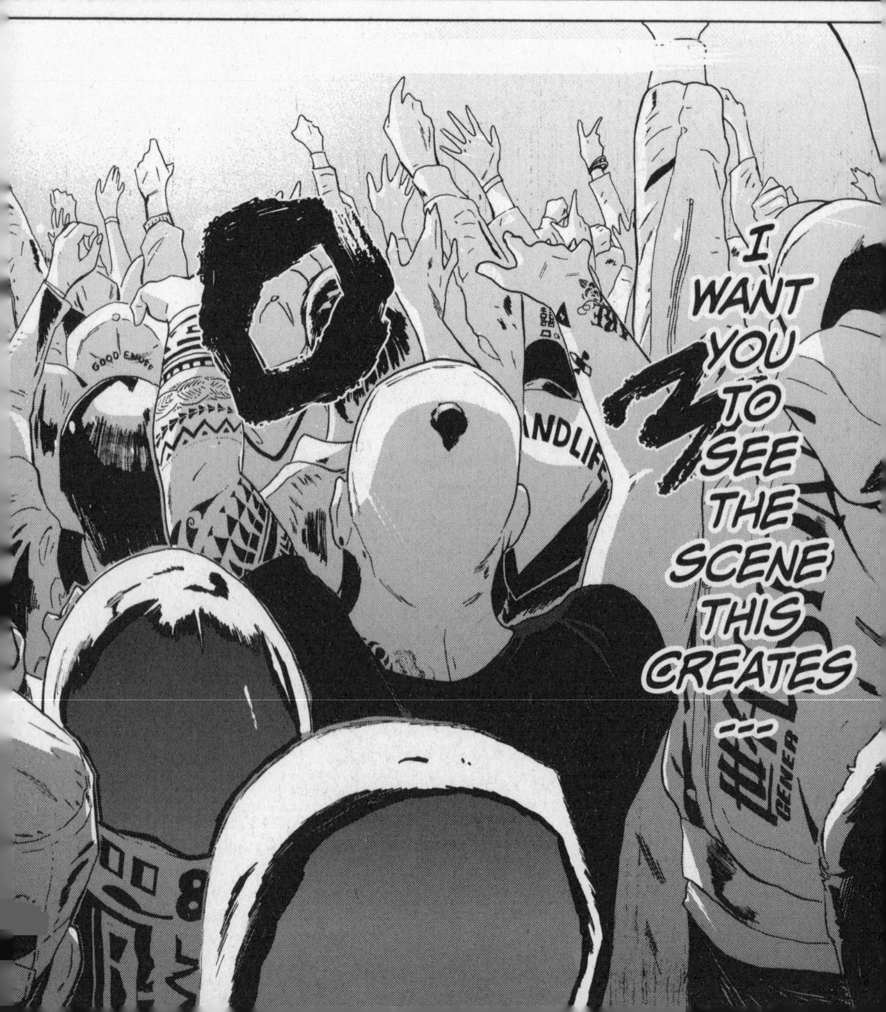
I WANT YOU TO SEE THE SCENE THIS CREATES...
GOOD ENUFF
ANDLIFE

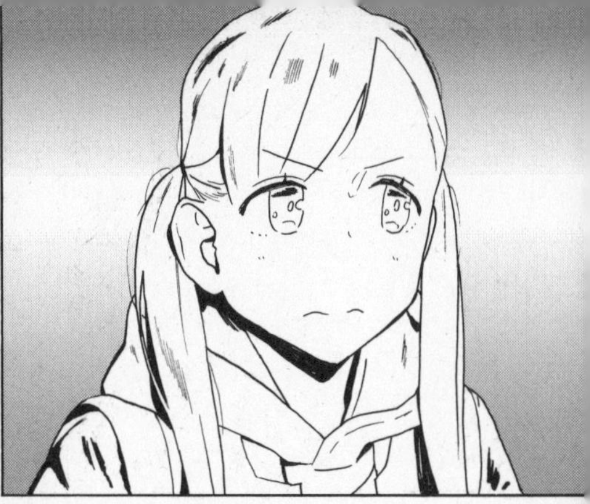
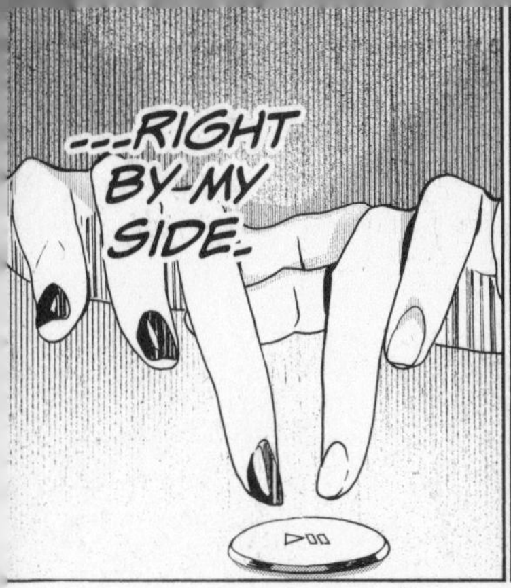
---RIGHT BY MY SIDE...
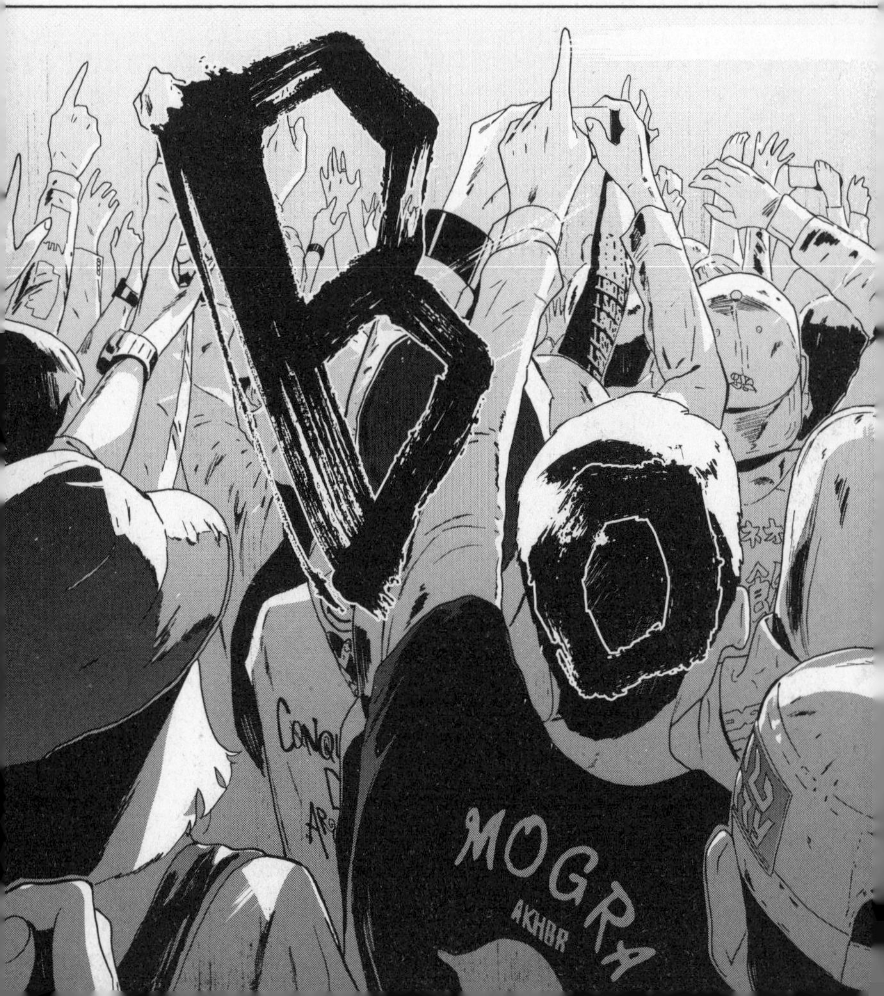
MOGRA
AKHBR

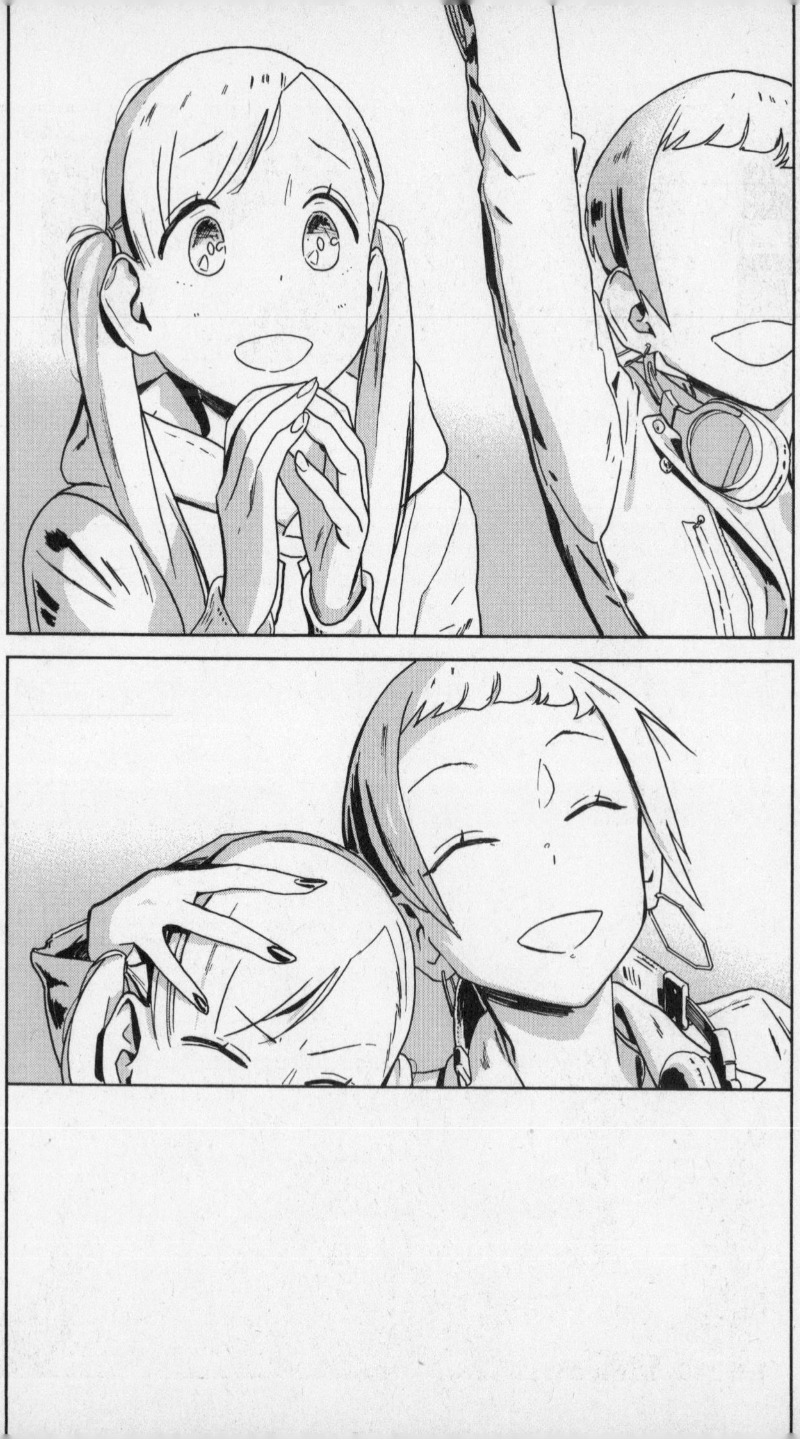

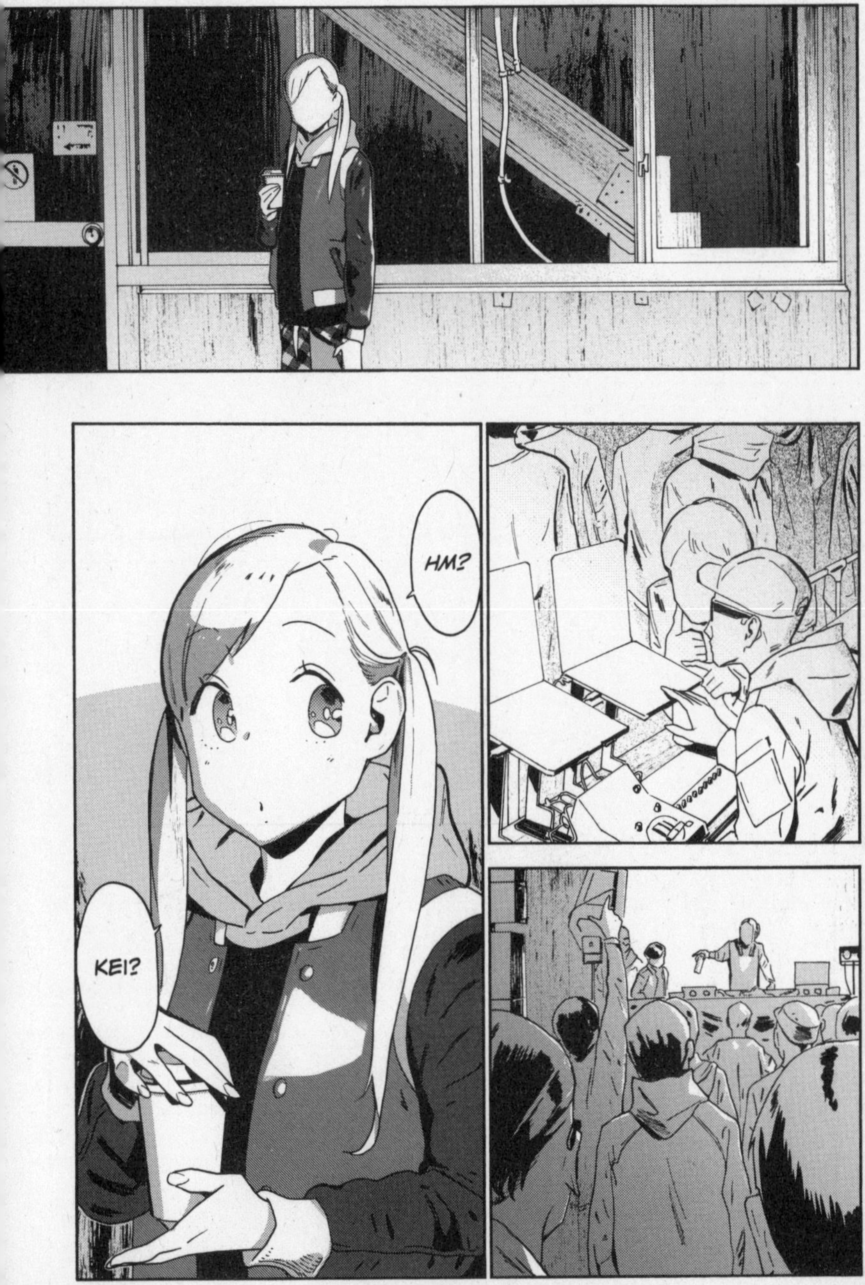
HM?
KEI?

VMM———M
VMM———M

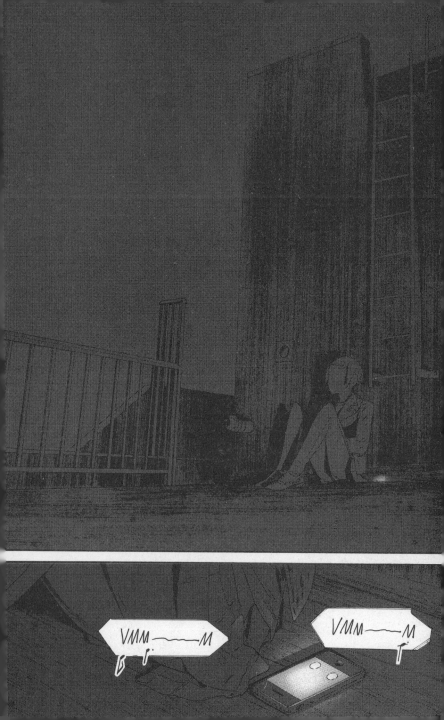

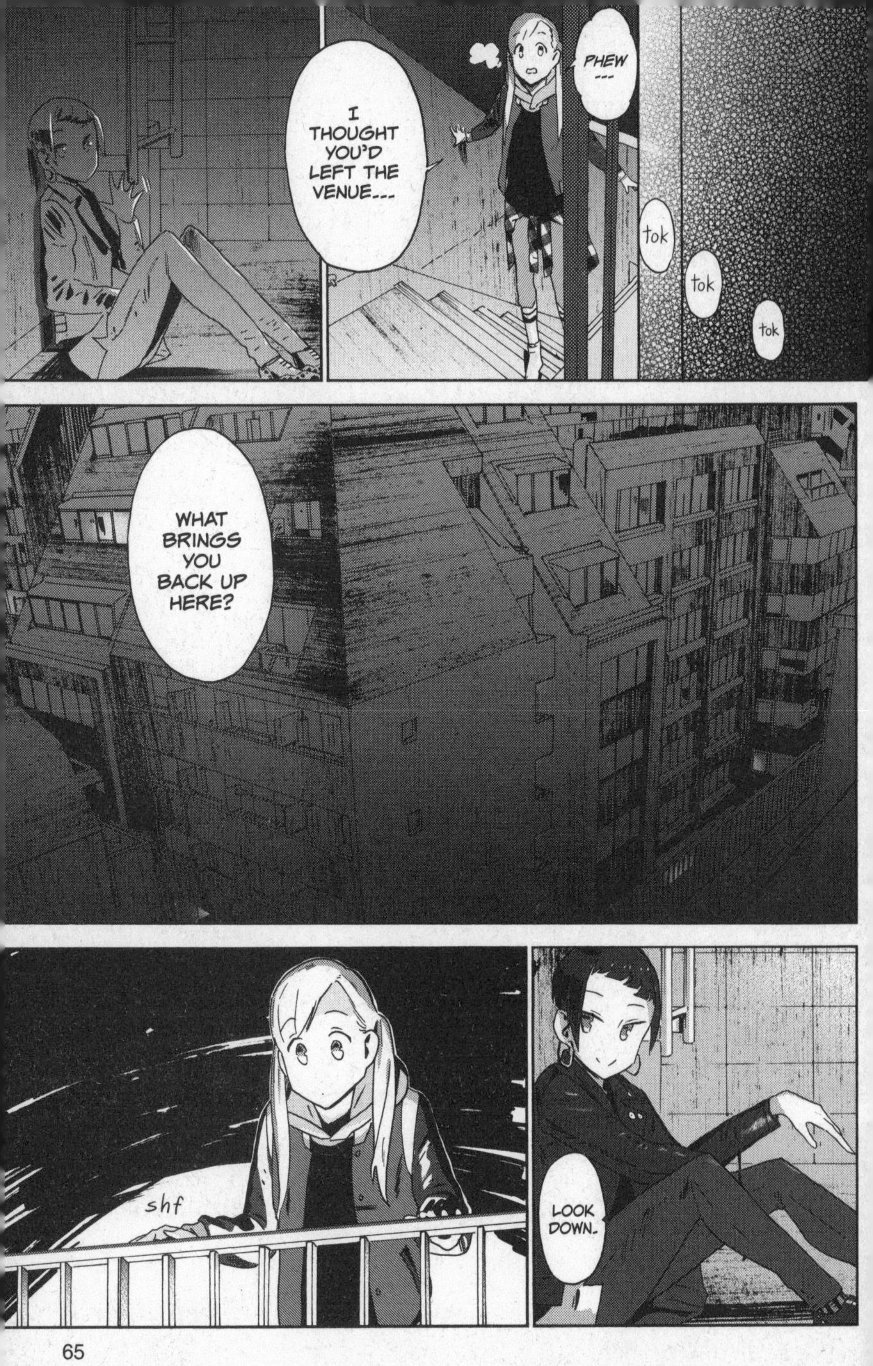
tok
tok
tok
PHEW ---
I THOUGHT YOU'D LEFT THE VENUE---
WHAT BRINGS YOU BACK UP HERE?
LOOK DOWN.
shf

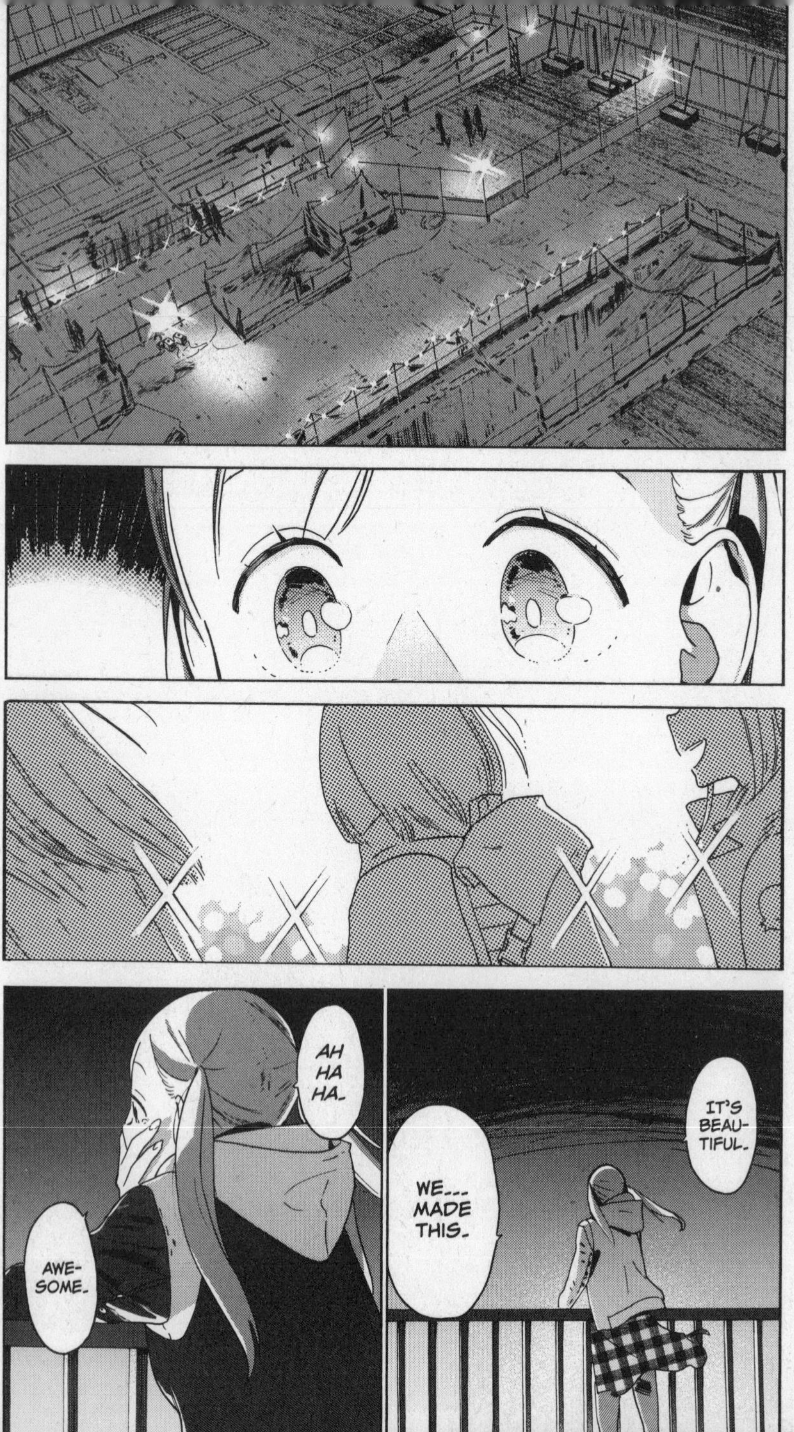
IT'S BEAU-TIFUL...
WE... MADE THIS...
AH HA HA...
AWE-SOME...

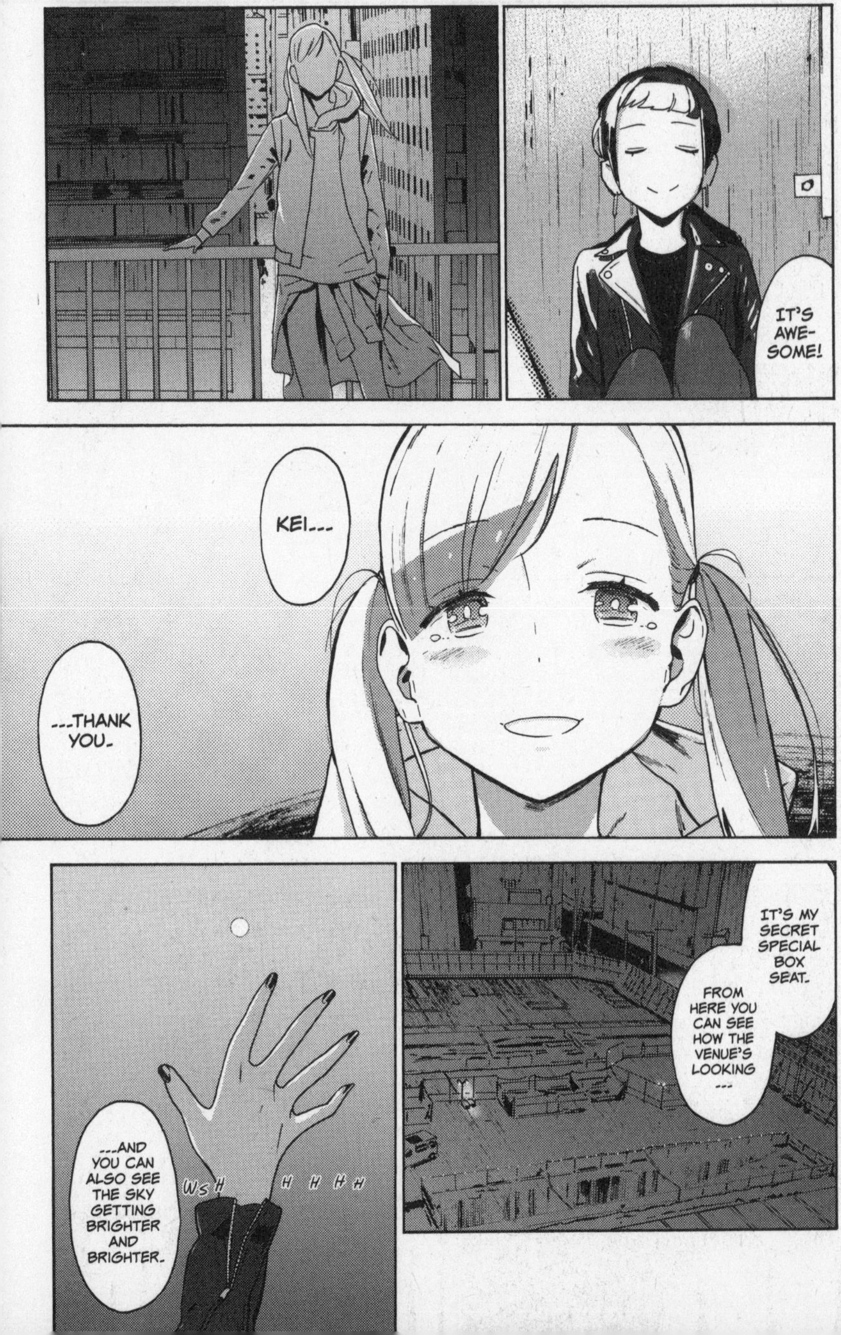
IT'S AWE-SOME!
KEI...
...THANK YOU.
IT'S MY SECRET SPECIAL BOX SEAT.
FROM HERE YOU CAN SEE HOW THE VENUE'S LOOKING...
...AND YOU CAN ALSO SEE THE SKY GETTING BRIGHTER AND BRIGHTER.
WSHHHHH

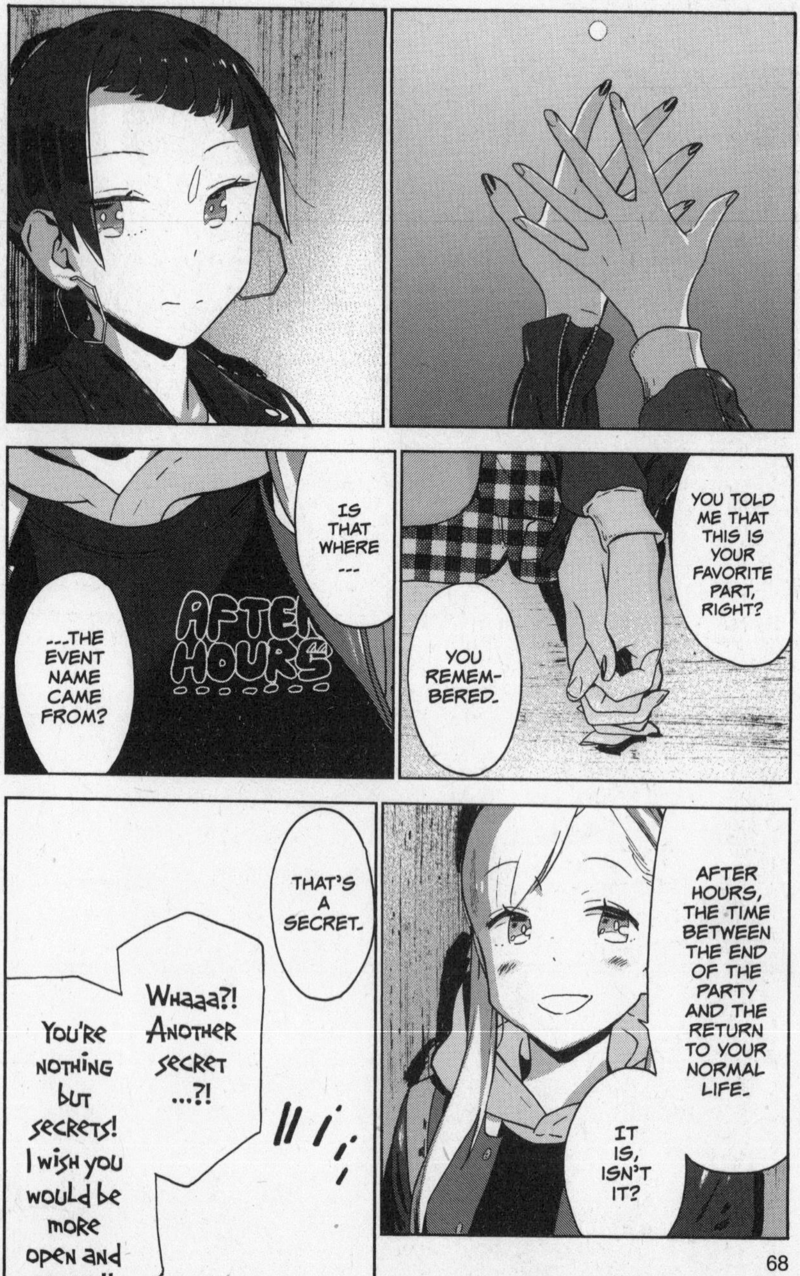
YOU TOLD ME THAT THIS IS YOUR FAVORITE PART, RIGHT?
YOU REMEMBERED.
IS THAT WHERE---
---THE EVENT NAME CAME FROM?
AFTER HOURS, THE TIME BETWEEN THE END OF THE PARTY AND THE RETURN TO YOUR NORMAL LIFE.
IT IS, ISN'T IT?
THAT'S A SECRET.
Whaaa?! Another secret ...?!
You're nothing but secrets! I wish you would be more open and honest!!

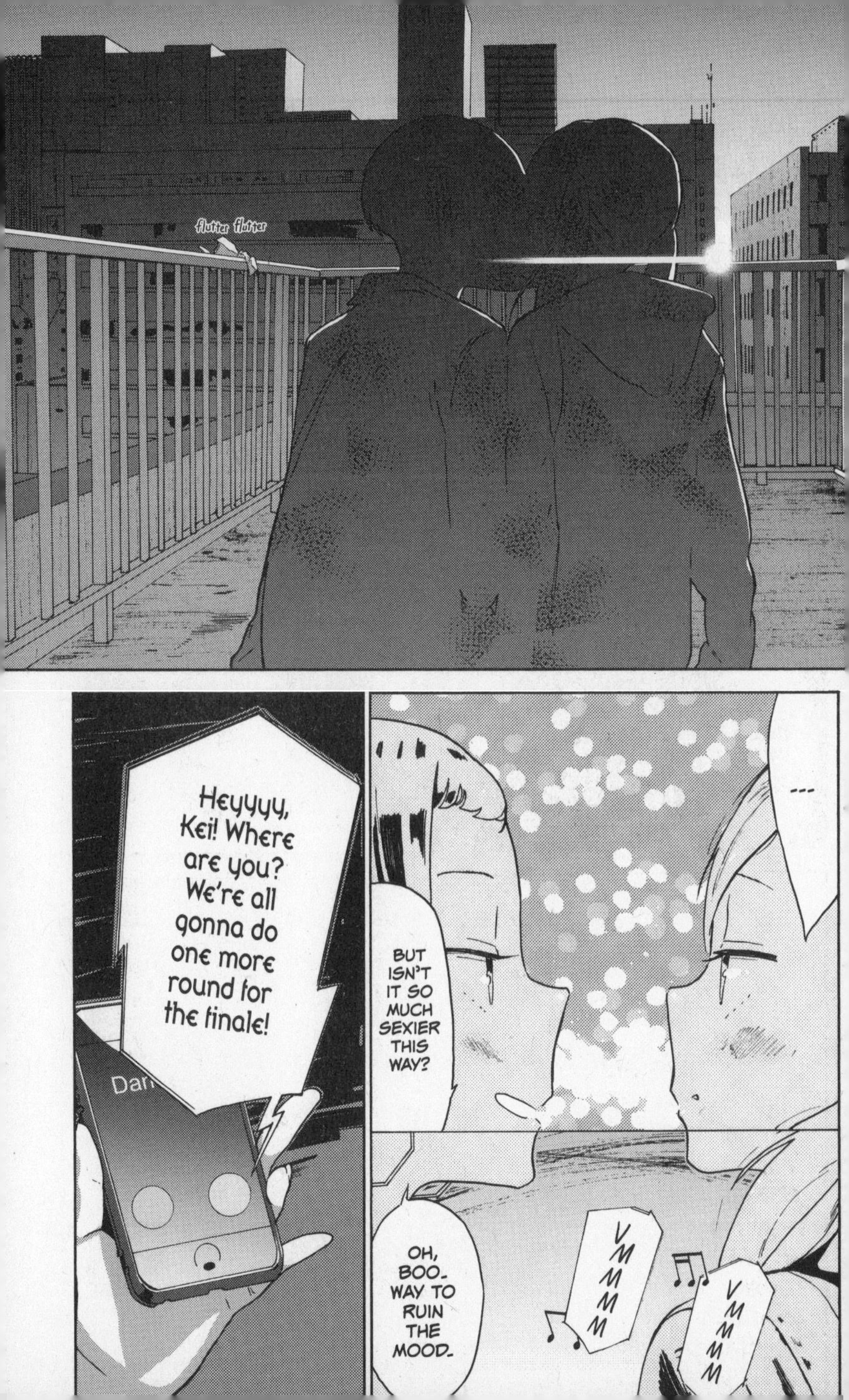
flutter flutter

BUT ISN'T IT SO MUCH SEXIER THIS WAY?
VMMMM
VMMMM
OH, BOO- WAY TO RUIN THE MOOD.
Heyyyy, Kei! Where are you? We're all gonna do one more round for the finale!

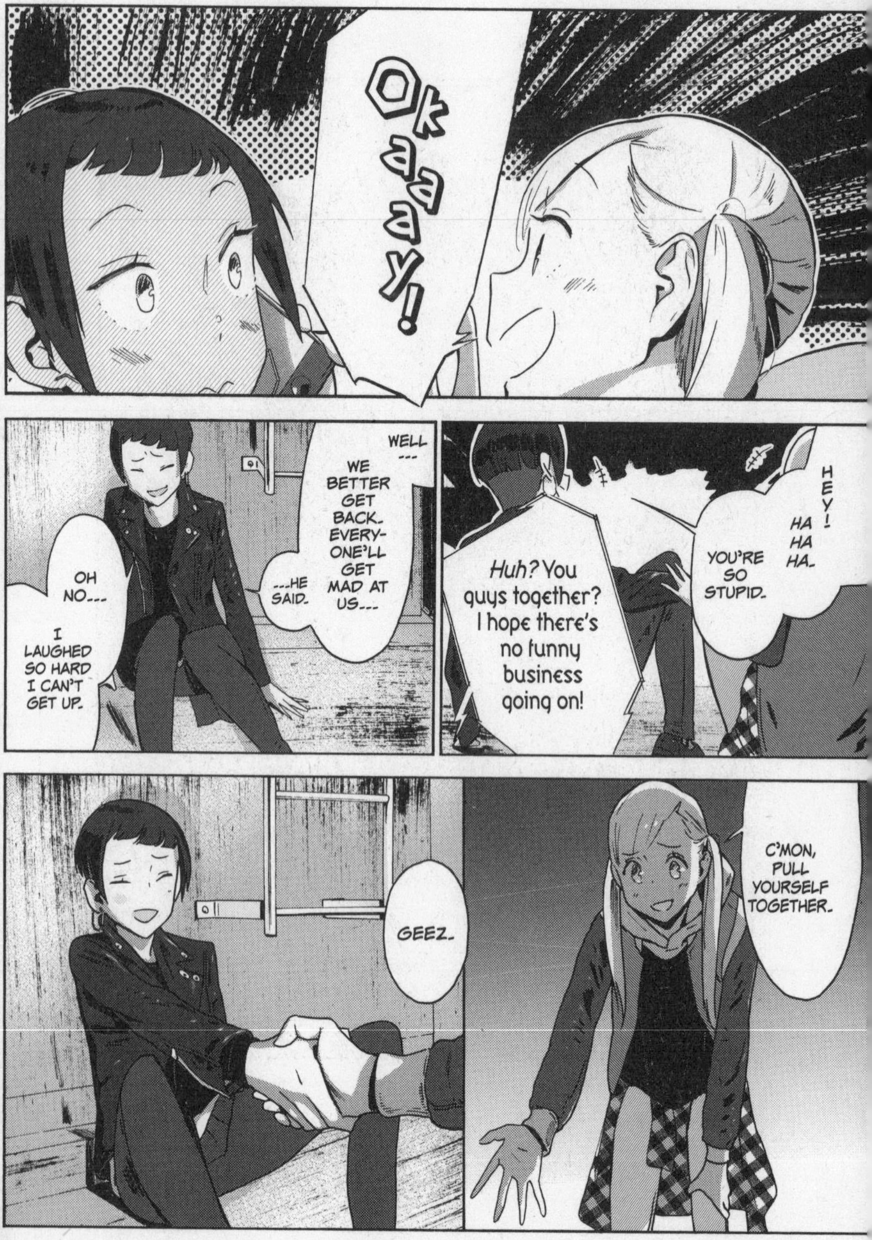
Okaaay!
HEY!
HA HA HA.
YOU'RE SO STUPID.
Huh? You guys together? I hope there's no funny business going on!
WELL--- WE BETTER GET BACK. EVERYONE'LL GET MAD AT US---
---HE SAID.
OH NO--- I LAUGHED SO HARD I CAN'T GET UP.
C'MON, PULL YOURSELF TOGETHER.
GEEZ.

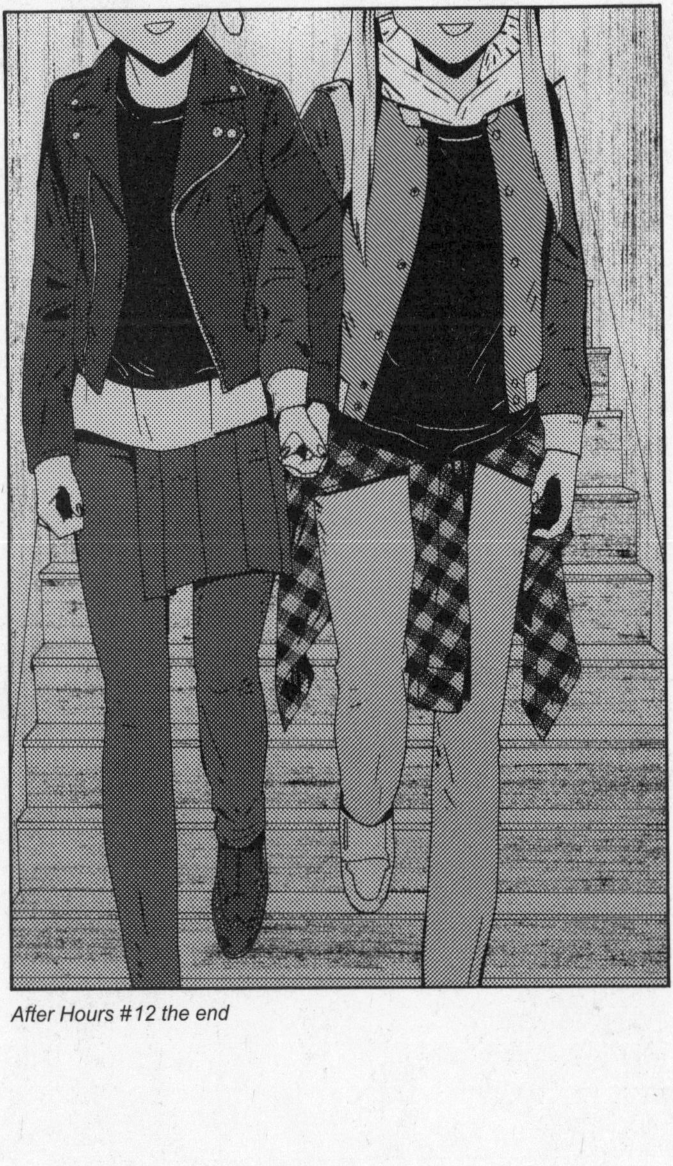

After Hours #12 the end

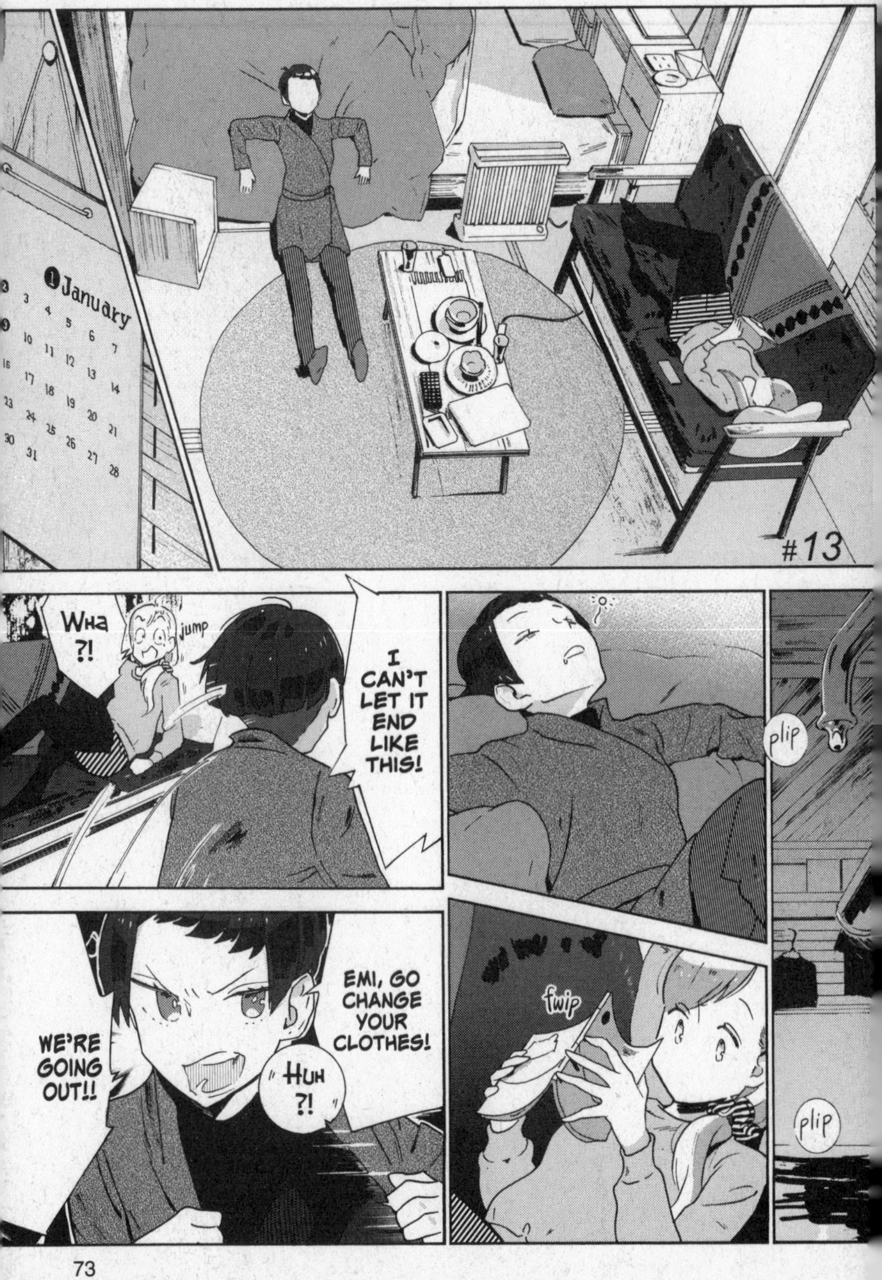
January
#13
plip
I CAN'T LET IT END LIKE THIS!
WHA ?!
jump
plip
fwip
EMI, GO CHANGE YOUR CLOTHES!
HUH ?!
WE'RE GOING OUT!!

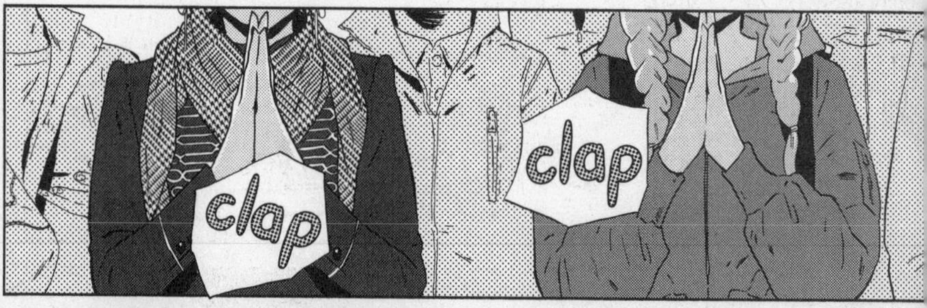
clap
clap

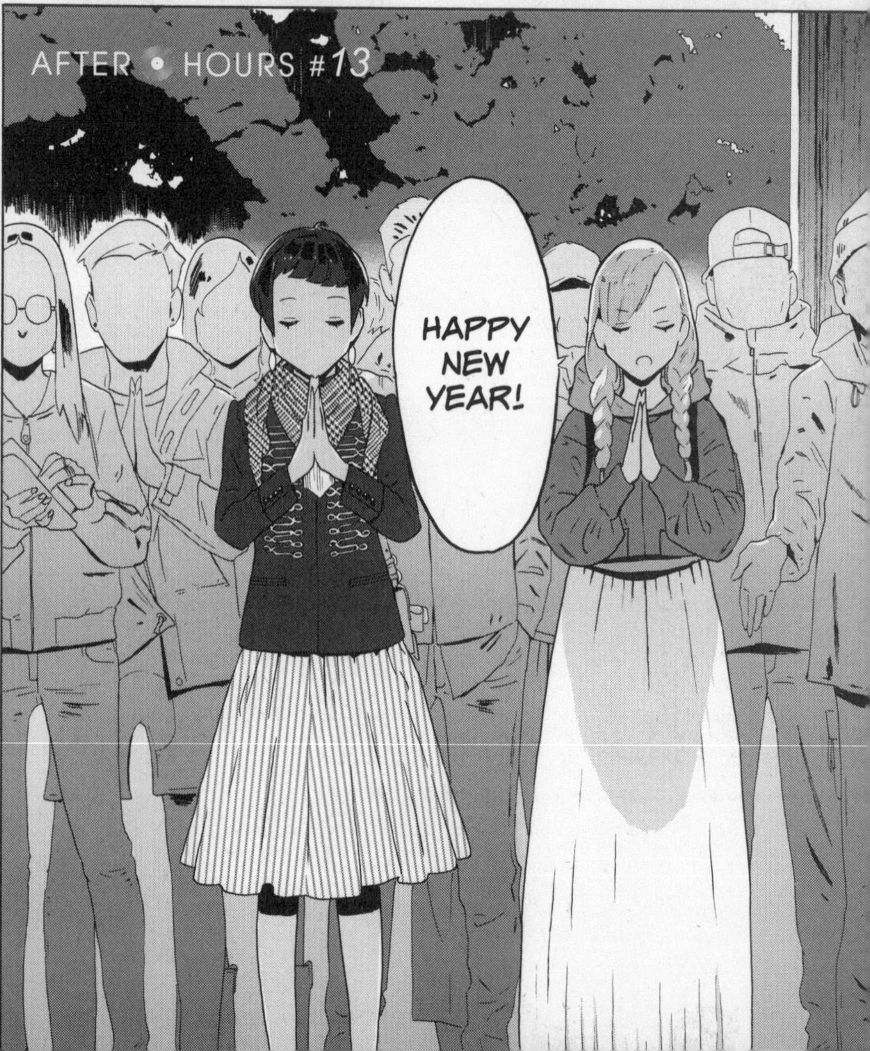
AFTER HOURS #13
HAPPY NEW YEAR!

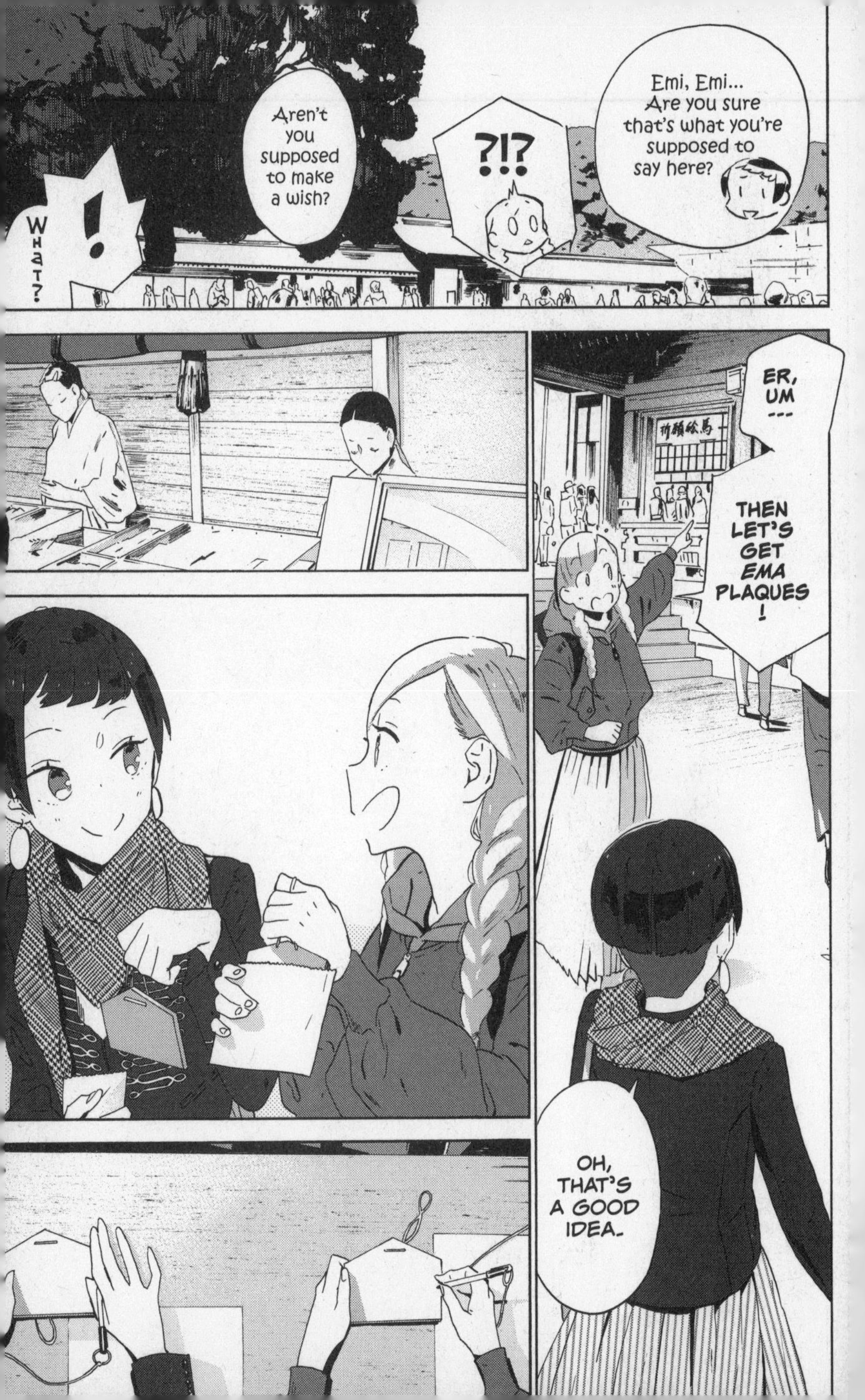
Emi, Emi... Are you sure that's what you're supposed to say here?
?!?
Aren't you supposed to make a wish?
!
What?
ER, UM ---
祈願絵馬
THEN LET'S GET EMA PLAQUES!
OH, THAT'S A GOOD IDEA.

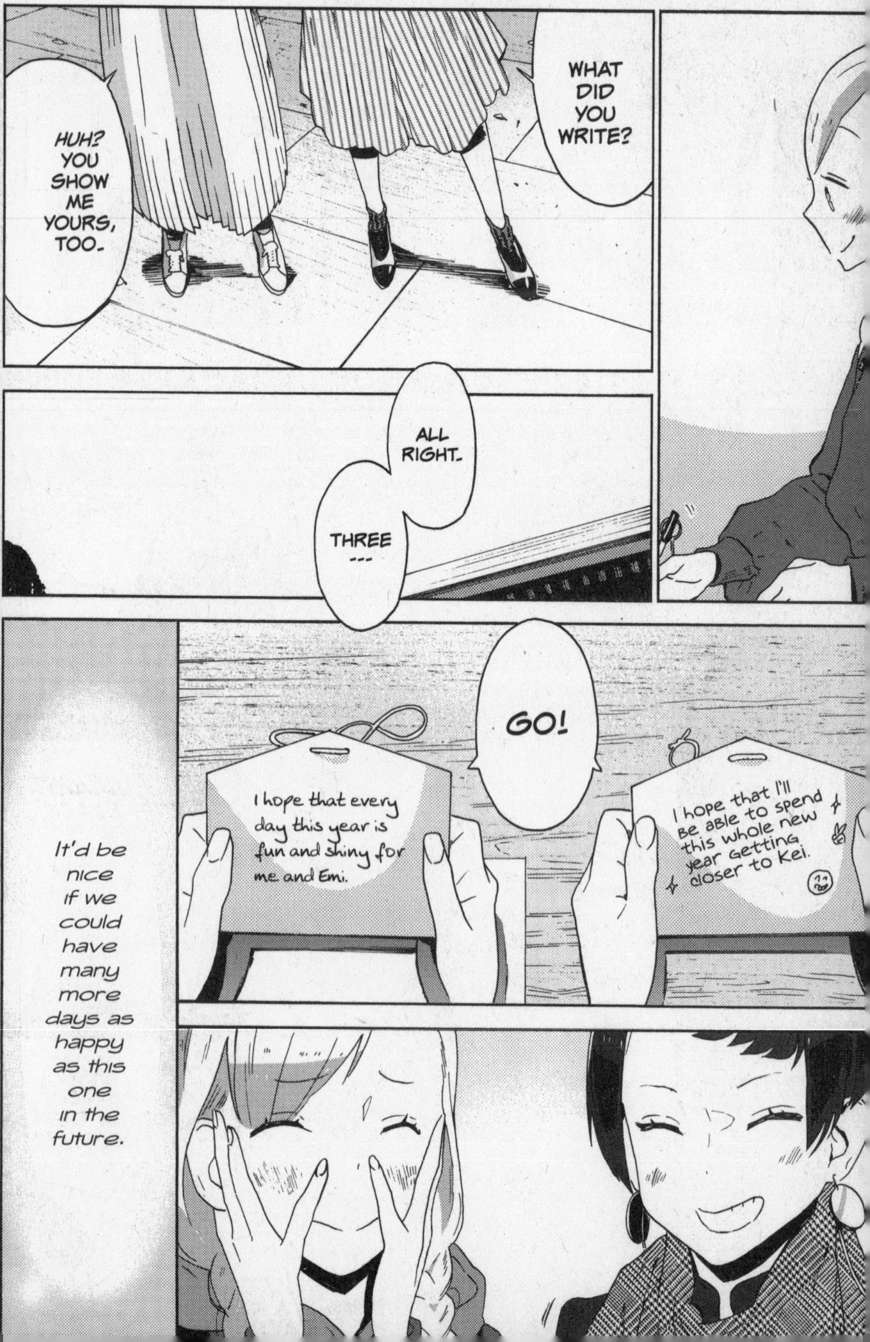
WHAT DID YOU WRITE?
HUH? YOU SHOW ME YOURS, TOO.
ALL RIGHT.
THREE ---
GO!
I hope that I'll be able to spend this whole new year getting closer to Kei.
I hope that every day this year is fun and shiny for me and Emi.
It'd be nice if we could have many more days as happy as this one in the future.

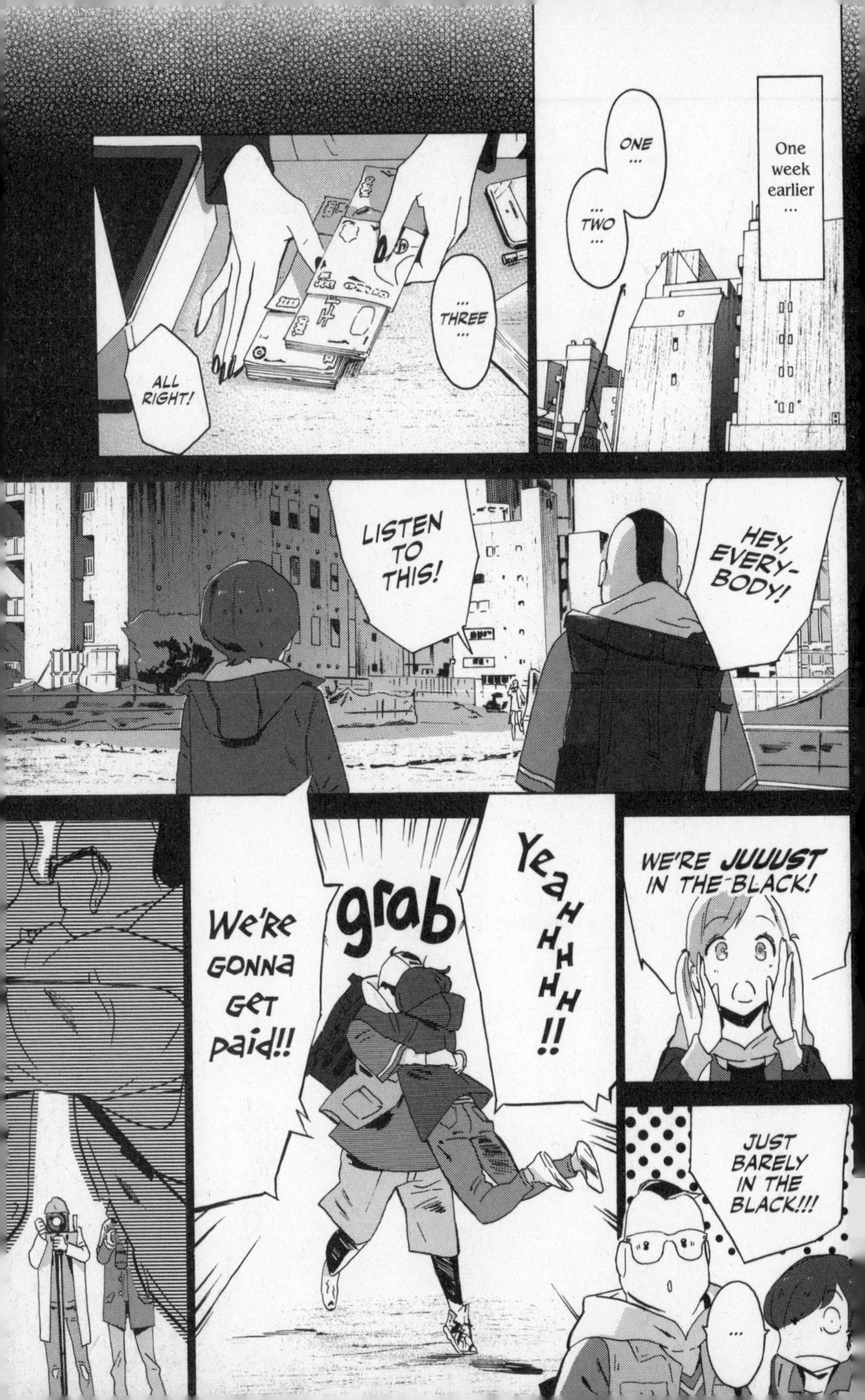
One week earlier ...
ONE ...
... TWO ...
... THREE ...
ALL RIGHT!
HEY, EVERYBODY!
LISTEN TO THIS!
WE'RE JUUUST IN THE BLACK!
JUST BARELY IN THE BLACK!!!
...
YeaHHHHH!!
grab
We're GONNA GET paid!!

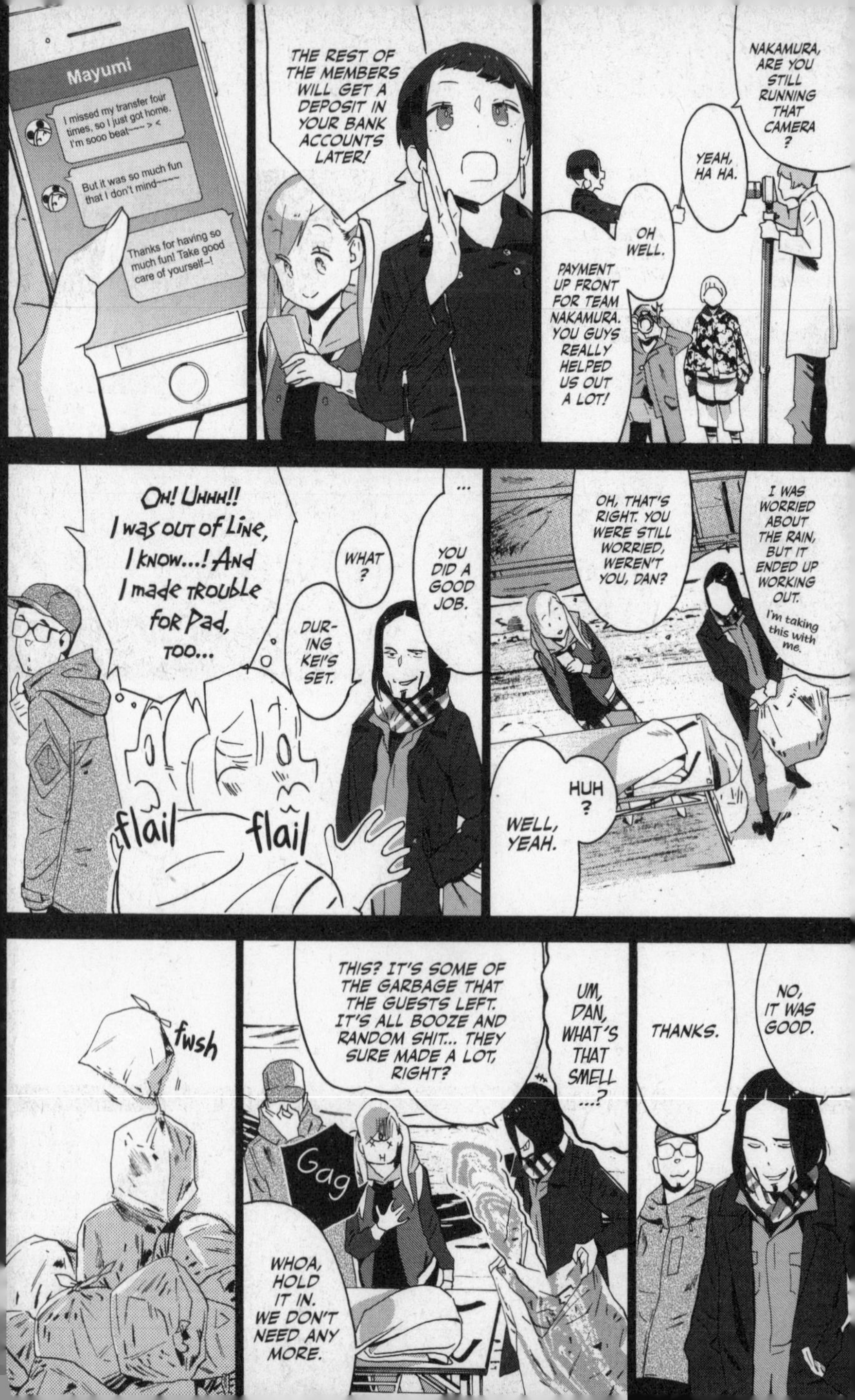
NAKAMURA, ARE YOU STILL RUNNING THAT CAMERA?
YEAH, HA HA.
OH WELL.
PAYMENT UP FRONT FOR TEAM NAKAMURA. YOU GUYS REALLY HELPED US OUT A LOT!
THE REST OF THE MEMBERS WILL GET A DEPOSIT IN YOUR BANK ACCOUNTS LATER!
Mayumi
I missed my transfer four times, so I just got home. I'm sooo beat~~~ > <
But it was so much fun that I don't mind~~~~
Thanks for having so much fun! Take good care of yourself~!
I WAS WORRIED ABOUT THE RAIN, BUT IT ENDED UP WORKING OUT.
I'm taking this with me.
OH, THAT'S RIGHT. YOU WERE STILL WORRIED, WEREN'T YOU, DAN?
HUH?
WELL, YEAH.
...
YOU DID A GOOD JOB.
WHAT?
DUR-ING KEI'S SET.
OH! UHHH!! I was out of line, I know...! And I made trouble for Dad, too...
flail
flail
NO, IT WAS GOOD.
THANKS.
UM, DAN, WHAT'S THAT SMELL...?
THIS? IT'S SOME OF THE GARBAGE THAT THE GUESTS LEFT. IT'S ALL BOOZE AND RANDOM SHIT... THEY SURE MADE A LOT, RIGHT?
Gag
WHOA, HOLD IT IN. WE DON'T NEED ANY MORE.
fwsh

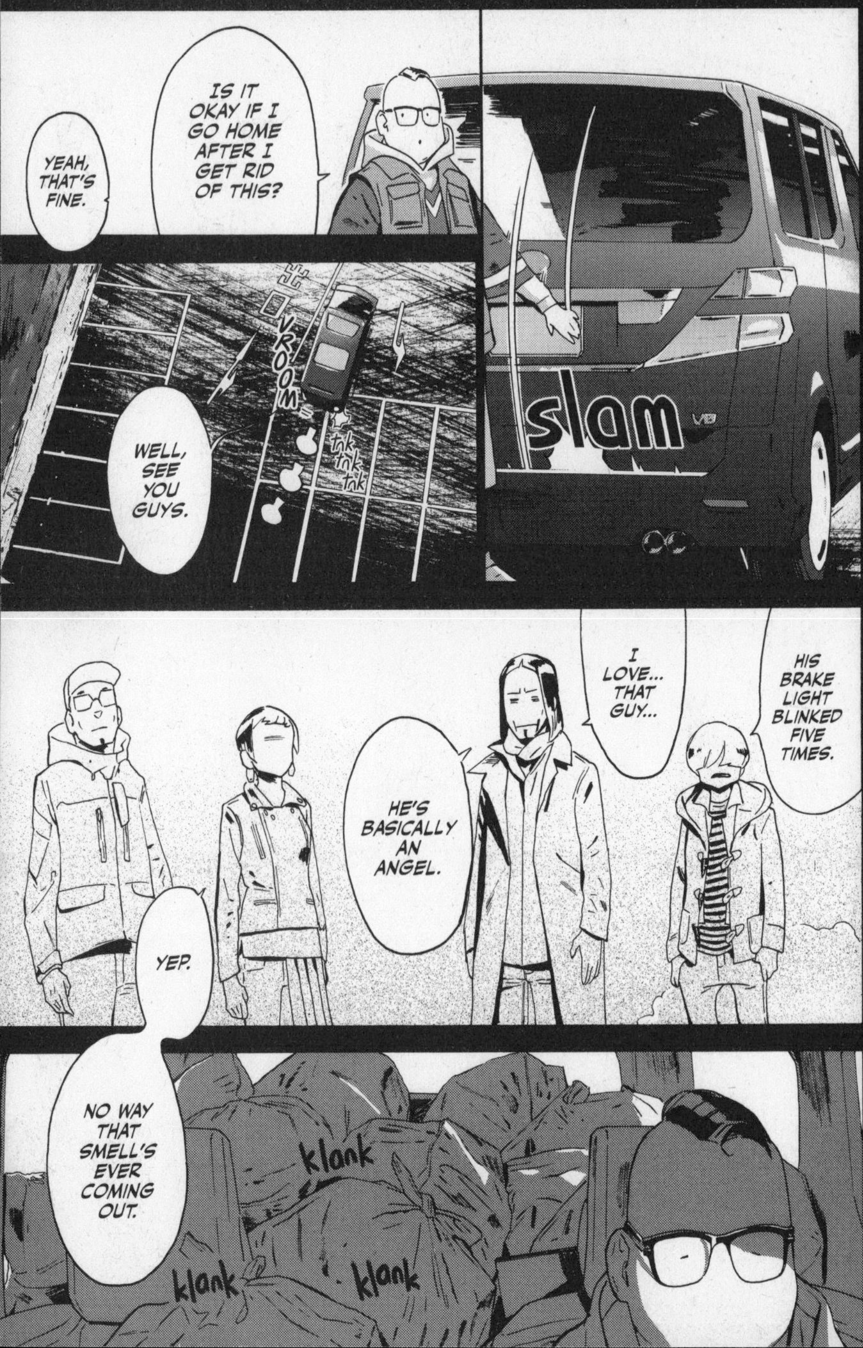
IS IT OKAY IF I GO HOME AFTER I GET RID OF THIS?
YEAH, THAT'S FINE.
slam
出口
VROOM
tnk tnk tnk
WELL, SEE YOU GUYS.
HIS BRAKE LIGHT BLINKED FIVE TIMES.
I LOVE... THAT GUY...
HE'S BASICALLY AN ANGEL.
YEP.
NO WAY THAT SMELL'S EVER COMING OUT.
klank
klank
klank

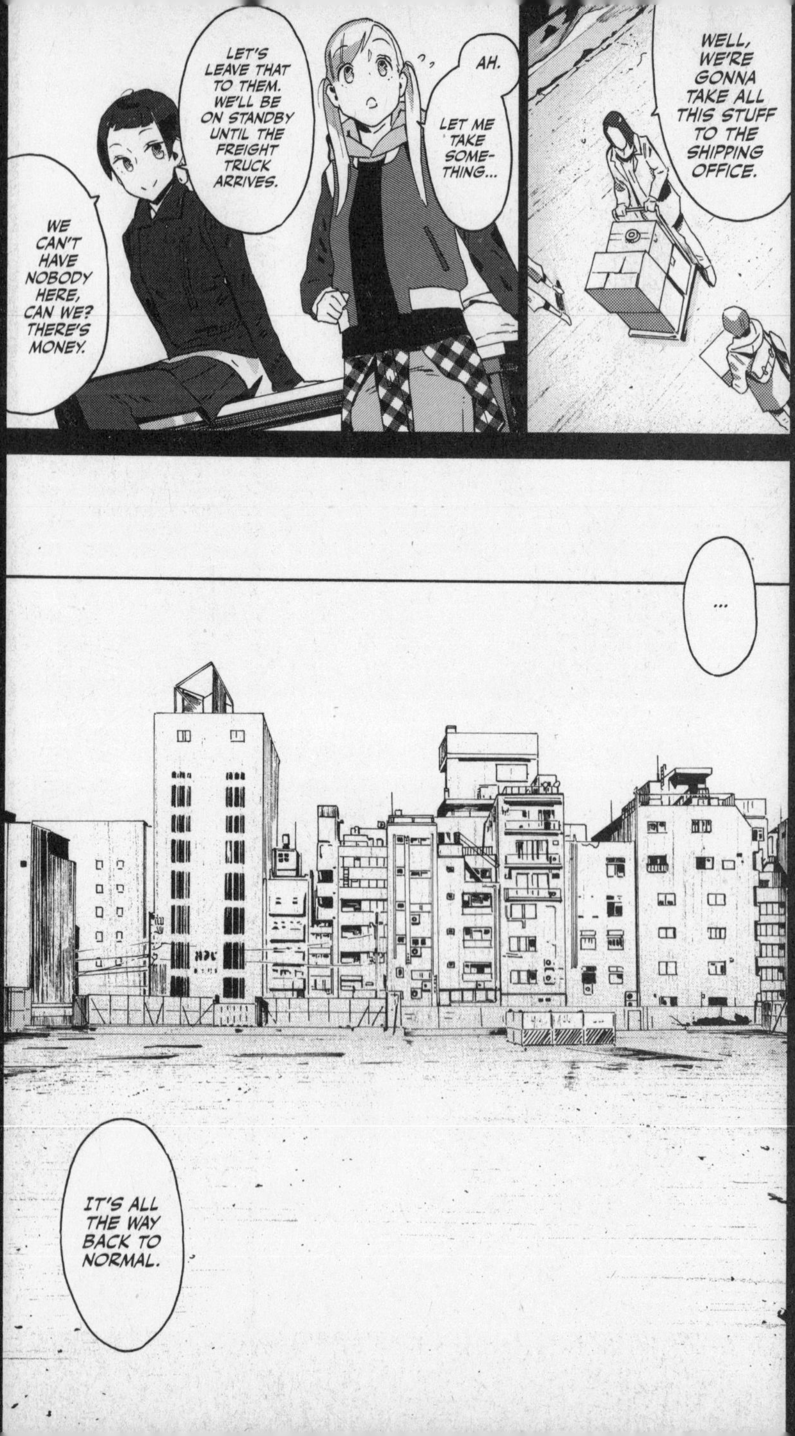
WELL, WE'RE GONNA TAKE ALL THIS STUFF TO THE SHIPPING OFFICE.
AH.
LET ME TAKE SOME-THING...
LET'S LEAVE THAT TO THEM. WE'LL BE ON STANDBY UNTIL THE FREIGHT TRUCK ARRIVES.
WE CAN'T HAVE NOBODY HERE, CAN WE? THERE'S MONEY.
...
IT'S ALL THE WAY BACK TO NORMAL.

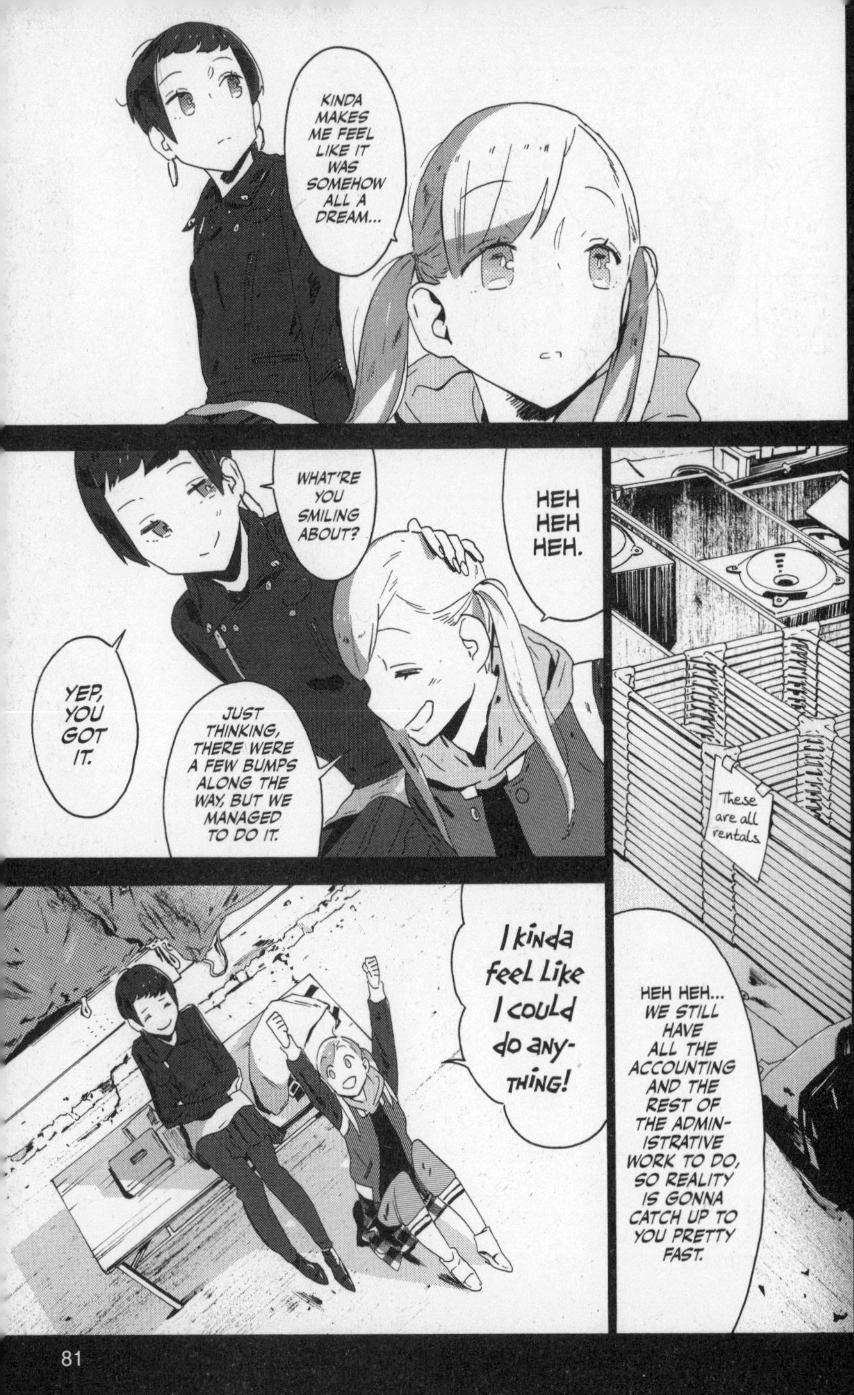
KINDA MAKES ME FEEL LIKE IT WAS SOMEHOW ALL A DREAM...
HEH HEH HEH.
WHAT'RE YOU SMILING ABOUT?
JUST THINKING, THERE WERE A FEW BUMPS ALONG THE WAY, BUT WE MANAGED TO DO IT.
YEP, YOU GOT IT.
I kinda feel like I could do any-THING!
These are all rentals
HEH HEH... WE STILL HAVE ALL THE ACCOUNTING AND THE REST OF THE ADMIN-ISTRATIVE WORK TO DO, SO REALITY IS GONNA CATCH UP TO YOU PRETTY FAST.

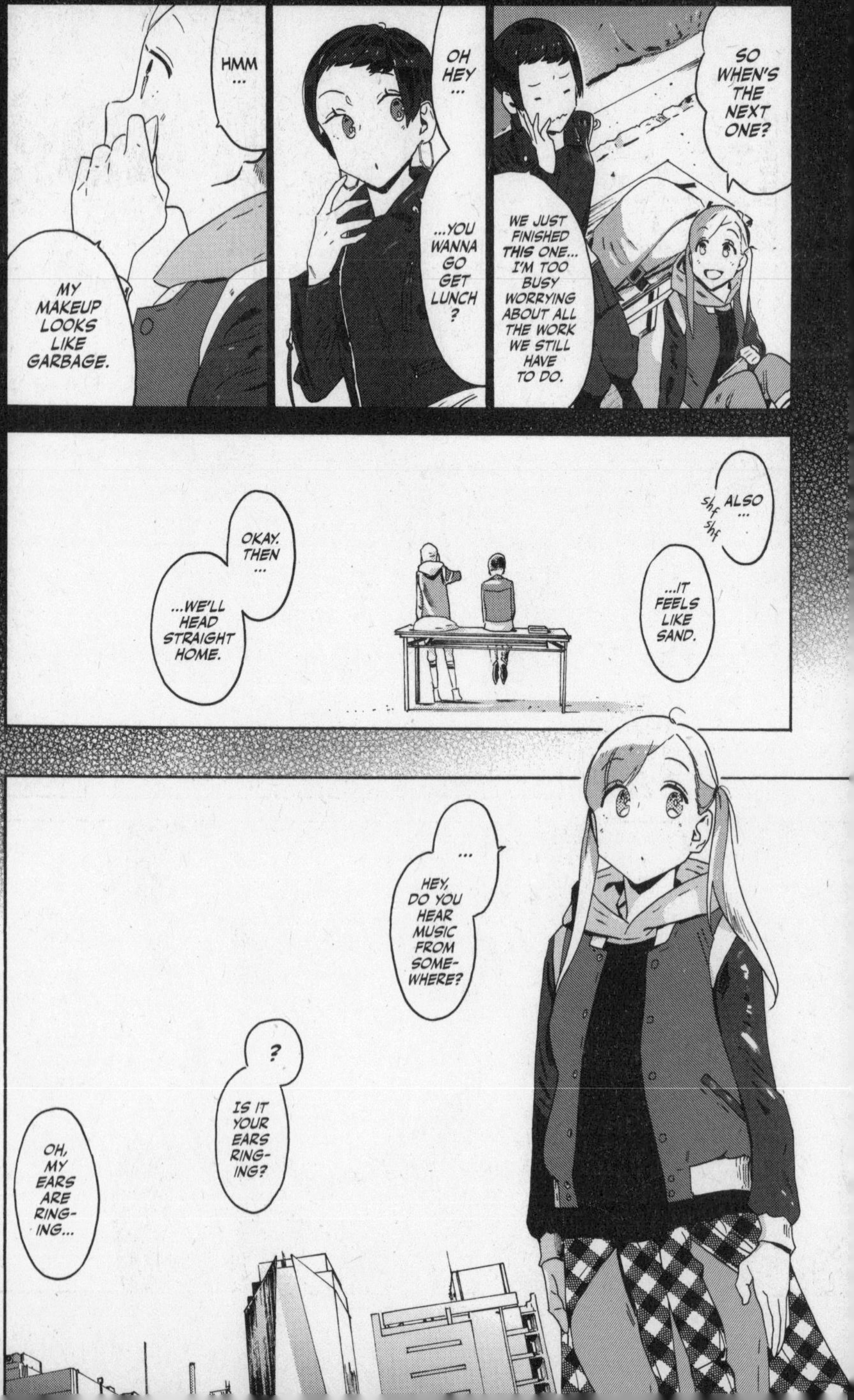
SO WHEN'S THE NEXT ONE?
WE JUST FINISHED THIS ONE... I'M TOO BUSY WORRYING ABOUT ALL THE WORK WE STILL HAVE TO DO.
OH HEY ...
...YOU WANNA GO GET LUNCH?
HMM ...
MY MAKEUP LOOKS LIKE GARBAGE.
ALSO ...
shf shf
...IT FEELS LIKE SAND.
OKAY. THEN ...
...WE'LL HEAD STRAIGHT HOME.
...
HEY, DO YOU HEAR MUSIC FROM SOME-WHERE?
?
IS IT YOUR EARS RING-ING?
OH, MY EARS ARE RING-ING...

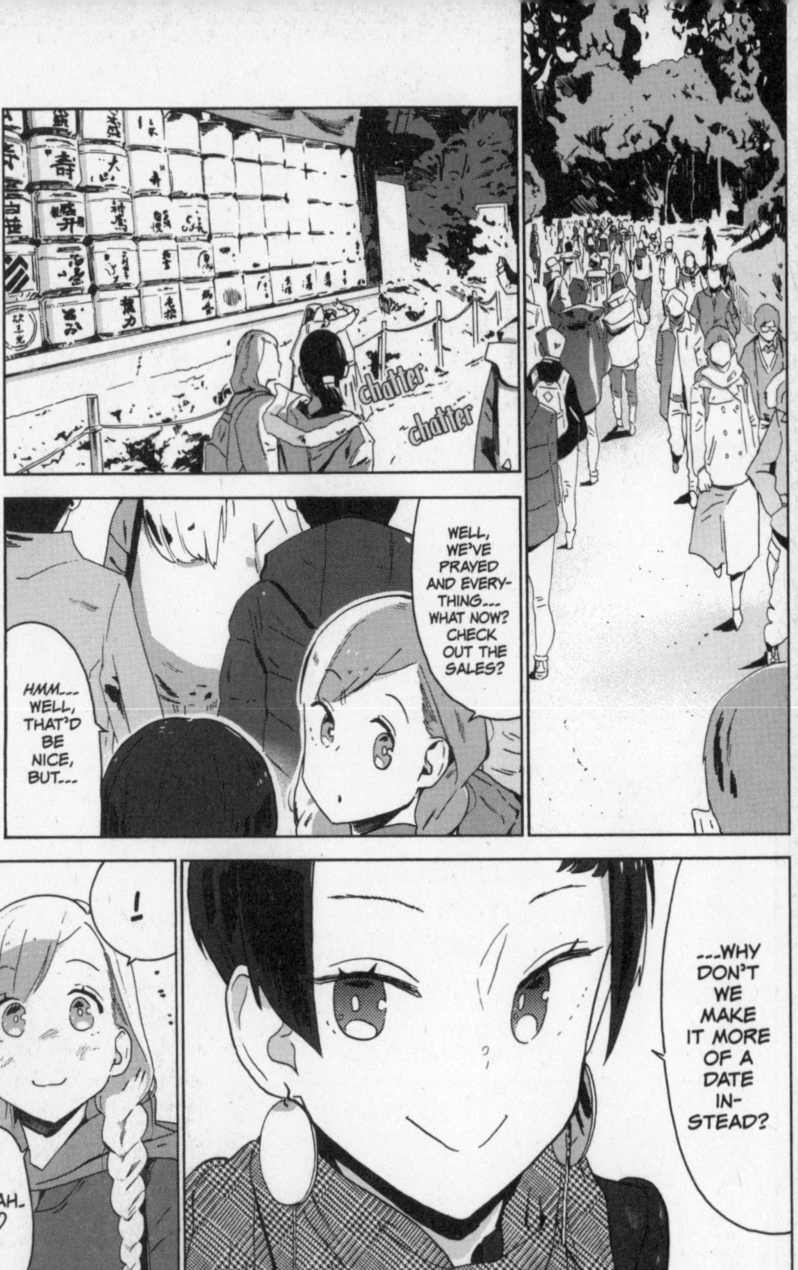
chatter
chatter
WELL, WE'VE PRAYED AND EVERY-THING... WHAT NOW? CHECK OUT THE SALES?
HMM... WELL, THAT'D BE NICE, BUT...
...WHY DON'T WE MAKE IT MORE OF A DATE IN-STEAD?
!
YEAH.♡

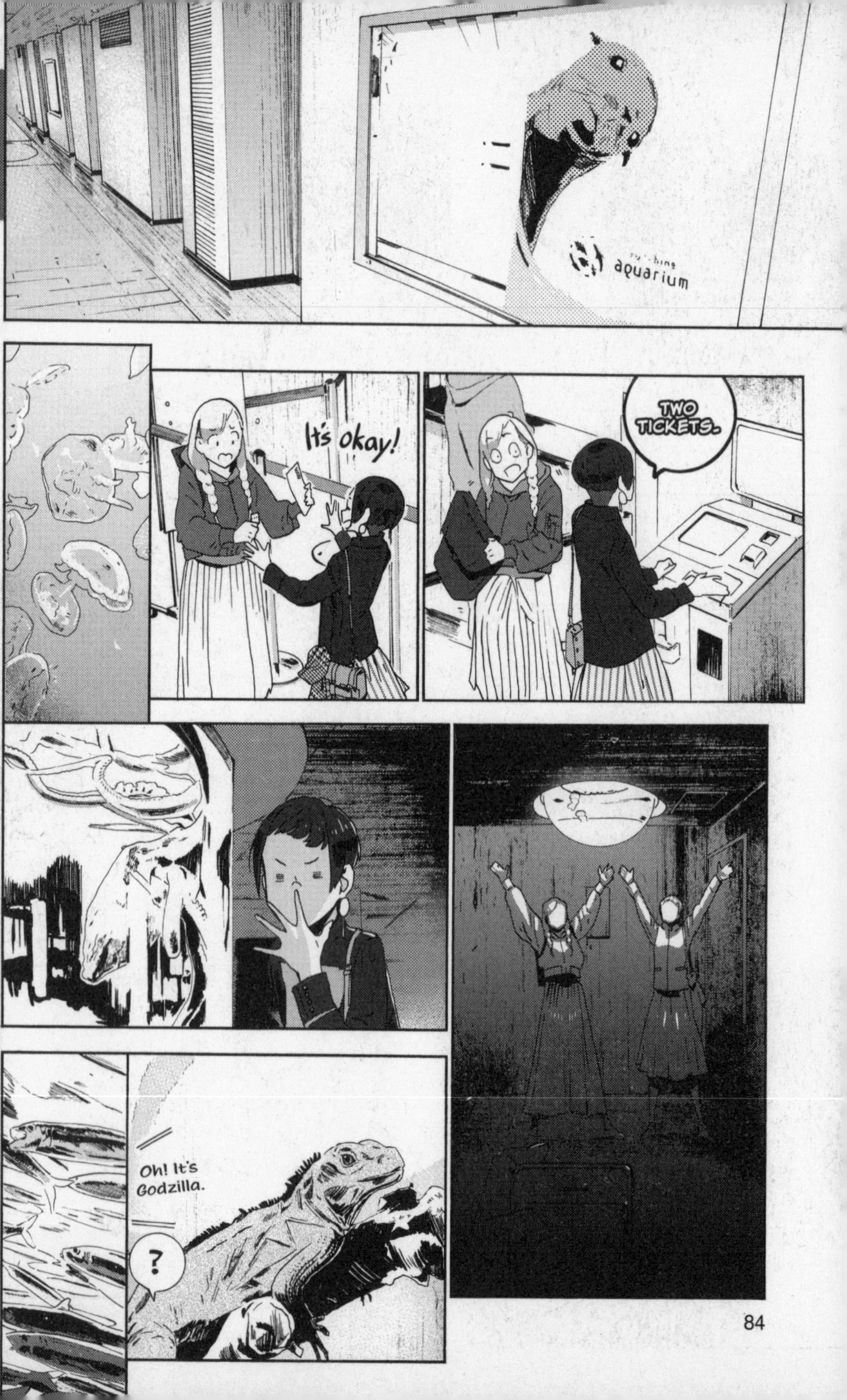
aquarium
TWO TICKETS.
It's okay!
Oh! It's Godzilla.
?

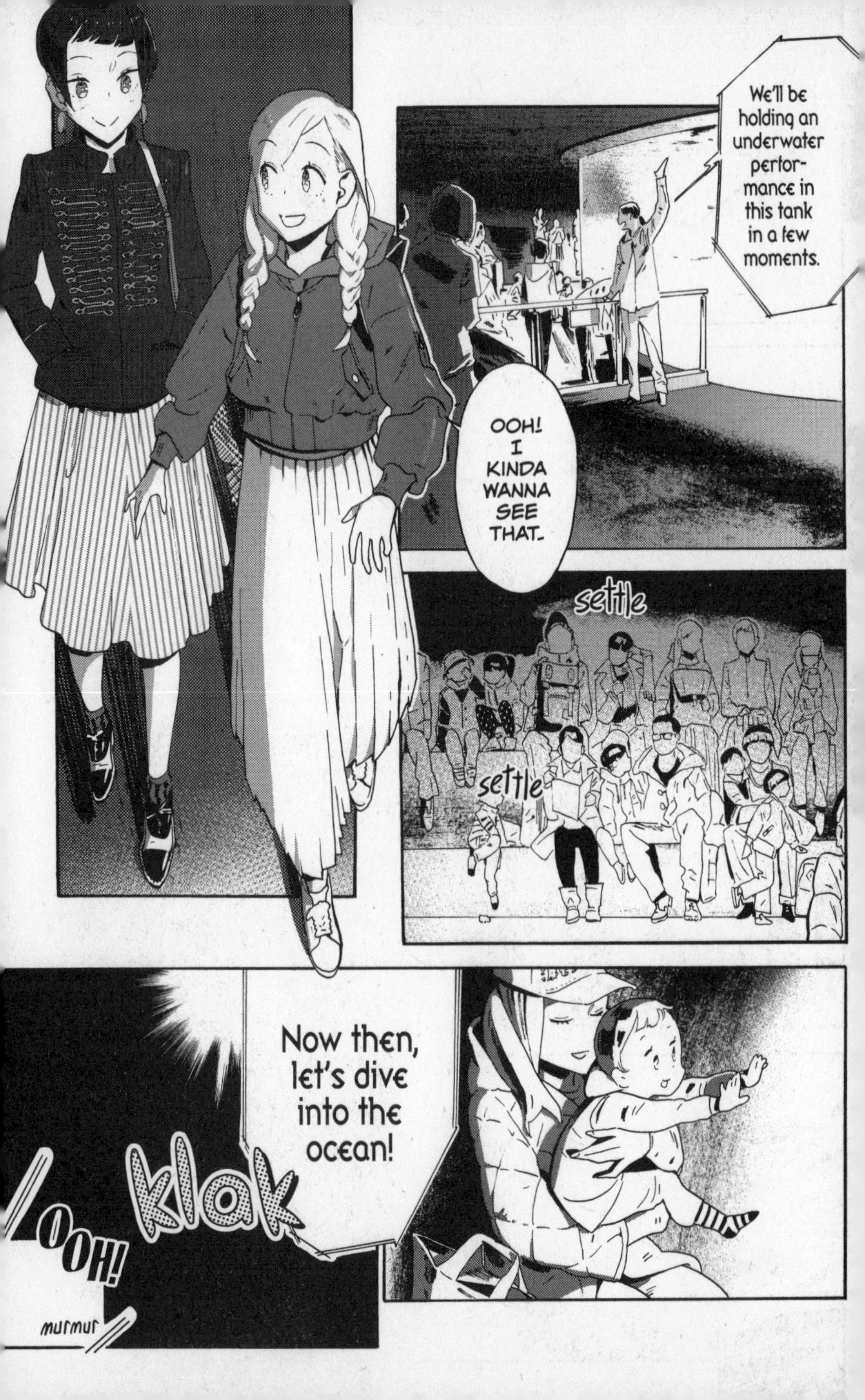
We'll be holding an underwater performance in this tank in a few moments.
OOH! I KINDA WANNA SEE THAT.
settle
settle
Now then, let's dive into the ocean!
klak
OOH!
murmur

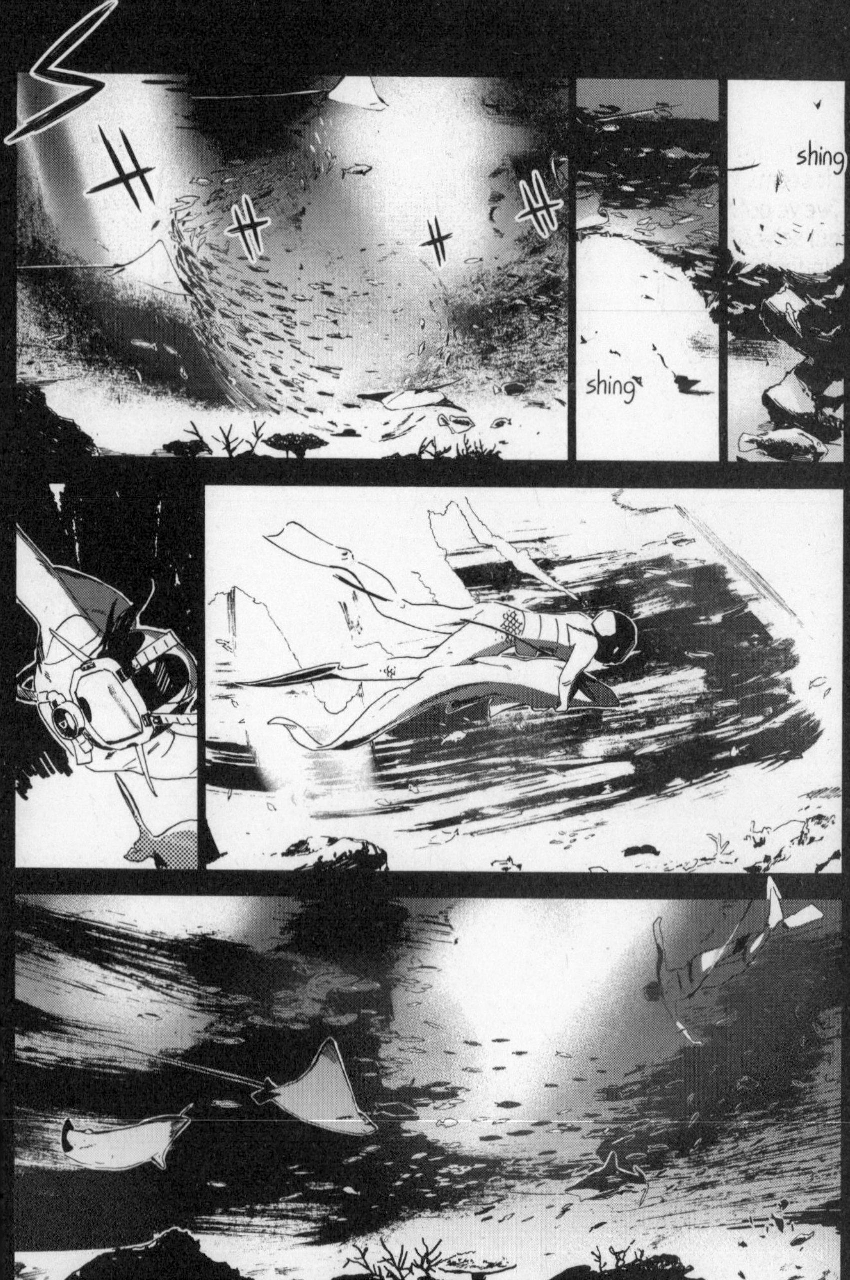
shing
shing

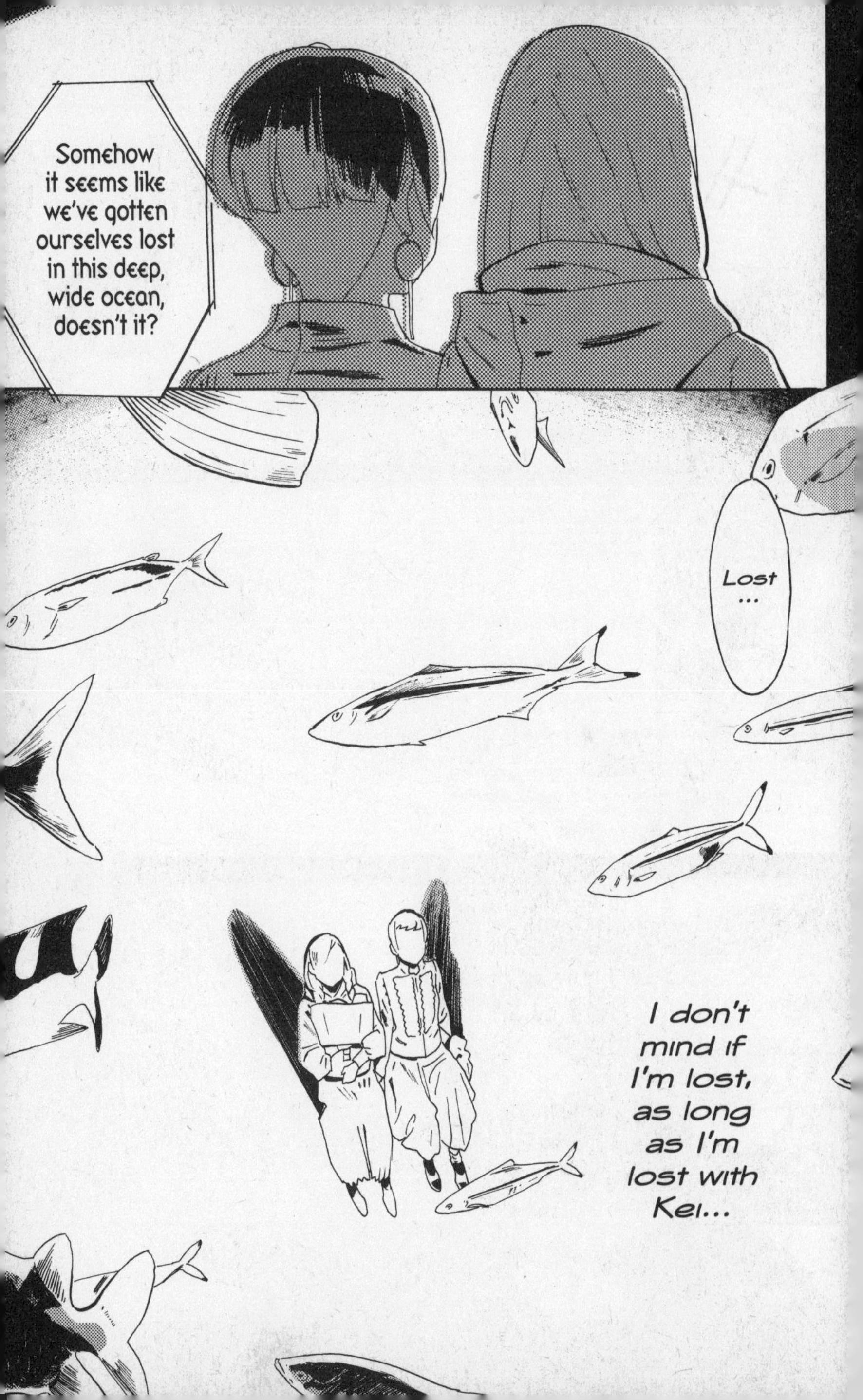
Somehow it seems like we've gotten ourselves lost in this deep, wide ocean, doesn't it?
Lost...
I don't mind if I'm lost, as long as I'm lost with Kei...

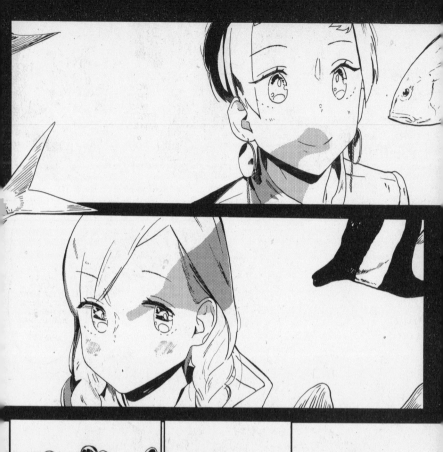

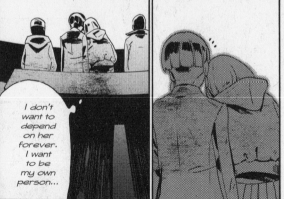

But if things stay that way, she'll never ever see me as an equal.
I don't want to depend on her forever. I want to be my own person...

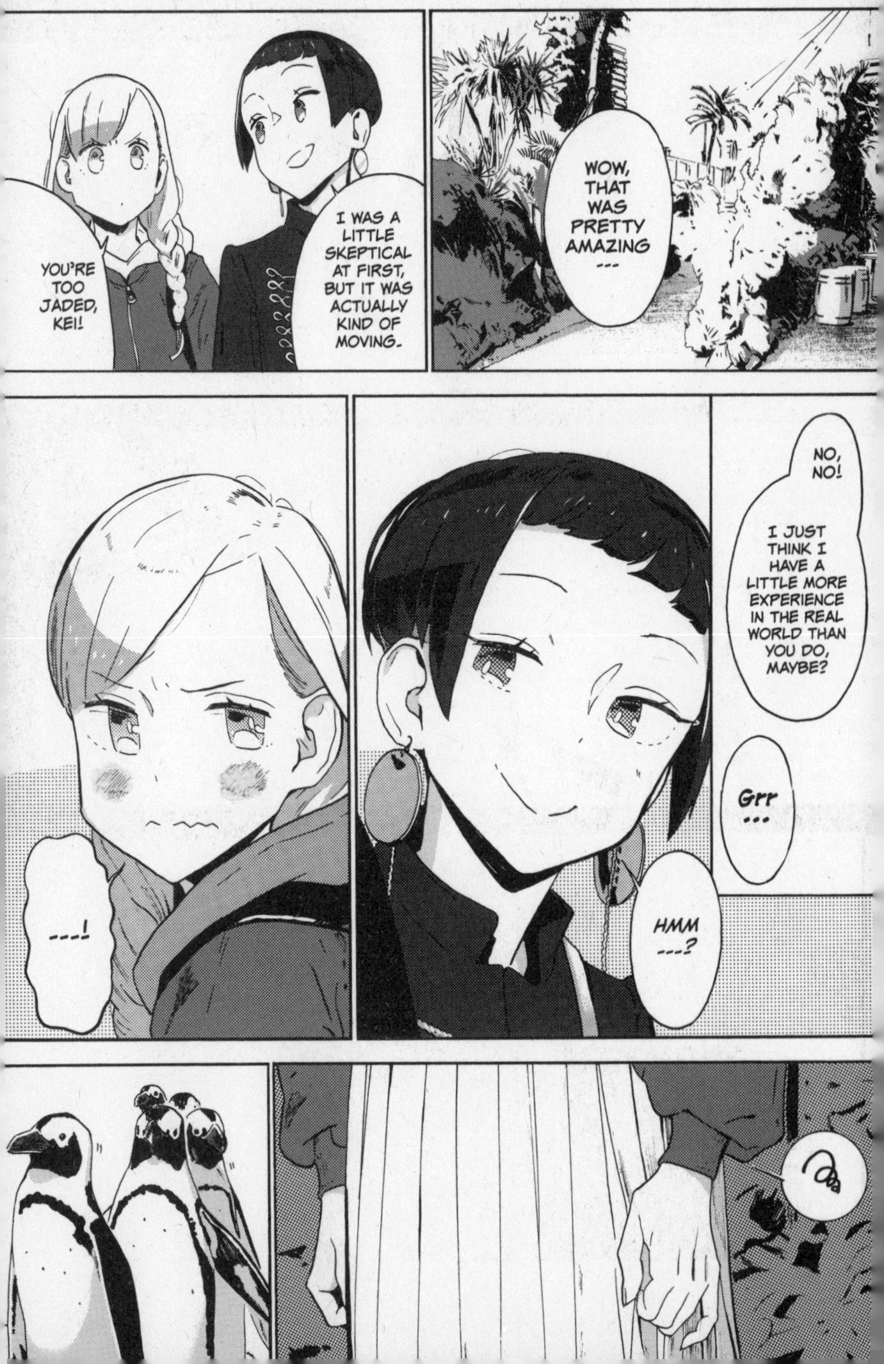
WOW, THAT WAS PRETTY AMAZING---
I WAS A LITTLE SKEPTICAL AT FIRST, BUT IT WAS ACTUALLY KIND OF MOVING.
YOU'RE TOO JADED, KEI!
NO, NO!
I JUST THINK I HAVE A LITTLE MORE EXPERIENCE IN THE REAL WORLD THAN YOU DO, MAYBE?
Grr...
HMM---?
---!

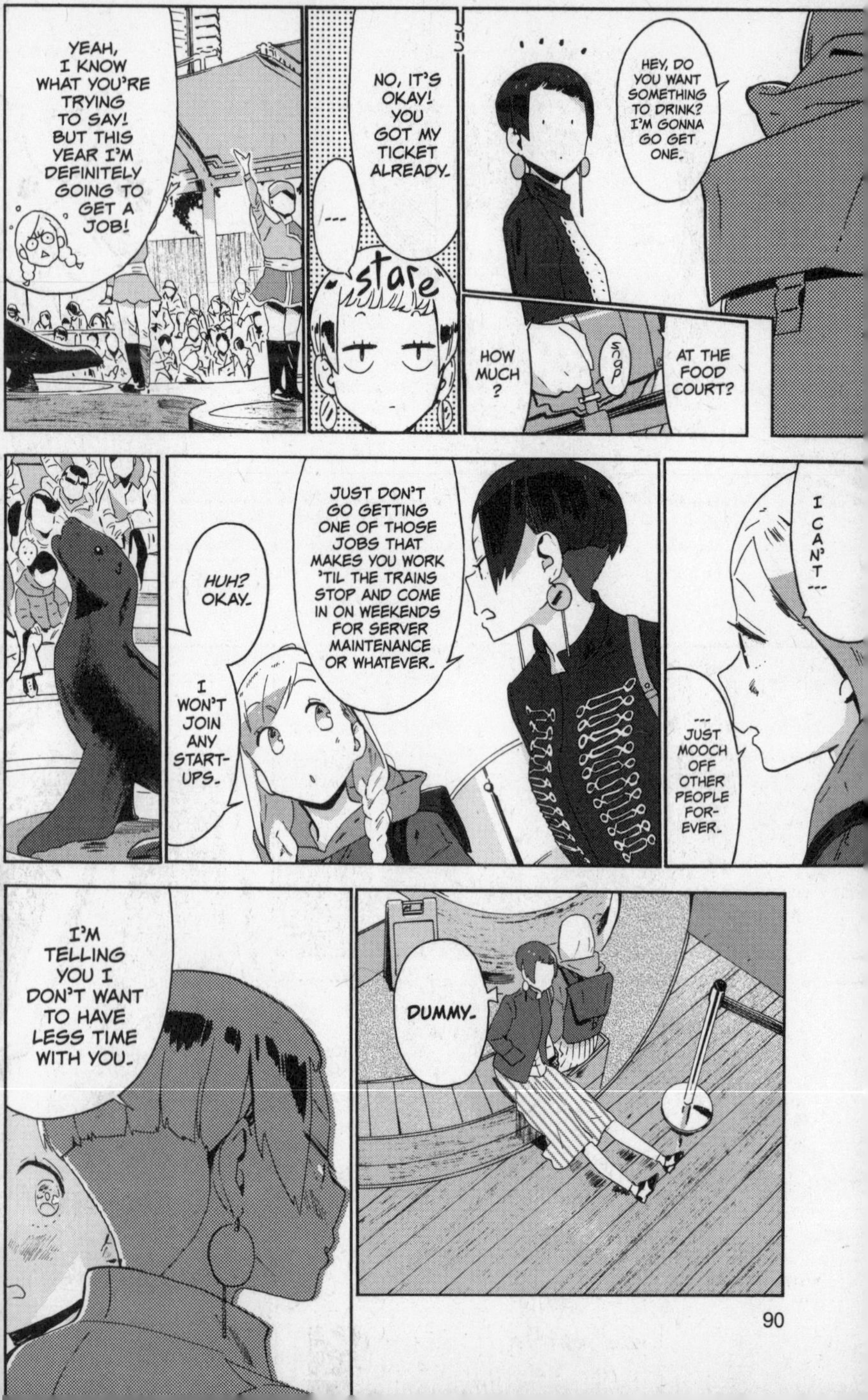

HEY, DO YOU WANT SOMETHING TO DRINK? I'M GONNA GO GET ONE.
AT THE FOOD COURT?
snap
HOW MUCH?
NO, IT'S OKAY! YOU GOT MY TICKET ALREADY.
...
stare
YEAH, I KNOW WHAT YOU'RE TRYING TO SAY! BUT THIS YEAR I'M DEFINITELY GOING TO GET A JOB!
I CAN'T...
...JUST MOOCH OFF OTHER PEOPLE FOREVER.
JUST DON'T GO GETTING ONE OF THOSE JOBS THAT MAKES YOU WORK 'TIL THE TRAINS STOP AND COME IN ON WEEKENDS FOR SERVER MAINTENANCE OR WHATEVER.
HUH? OKAY.
I WON'T JOIN ANY START-UPS.
DUMMY.
I'M TELLING YOU I DON'T WANT TO HAVE LESS TIME WITH YOU.

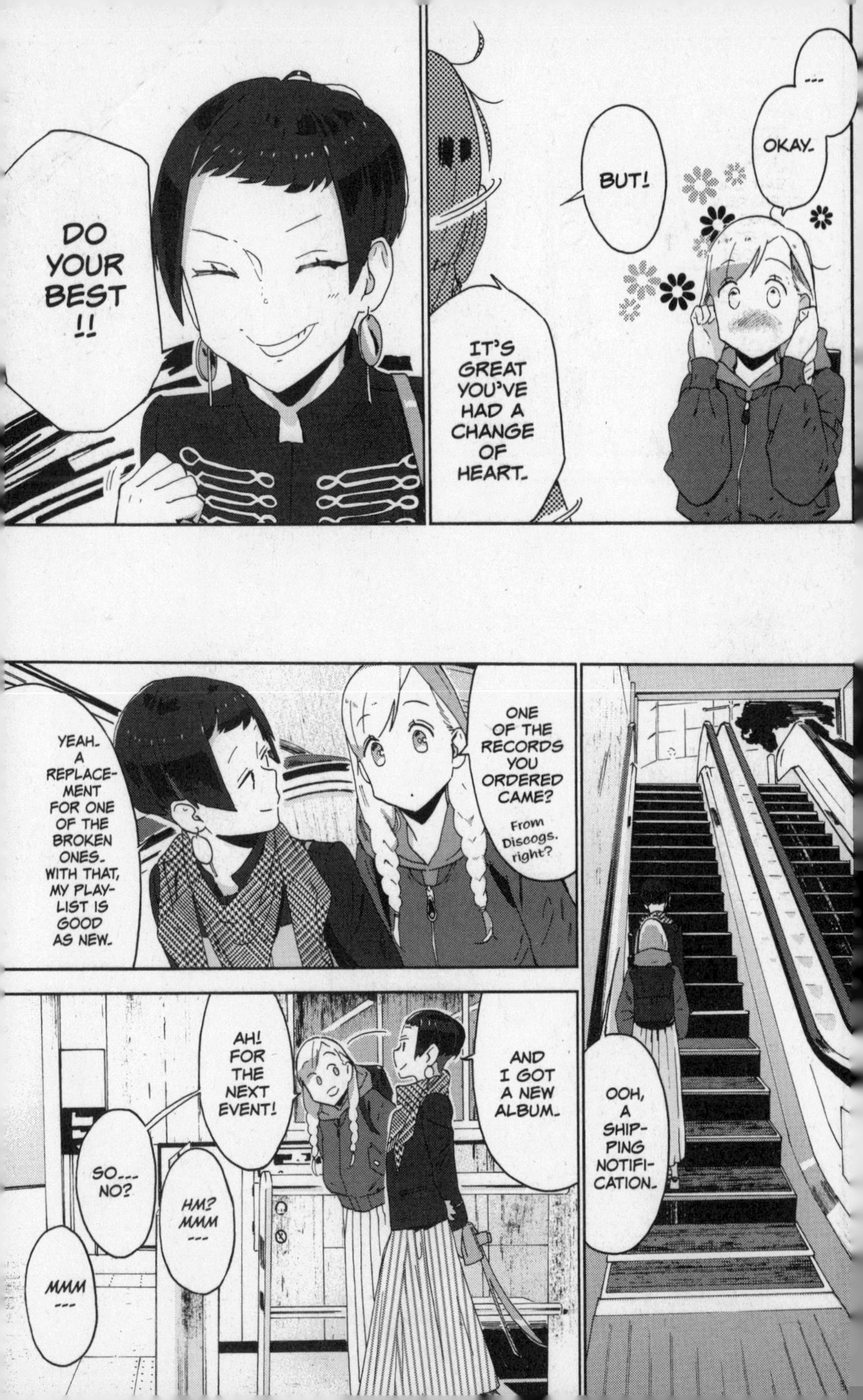
...
OKAY.
BUT!
IT'S GREAT YOU'VE HAD A CHANGE OF HEART.
DO YOUR BEST!!
OOH, A SHIP-PING NOTIFI-CATION.
ONE OF THE RECORDS YOU ORDERED CAME?
From Discogs, right?
YEAH. A REPLACE-MENT FOR ONE OF THE BROKEN ONES. WITH THAT, MY PLAY-LIST IS GOOD AS NEW.
AND I GOT A NEW ALBUM.
AH! FOR THE NEXT EVENT!
HM? MMM...
SO... NO?
MMM...

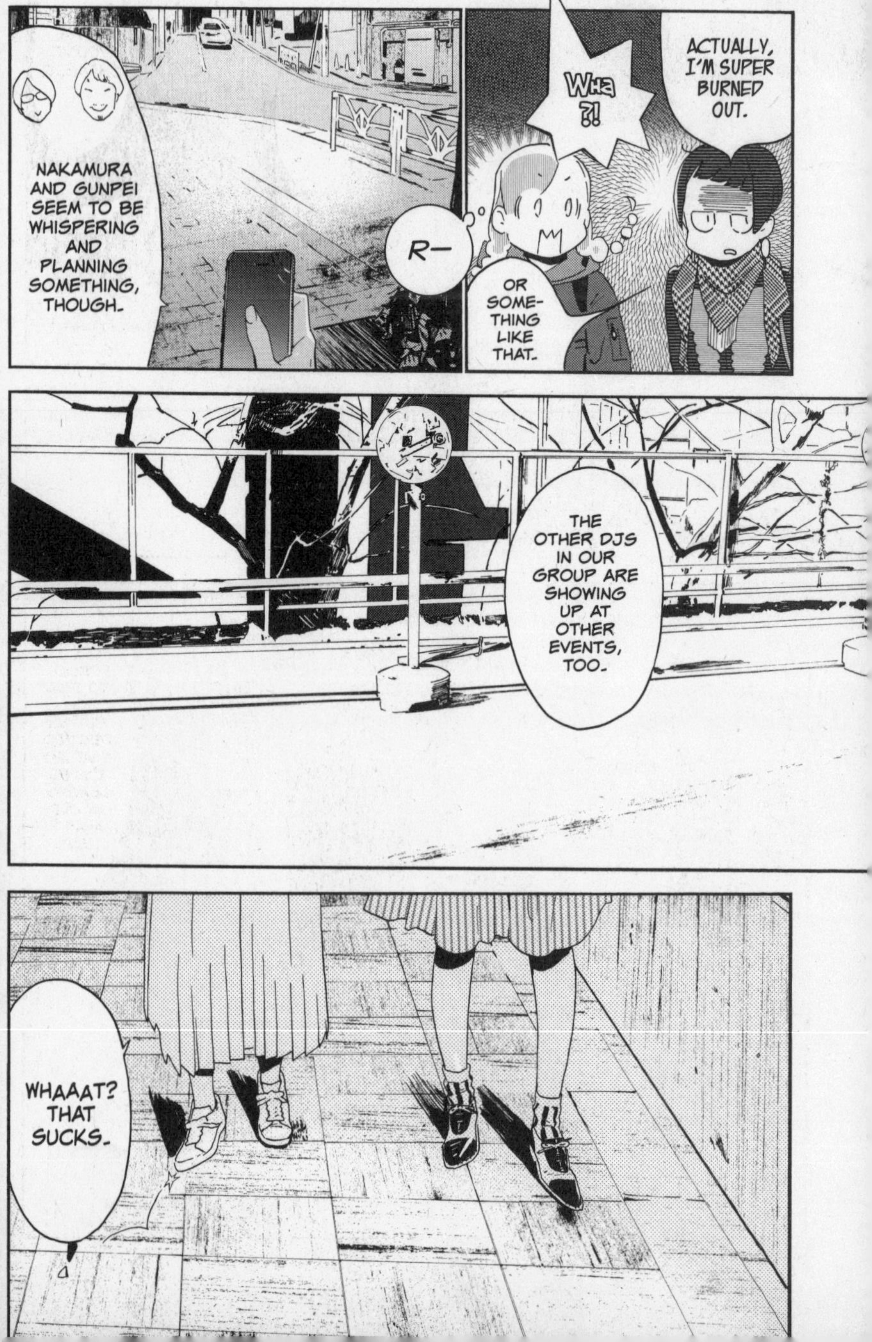
ACTUALLY, I'M SUPER BURNED OUT.
WHA ?!
R—
OR SOME-THING LIKE THAT.
NAKAMURA AND GUNPEI SEEM TO BE WHISPERING AND PLANNING SOMETHING, THOUGH.
THE OTHER DJS IN OUR GROUP ARE SHOWING UP AT OTHER EVENTS, TOO.
WHAAAT? THAT SUCKS.

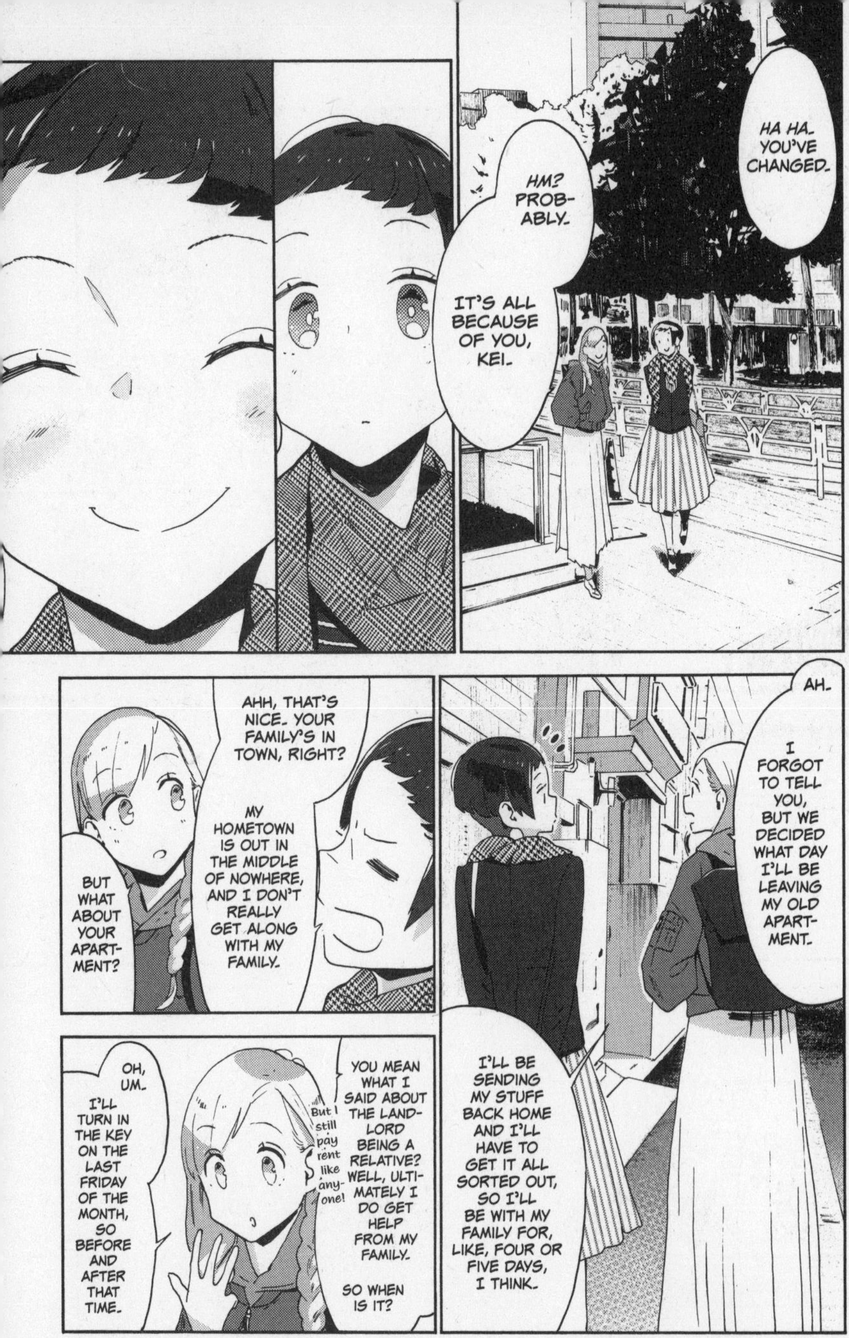
HA HA. YOU'VE CHANGED.
HM? PROBABLY.
IT'S ALL BECAUSE OF YOU, KEI.
AH.
I FORGOT TO TELL YOU, BUT WE DECIDED WHAT DAY I'LL BE LEAVING MY OLD APARTMENT.
I'LL BE SENDING MY STUFF BACK HOME AND I'LL HAVE TO GET IT ALL SORTED OUT, SO I'LL BE WITH MY FAMILY FOR, LIKE, FOUR OR FIVE DAYS, I THINK.
AHH, THAT'S NICE. YOUR FAMILY'S IN TOWN, RIGHT?
MY HOMETOWN IS OUT IN THE MIDDLE OF NOWHERE, AND I DON'T REALLY GET ALONG WITH MY FAMILY.
BUT WHAT ABOUT YOUR APARTMENT?
YOU MEAN WHAT I SAID ABOUT THE LANDLORD BEING A RELATIVE? WELL, ULTIMATELY I DO GET HELP FROM MY FAMILY.
But I still pay rent like anyone!
SO WHEN IS IT?
OH, UM.
I'LL TURN IN THE KEY ON THE LAST FRIDAY OF THE MONTH, SO BEFORE AND AFTER THAT TIME.

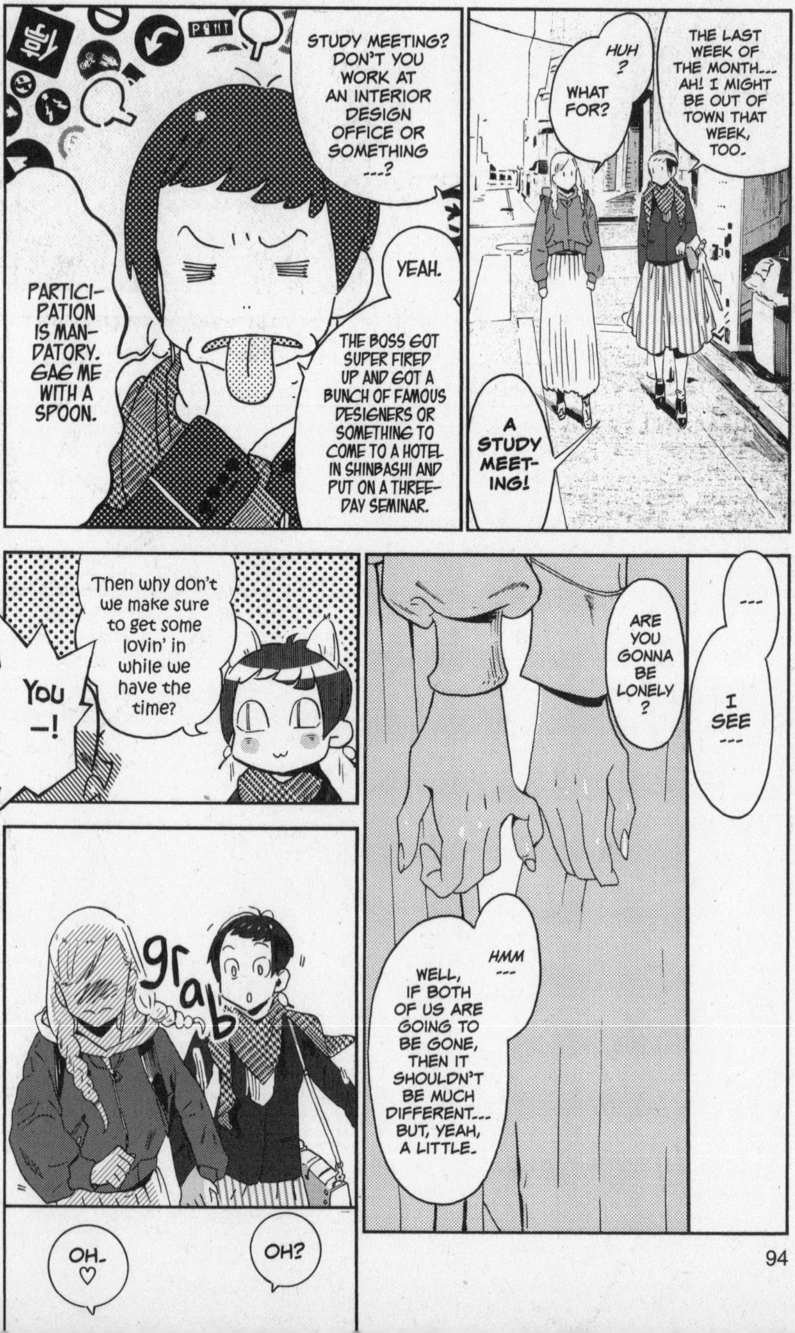
THE LAST WEEK OF THE MONTH... AH! I MIGHT BE OUT OF TOWN THAT WEEK, TOO.
HUH? WHAT FOR?
A STUDY MEETING!
STUDY MEETING? DON'T YOU WORK AT AN INTERIOR DESIGN OFFICE OR SOMETHING...?
YEAH.
THE BOSS GOT SUPER FIRED UP AND GOT A BUNCH OF FAMOUS DESIGNERS OR SOMETHING TO COME TO A HOTEL IN SHINBASHI AND PUT ON A THREE-DAY SEMINAR.
PARTICIPATION IS MANDATORY. GAG ME WITH A SPOON.
...
I SEE...
ARE YOU GONNA BE LONELY?
HMM...
WELL, IF BOTH OF US ARE GOING TO BE GONE, THEN IT SHOULDN'T BE MUCH DIFFERENT... BUT, YEAH, A LITTLE.
Then why don't we make sure to get some lovin' in while we have the time?
YOU—!
grab
OH?
OH.♡

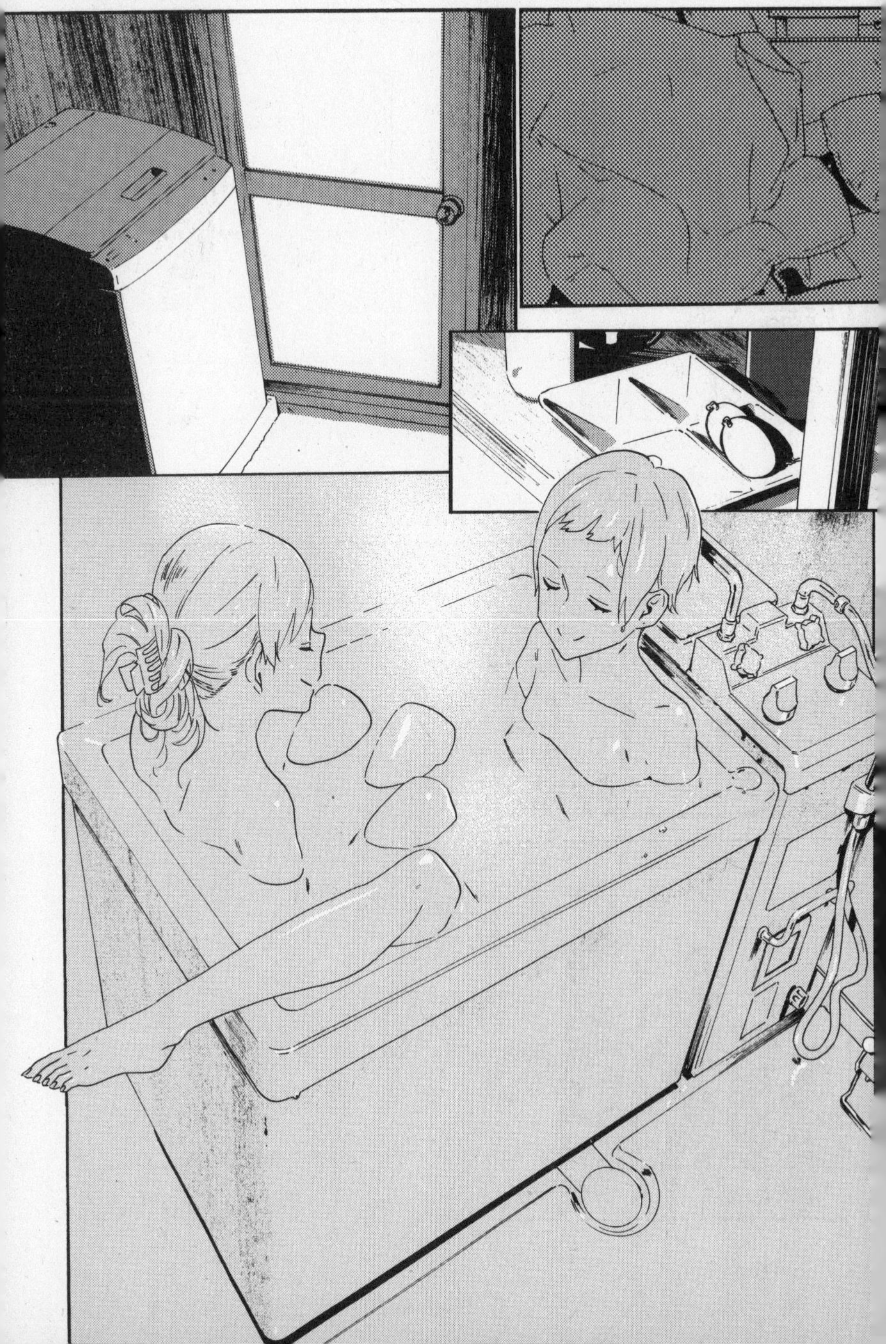

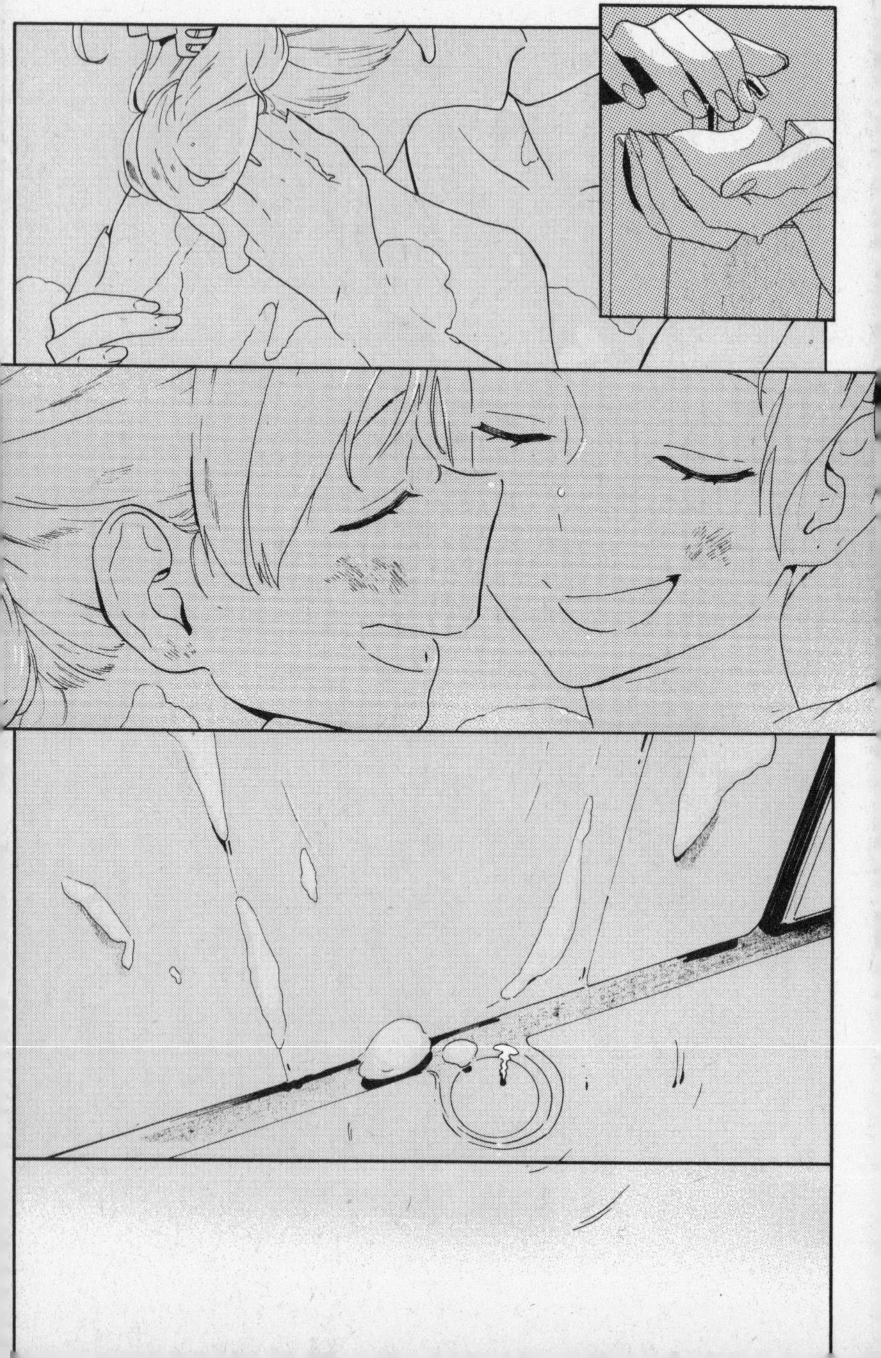

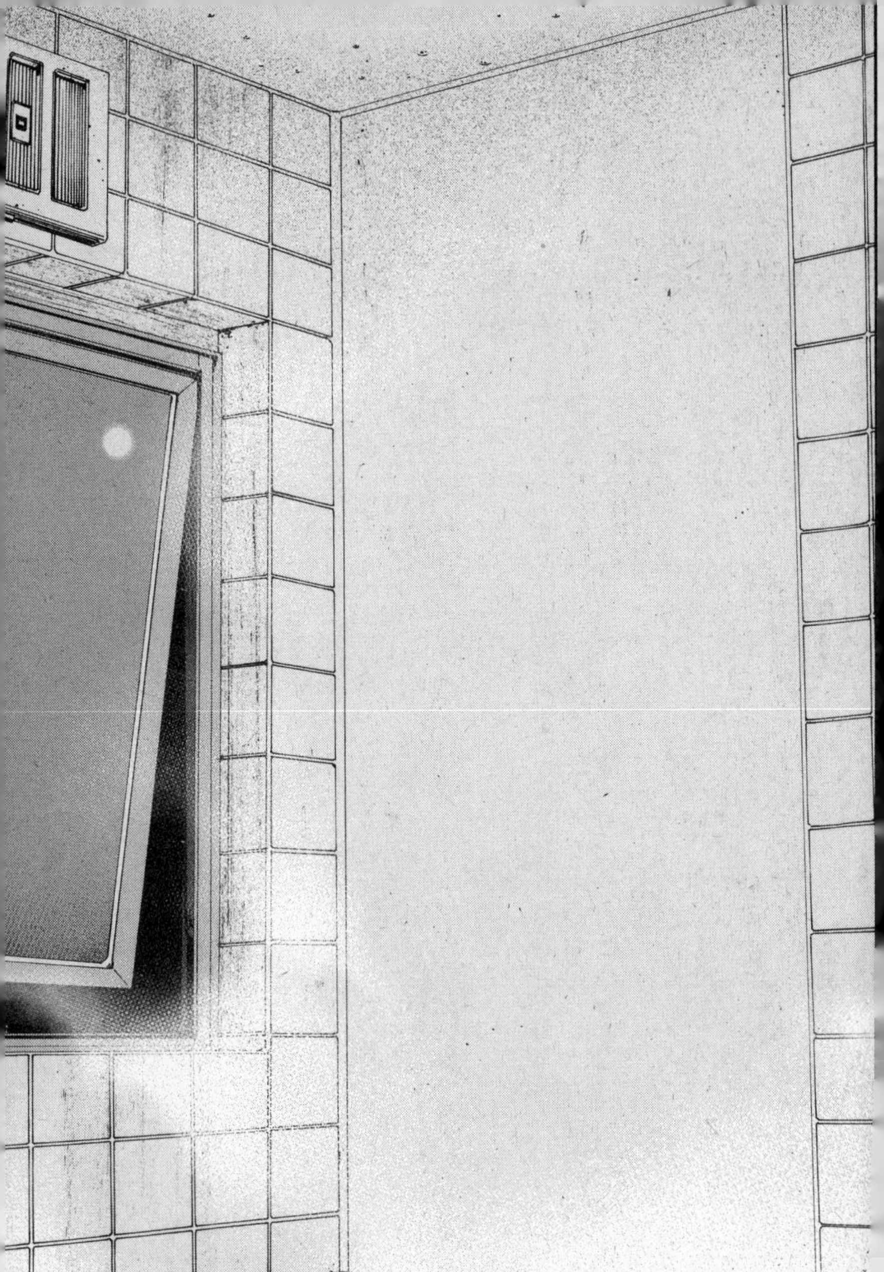

beep beep beep

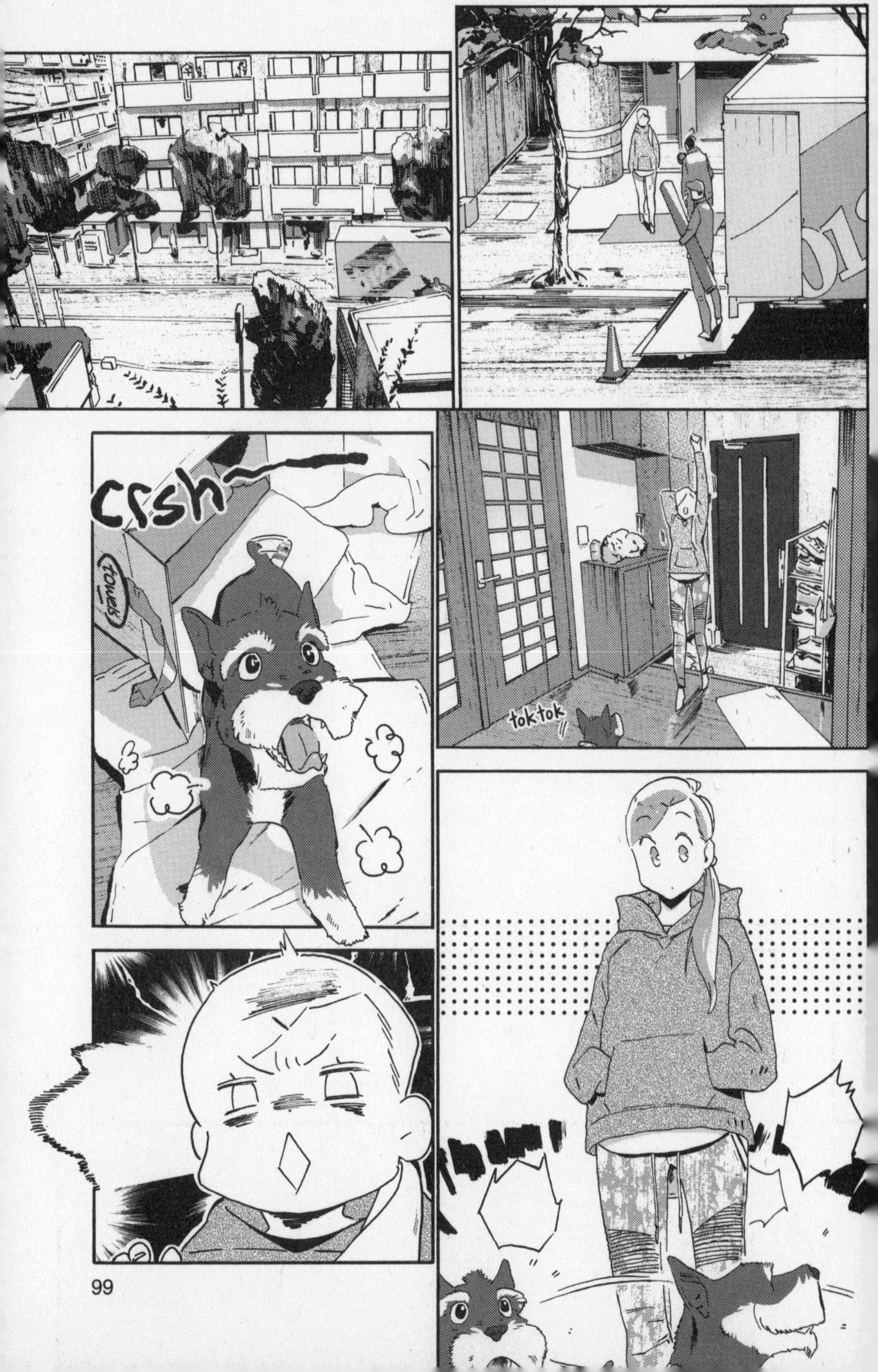
tok tok
Crsh~
towels

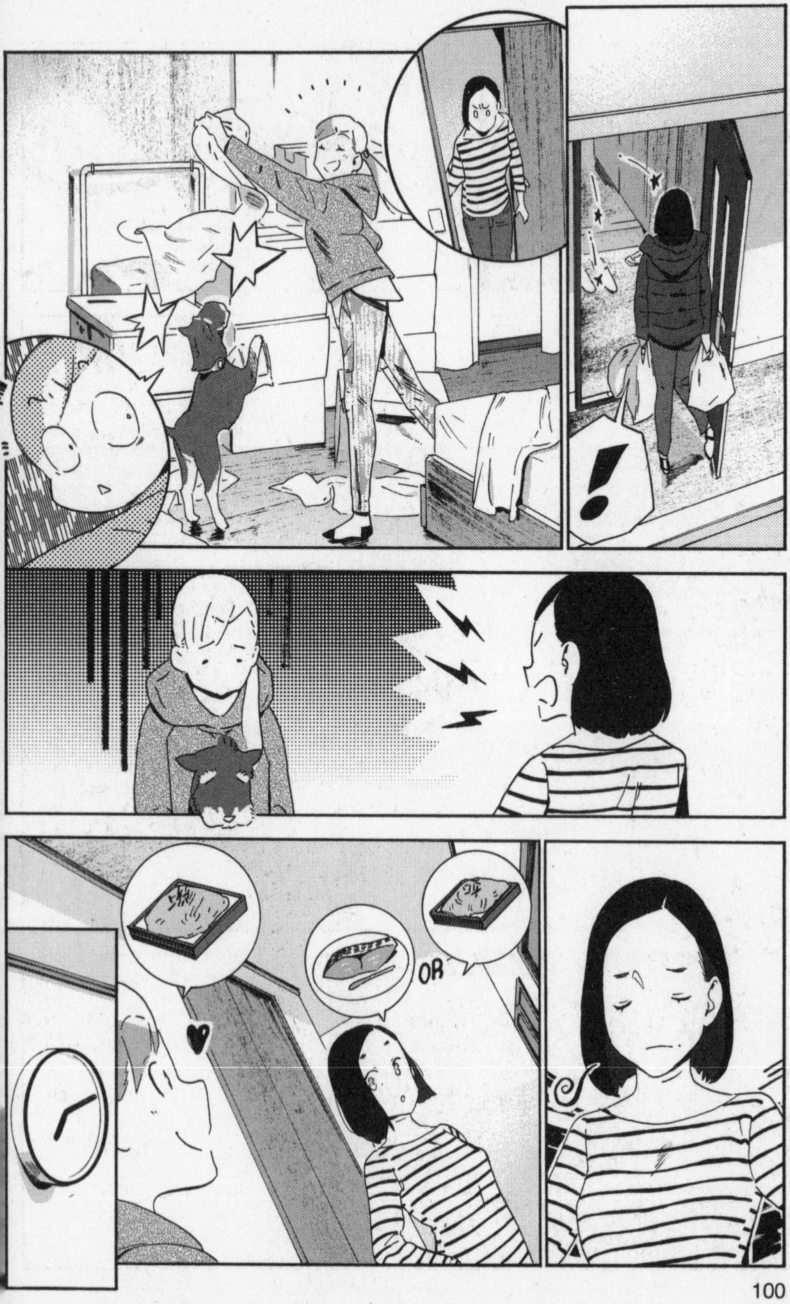
!
OR

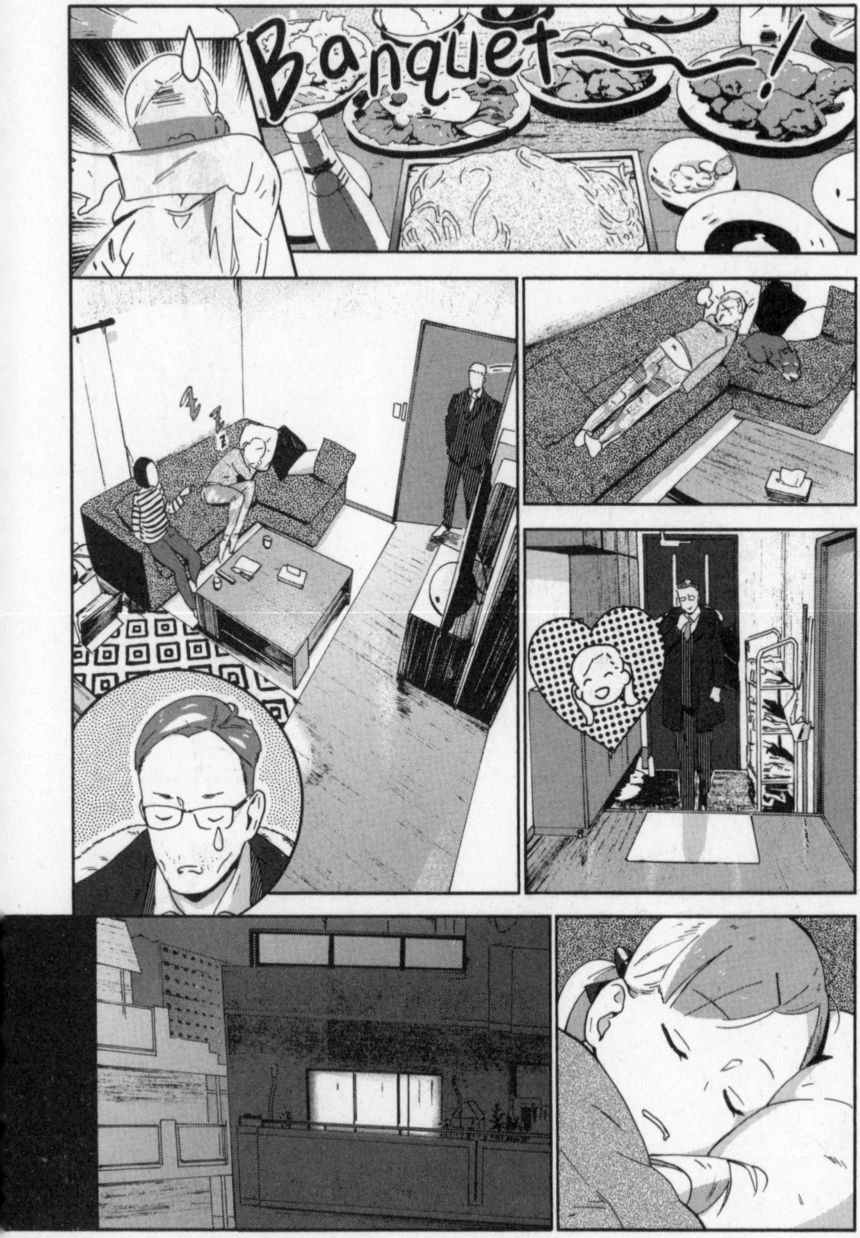
Banquet~~~!

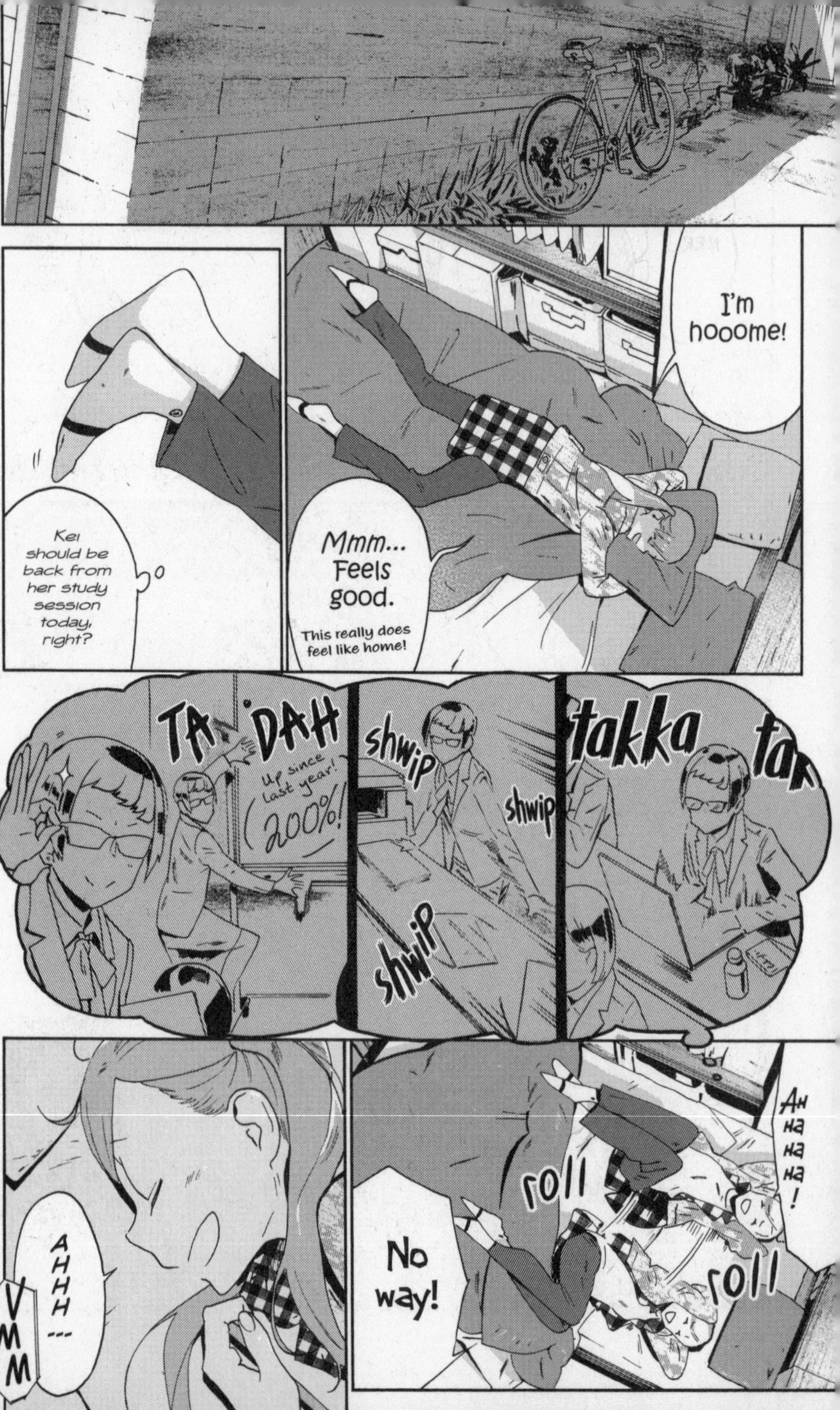
I'm hooome!
Mmm... Feels good.
This really does feel like home!
Kei should be back from her study session today, right?
takka tak
shwip
shwip
shwip
TA DAH
Up since last year!
200%!
AH HA HA HA!
roll
roll
No way!
AHHH...
VMM

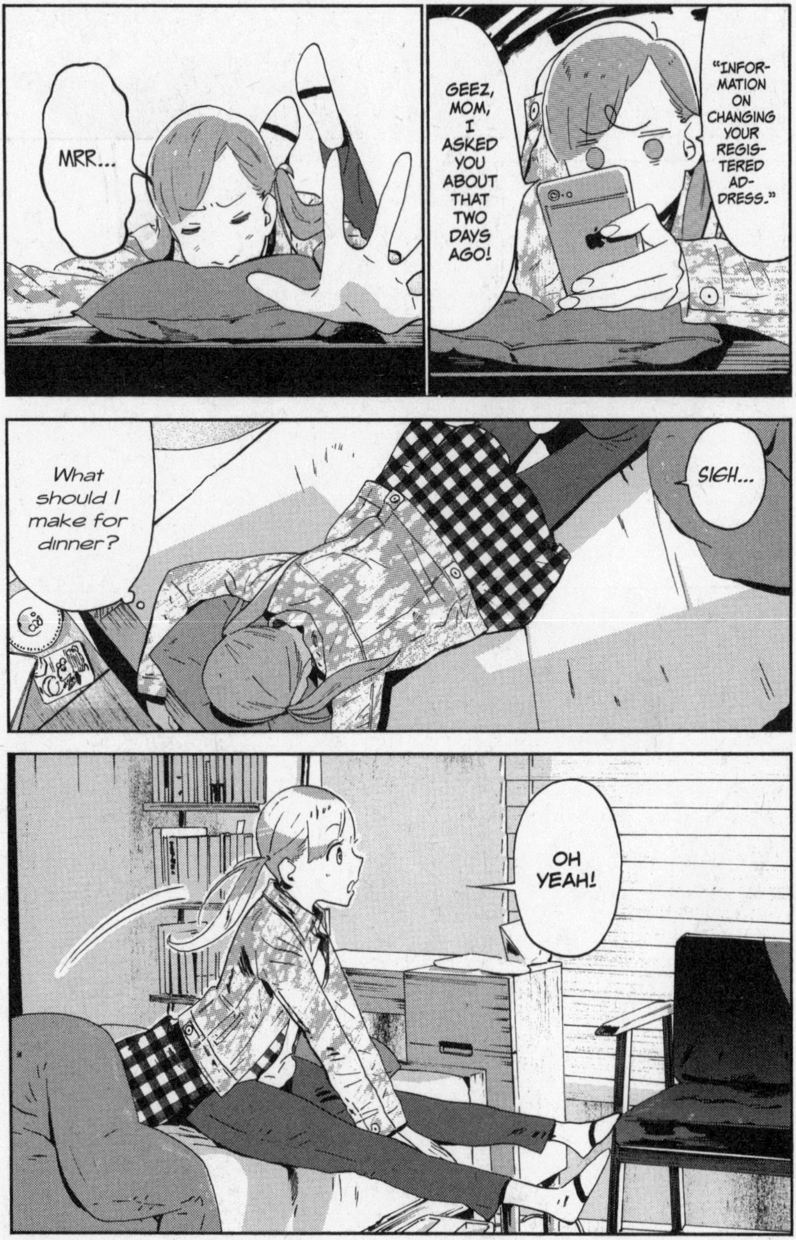
"INFORMATION ON CHANGING YOUR REGISTERED ADDRESS."
GEEZ, MOM, I ASKED YOU ABOUT THAT TWO DAYS AGO!
MRR...
SIGH...
What should I make for dinner?
OH YEAH!

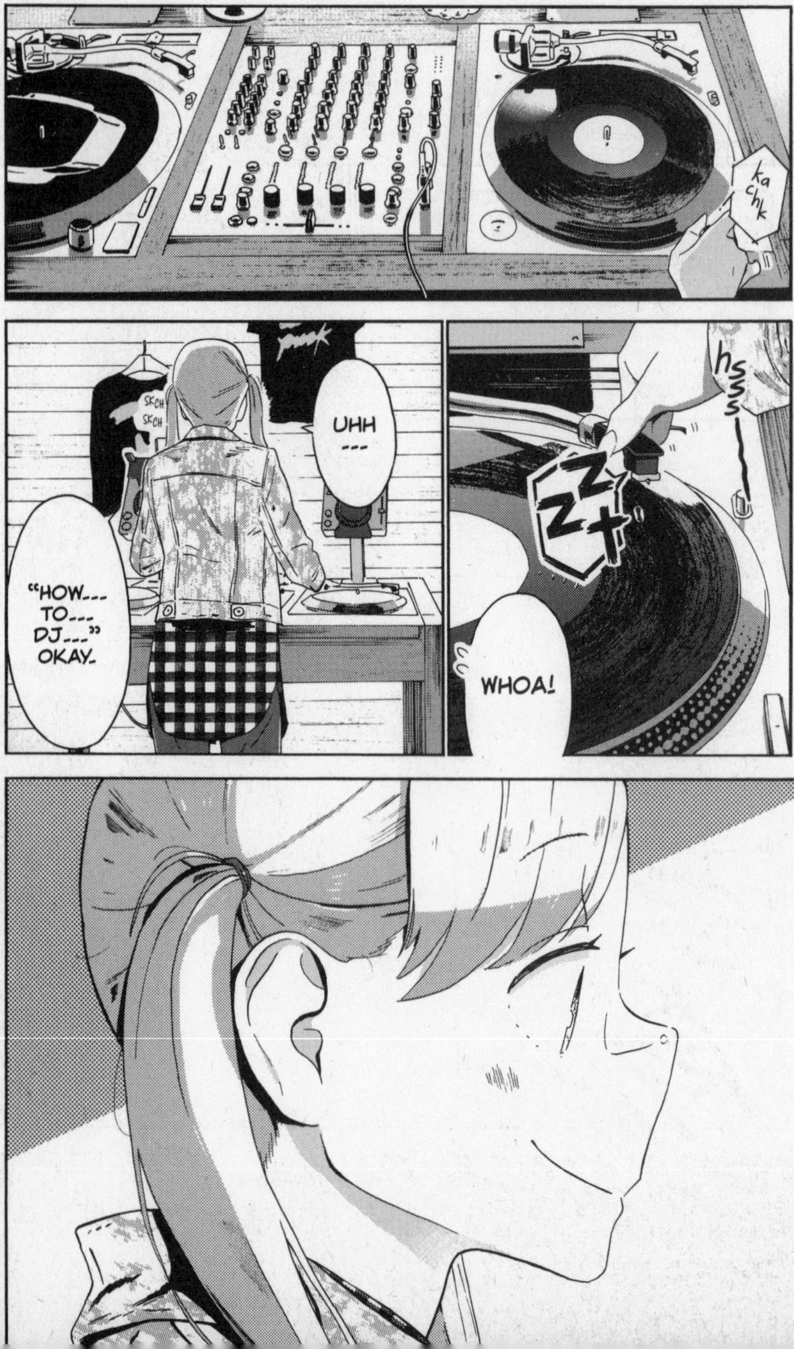
ka chk
hsss—
WHOA!
UHH ---
"HOW--- TO--- DJ---" OKAY.
SKCH SKCH

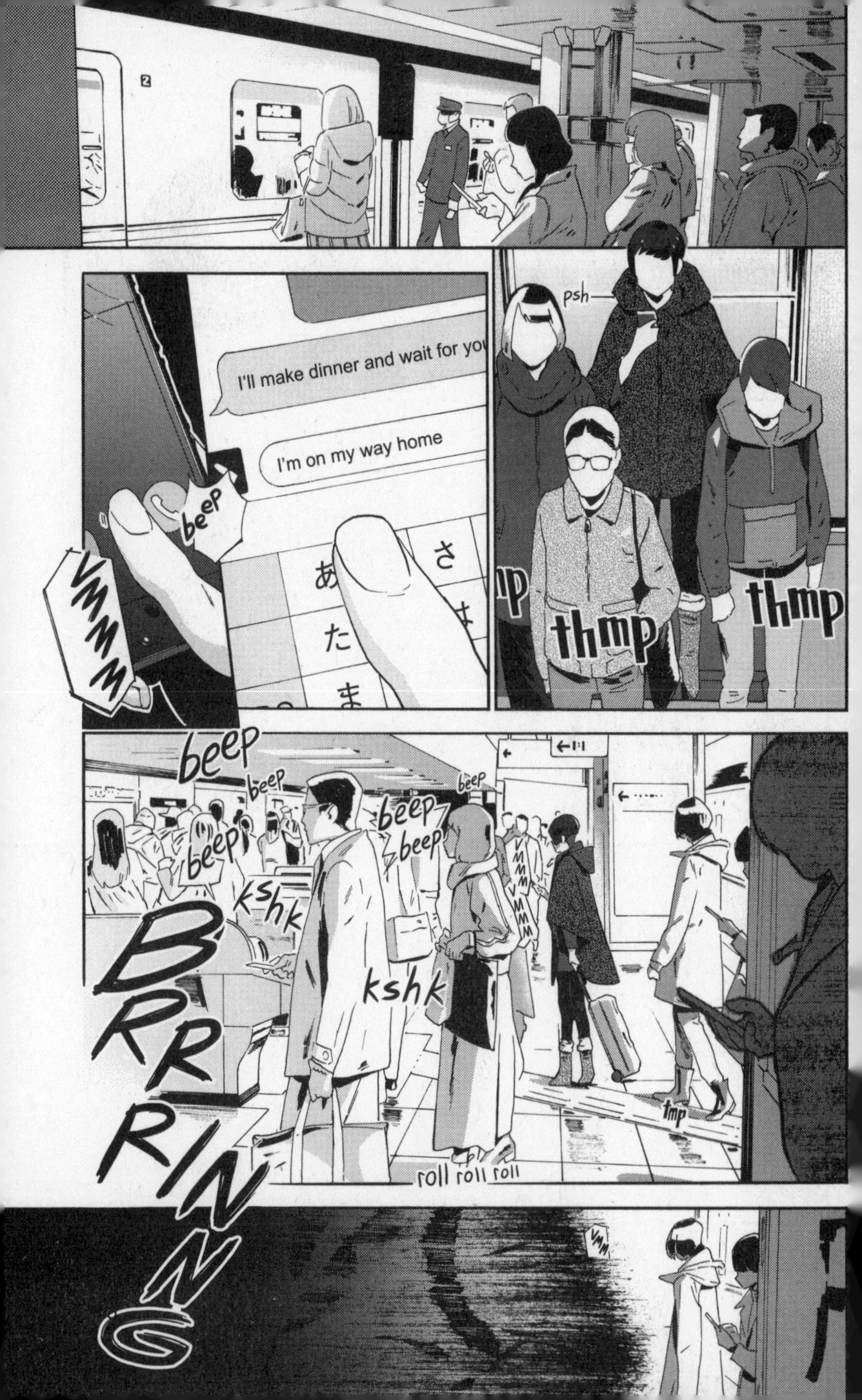
2
psh
thmp
thmp
mp
I'll make dinner and wait for yo
I'm on my way home
beep
あ
さ
た
ま
VMMMM
beep
beep
beep
beep
beep
beep
kshk
kshk
VMMM
VMMMM
tmp
roll roll roll
BRRRINNG
VMM

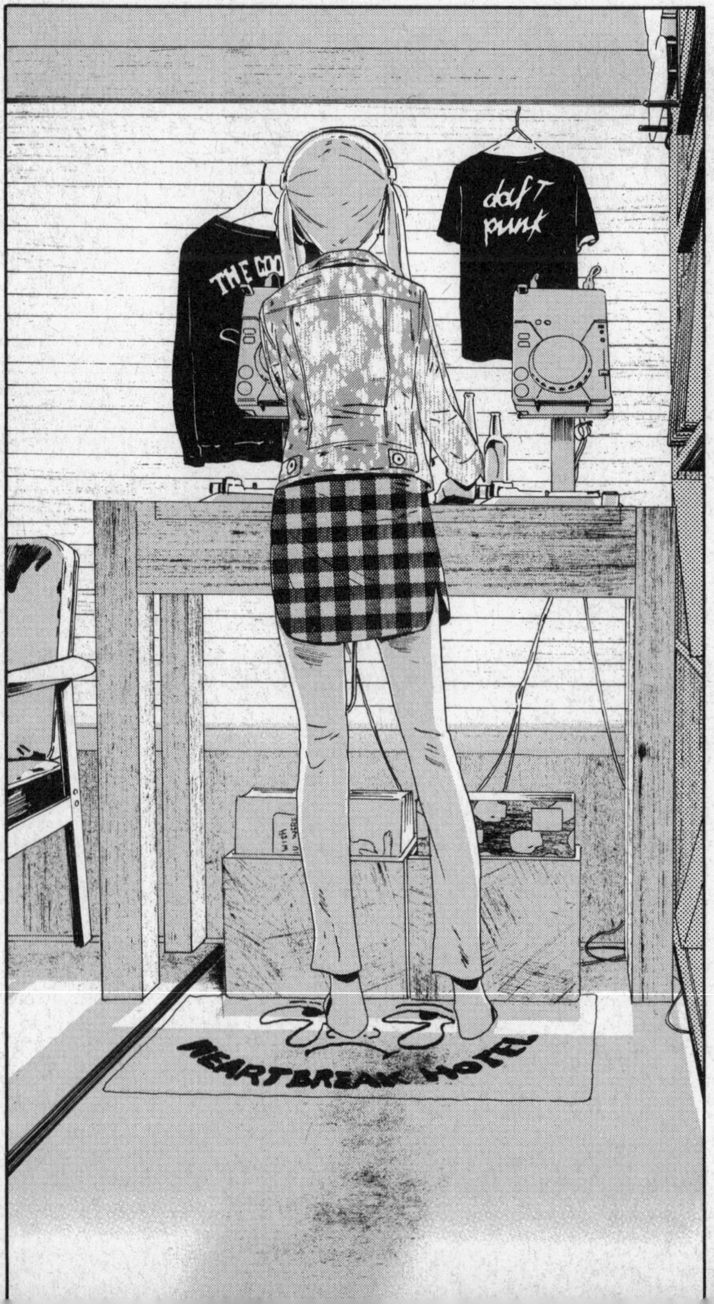
daft punk
HEARTBREAK HOTEL

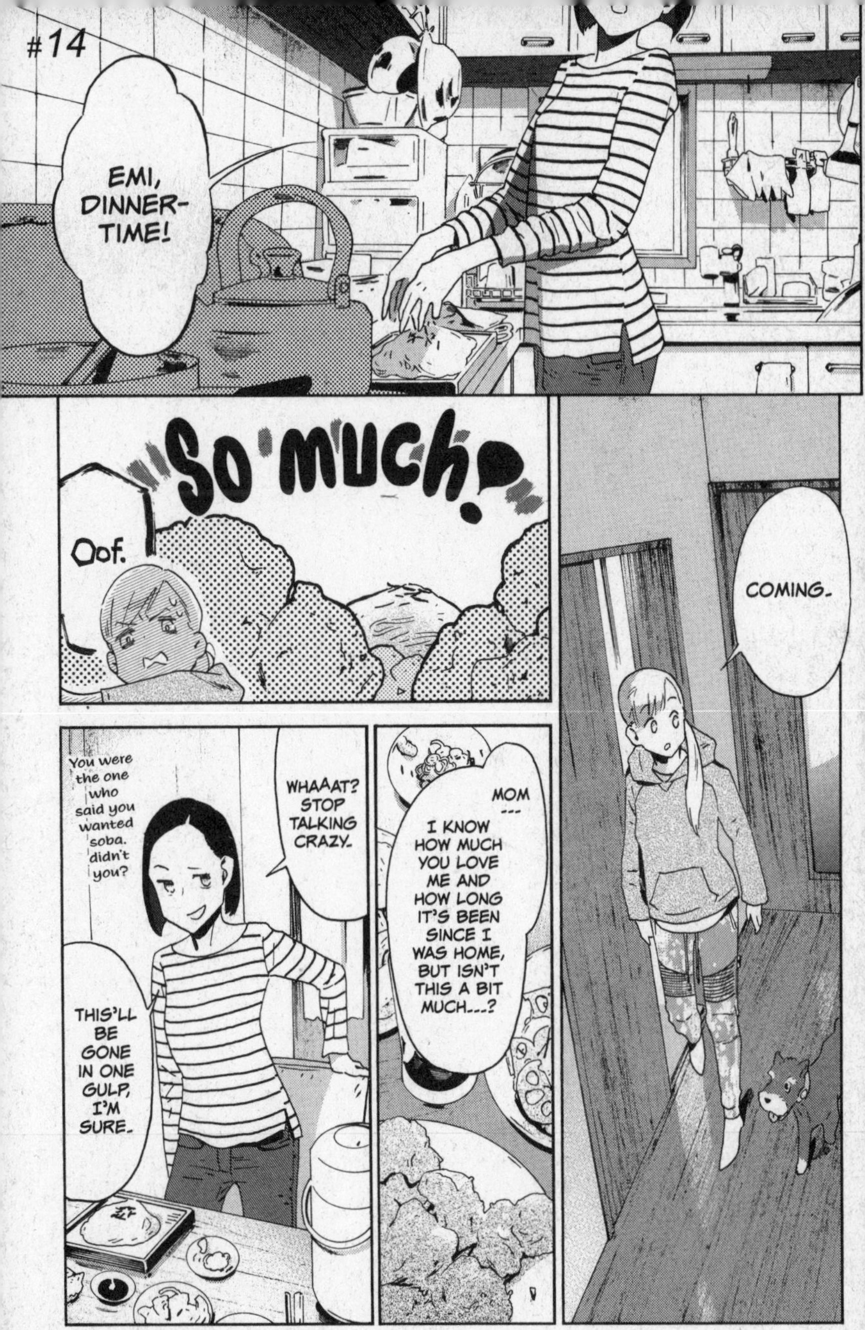
#14
EMI, DINNER-TIME!
COMING.
So much!
Oof.
MOM... I KNOW HOW MUCH YOU LOVE ME AND HOW LONG IT'S BEEN SINCE I WAS HOME, BUT ISN'T THIS A BIT MUCH...?
WHAAAT? STOP TALKING CRAZY.
You were the one who said you wanted soba, didn't you?
THIS'LL BE GONE IN ONE GULP, I'M SURE.

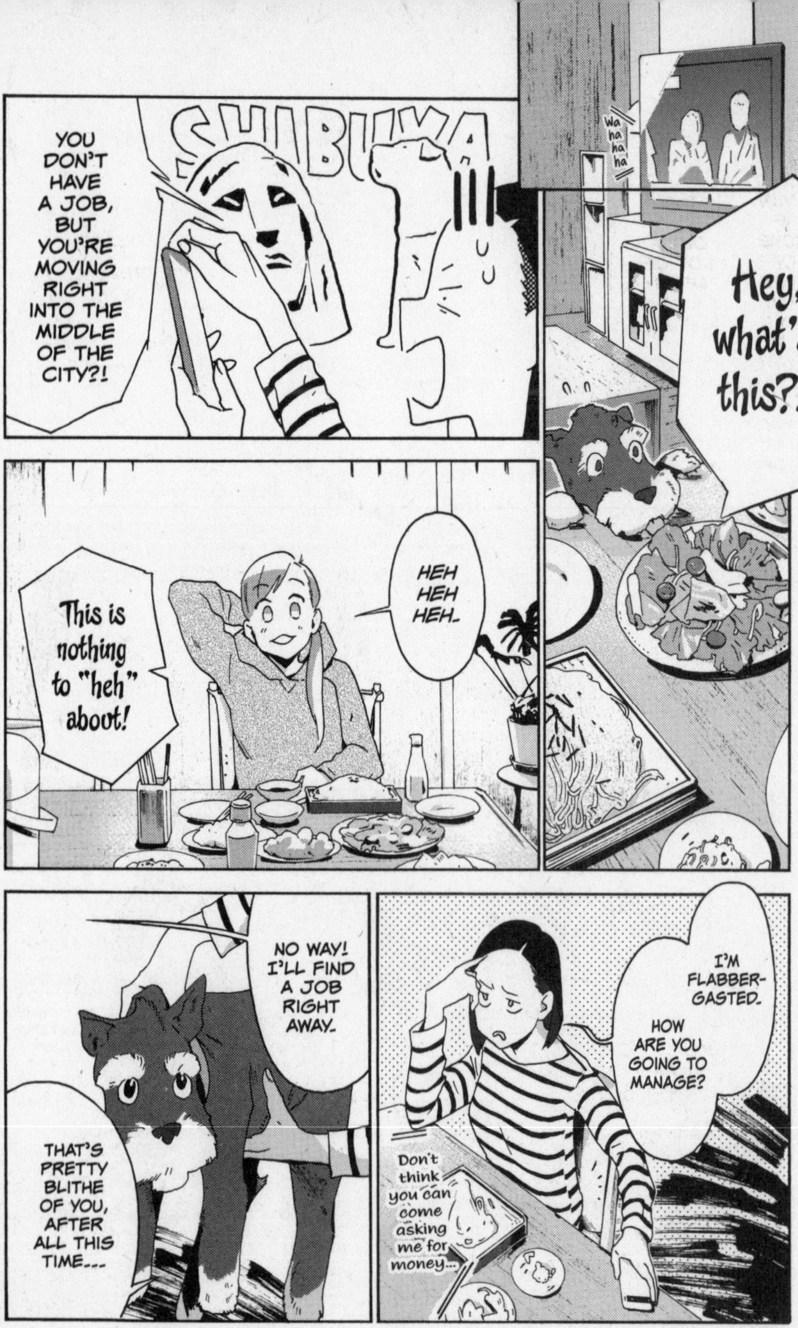
Wa ha ha ha
Hey, what's this?!
SHIBUYA
YOU DON'T HAVE A JOB, BUT YOU'RE MOVING RIGHT INTO THE MIDDLE OF THE CITY?!
HEH HEH HEH.
This is nothing to "heh" about!
I'M FLABBERGASTED.
HOW ARE YOU GOING TO MANAGE?
Don't think you can come asking me for money...
NO WAY! I'LL FIND A JOB RIGHT AWAY.
THAT'S PRETTY BLITHE OF YOU, AFTER ALL THIS TIME...

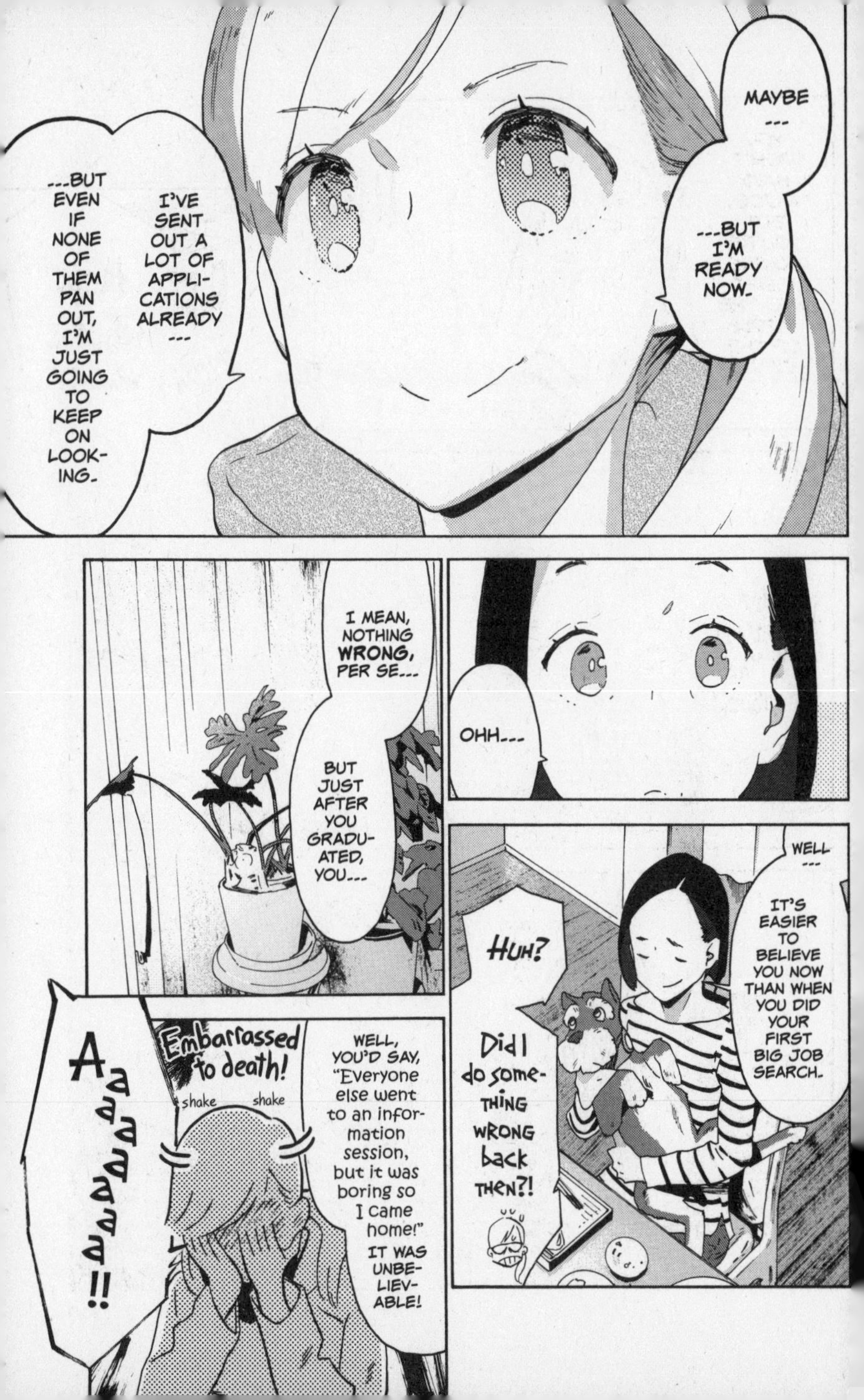
MAYBE---
---BUT I'M READY NOW.
I'VE SENT OUT A LOT OF APPLICATIONS ALREADY---
---BUT EVEN IF NONE OF THEM PAN OUT, I'M JUST GOING TO KEEP ON LOOKING.
OHH...
WELL---
IT'S EASIER TO BELIEVE YOU NOW THAN WHEN YOU DID YOUR FIRST BIG JOB SEARCH.
HUH?
Did I do some-thing wrong back then?!
I MEAN, NOTHING WRONG, PER SE...
BUT JUST AFTER YOU GRADUATED, YOU...
WELL, YOU'D SAY, "Everyone else went to an information session, but it was boring so I came home!" IT WAS UNBELIEVABLE!
shake shake
Embarrassed to death!
Aaaaaaaaaaaa!!

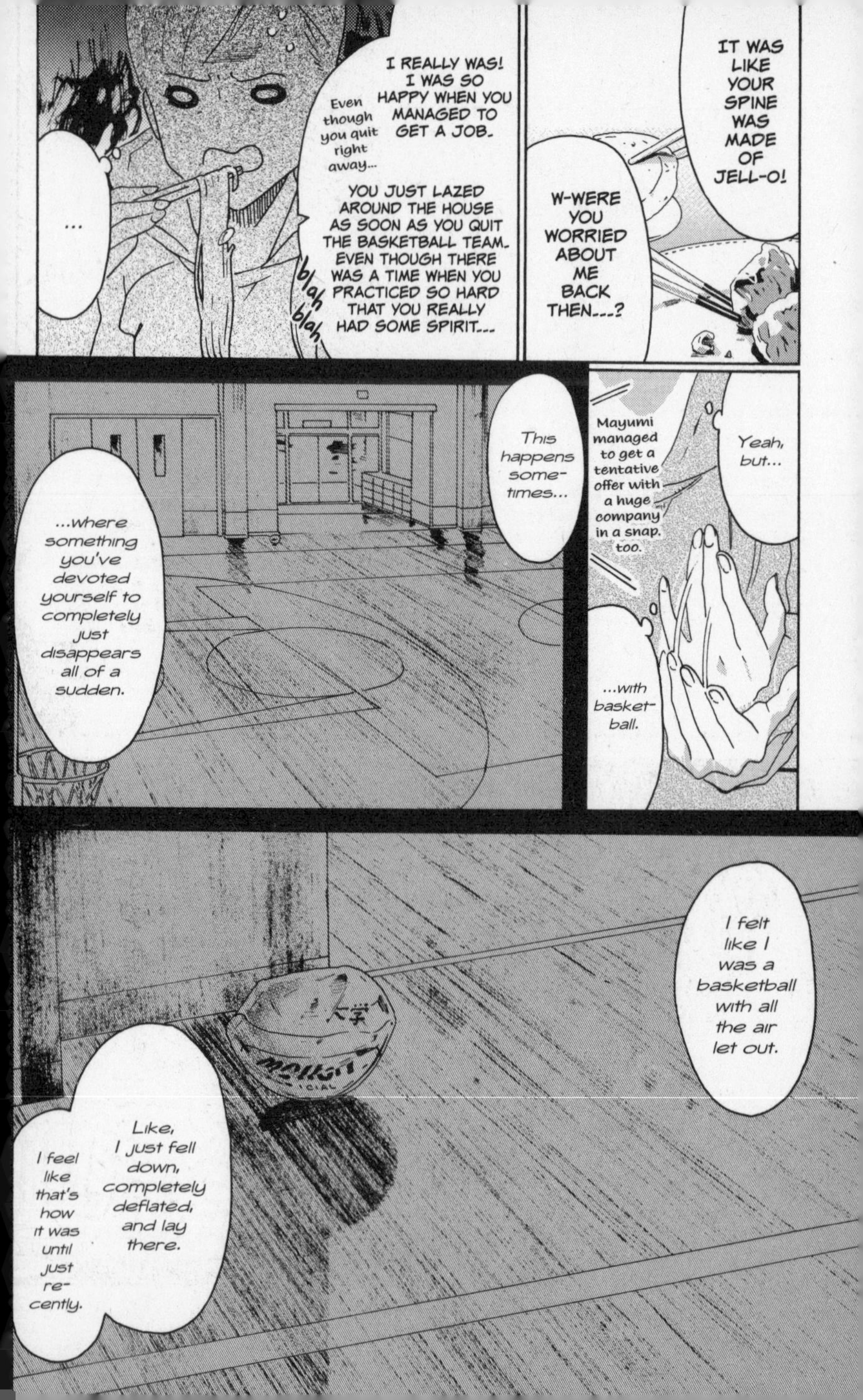
IT WAS LIKE YOUR SPINE WAS MADE OF JELL-O!
W-WERE YOU WORRIED ABOUT ME BACK THEN...?
I REALLY WAS! I WAS SO HAPPY WHEN YOU MANAGED TO GET A JOB.
Even though you quit right away...
YOU JUST LAZED AROUND THE HOUSE AS SOON AS YOU QUIT THE BASKETBALL TEAM. EVEN THOUGH THERE WAS A TIME WHEN YOU PRACTICED SO HARD THAT YOU REALLY HAD SOME SPIRIT...
blah blah
...
Yeah, but...
Mayumi managed to get a tentative offer with a huge company in a snap, too.
...with basketball.
This happens sometimes...
...where something you've devoted yourself to completely just disappears all of a sudden.
I felt like I was a basketball with all the air let out.
Like, I just fell down, completely deflated, and lay there.
I feel like that's how it was until just recently.

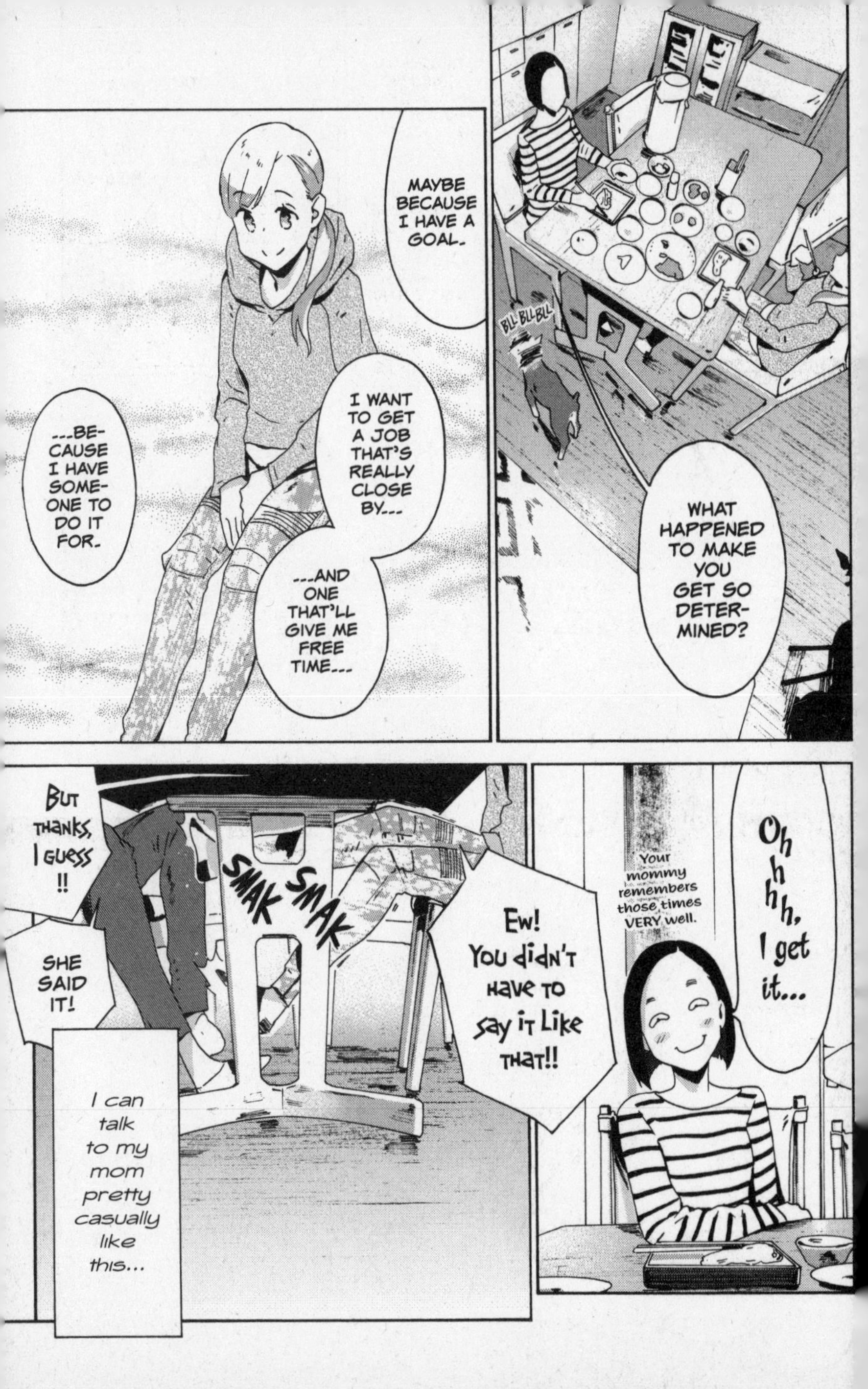
BLL BLL BLL
WHAT HAPPENED TO MAKE YOU GET SO DETERMINED?
MAYBE BECAUSE I HAVE A GOAL.
I WANT TO GET A JOB THAT'S REALLY CLOSE BY...
...AND ONE THAT'LL GIVE ME FREE TIME...
...BECAUSE I HAVE SOMEONE TO DO IT FOR.
Ohhhh, I get it...
Your mommy remembers those times VERY well.
Ew! You didn't have to say it like that!!
SMAK SMAK
But thanks, I guess!!
SHE SAID IT!
I can talk to my mom pretty casually like this...

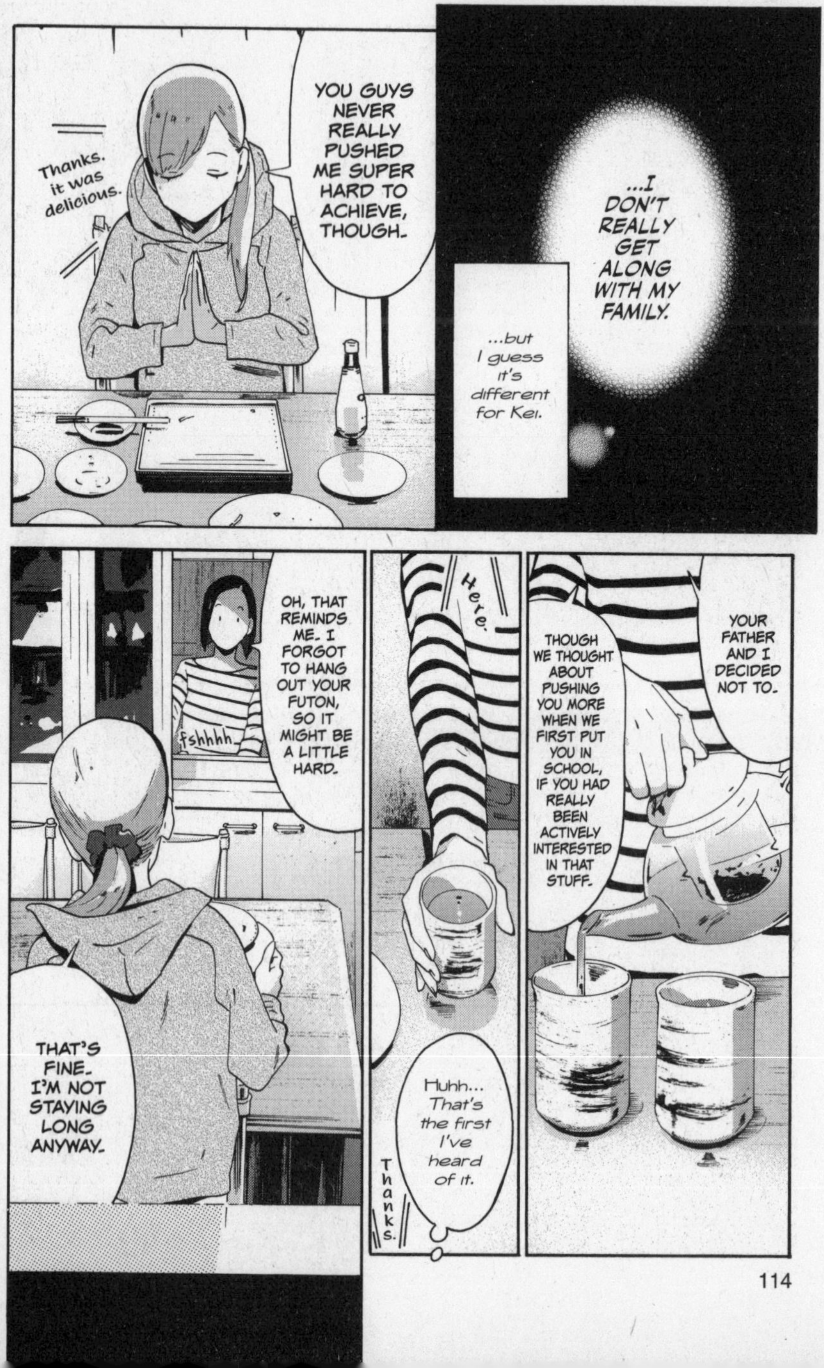
...I DON'T REALLY GET ALONG WITH MY FAMILY.
...but I guess it's different for Kei.
YOU GUYS NEVER REALLY PUSHED ME SUPER HARD TO ACHIEVE, THOUGH.
Thanks. it was delicious.
YOUR FATHER AND I DECIDED NOT TO.
THOUGH WE THOUGHT ABOUT PUSHING YOU MORE WHEN WE FIRST PUT YOU IN SCHOOL, IF YOU HAD REALLY BEEN ACTIVELY INTERESTED IN THAT STUFF.
Here.
Huhh... That's the first I've heard of it.
Thanks.
OH, THAT REMINDS ME. I FORGOT TO HANG OUT YOUR FUTON, SO IT MIGHT BE A LITTLE HARD.
fshhhh
THAT'S FINE. I'M NOT STAYING LONG ANYWAY.

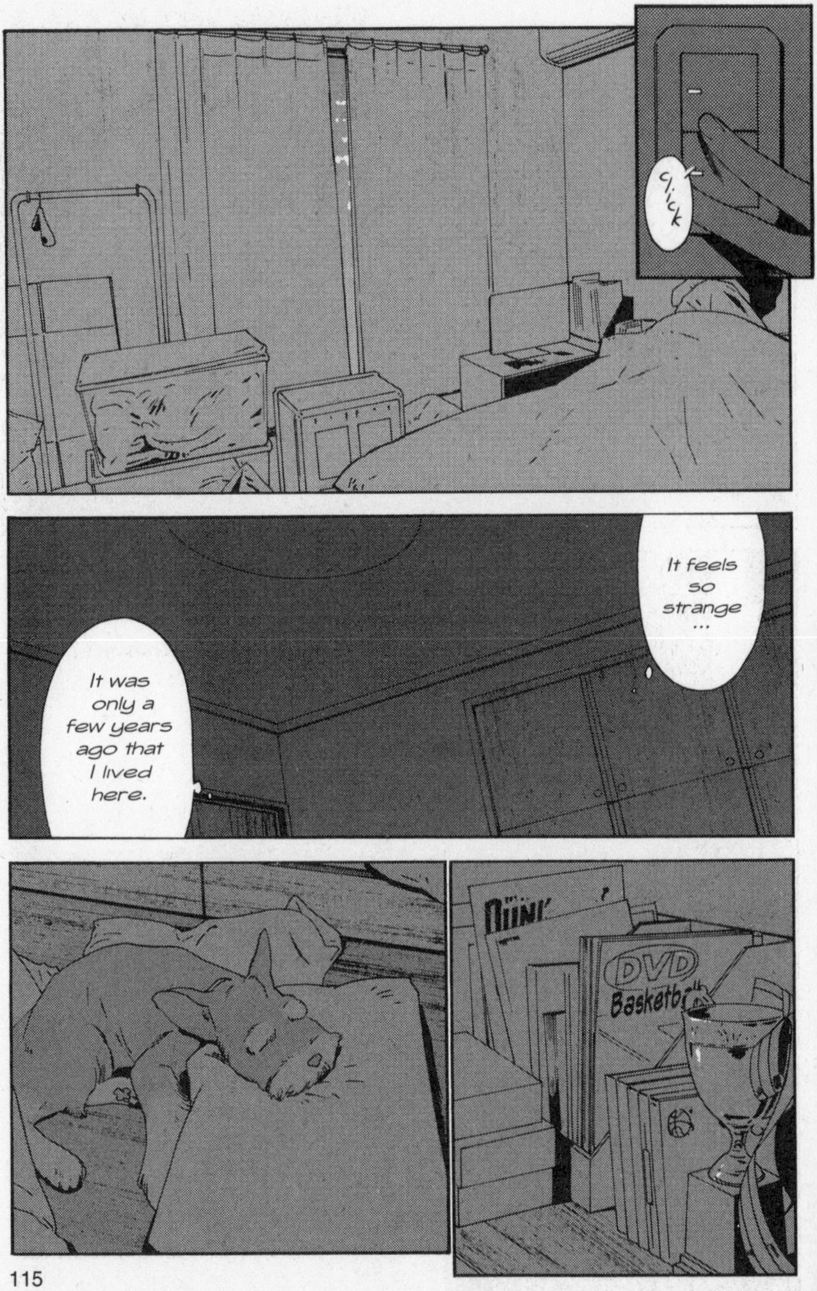
click
It feels so strange …
It was only a few years ago that I lived here.
DVD

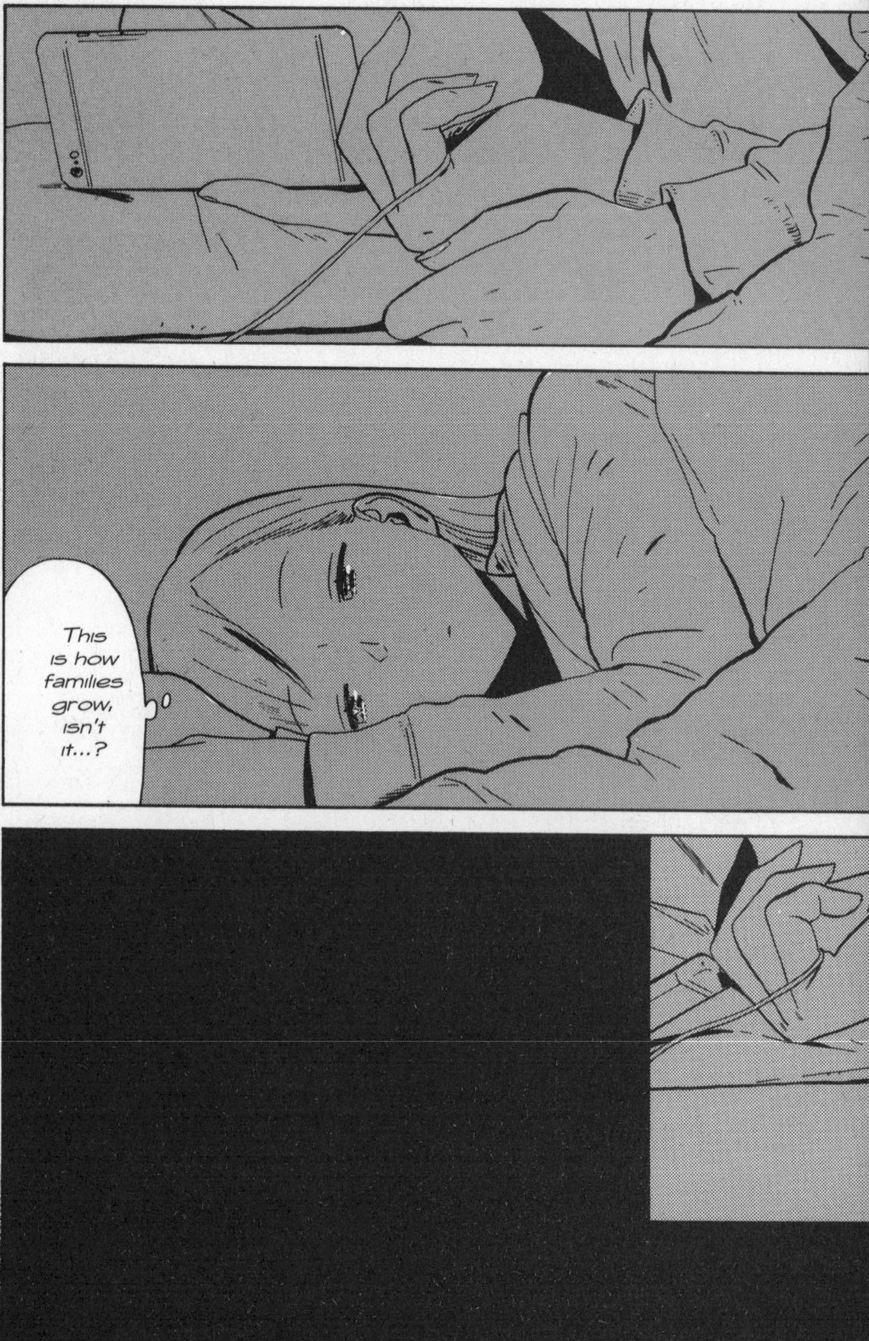
This is how families grow, isn't it...?

AFTER HOURS #14

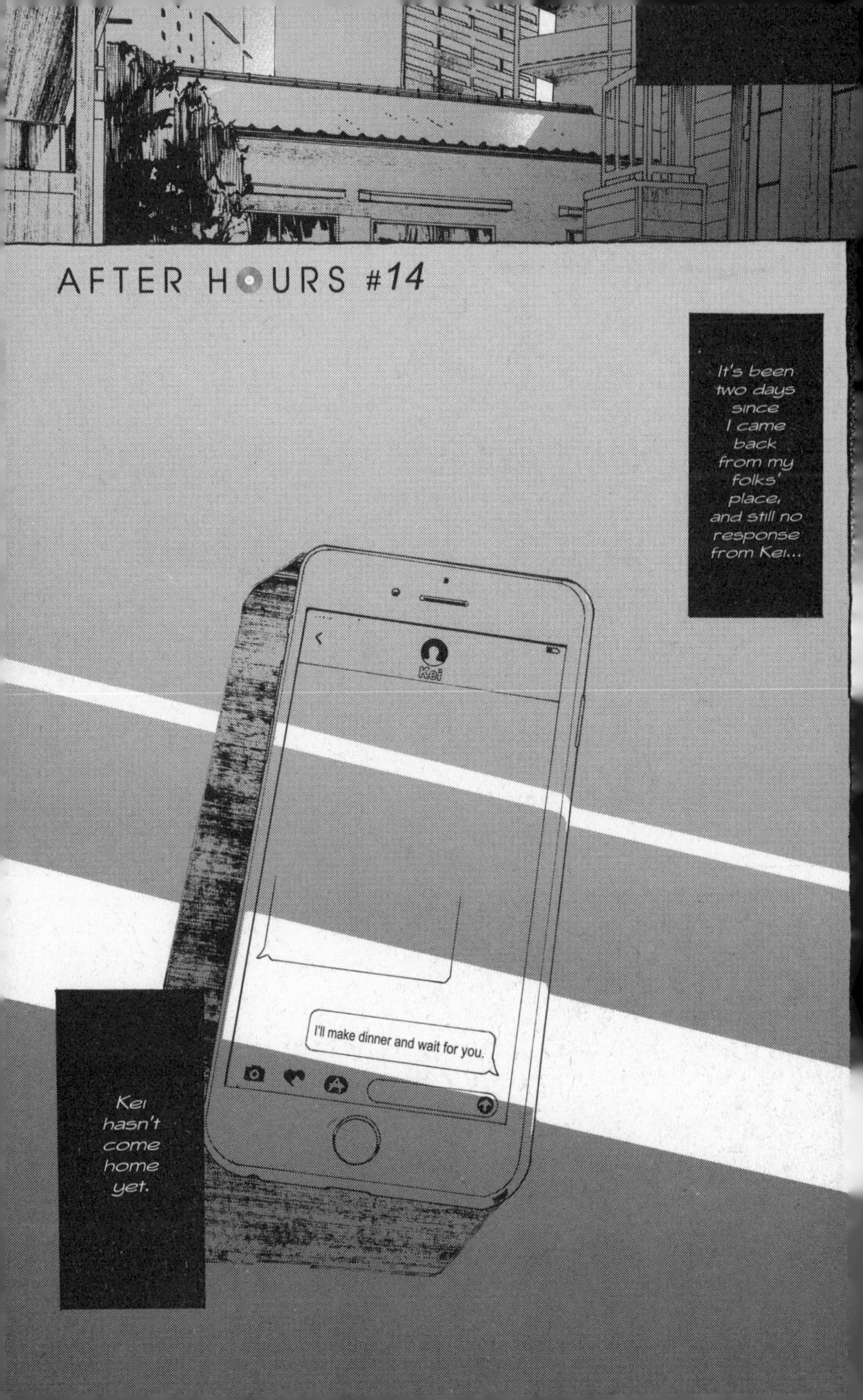
It's been two days since I came back from my folks' place, and still no response from Kei...
Kei
I'll make dinner and wait for you.
Kei hasn't come home yet.

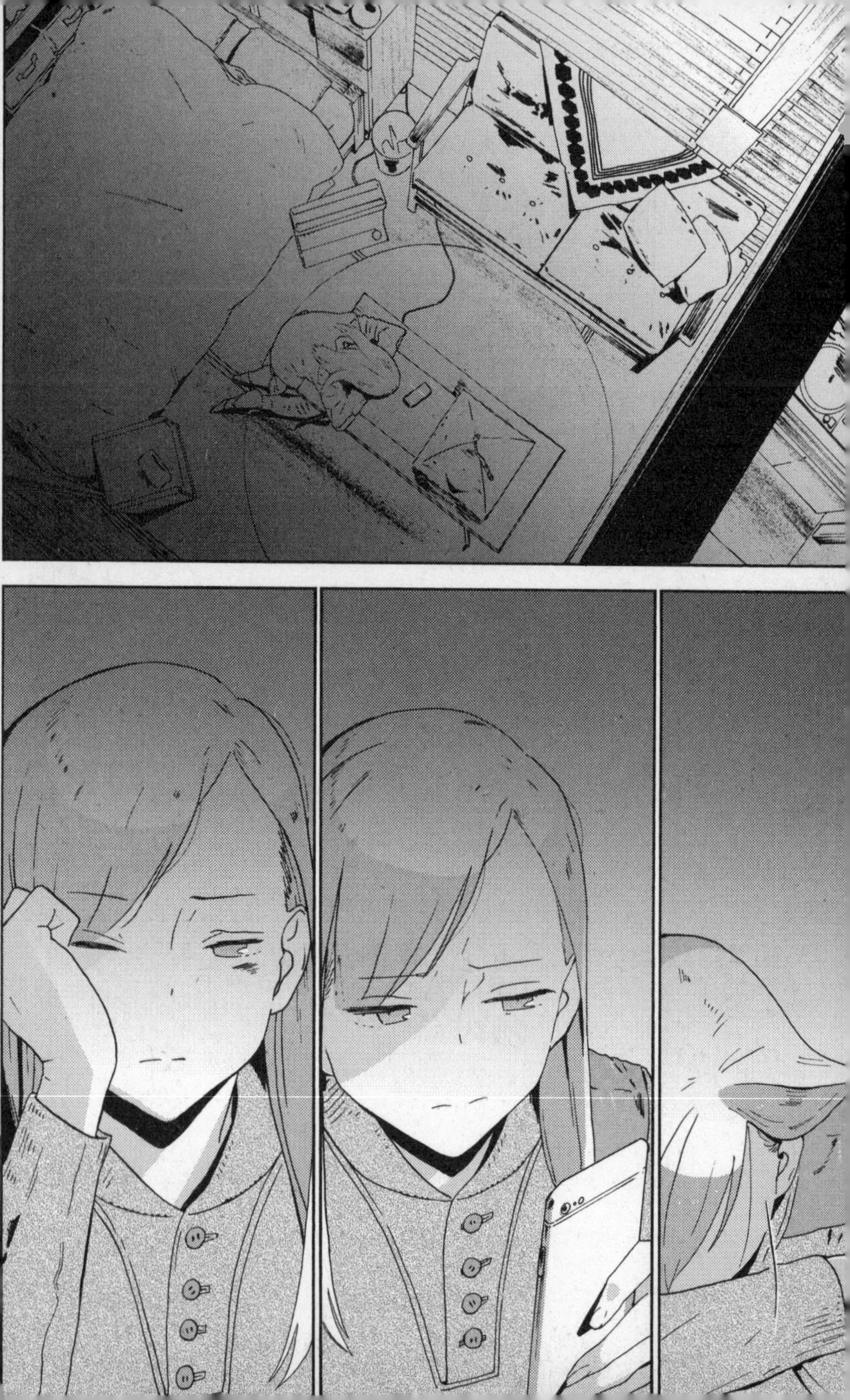

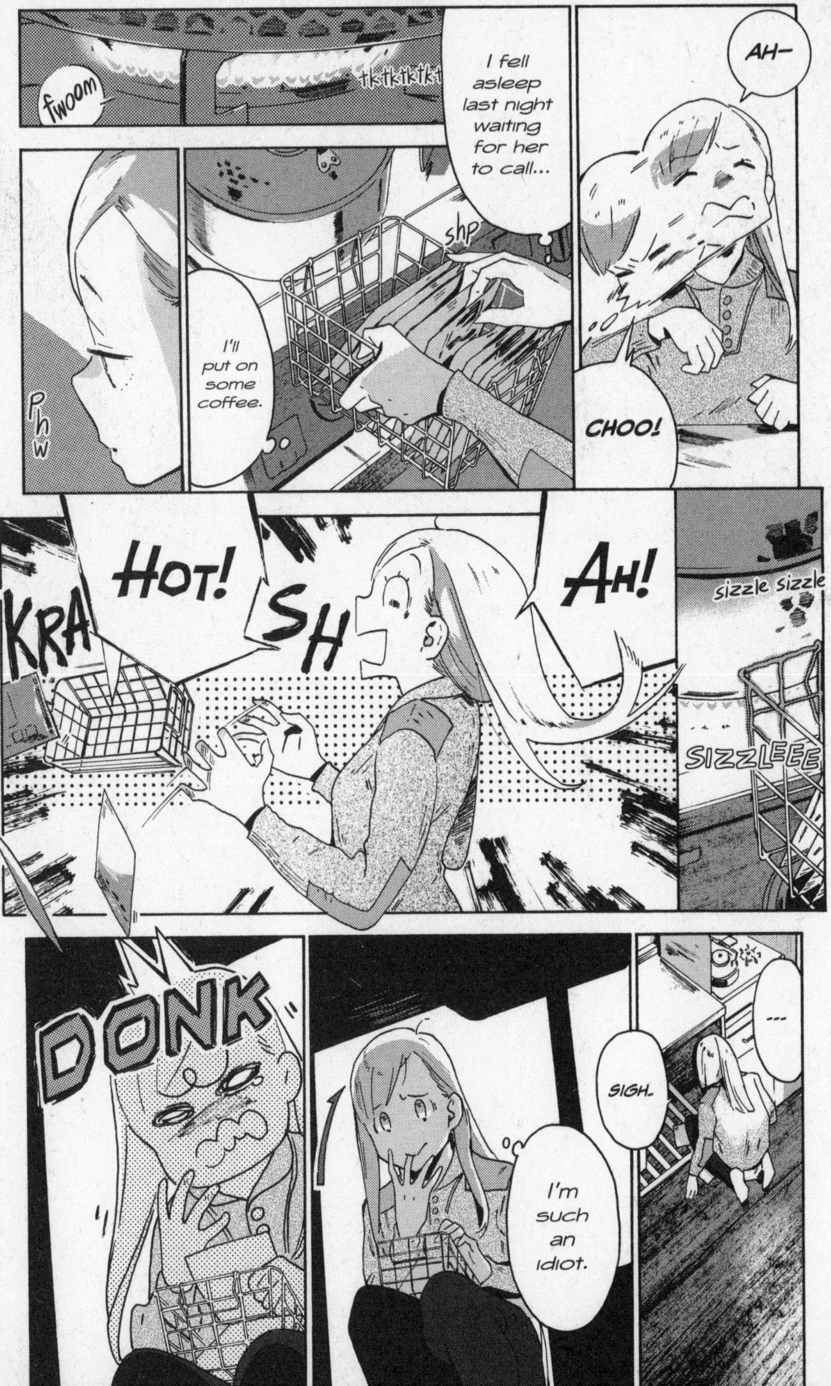
AH—
CHOO!
tktktktkt
fwoom
I fell asleep last night waiting for her to call...
shp
I'll put on some coffee.
phw
sizzle sizzle
SIZZLEEE
AH!
SH
HOT!
KRA
...
SIGH.
I'm such an idiot.
DONK

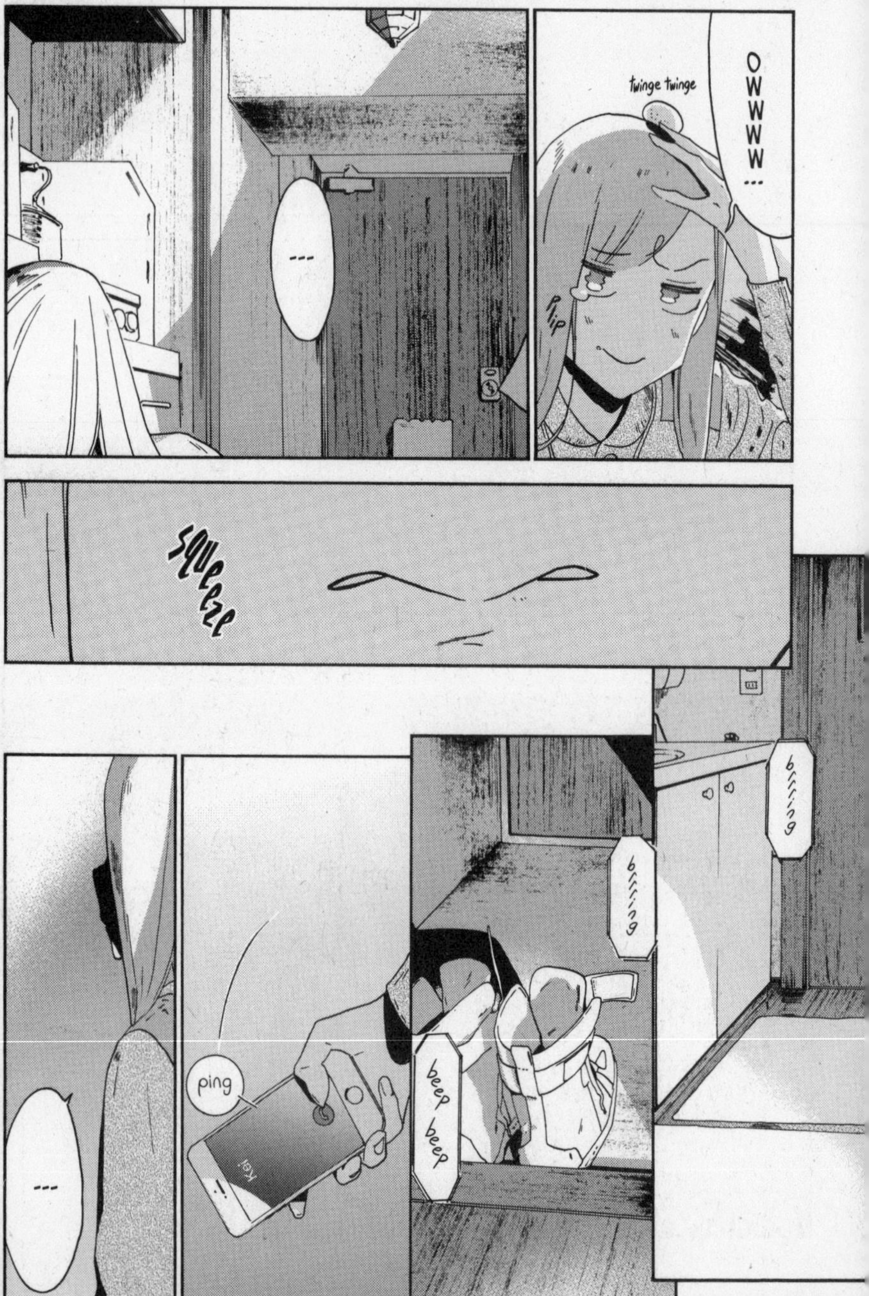
OWWWW...
twinge twinge
...
squeeze
brrring
brrring
beep beep
ping
...

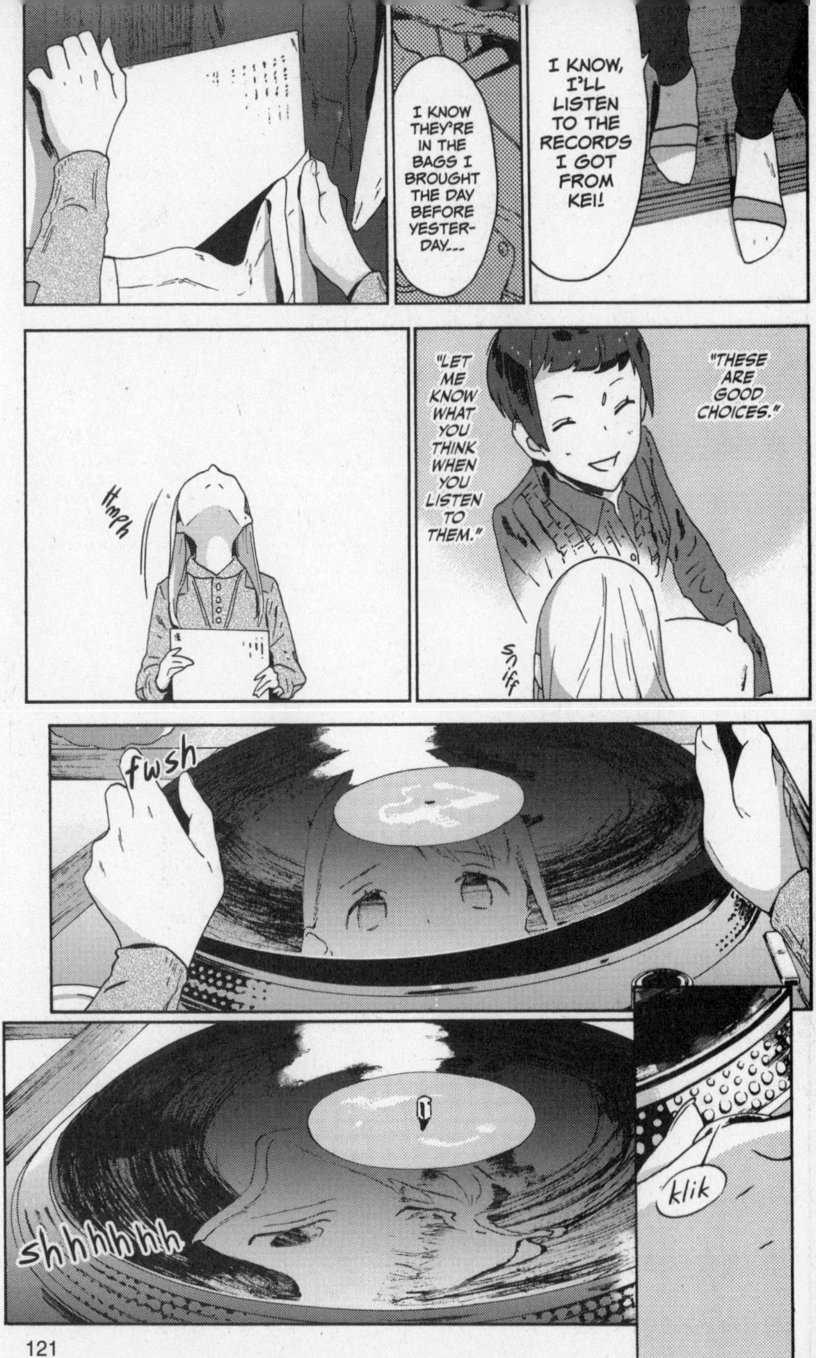
I KNOW, I'LL LISTEN TO THE RECORDS I GOT FROM KEI!
I KNOW THEY'RE IN THE BAGS I BROUGHT THE DAY BEFORE YESTER-DAY...
"THESE ARE GOOD CHOICES."
"LET ME KNOW WHAT YOU THINK WHEN YOU LISTEN TO THEM."
sniff
Hmph
fwsh
klik
shhhhhh

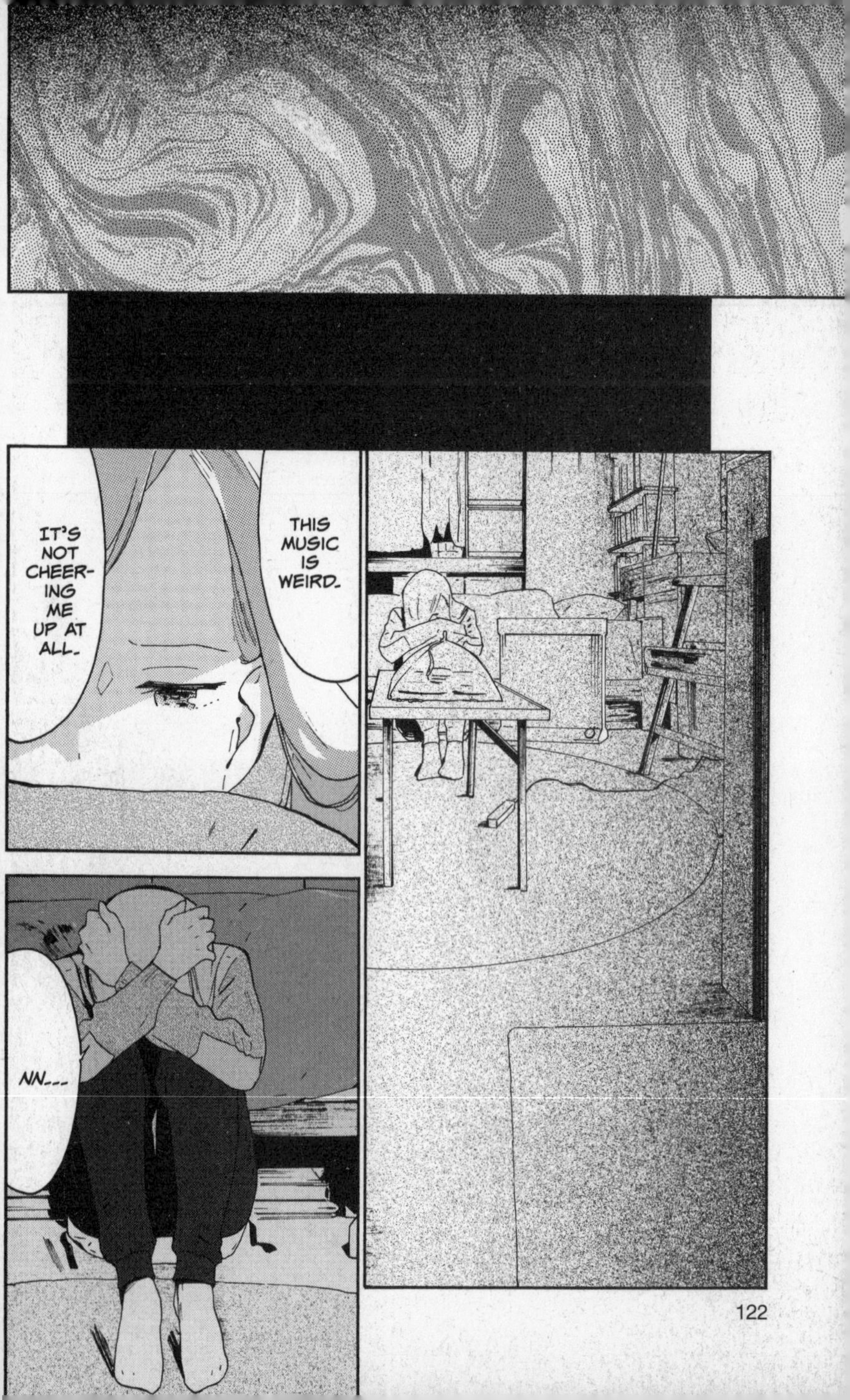
THIS MUSIC IS WEIRD.
IT'S NOT CHEERING ME UP AT ALL.
NN...

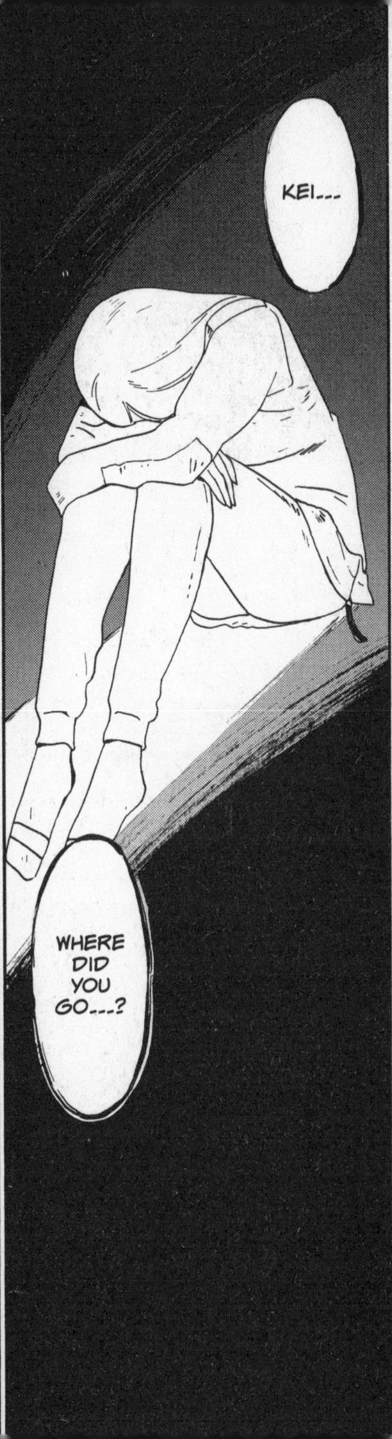
KEI...
WHERE DID YOU GO...?

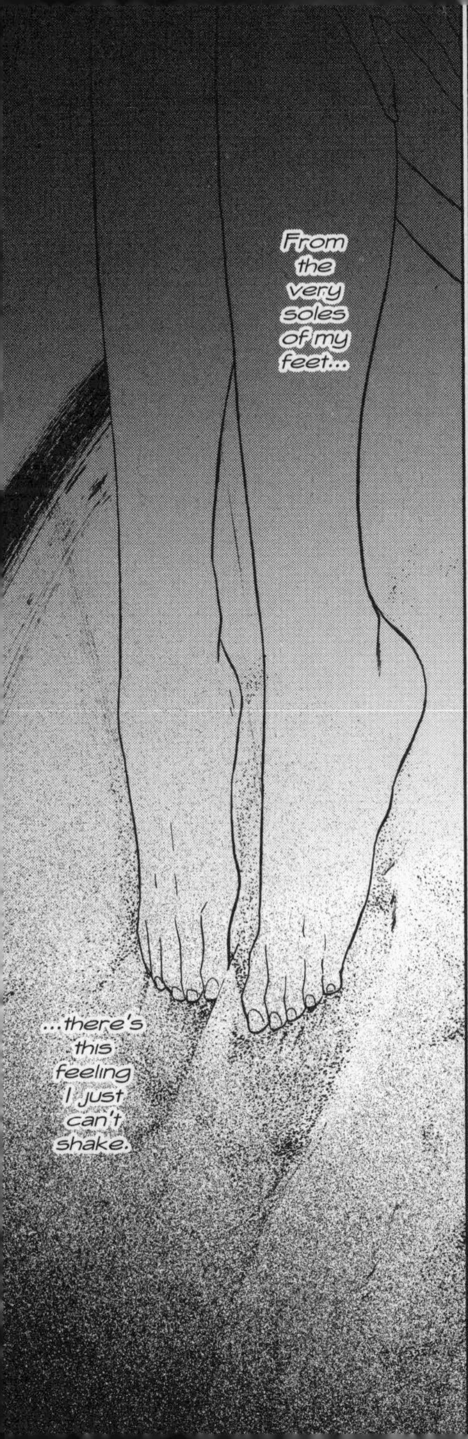
From the very soles of my feet...
...there's this feeling I just can't shake.

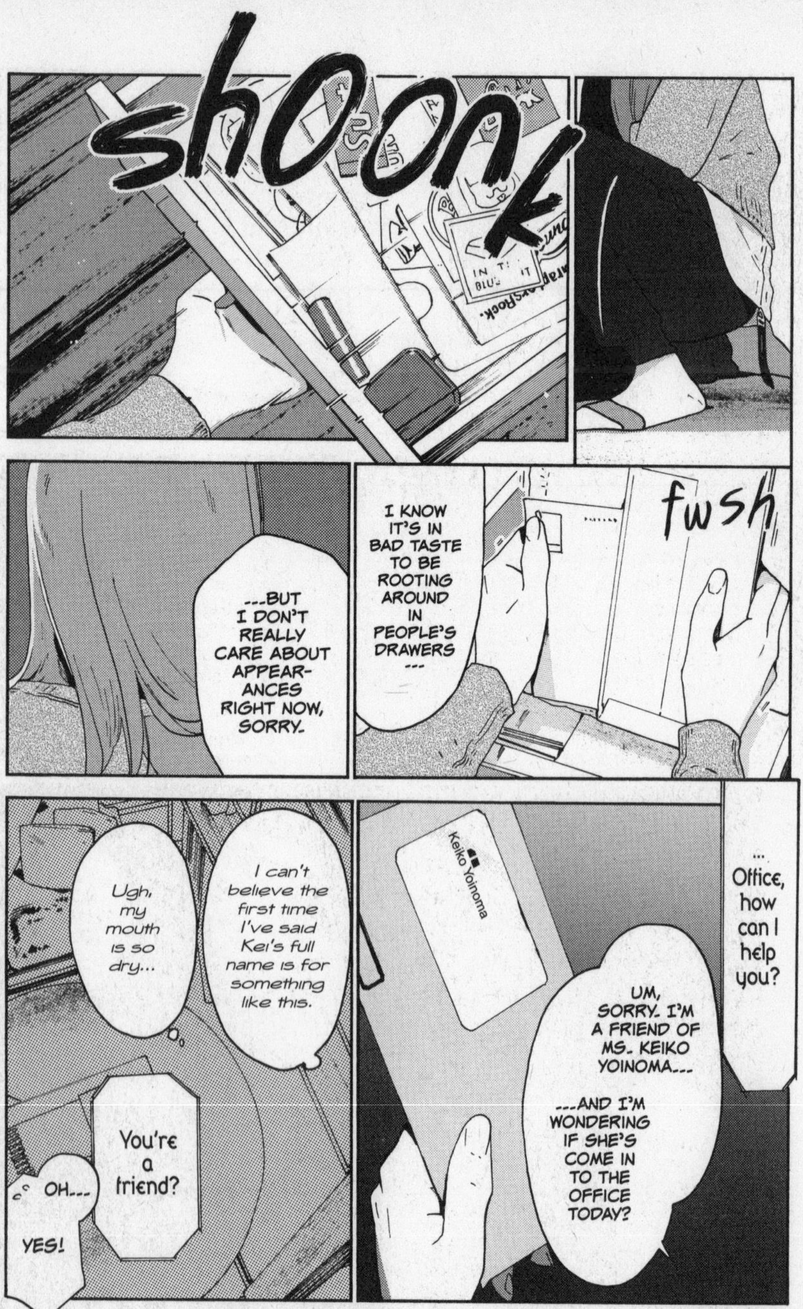
shOOnk
IN TH IT
BLU IT
fwsh
I KNOW IT'S IN BAD TASTE TO BE ROOTING AROUND IN PEOPLE'S DRAWERS...
...BUT I DON'T REALLY CARE ABOUT APPEARANCES RIGHT NOW, SORRY.
...Office, how can I help you?
Keiko Yoinoma
UM, SORRY. I'M A FRIEND OF MS. KEIKO YOINOMA...
...AND I'M WONDERING IF SHE'S COME IN TO THE OFFICE TODAY?
You're a friend?
OH... YES!
I can't believe the first time I've said Kei's full name is for something like this.
Ugh, my mouth is so dry...

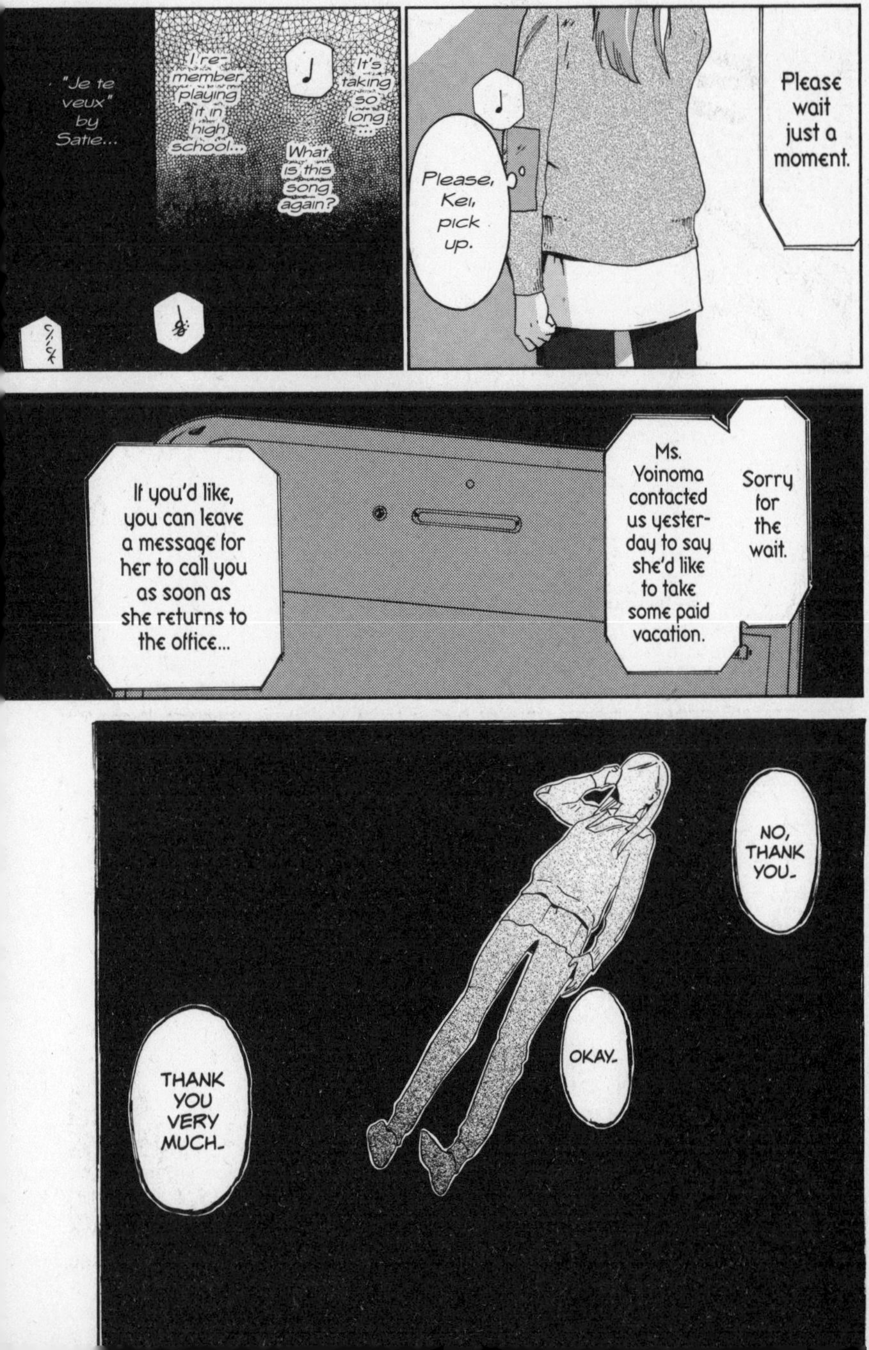
Please wait just a moment.
Please, Kei, pick up.
It's taking so long...
What is this song again?
I re-member playing it in high school...
"Je te veux" by Satie...
Click
Sorry for the wait.
Ms. Yoinoma contacted us yester-day to say she'd like to take some paid vacation.
If you'd like, you can leave a message for her to call you as soon as she returns to the office...
NO, THANK YOU.
OKAY.
THANK YOU VERY MUCH.

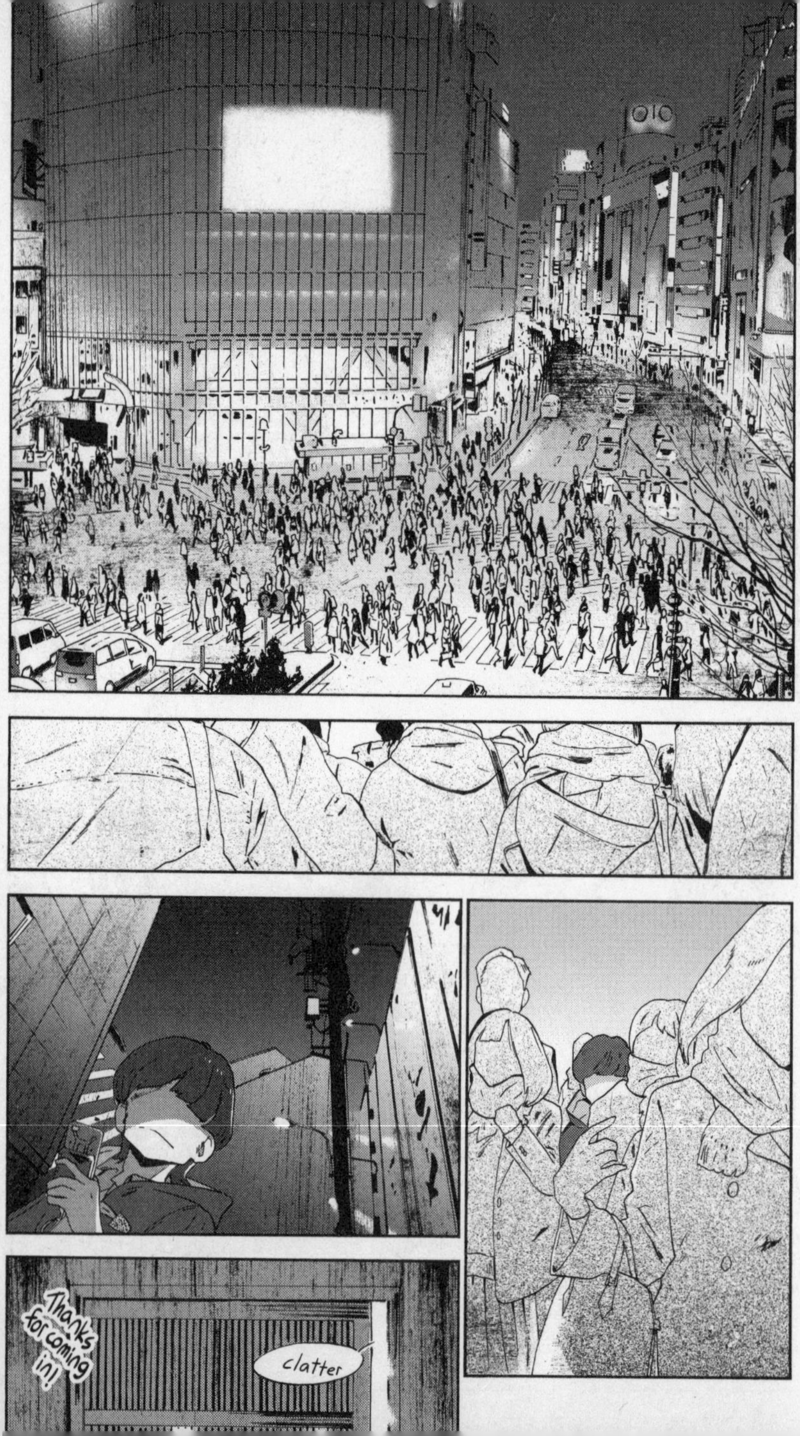
Thanks for coming in!
clatter

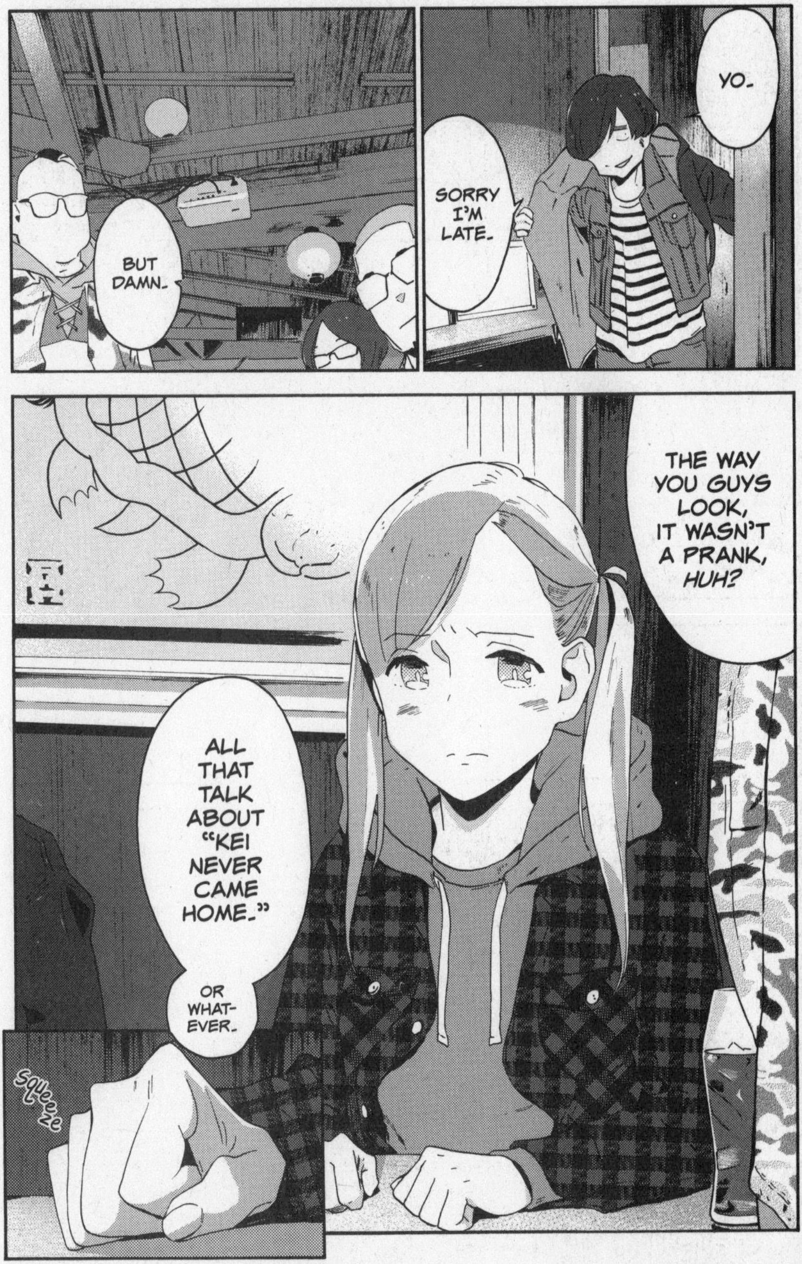
YO.
SORRY I'M LATE.
BUT DAMN.
THE WAY YOU GUYS LOOK, IT WASN'T A PRANK, HUH?
ALL THAT TALK ABOUT "KEI NEVER CAME HOME."
OR WHATEVER.
squeeze

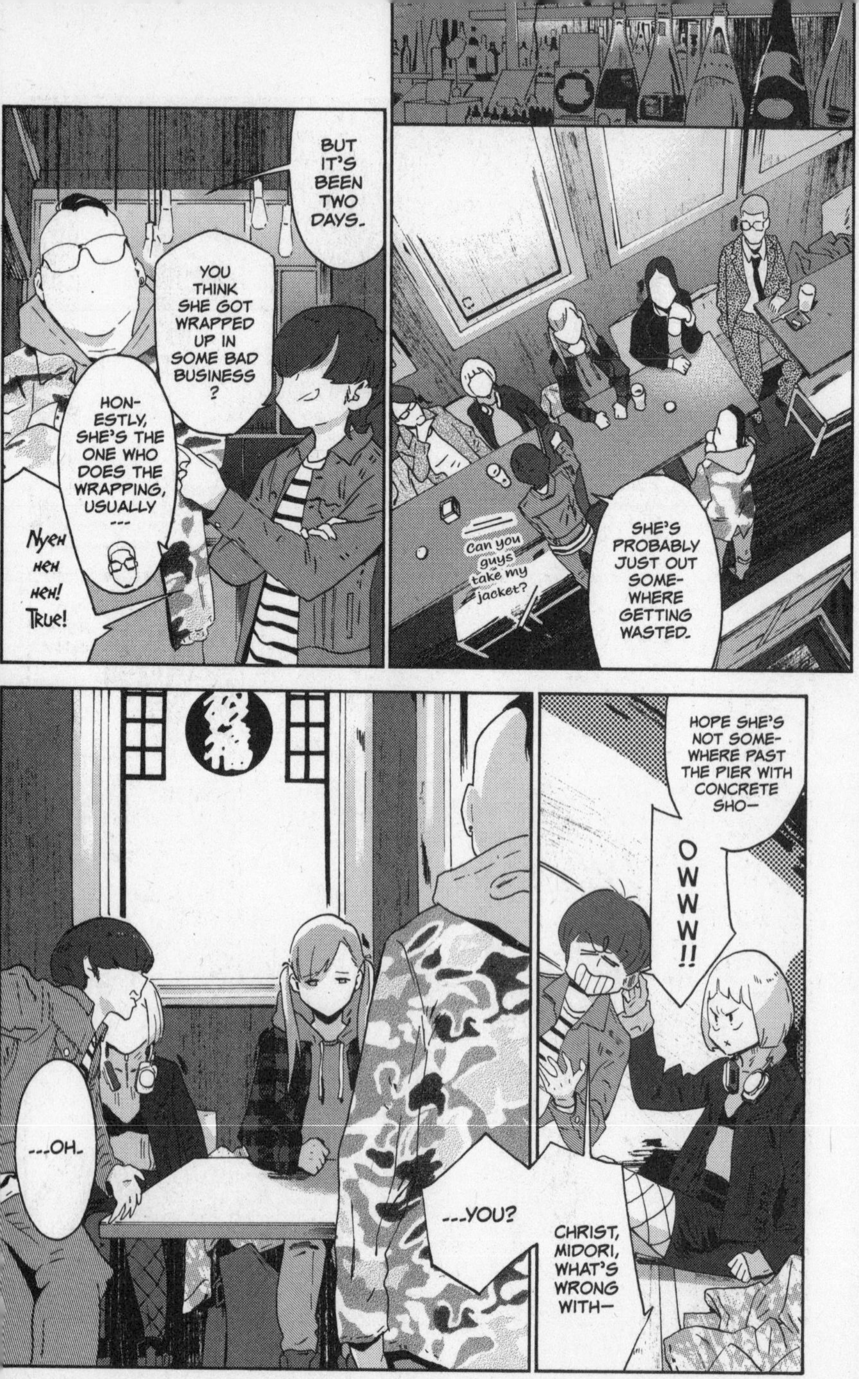
Can you guys take my jacket?
SHE'S PROBABLY JUST OUT SOMEWHERE GETTING WASTED.
BUT IT'S BEEN TWO DAYS.
YOU THINK SHE GOT WRAPPED UP IN SOME BAD BUSINESS?
HONESTLY, SHE'S THE ONE WHO DOES THE WRAPPING, USUALLY...
Nyeh heh heh! True!
HOPE SHE'S NOT SOMEWHERE PAST THE PIER WITH CONCRETE SHO—
OWWW!!
CHRIST, MIDORI, WHAT'S WRONG WITH—
...YOU?
...OH.

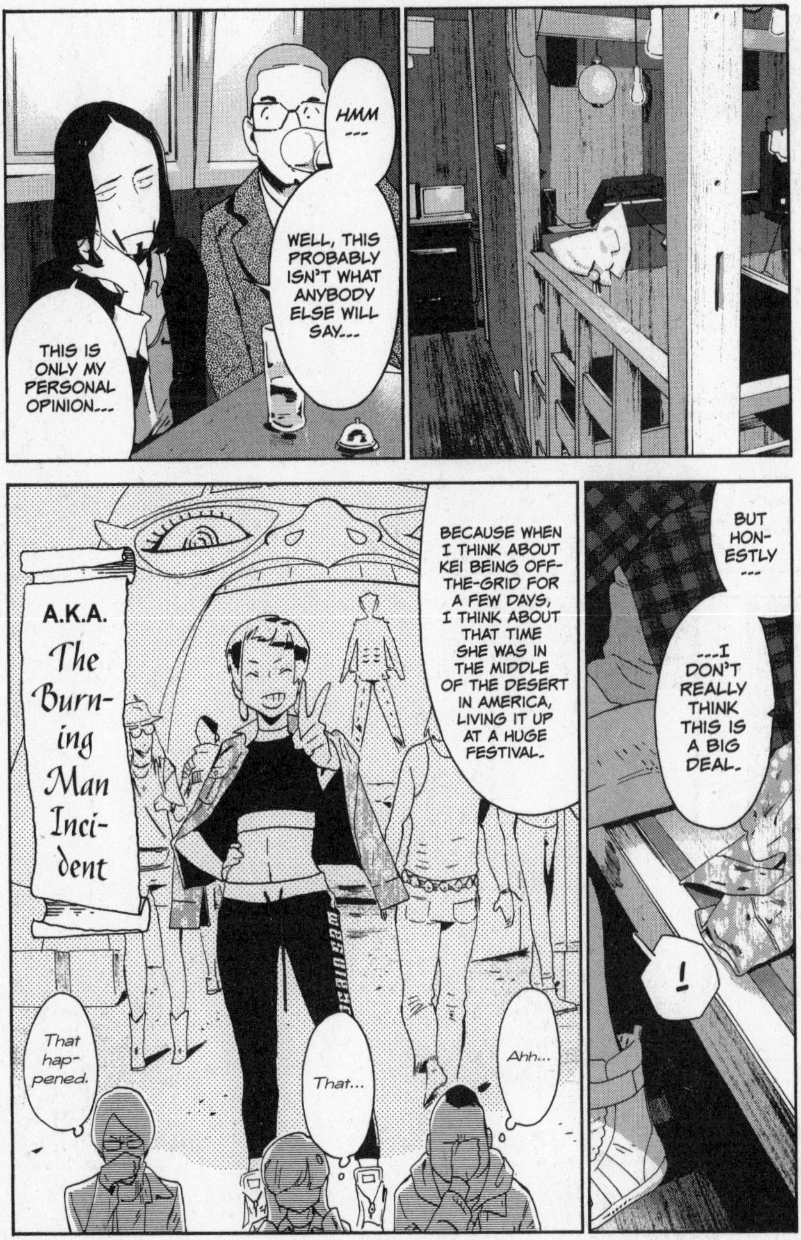
HMM---
WELL, THIS PROBABLY ISN'T WHAT ANYBODY ELSE WILL SAY---
THIS IS ONLY MY PERSONAL OPINION---
BUT HON-ESTLY---
---I DON'T REALLY THINK THIS IS A BIG DEAL.
!
BECAUSE WHEN I THINK ABOUT KEI BEING OFF-THE-GRID FOR A FEW DAYS, I THINK ABOUT THAT TIME SHE WAS IN THE MIDDLE OF THE DESERT IN AMERICA, LIVING IT UP AT A HUGE FESTIVAL.
A.K.A. The Burning Man Incident
Ahh...
That...
That hap-pened.

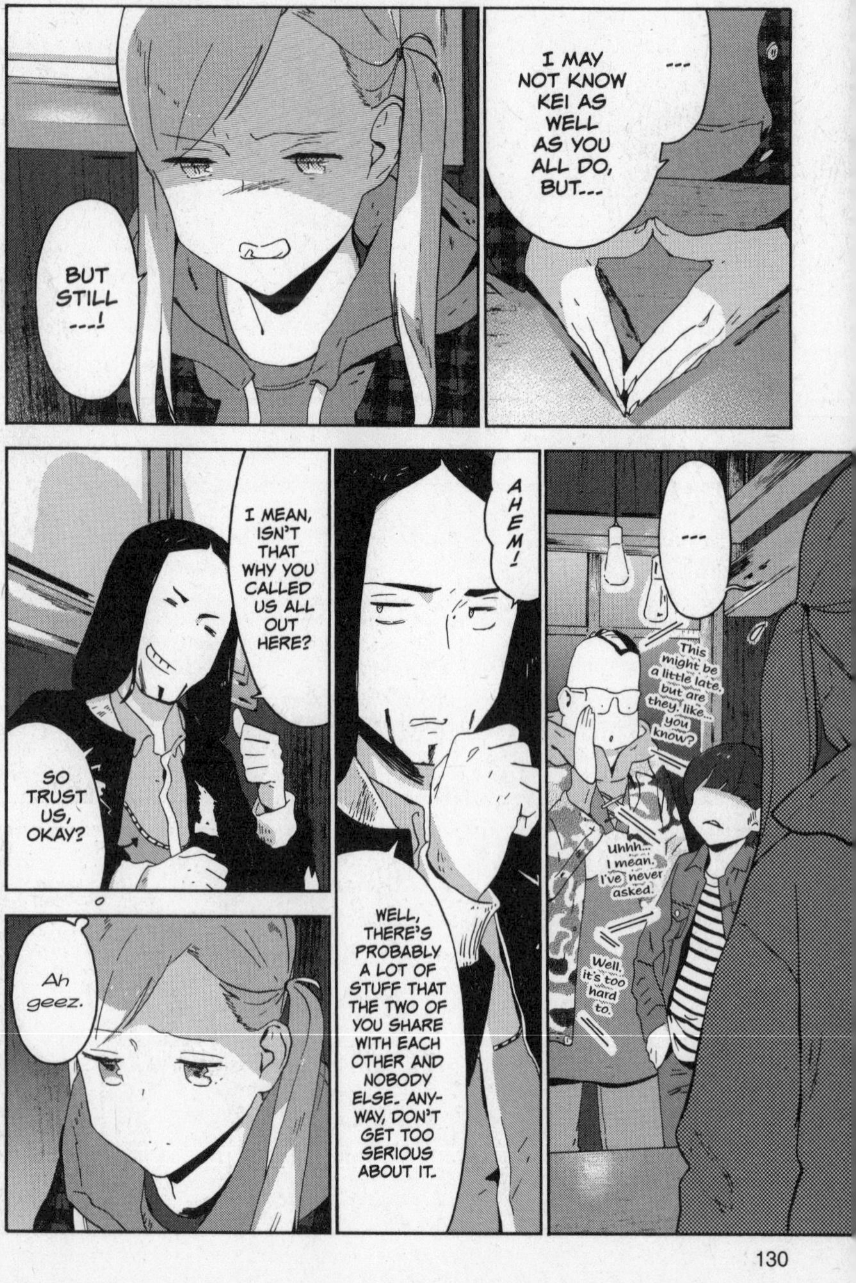
...
I MAY NOT KNOW KEI AS WELL AS YOU ALL DO, BUT...
BUT STILL...!
...
This might be a little late, but are they, like... you know?
Uhhh... I mean, I've never asked.
Well, it's too hard to.
AHEM!
WELL, THERE'S PROBABLY A LOT OF STUFF THAT THE TWO OF YOU SHARE WITH EACH OTHER AND NOBODY ELSE. ANY-WAY, DON'T GET TOO SERIOUS ABOUT IT.
I MEAN, ISN'T THAT WHY YOU CALLED US ALL OUT HERE?
SO TRUST US, OKAY?
Ah geez.

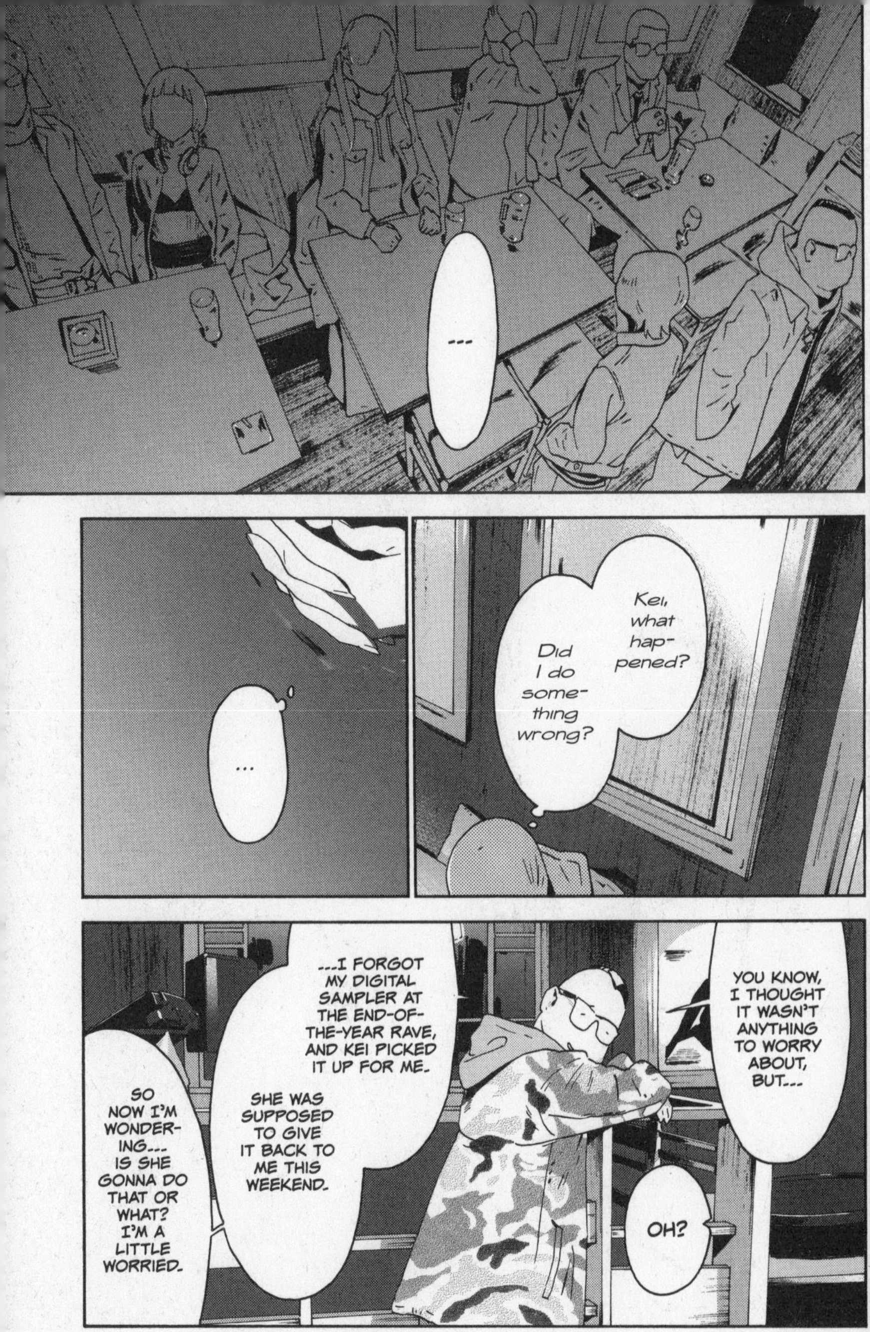
...
Kei, what happened? Did I do something wrong?
...
YOU KNOW, I THOUGHT IT WASN'T ANYTHING TO WORRY ABOUT, BUT...
OH?
...I FORGOT MY DIGITAL SAMPLER AT THE END-OF-THE-YEAR RAVE, AND KEI PICKED IT UP FOR ME.
SHE WAS SUPPOSED TO GIVE IT BACK TO ME THIS WEEKEND.
SO NOW I'M WONDERING... IS SHE GONNA DO THAT OR WHAT? I'M A LITTLE WORRIED.

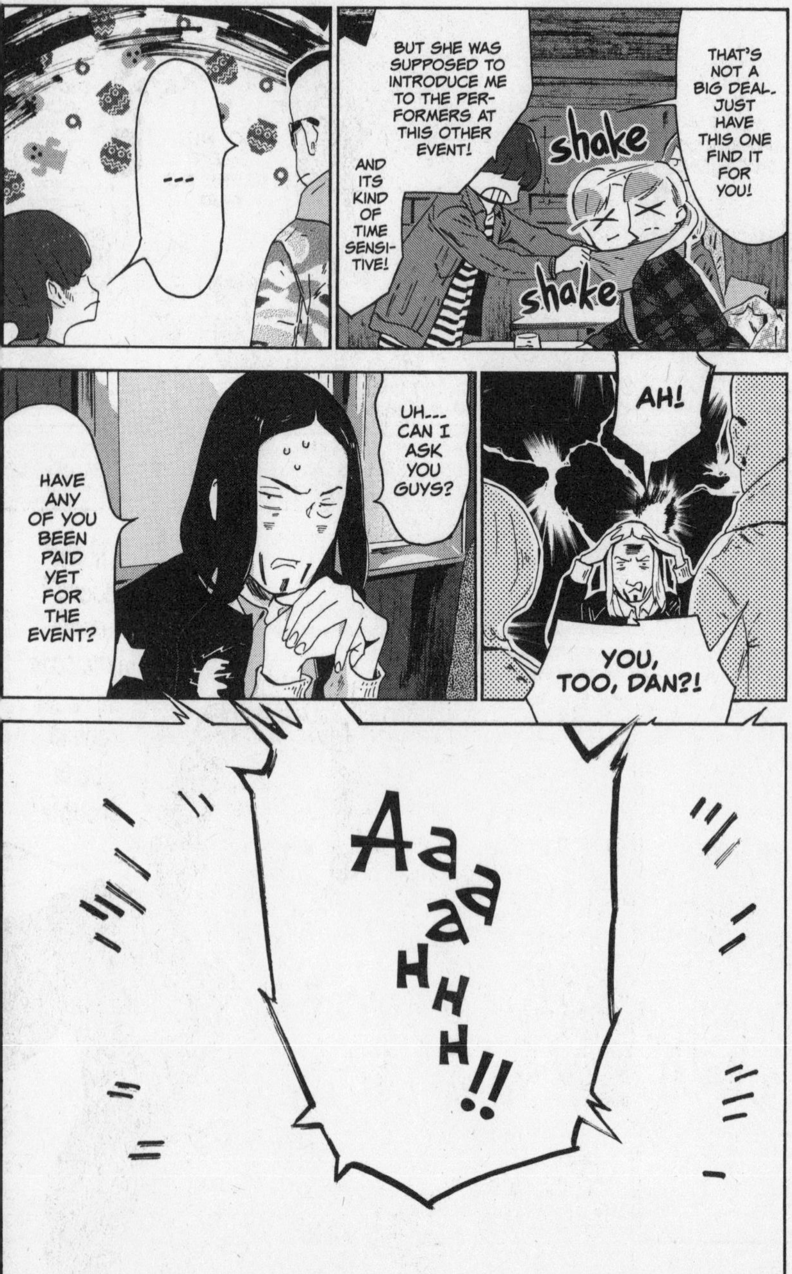

...
BUT SHE WAS SUPPOSED TO INTRODUCE ME TO THE PER-FORMERS AT THIS OTHER EVENT!
AND ITS KIND OF TIME SENSI-TIVE!
shake
shake
THAT'S NOT A BIG DEAL. JUST HAVE THIS ONE FIND IT FOR YOU!
UH... CAN I ASK YOU GUYS?
HAVE ANY OF YOU BEEN PAID YET FOR THE EVENT?
AH!
YOU, TOO, DAN?!
AaaaHHH!!

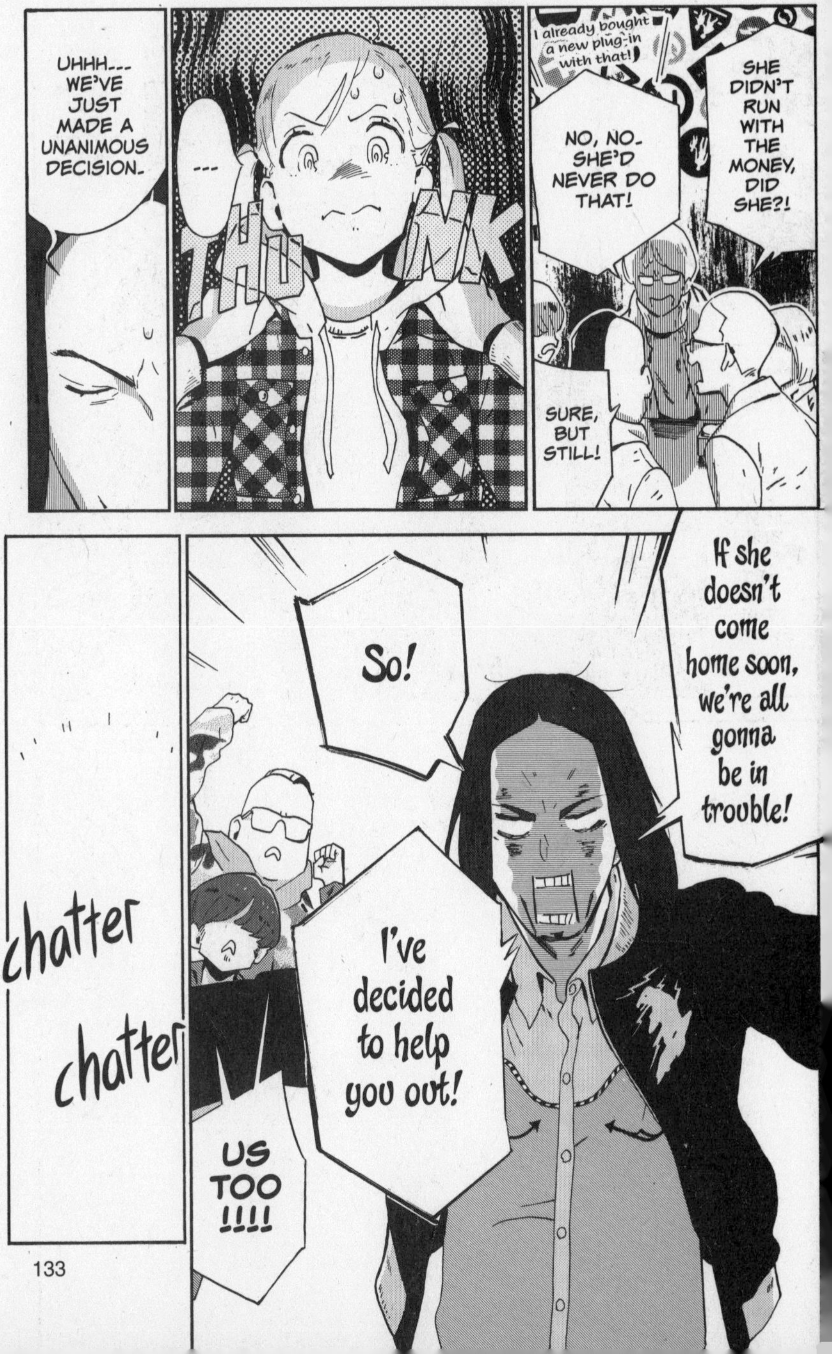

SHE DIDN'T RUN WITH THE MONEY, DID SHE?!
I already bought a new plug-in with that!
NO, NO. SHE'D NEVER DO THAT!
SURE, BUT STILL!
...
THUNK
UHHH... WE'VE JUST MADE A UNANIMOUS DECISION.
If she doesn't come home soon, we're all gonna be in trouble!
So!
I've decided to help you out!
US TOO!!!!
chatter
chatter

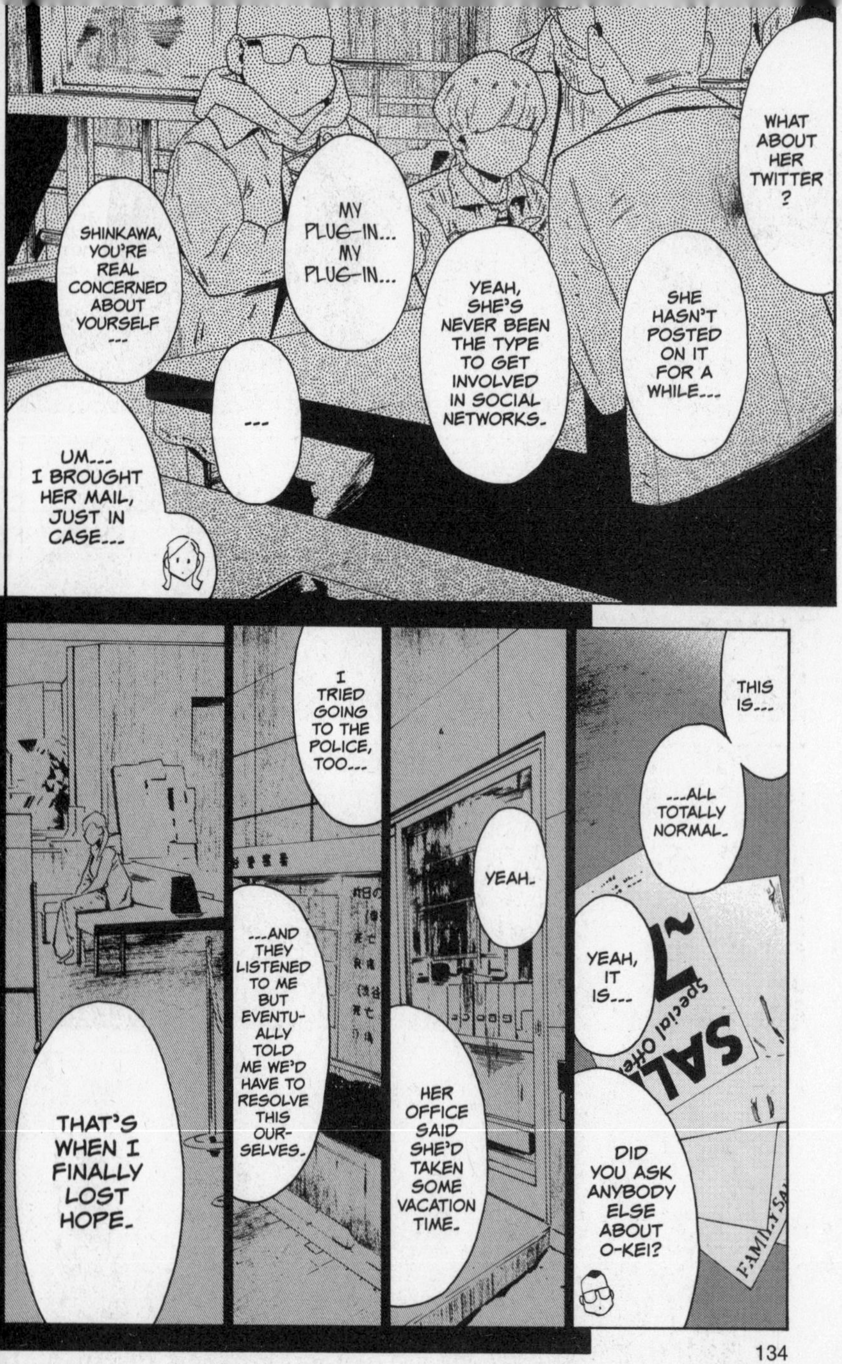
WHAT ABOUT HER TWITTER?
SHE HASN'T POSTED ON IT FOR A WHILE...
YEAH, SHE'S NEVER BEEN THE TYPE TO GET INVOLVED IN SOCIAL NETWORKS.
MY PLUG-IN... MY PLUG-IN...
SHINKAWA, YOU'RE REAL CONCERNED ABOUT YOURSELF...
...
UM... I BROUGHT HER MAIL, JUST IN CASE...
THIS IS...
...ALL TOTALLY NORMAL.
YEAH, IT IS...
DID YOU ASK ANYBODY ELSE ABOUT O-KEI?
YEAH.
HER OFFICE SAID SHE'D TAKEN SOME VACATION TIME.
I TRIED GOING TO THE POLICE, TOO...
...AND THEY LISTENED TO ME BUT EVENTU-ALLY TOLD ME WE'D HAVE TO RESOLVE THIS OUR-SELVES.
THAT'S WHEN I FINALLY LOST HOPE.

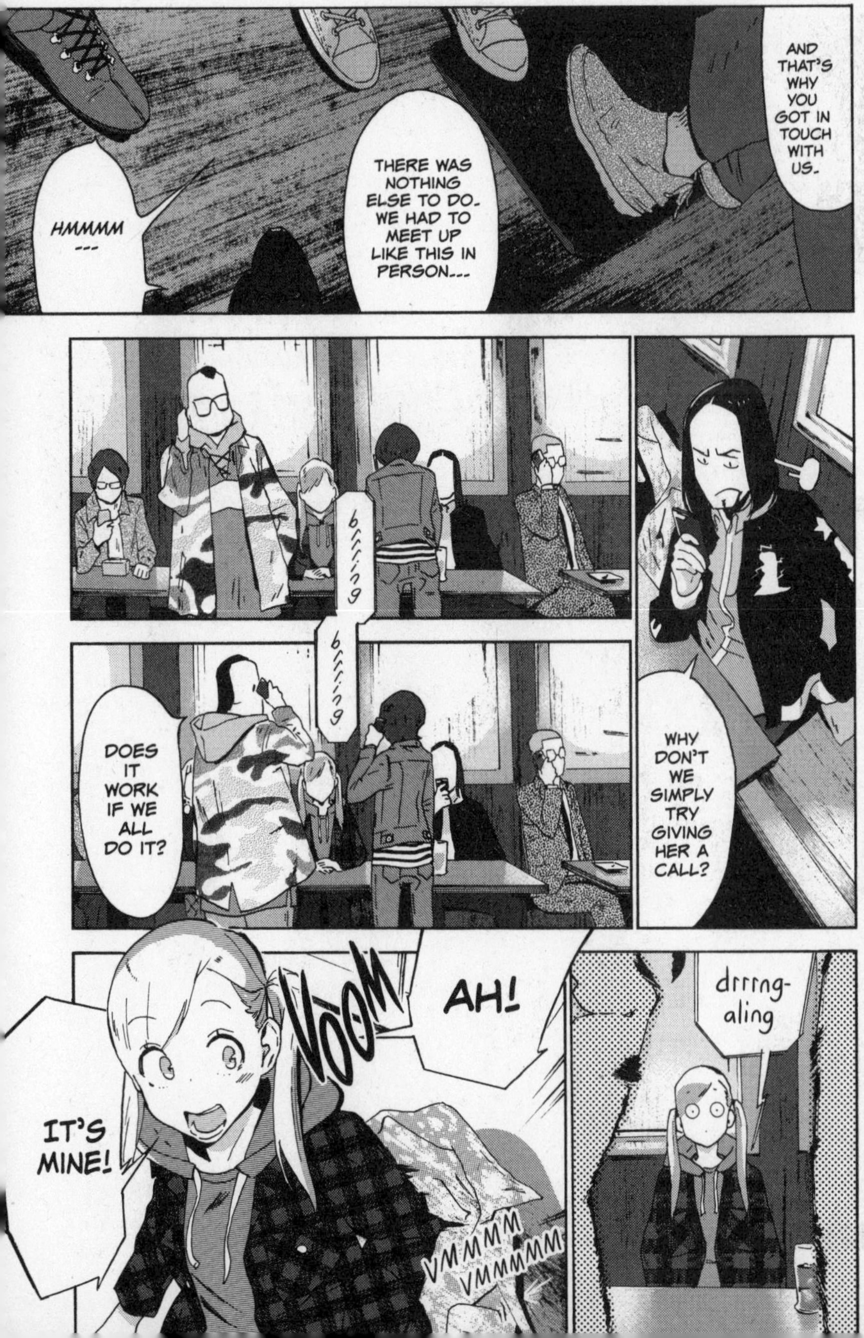
AND THAT'S WHY YOU GOT IN TOUCH WITH US.
THERE WAS NOTHING ELSE TO DO. WE HAD TO MEET UP LIKE THIS IN PERSON...
HMMMM ---
WHY DON'T WE SIMPLY TRY GIVING HER A CALL?
brrring
brrring
DOES IT WORK IF WE ALL DO IT?
drrrng-aling
AH!
VOOM
IT'S MINE!
VMMMM
VMMMMM

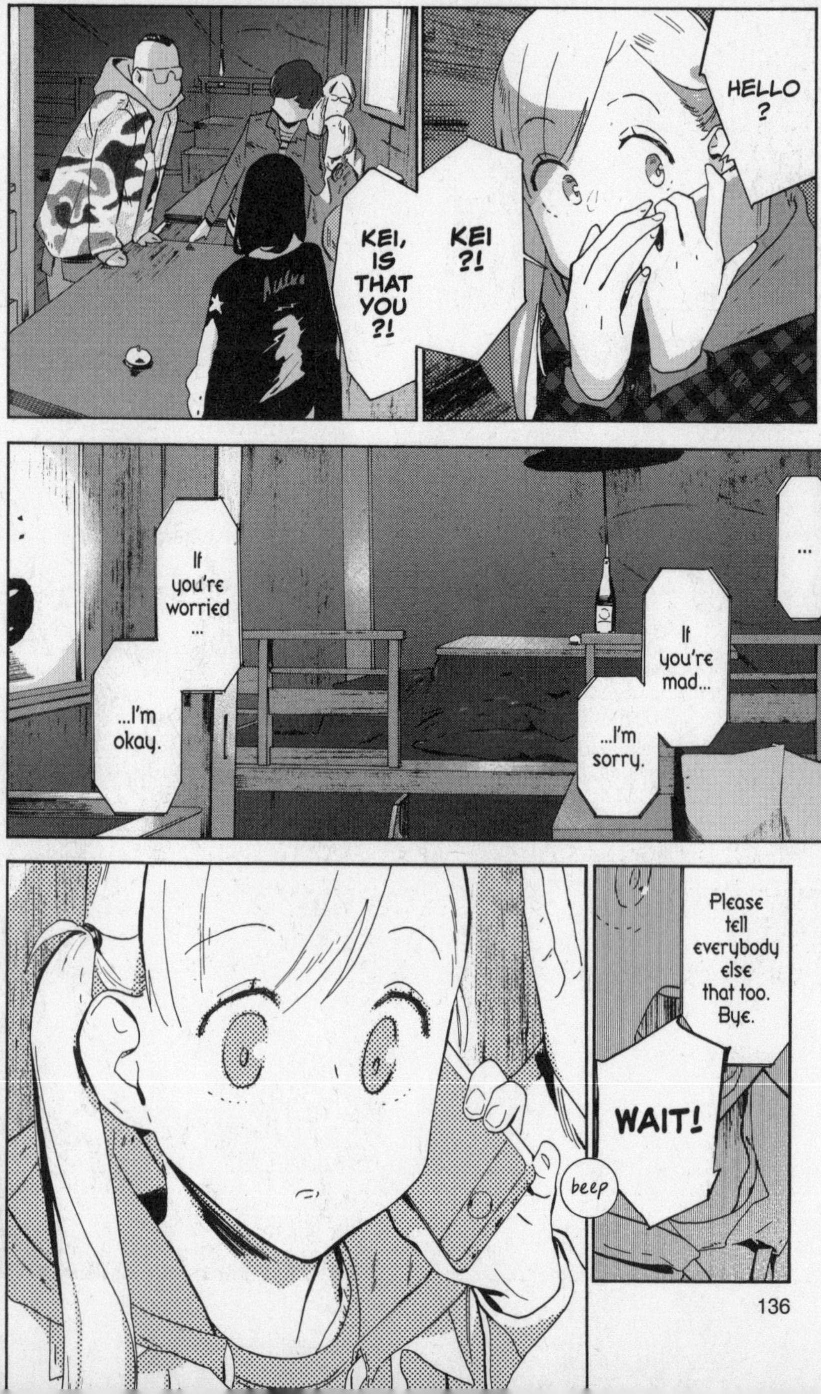
HELLO ?
KEI ?!
KEI, IS THAT YOU ?!
...
If you're mad...
...I'm sorry.
If you're worried ...
...I'm okay.
Please tell everybody else that too. Bye.
WAIT!
beep

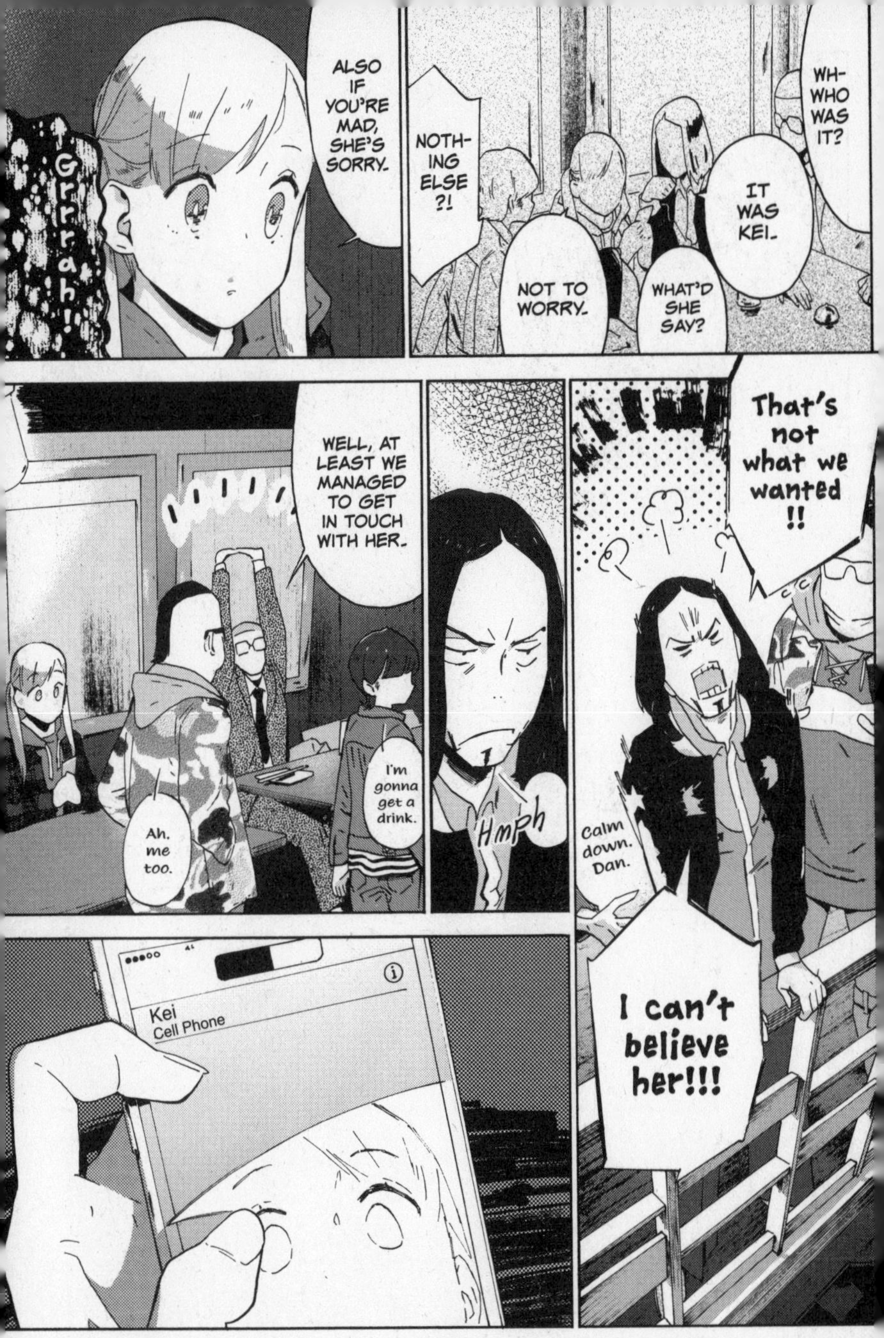
WH- WHO WAS IT?
IT WAS KEI.
WHAT'D SHE SAY?
NOT TO WORRY.
NOTH- ING ELSE ?!
ALSO IF YOU'RE MAD, SHE'S SORRY.
Grrrah!
That's not what we wanted !!
Calm down. Dan.
I can't believe her!!!
Hmph
WELL, AT LEAST WE MANAGED TO GET IN TOUCH WITH HER.
I'm gonna get a drink.
Ah. me too.
Kei
Cell Phone

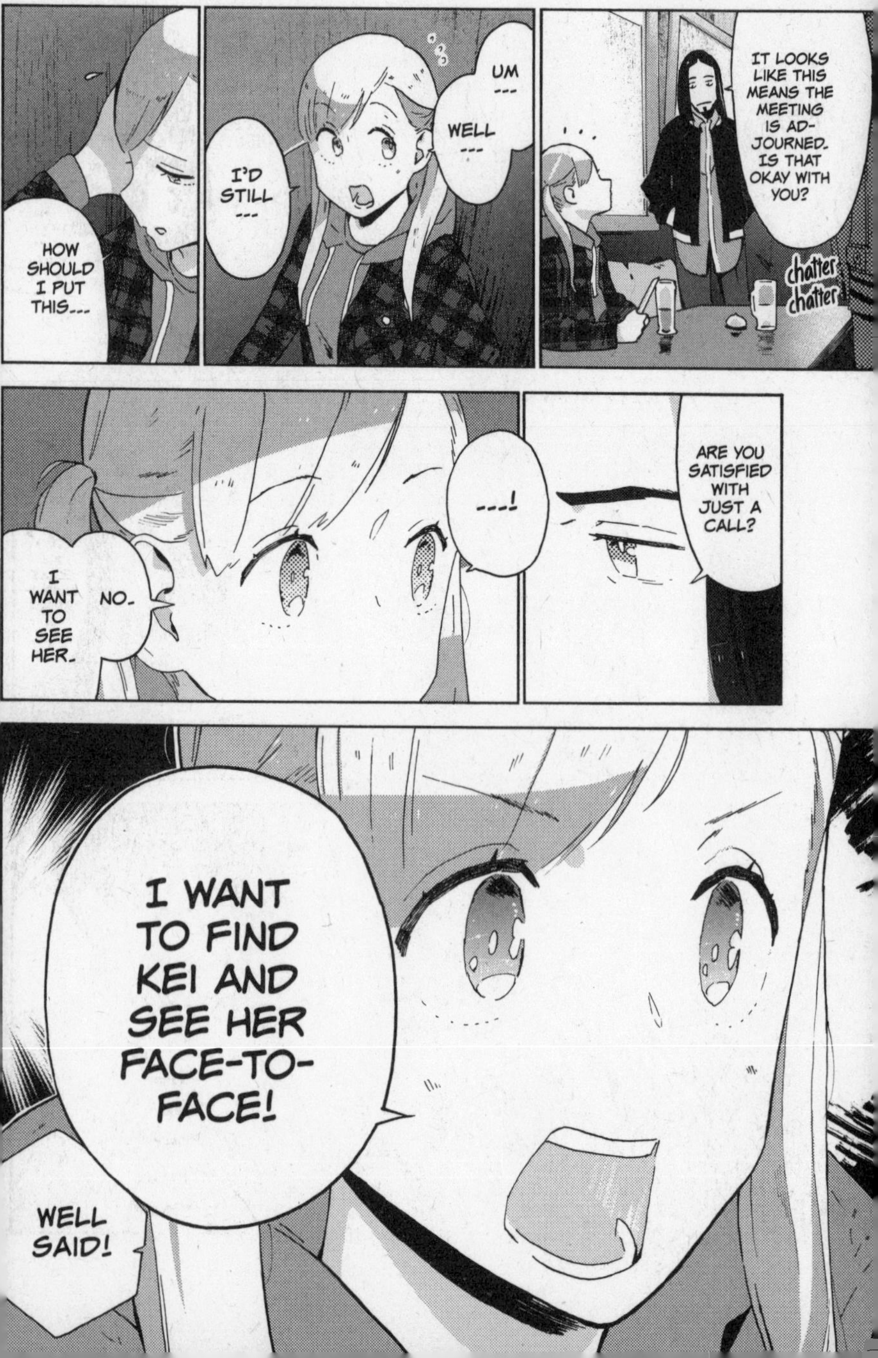
IT LOOKS LIKE THIS MEANS THE MEETING IS AD-JOURNED. IS THAT OKAY WITH YOU?
chatter chatter
UM ---
WELL ---
I'D STILL ---
HOW SHOULD I PUT THIS...
ARE YOU SATISFIED WITH JUST A CALL?
---!
NO.
I WANT TO SEE HER.
I WANT TO FIND KEI AND SEE HER FACE-TO-FACE!
WELL SAID!

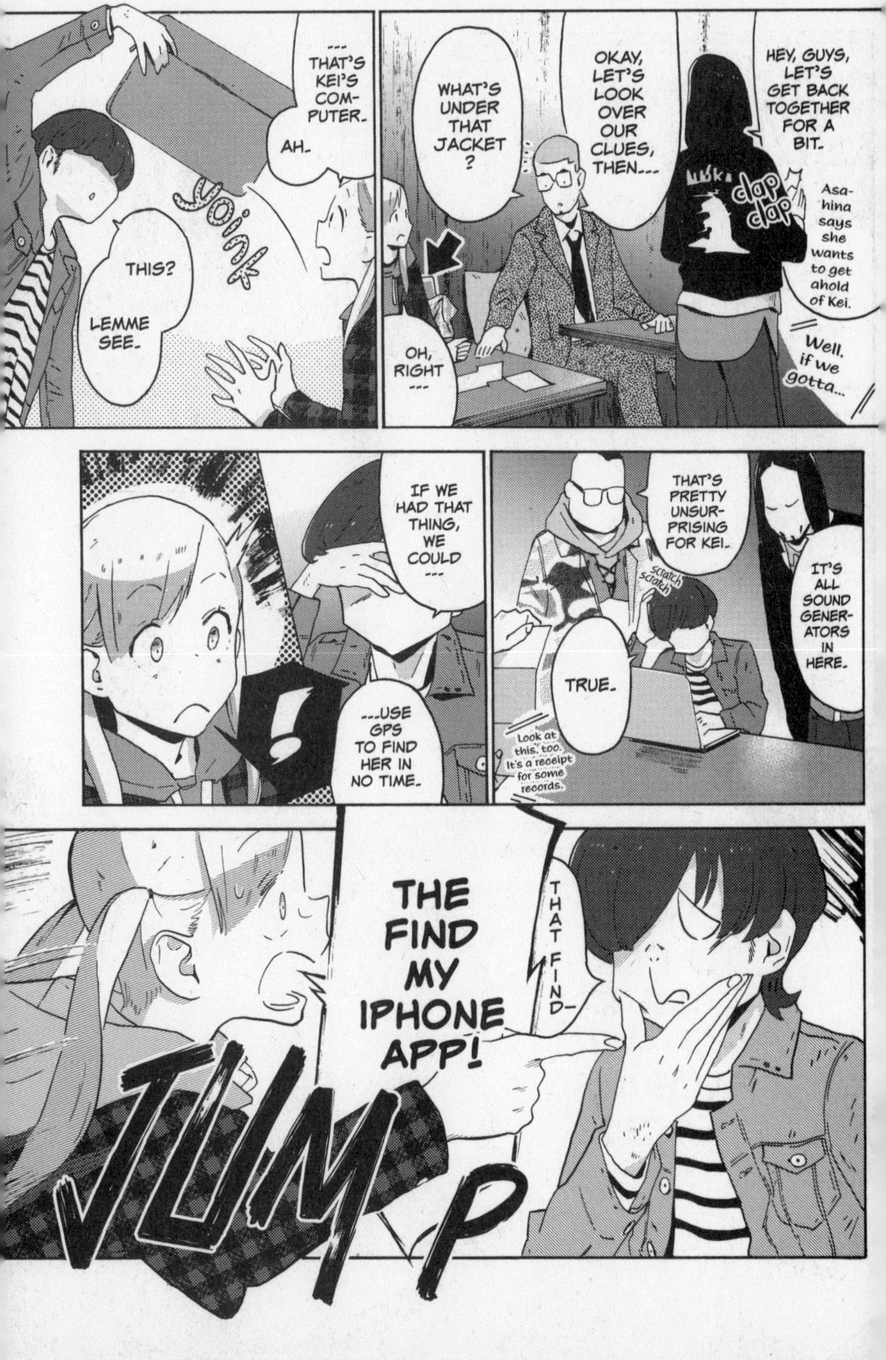
HEY, GUYS, LET'S GET BACK TOGETHER FOR A BIT.
clap clap
Asahina says she wants to get ahold of Kei.
Well, if we gotta...
OKAY, LET'S LOOK OVER OUR CLUES, THEN...
WHAT'S UNDER THAT JACKET?
OH, RIGHT...
...THAT'S KEI'S COMPUTER.
AH.
yoink
THIS?
LEMME SEE.
THAT'S PRETTY UNSURPRISING FOR KEI.
IT'S ALL SOUND GENERATORS IN HERE.
scratch scratch
TRUE.
Look at this, too. It's a receipt for some records.
IF WE HAD THAT THING, WE COULD...
...USE GPS TO FIND HER IN NO TIME.
THAT FIND—
THE FIND MY IPHONE APP!
JUMP

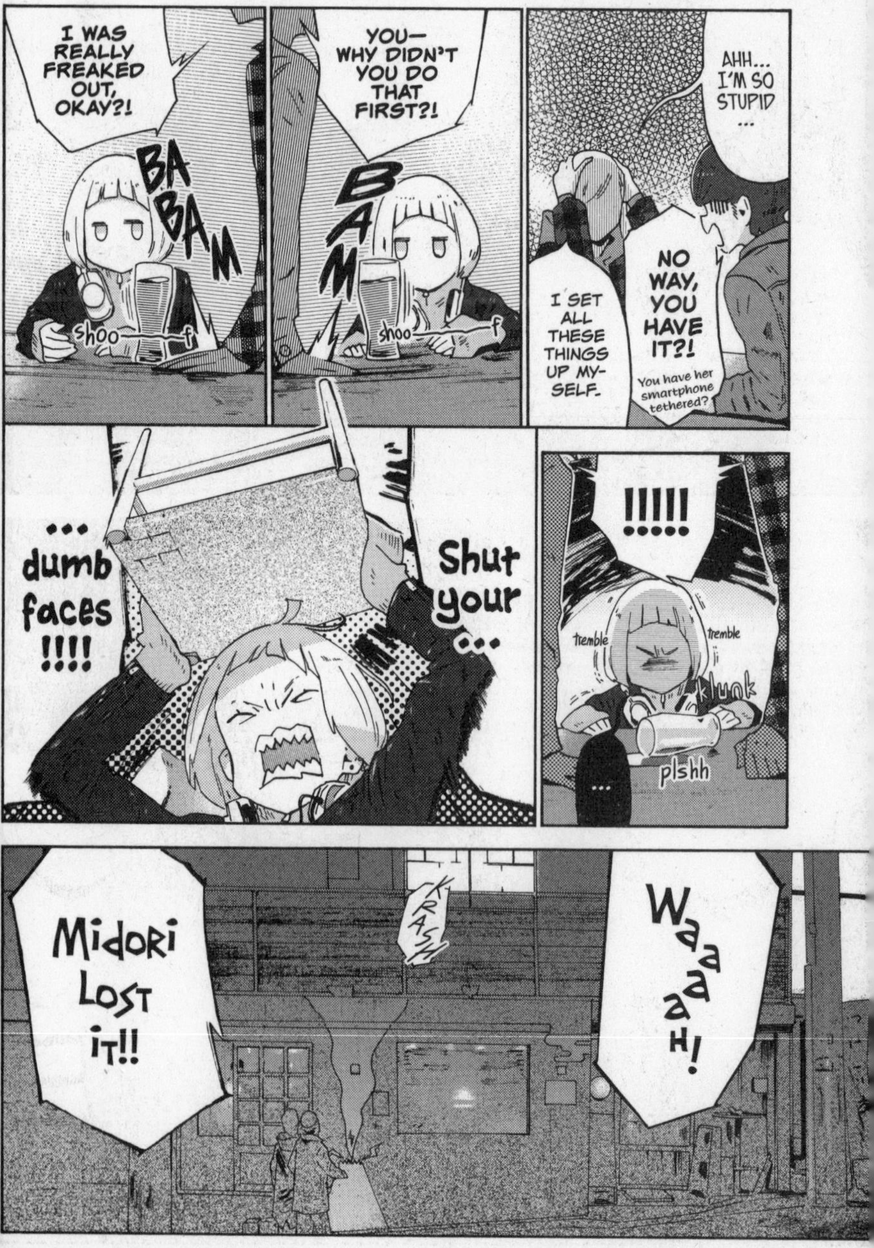
AHH... I'M SO STUPID ...
NO WAY, YOU HAVE IT?!
You have her smartphone tethered?
I SET ALL THESE THINGS UP MY-SELF.
YOU— WHY DIDN'T YOU DO THAT FIRST?!
BAMM
shoo—f
I WAS REALLY FREAKED OUT, OKAY?!
BABAM
shoo—f
!!!!!
tremble
tremble
klunk
plshh
Shut your...
...dumb faces!!!!
Waaaah!
KRASH
Midori LOST it!!

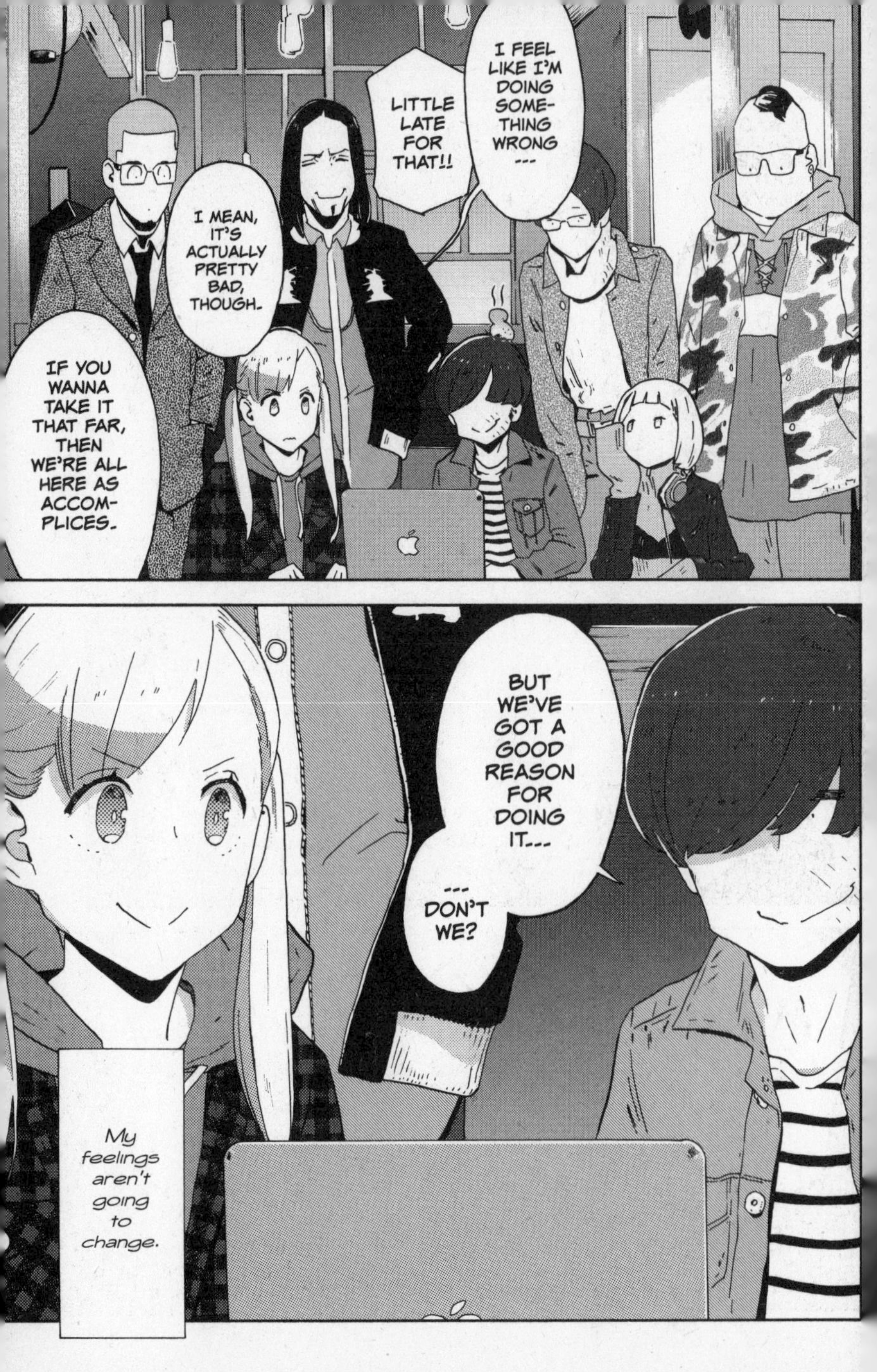
I FEEL LIKE I'M DOING SOMETHING WRONG...
LITTLE LATE FOR THAT!!
I MEAN, IT'S ACTUALLY PRETTY BAD, THOUGH.
IF YOU WANNA TAKE IT THAT FAR, THEN WE'RE ALL HERE AS ACCOMPLICES.
BUT WE'VE GOT A GOOD REASON FOR DOING IT...
...DON'T WE?
My feelings aren't going to change.

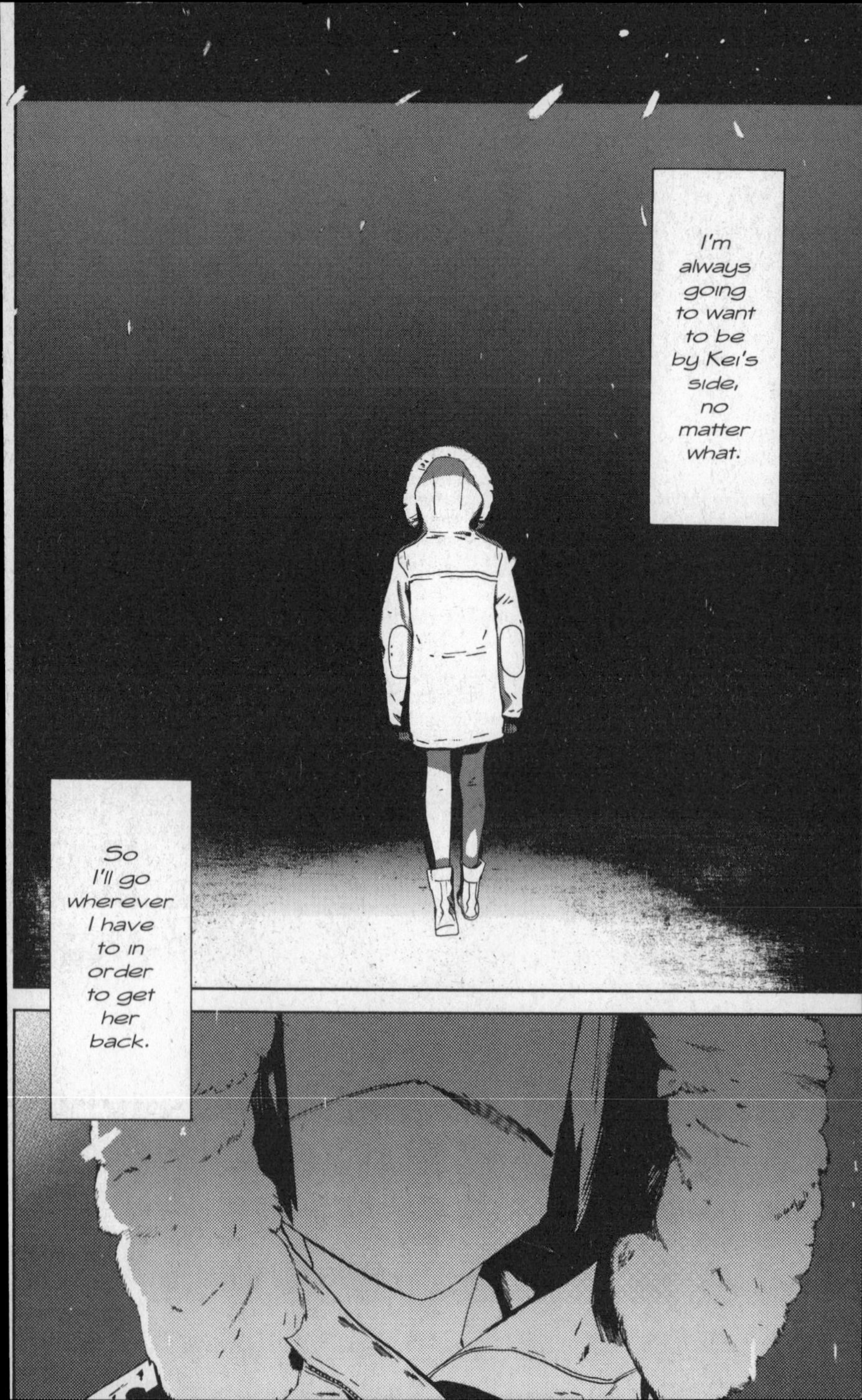
I'm always going to want to be by Kei's side, no matter what.
So I'll go wherever I have to in order to get her back.

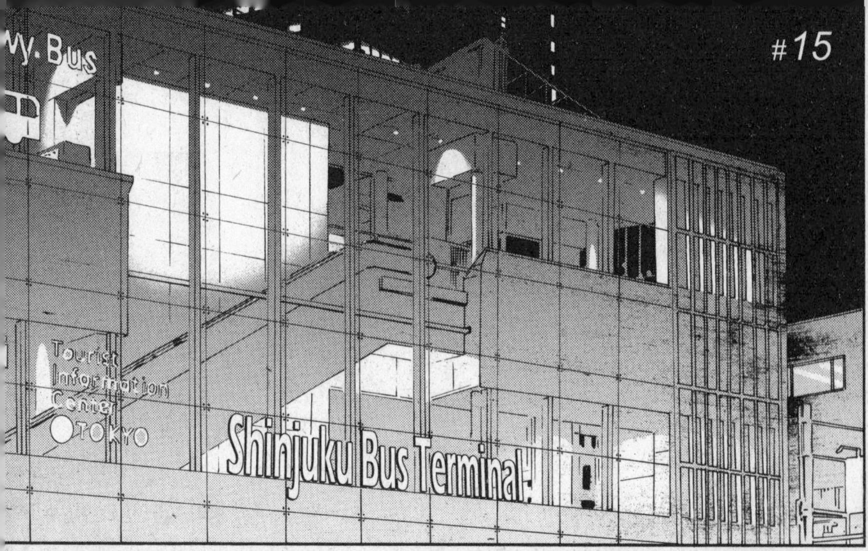
#15
Tourist Information Center
TOKYO
Shinjuku Bus Terminal

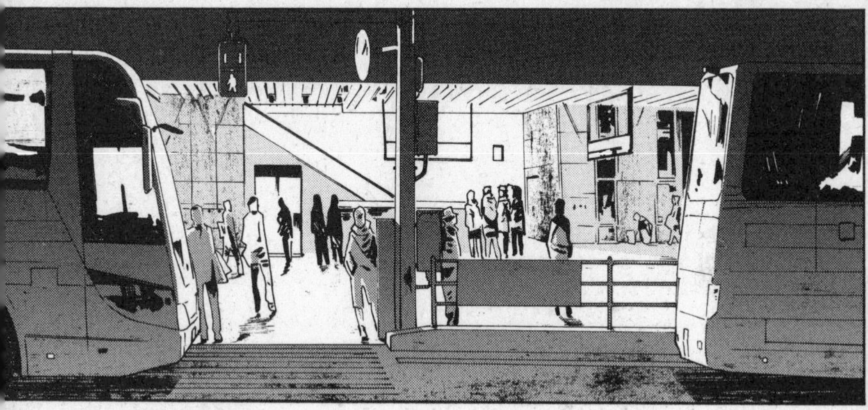

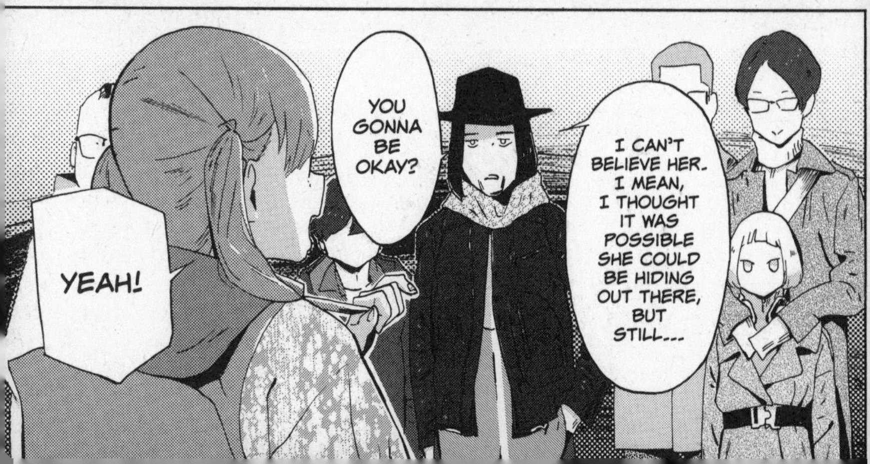
I CAN'T BELIEVE HER. I MEAN, I THOUGHT IT WAS POSSIBLE SHE COULD BE HIDING OUT THERE, BUT STILL...
YOU GONNA BE OKAY?
YEAH!

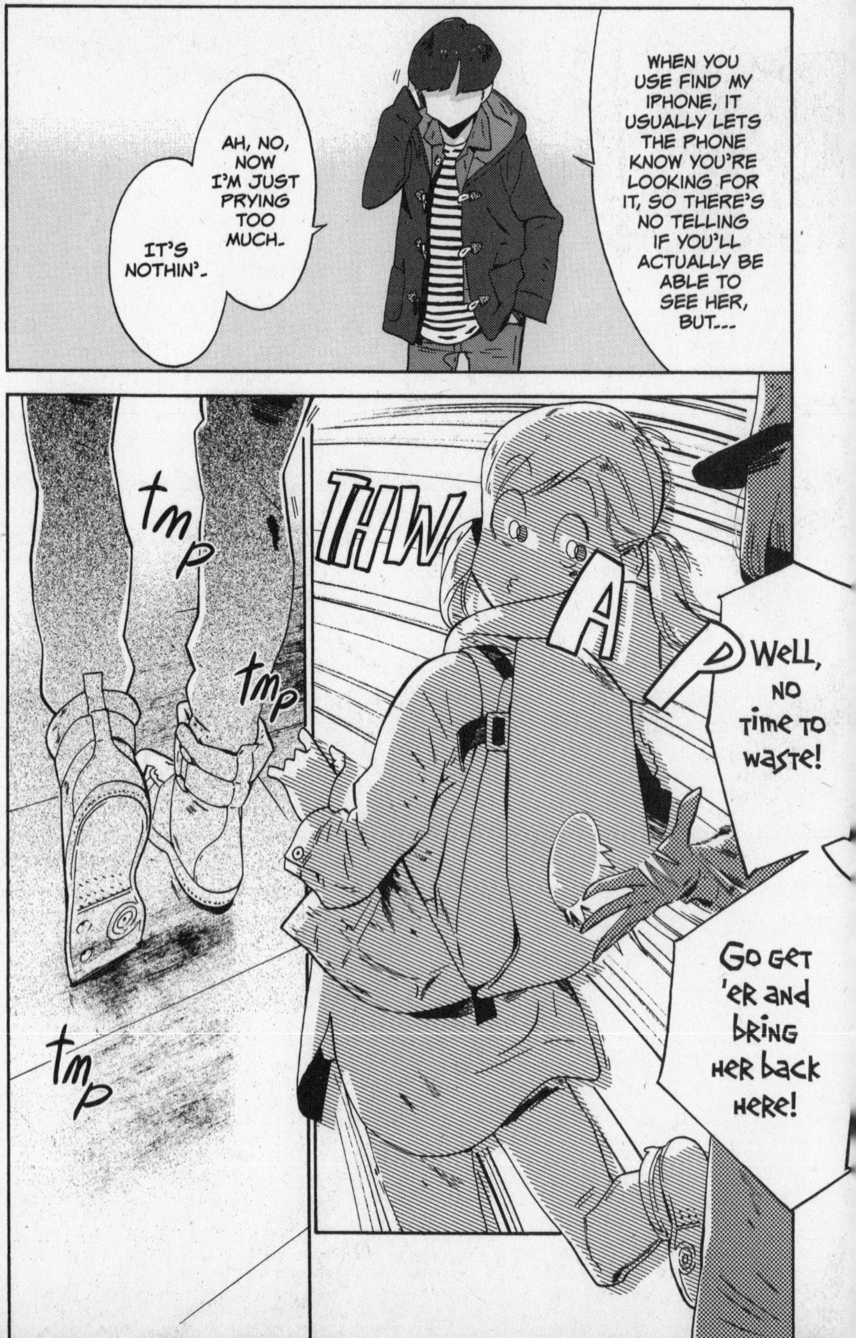
WHEN YOU USE FIND MY IPHONE, IT USUALLY LETS THE PHONE KNOW YOU'RE LOOKING FOR IT, SO THERE'S NO TELLING IF YOU'LL ACTUALLY BE ABLE TO SEE HER, BUT...
AH, NO, NOW I'M JUST PRYING TOO MUCH.
IT'S NOTHIN'.
THWAP
Well, no time to waste!
Go get 'er and bring her back here!
tmp
tmp
tmp

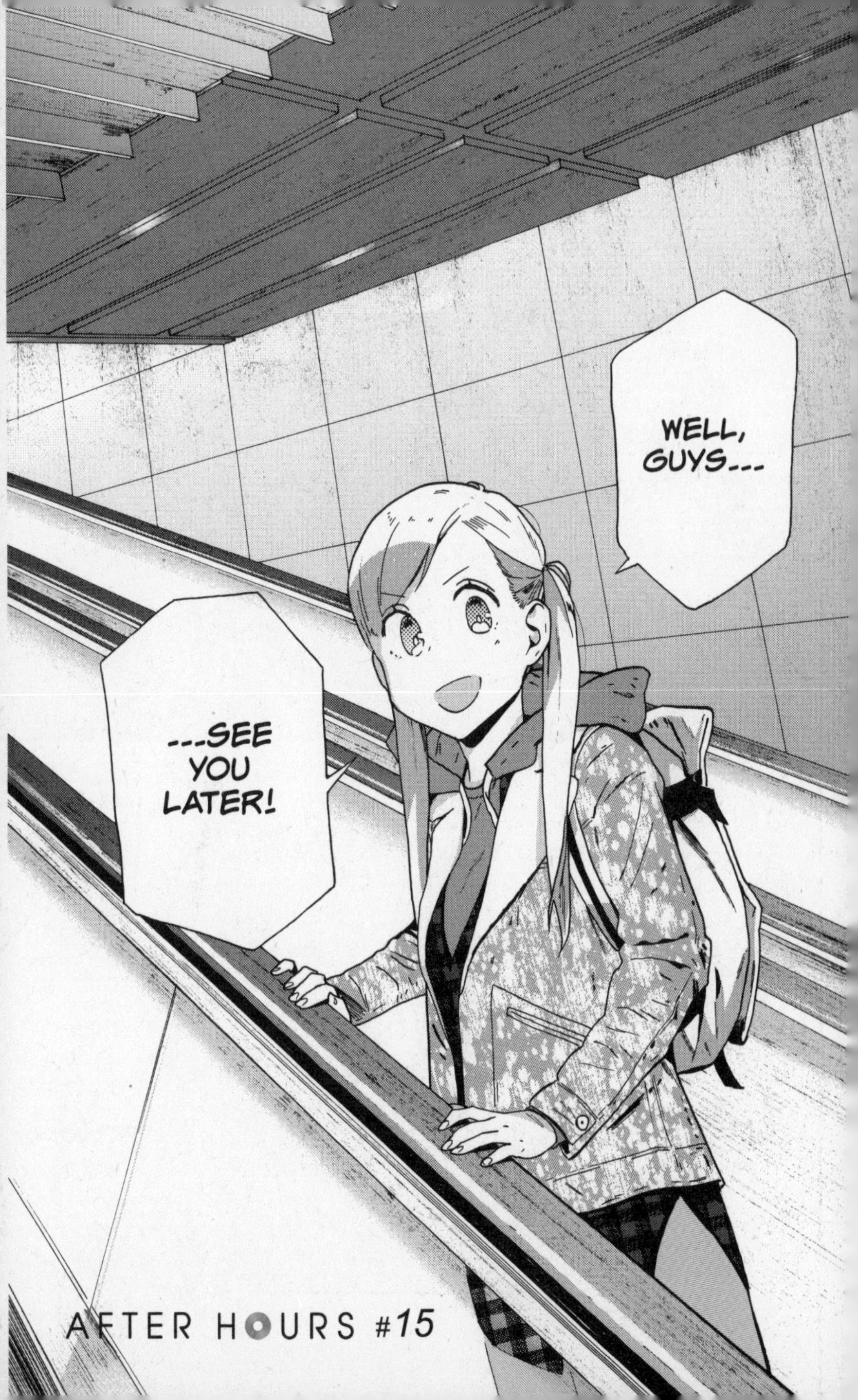
WELL, GUYS...
...SEE YOU LATER!
AFTER HOURS #15

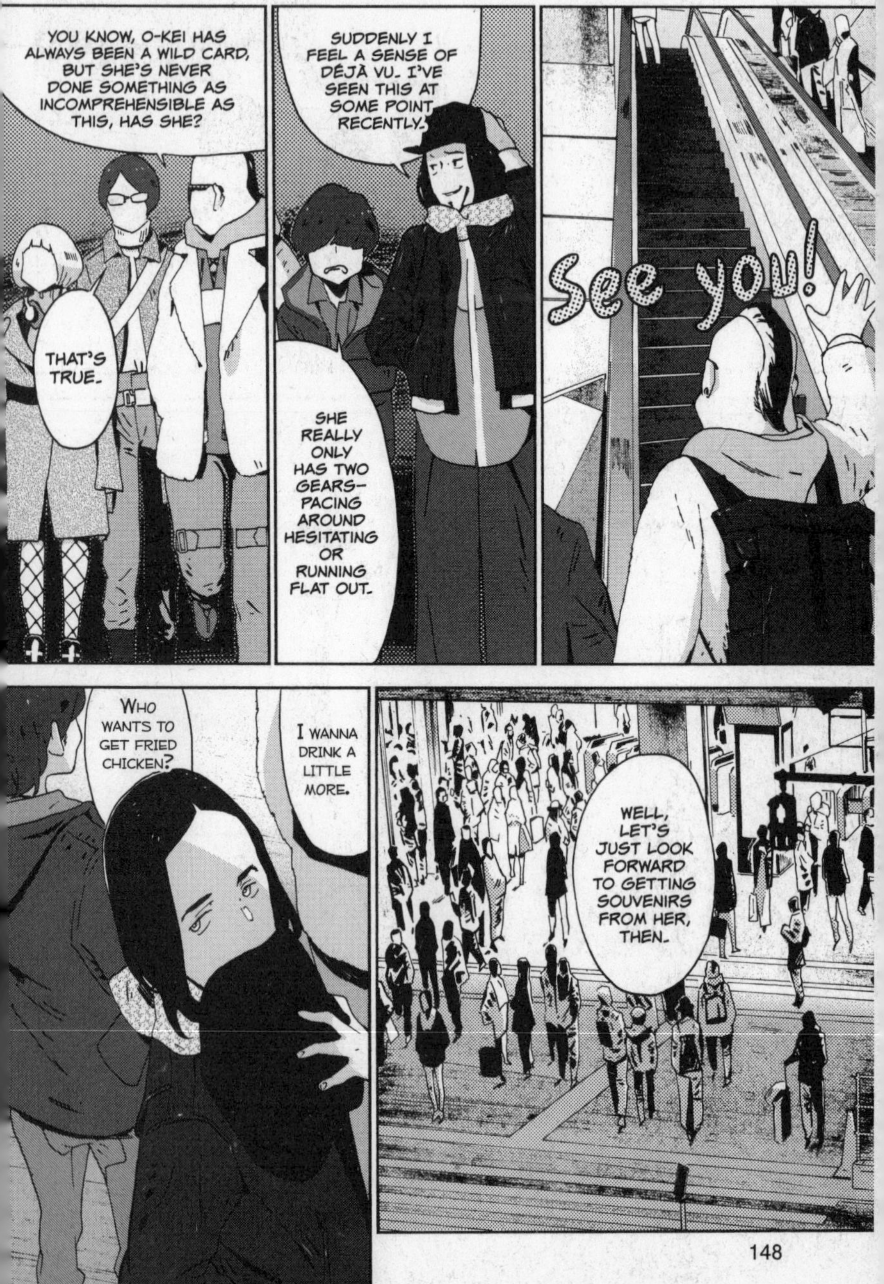
See you!
SUDDENLY I FEEL A SENSE OF DÉJÀ VU. I'VE SEEN THIS AT SOME POINT RECENTLY.
SHE REALLY ONLY HAS TWO GEARS– PACING AROUND HESITATING OR RUNNING FLAT OUT.
YOU KNOW, O-KEI HAS ALWAYS BEEN A WILD CARD, BUT SHE'S NEVER DONE SOMETHING AS INCOMPREHENSIBLE AS THIS, HAS SHE?
THAT'S TRUE.
WELL, LET'S JUST LOOK FORWARD TO GETTING SOUVENIRS FROM HER, THEN.
I WANNA DRINK A LITTLE MORE.
WHO WANTS TO GET FRIED CHICKEN?

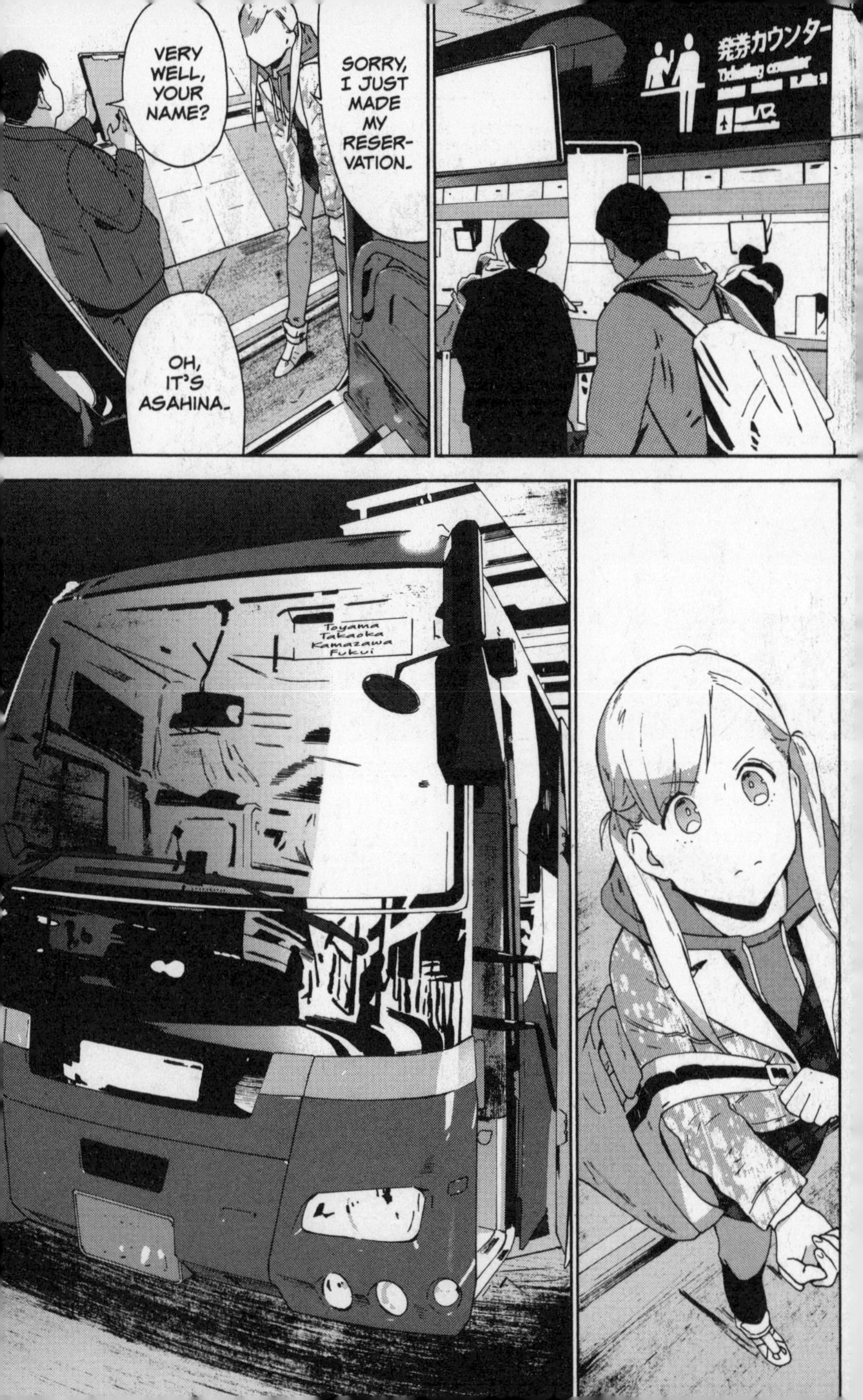
発券カウンター
SORRY, I JUST MADE MY RESERVATION.
VERY WELL, YOUR NAME?
OH, IT'S ASAHINA.
Toyama
Takaoka
Kamazawa
Fukui

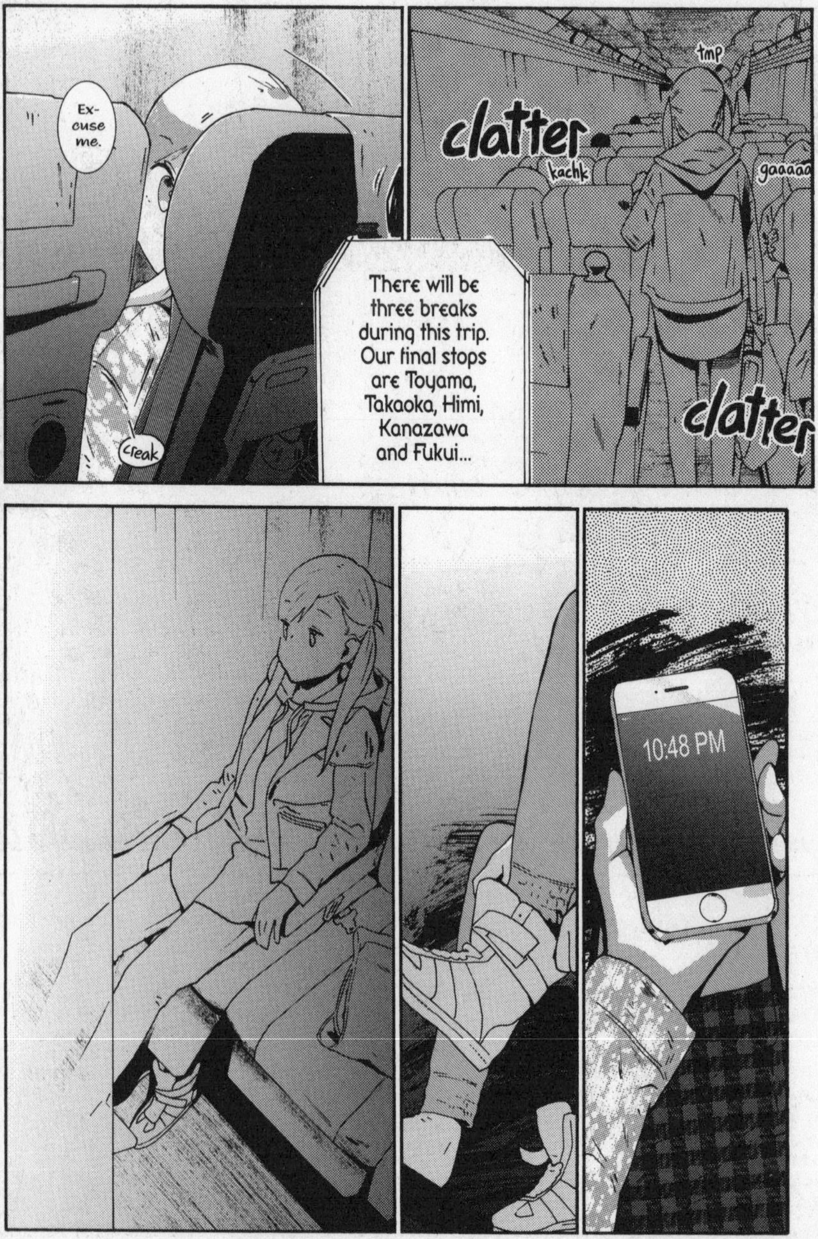
tmp
clatter
kachk
gaaaaa
There will be three breaks during this trip. Our final stops are Toyama, Takaoka, Himi, Kanazawa and Fukui...
clatter
Ex-cuse me.
creak
10:48 PM

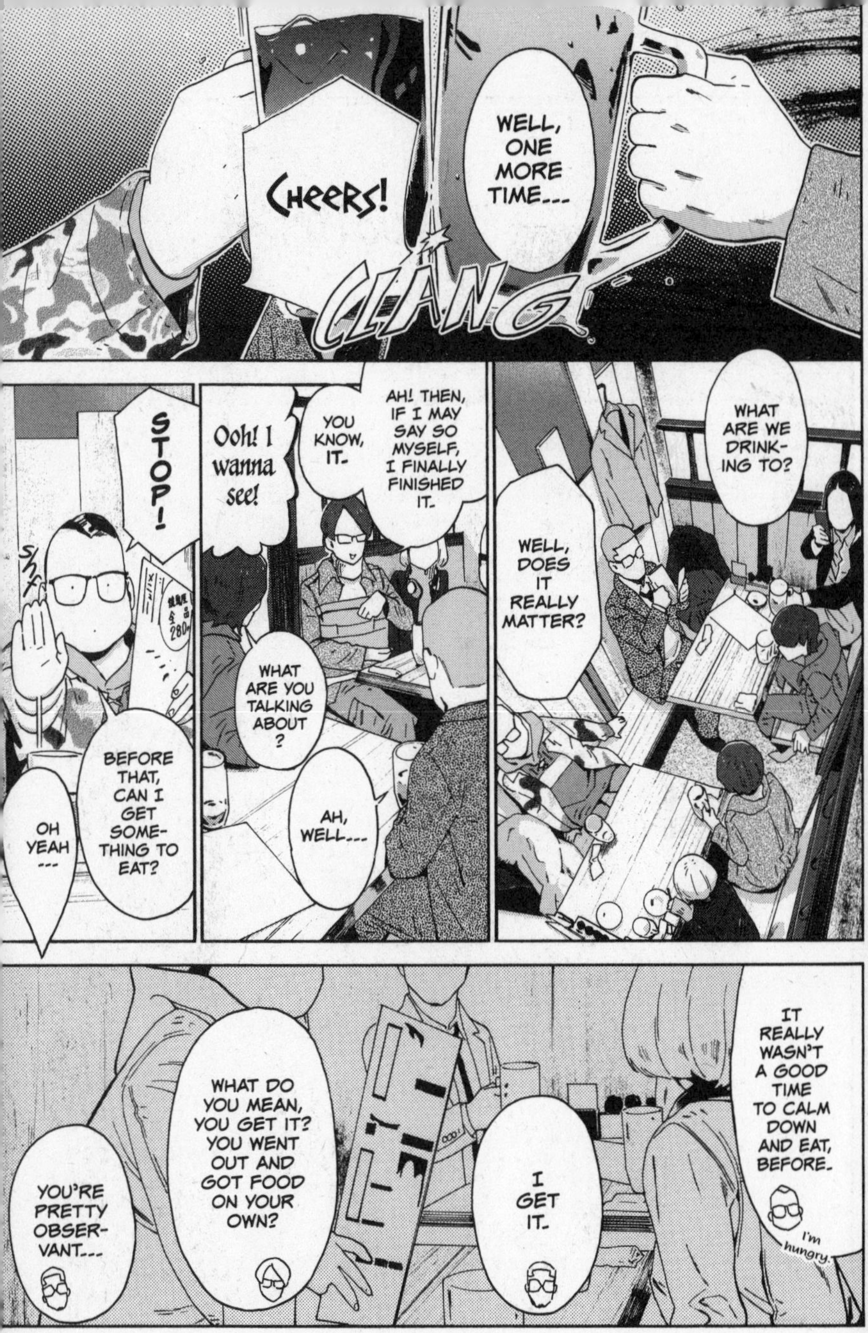
WELL, ONE MORE TIME...
Cheers!
CLANG
WHAT ARE WE DRINKING TO?
WELL, DOES IT REALLY MATTER?
AH! THEN, IF I MAY SAY SO MYSELF, I FINALLY FINISHED IT.
YOU KNOW, IT.
Ooh! I wanna see!
WHAT ARE YOU TALKING ABOUT?
AH, WELL...
STOP!
BEFORE THAT, CAN I GET SOMETHING TO EAT?
OH YEAH...
IT REALLY WASN'T A GOOD TIME TO CALM DOWN AND EAT, BEFORE.
I'm hungry.
I GET IT.
WHAT DO YOU MEAN, YOU GET IT? YOU WENT OUT AND GOT FOOD ON YOUR OWN?
YOU'RE PRETTY OBSERVANT...

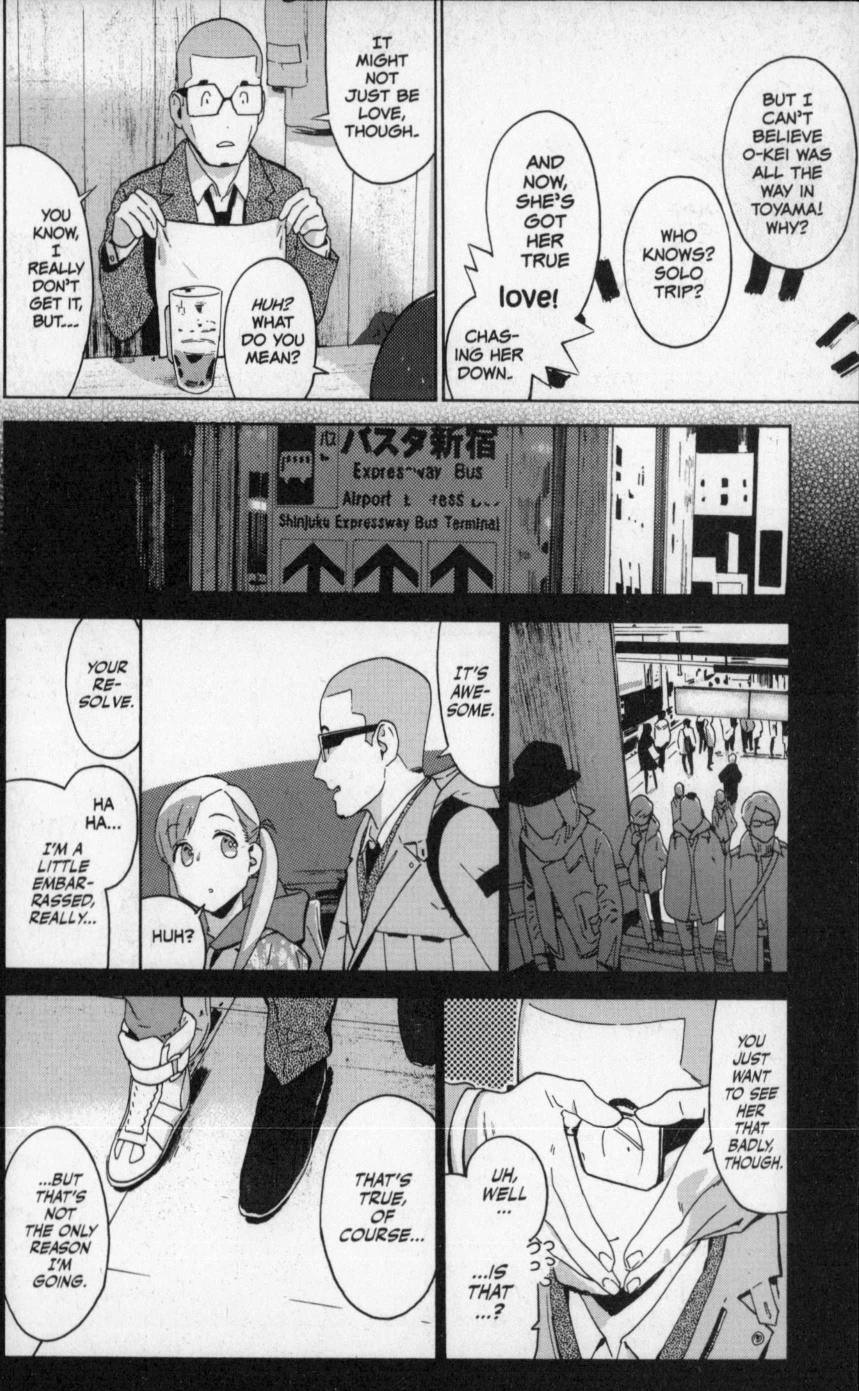
BUT I CAN'T BELIEVE O-KEI WAS ALL THE WAY IN TOYAMA! WHY?
WHO KNOWS? SOLO TRIP?
AND NOW, SHE'S GOT HER TRUE love!
CHASING HER DOWN..
IT MIGHT NOT JUST BE LOVE, THOUGH..
HUH? WHAT DO YOU MEAN?
YOU KNOW, I REALLY DON'T GET IT, BUT...
バスタ新宿
Shinjuku Expressway Bus Terminal
IT'S AWESOME.
YOUR RESOLVE.
HUH?
HA HA... I'M A LITTLE EMBARRASSED, REALLY...
YOU JUST WANT TO SEE HER THAT BADLY, THOUGH.
UH, WELL...
...IS THAT...?
THAT'S TRUE, OF COURSE...
...BUT THAT'S NOT THE ONLY REASON I'M GOING.

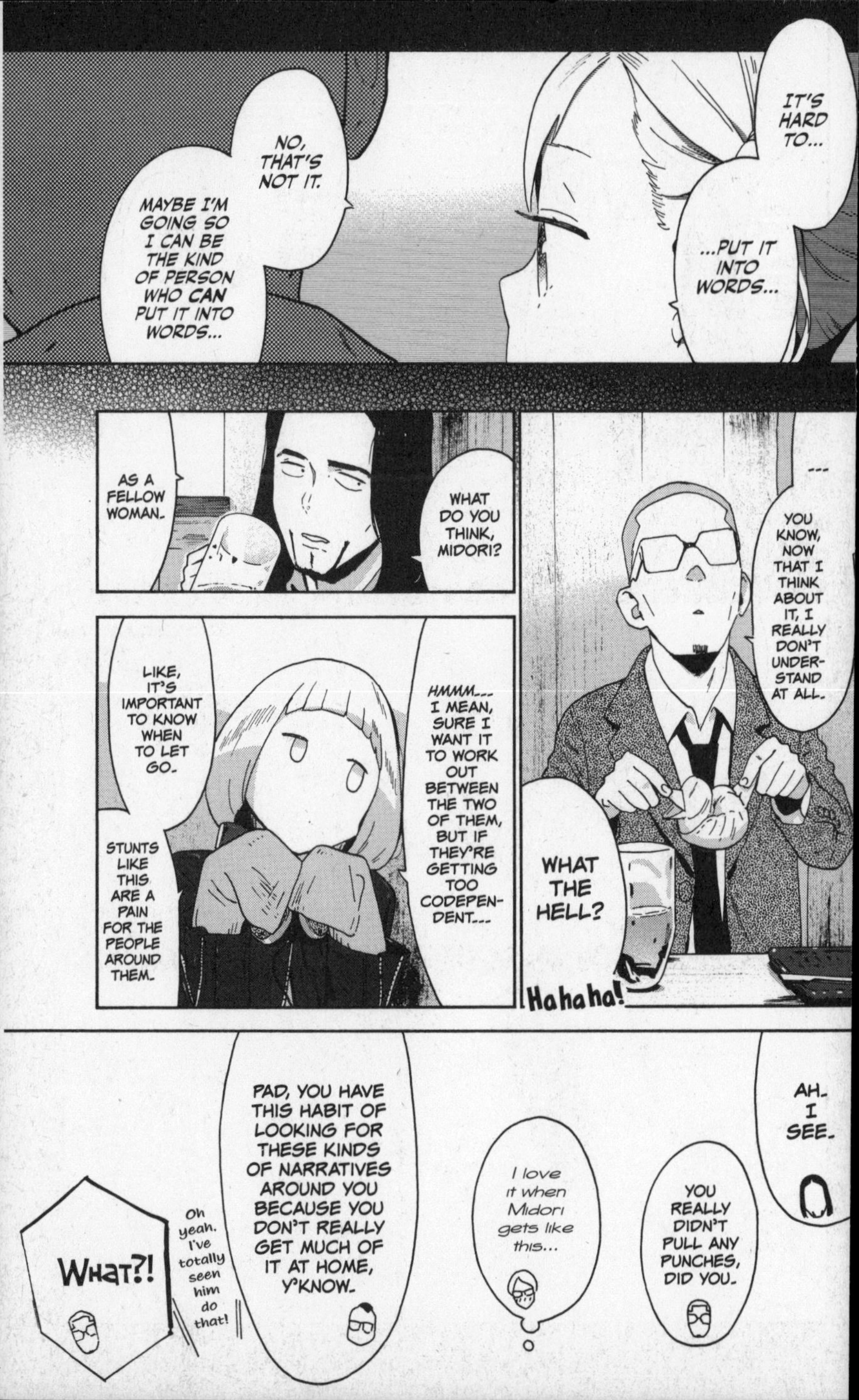
IT'S HARD TO...
...PUT IT INTO WORDS...
NO, THAT'S NOT IT.
MAYBE I'M GOING SO I CAN BE THE KIND OF PERSON WHO CAN PUT IT INTO WORDS...
...
YOU KNOW, NOW THAT I THINK ABOUT IT, I REALLY DON'T UNDERSTAND AT ALL.
WHAT THE HELL?
Hahaha!
WHAT DO YOU THINK, MIDORI?
AS A FELLOW WOMAN.
HMMM... I MEAN, SURE I WANT IT TO WORK OUT BETWEEN THE TWO OF THEM, BUT IF THEY'RE GETTING TOO CODEPENDENT...
LIKE, IT'S IMPORTANT TO KNOW WHEN TO LET GO.
STUNTS LIKE THIS ARE A PAIN FOR THE PEOPLE AROUND THEM.
AH. I SEE.
YOU REALLY DIDN'T PULL ANY PUNCHES, DID YOU.
I love it when Midori gets like this...
DAD, YOU HAVE THIS HABIT OF LOOKING FOR THESE KINDS OF NARRATIVES AROUND YOU BECAUSE YOU DON'T REALLY GET MUCH OF IT AT HOME, Y'KNOW.
Oh yeah. I've totally seen him do that!
WHAT?!

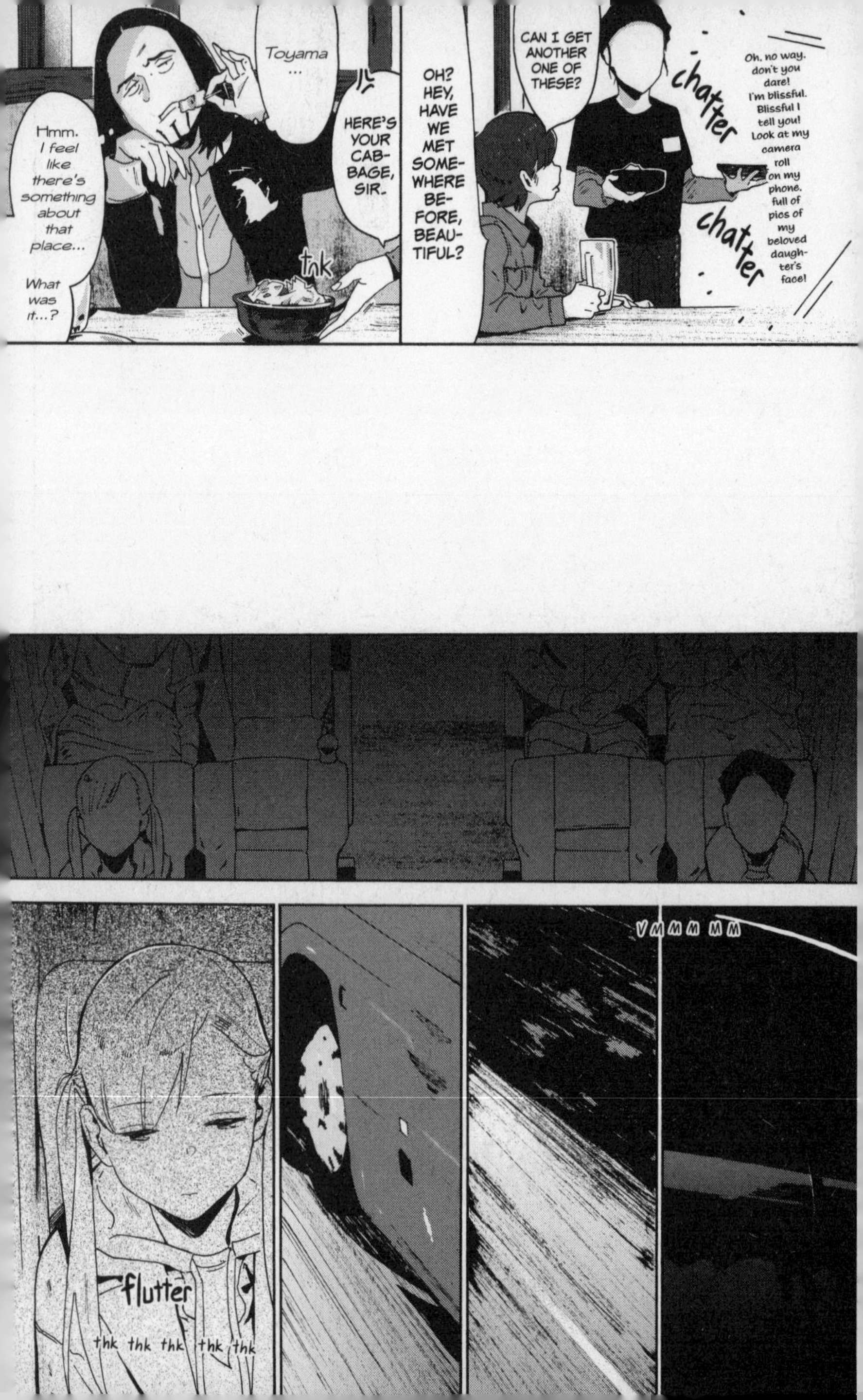
Oh, no way. don't you dare! I'm blissful. Blissful I tell you! Look at my camera roll on my phone. full of pics of my beloved daughter's face!
chatter
chatter
CAN I GET ANOTHER ONE OF THESE?
OH? HEY, HAVE WE MET SOMEWHERE BEFORE, BEAUTIFUL?
HERE'S YOUR CABBAGE, SIR.
Toyama ...
tnk
Hmm. I feel like there's something about that place...
What was it...?
VMMM MM
flutter
thk thk thk thk thk

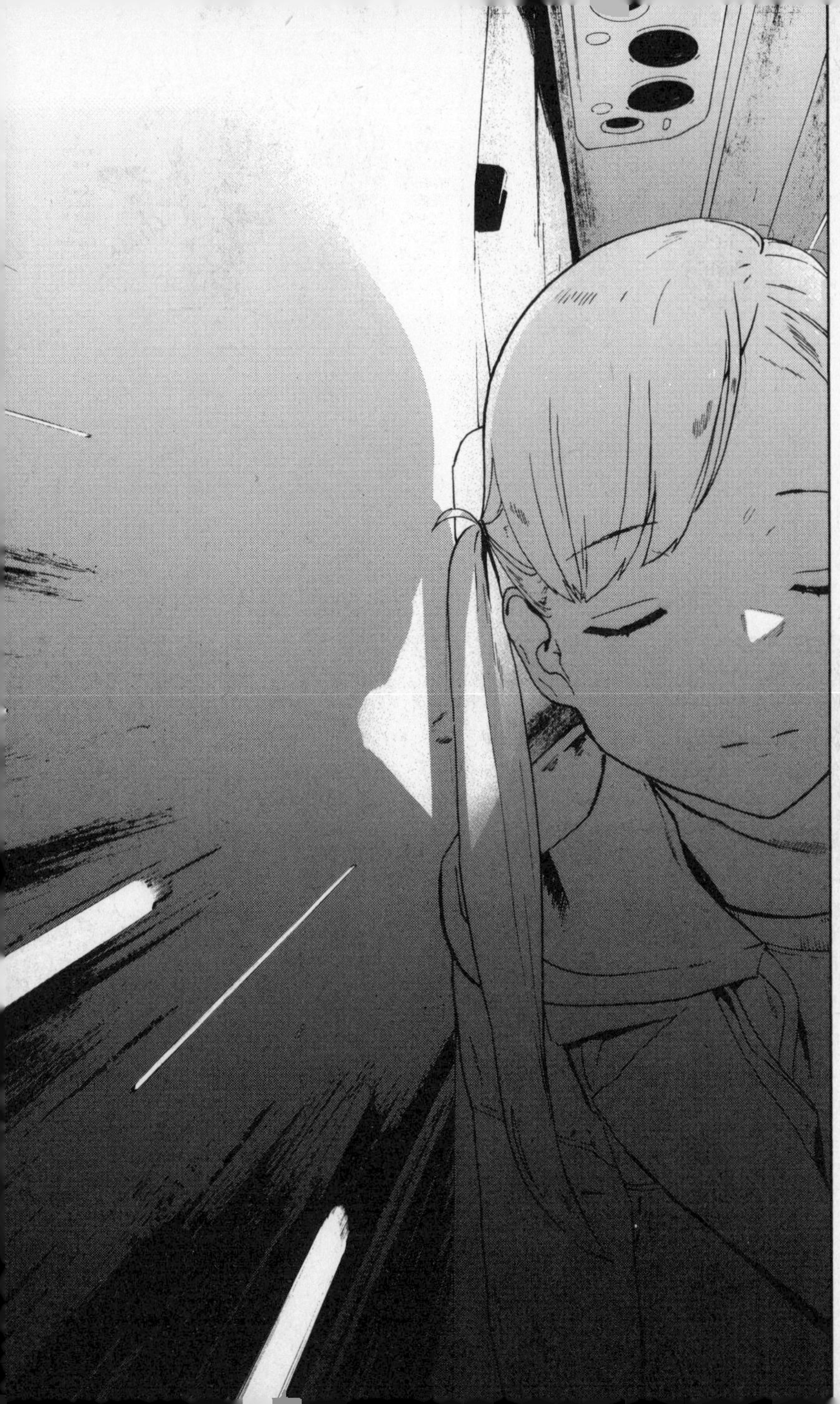

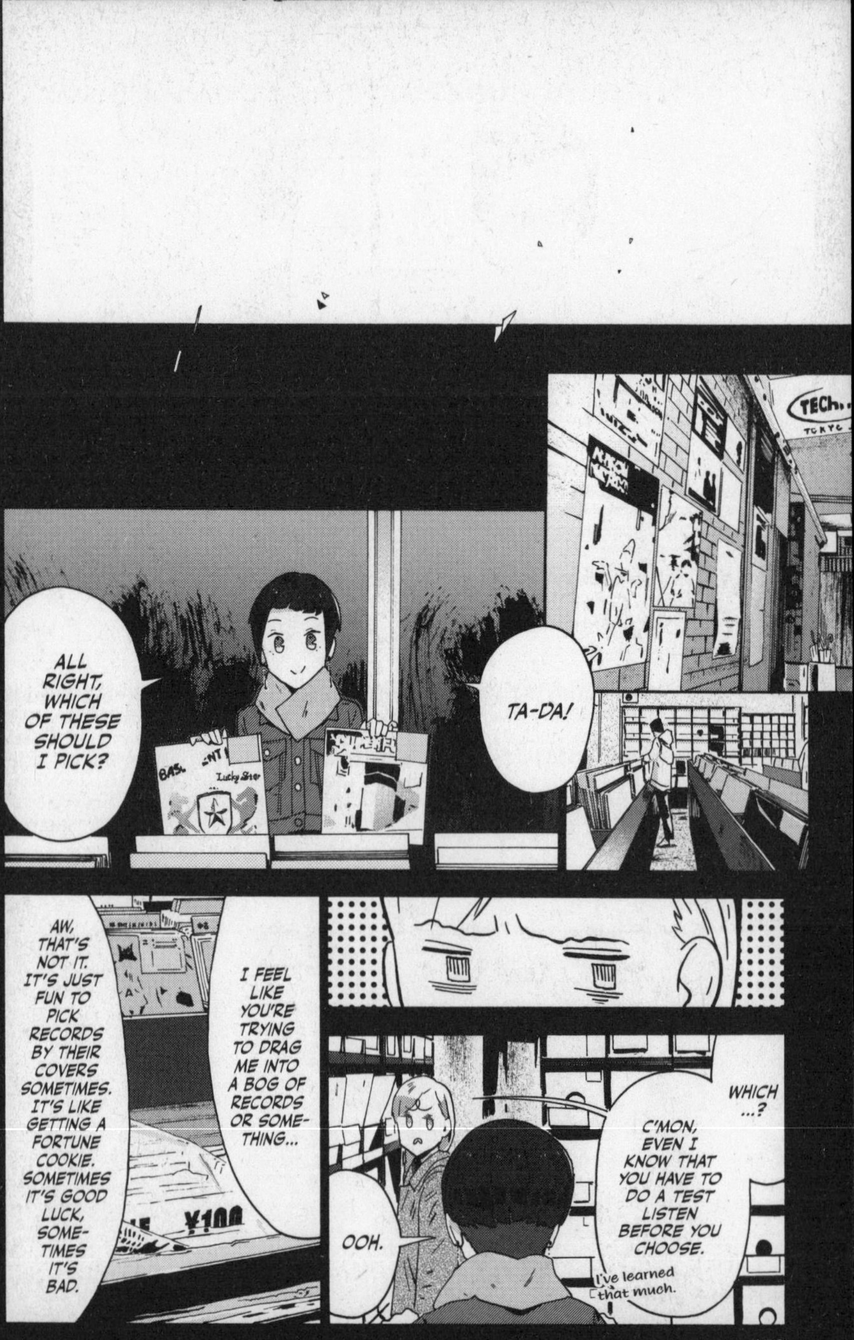
TECH...
TA-DA!
ALL RIGHT, WHICH OF THESE SHOULD I PICK?
Lucky Star
WHICH ...?
C'MON, EVEN I KNOW THAT YOU HAVE TO DO A TEST LISTEN BEFORE YOU CHOOSE.
I've learned that much.
OOH.
I FEEL LIKE YOU'RE TRYING TO DRAG ME INTO A BOG OF RECORDS OR SOME-THING...
AW, THAT'S NOT IT. IT'S JUST FUN TO PICK RECORDS BY THEIR COVERS SOMETIMES. IT'S LIKE GETTING A FORTUNE COOKIE. SOMETIMES IT'S GOOD LUCK, SOME-TIMES IT'S BAD.
¥100

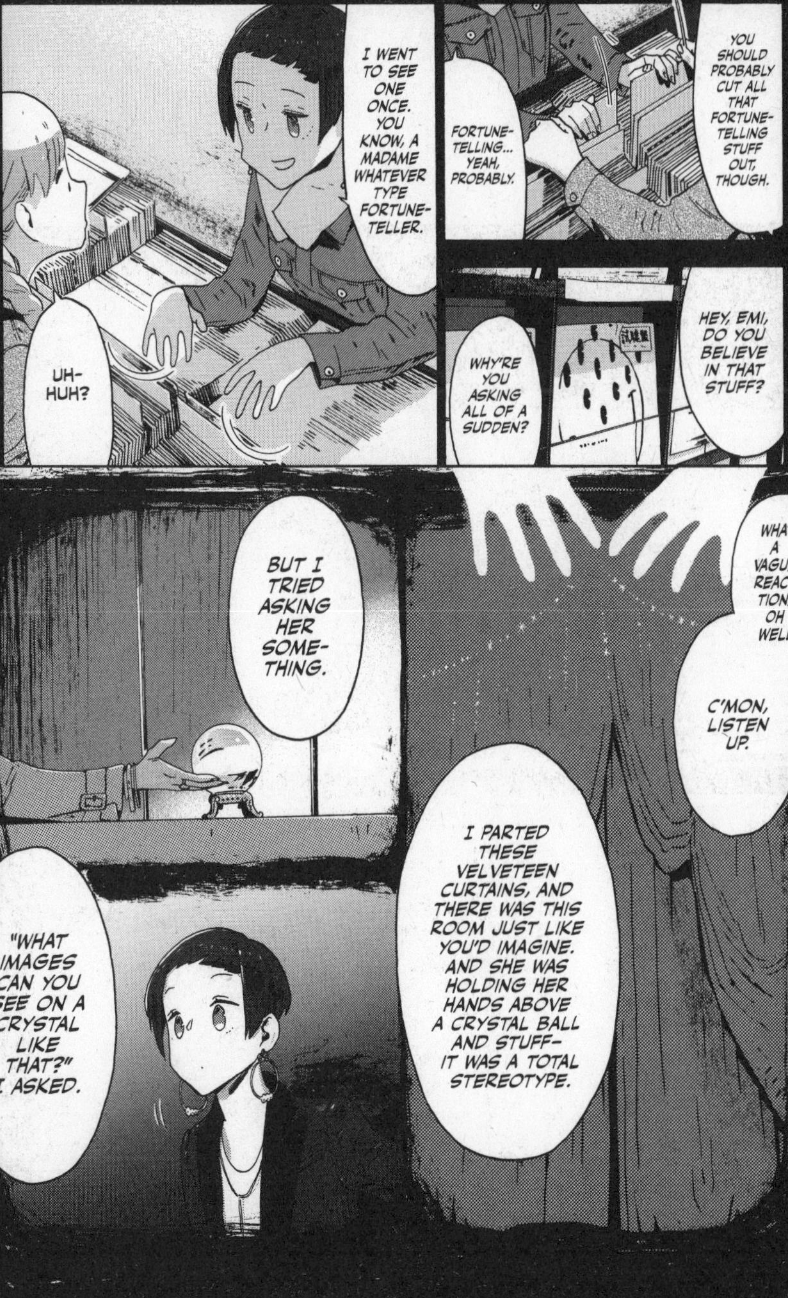
YOU SHOULD PROBABLY CUT ALL THAT FORTUNE-TELLING STUFF OUT, THOUGH.
FORTUNE-TELLING... YEAH, PROBABLY.
HEY, EMI, DO YOU BELIEVE IN THAT STUFF?
WHY'RE YOU ASKING ALL OF A SUDDEN?
I WENT TO SEE ONE ONCE. YOU KNOW, A MADAME WHATEVER TYPE FORTUNE-TELLER.
UH-HUH?
WHAT A VAGUE REACTION! OH WELL.
C'MON, LISTEN UP.
I PARTED THESE VELVETEEN CURTAINS, AND THERE WAS THIS ROOM JUST LIKE YOU'D IMAGINE. AND SHE WAS HOLDING HER HANDS ABOVE A CRYSTAL BALL AND STUFF– IT WAS A TOTAL STEREOTYPE.
BUT I TRIED ASKING HER SOMETHING.
"WHAT IMAGES CAN YOU SEE ON A CRYSTAL LIKE THAT?" I ASKED.

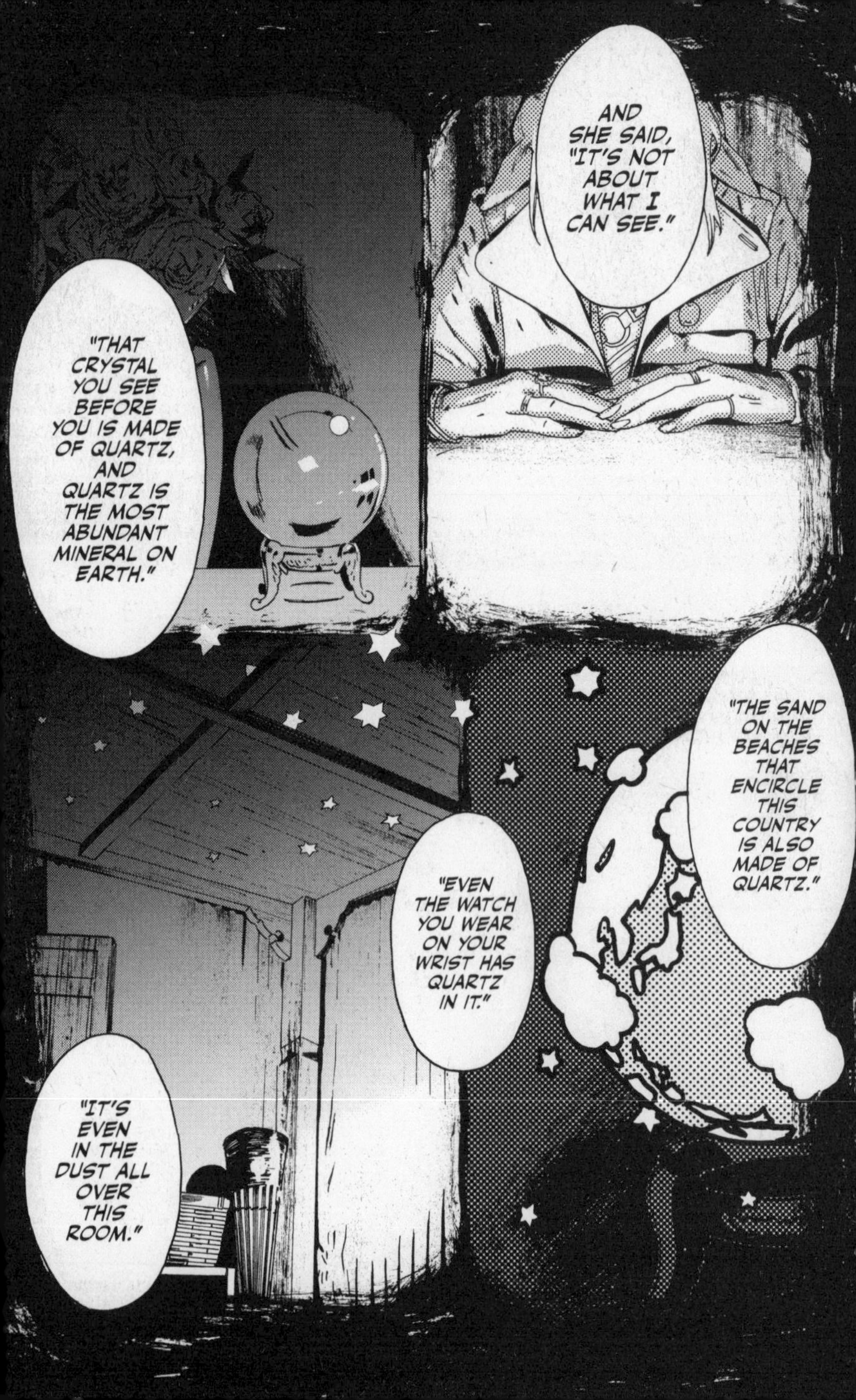
AND SHE SAID, "IT'S NOT ABOUT WHAT I CAN SEE."
"THAT CRYSTAL YOU SEE BEFORE YOU IS MADE OF QUARTZ, AND QUARTZ IS THE MOST ABUNDANT MINERAL ON EARTH."
"THE SAND ON THE BEACHES THAT ENCIRCLE THIS COUNTRY IS ALSO MADE OF QUARTZ."
"EVEN THE WATCH YOU WEAR ON YOUR WRIST HAS QUARTZ IN IT."
"IT'S EVEN IN THE DUST ALL OVER THIS ROOM."

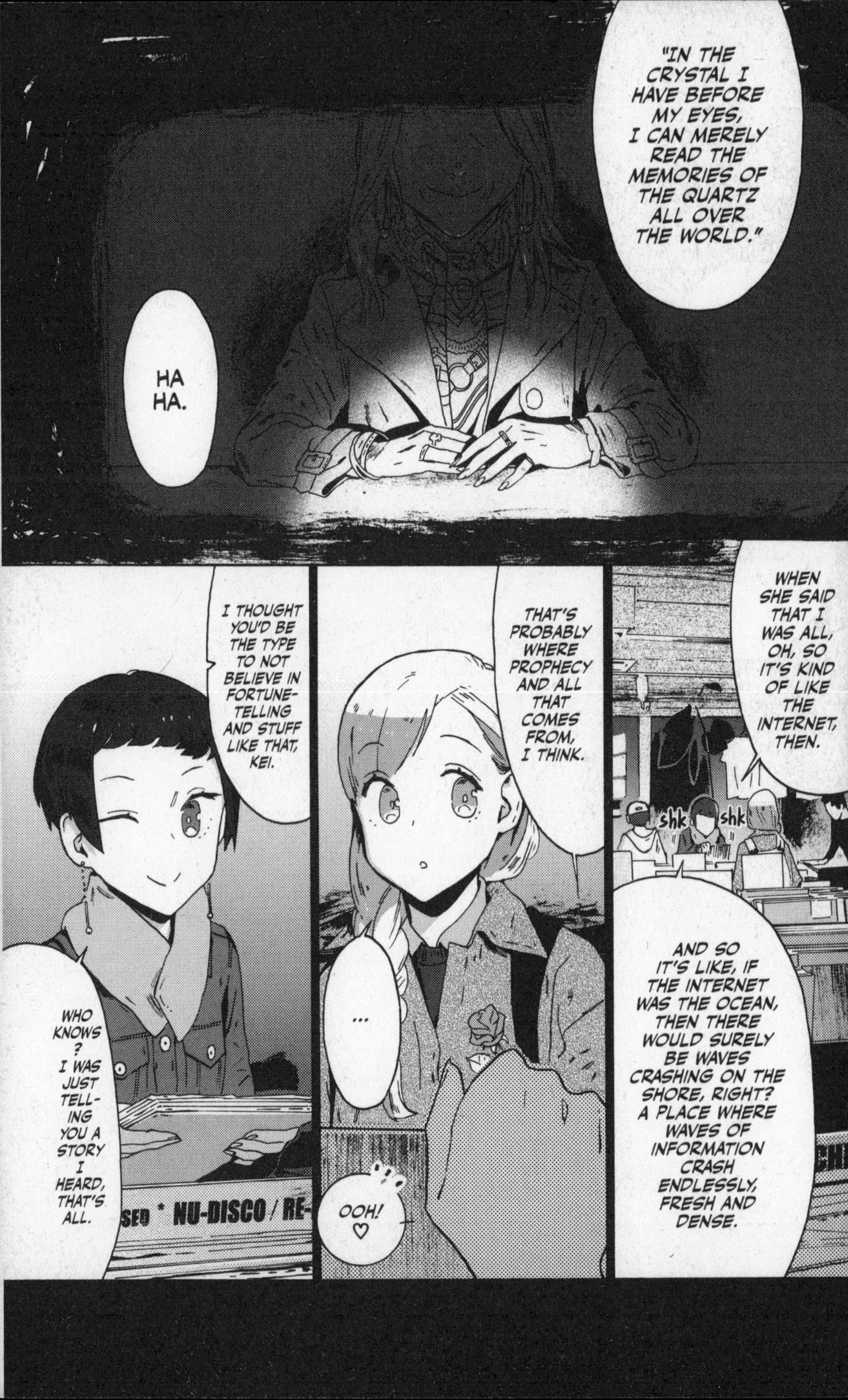
"IN THE CRYSTAL I HAVE BEFORE MY EYES, I CAN MERELY READ THE MEMORIES OF THE QUARTZ ALL OVER THE WORLD."
HA HA.
WHEN SHE SAID THAT I WAS ALL, OH, SO IT'S KIND OF LIKE THE INTERNET, THEN.
shk shk
AND SO IT'S LIKE, IF THE INTERNET WAS THE OCEAN, THEN THERE WOULD SURELY BE WAVES CRASHING ON THE SHORE, RIGHT? A PLACE WHERE WAVES OF INFORMATION CRASH ENDLESSLY, FRESH AND DENSE.
THAT'S PROBABLY WHERE PROPHECY AND ALL THAT COMES FROM, I THINK.
...
OOH! ♥
I THOUGHT YOU'D BE THE TYPE TO NOT BELIEVE IN FORTUNE-TELLING AND STUFF LIKE THAT, KEI.
WHO KNOWS? I WAS JUST TELLING YOU A STORY I HEARD, THAT'S ALL.
NU-DISCO / RE-

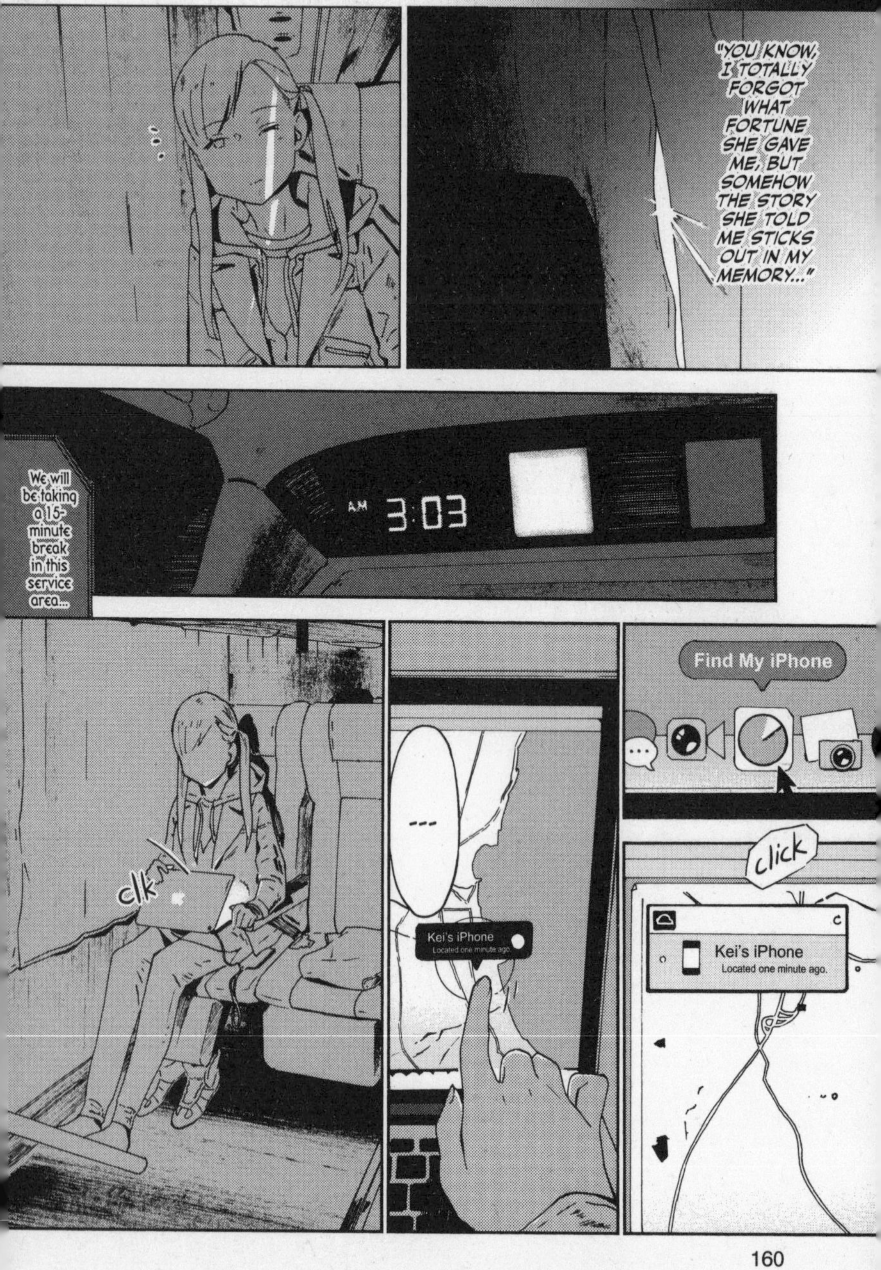
"YOU KNOW, I TOTALLY FORGOT WHAT FORTUNE SHE GAVE ME, BUT SOMEHOW THE STORY SHE TOLD ME STICKS OUT IN MY MEMORY..."
AM 3:03
We will be taking a 15-minute break in this service area...
Find My iPhone
click
Kei's iPhone
Located one minute ago.

Kei's iPhone
Located one minute ago.
clk

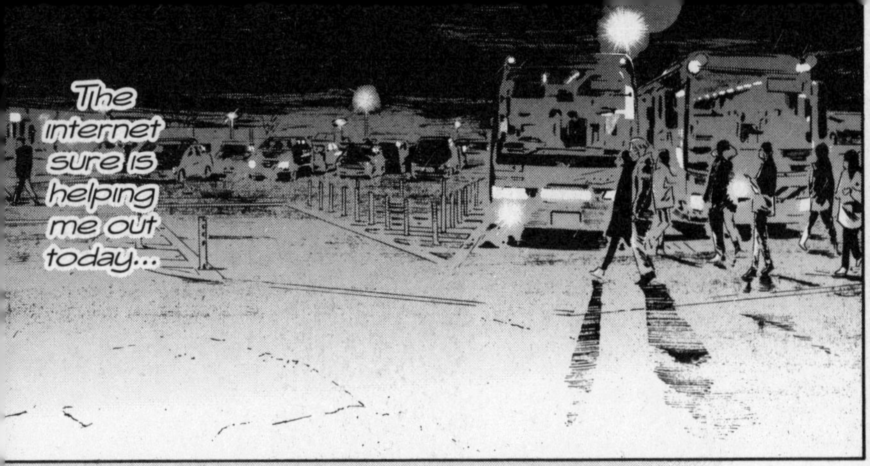
The internet sure is helping me out today...
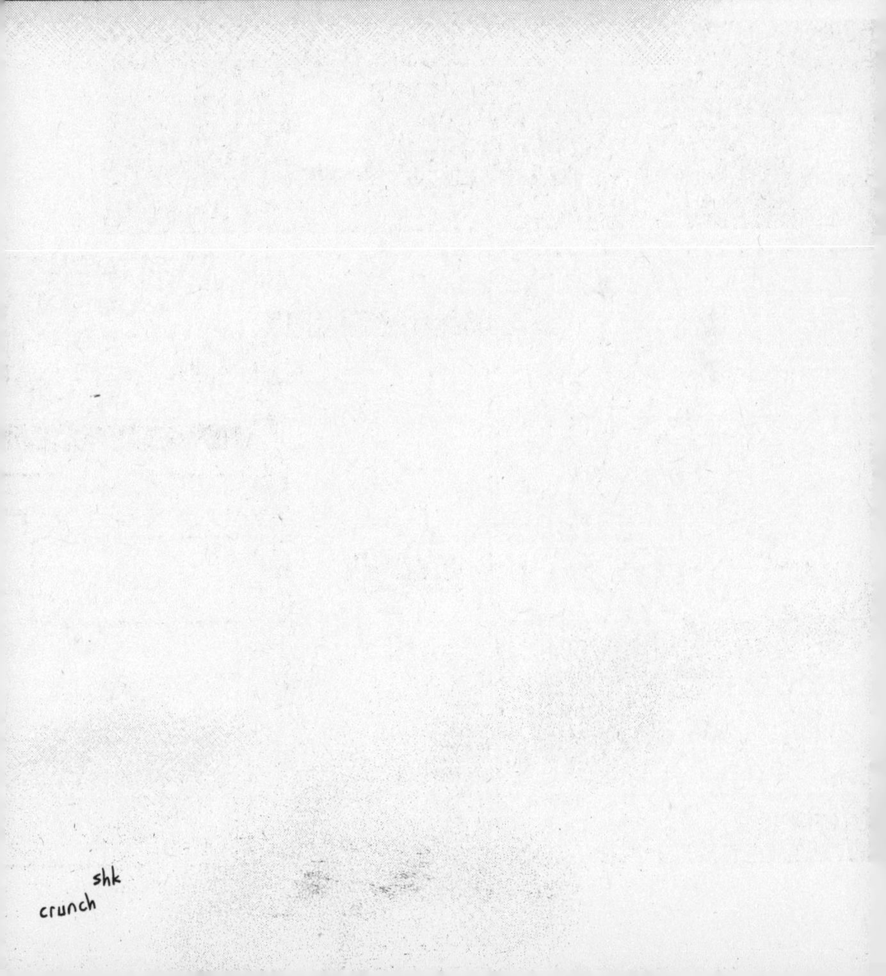
shk
crunch

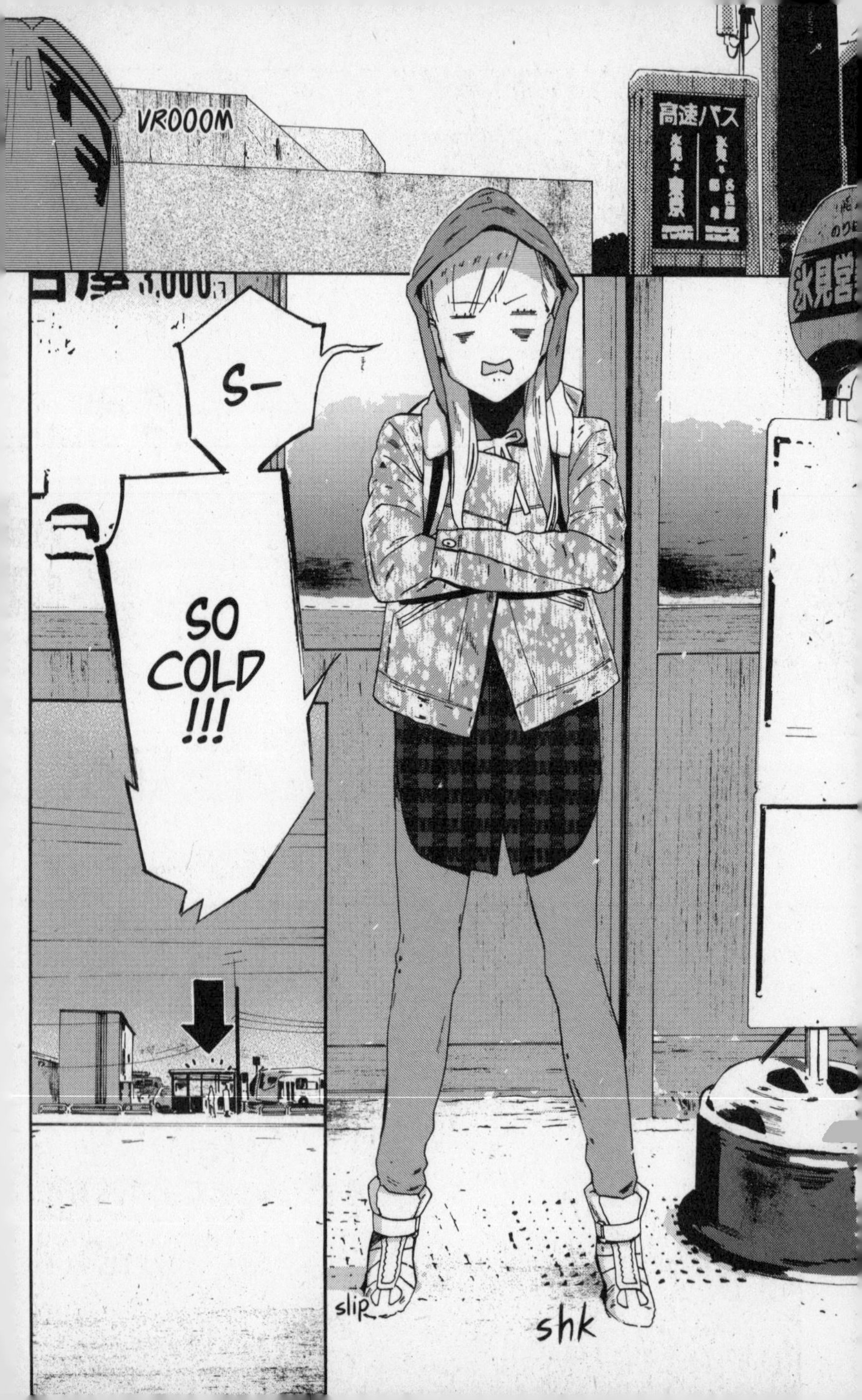
VROOOM
高速バス
S—
SO COLD!!!
slip
shk

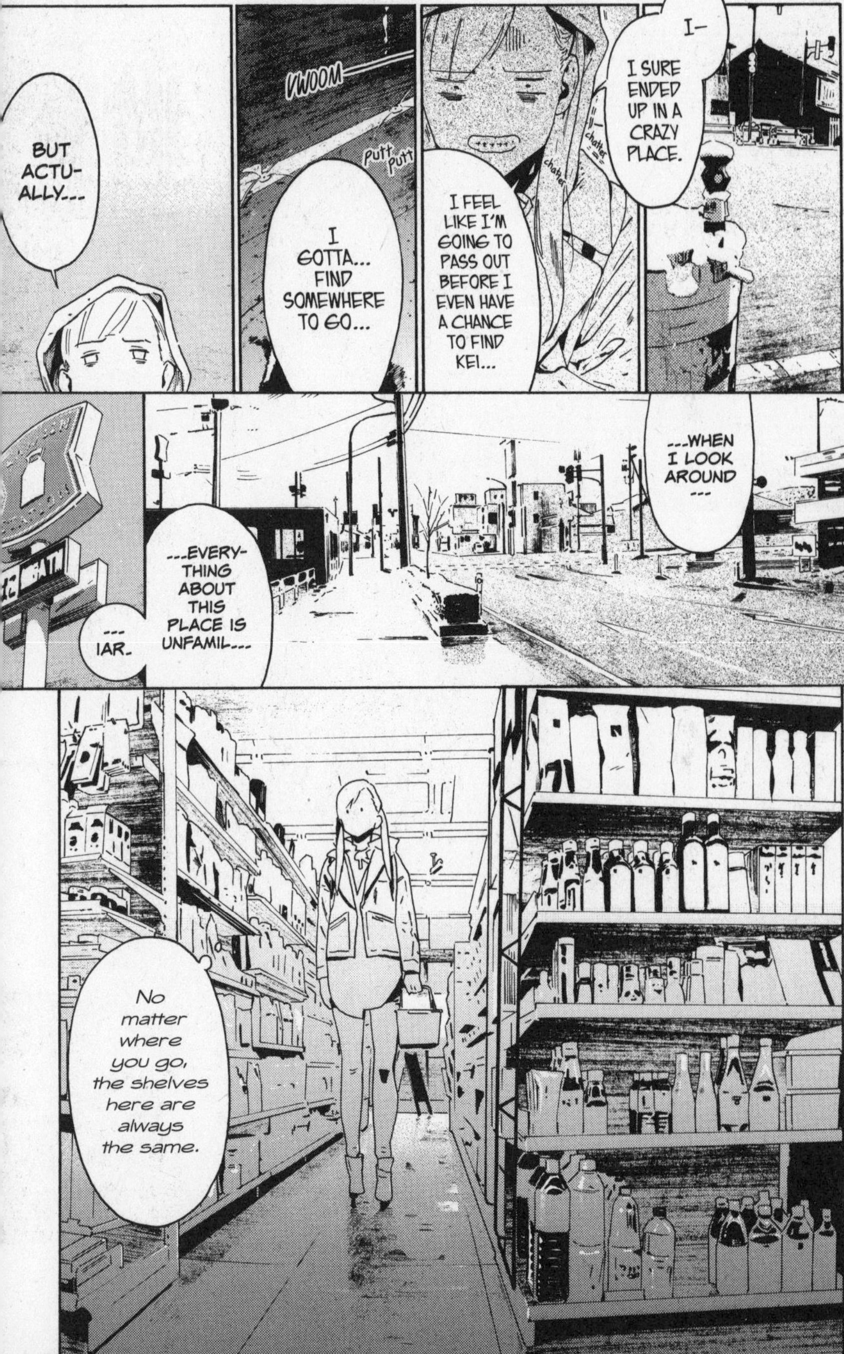
I—
I SURE ENDED UP IN A CRAZY PLACE.
chatter chatter
I FEEL LIKE I'M GOING TO PASS OUT BEFORE I EVEN HAVE A CHANCE TO FIND KEI...
VWOOM
Putt putt
I GOTTA... FIND SOMEWHERE TO GO...
BUT ACTU-ALLY...
...WHEN I LOOK AROUND ...
...EVERY-THING ABOUT THIS PLACE IS UNFAMIL...
...IAR.
No matter where you go, the shelves here are always the same.

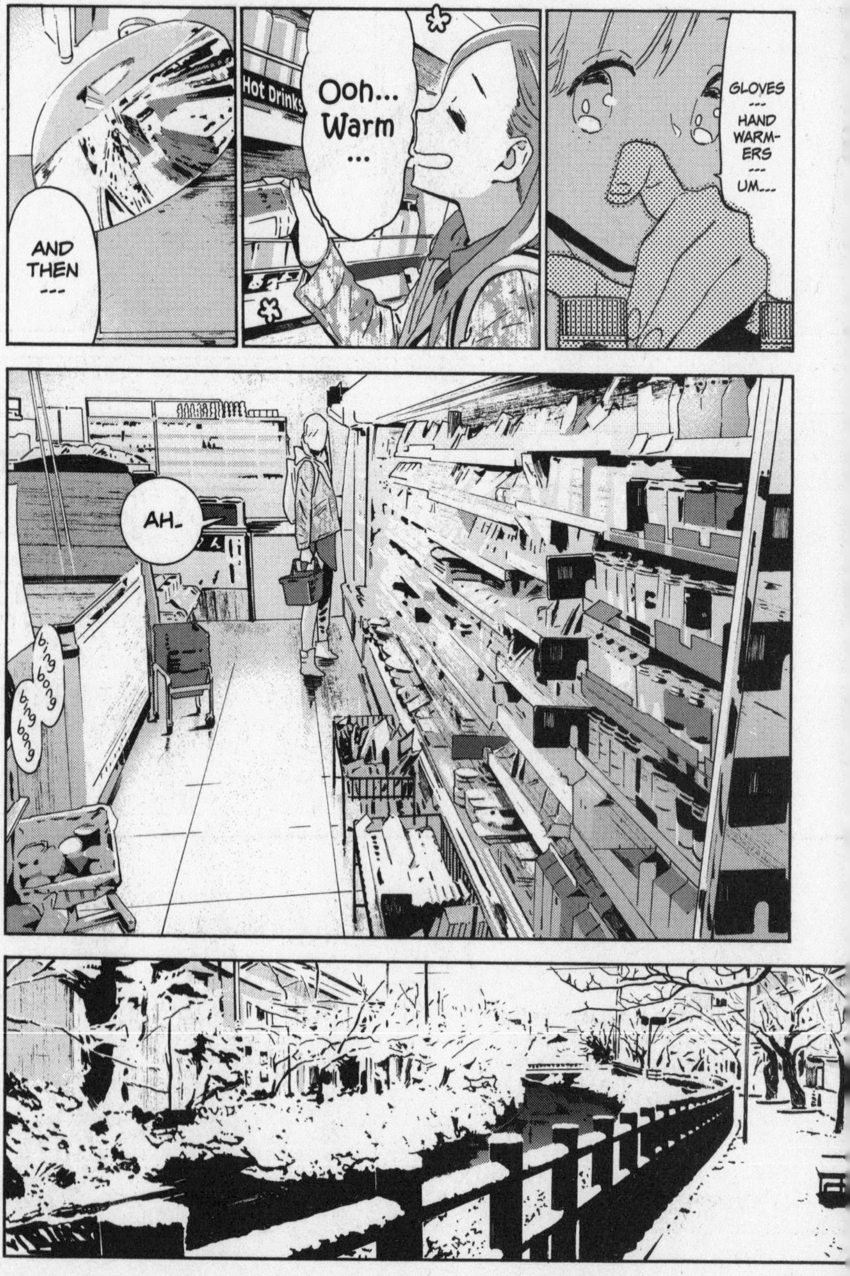
GLOVES --- HAND WARMERS --- UM---
Ooh... Warm ...
Hot Drinks
AND THEN ---
AH_
bing bong
bing bong

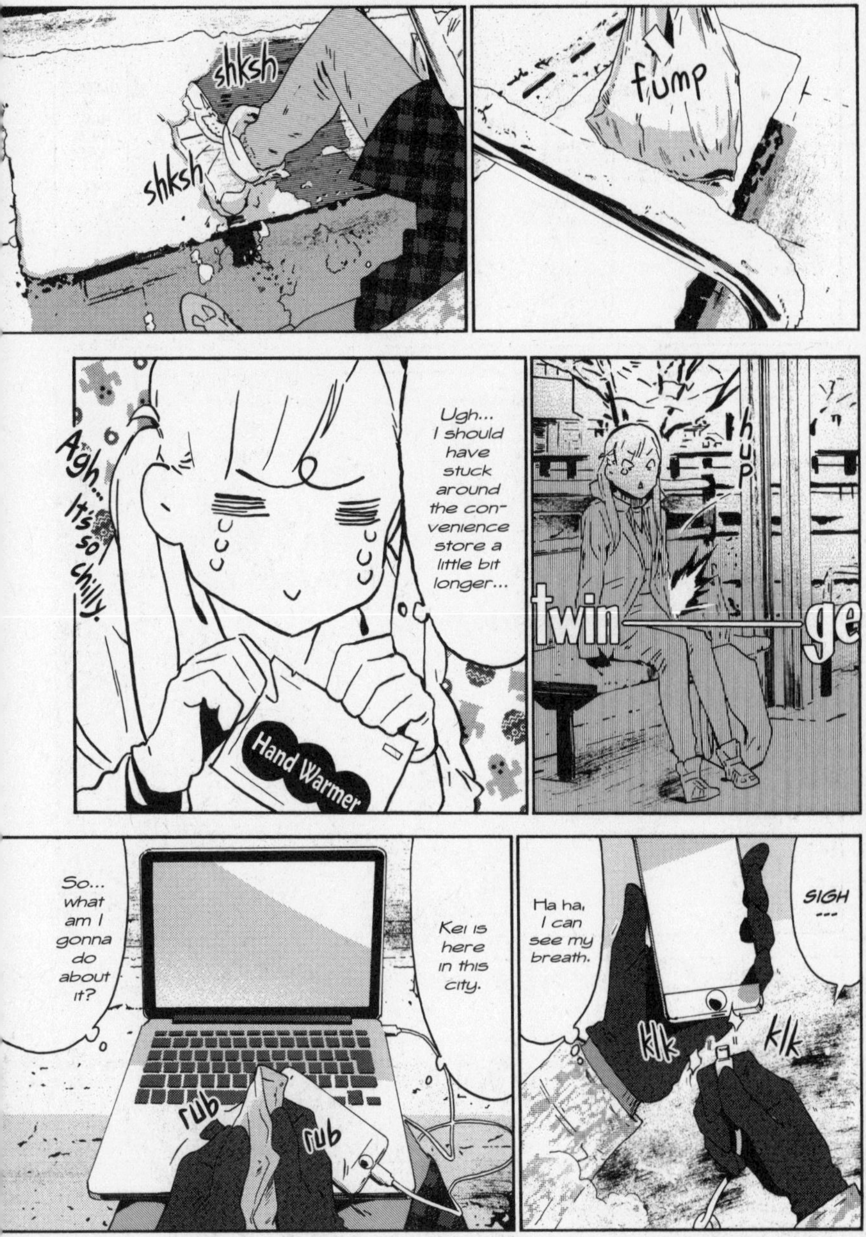
fump
shksh
shksh
hup
twinge
Ugh... I should have stuck around the convenience store a little bit longer...
Agh... It's so chilly.
Hand Warmer
SIGH...
Ha ha, I can see my breath.
klk
klk
Kei is here in this city.
So... what am I gonna do about it?
rub
rub

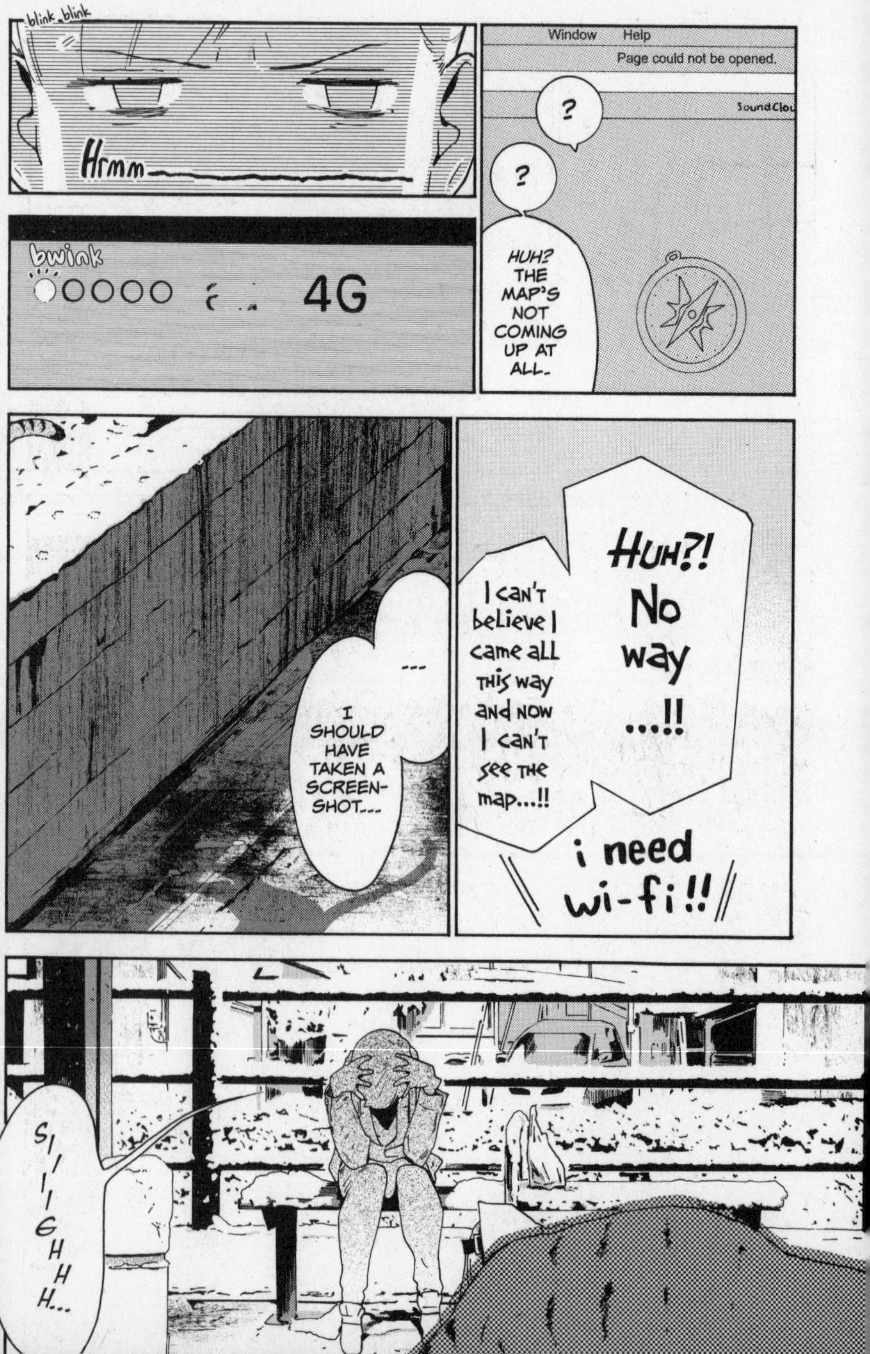
blink blink
Hrmm
bwink
4G
Window Help
Page could not be opened.
SoundClou
?
?
HUH? THE MAP'S NOT COMING UP AT ALL.
HUH?! No way ...!!
I can't believe I came all this way and now I can't see the map...!!
i need wi-fi!!
...
I SHOULD HAVE TAKEN A SCREEN-SHOT...
SIIIIGHHHH...

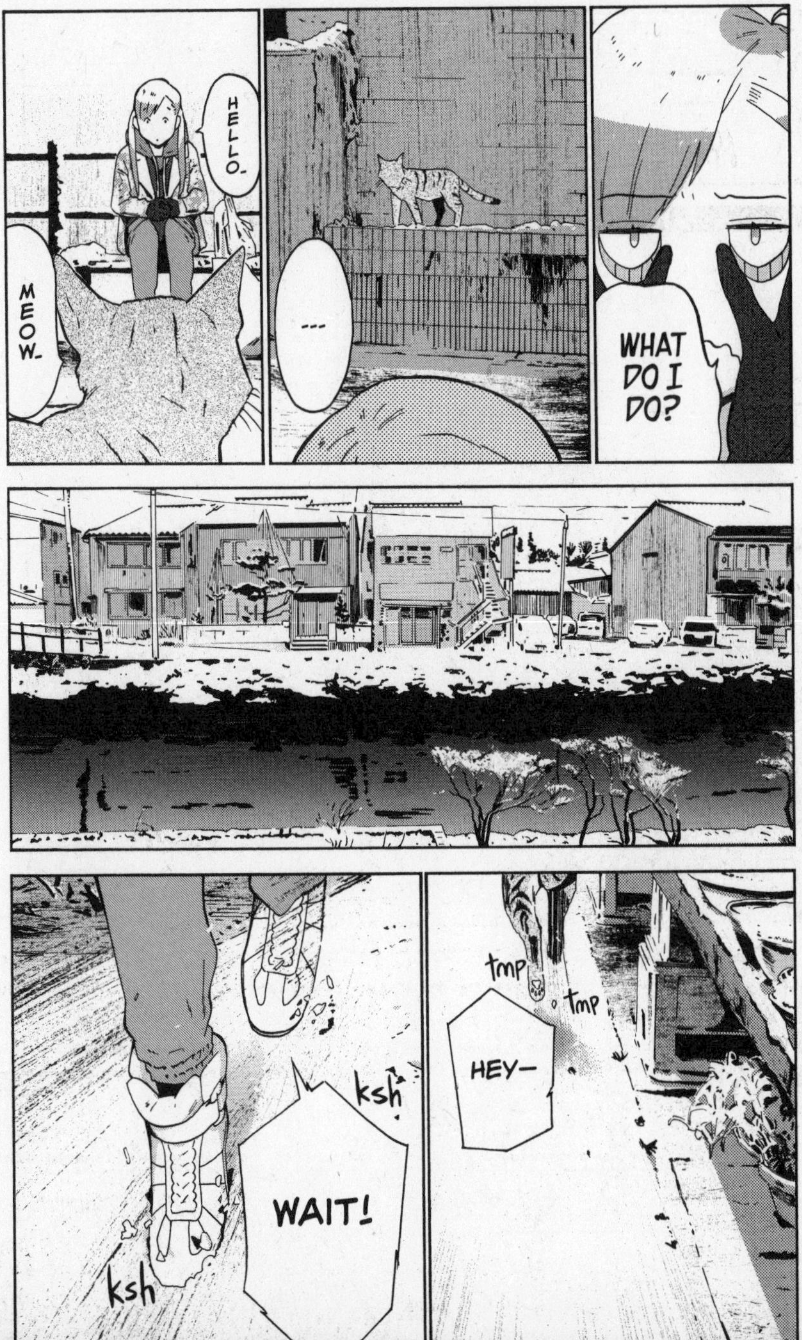
WHAT DO I DO?
...
HELLO_
MEOW_
tmp
tmp
HEY—
ksh
WAIT!
ksh

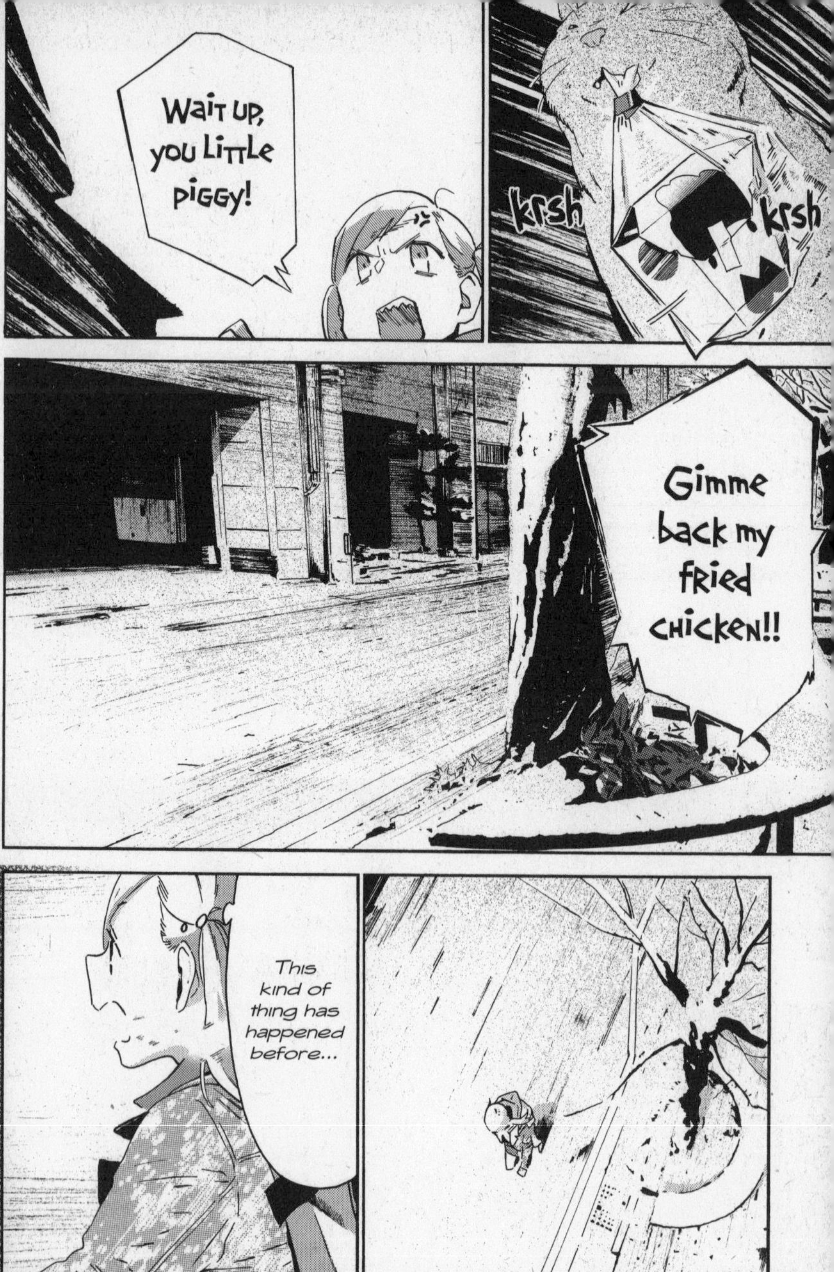
krsh krsh
Wait up, you little piggy!
Gimme back my fried chicken!!
This kind of thing has happened before...

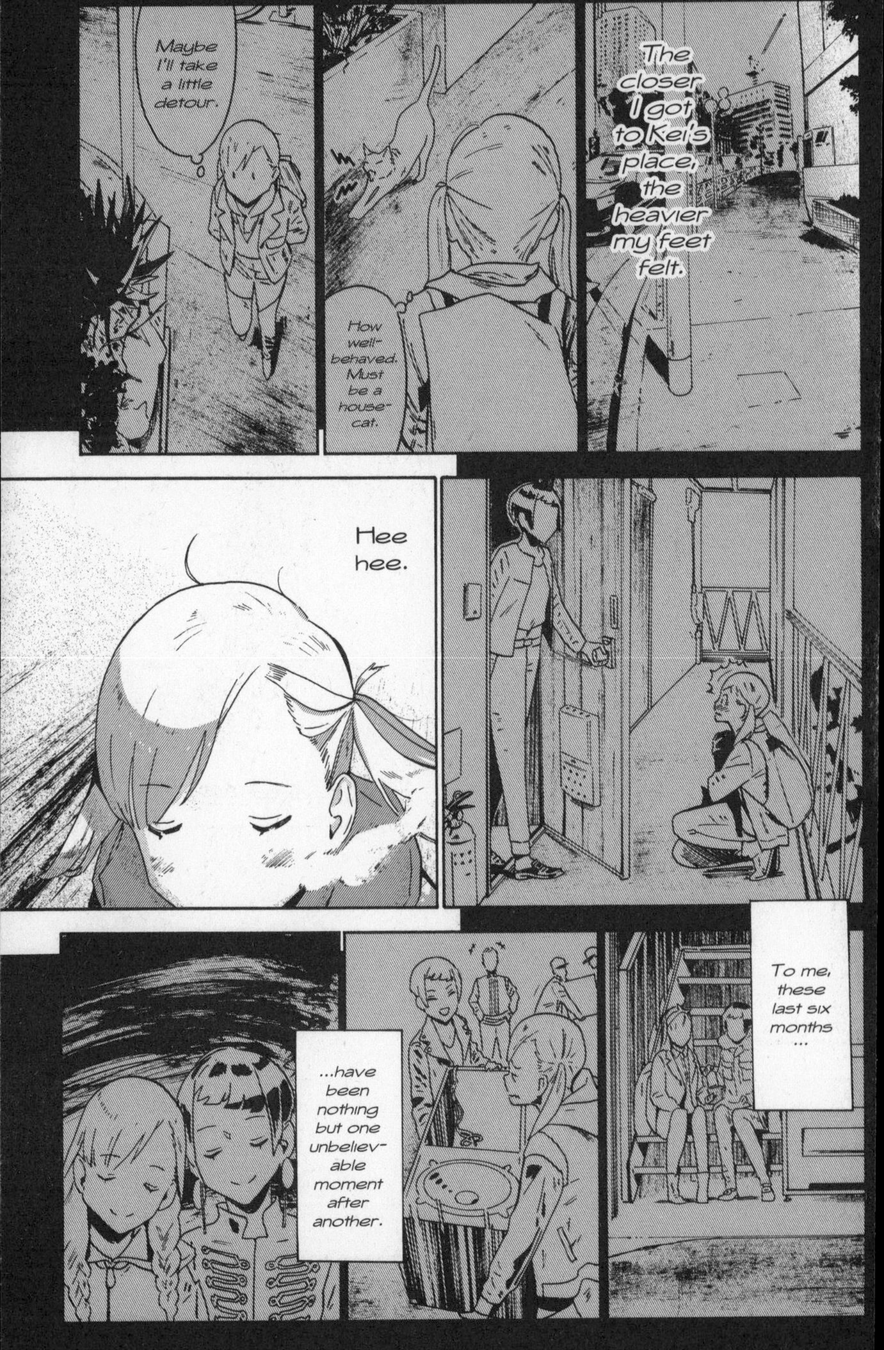
The closer I got to Kei's place, the heavier my feet felt.
How well-behaved. Must be a house-cat.
Maybe I'll take a little detour.
Hee hee.
To me, these last six months ...
...have been nothing but one unbelievable moment after another.

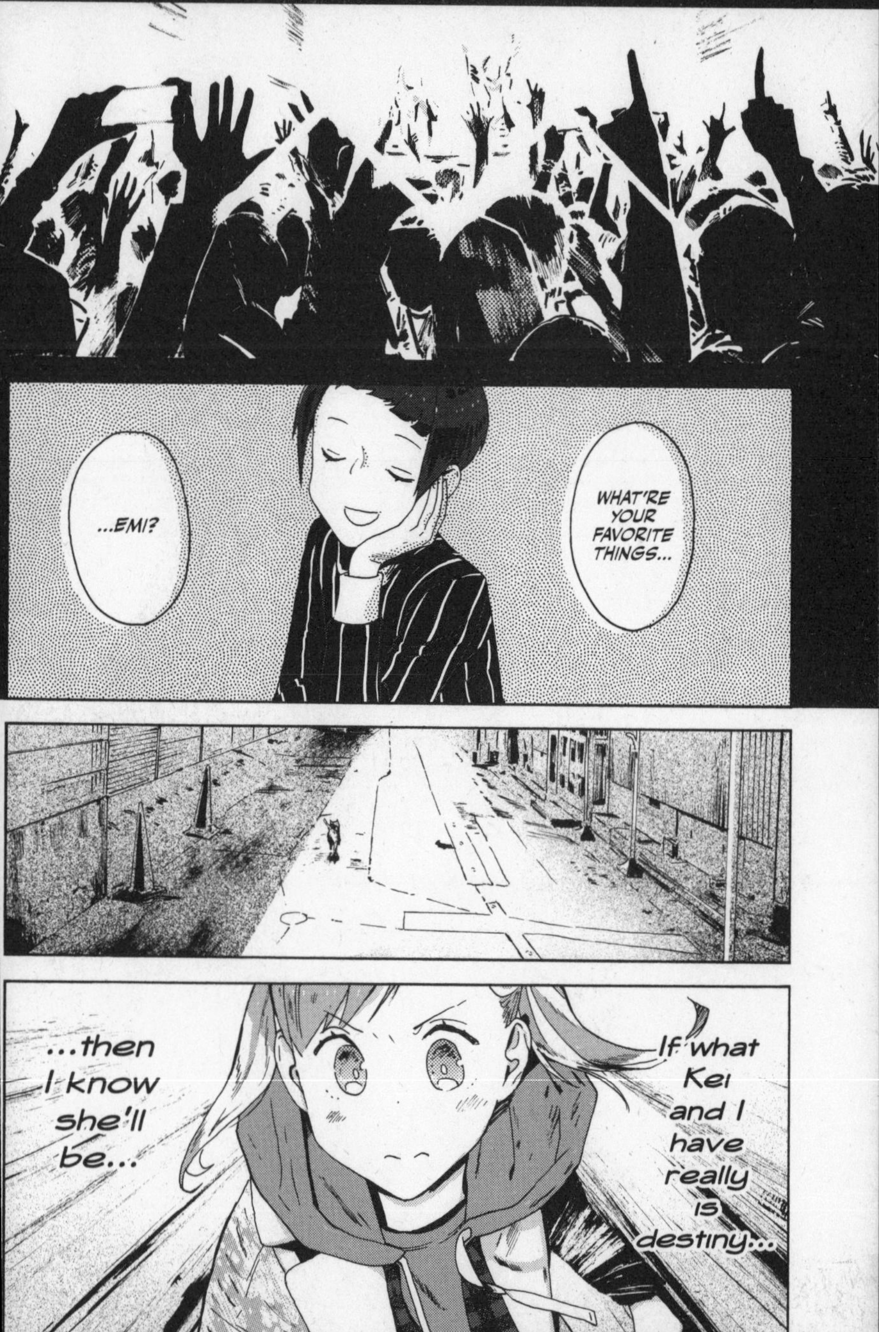
WHAT'RE YOUR FAVORITE THINGS...
...EMI?
If what Kei and I have really is destiny...
...then I know she'll be...

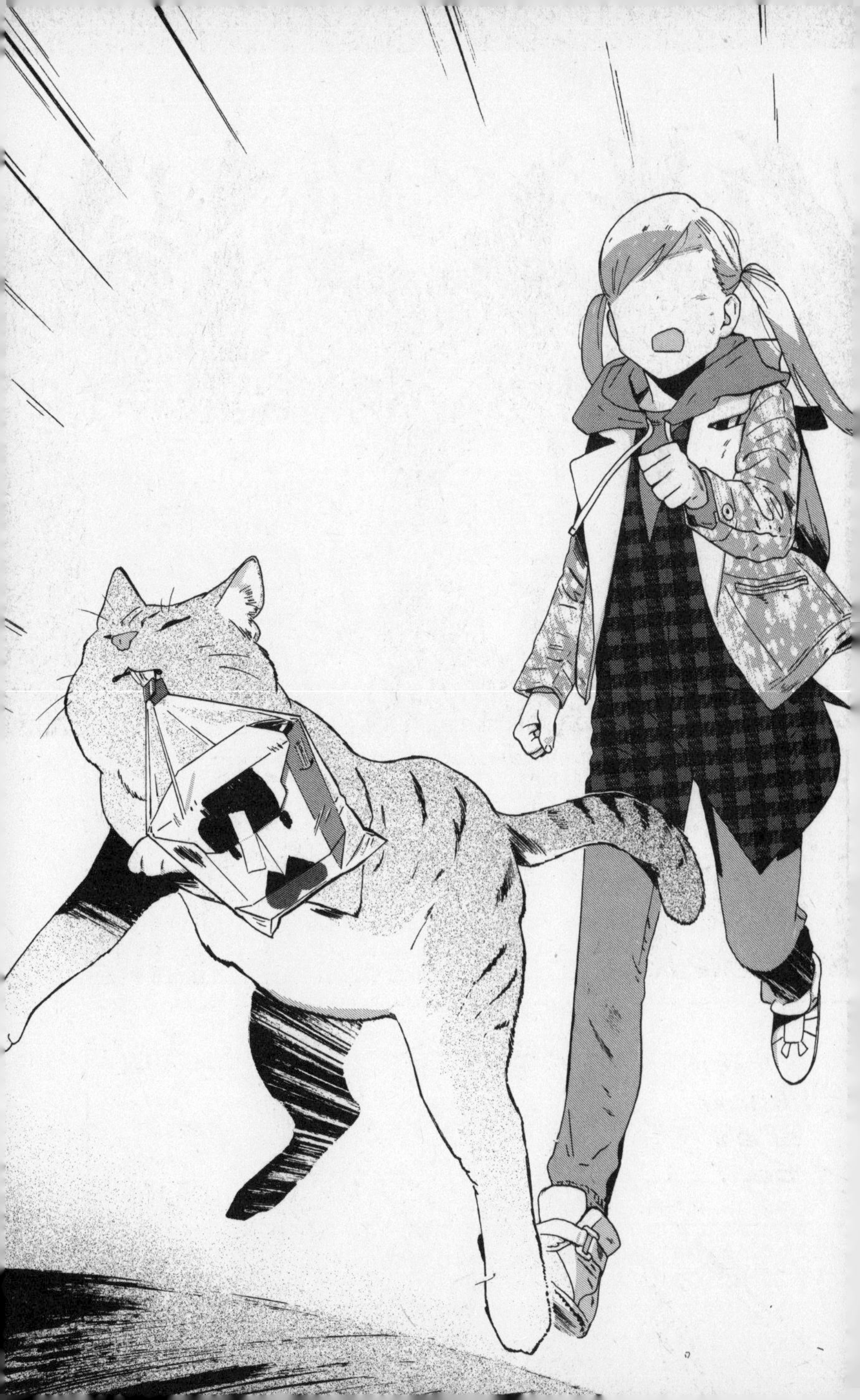

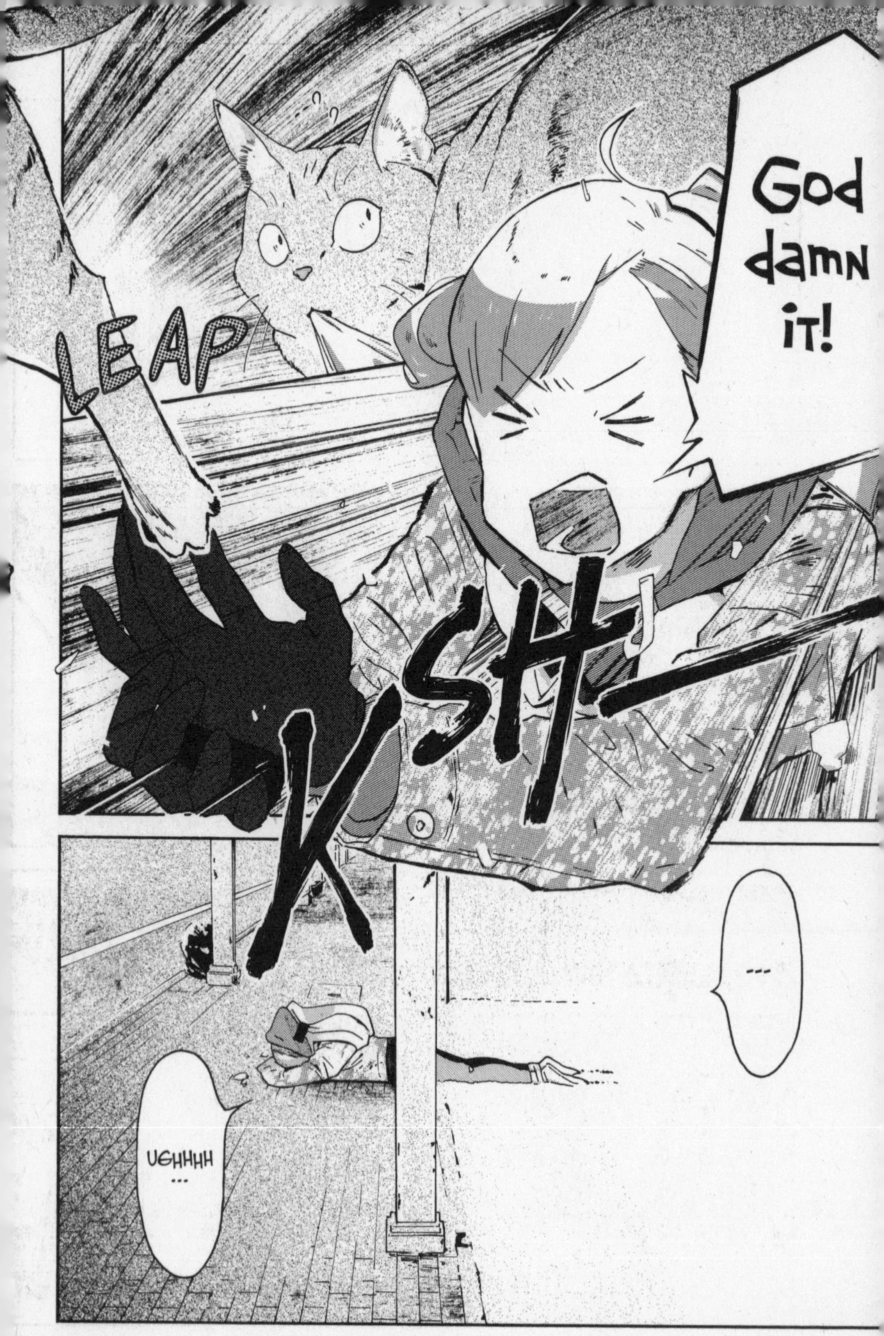
God damn it!
LEAP
KSH
...
UGHHHH ...

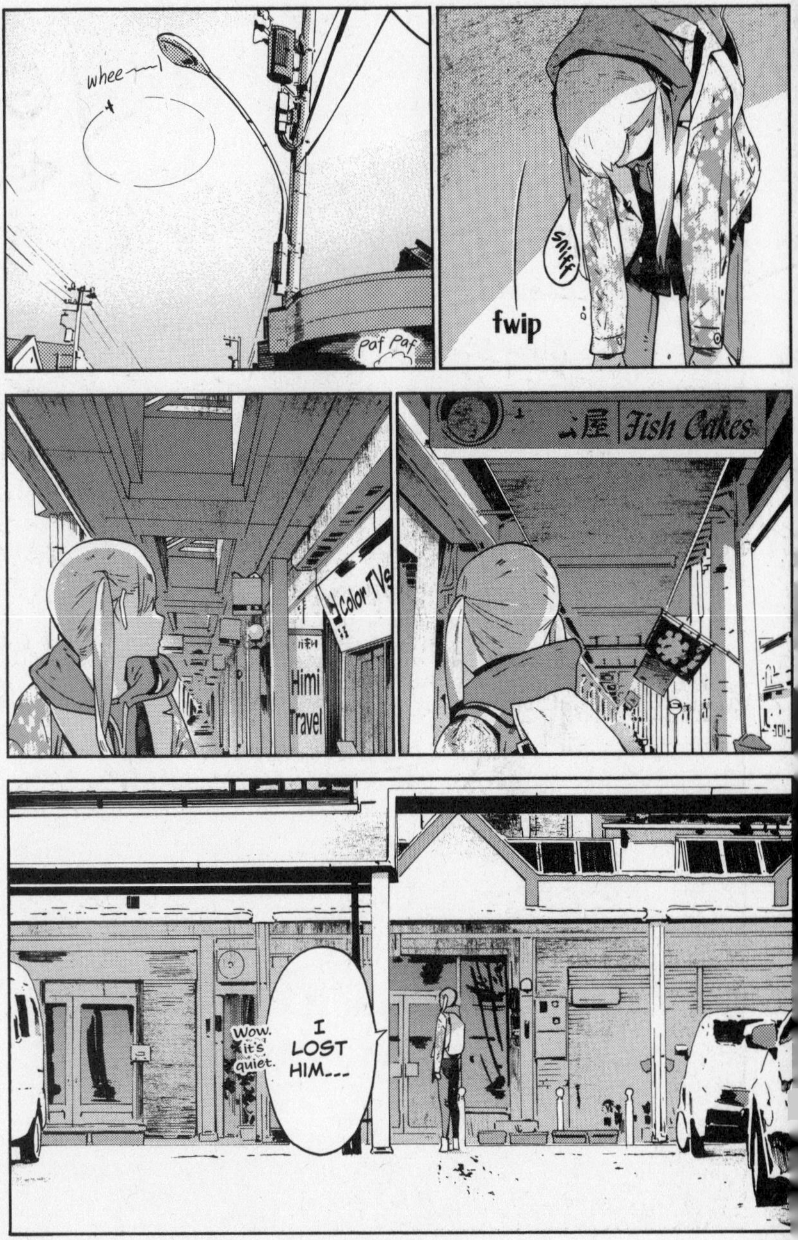
sniff
fwip
whee
Paf Paf
Fish Cakes
Color TVs
Himi Travel
I LOST HIM...
Wow. it's quiet.

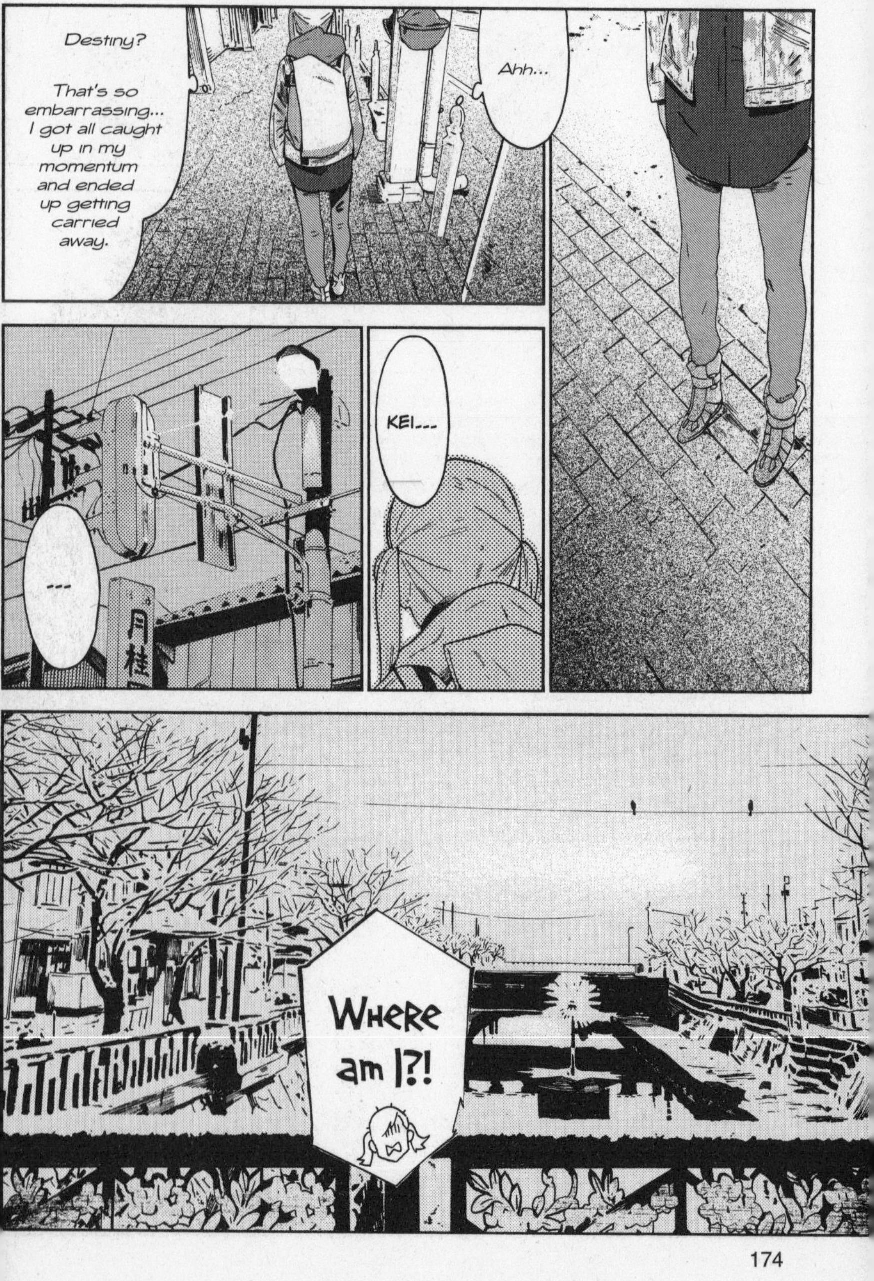
Ahh...
Destiny?
That's so embarrassing... I got all caught up in my momentum and ended up getting carried away.
KEI...
...
月桂
Where am I?!

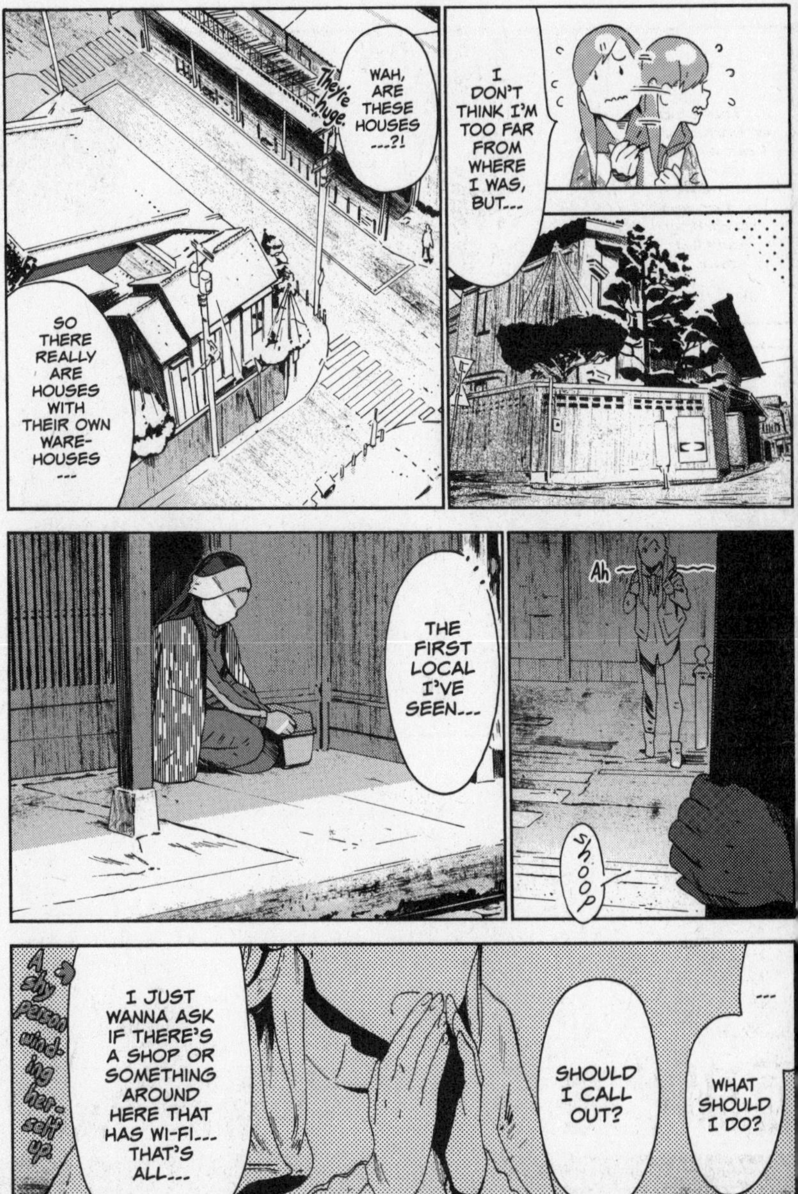
I DON'T THINK I'M TOO FAR FROM WHERE I WAS, BUT...
WAH, ARE THESE HOUSES...?!
They're huge.
SO THERE REALLY ARE HOUSES WITH THEIR OWN WARE-HOUSES...
Ah~~~
SHOOP
THE FIRST LOCAL I'VE SEEN...
...
WHAT SHOULD I DO?
SHOULD I CALL OUT?
I JUST WANNA ASK IF THERE'S A SHOP OR SOMETHING AROUND HERE THAT HAS WI-FI... THAT'S ALL...
A shy person winding herself up.

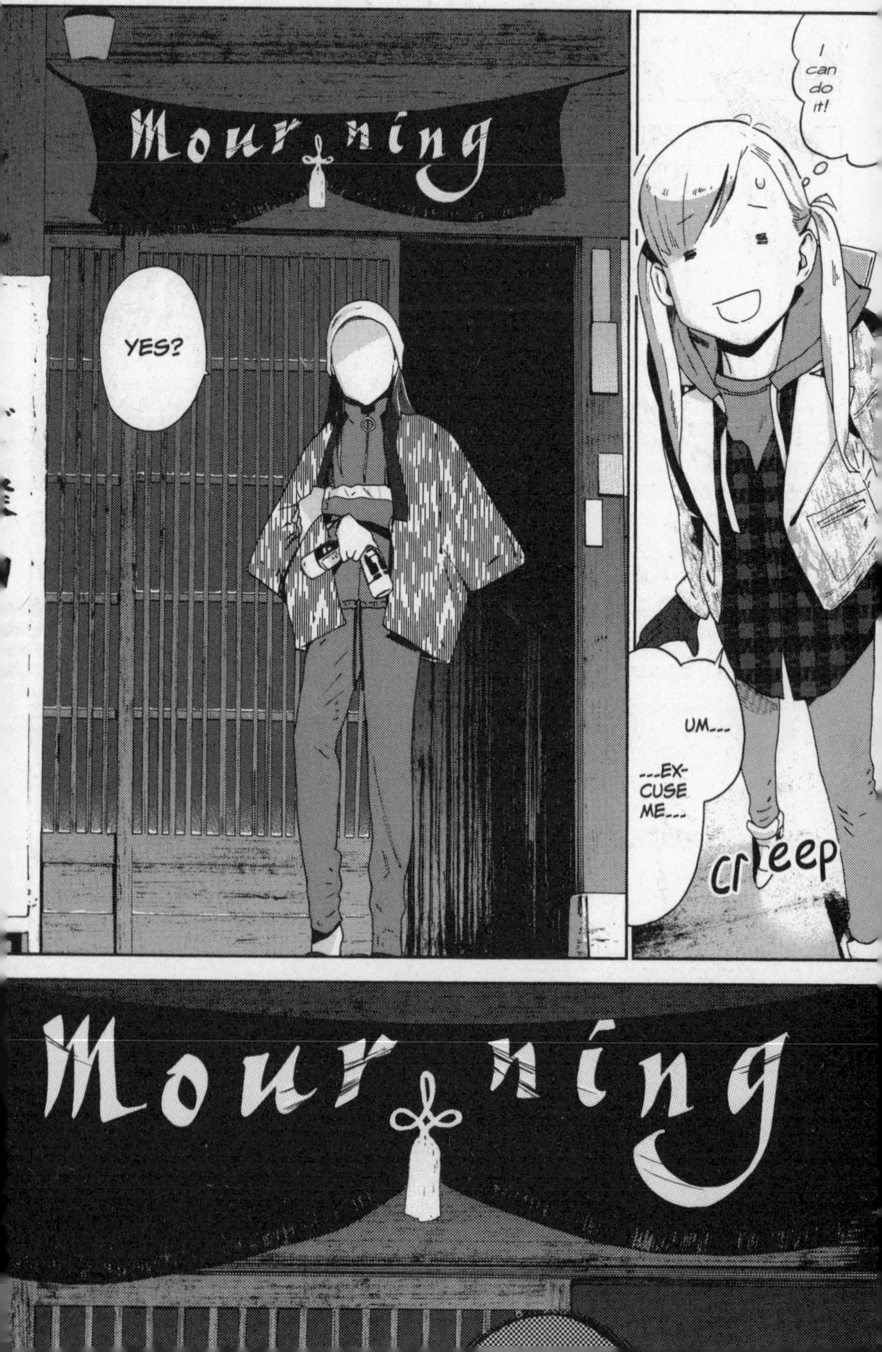
I can do it!
UM...
...EX-CUSE ME...
creep
Mourning
YES?
Mourning

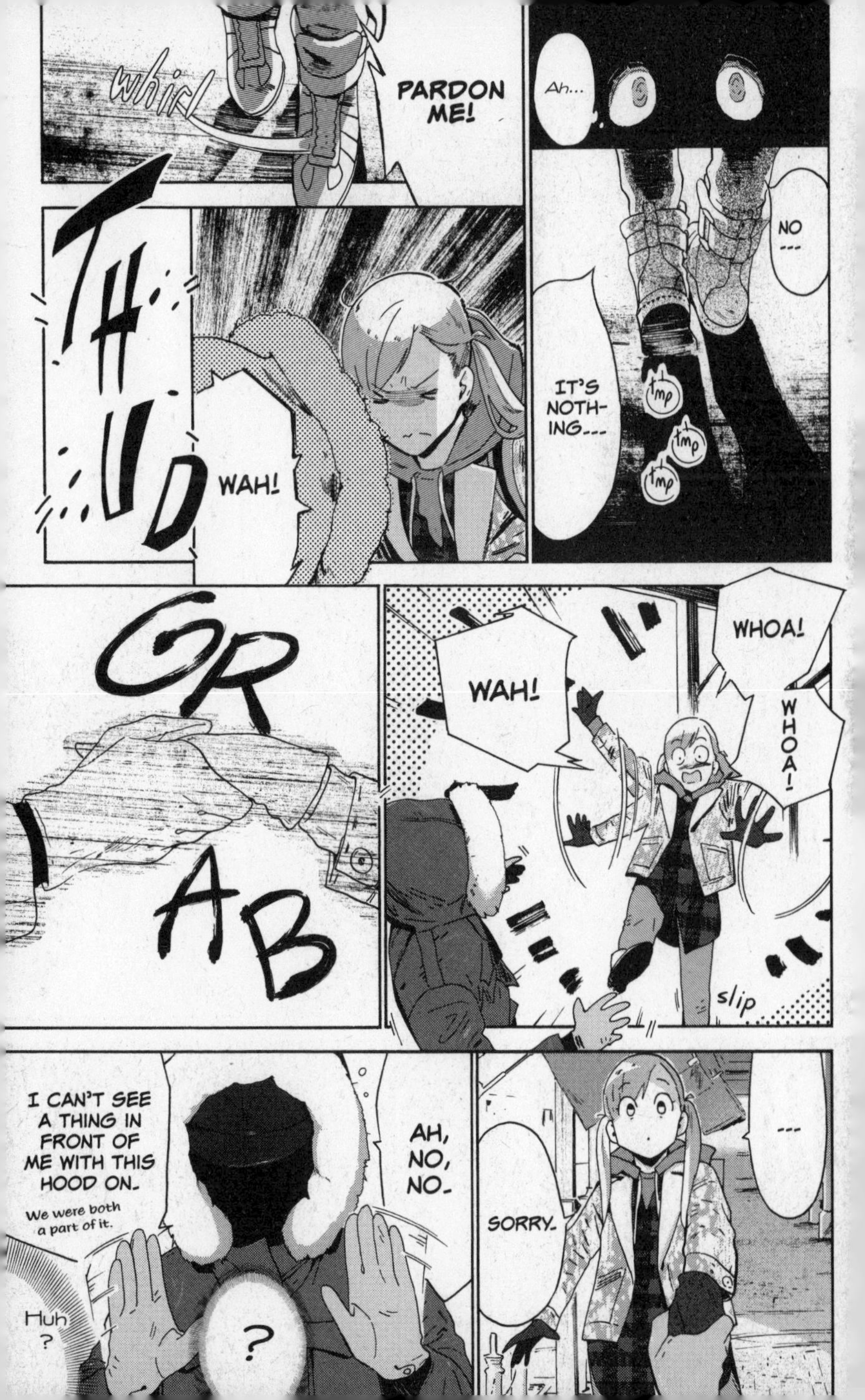
Ah...
NO---
IT'S NOTHING---
tmp
tmp
tmp
whirl
PARDON ME!
THUD
WAH!
WHOA!
WHOA!
WAH!
slip
GRAB

SORRY.
AH, NO, NO.
I CAN'T SEE A THING IN FRONT OF ME WITH THIS HOOD ON.
We were both a part of it.
Huh?
?

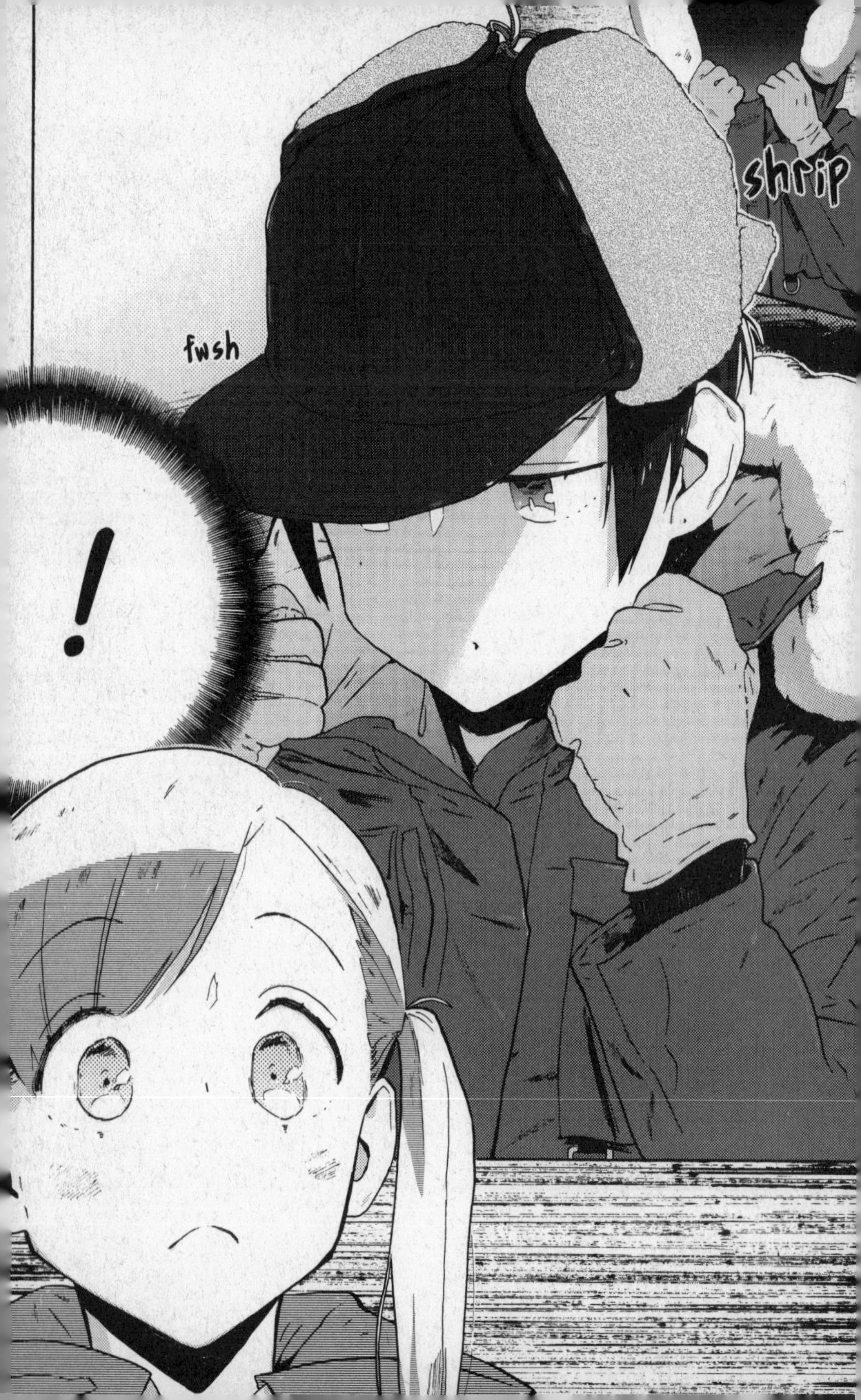
shrip
fwsh
!

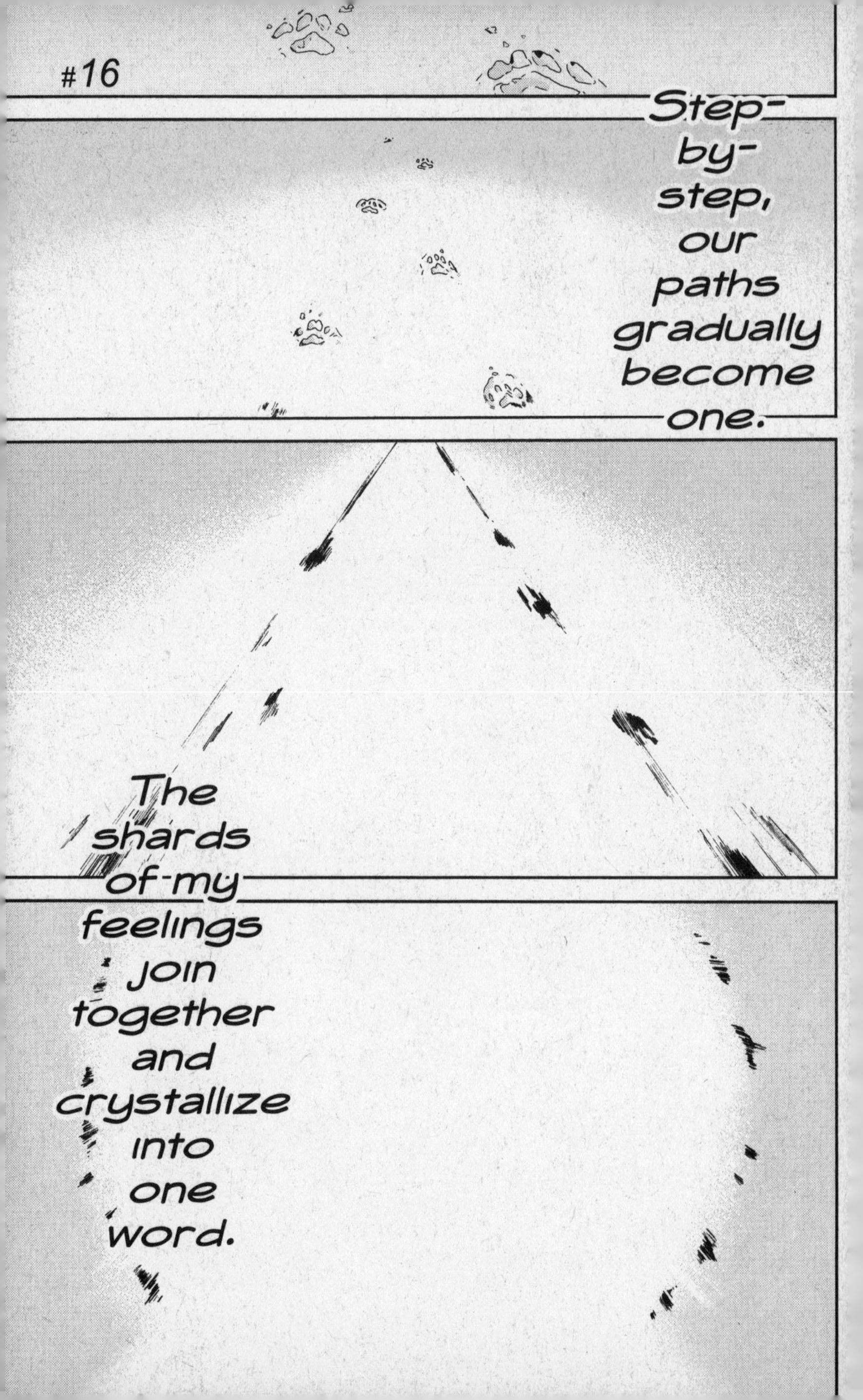
#16
Step-by-step, our paths gradually become one.
The shards of my feelings join together and crystallize into one word.

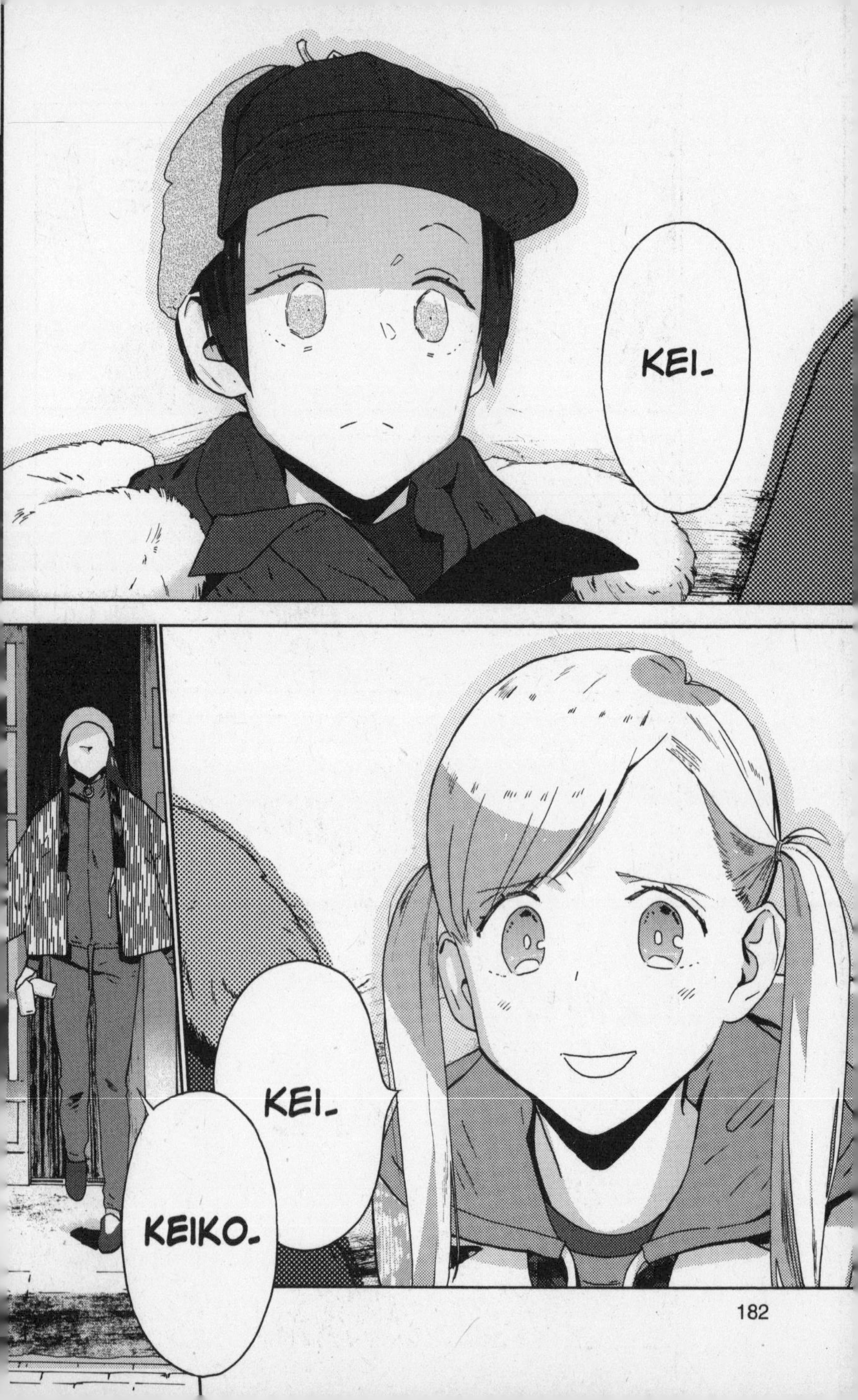
KEI_
KEI_
KEIKO_

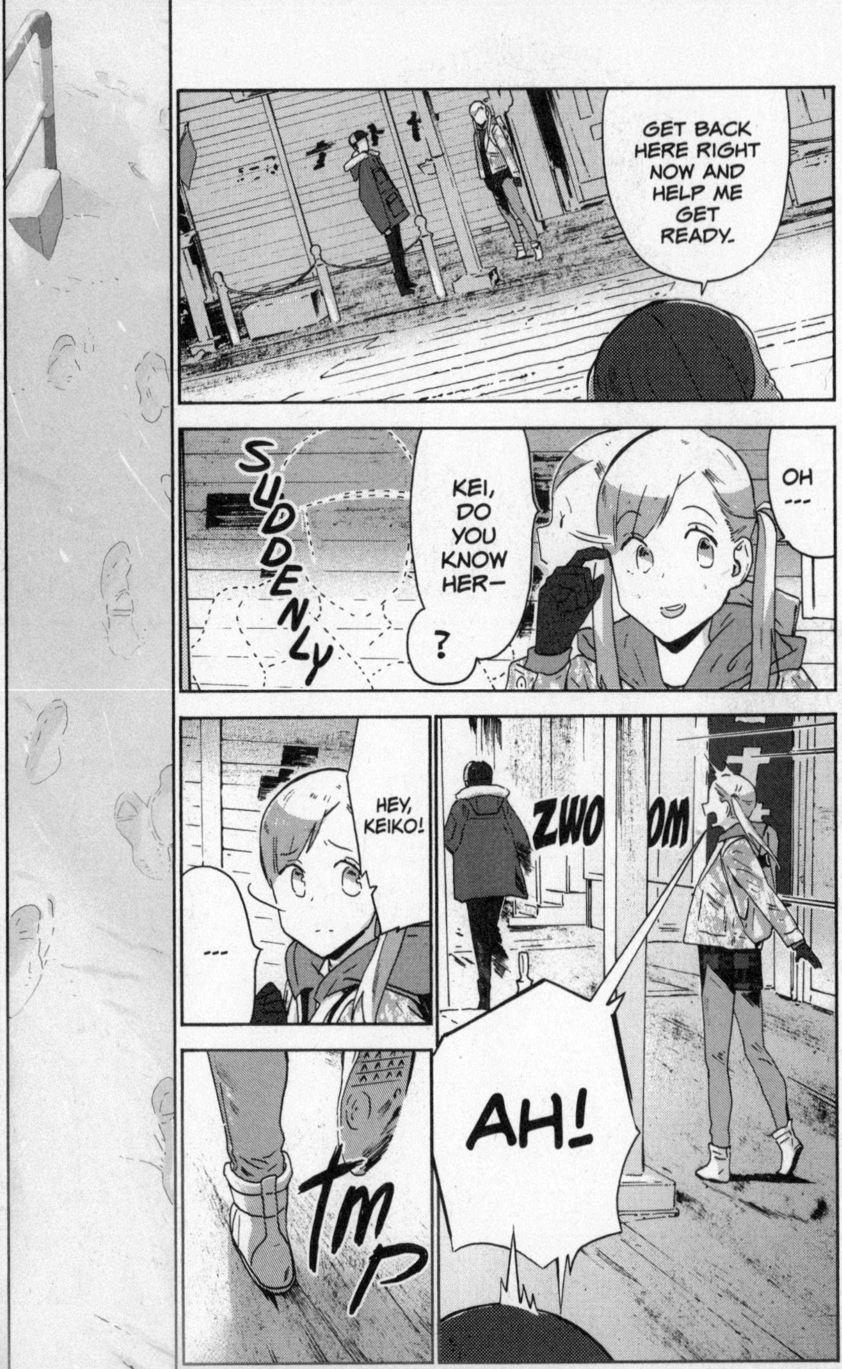
GET BACK HERE RIGHT NOW AND HELP ME GET READY.
OH ---
KEI, DO YOU KNOW HER— ?
SUDDENLY
ZWOOM
HEY, KEIKO!

AH!
tmp

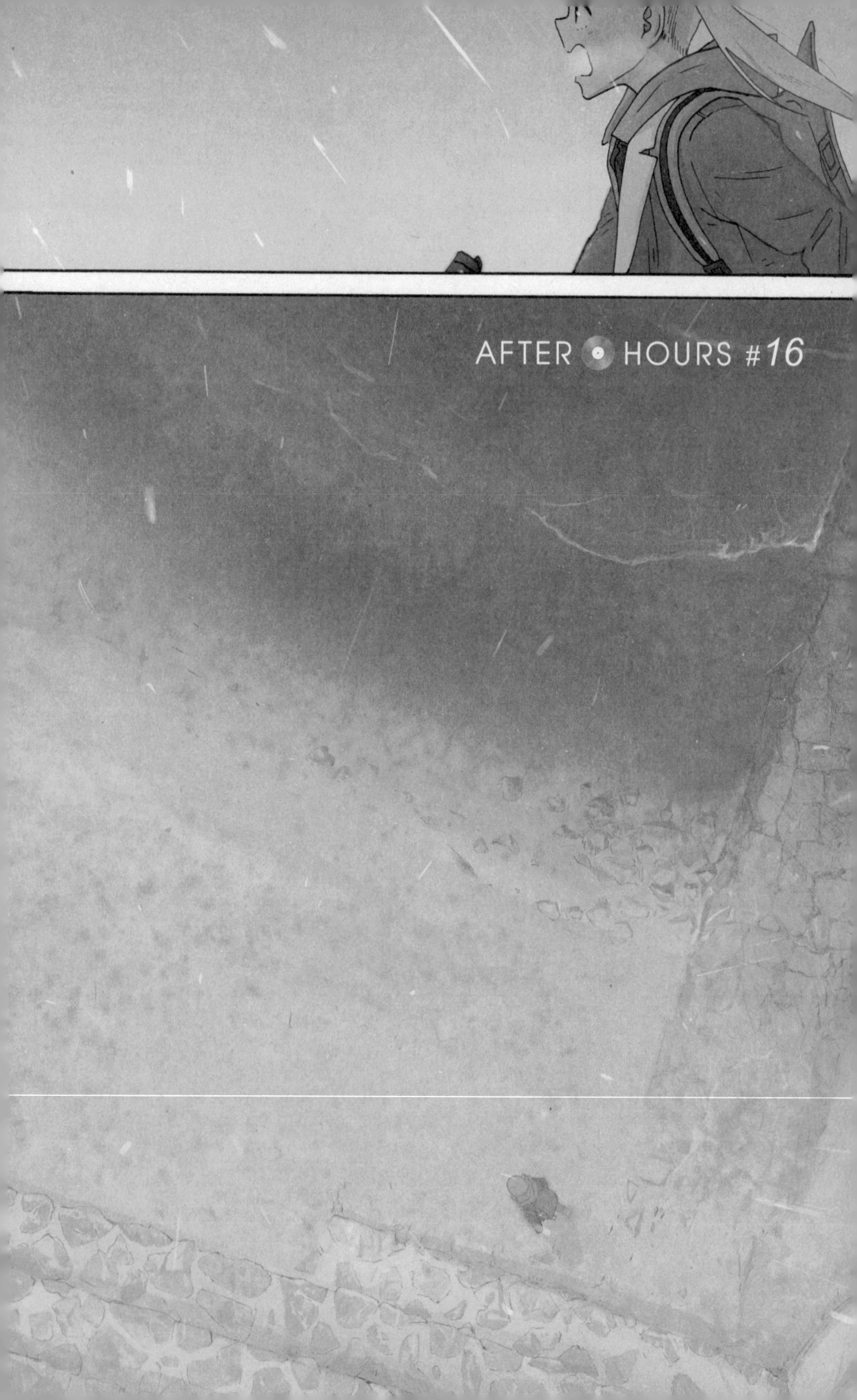
AFTER HOURS #16

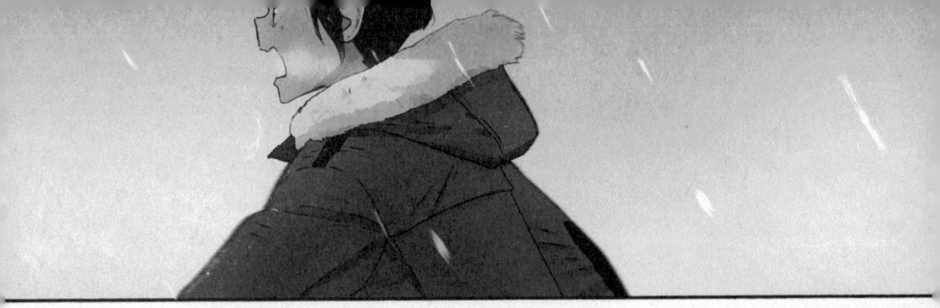
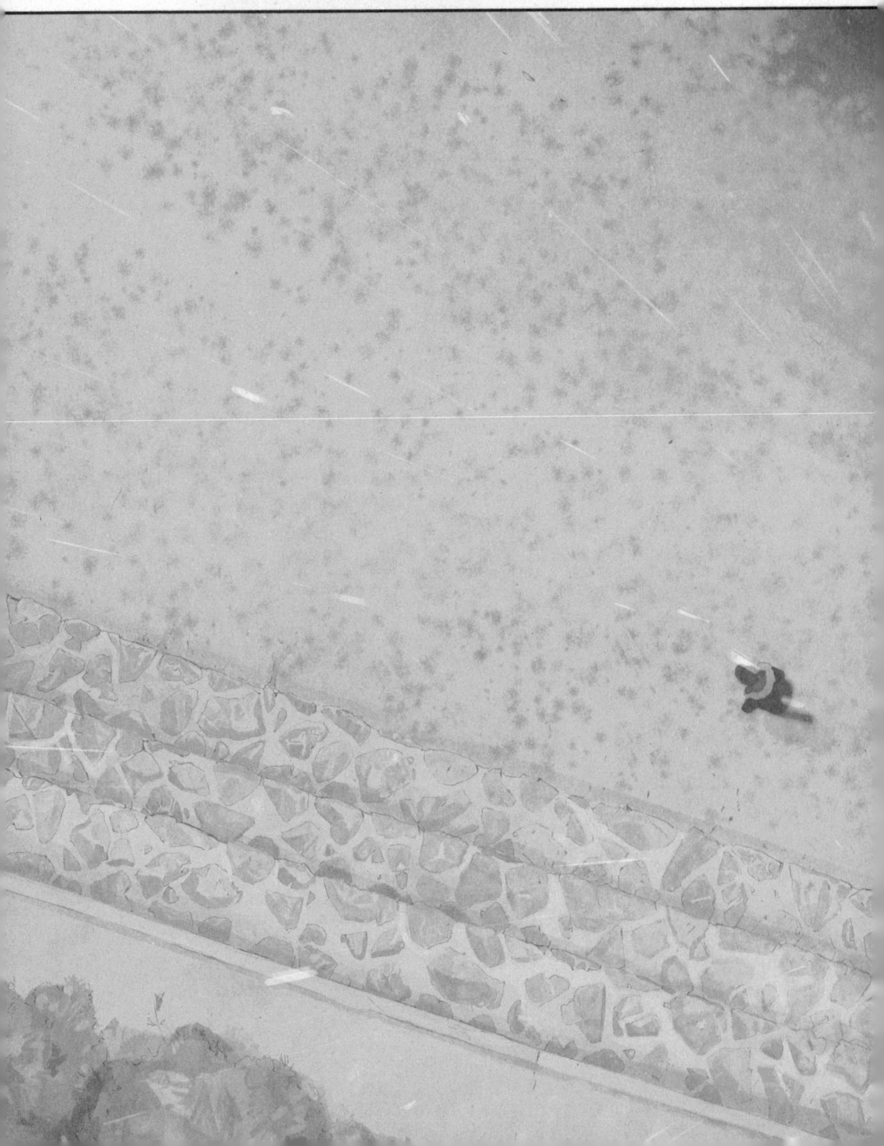

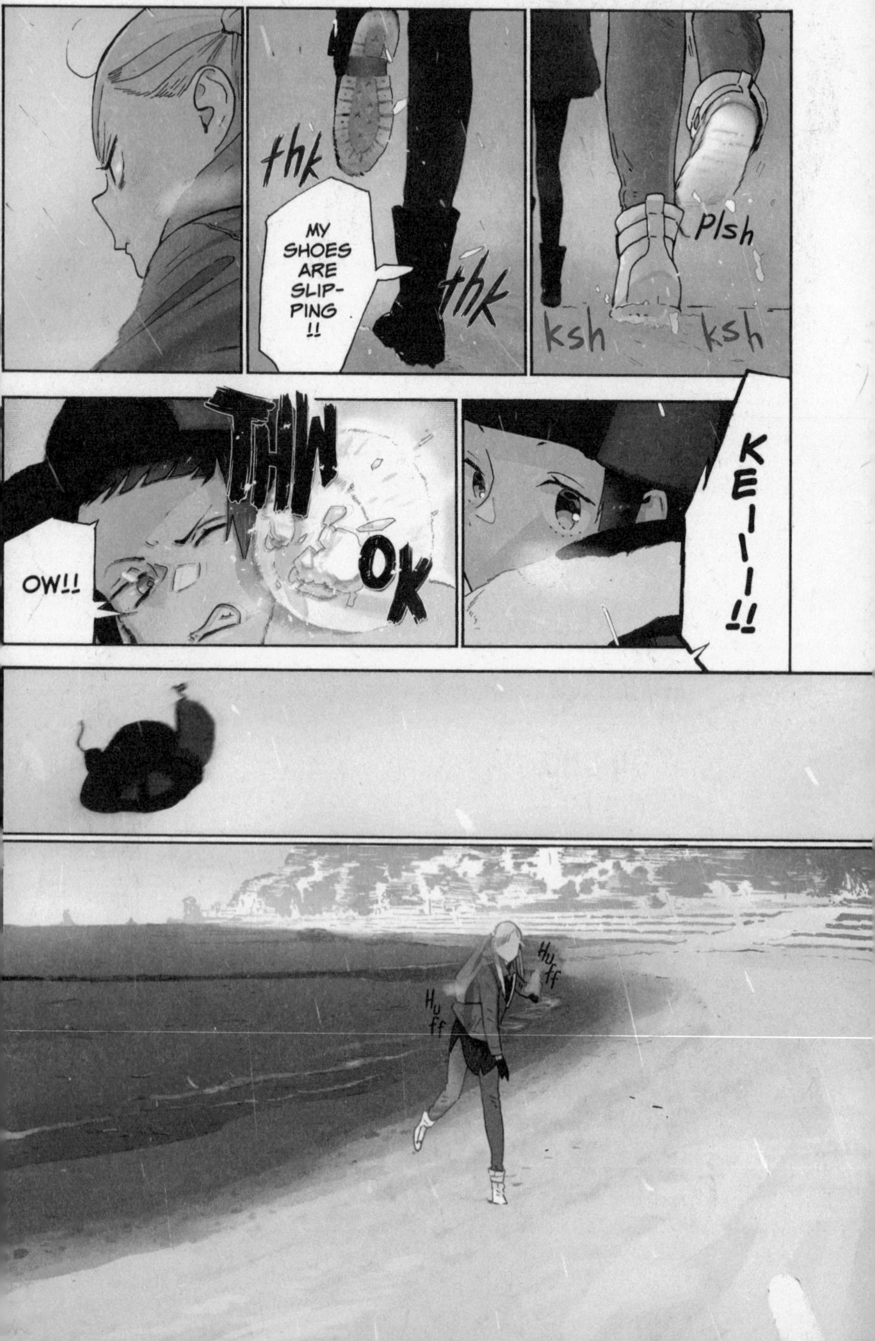
Plsh
ksh ksh
thk
MY SHOES ARE SLIP-PING!!
thk
KEIII!!
THWOK
OW!!
Huff
Huff

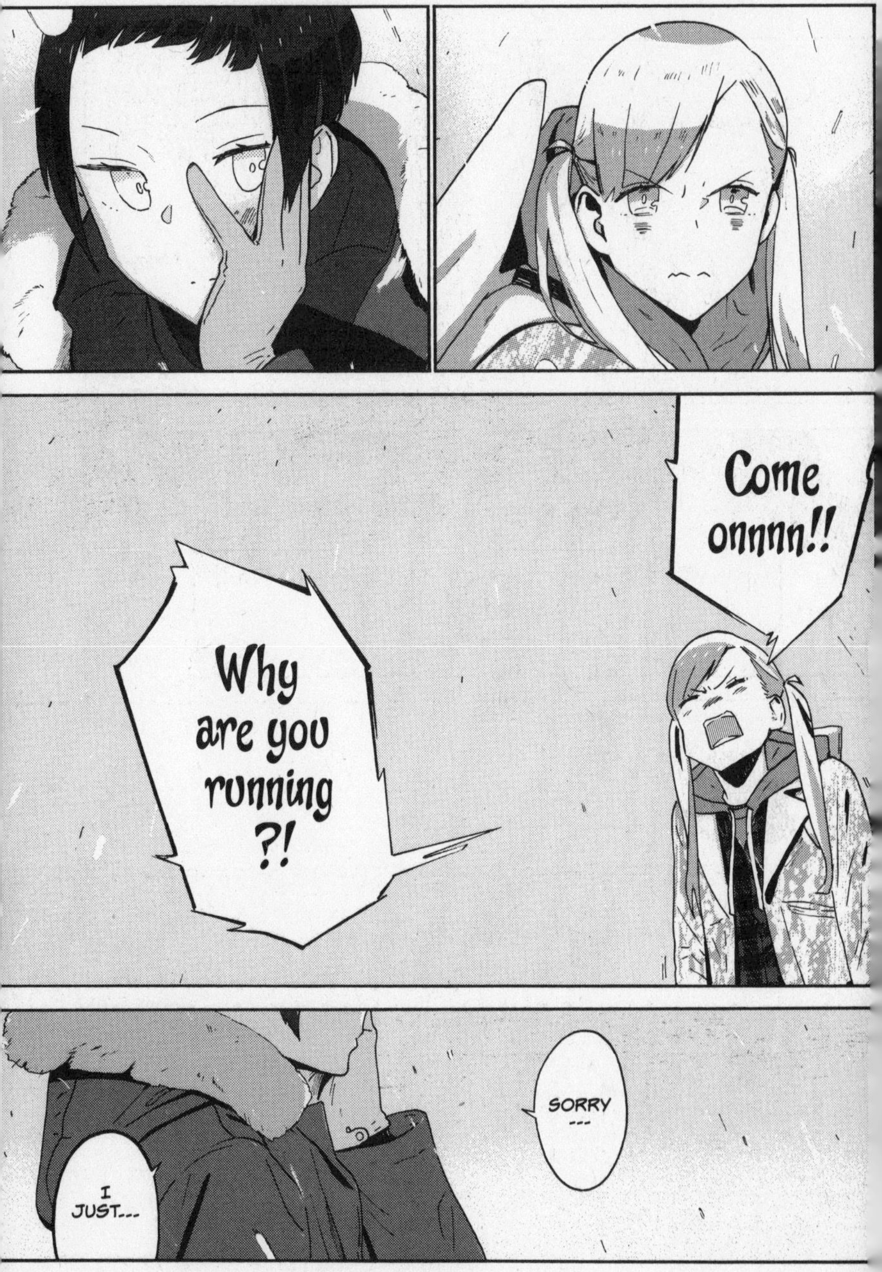
Come onnnn!!
Why are you running ?!
SORRY ...
I JUST...

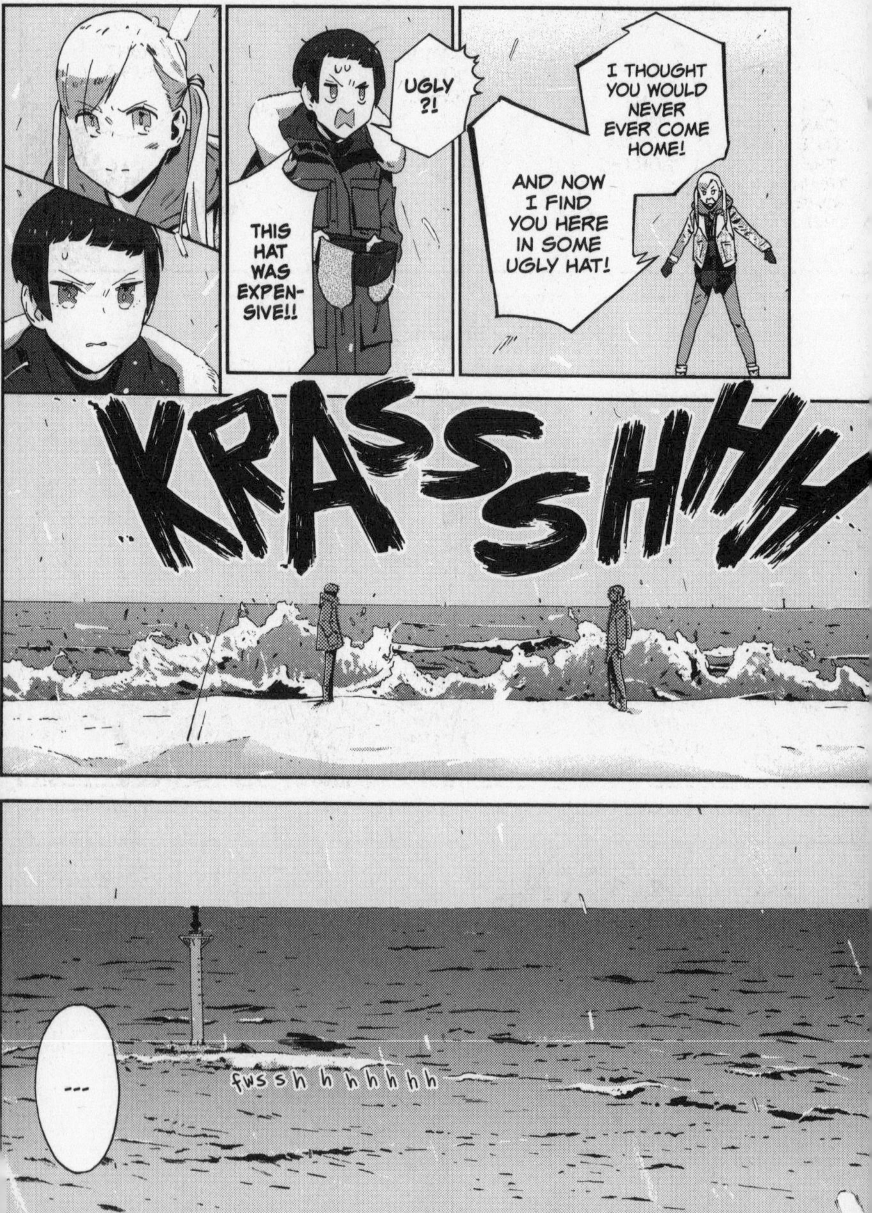
I THOUGHT YOU WOULD NEVER EVER COME HOME!
AND NOW I FIND YOU HERE IN SOME UGLY HAT!
UGLY ?!
THIS HAT WAS EXPEN-SIVE!!
KRASSHHH
fwsshhhhhhh

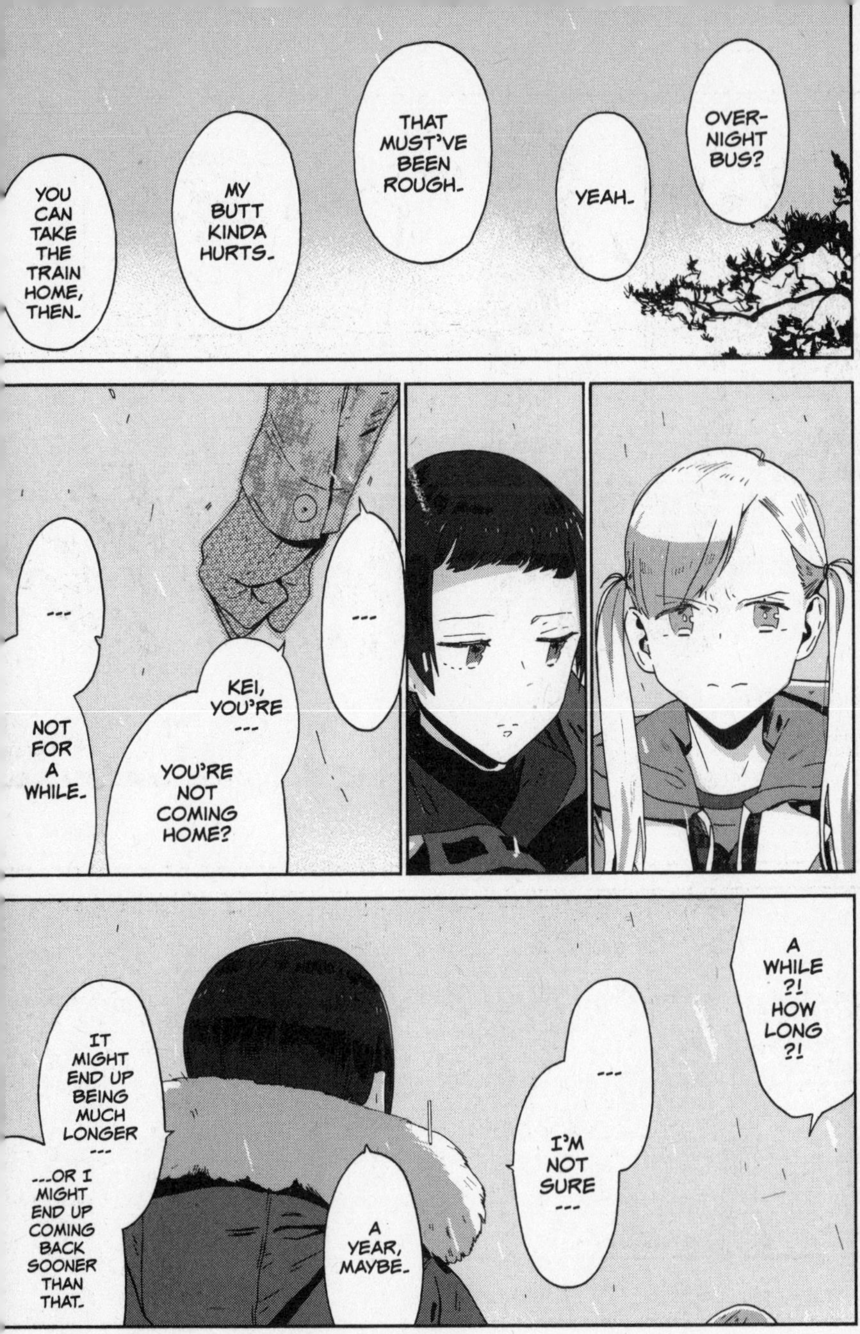
OVER-NIGHT BUS?
YEAH.
THAT MUST'VE BEEN ROUGH.
MY BUTT KINDA HURTS.
YOU CAN TAKE THE TRAIN HOME, THEN.
...
KEI, YOU'RE...
YOU'RE NOT COMING HOME?
...
NOT FOR A WHILE.
A WHILE?! HOW LONG?!
...
I'M NOT SURE...
A YEAR, MAYBE.
IT MIGHT END UP BEING MUCH LONGER...
...OR I MIGHT END UP COMING BACK SOONER THAN THAT.

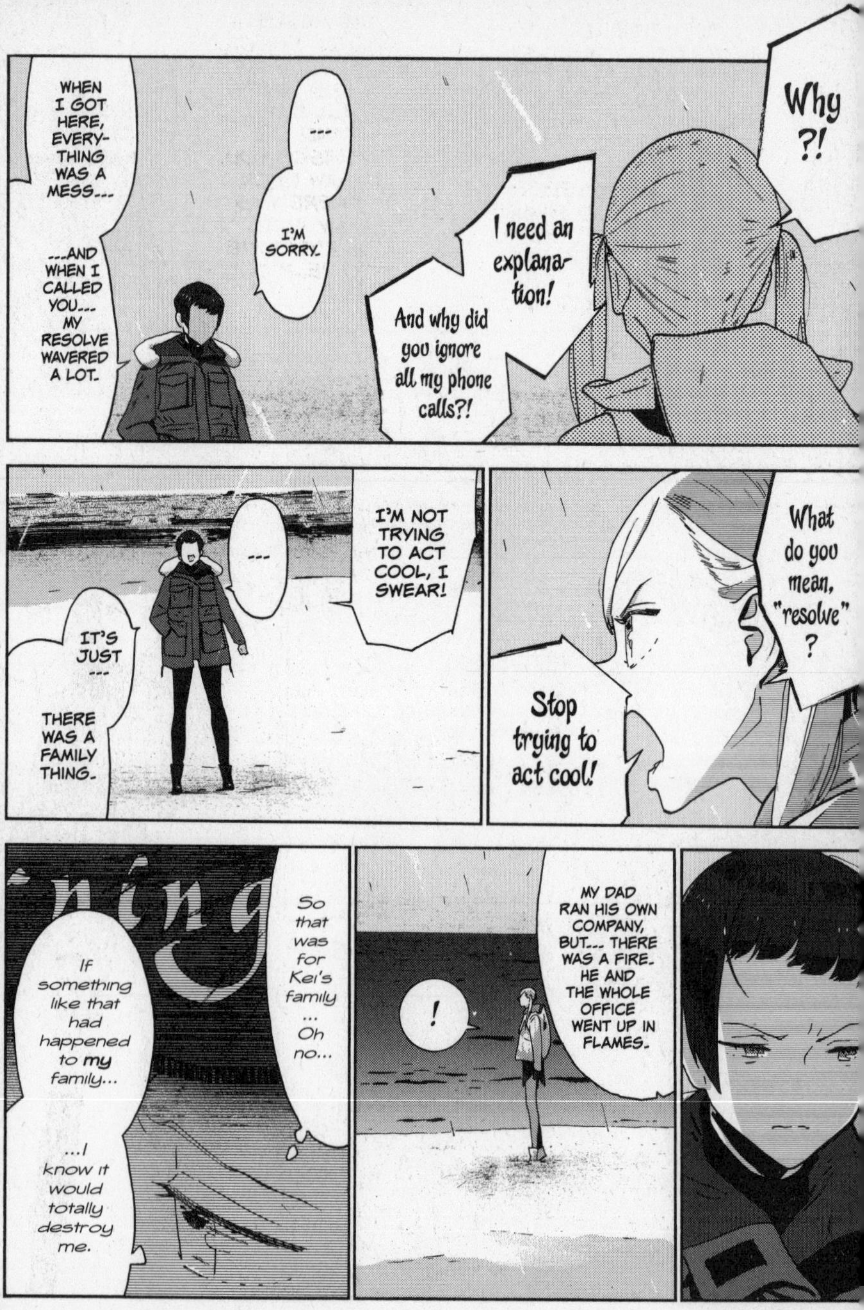
Why?!
I need an explanation!
And why did you ignore all my phone calls?!
...
I'M SORRY.
WHEN I GOT HERE, EVERYTHING WAS A MESS...
...AND WHEN I CALLED YOU... MY RESOLVE WAVERED A LOT.
What do you mean, "resolve"?
Stop trying to act cool!
I'M NOT TRYING TO ACT COOL, I SWEAR!
...
IT'S JUST...
THERE WAS A FAMILY THING.
MY DAD RAN HIS OWN COMPANY, BUT... THERE WAS A FIRE. HE AND THE WHOLE OFFICE WENT UP IN FLAMES.
!
So that was for Kei's family... Oh no...
If something like that had happened to my family...
...I know it would totally destroy me.

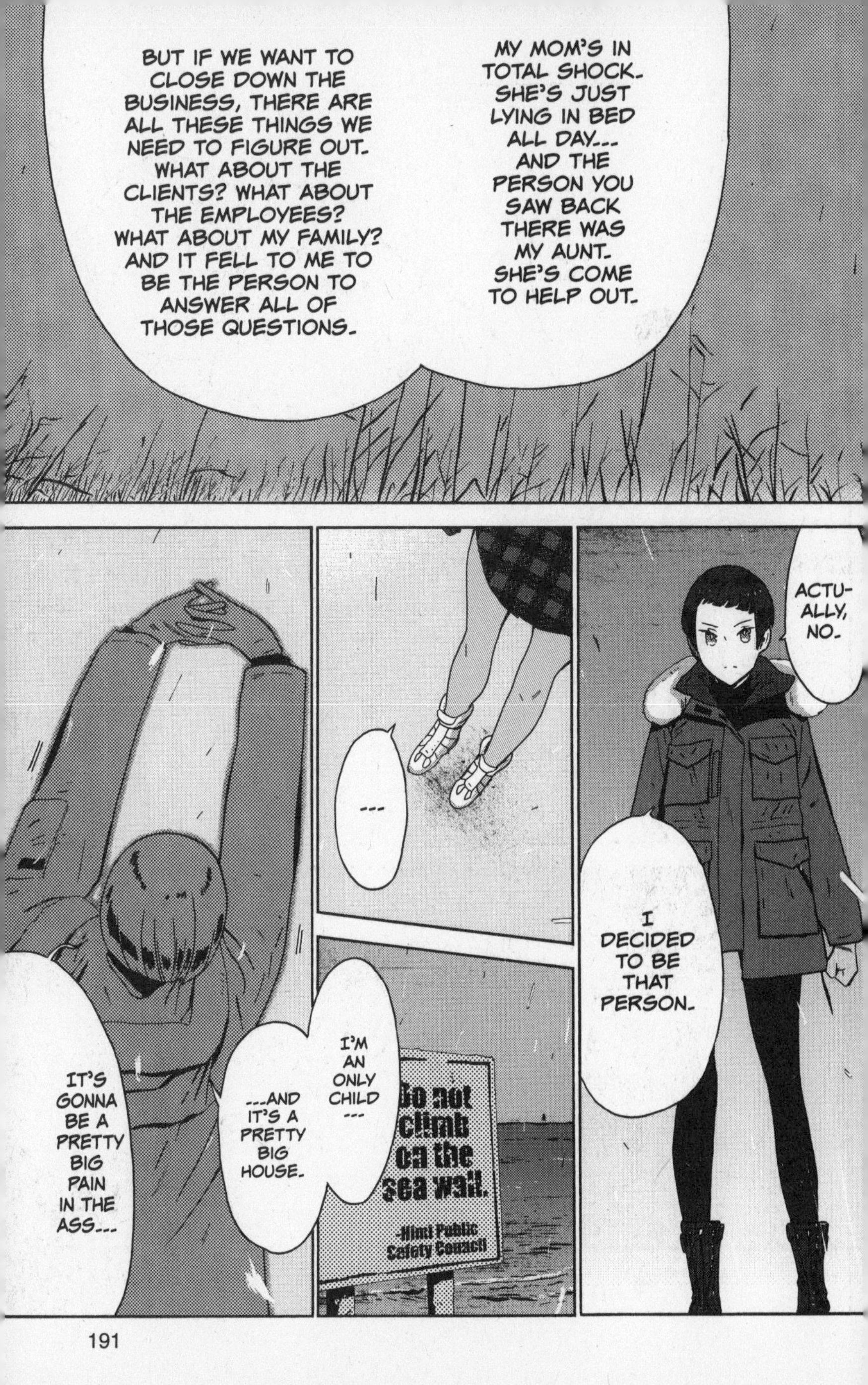
MY MOM'S IN TOTAL SHOCK. SHE'S JUST LYING IN BED ALL DAY... AND THE PERSON YOU SAW BACK THERE WAS MY AUNT. SHE'S COME TO HELP OUT.
BUT IF WE WANT TO CLOSE DOWN THE BUSINESS, THERE ARE ALL THESE THINGS WE NEED TO FIGURE OUT. WHAT ABOUT THE CLIENTS? WHAT ABOUT THE EMPLOYEES? WHAT ABOUT MY FAMILY? AND IT FELL TO ME TO BE THE PERSON TO ANSWER ALL OF THOSE QUESTIONS.
ACTUALLY, NO.
I DECIDED TO BE THAT PERSON.
...
I'M AN ONLY CHILD...
...AND IT'S A PRETTY BIG HOUSE.
Do not climb on the sea wall.
-Himi Public Safety Council
IT'S GONNA BE A PRETTY BIG PAIN IN THE ASS...

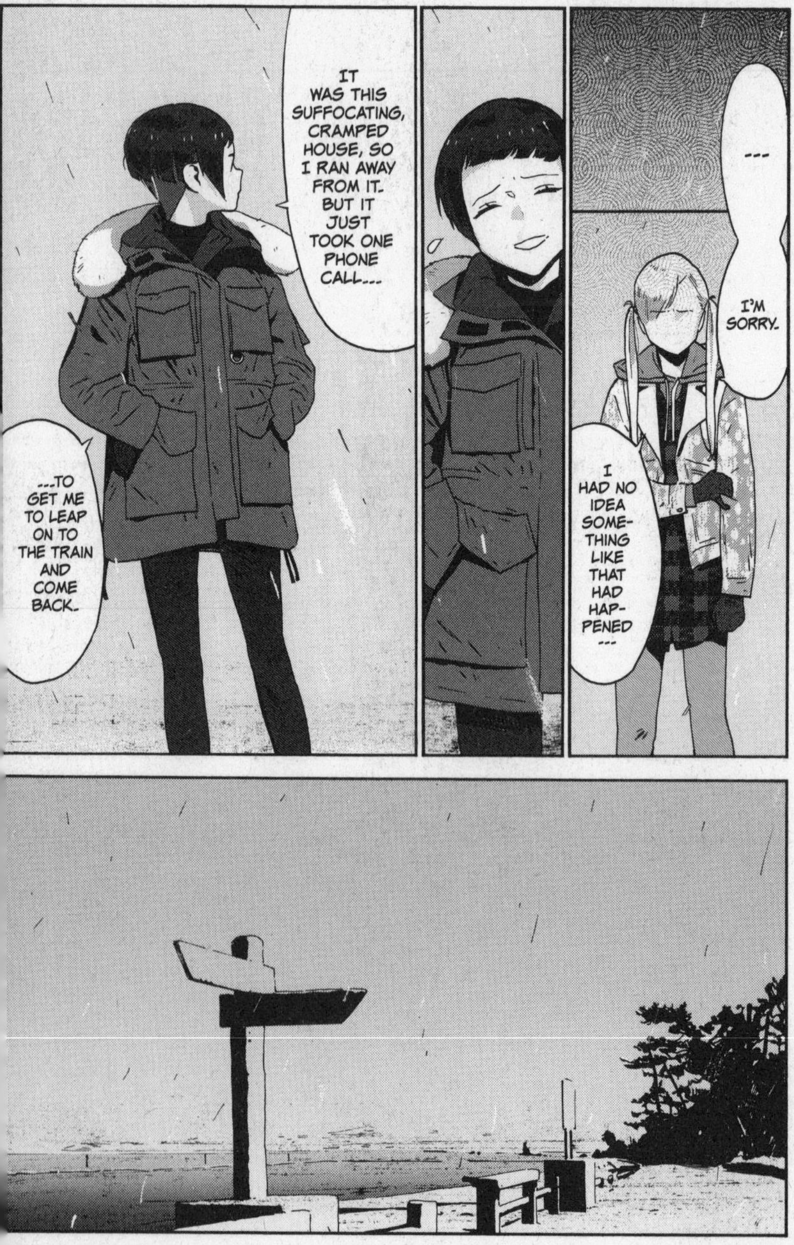
...
I'M SORRY.
I HAD NO IDEA SOMETHING LIKE THAT HAD HAPPENED...
IT WAS THIS SUFFOCATING, CRAMPED HOUSE, SO I RAN AWAY FROM IT. BUT IT JUST TOOK ONE PHONE CALL...
...TO GET ME TO LEAP ON TO THE TRAIN AND COME BACK.

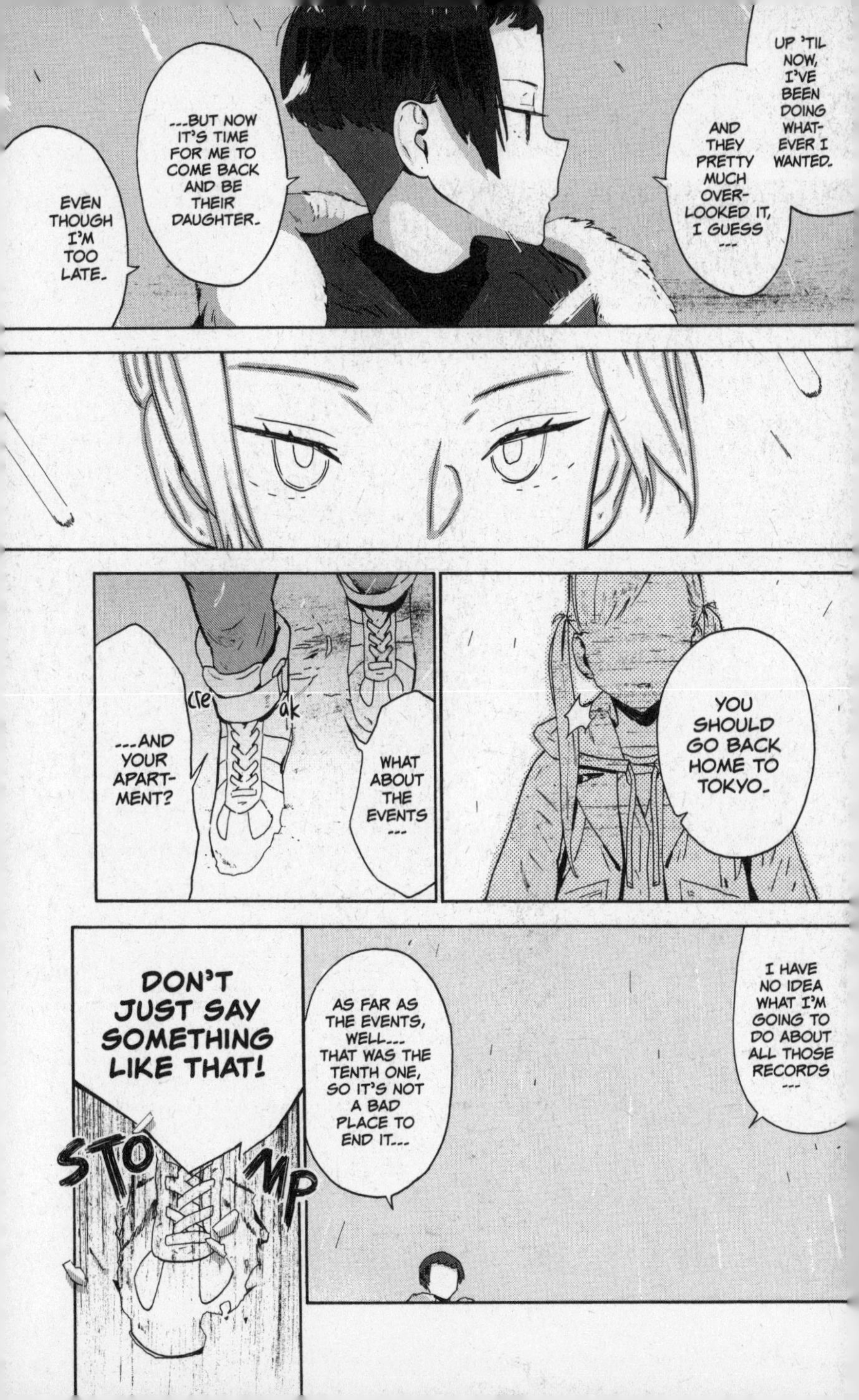
UP 'TIL NOW, I'VE BEEN DOING WHAT-EVER I WANTED.
AND THEY PRETTY MUCH OVER-LOOKED IT, I GUESS ...
...BUT NOW IT'S TIME FOR ME TO COME BACK AND BE THEIR DAUGHTER.
EVEN THOUGH I'M TOO LATE.
YOU SHOULD GO BACK HOME TO TOKYO.
WHAT ABOUT THE EVENTS ...
...AND YOUR APART-MENT?
creak
I HAVE NO IDEA WHAT I'M GOING TO DO ABOUT ALL THOSE RECORDS ...
AS FAR AS THE EVENTS, WELL... THAT WAS THE TENTH ONE, SO IT'S NOT A BAD PLACE TO END IT...
DON'T JUST SAY SOMETHING LIKE THAT!
STOMP

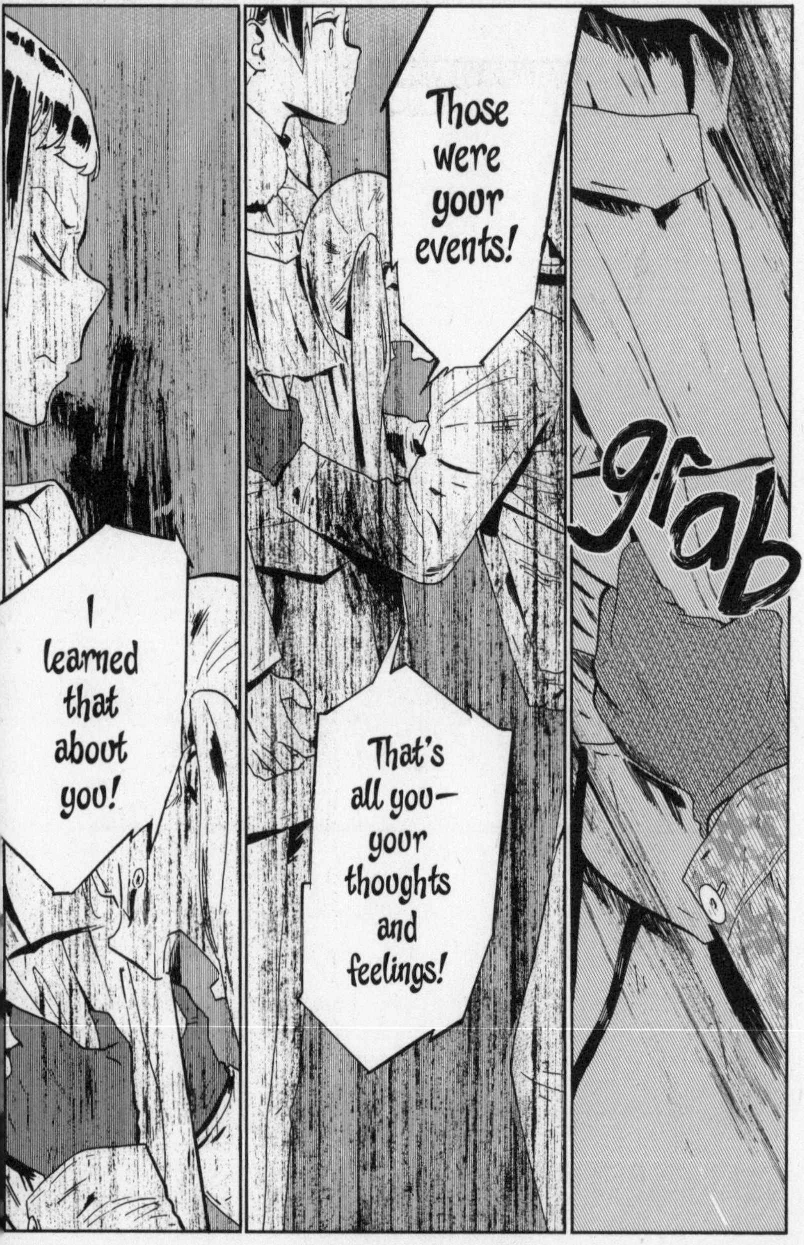
grab
Those were your events!
That's all you— your thoughts and feelings!
I learned that about you!

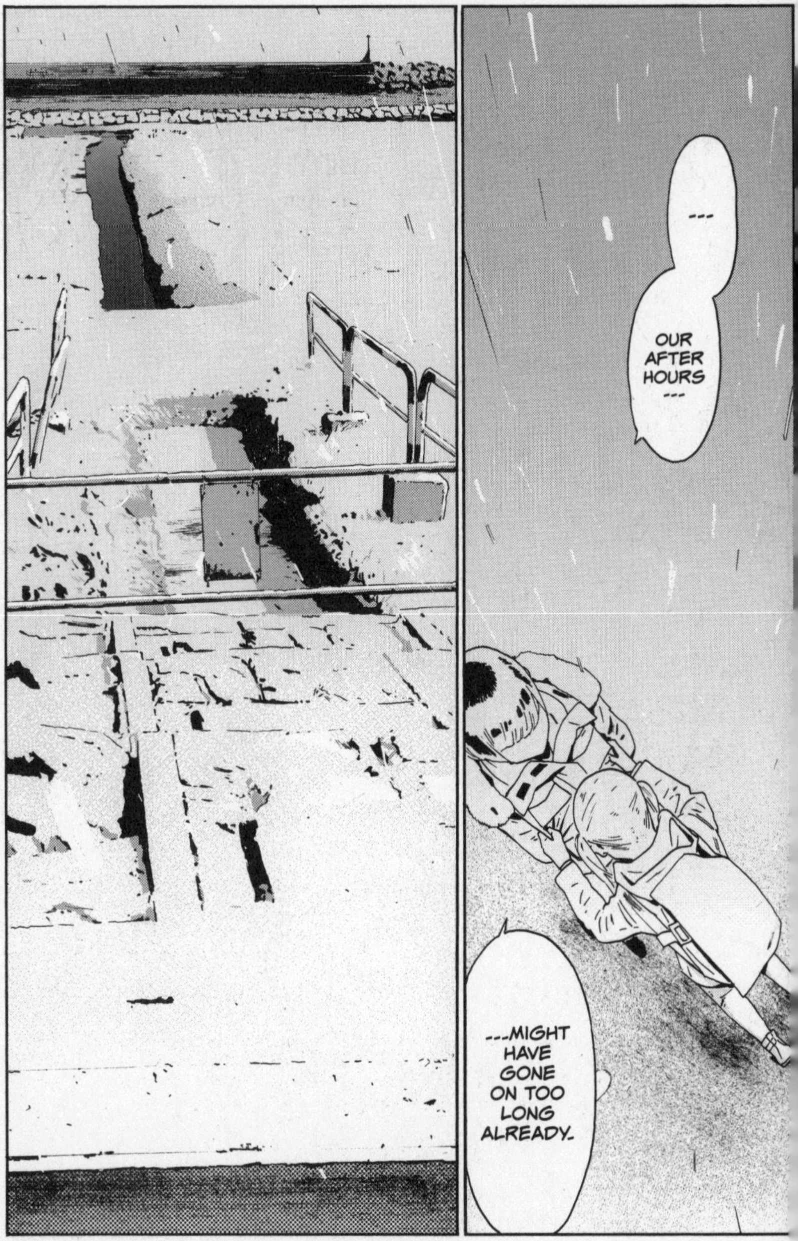

OUR AFTER HOURS ---
---MIGHT HAVE GONE ON TOO LONG ALREADY.

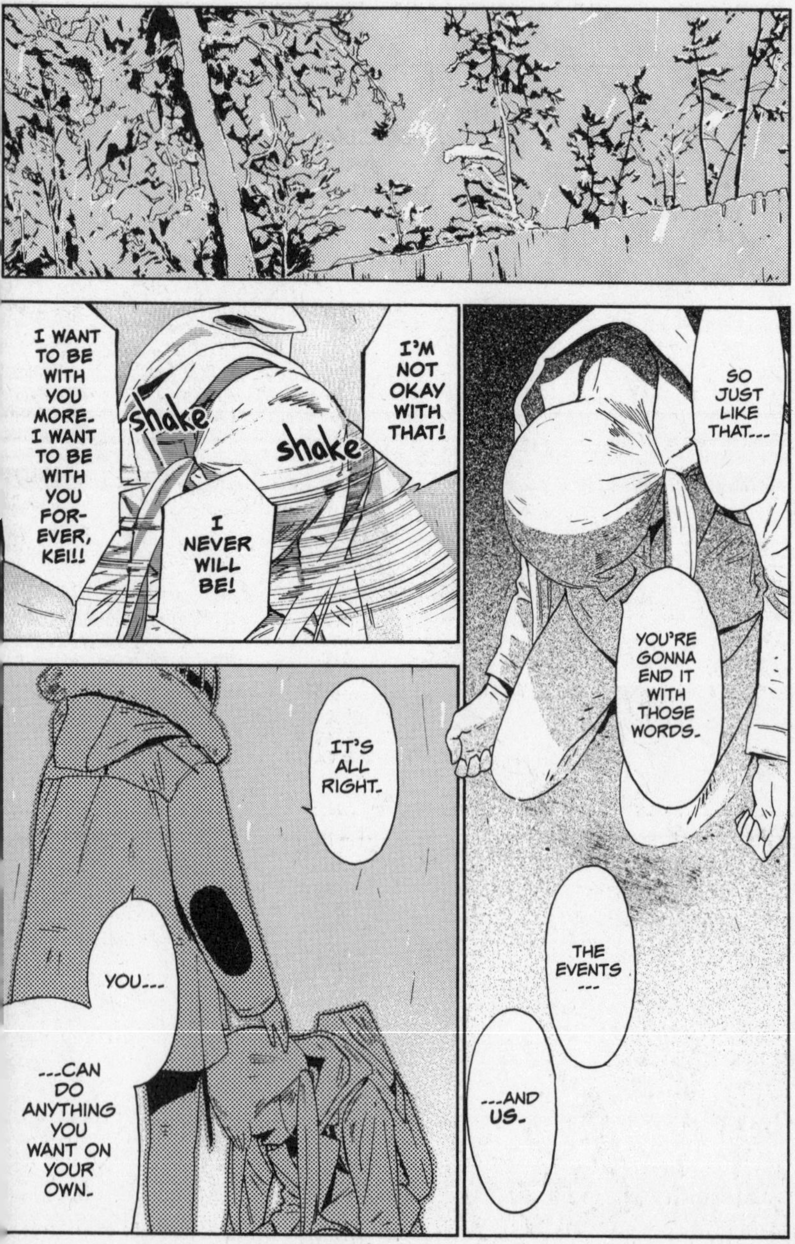
SO JUST LIKE THAT...
YOU'RE GONNA END IT WITH THOSE WORDS.
THE EVENTS ---
...AND US.
I'M NOT OKAY WITH THAT!
shake
shake
I NEVER WILL BE!
I WANT TO BE WITH YOU MORE. I WANT TO BE WITH YOU FOR-EVER, KEI!!
IT'S ALL RIGHT.
YOU...
...CAN DO ANYTHING YOU WANT ON YOUR OWN.

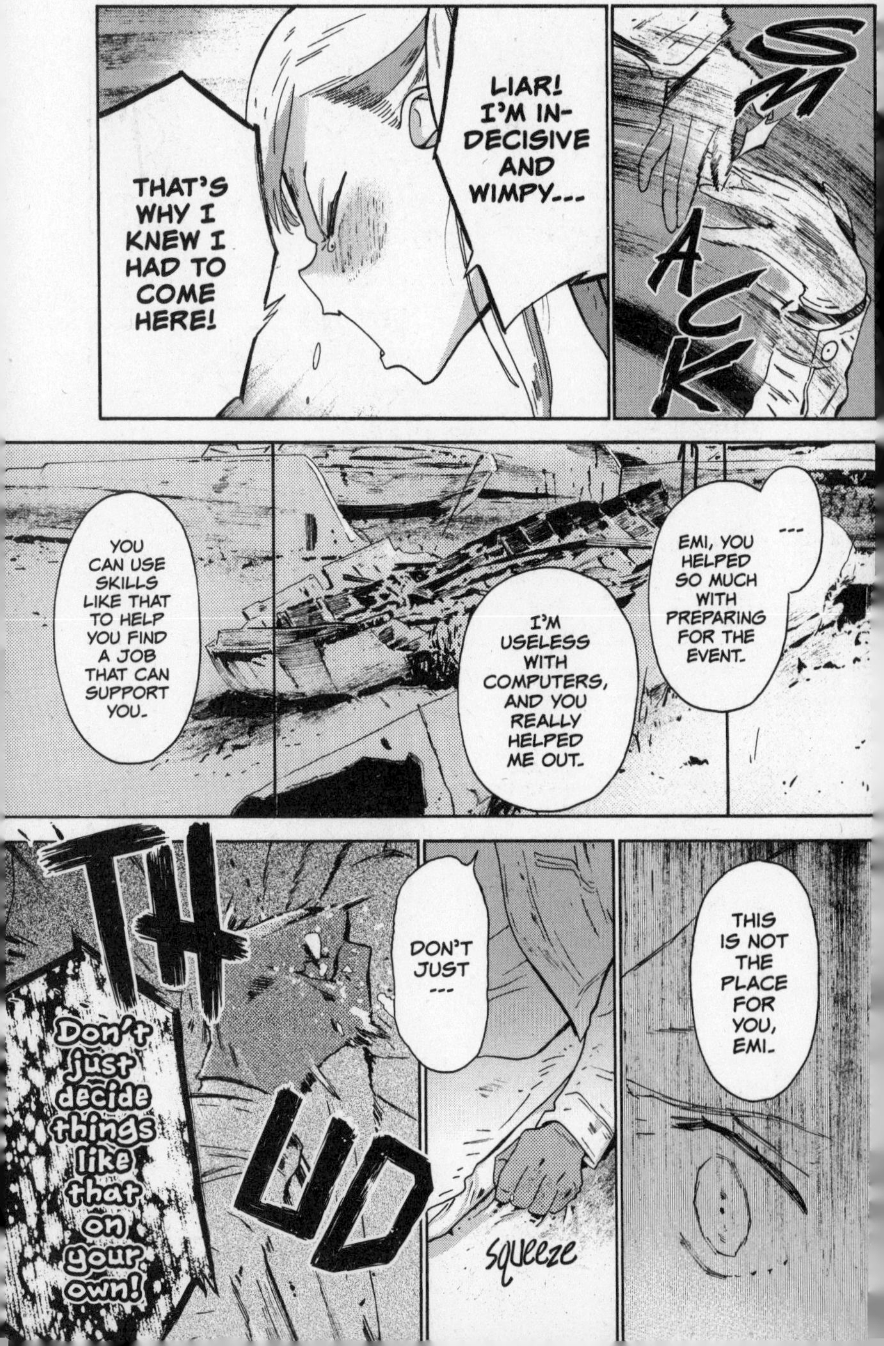
SMACK
LIAR! I'M INDECISIVE AND WIMPY...
THAT'S WHY I KNEW I HAD TO COME HERE!
...
EMI, YOU HELPED SO MUCH WITH PREPARING FOR THE EVENT.
I'M USELESS WITH COMPUTERS, AND YOU REALLY HELPED ME OUT.
YOU CAN USE SKILLS LIKE THAT TO HELP YOU FIND A JOB THAT CAN SUPPORT YOU.
THIS IS NOT THE PLACE FOR YOU, EMI.
DON'T JUST ...
squeeze
THUD
Don't just decide things like that on your own!

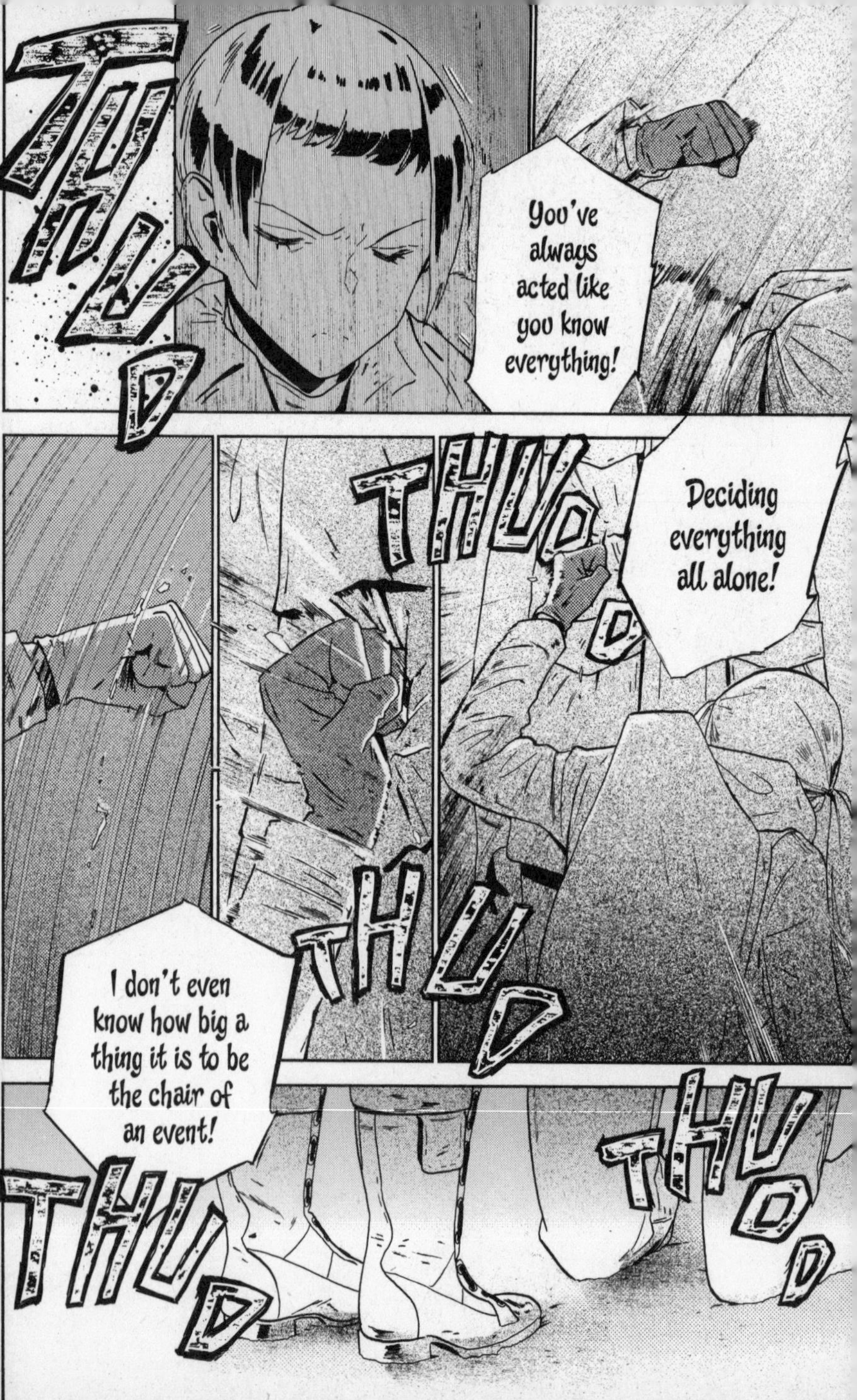
You've always acted like you know everything!
THUD
Deciding everything all alone!
THUD
THUD
I don't even know how big a thing it is to be the chair of an event!
THUD
THUD

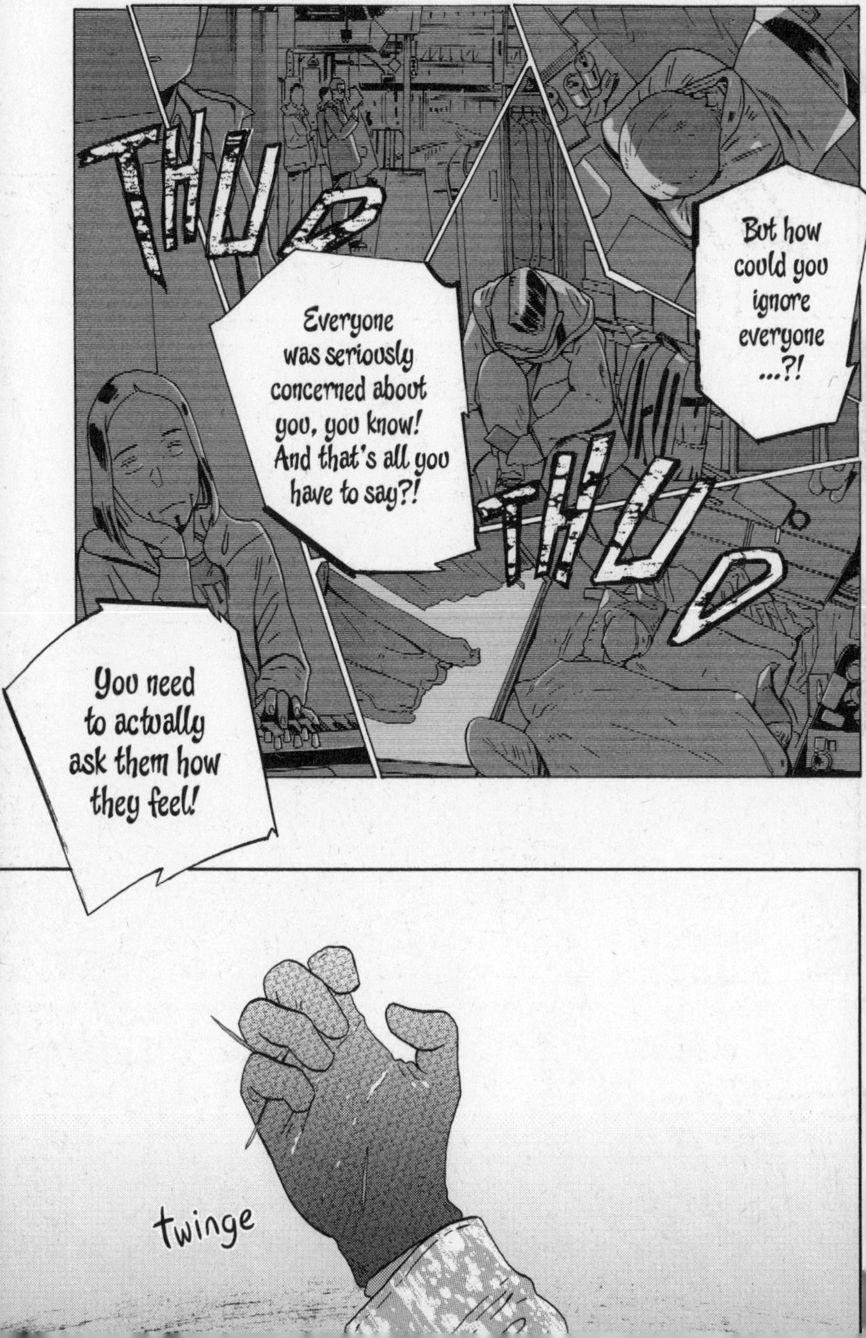
THUD
But how could you ignore everyone ...?!
Everyone was seriously concerned about you, you know! And that's all you have to say?!
THUD
You need to actually ask them how they feel!
twinge

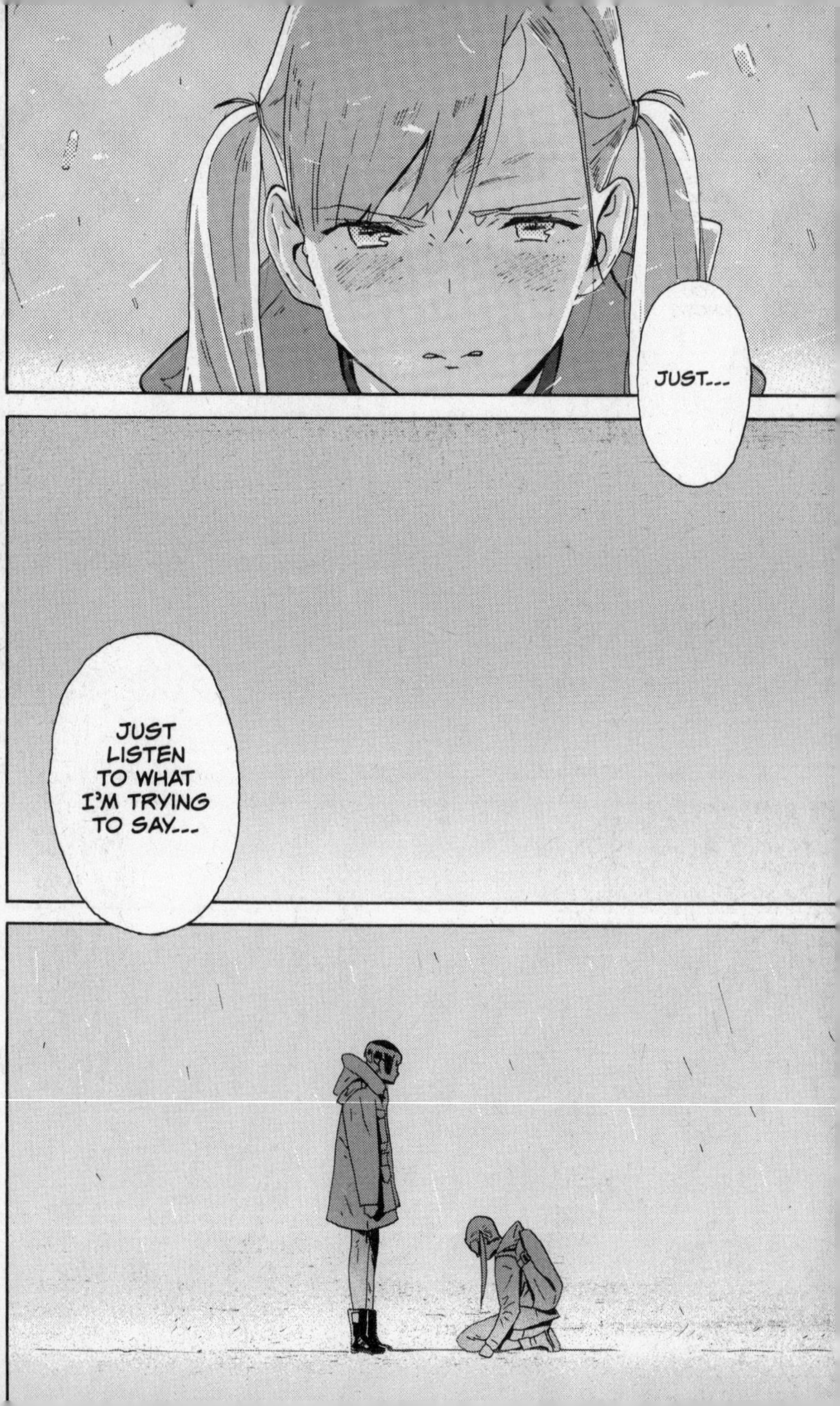
JUST...
JUST LISTEN TO WHAT I'M TRYING TO SAY...

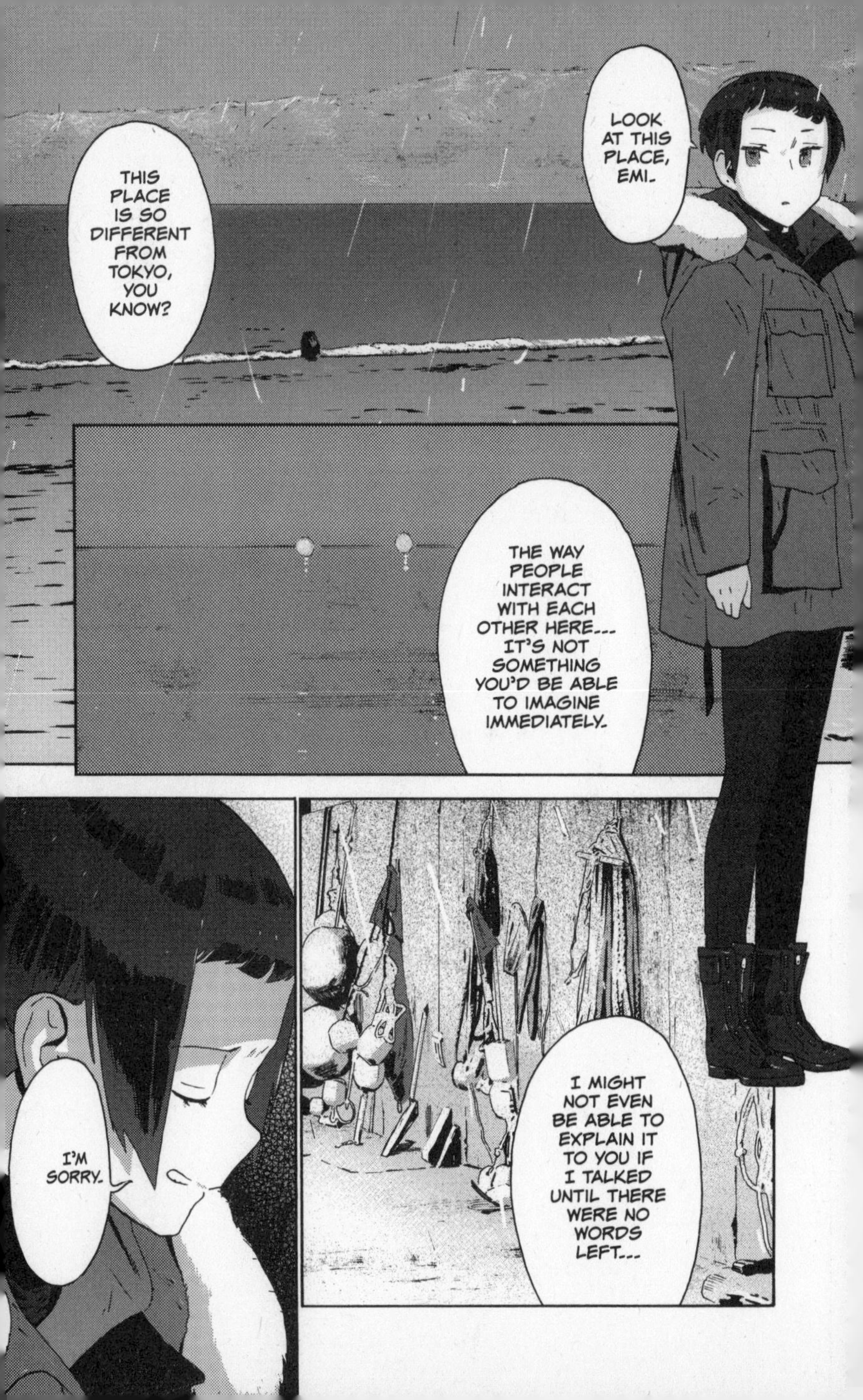
LOOK AT THIS PLACE, EMI.
THIS PLACE IS SO DIFFERENT FROM TOKYO, YOU KNOW?
THE WAY PEOPLE INTERACT WITH EACH OTHER HERE... IT'S NOT SOMETHING YOU'D BE ABLE TO IMAGINE IMMEDIATELY.
I MIGHT NOT EVEN BE ABLE TO EXPLAIN IT TO YOU IF I TALKED UNTIL THERE WERE NO WORDS LEFT...
I'M SORRY.

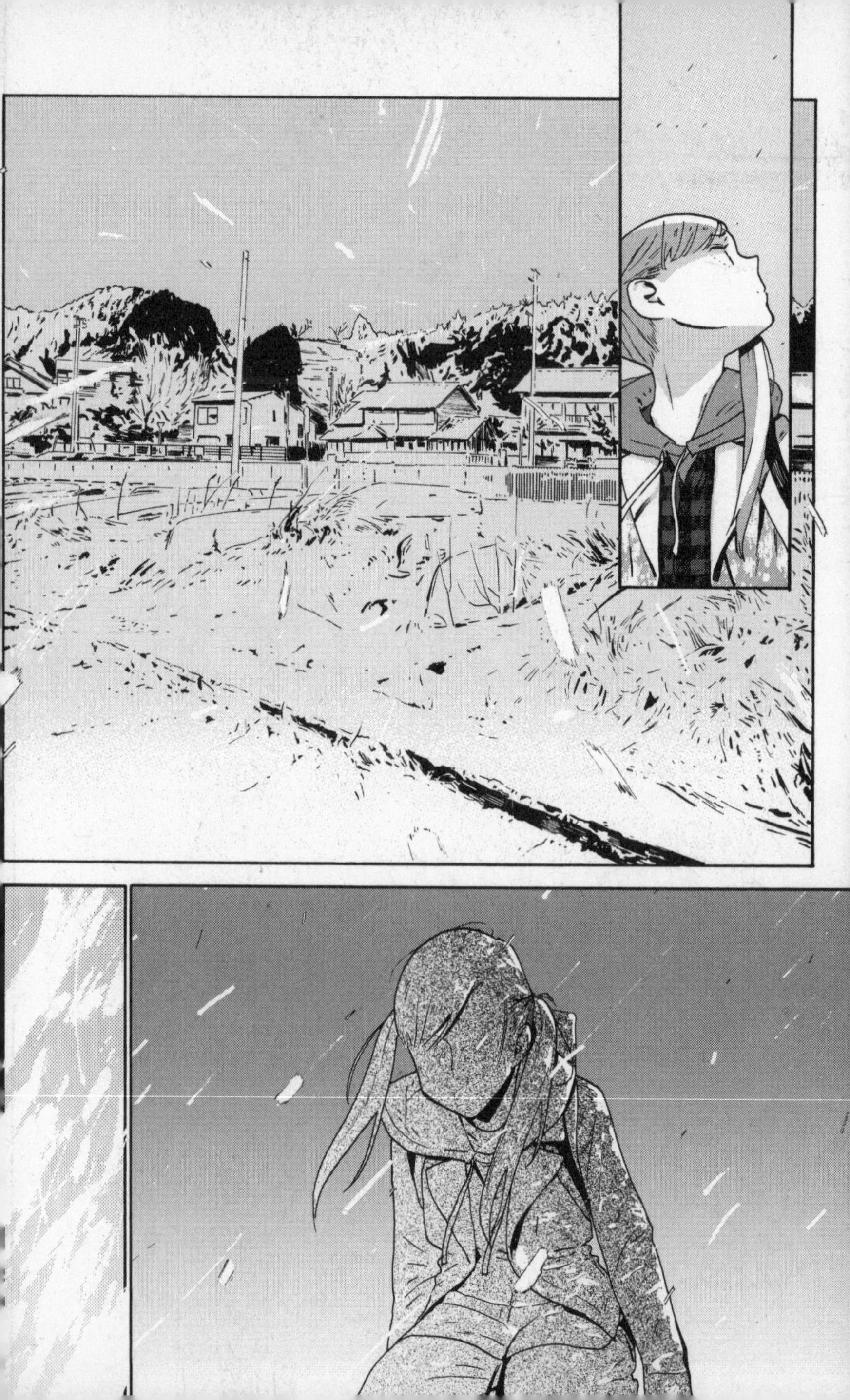

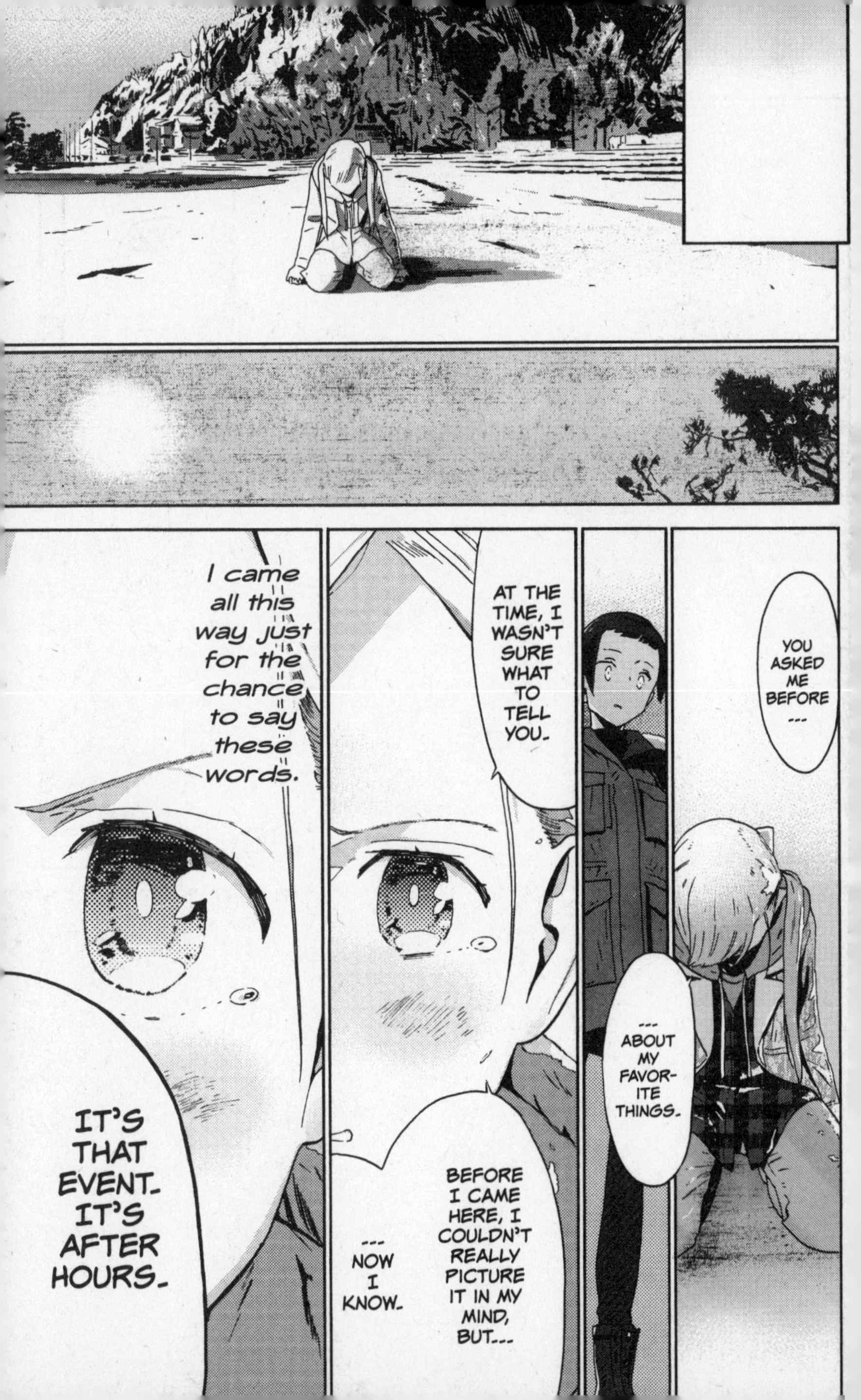
YOU ASKED ME BEFORE---
---ABOUT MY FAVOR-ITE THINGS.
AT THE TIME, I WASN'T SURE WHAT TO TELL YOU.
BEFORE I CAME HERE, I COULDN'T REALLY PICTURE IT IN MY MIND, BUT...
---NOW I KNOW.
I came all this way just for the chance to say these words.
IT'S THAT EVENT. IT'S AFTER HOURS.

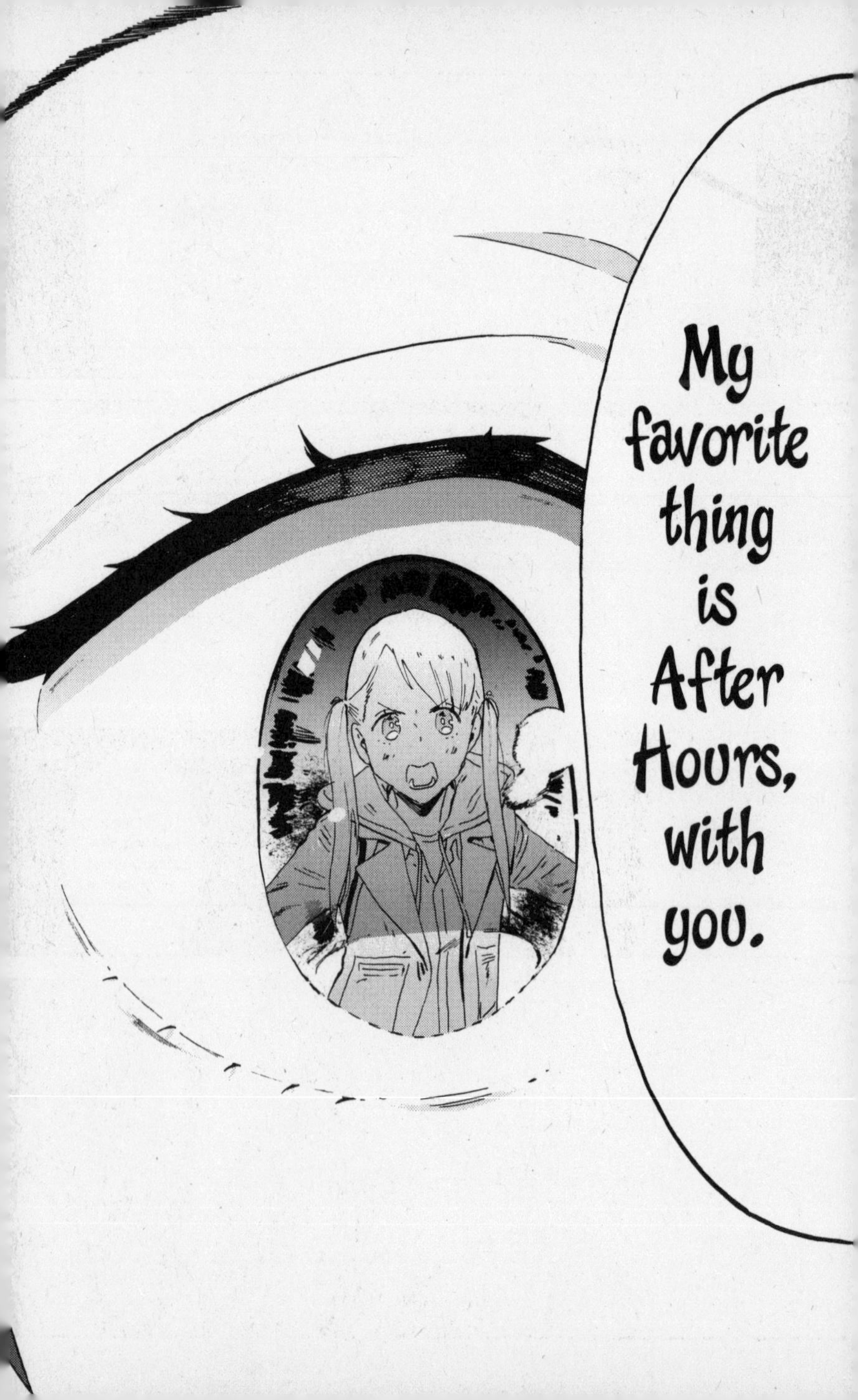
My favorite thing is After Hours, with you.

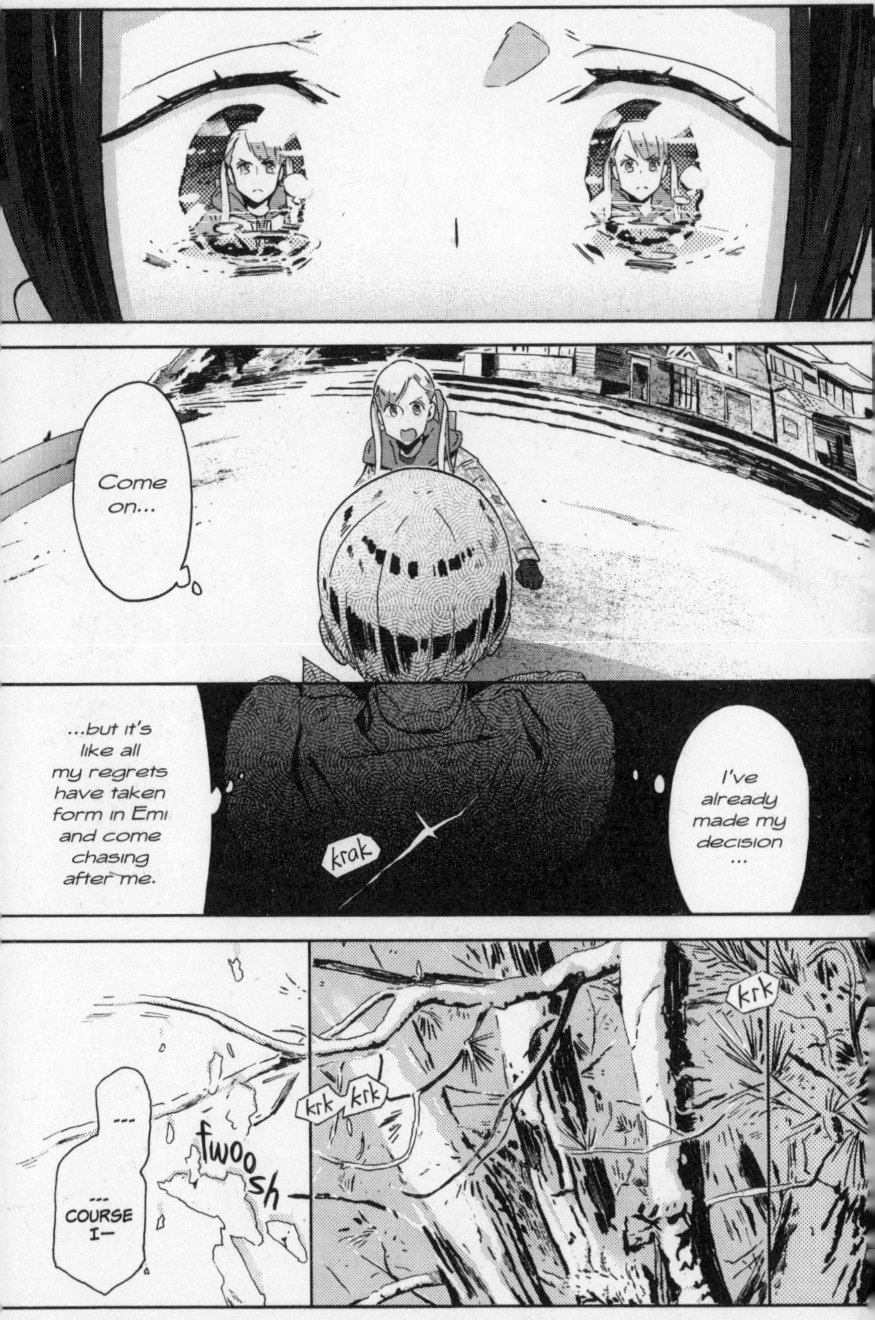
Come on...
I've already made my decision ...
krak
...but it's like all my regrets have taken form in Emi and come chasing after me.
krk
krk
krk
fwoosh
--- --- COURSE I—

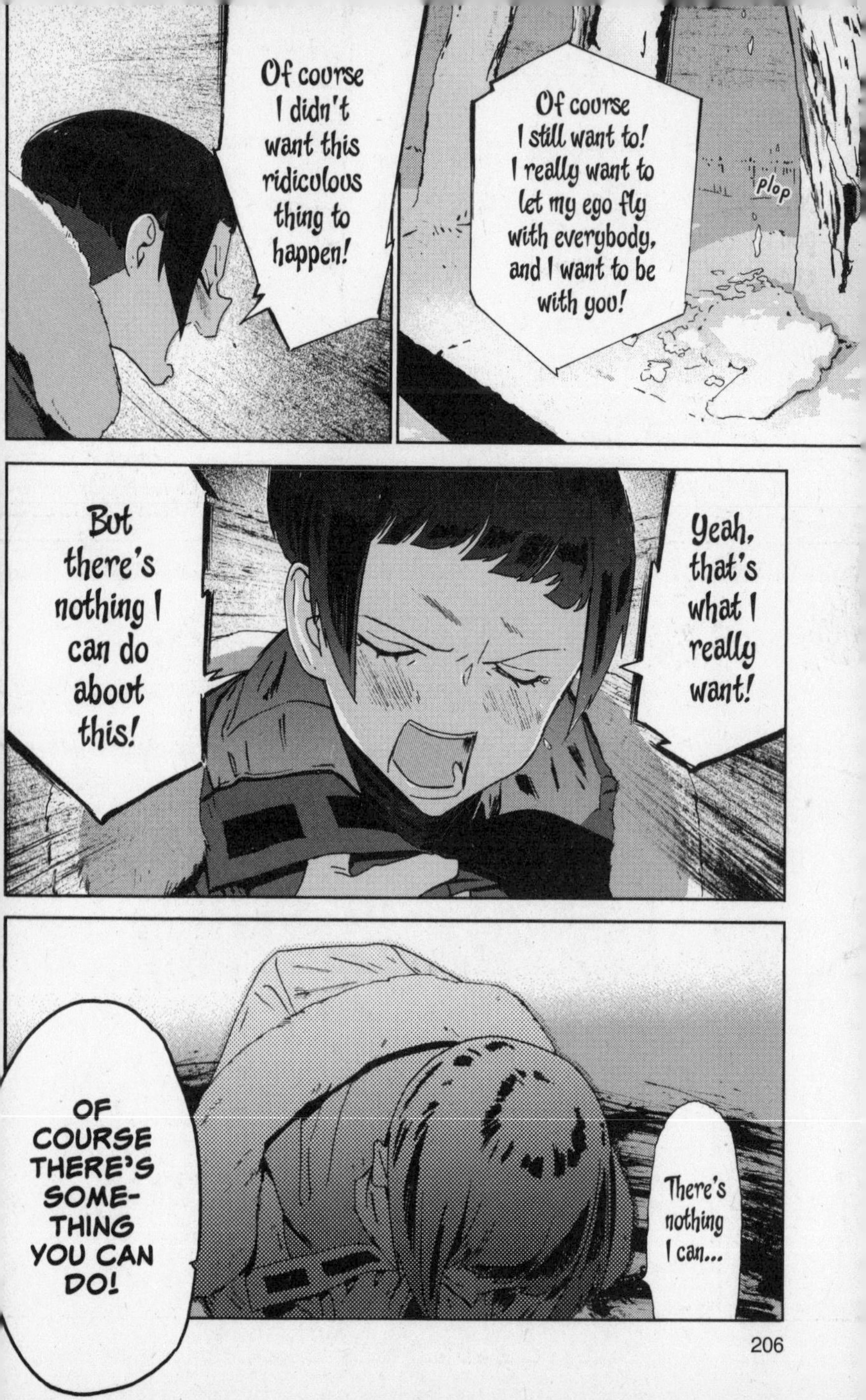
Of course I still want to! I really want to let my ego fly with everybody, and I want to be with you!
Plop
Of course I didn't want this ridiculous thing to happen!
Yeah, that's what I really want!
But there's nothing I can do about this!
There's nothing I can...
OF COURSE THERE'S SOME-THING YOU CAN DO!

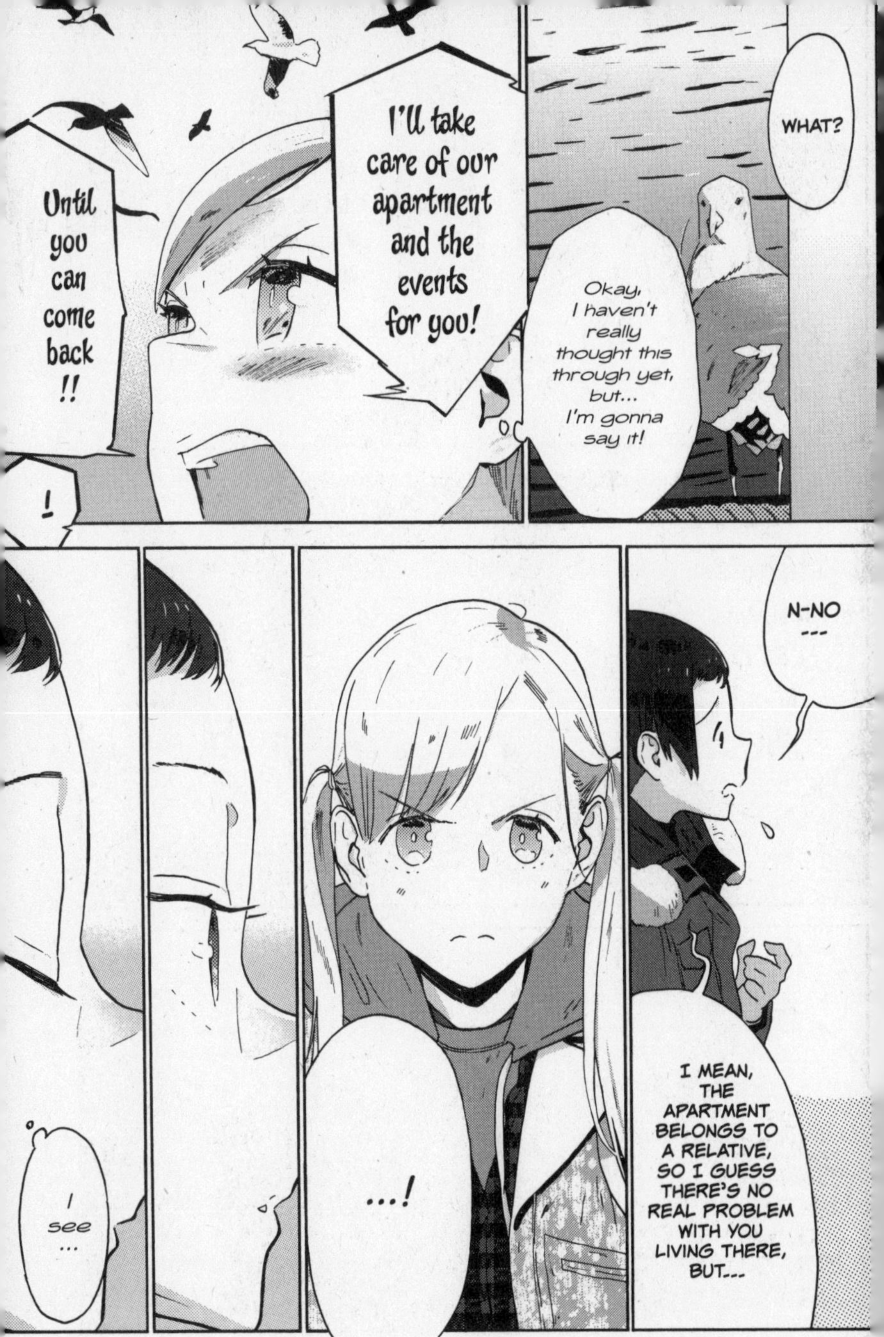
WHAT?
Okay, I haven't really thought this through yet, but... I'm gonna say it!
I'll take care of our apartment and the events for you!
Until you can come back !!
!
N-NO ---
I MEAN, THE APARTMENT BELONGS TO A RELATIVE, SO I GUESS THERE'S NO REAL PROBLEM WITH YOU LIVING THERE, BUT---
...!
I see ...

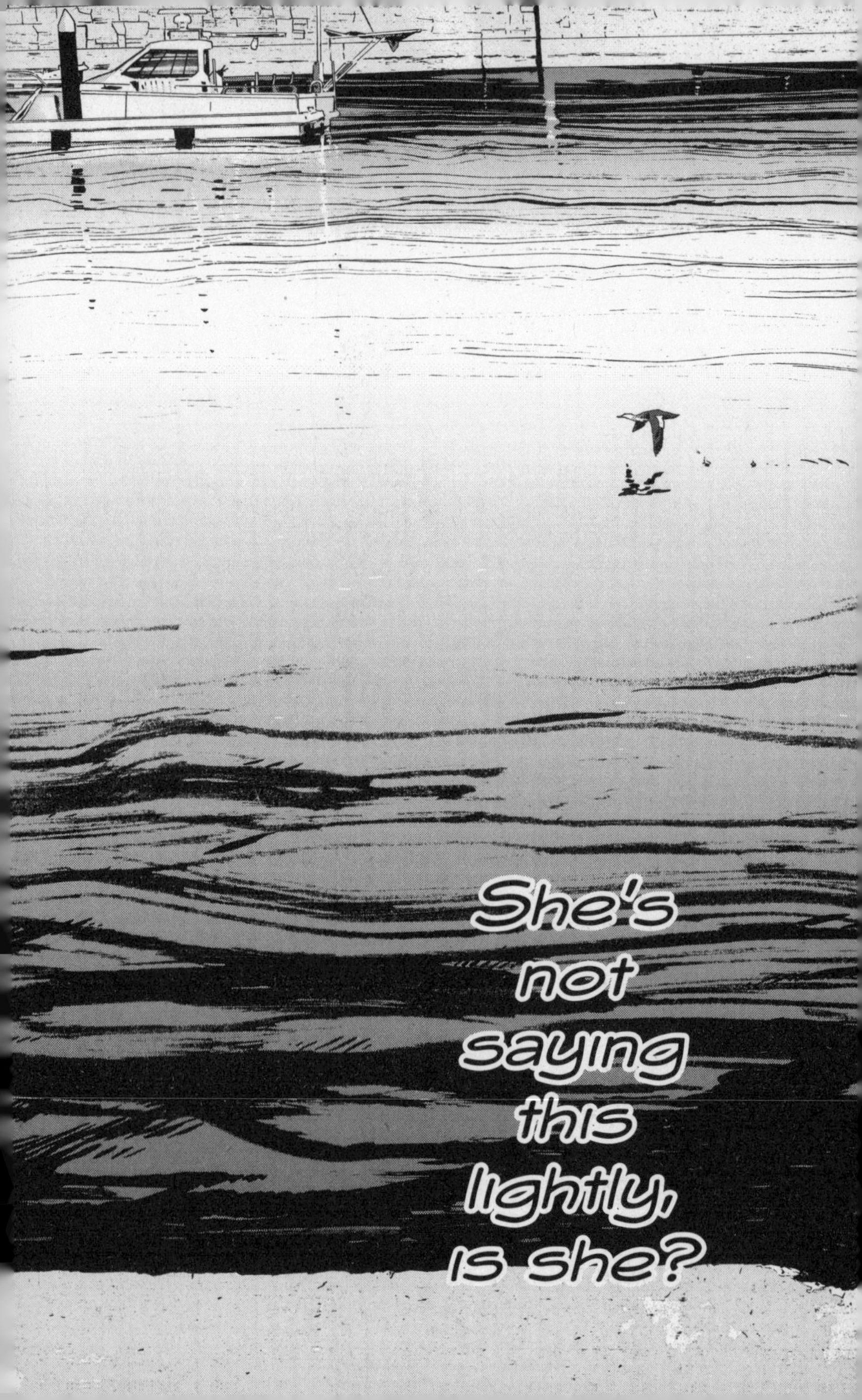
She's not saying this lightly, is she?

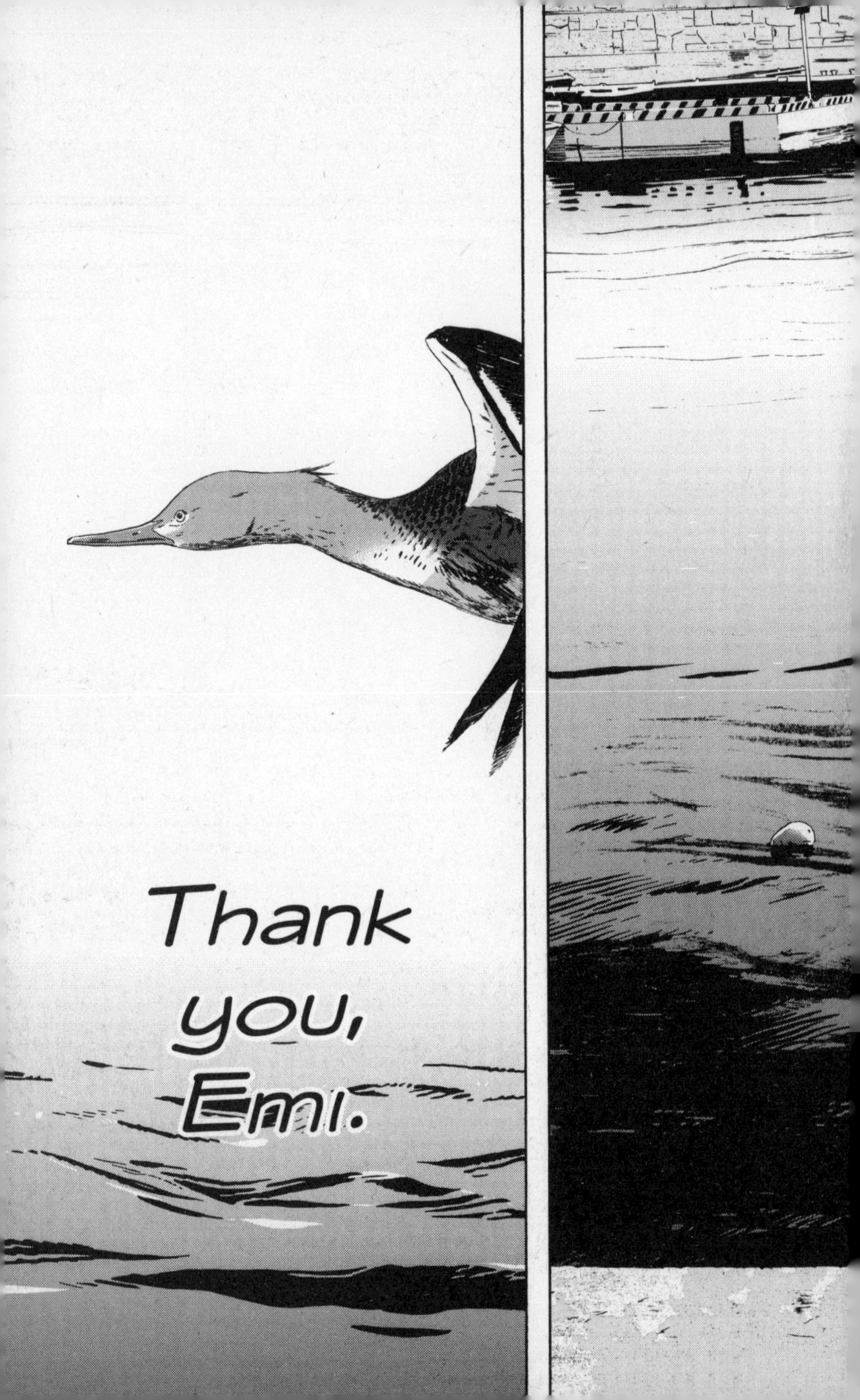
Thank you, Emi.

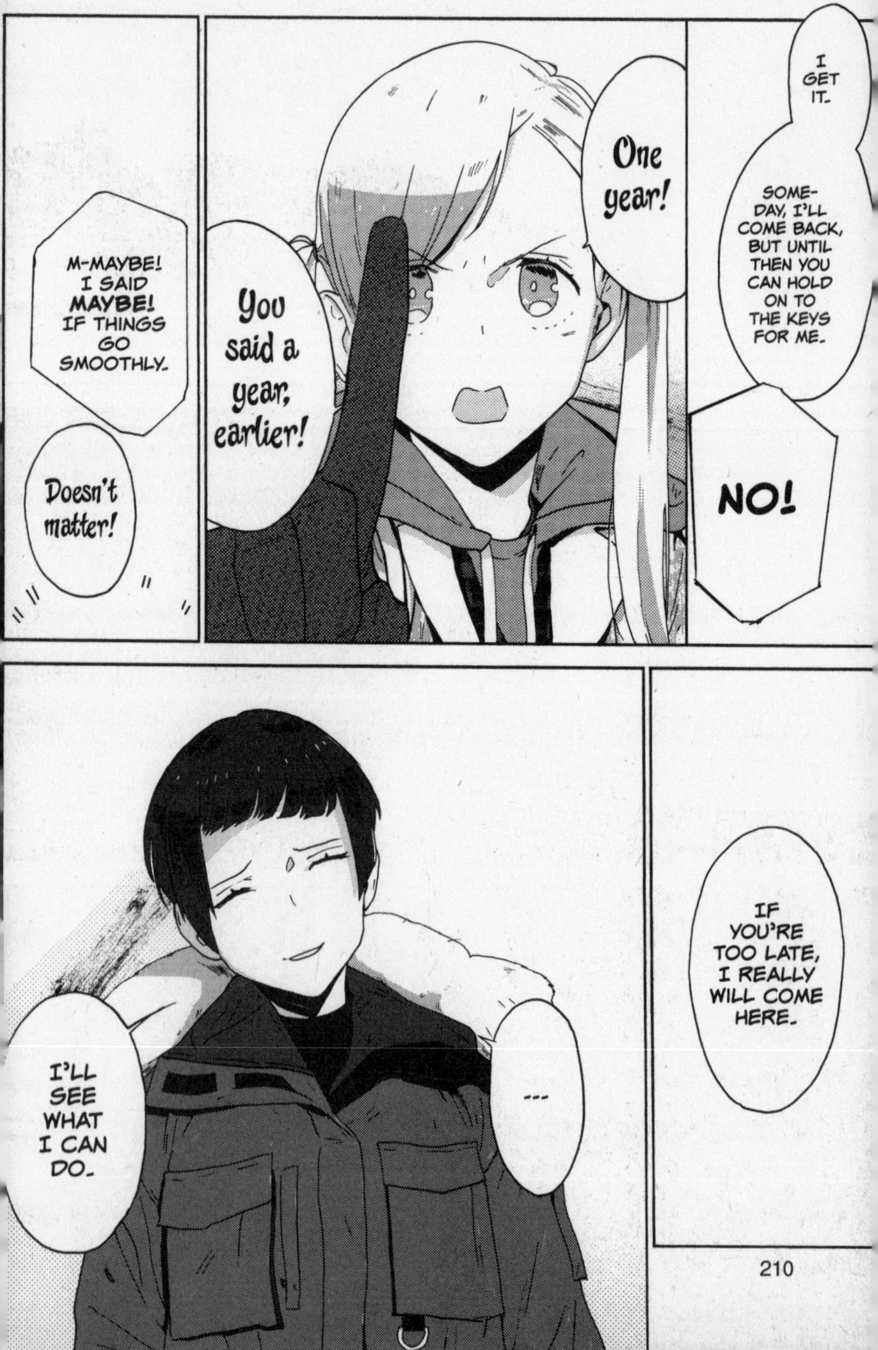
I GET IT.
SOMEDAY, I'LL COME BACK, BUT UNTIL THEN YOU CAN HOLD ON TO THE KEYS FOR ME.
NO!
One year!
You said a year, earlier!
M-MAYBE! I SAID MAYBE! IF THINGS GO SMOOTHLY.
Doesn't matter!
IF YOU'RE TOO LATE, I REALLY WILL COME HERE.
...
I'LL SEE WHAT I CAN DO.

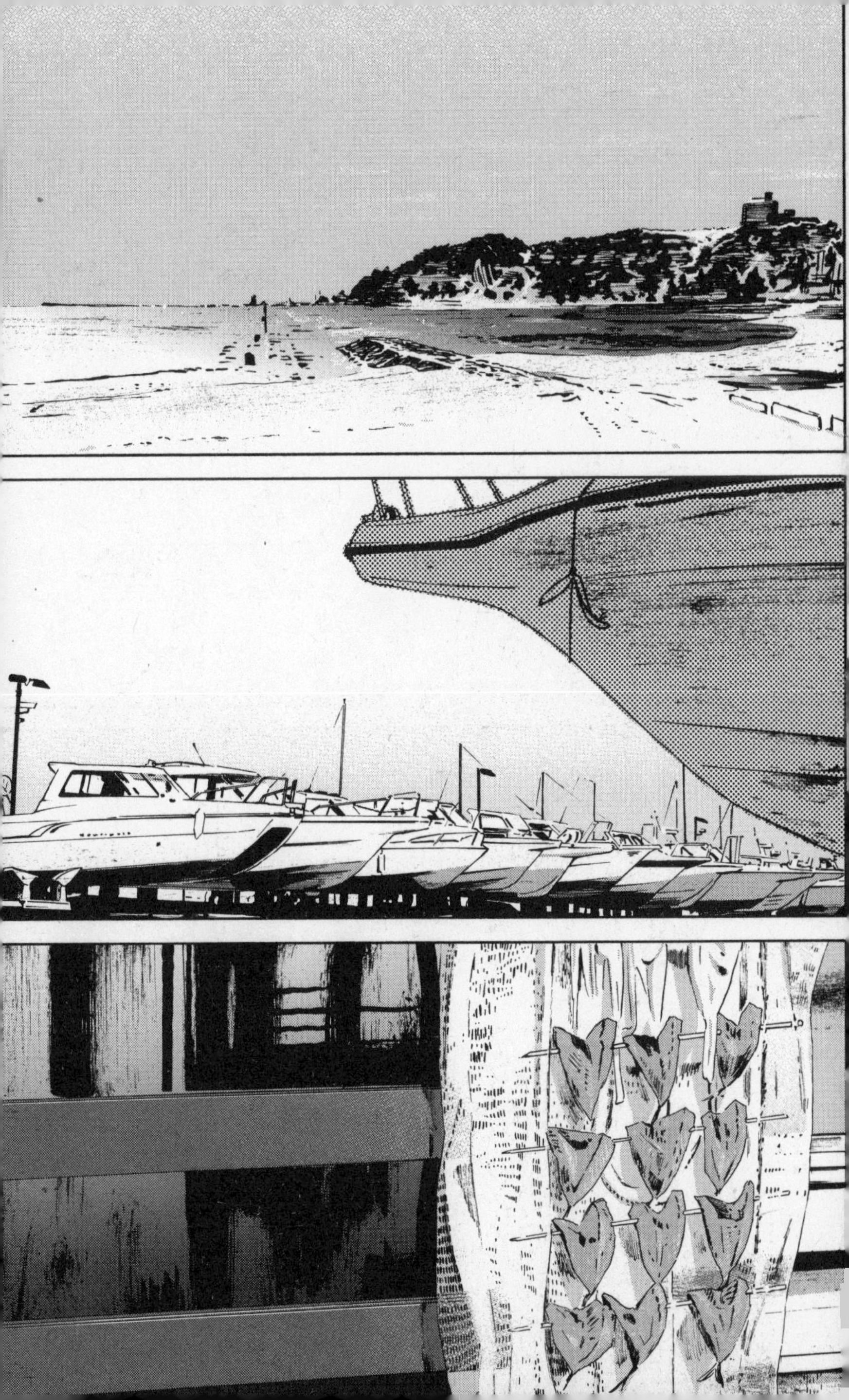

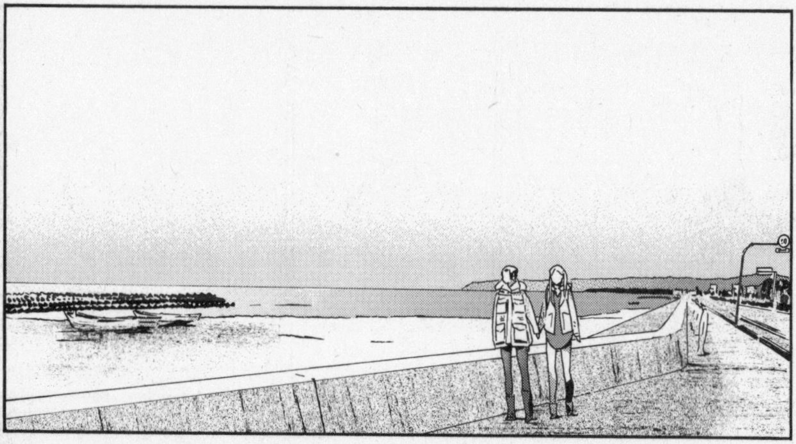
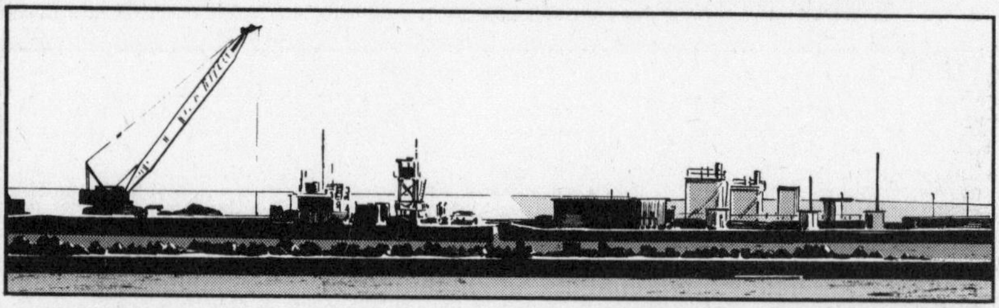
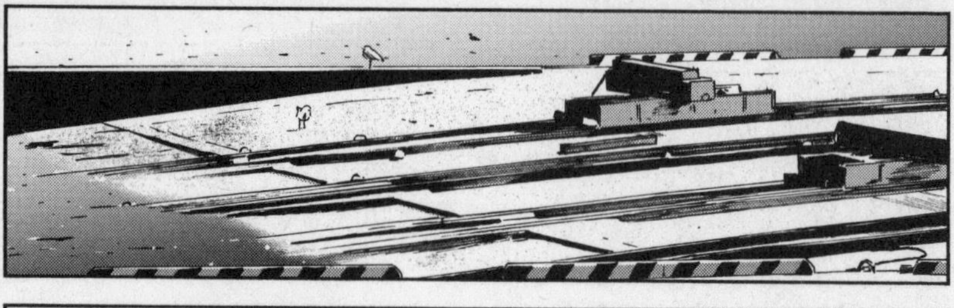
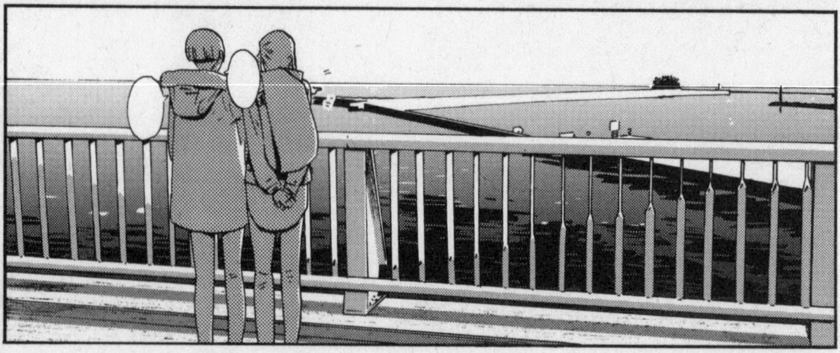

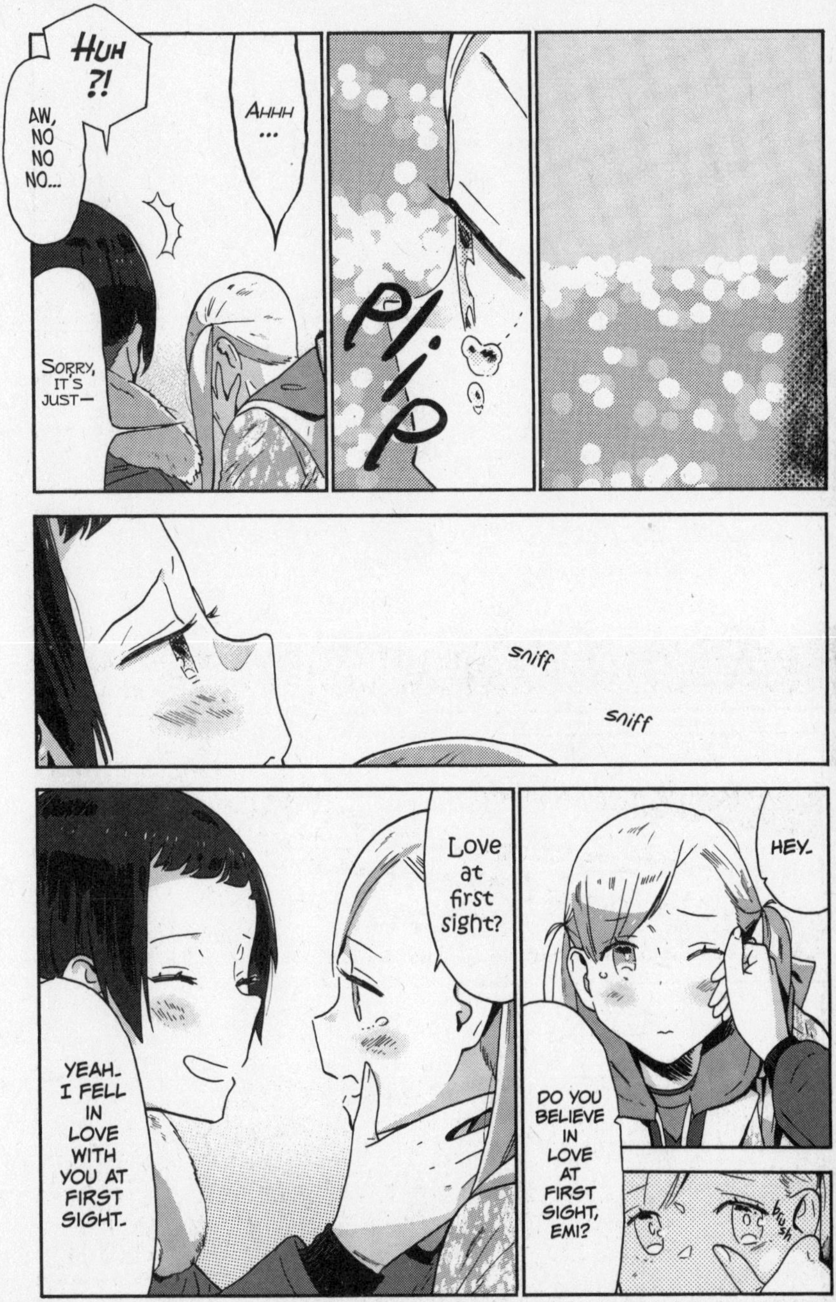
PLIP
AHHH...
HUH?!
AW, NO NO NO NO...
SORRY, IT'S JUST—
sniff
sniff
HEY.
DO YOU BELIEVE IN LOVE AT FIRST SIGHT, EMI?
brush
Love at first sight?
YEAH. I FELL IN LOVE WITH YOU AT FIRST SIGHT.

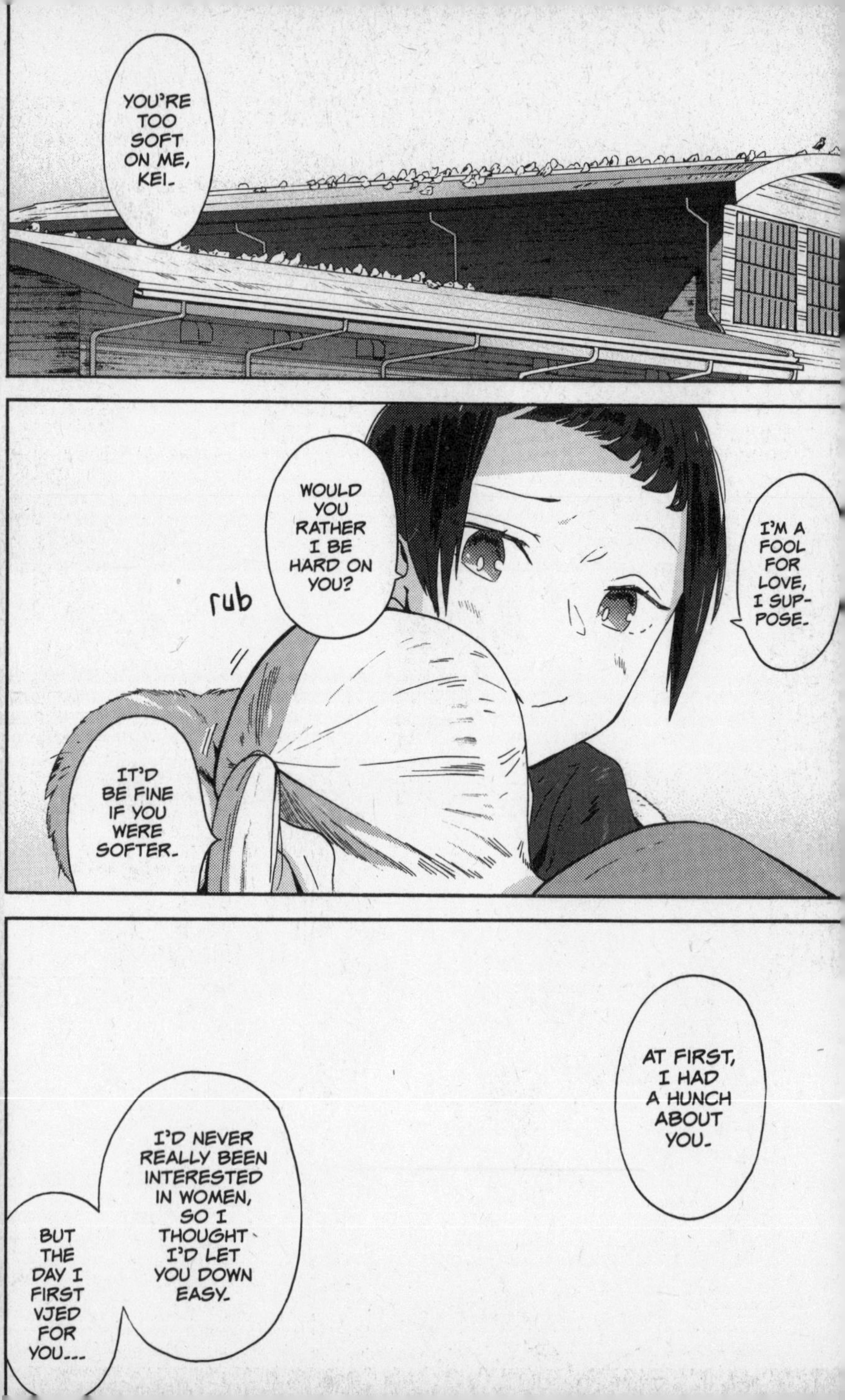
YOU'RE TOO SOFT ON ME, KEI.
I'M A FOOL FOR LOVE, I SUPPOSE.
WOULD YOU RATHER I BE HARD ON YOU?
rub
IT'D BE FINE IF YOU WERE SOFTER.
AT FIRST, I HAD A HUNCH ABOUT YOU.
I'D NEVER REALLY BEEN INTERESTED IN WOMEN, SO I THOUGHT I'D LET YOU DOWN EASY.
BUT THE DAY I FIRST VJED FOR YOU...

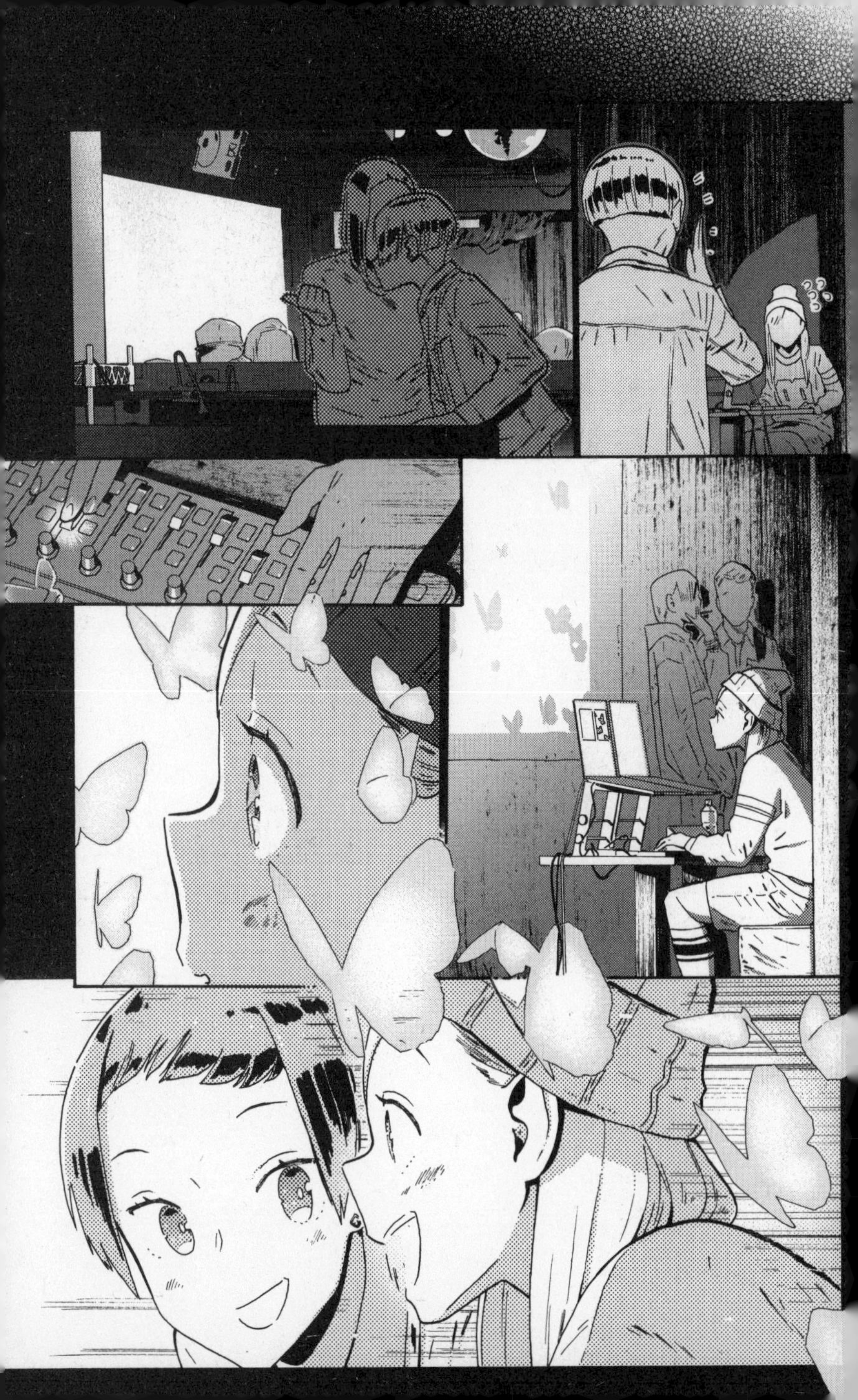

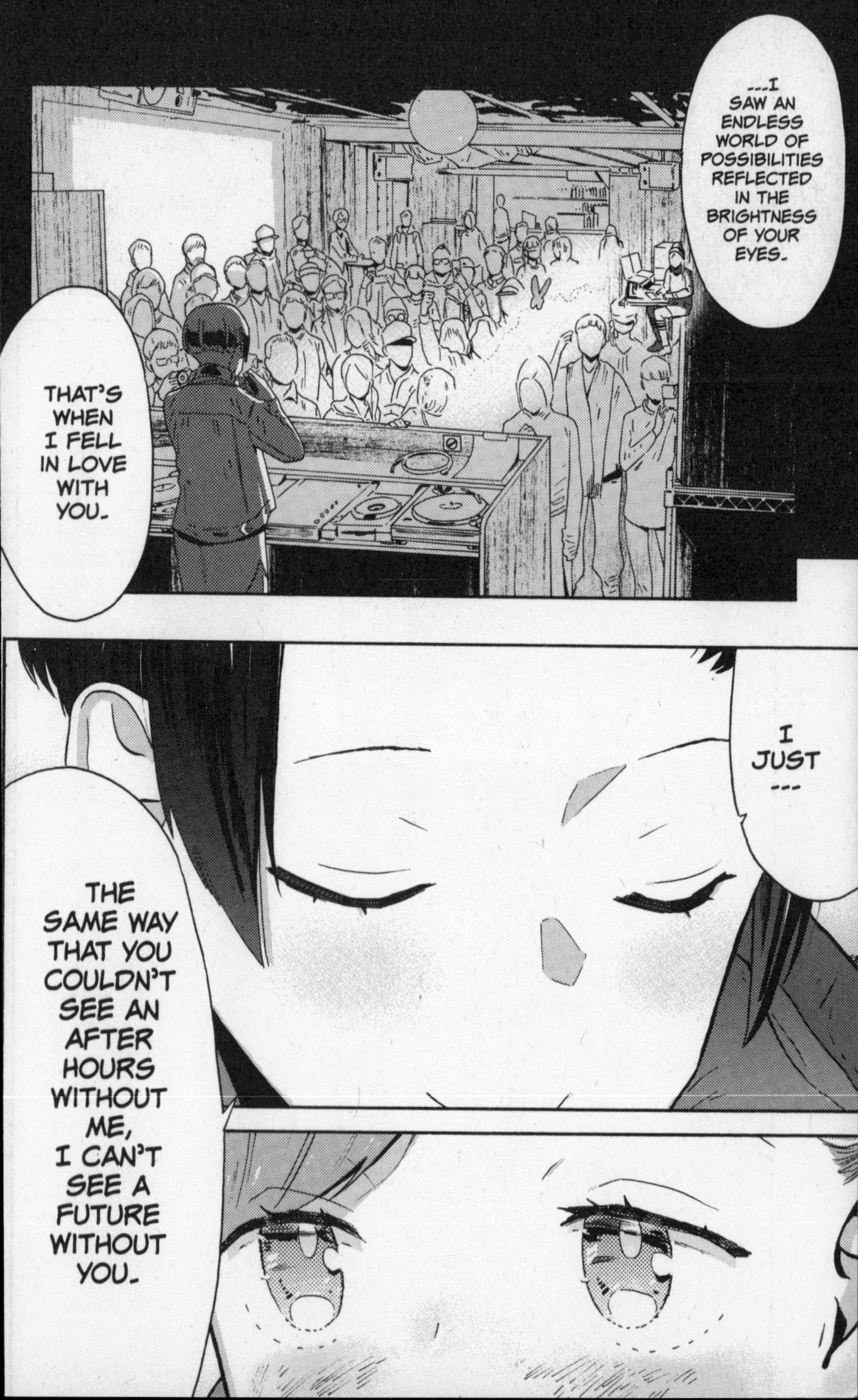
...I SAW AN ENDLESS WORLD OF POSSIBILITIES REFLECTED IN THE BRIGHTNESS OF YOUR EYES.
THAT'S WHEN I FELL IN LOVE WITH YOU.
I JUST ...
THE SAME WAY THAT YOU COULDN'T SEE AN AFTER HOURS WITHOUT ME, I CAN'T SEE A FUTURE WITHOUT YOU.

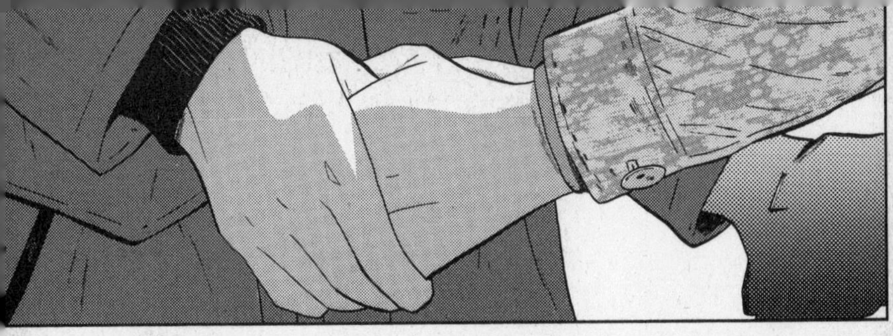
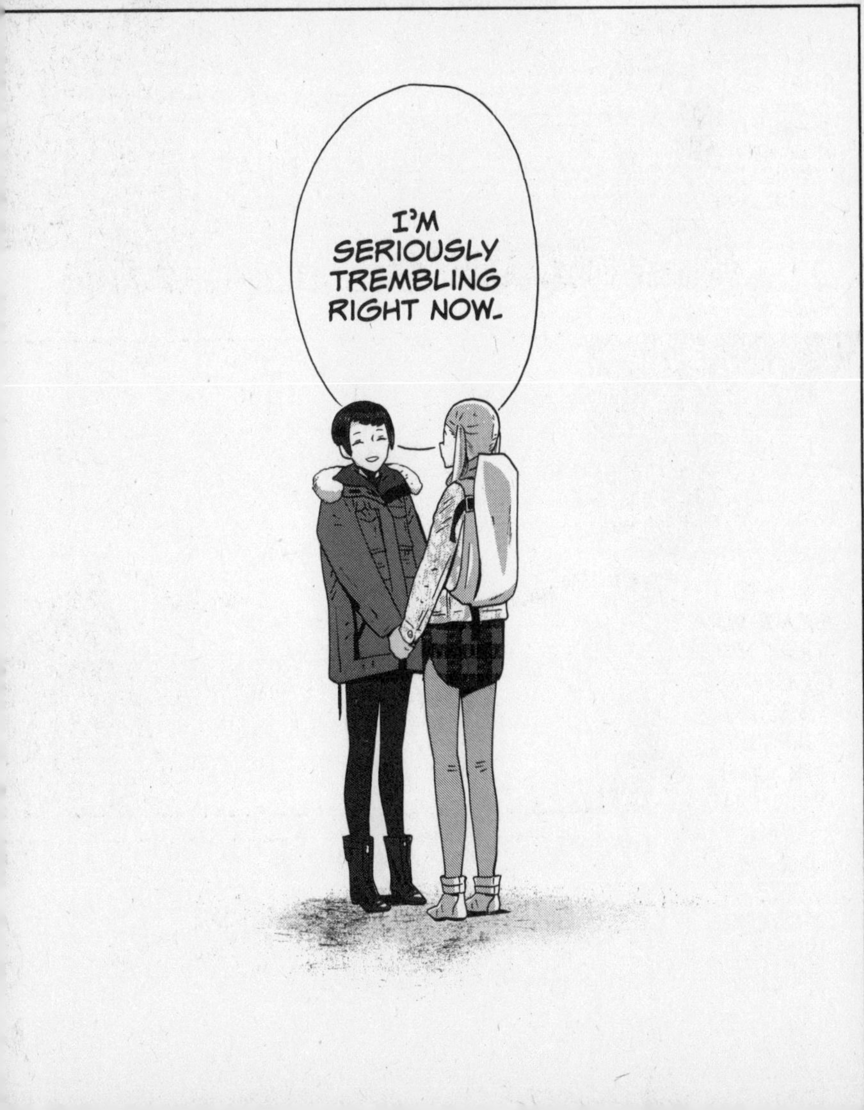
I'M SERIOUSLY TREMBLING RIGHT NOW.

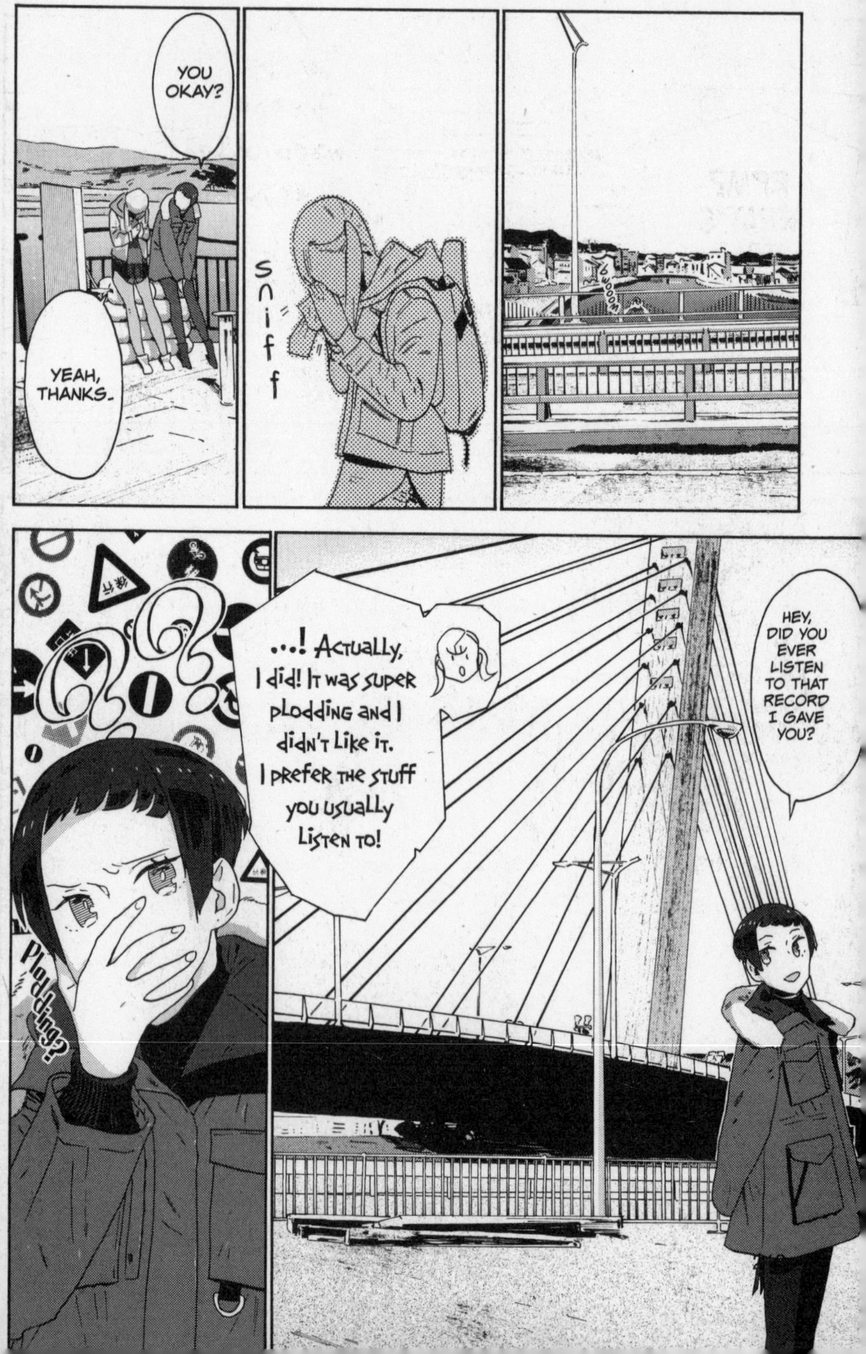
BWOOOM
SNIFF
YOU OKAY?
YEAH, THANKS_
HEY, DID YOU EVER LISTEN TO THAT RECORD I GAVE YOU?
...! Actually, I did! It was super plodding and I didn't like it. I prefer the stuff you usually listen to!
Plodding?

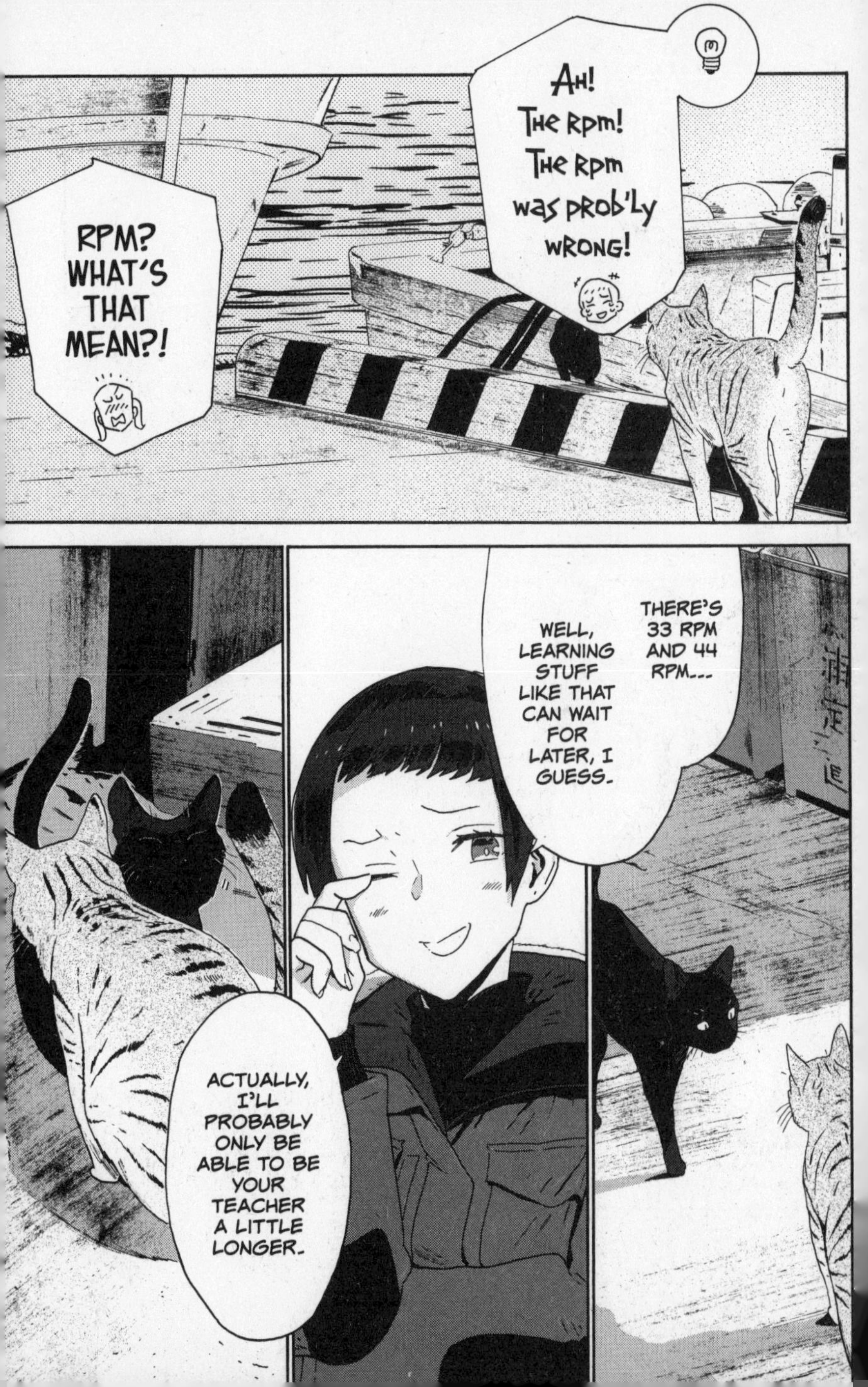
AH! THE RPM! THE RPM WAS PROB'LY WRONG!
RPM? WHAT'S THAT MEAN?!
THERE'S 33 RPM AND 44 RPM...
WELL, LEARNING STUFF LIKE THAT CAN WAIT FOR LATER, I GUESS.
ACTUALLY, I'LL PROBABLY ONLY BE ABLE TO BE YOUR TEACHER A LITTLE LONGER.

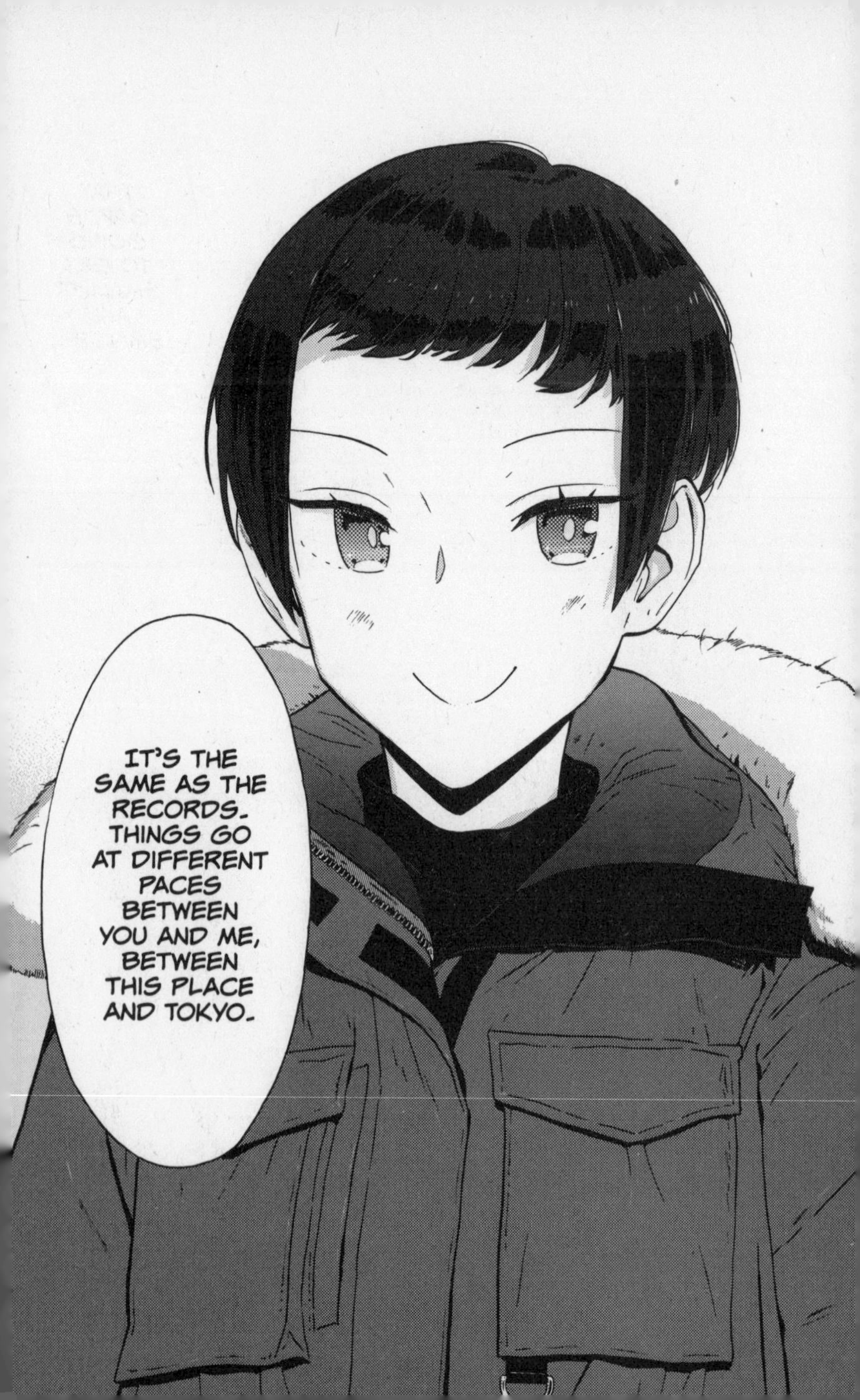
IT'S THE SAME AS THE RECORDS. THINGS GO AT DIFFERENT PACES BETWEEN YOU AND ME, BETWEEN THIS PLACE AND TOKYO.

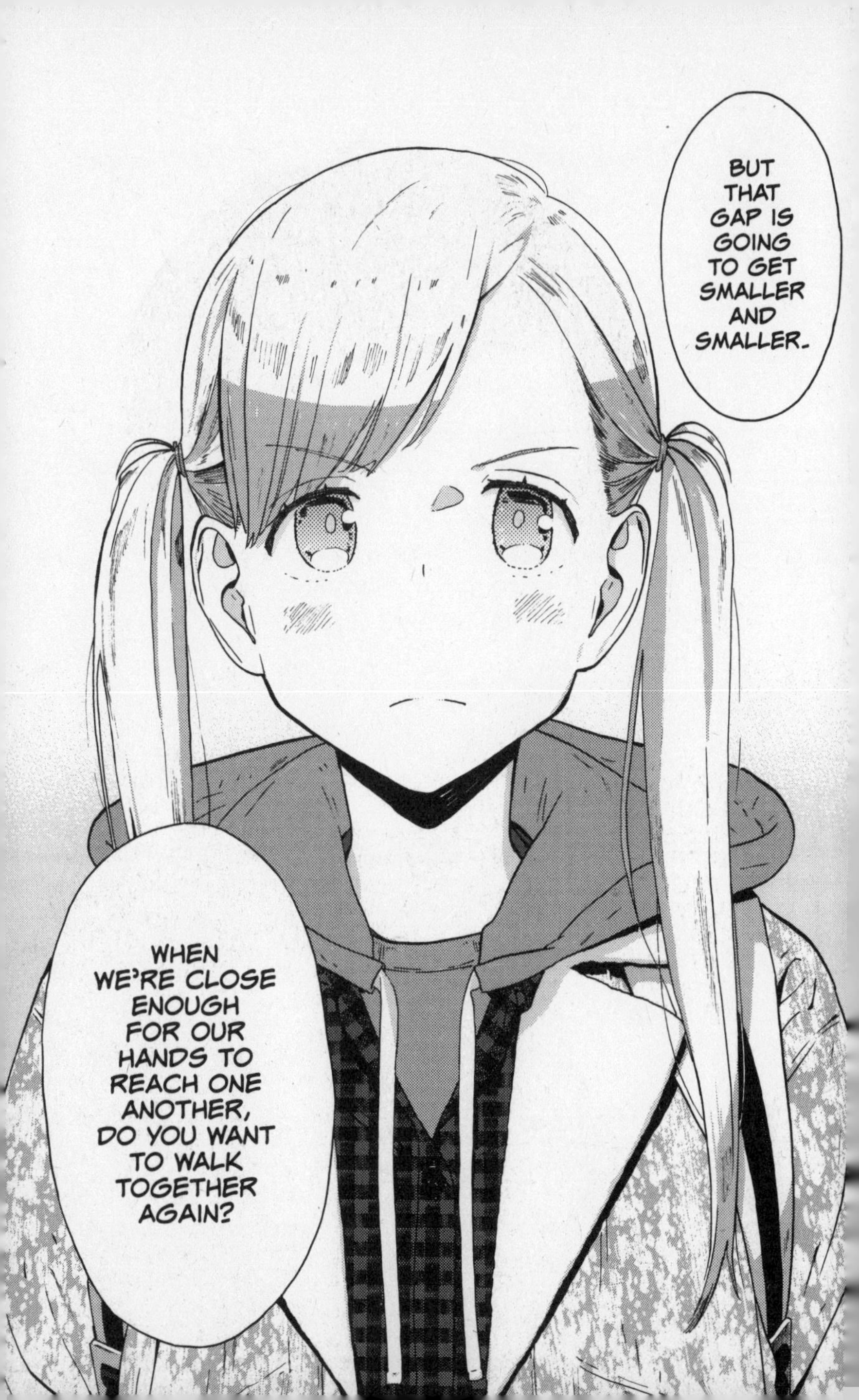
BUT THAT GAP IS GOING TO GET SMALLER AND SMALLER...
WHEN WE'RE CLOSE ENOUGH FOR OUR HANDS TO REACH ONE ANOTHER, DO YOU WANT TO WALK TOGETHER AGAIN?

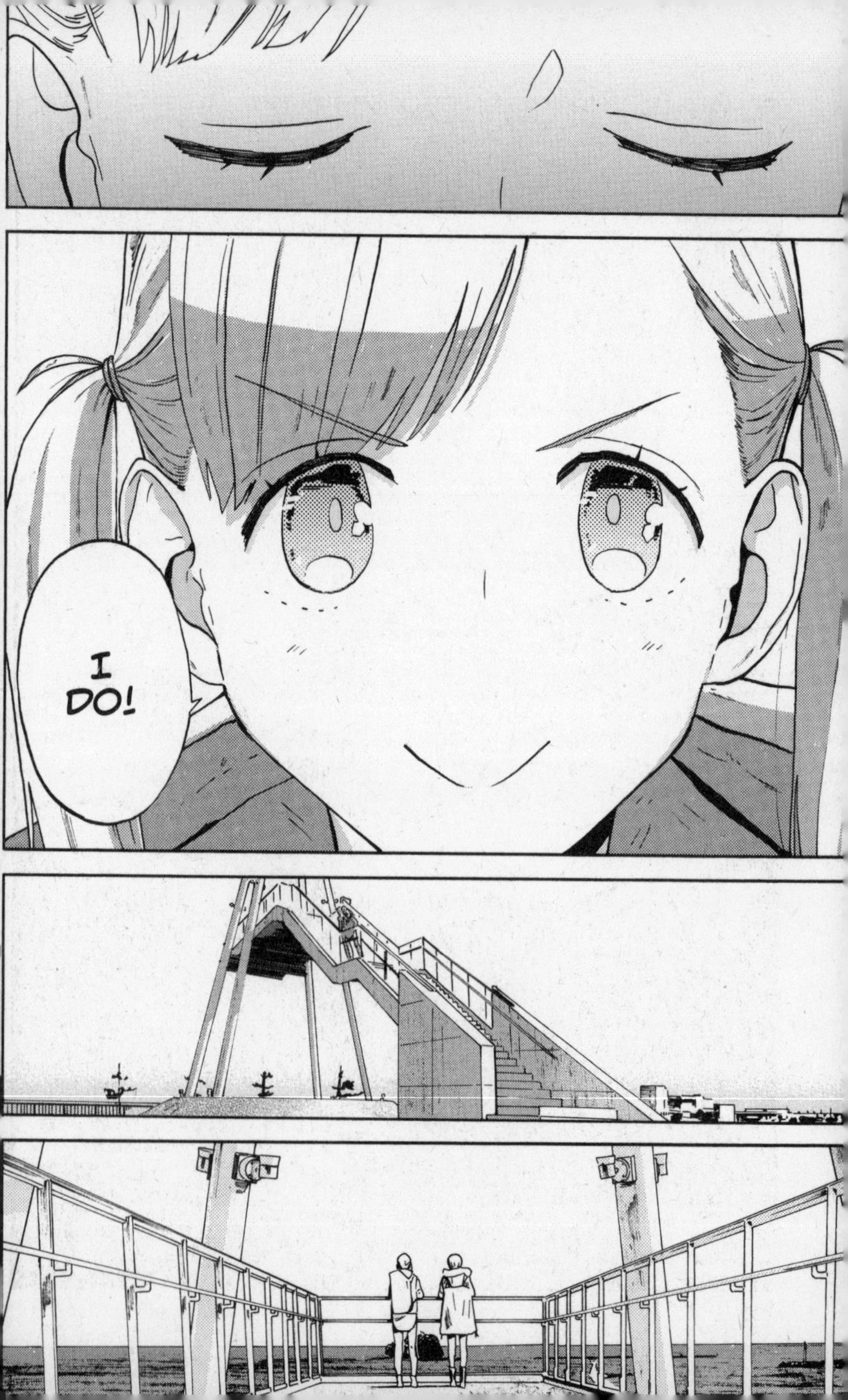
I DO!

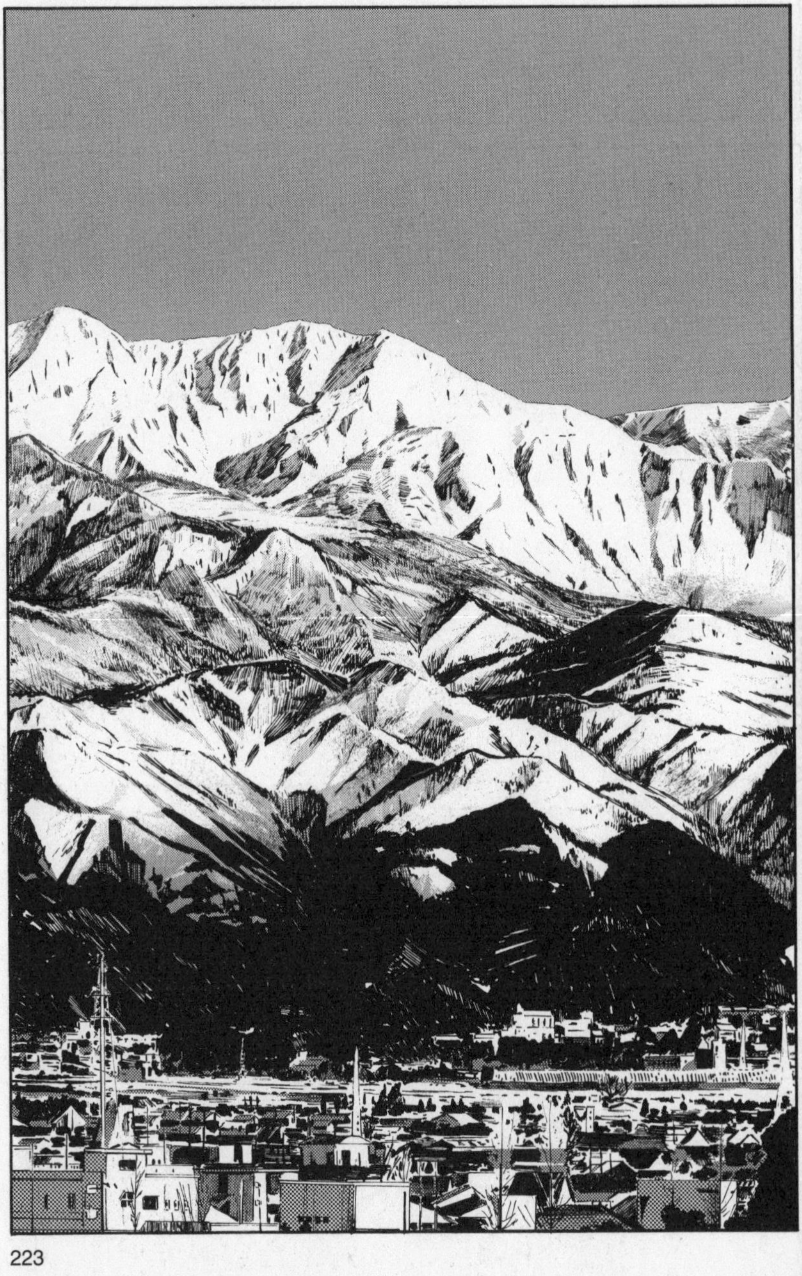

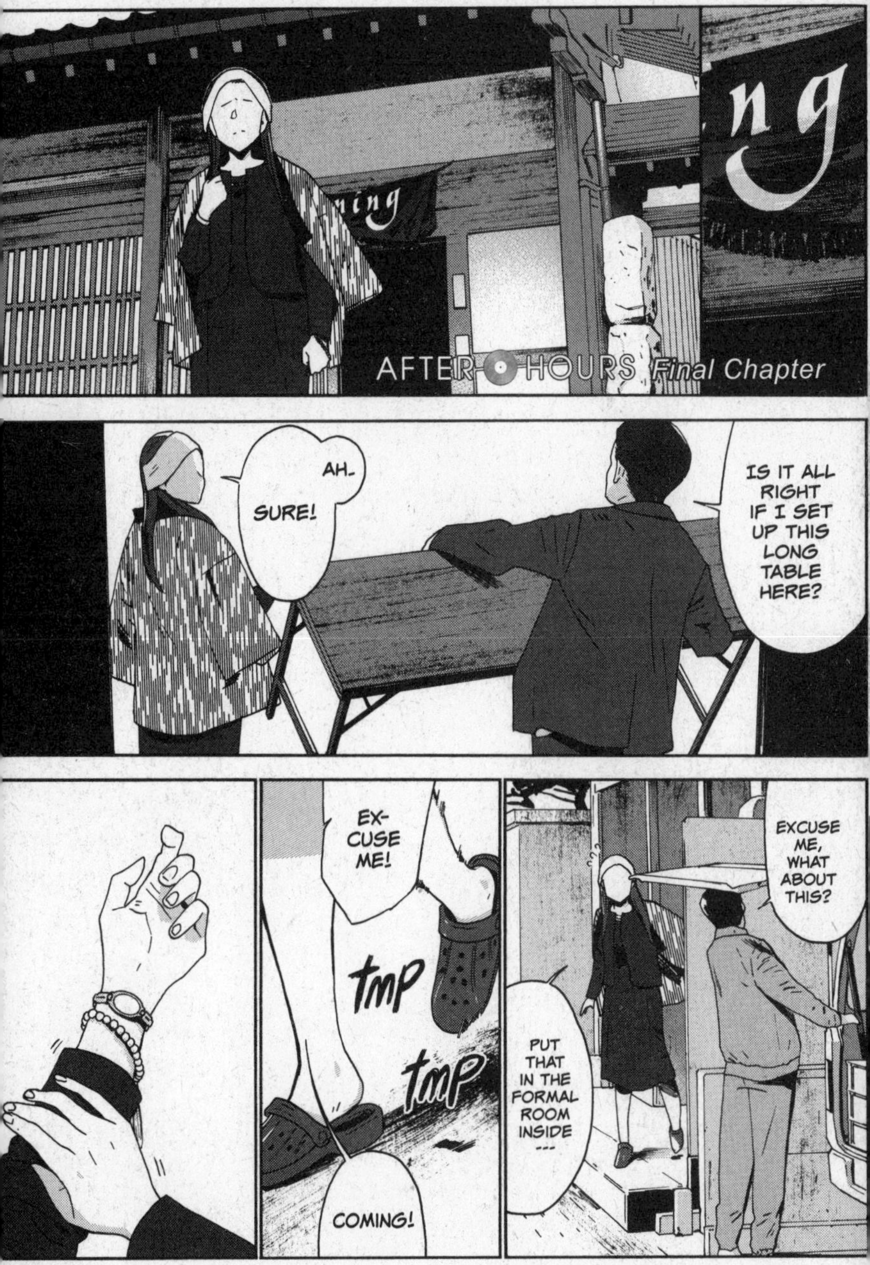
AFTER HOURS Final Chapter
IS IT ALL RIGHT IF I SET UP THIS LONG TABLE HERE?
AH. SURE!
EXCUSE ME, WHAT ABOUT THIS?
PUT THAT IN THE FORMAL ROOM INSIDE---
EX-CUSE ME!
tmp
tmp
COMING!

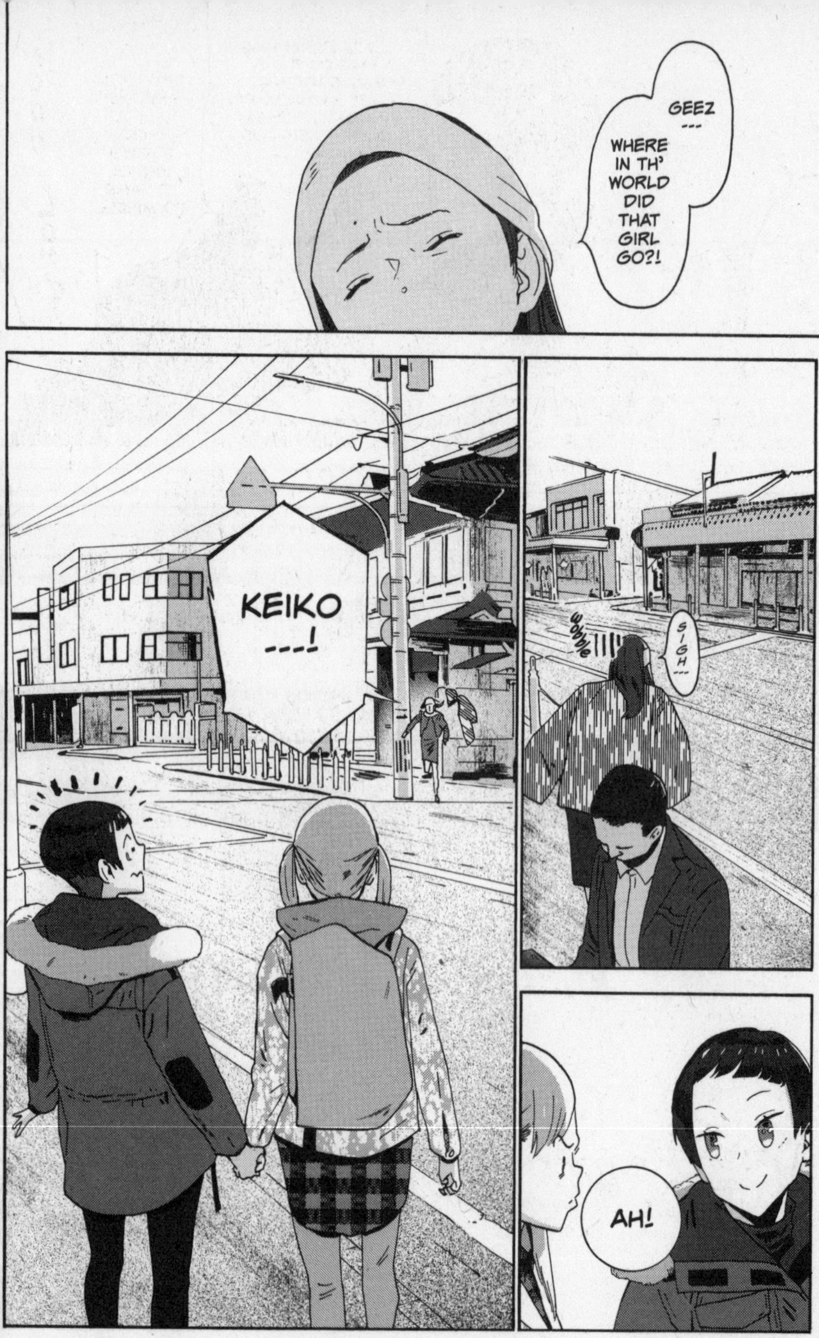
GEEZ --- WHERE IN TH' WORLD DID THAT GIRL GO?!
WOBBLE
SIGH ---
AH!
KEIKO ---!

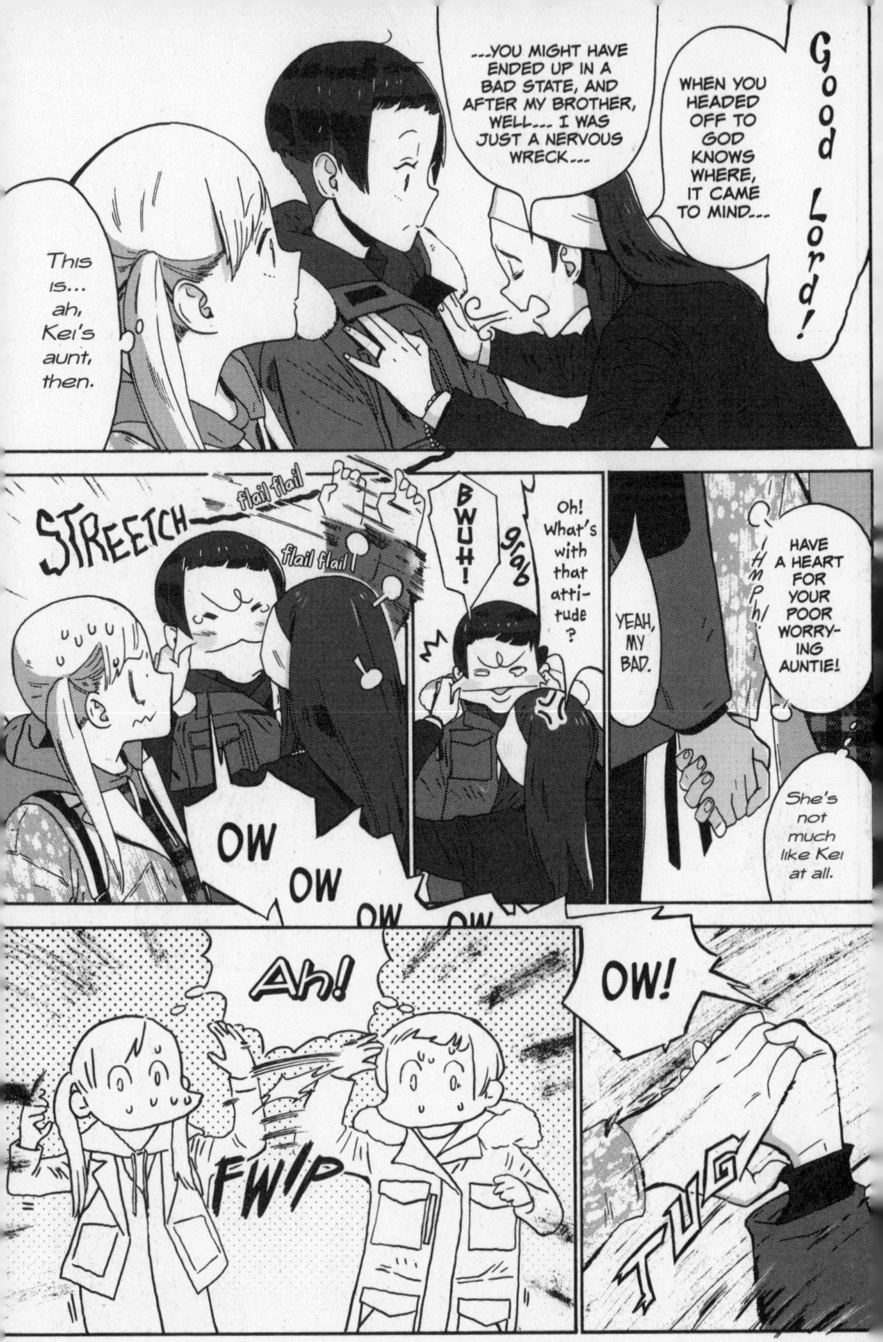
Good Lord!
WHEN YOU HEADED OFF TO GOD KNOWS WHERE, IT CAME TO MIND...
...YOU MIGHT HAVE ENDED UP IN A BAD STATE, AND AFTER MY BROTHER, WELL... I WAS JUST A NERVOUS WRECK...
This is... ah, Kei's aunt, then.
HMPH!
HAVE A HEART FOR YOUR POOR WORRYING AUNTIE!
YEAH, MY BAD.
She's not much like Kei at all.
Oh! What's with that atti-tude?
grab
BWUH!
STREETCH
flail flail
flail flail
OW
OW
OW
OW
OW!
TUG
Ah!
FWIP

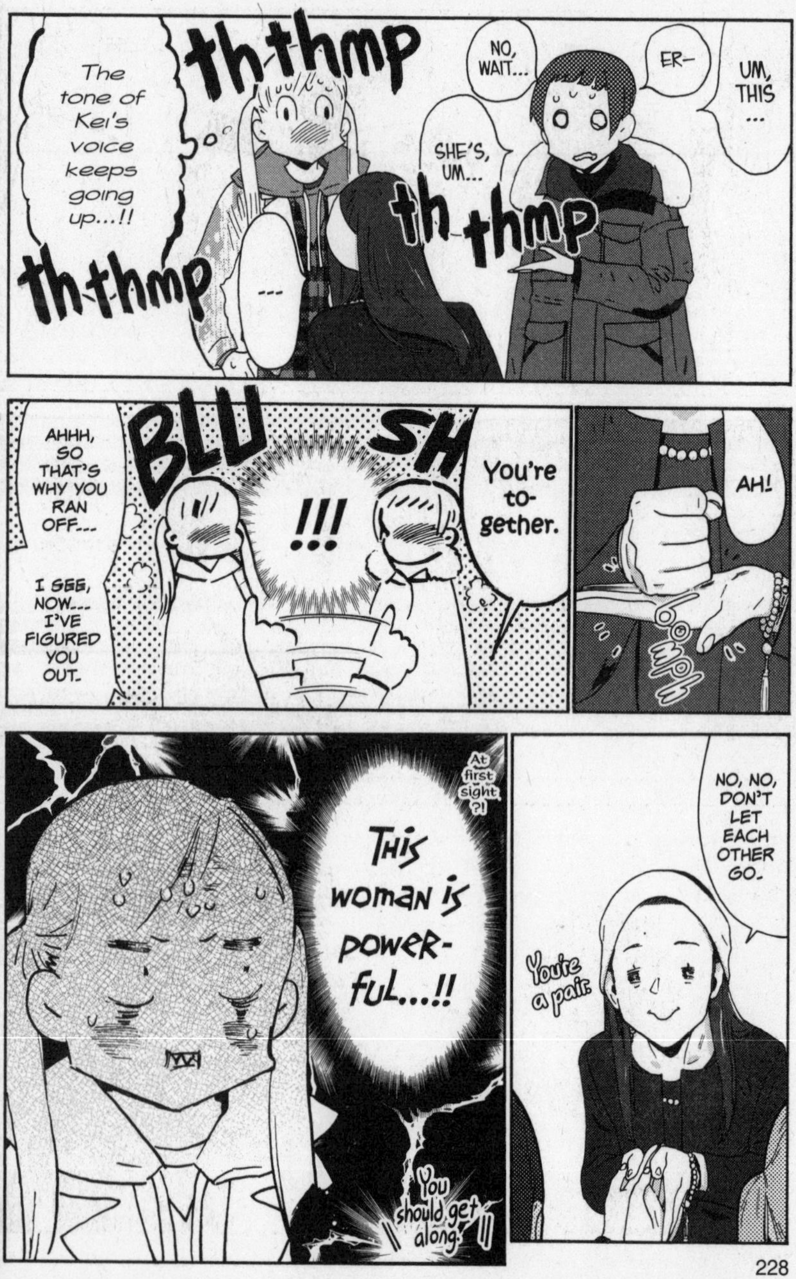
UM, THIS ...
ER—
NO, WAIT...
SHE'S, UM...
th-thmp
th thmp
th-t-hmp
...
The tone of Kei's voice keeps going up...!!
AH!
bomph
You're to-gether.
BLU SH
!!!
AHHH, SO THAT'S WHY YOU RAN OFF...
I SEE, NOW... I'VE FIGURED YOU OUT.
NO, NO, DON'T LET EACH OTHER GO.
You're a pair.
At first sight?!
THIS woman is power-ful...!!
You should get along.

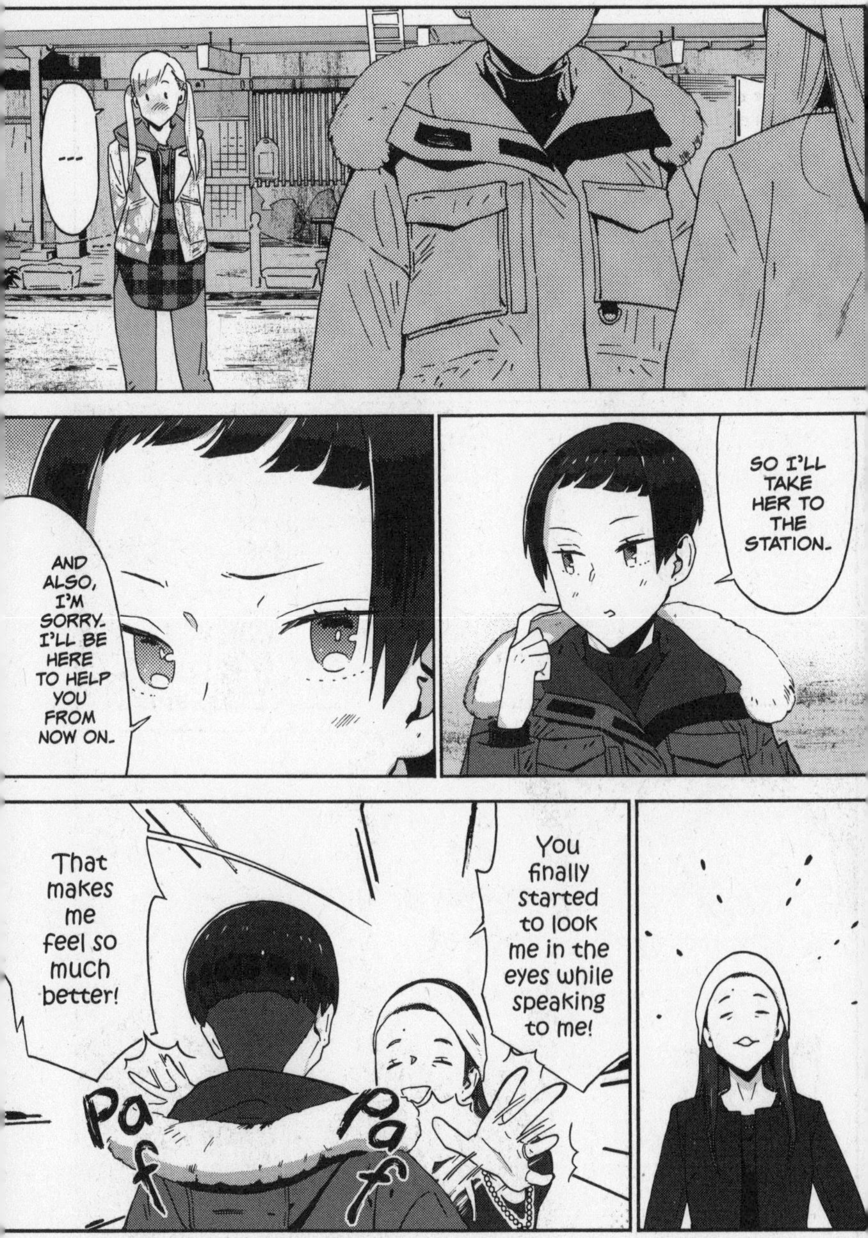
...
SO I'LL TAKE HER TO THE STATION.
AND ALSO, I'M SORRY. I'LL BE HERE TO HELP YOU FROM NOW ON.
You finally started to look me in the eyes while speaking to me!
That makes me feel so much better!
Paf
Paf

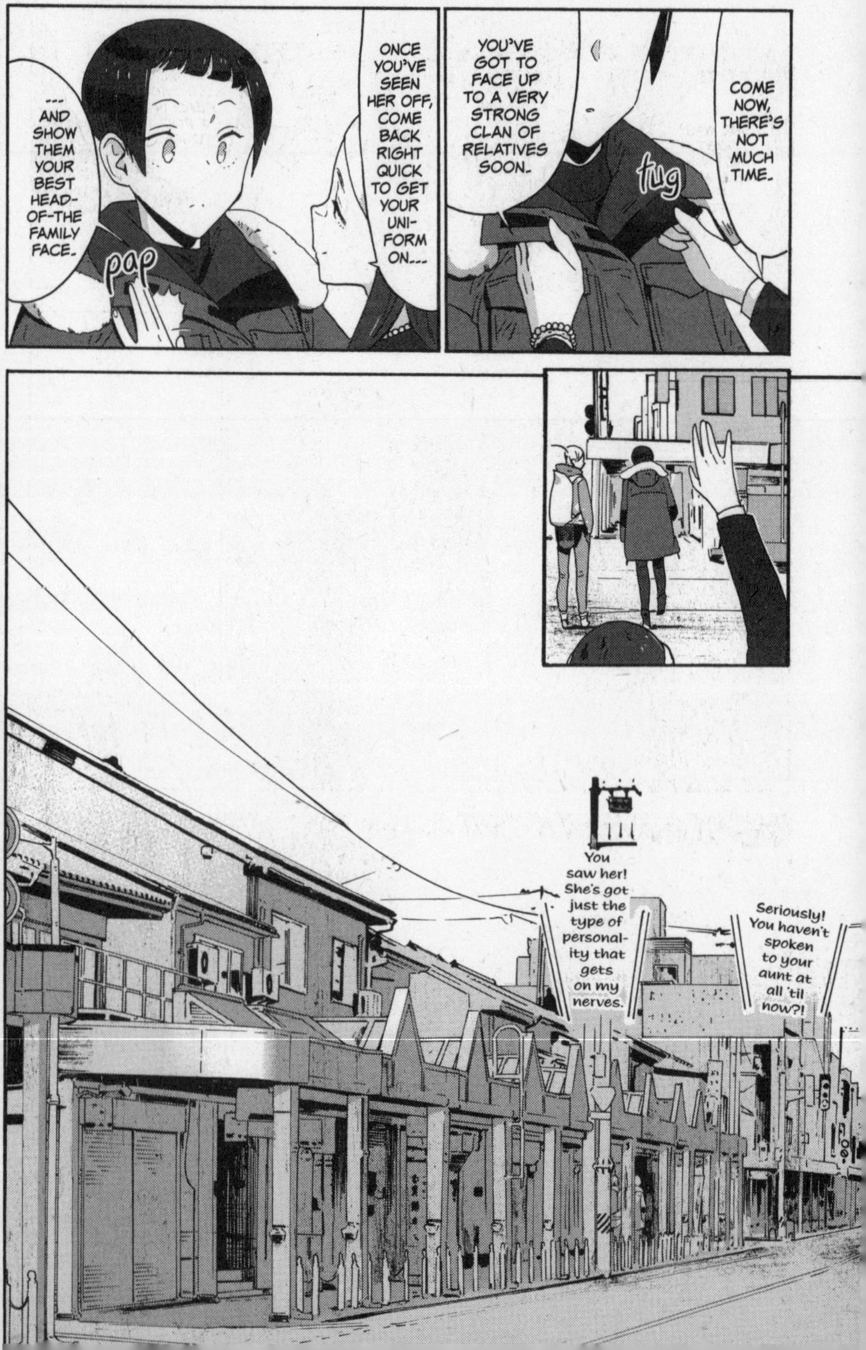
COME NOW, THERE'S NOT MUCH TIME.
YOU'VE GOT TO FACE UP TO A VERY STRONG CLAN OF RELATIVES SOON.
tug
ONCE YOU'VE SEEN HER OFF, COME BACK RIGHT QUICK TO GET YOUR UNI-FORM ON...
...AND SHOW THEM YOUR BEST HEAD-OF-THE FAMILY FACE.
pap
Seriously! You haven't spoken to your aunt at all 'til now?!
You saw her! She's got just the type of personal-ity that gets on my nerves.

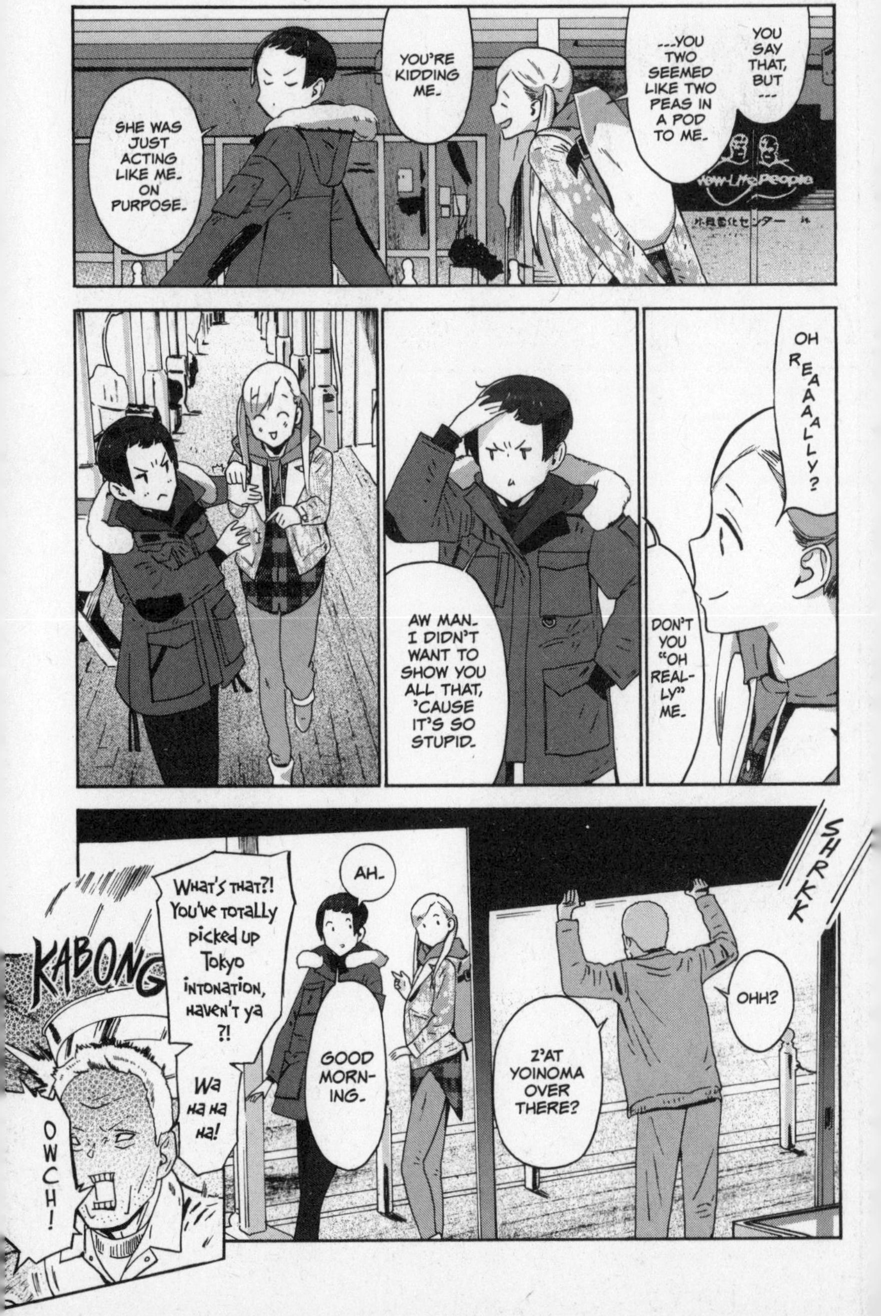
YOU SAY THAT, BUT...
...YOU TWO SEEMED LIKE TWO PEAS IN A POD TO ME.
YOU'RE KIDDING ME.
SHE WAS JUST ACTING LIKE ME. ON PURPOSE.
OH REAAAAALLY?
DON'T YOU "OH REALLY" ME.
AW MAN. I DIDN'T WANT TO SHOW YOU ALL THAT, 'CAUSE IT'S SO STUPID.
SHRKK
OHH?
Z'AT YOINOMA OVER THERE?
AH.
GOOD MORNING.
What's that?! You've totally picked up Tokyo intonation, haven't ya?!
Wa ha ha ha!
KABONG
OWCH!

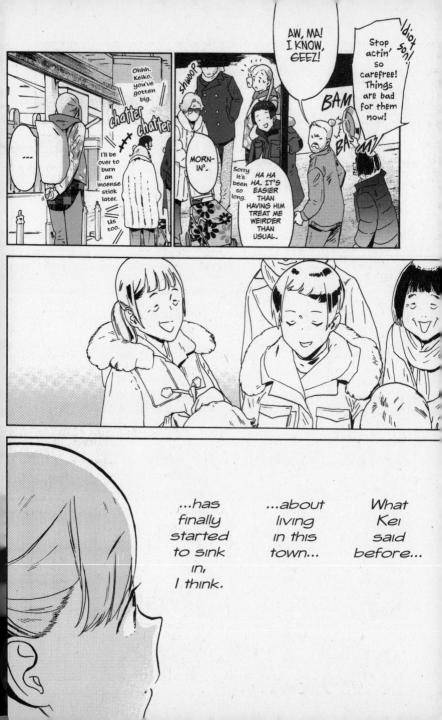

Idiot son!
Stop actin' so carefree! Things are bad for them now!
BAM
BAM
AW, MA! I KNOW, GEEZ!
HA HA HA. IT'S EASIER THAN HAVING HIM TREAT ME WEIRDER THAN USUAL.
Sorry it's been so long.
MORN-IN'.
shwoop
Ohhh. Keiko, you've gotten big.
chatter chatter
I'll be over to burn an incense stick later.
Us too.
...
What Kei said before...
...about living in this town...
...has finally started to sink in, I think.

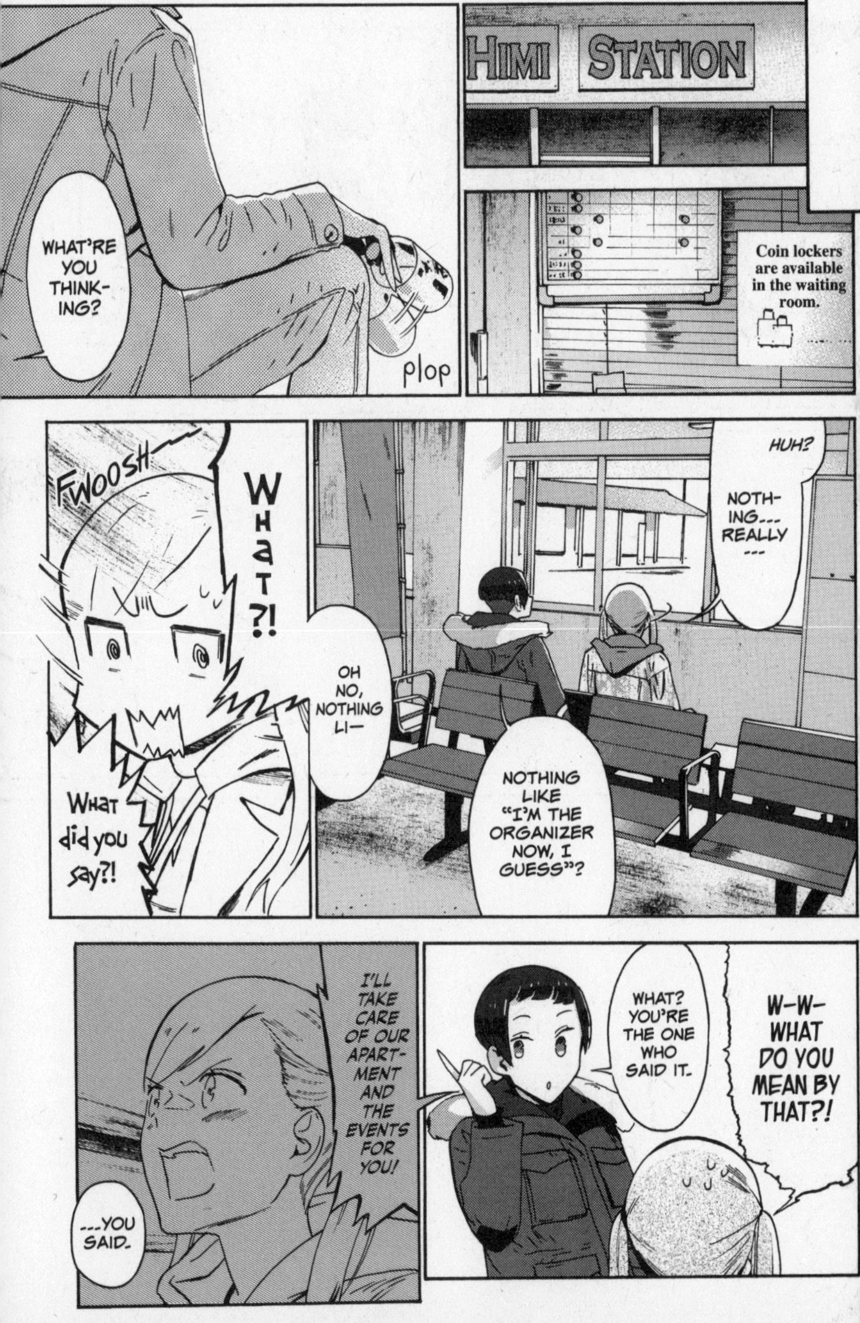
HIMI STATION
Coin lockers are available in the waiting room.
WHAT'RE YOU THINKING?
plop
HUH? NOTHING... REALLY...
NOTHING LIKE "I'M THE ORGANIZER NOW, I GUESS"?
OH NO, NOTHING LI—
FWOOSH
WHAT?!
What did you say?!
WHAT? YOU'RE THE ONE WHO SAID IT.
W-W-WHAT DO YOU MEAN BY THAT?!
I'LL TAKE CARE OF OUR APARTMENT AND THE EVENTS FOR YOU!
...YOU SAID.

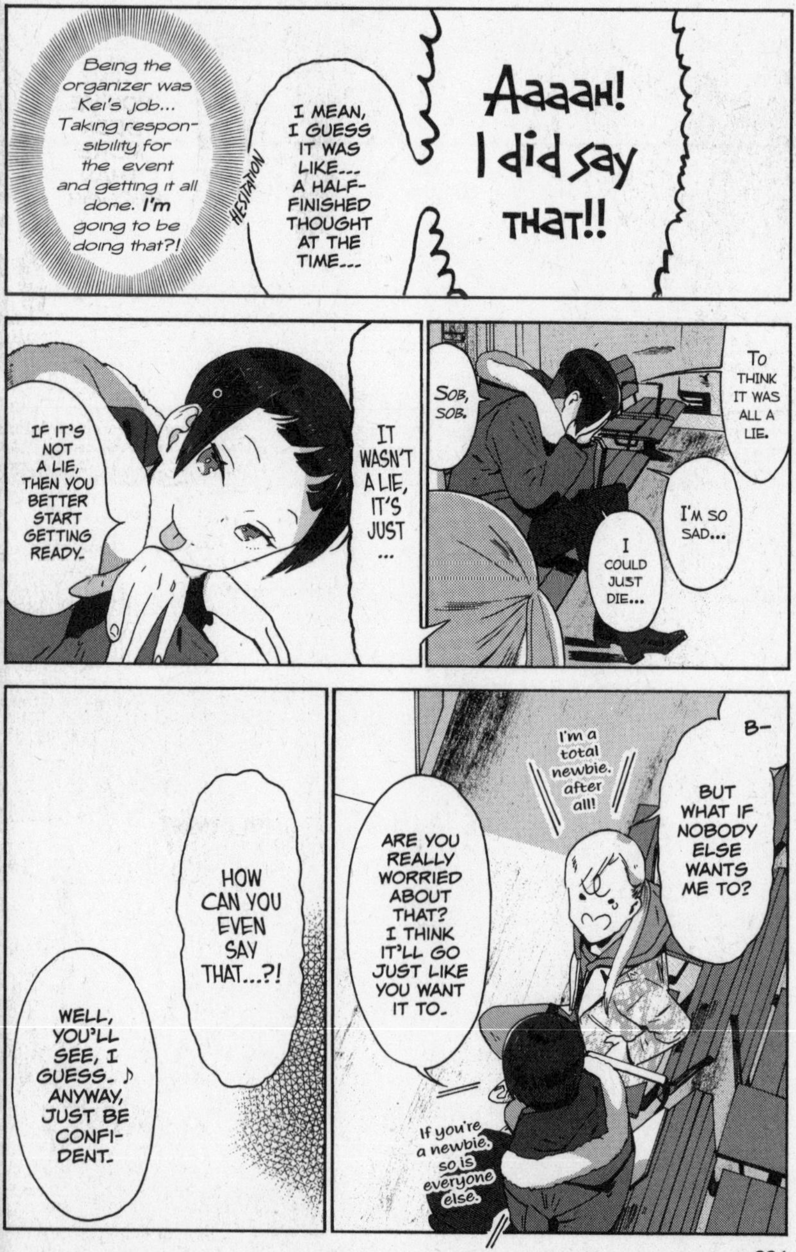
Aaaah! I did say that!!
I MEAN, I GUESS IT WAS LIKE... A HALF-FINISHED THOUGHT AT THE TIME...
HESITATION
Being the organizer was Kei's job... Taking responsibility for the event and getting it all done. I'm going to be doing that?!
TO THINK IT WAS ALL A LIE.
SOB, SOB.
I'M SO SAD...
I COULD JUST DIE...
IT WASN'T A LIE, IT'S JUST ...
IF IT'S NOT A LIE, THEN YOU BETTER START GETTING READY.
B- BUT WHAT IF NOBODY ELSE WANTS ME TO?
I'm a total newbie, after all!
ARE YOU REALLY WORRIED ABOUT THAT? I THINK IT'LL GO JUST LIKE YOU WANT IT TO.
If you're a newbie, so is everyone else.
HOW CAN YOU EVEN SAY THAT...?!
WELL, YOU'LL SEE, I GUESS. ♪ ANYWAY, JUST BE CONFIDENT.

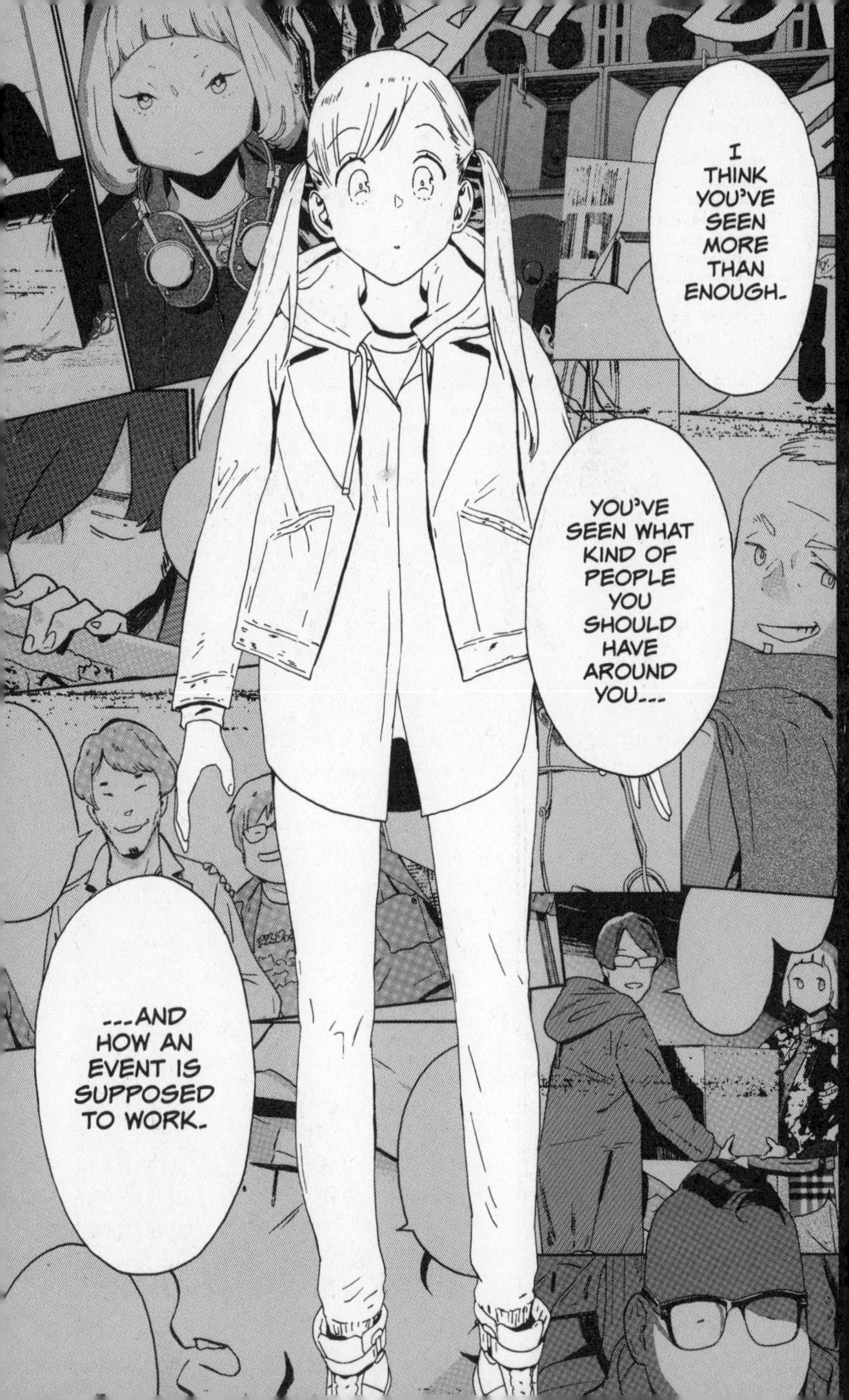
I THINK YOU'VE SEEN MORE THAN ENOUGH.
YOU'VE SEEN WHAT KIND OF PEOPLE YOU SHOULD HAVE AROUND YOU...
...AND HOW AN EVENT IS SUPPOSED TO WORK.

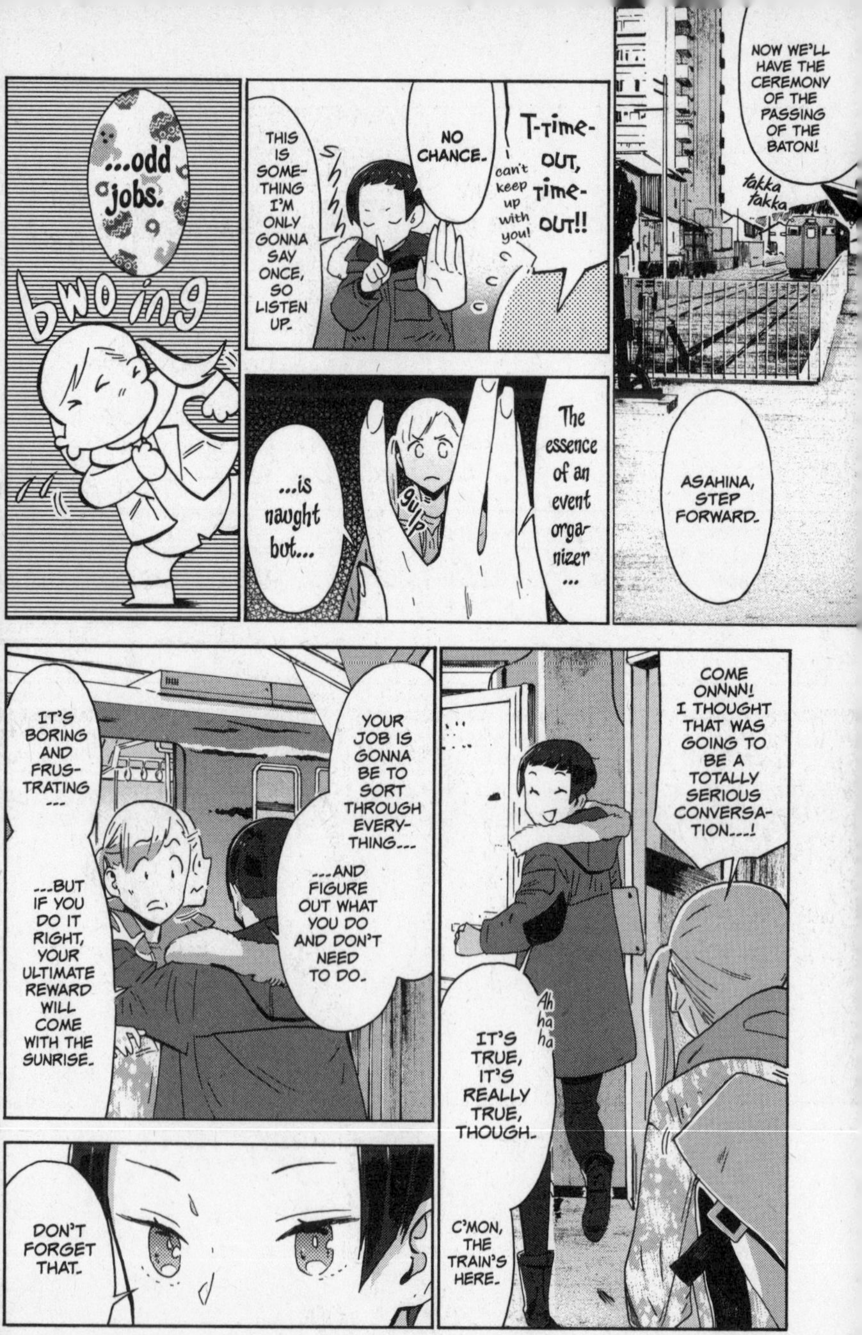
NOW WE'LL HAVE THE CEREMONY OF THE PASSING OF THE BATON!
takka takka
ASAHINA, STEP FORWARD.
T-time-OUT, time-OUT!!
can't keep up with you!
NO CHANCE.
THIS IS SOME-THING I'M ONLY GONNA SAY ONCE, SO LISTEN UP.
The essence of an event orga-nizer...
gulp
...is naught but...
...odd jobs.
bwo ing
YOUR JOB IS GONNA BE TO SORT THROUGH EVERY-THING...
...AND FIGURE OUT WHAT YOU DO AND DON'T NEED TO DO.
IT'S BORING AND FRUS-TRATING...
...BUT IF YOU DO IT RIGHT, YOUR ULTIMATE REWARD WILL COME WITH THE SUNRISE.
DON'T FORGET THAT.
COME ONNNN! I THOUGHT THAT WAS GOING TO BE A TOTALLY SERIOUS CONVERSA-TION...!
Ahhaha
IT'S TRUE, IT'S REALLY TRUE, THOUGH.
C'MON, THE TRAIN'S HERE.

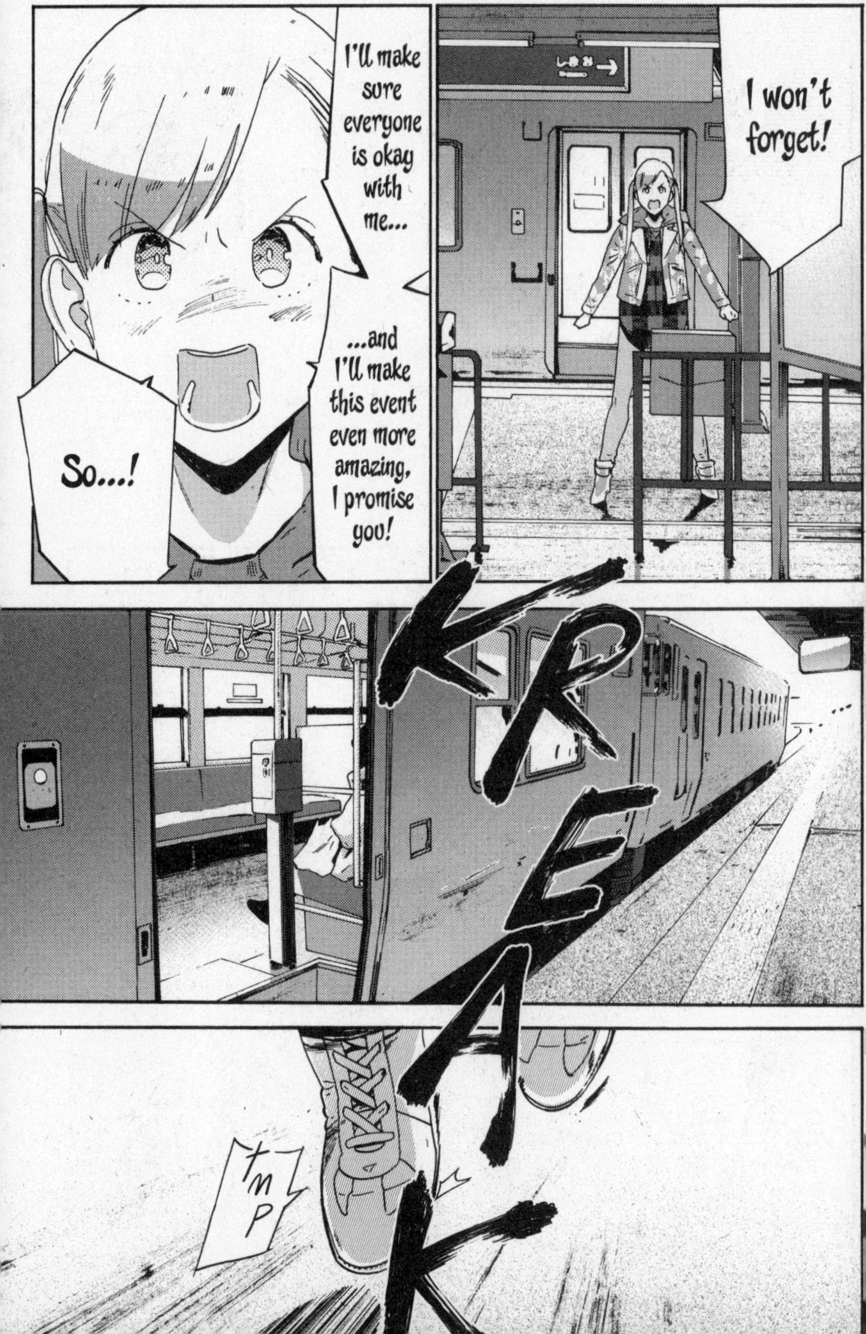
I won't forget!
I'll make sure everyone is okay with me...
...and I'll make this event even more amazing, I promise you!
So...!
KREAK
TMP

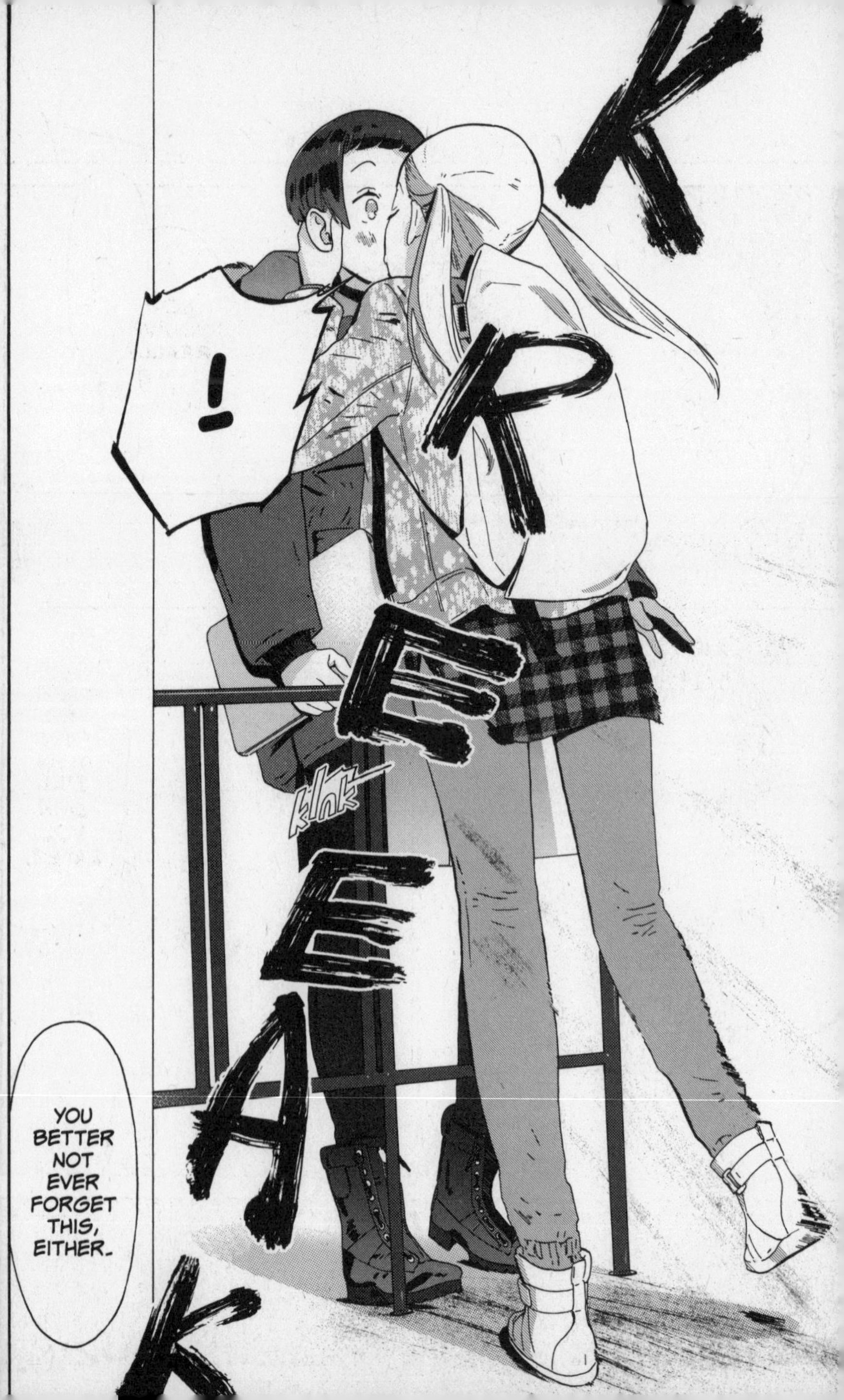
!
KREEAK
klink
YOU BETTER NOT EVER FORGET THIS, EITHER..

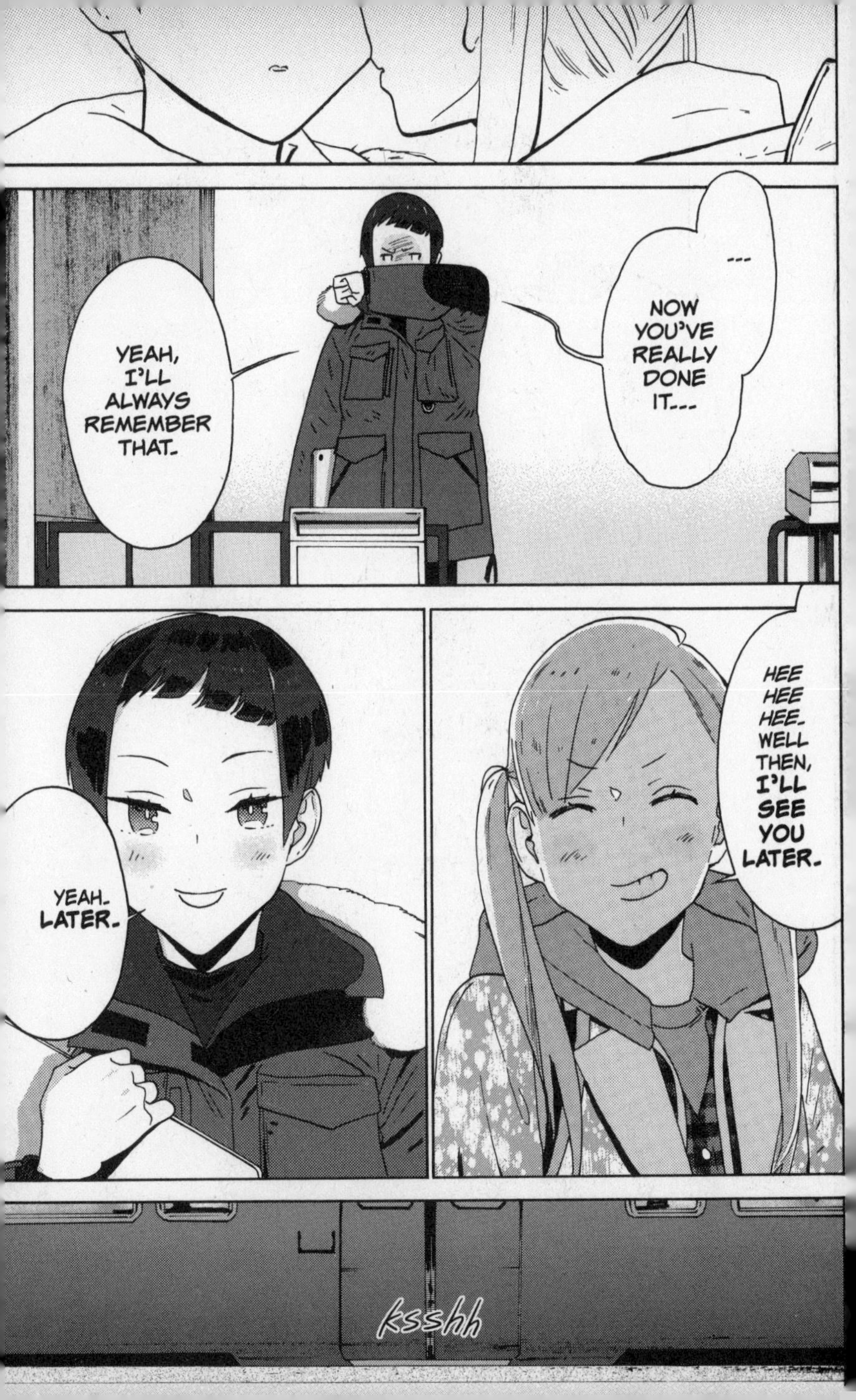
...
NOW YOU'VE REALLY DONE IT...
YEAH, I'LL ALWAYS REMEMBER THAT.
HEE HEE HEE. WELL THEN, I'LL SEE YOU LATER.
YEAH. LATER.
ksshh

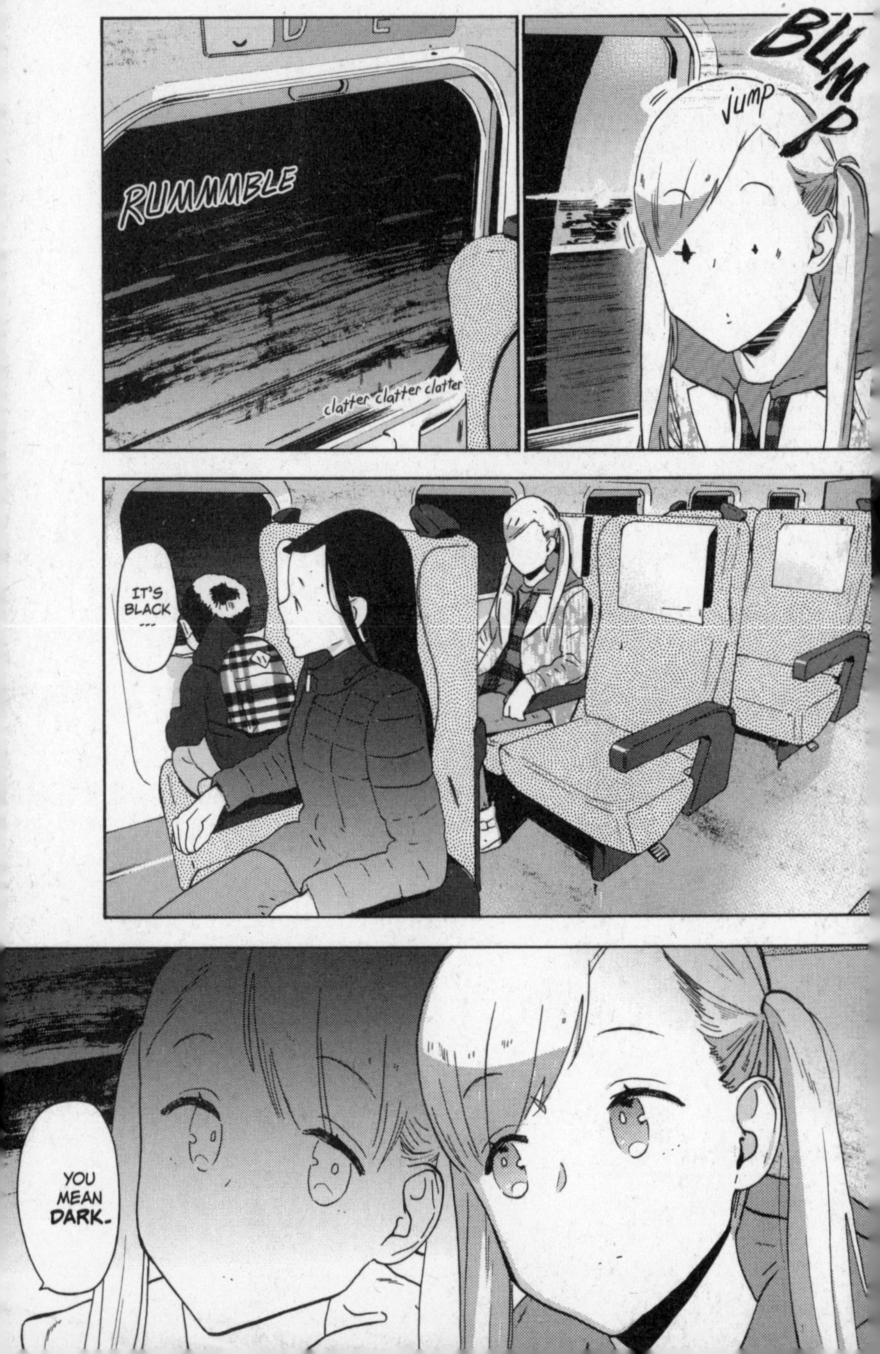
BUMP
jump
RUMMMBLE
clatter clatter clatter
IT'S BLACK ...
YOU MEAN DARK.

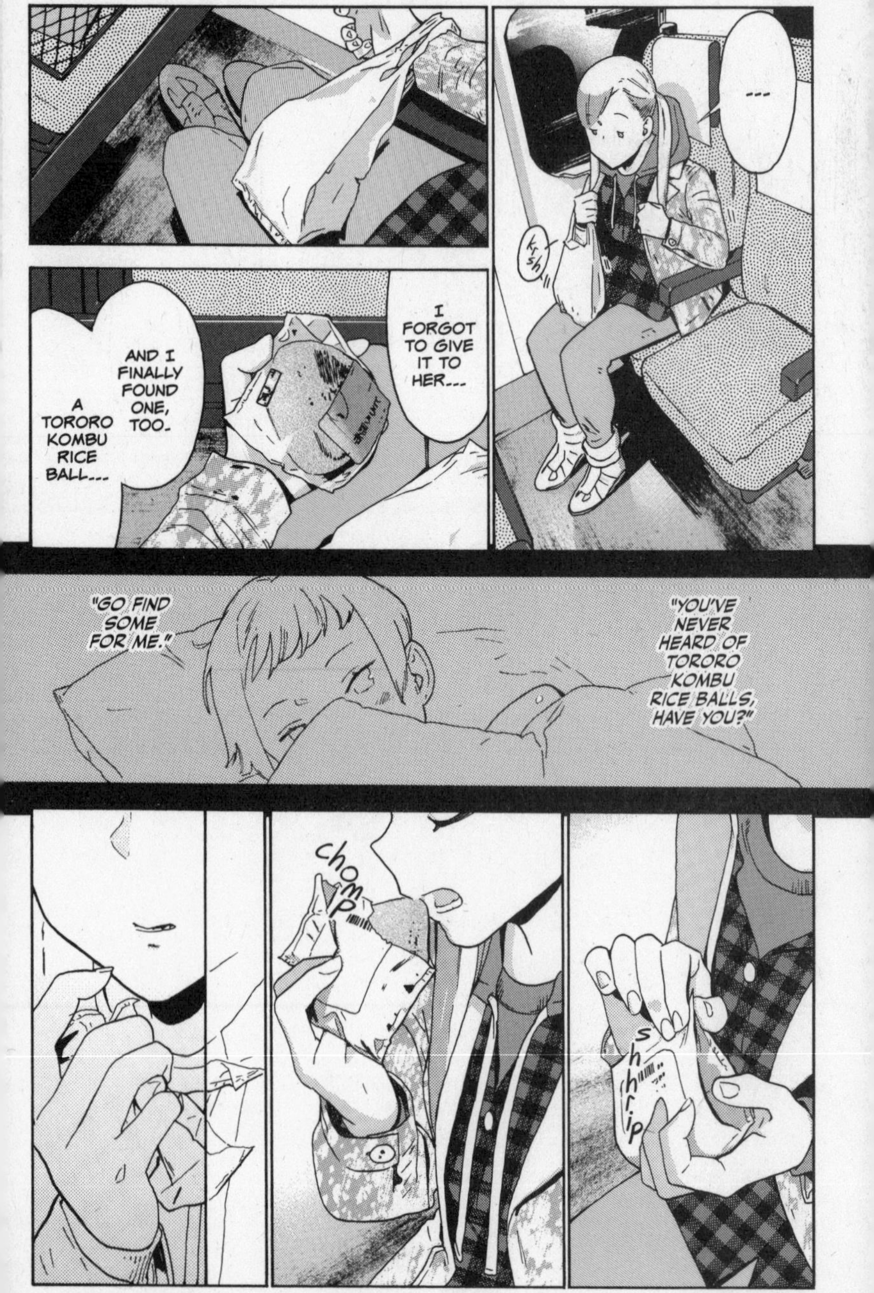
...
krsh
I FORGOT TO GIVE IT TO HER...
AND I FINALLY FOUND ONE, TOO.
A TORORO KOMBU RICE BALL...
"YOU'VE NEVER HEARD OF TORORO KOMBU RICE BALLS, HAVE YOU?"
"GO FIND SOME FOR ME."
shhrip
chomp

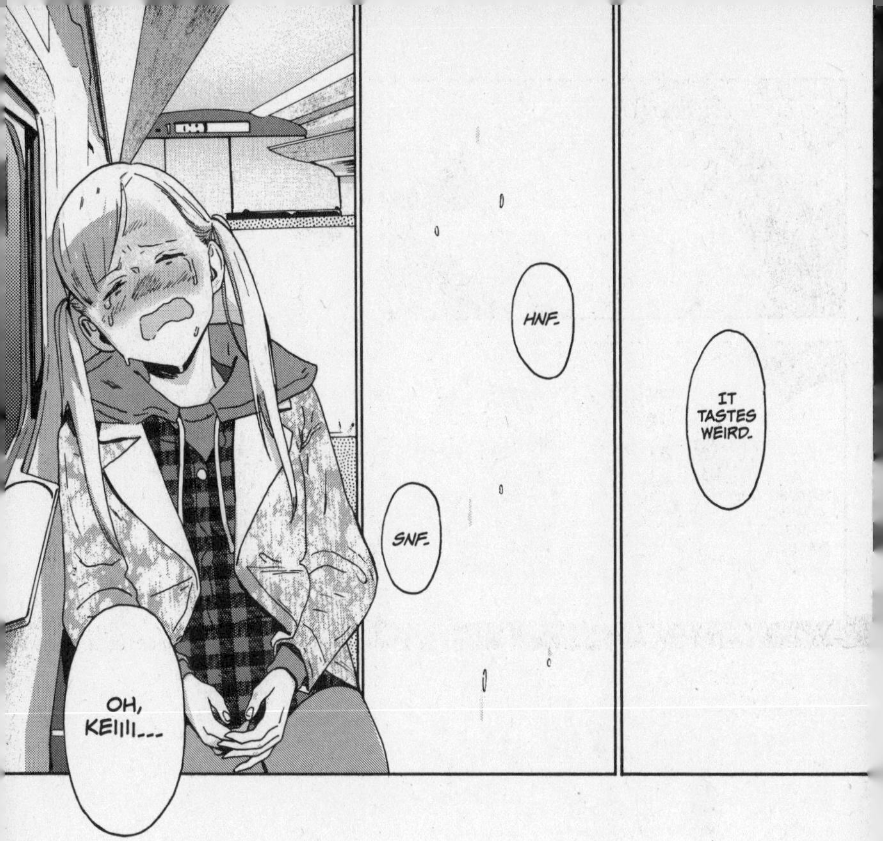
IT TASTES WEIRD...
HNF...
SNF...
OH, KEIIII...

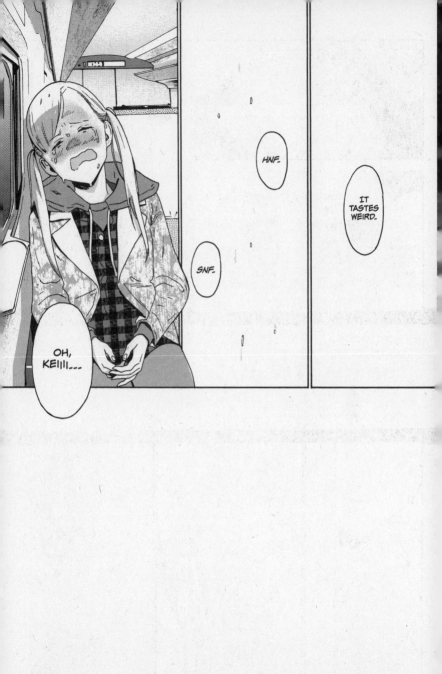

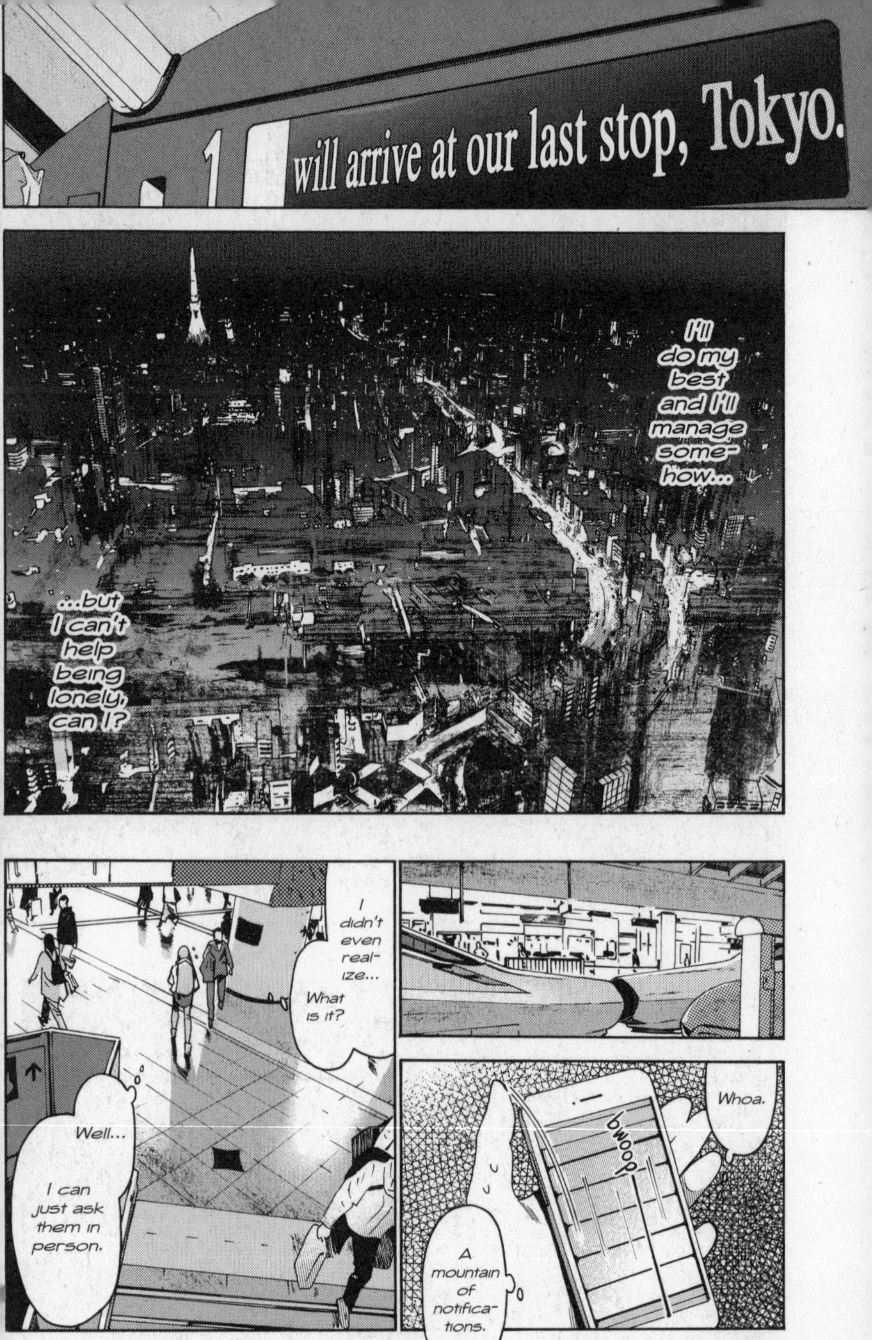
will arrive at our last stop, Tokyo.
I'll do my best and I'll manage some-how...
...but I can't help being lonely, can I?
Whoa.
bwoop
A mountain of notifica-tions.
I didn't even real-ize...
What is it?
Well...
I can just ask them in person.

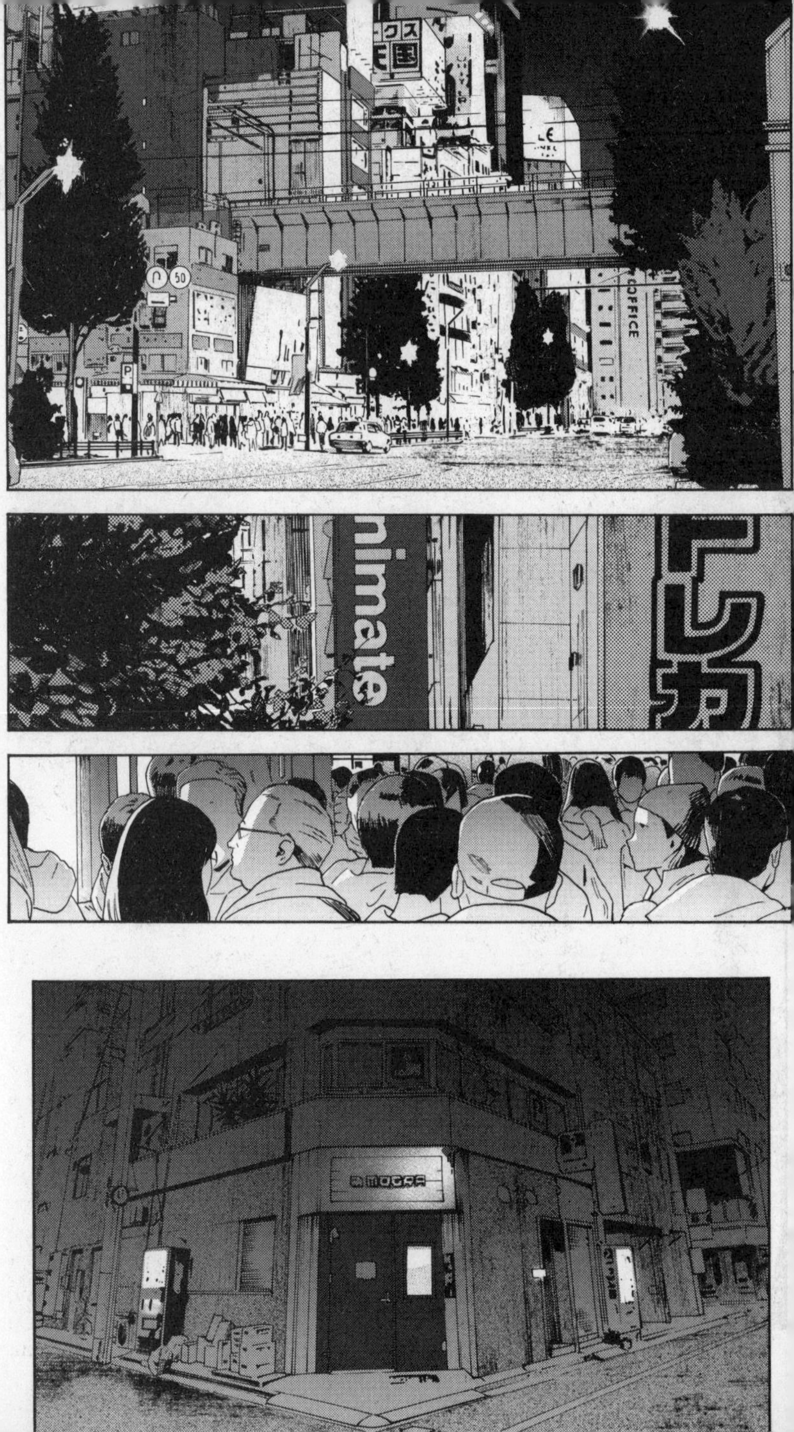
OFFICE
nimate
MOGRA

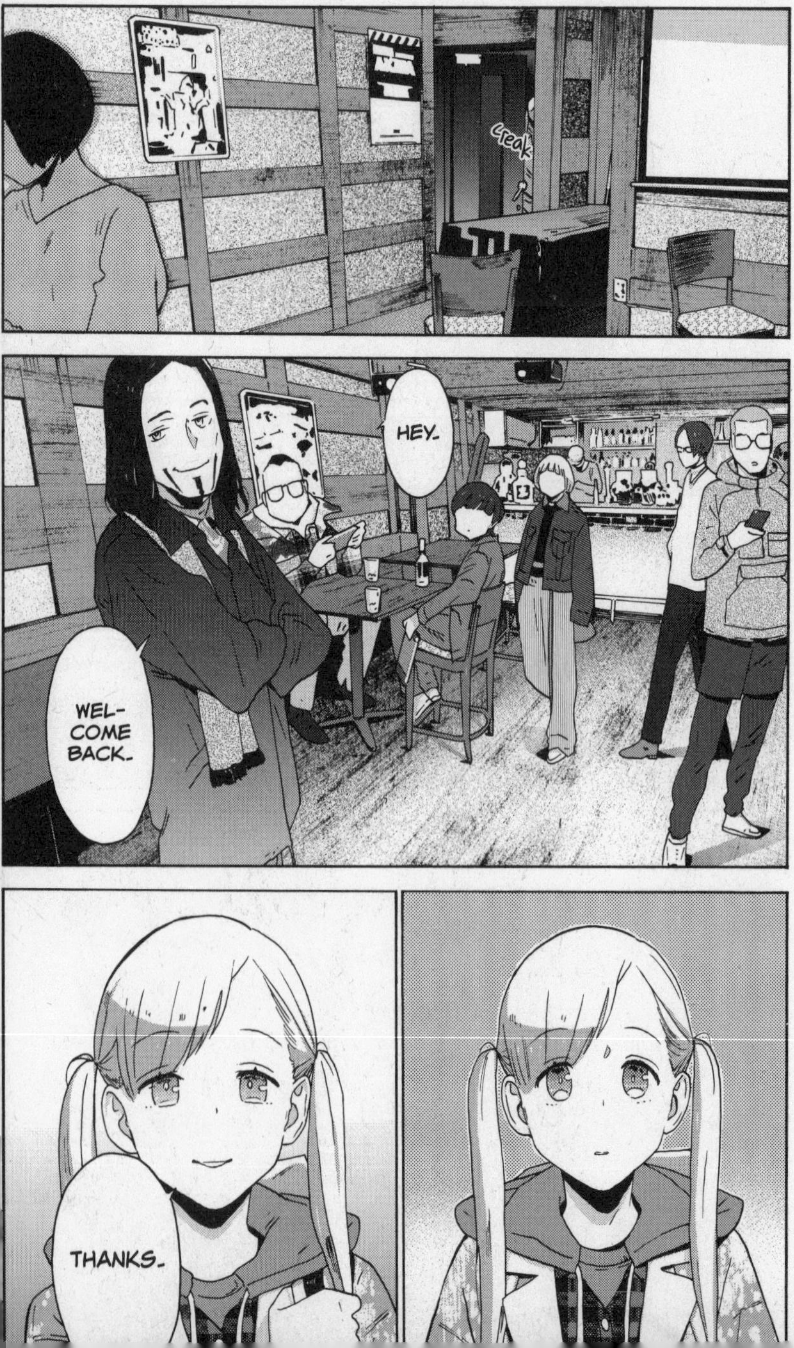
creak
HEY.
WEL-COME BACK.
THANKS.

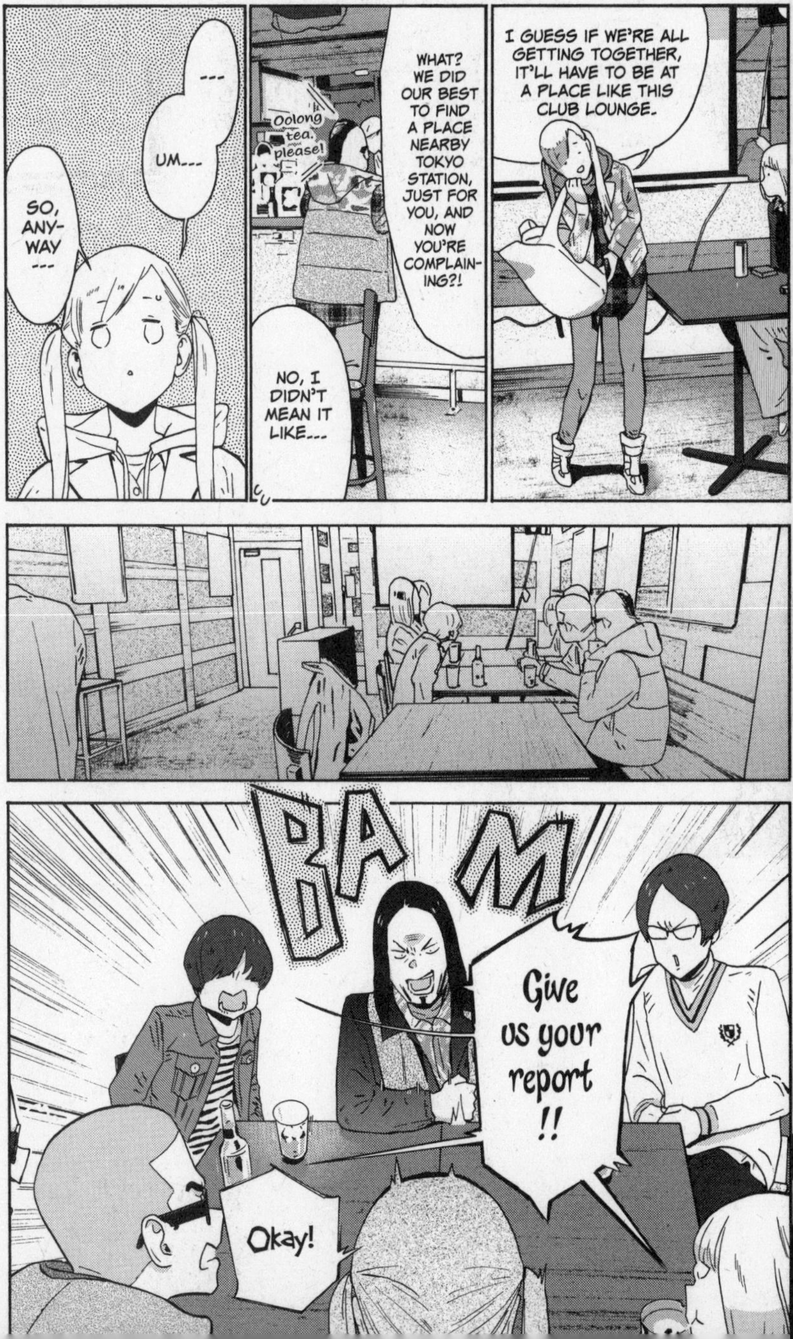
I GUESS IF WE'RE ALL GETTING TOGETHER, IT'LL HAVE TO BE AT A PLACE LIKE THIS CLUB LOUNGE.
WHAT? WE DID OUR BEST TO FIND A PLACE NEARBY TOKYO STATION, JUST FOR YOU, AND NOW YOU'RE COMPLAINING?!
Oolong tea, please!
NO, I DIDN'T MEAN IT LIKE...
...
UM...
SO, ANYWAY...
BAM
Give us your report !!
Okay!

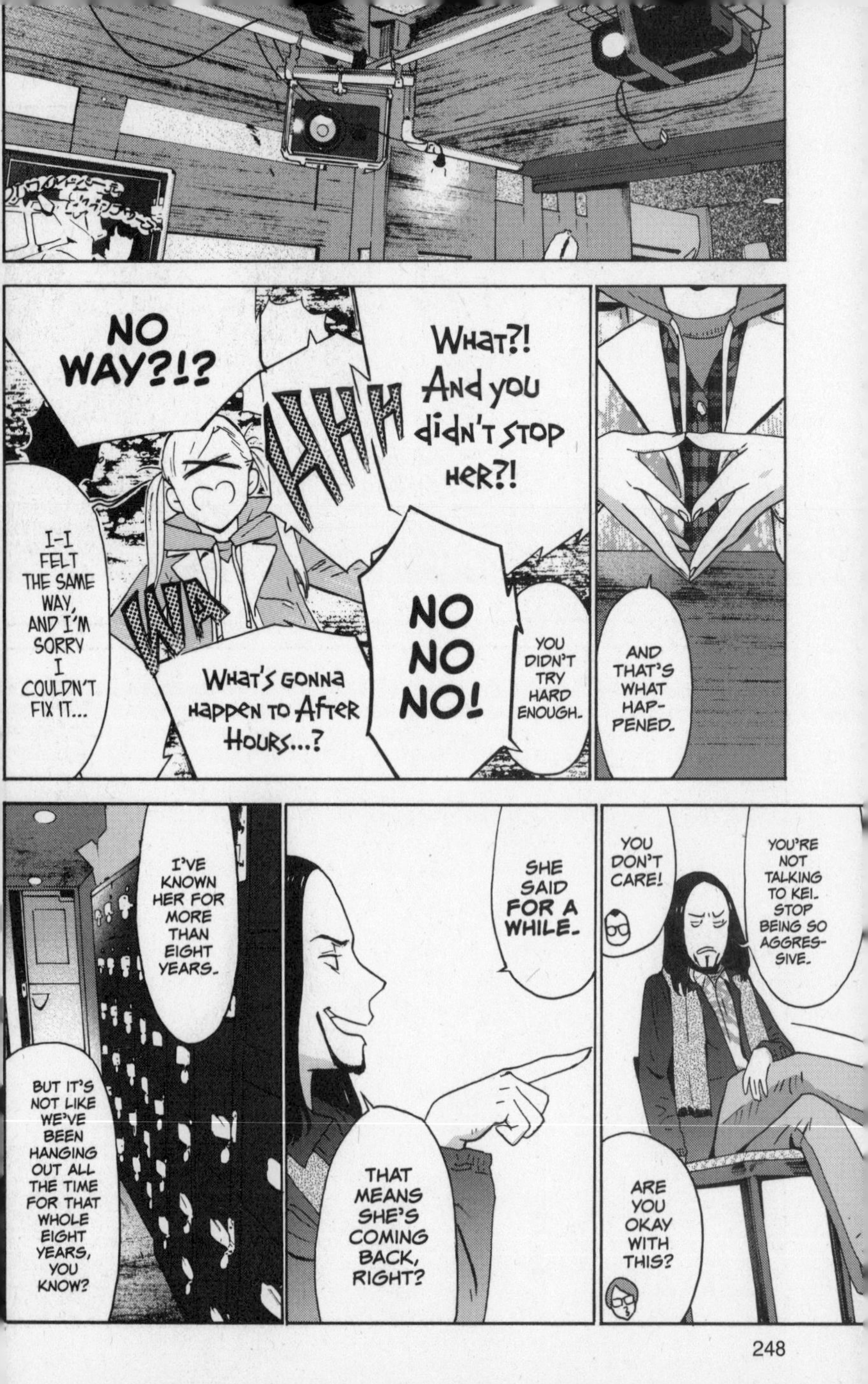
AND THAT'S WHAT HAP-PENED.
WHAT?! And you didn't STOP her?!
NO WAY?!?
YOU DIDN'T TRY HARD ENOUGH.
NO NO NO!
What's gonna happen to After Hours...?
I-I FELT THE SAME WAY, AND I'M SORRY I COULDN'T FIX IT...
YOU'RE NOT TALKING TO KEI. STOP BEING SO AGGRES-SIVE.
YOU DON'T CARE!
ARE YOU OKAY WITH THIS?
SHE SAID FOR A WHILE.
THAT MEANS SHE'S COMING BACK, RIGHT?
I'VE KNOWN HER FOR MORE THAN EIGHT YEARS.
BUT IT'S NOT LIKE WE'VE BEEN HANGING OUT ALL THE TIME FOR THAT WHOLE EIGHT YEARS, YOU KNOW?

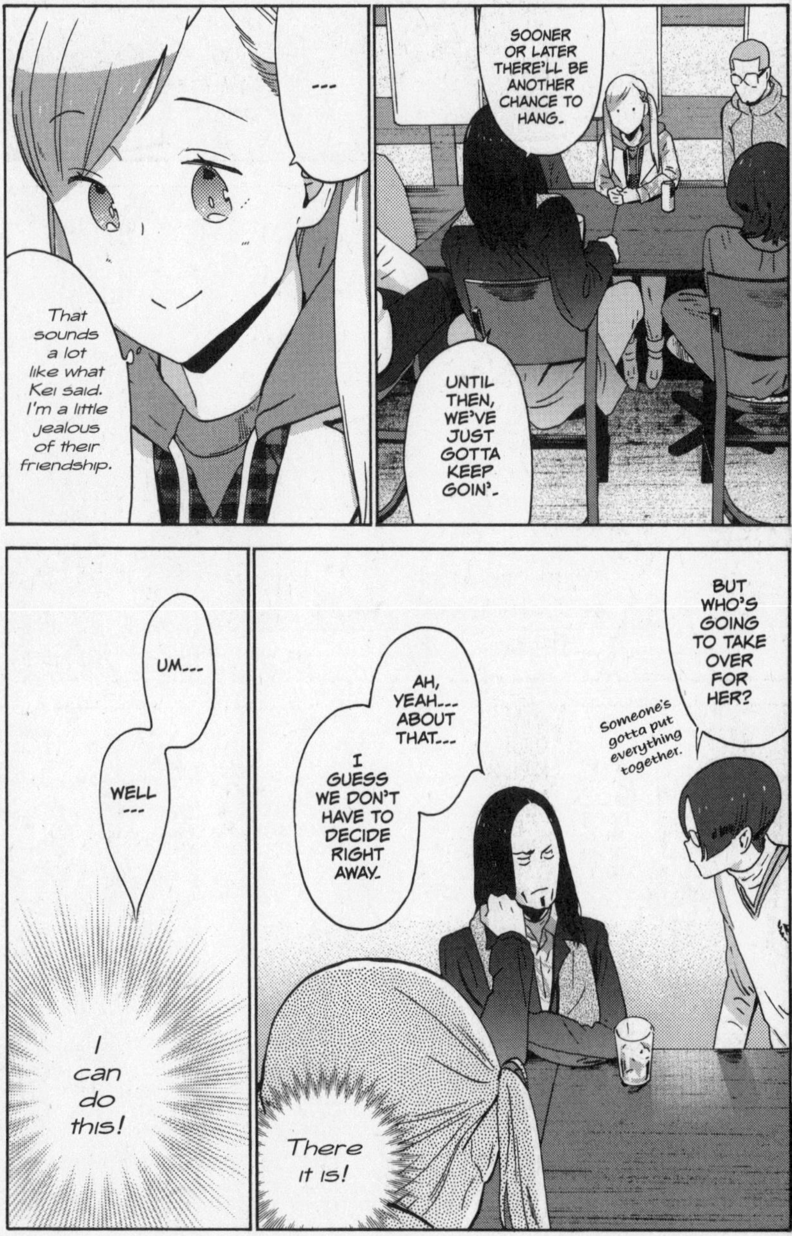
SOONER OR LATER THERE'LL BE ANOTHER CHANCE TO HANG.
UNTIL THEN, WE'VE JUST GOTTA KEEP GOIN'.
...
That sounds a lot like what Kei said. I'm a little jealous of their friendship.
BUT WHO'S GOING TO TAKE OVER FOR HER?
Someone's gotta put everything together.
AH, YEAH... ABOUT THAT...
I GUESS WE DON'T HAVE TO DECIDE RIGHT AWAY.
There it is!
UM...
WELL...
I can do this!

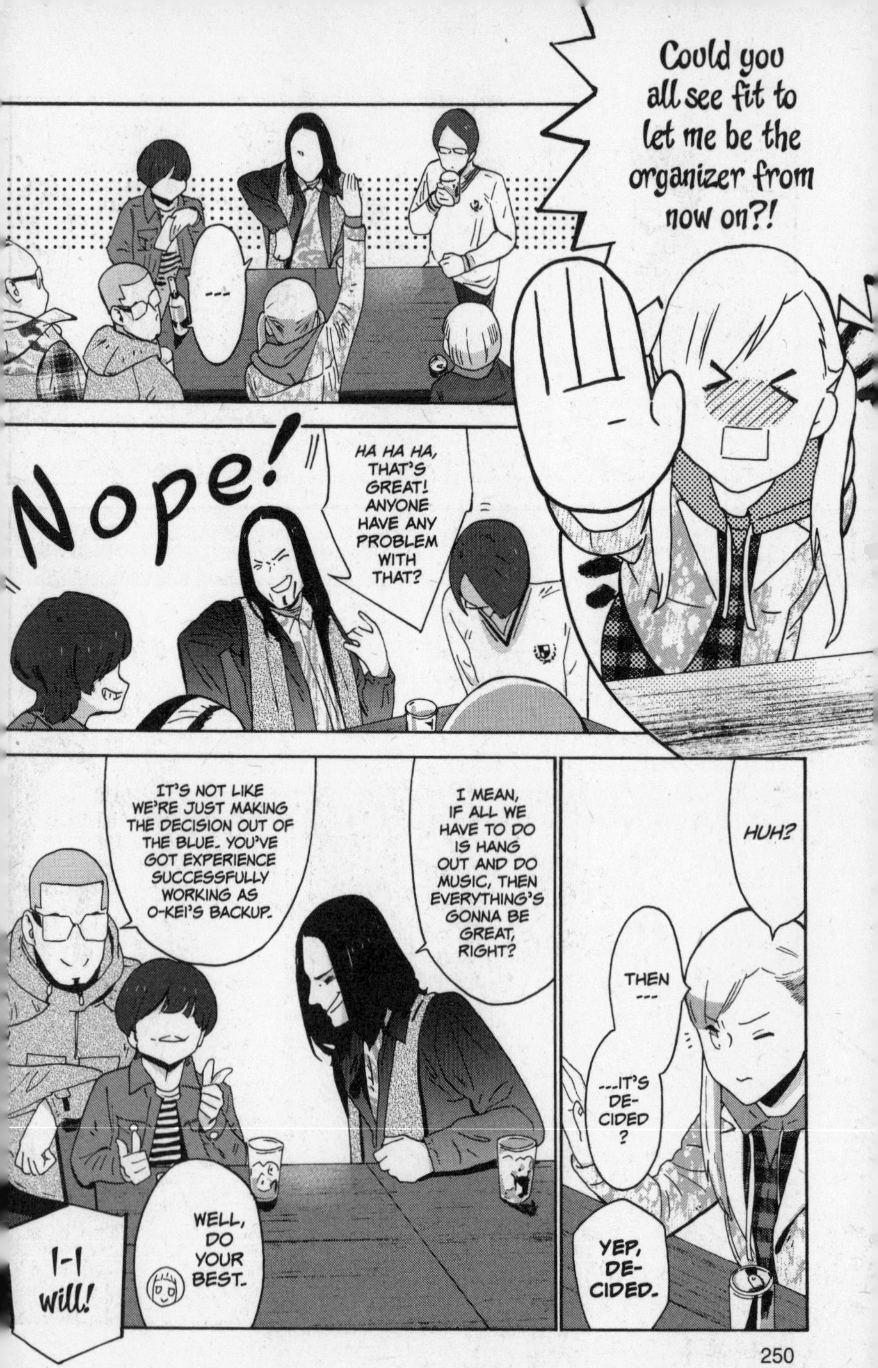
Could you all see fit to let me be the organizer from now on?!

HA HA HA, THAT'S GREAT! ANYONE HAVE ANY PROBLEM WITH THAT?
Nope!
HUH?
THEN ---
---IT'S DE-CIDED ?
YEP, DE-CIDED.
I MEAN, IF ALL WE HAVE TO DO IS HANG OUT AND DO MUSIC, THEN EVERYTHING'S GONNA BE GREAT, RIGHT?
IT'S NOT LIKE WE'RE JUST MAKING THE DECISION OUT OF THE BLUE. YOU'VE GOT EXPERIENCE SUCCESSFULLY WORKING AS O-KEI'S BACKUP.
WELL, DO YOUR BEST.
I-I will!

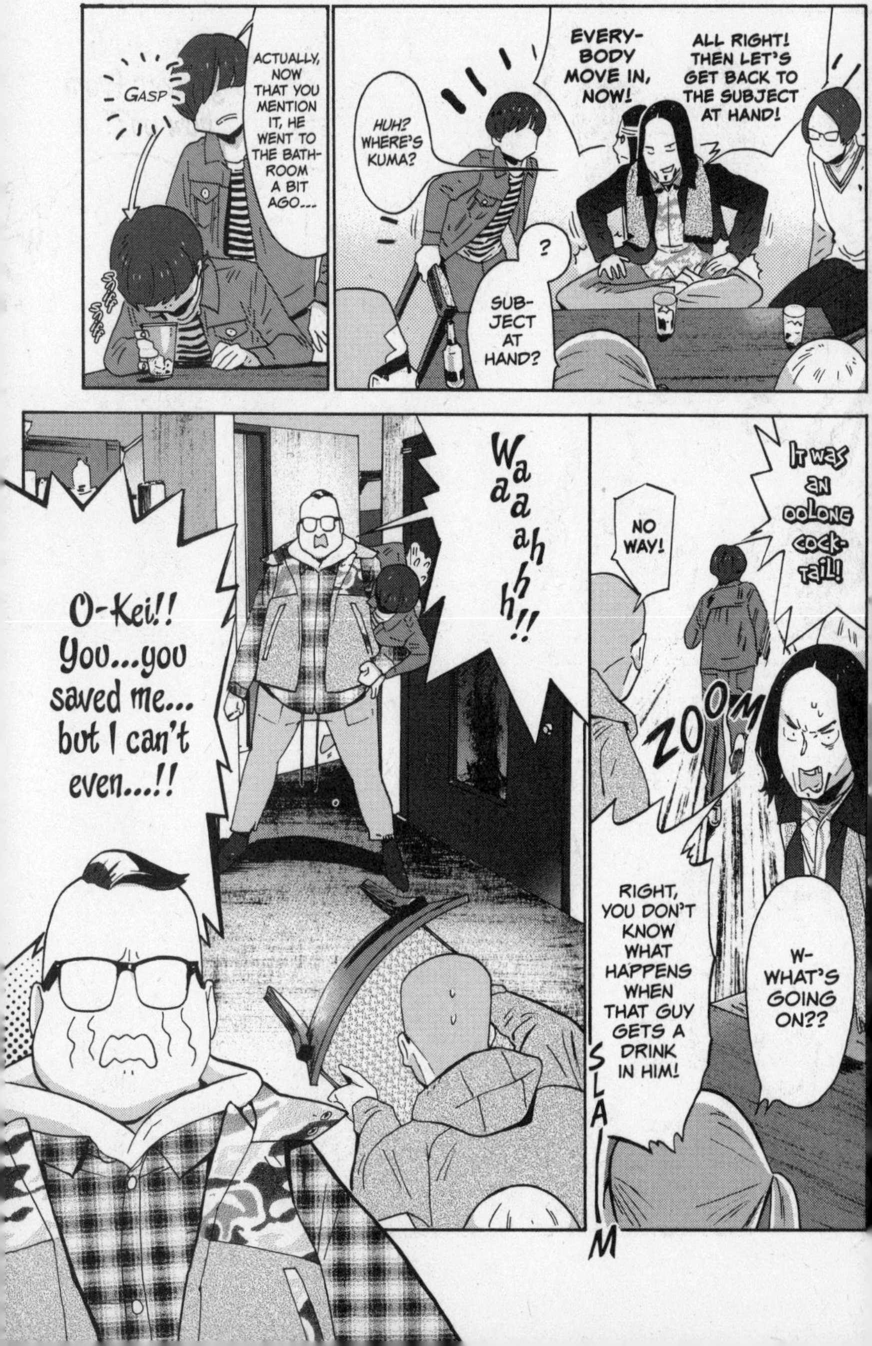
ALL RIGHT! THEN LET'S GET BACK TO THE SUBJECT AT HAND!
EVERY-BODY MOVE IN, NOW!
HUH? WHERE'S KUMA?
?
SUB-JECT AT HAND?
GASP
ACTUALLY, NOW THAT YOU MENTION IT, HE WENT TO THE BATH-ROOM A BIT AGO...
It was an oolong cock-tail!
NO WAY!
ZOOM
W-WHAT'S GOING ON??
RIGHT, YOU DON'T KNOW WHAT HAPPENS WHEN THAT GUY GETS A DRINK IN HIM!
SLAM
Waaaahhh!!
O-Kei!! You...you saved me... but I can't even...!!

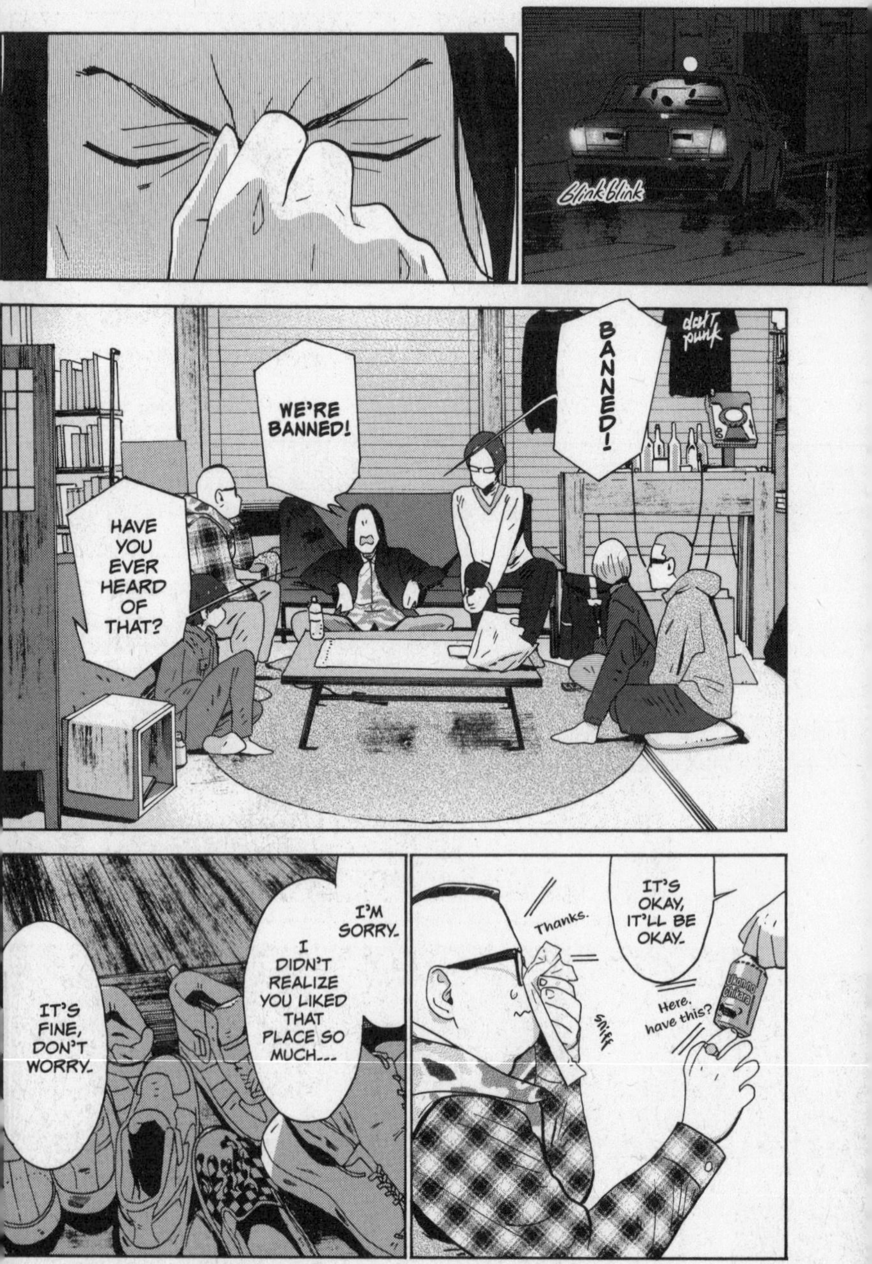
blinkblink
BANNED!
WE'RE BANNED!
HAVE YOU EVER HEARD OF THAT?
IT'S OKAY, IT'LL BE OKAY.
Thanks.
Here, have this?
Ukon no chikara
sniff
I'M SORRY.
I DIDN'T REALIZE YOU LIKED THAT PLACE SO MUCH...
IT'S FINE, DON'T WORRY.

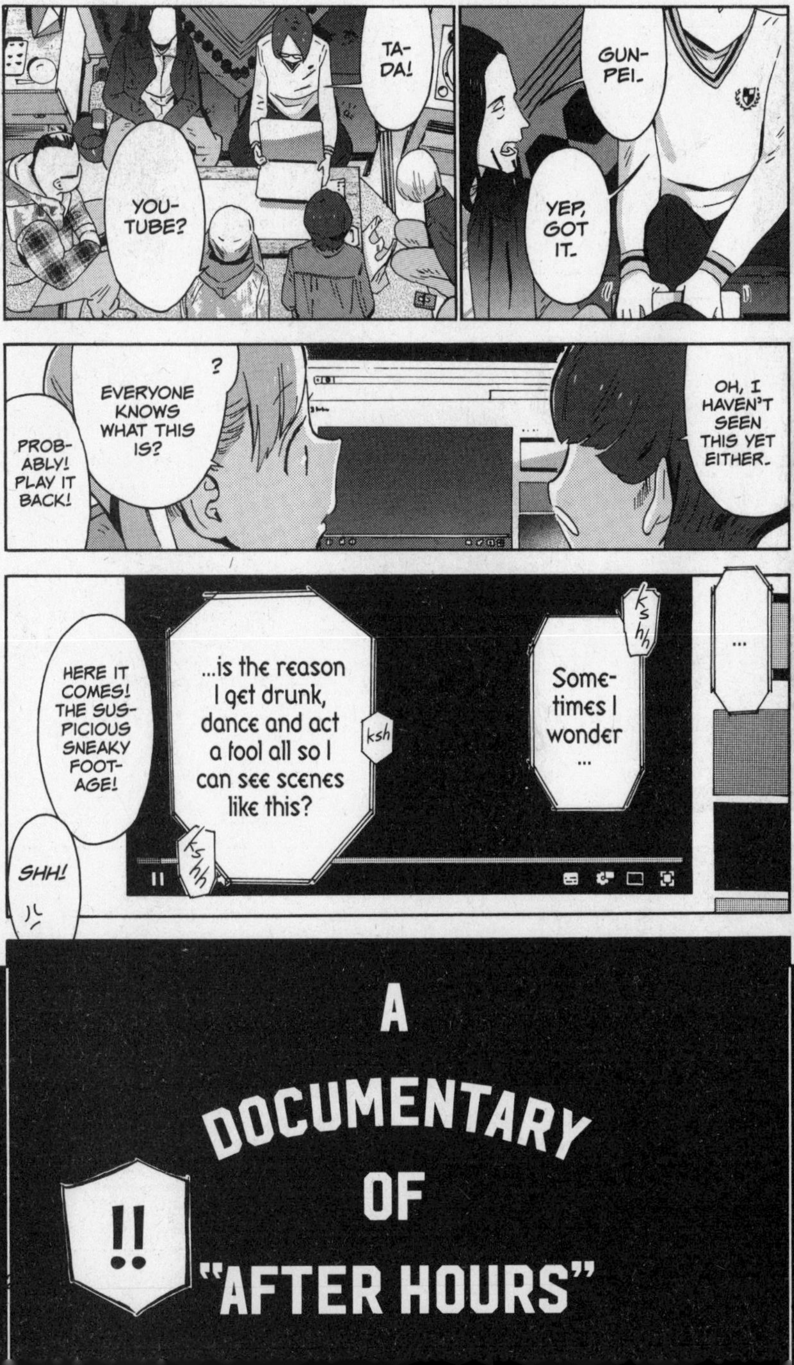
GUN-PEI.
YEP, GOT IT.
TA-DA!
YOU-TUBE?
OH, I HAVEN'T SEEN THIS YET EITHER.
?
EVERYONE KNOWS WHAT THIS IS?
PROBABLY! PLAY IT BACK!
...
Some-times I wonder...
kshhh
...is the reason I get drunk, dance and act a fool all so I can see scenes like this?
ksh
kshhh
HERE IT COMES! THE SUS-PICIOUS SNEAKY FOOT-AGE!
SHH!
!!
A DOCUMENTARY OF "AFTER HOURS"

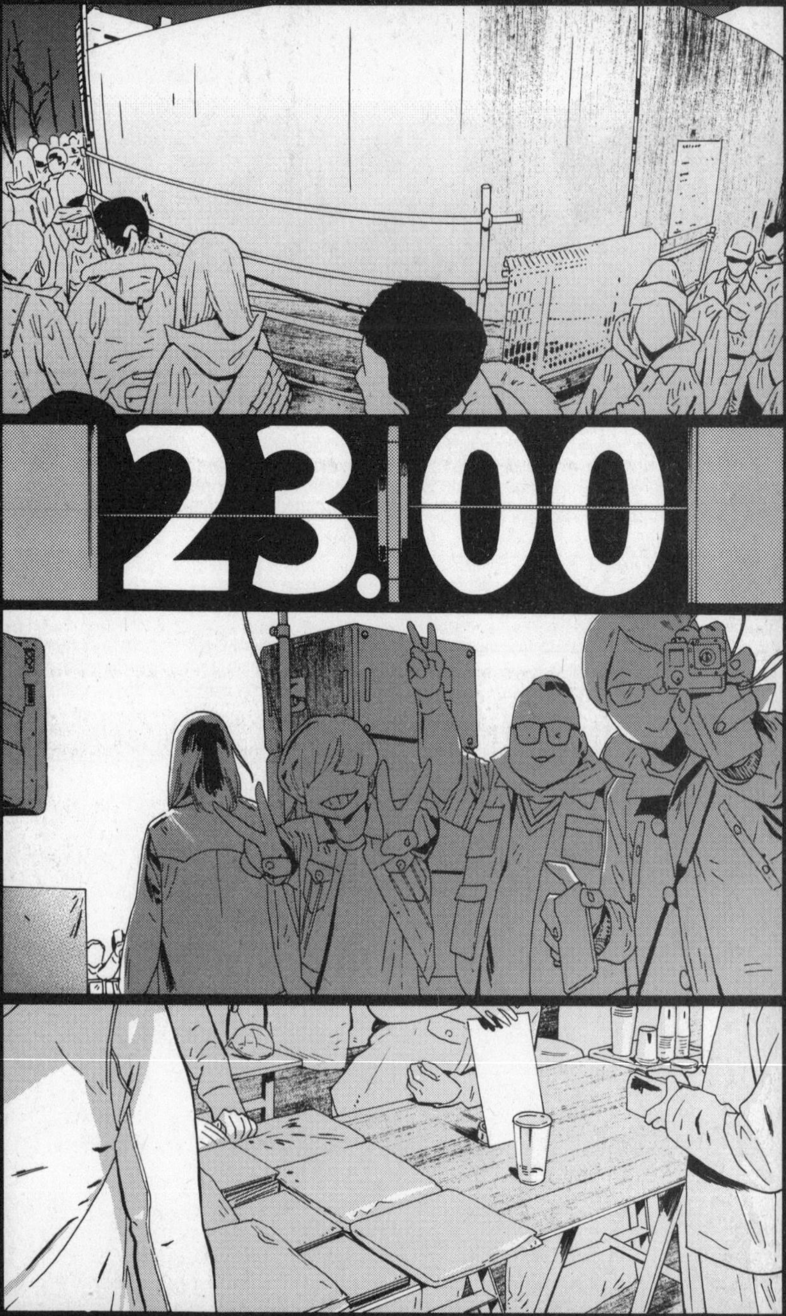
23.00

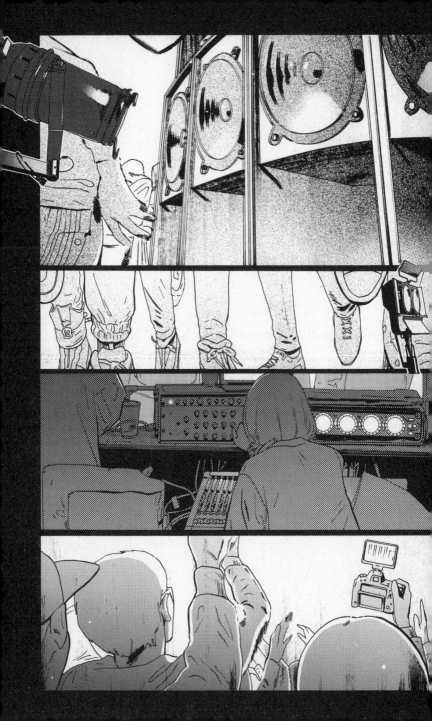

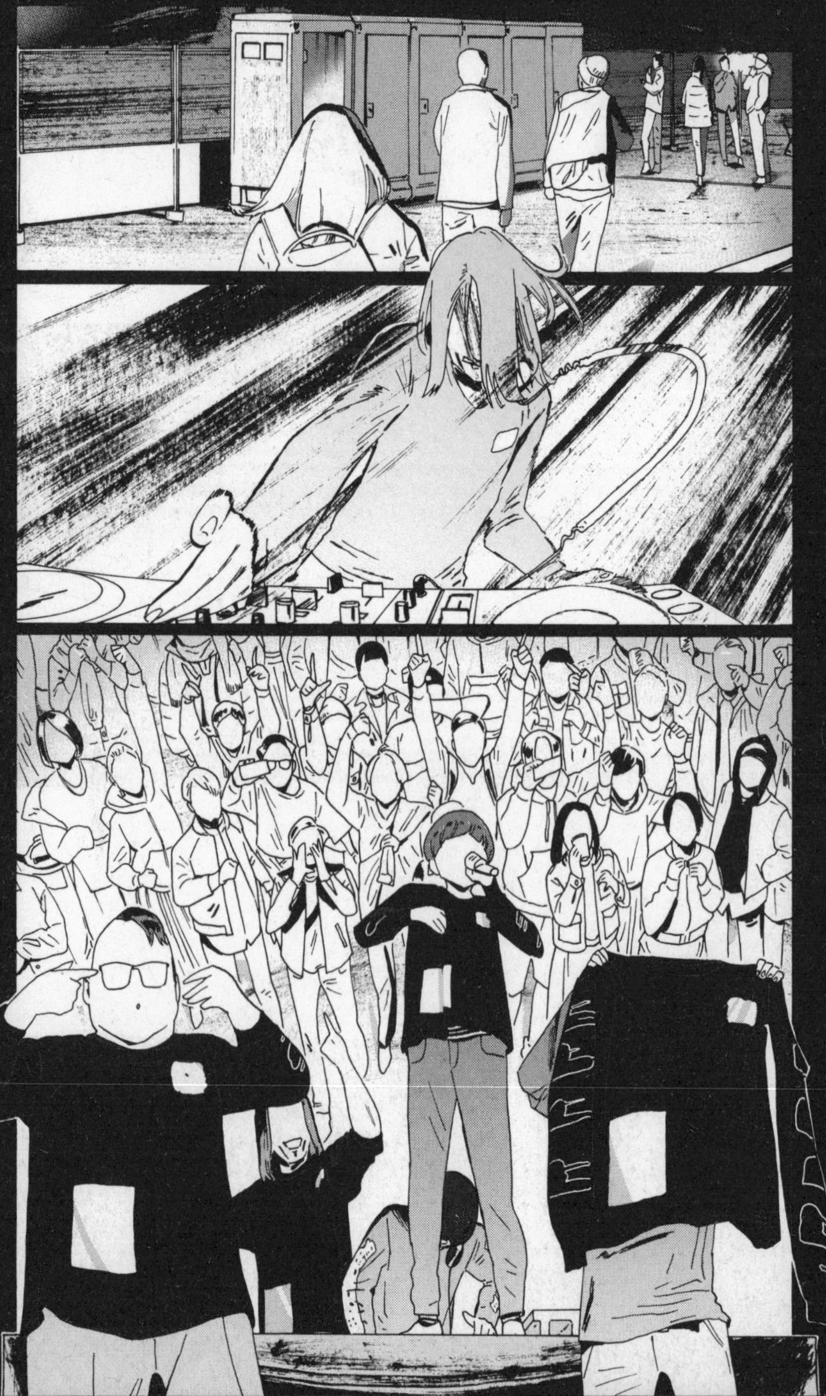

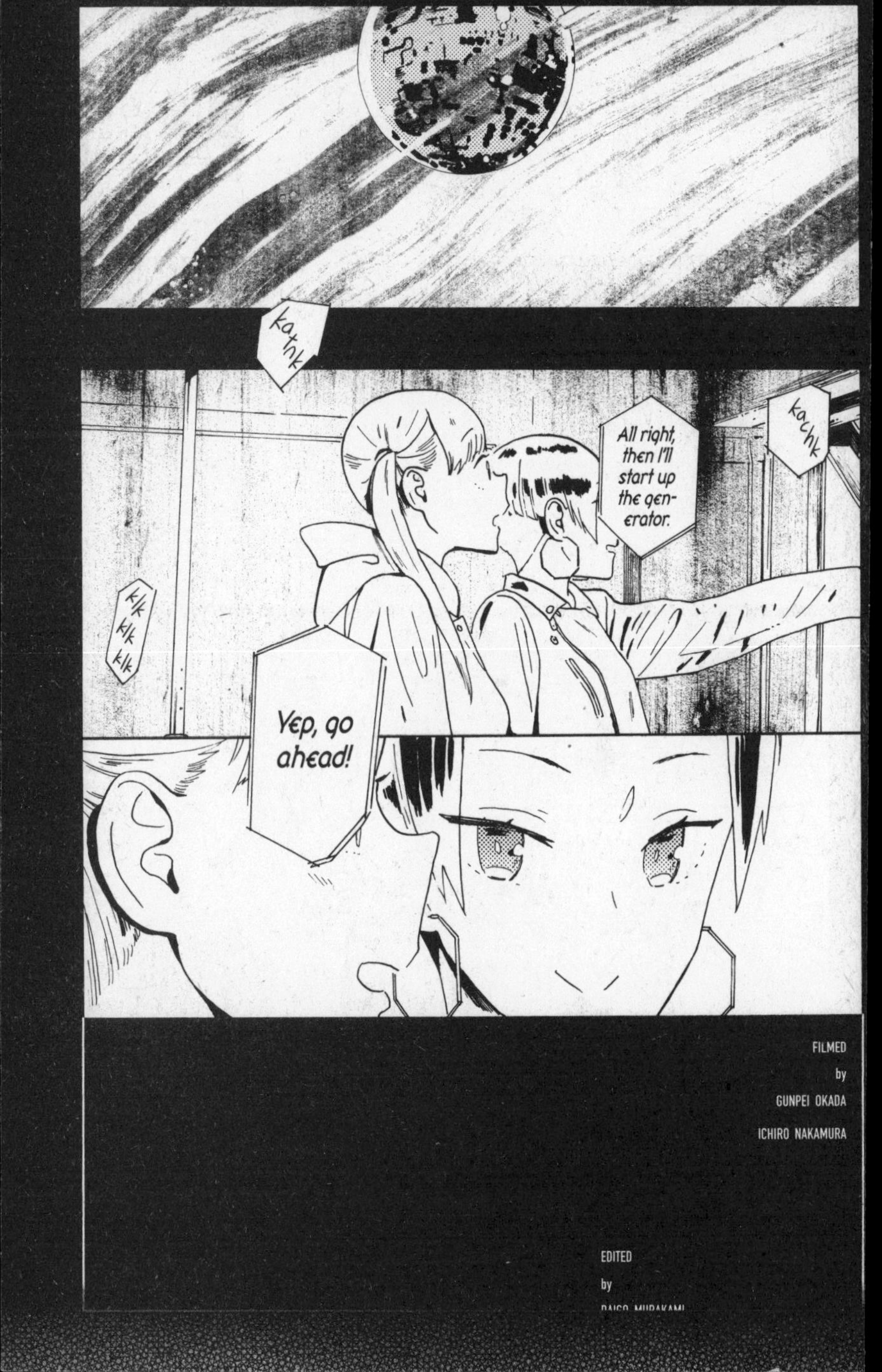
katnk
kachnk
All right, then I'll start up the gen-erator.
klk klk klk
Yep, go ahead!

FILMED

by

GUNPEI OKADA

ICHIRO NAKAMURA

EDITED

by

DAIGO MURAKAMI

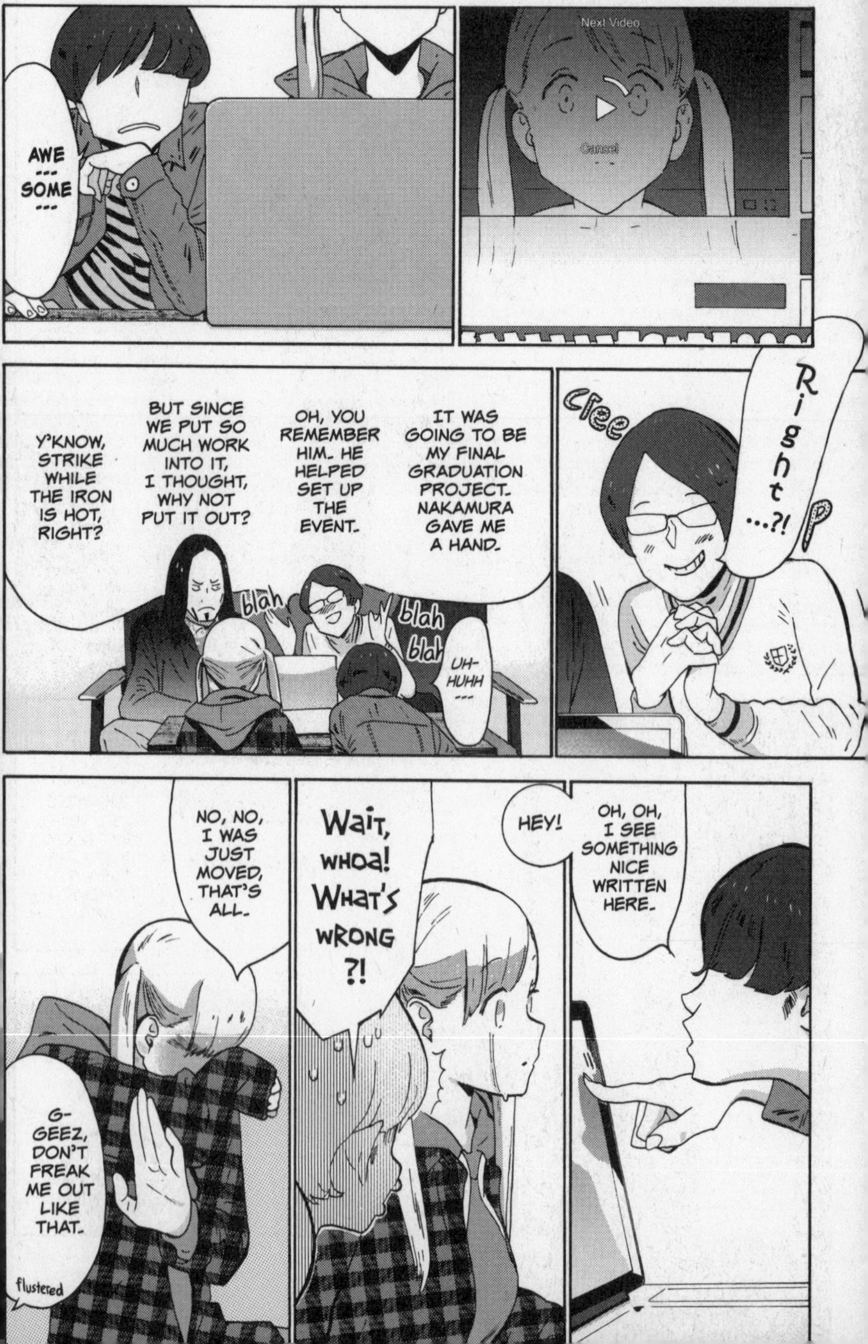
Next Video
Cancel
AWE... SOME...
Creee
Right...?!
IT WAS GOING TO BE MY FINAL GRADUATION PROJECT. NAKAMURA GAVE ME A HAND.
OH, YOU REMEMBER HIM. HE HELPED SET UP THE EVENT.
BUT SINCE WE PUT SO MUCH WORK INTO IT, I THOUGHT, WHY NOT PUT IT OUT?
Y'KNOW, STRIKE WHILE THE IRON IS HOT, RIGHT?
blah
blah
blah
UH-HUHH...
OH, OH, I SEE SOMETHING NICE WRITTEN HERE.
HEY!
Wait, whoa! What's wrong?!
NO, NO, I WAS JUST MOVED, THAT'S ALL.
G-GEEZ, DON'T FREAK ME OUT LIKE THAT.
flustered

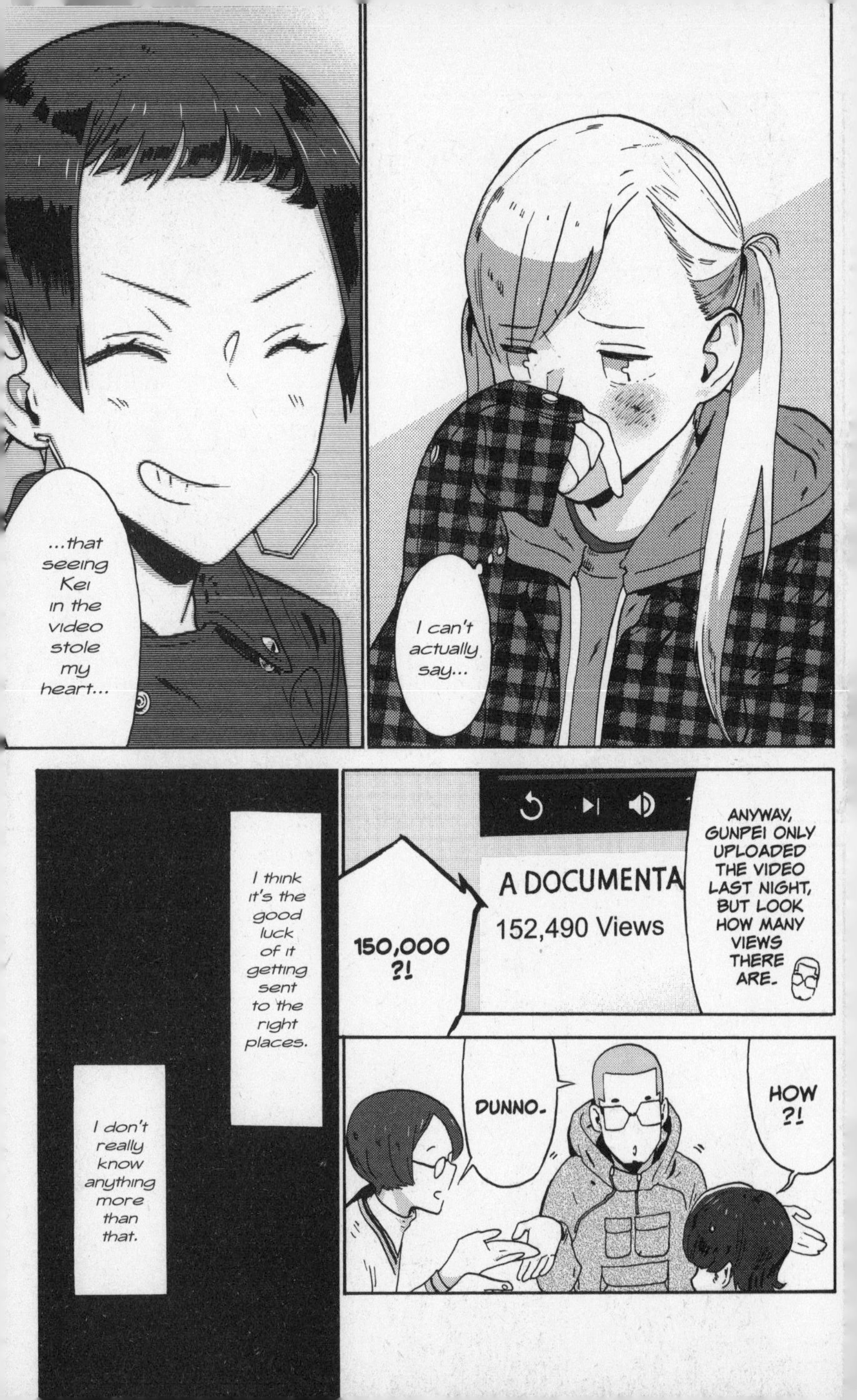
I can't actually say...
...that seeing Kei in the video stole my heart...
ANYWAY, GUNPEI ONLY UPLOADED THE VIDEO LAST NIGHT, BUT LOOK HOW MANY VIEWS THERE ARE.
A DOCUMENTA
152,490 Views
150,000 ?!
HOW ?!
DUNNO.
I think it's the good luck of it getting sent to the right places.
I don't really know anything more than that.

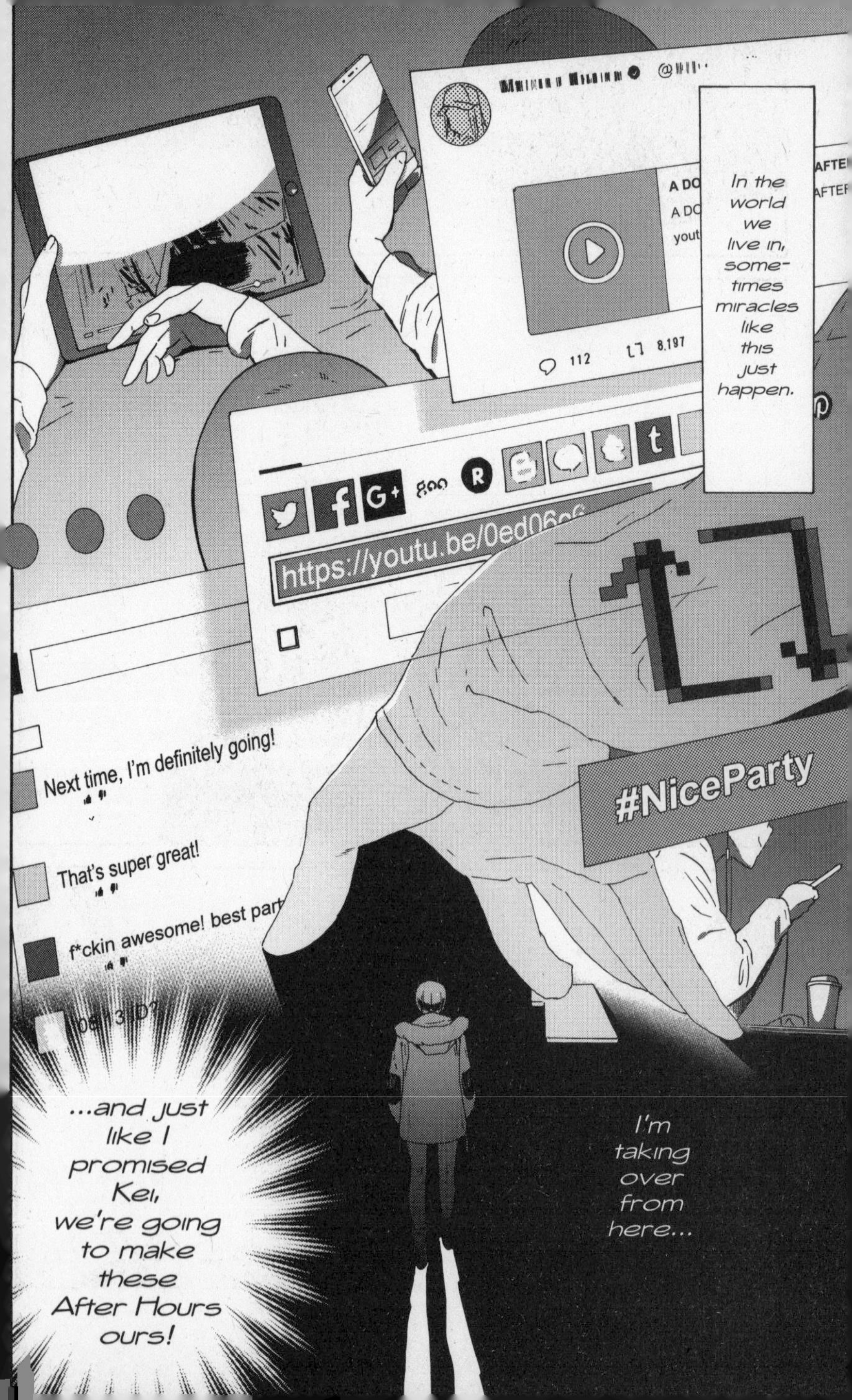
In the world we live in, sometimes miracles like this just happen.
112
8,197
https://youtu.be/0ed06
#NiceParty
Next time, I'm definitely going!
That's super great!
f*ckin awesome! best par
I'm taking over from here...
...and just like I promised Kei, we're going to make these After Hours ours!

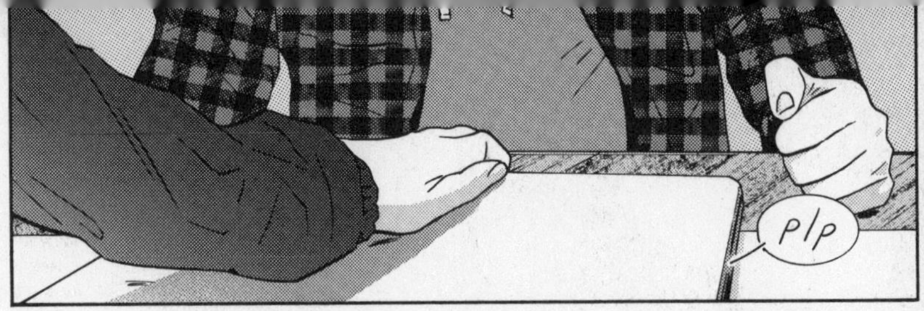
PIP

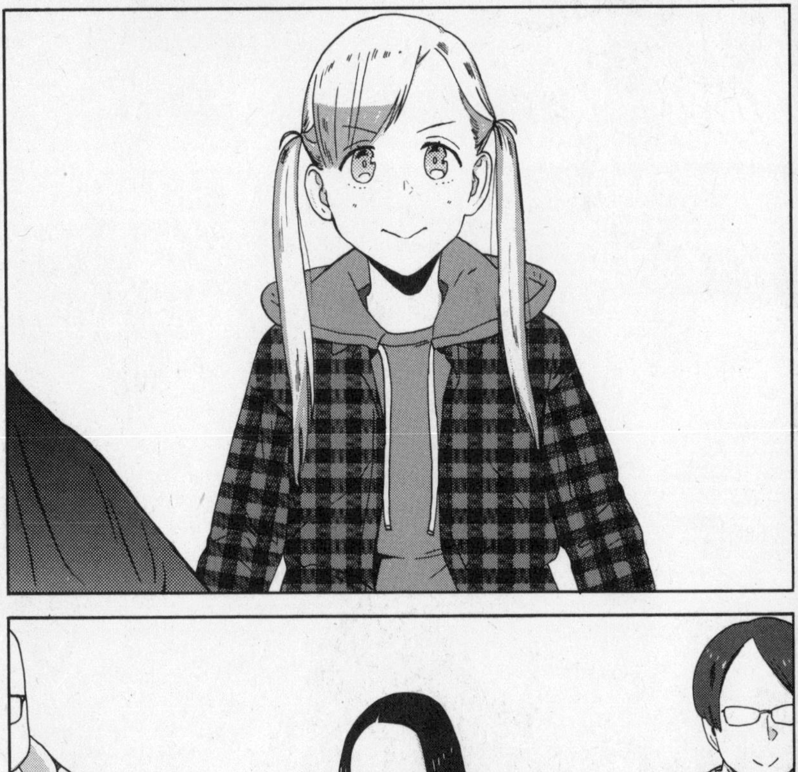

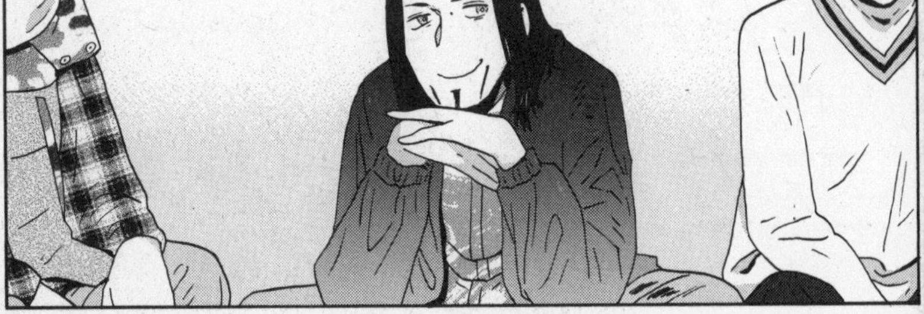

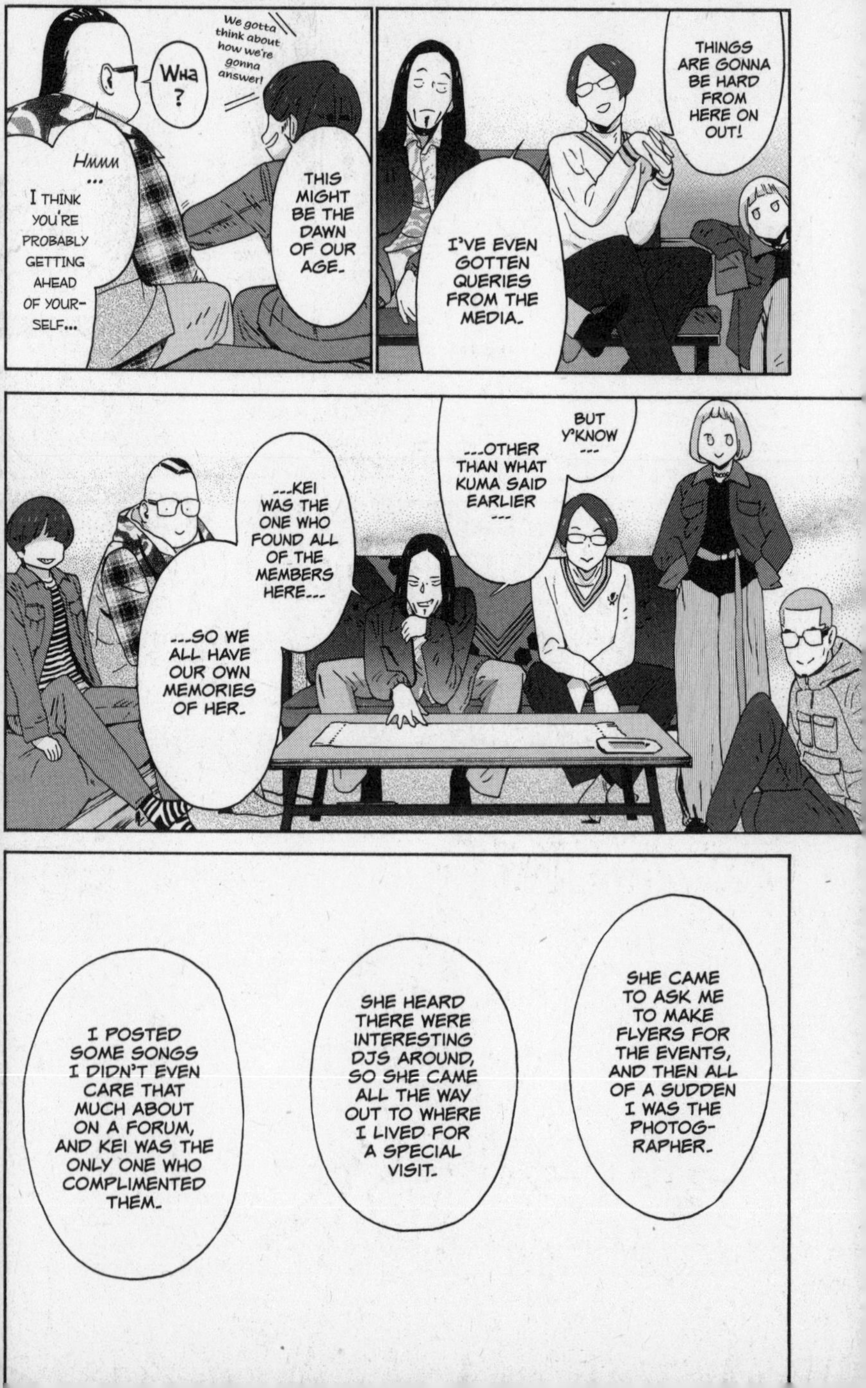
THINGS ARE GONNA BE HARD FROM HERE ON OUT!
I'VE EVEN GOTTEN QUERIES FROM THE MEDIA.
We gotta think about how we're gonna answer!
THIS MIGHT BE THE DAWN OF OUR AGE.
WHA?
HMMM... I THINK YOU'RE PROBABLY GETTING AHEAD OF YOURSELF...
BUT Y'KNOW---
---OTHER THAN WHAT KUMA SAID EARLIER---
---KEI WAS THE ONE WHO FOUND ALL OF THE MEMBERS HERE---
---SO WE ALL HAVE OUR OWN MEMORIES OF HER.
SHE CAME TO ASK ME TO MAKE FLYERS FOR THE EVENTS, AND THEN ALL OF A SUDDEN I WAS THE PHOTOGRAPHER.
SHE HEARD THERE WERE INTERESTING DJS AROUND, SO SHE CAME ALL THE WAY OUT TO WHERE I LIVED FOR A SPECIAL VISIT.
I POSTED SOME SONGS I DIDN'T EVEN CARE THAT MUCH ABOUT ON A FORUM, AND KEI WAS THE ONLY ONE WHO COMPLIMENTED THEM.

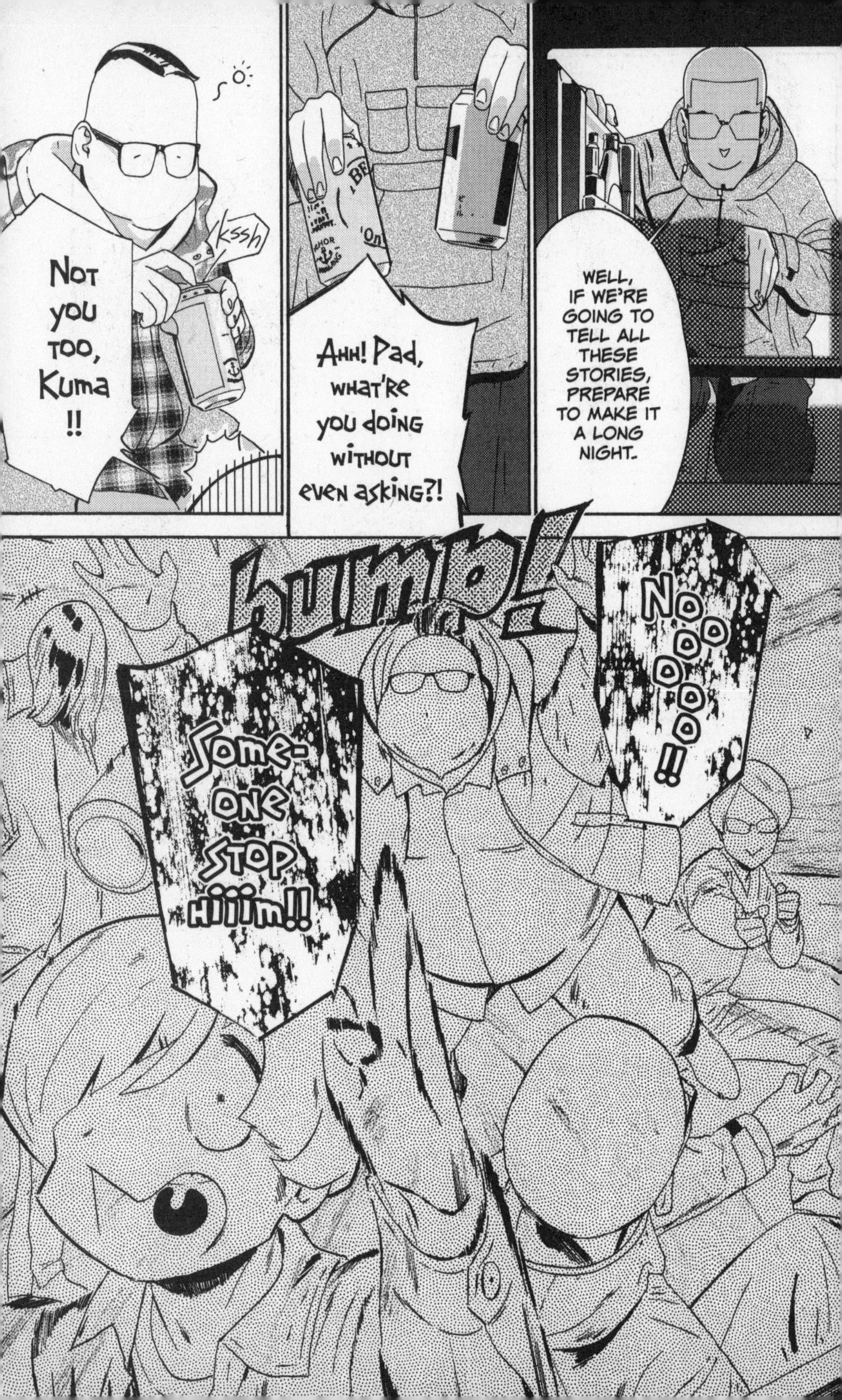
WELL, IF WE'RE GOING TO TELL ALL THESE STORIES, PREPARE TO MAKE IT A LONG NIGHT.
Ahh! Dad, what're you doing without even asking?!
kssh
Not you too, Kuma!!
bump!
NOOOOOO!!
Some-one stop hiiim!!

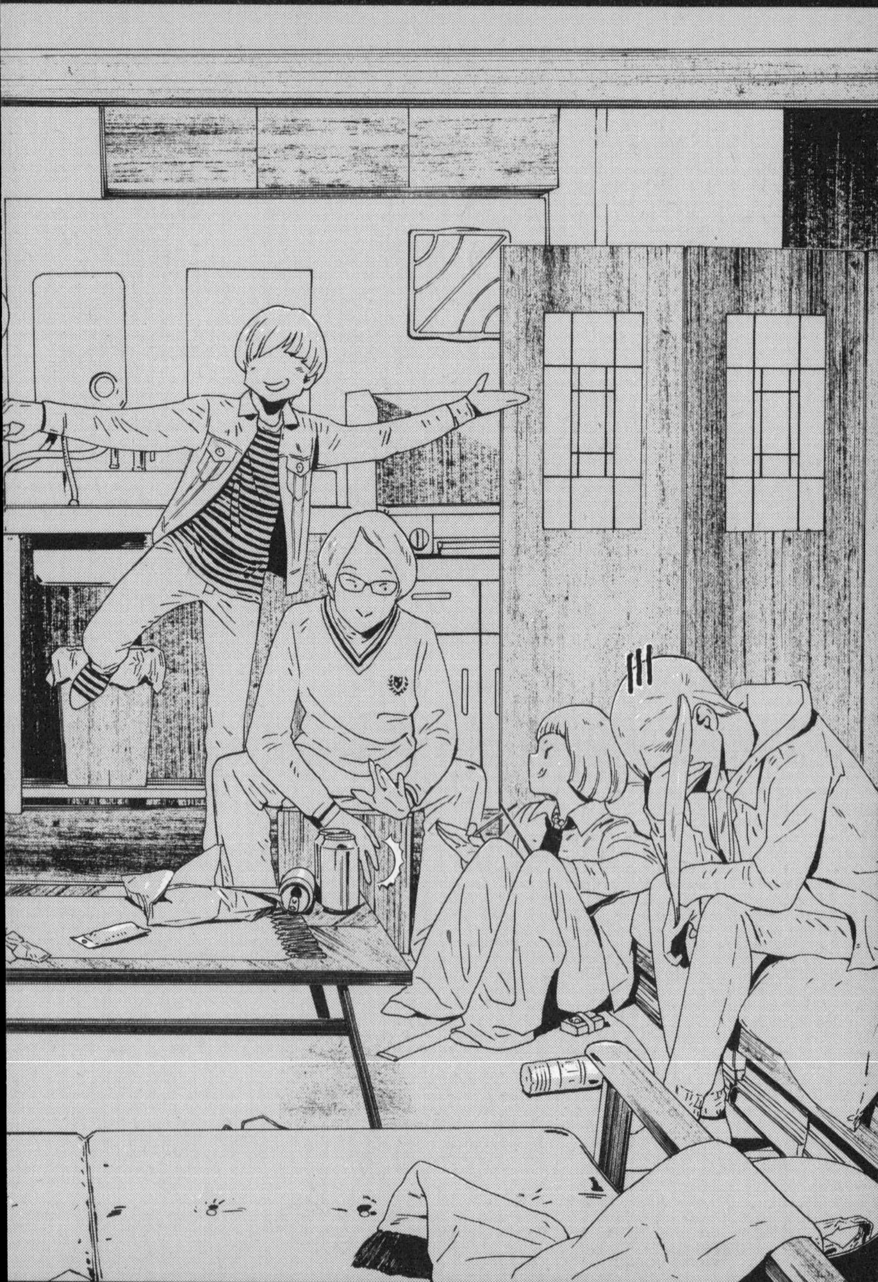

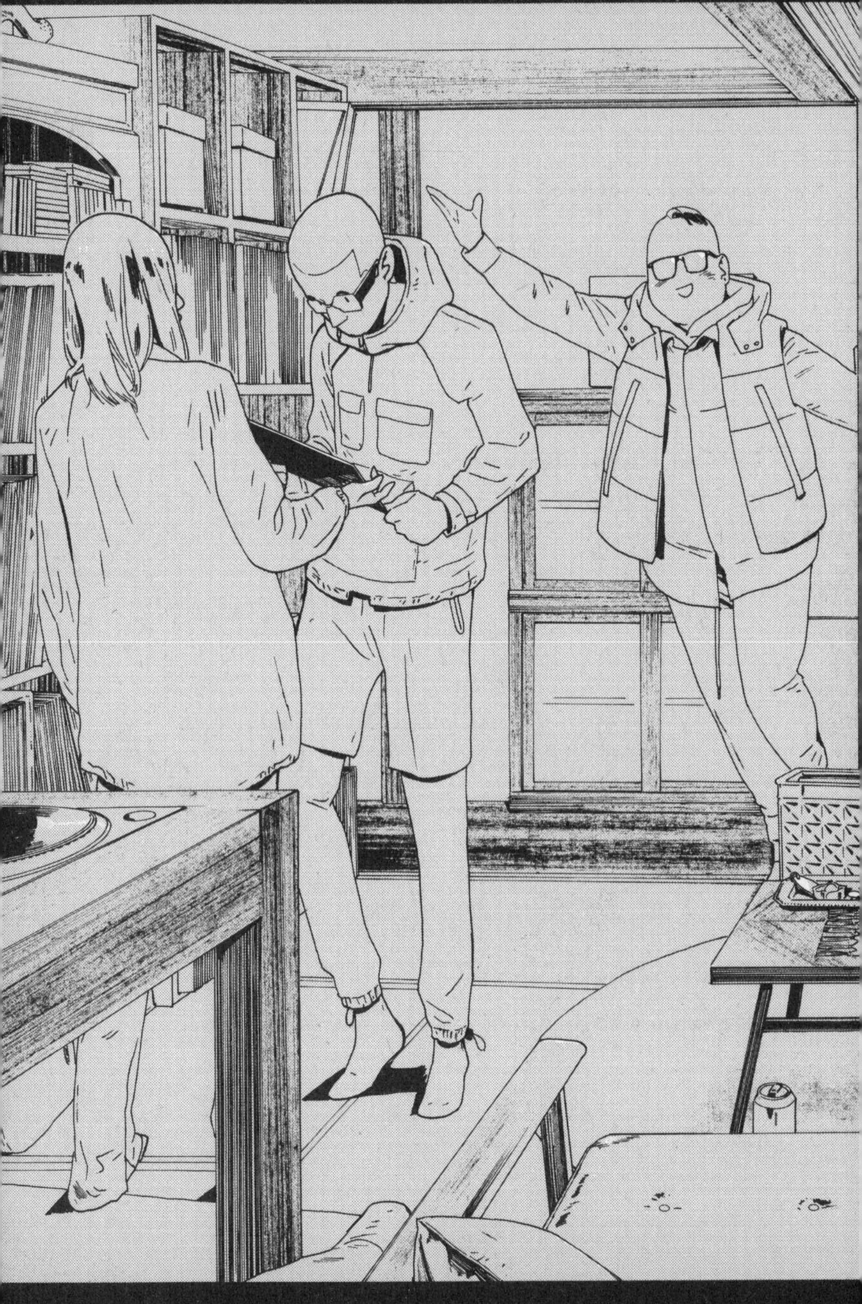

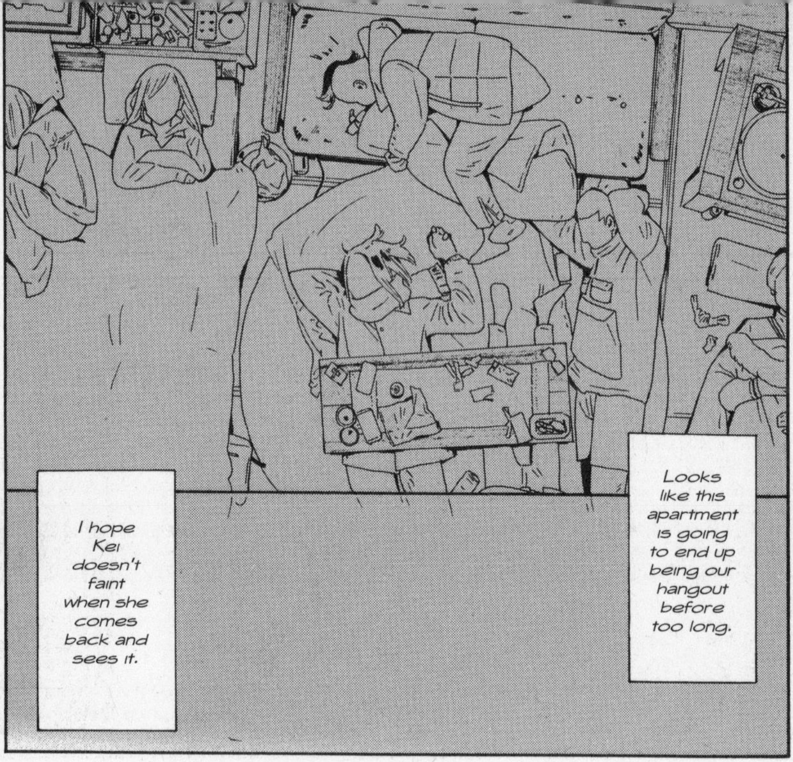
Looks like this apartment is going to end up being our hangout before too long.
I hope Kei doesn't faint when she comes back and sees it.

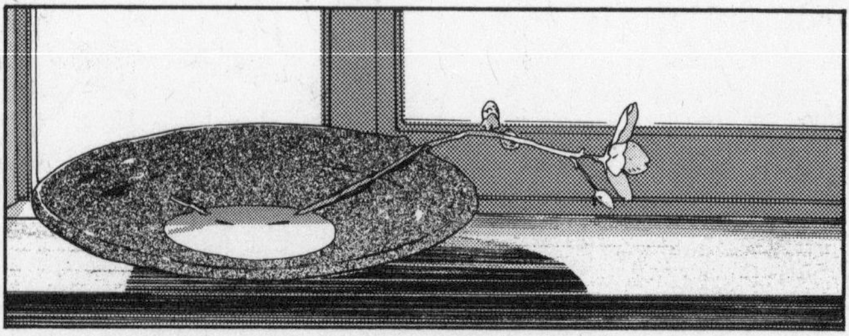

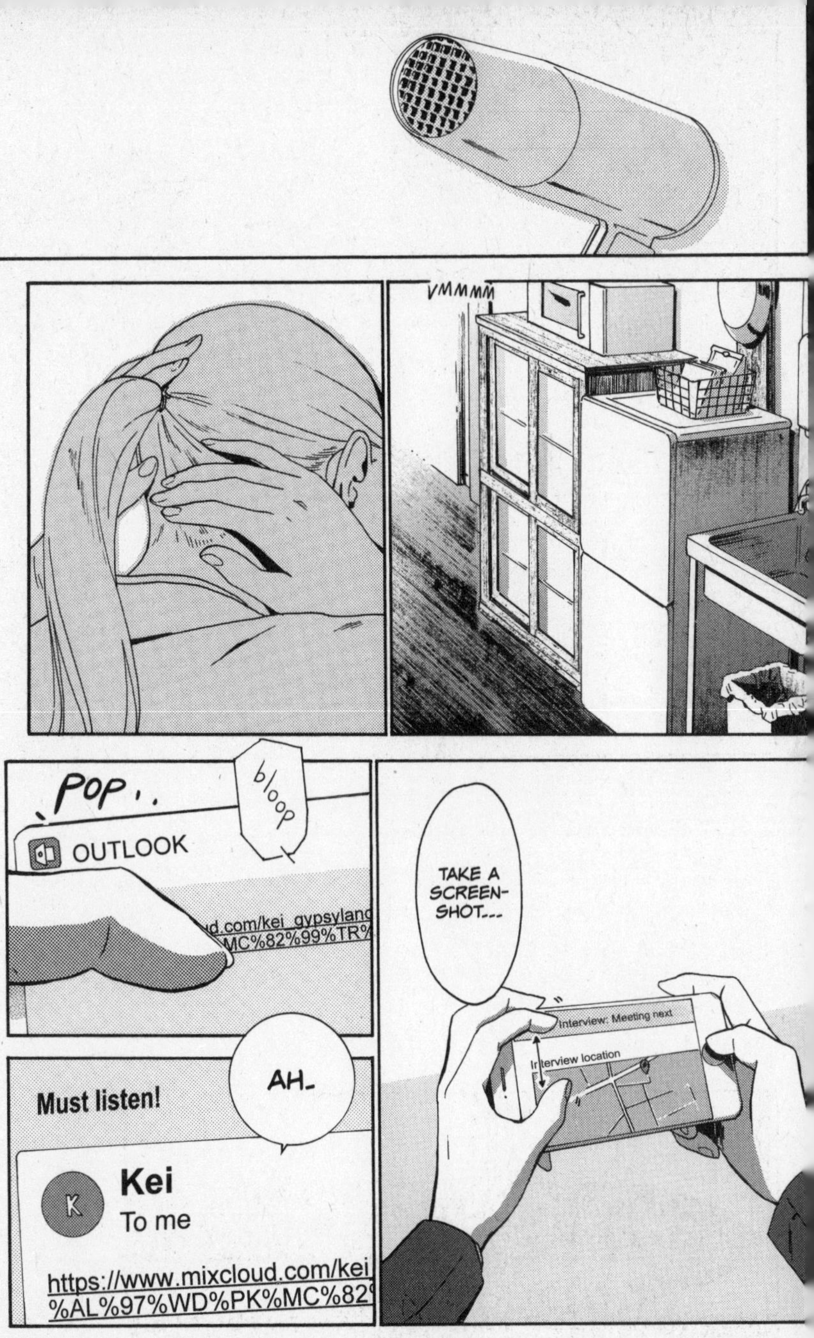
VMMMM
TAKE A SCREEN-SHOT...
Interview: Meeting next
Interview location
POP..
bloop
OUTLOOK
d.com/kei_gypsylan
MC%82%99%TR
AH...
Must listen!
Kei
To me
https://www.mixcloud.com/kei
%AL%97%WD%PK%MC%82

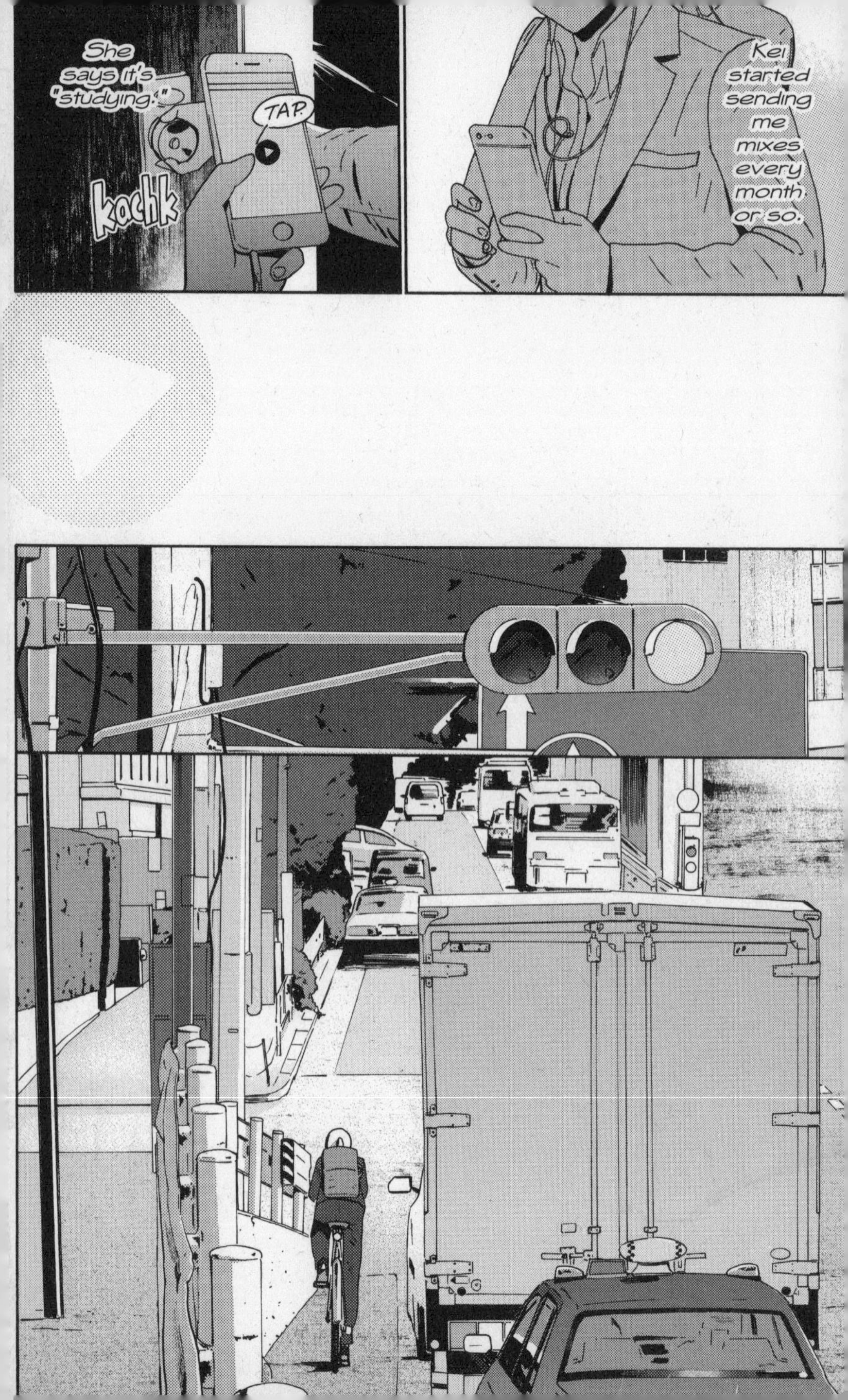
Kei started sending me mixes every month or so.
She says it's "studying."
TAP.
kachk

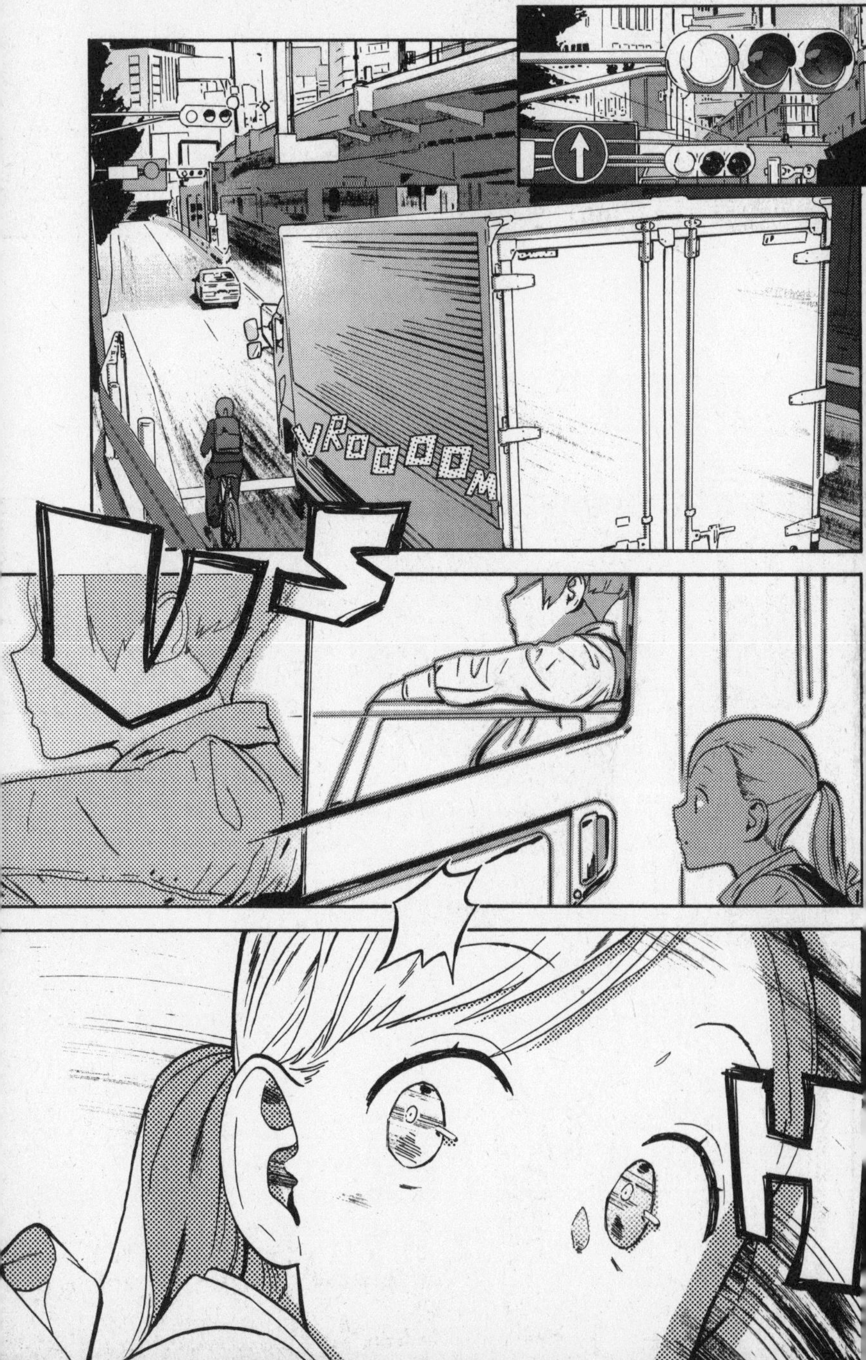
VROOOOM

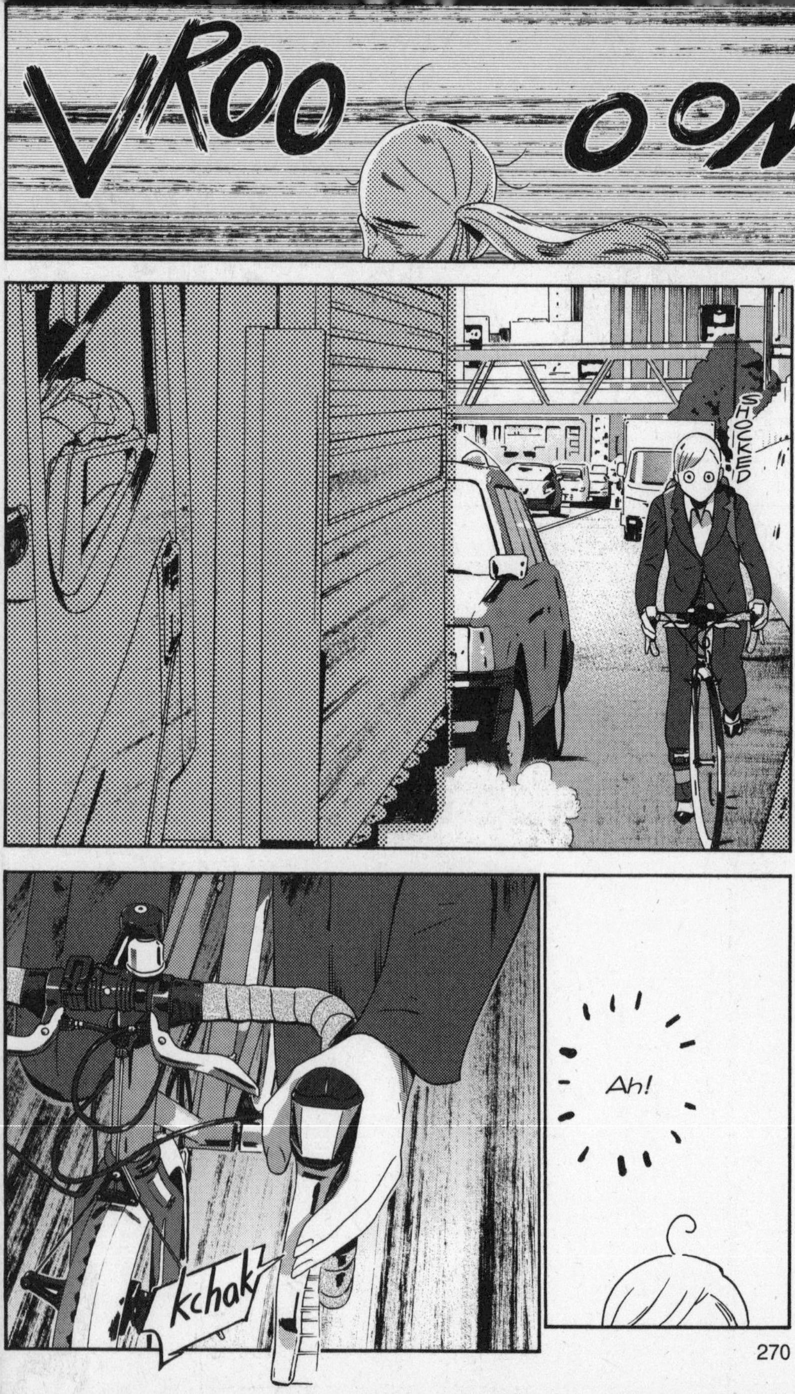
VROO OOM
SHOCKED
Ah!
kchak

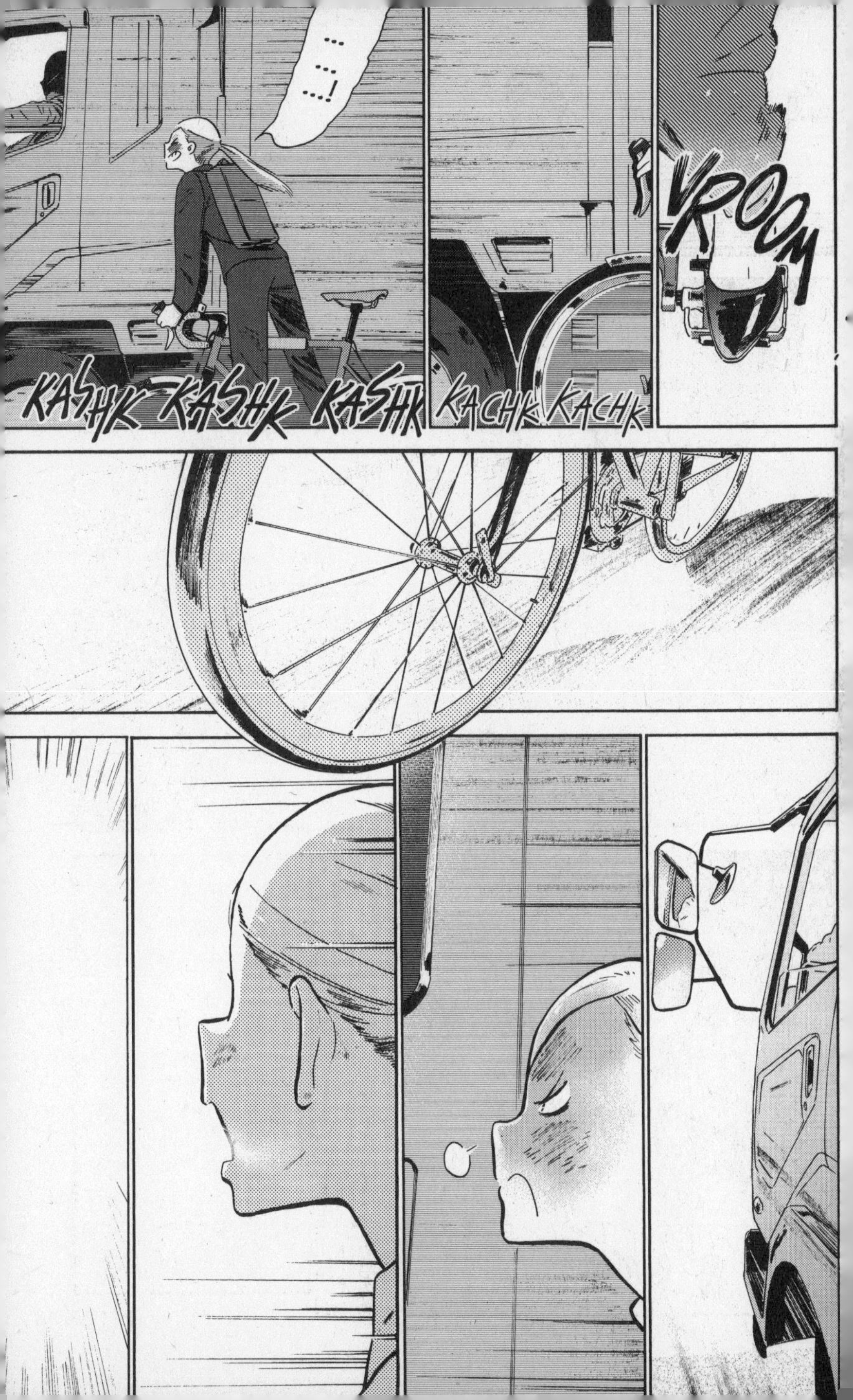
VROOM
KACHK KACHK
...
...
...!
KASHK KASHK KASHK

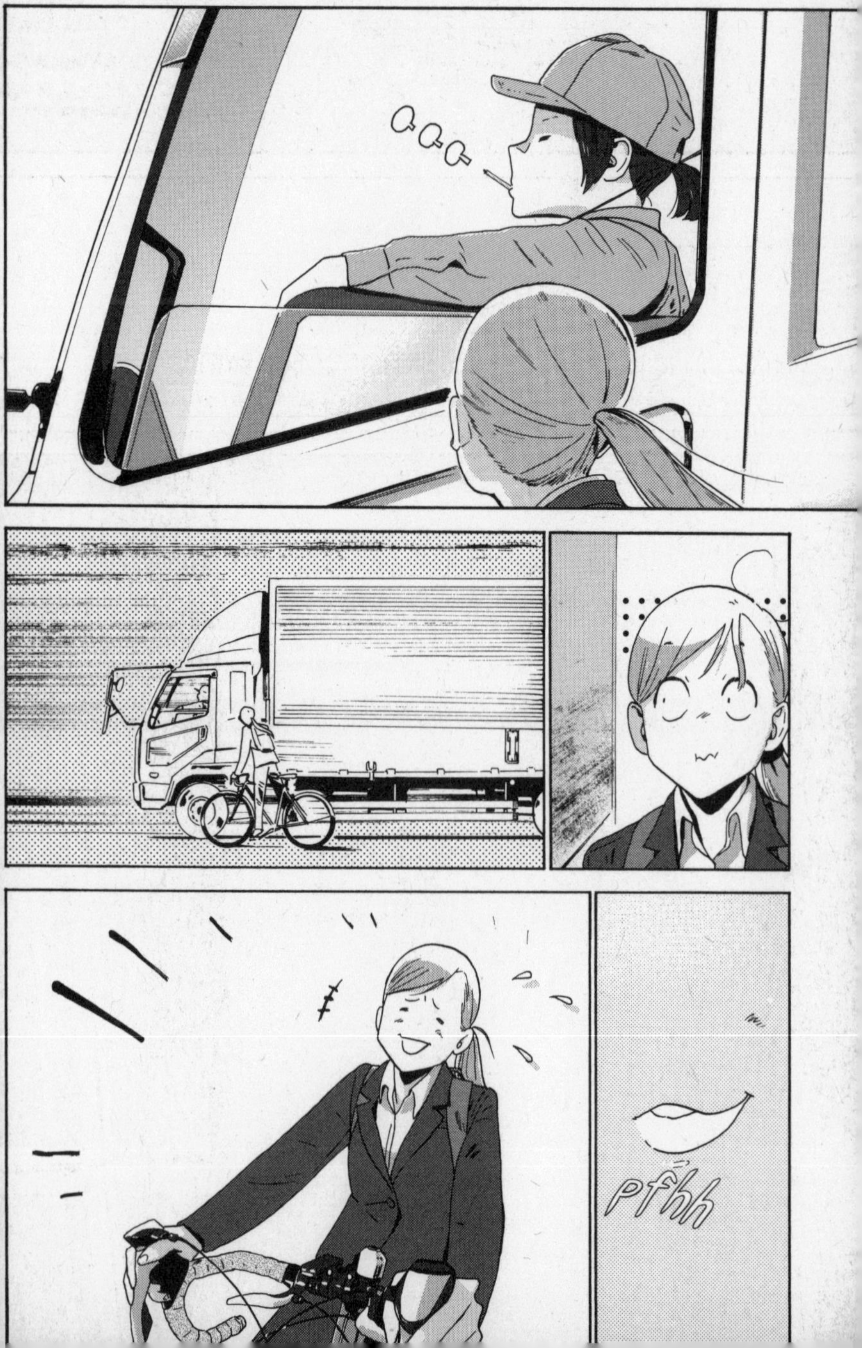
pfhh

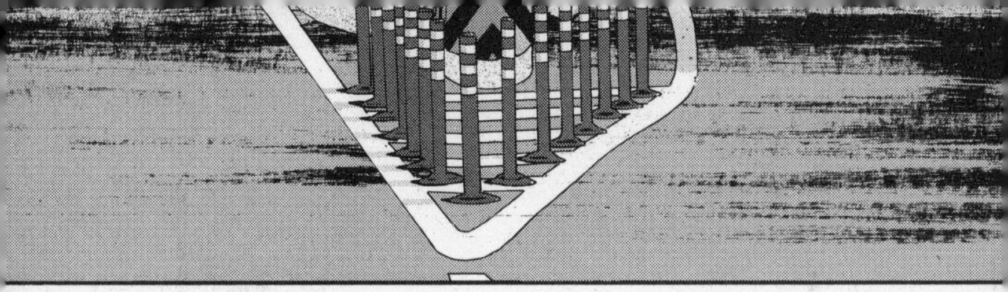
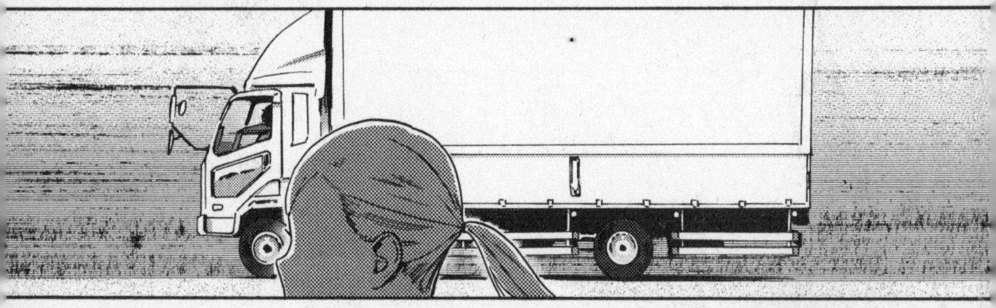
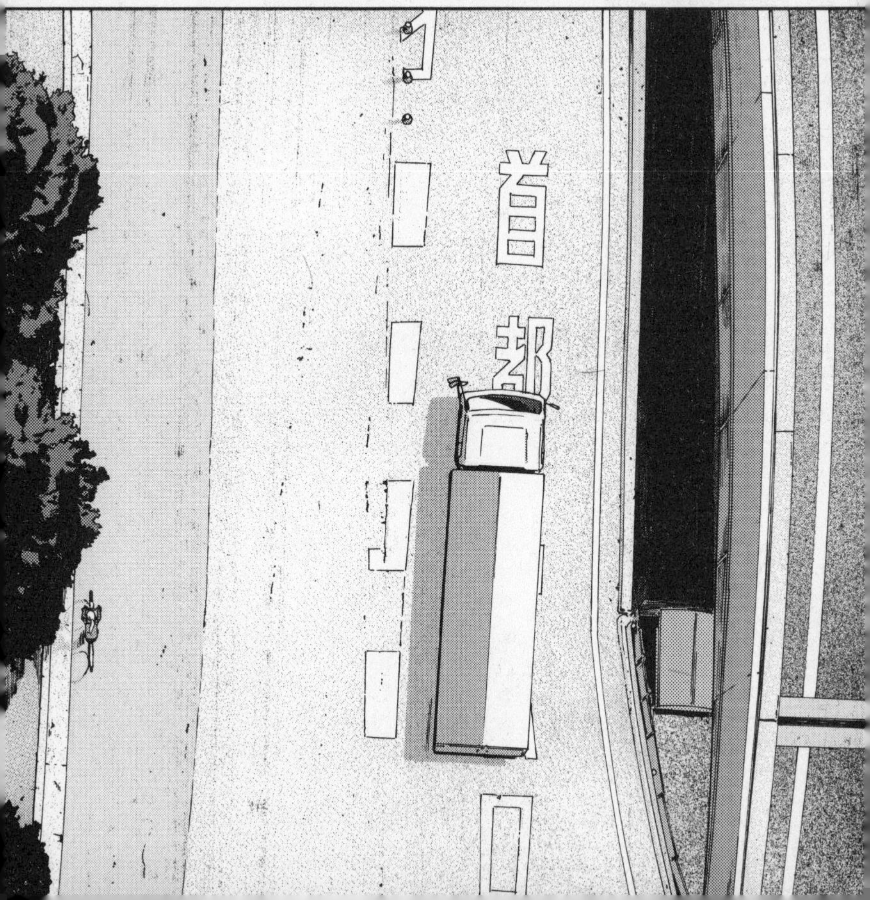

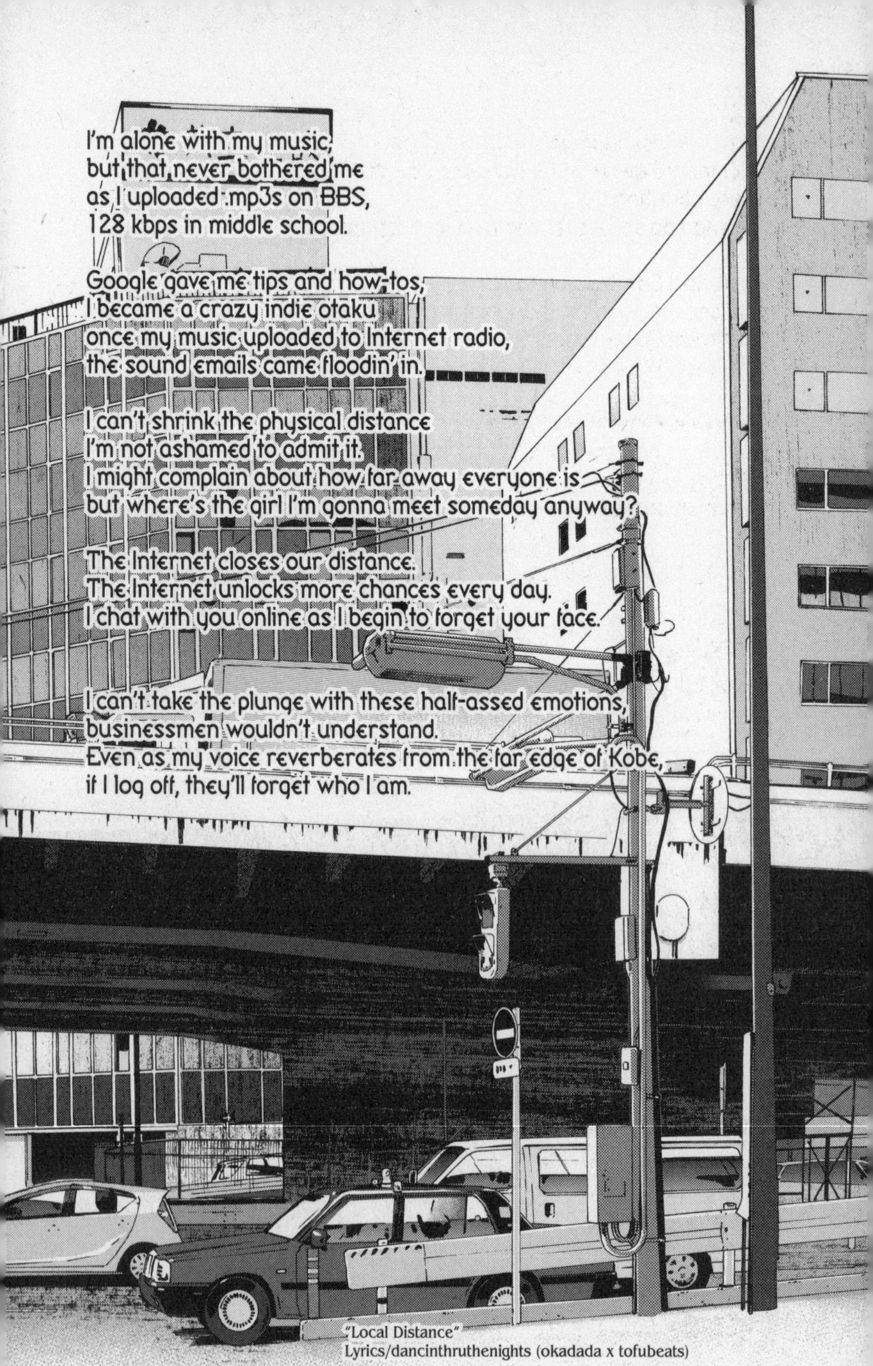
I'm alone with my music,
but that never bothered me
as I uploaded .mp3s on BBS,
128 kbps in middle school.

Google gave me tips and how-tos,
I became a crazy indie otaku
once my music uploaded to Internet radio,
the sound emails came floodin' in.

I can't shrink the physical distance
I'm not ashamed to admit it.
I might complain about how far away everyone is
but where's the girl I'm gonna meet someday anyway?

The Internet closes our distance.
The Internet unlocks more chances every day.
I chat with you online as I begin to forget your face.

I can't take the plunge with these half-assed emotions,
businessmen wouldn't understand.
Even as my voice reverberates from the far edge of Kobe,
if I log off, they'll forget who I am.

"Local Distance"
Lyrics/dancinthruthenights (okadada x tofubeats)

This town isn't big or small,
You moved away, but where are you now?
I keep counting up to 078,
serenading someone who isn't local anymore.

(distance) Can we sing too?
(distance) A timeline that connects all of Japan.
(distance) Can we stand out too?
(distance) We just want the praise.

(distance) We're always online.
(distance) Sometimes we're offline.
(distance) We should meet up and shake hands.
Distance, distance...

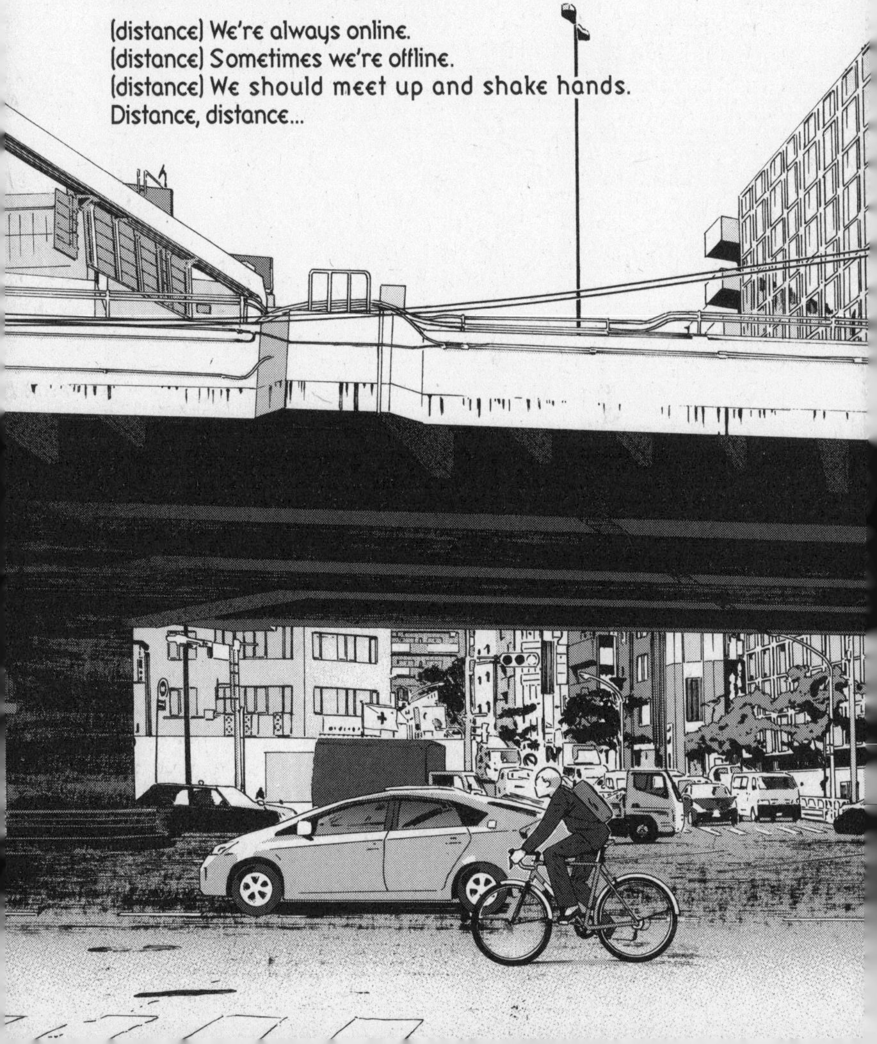

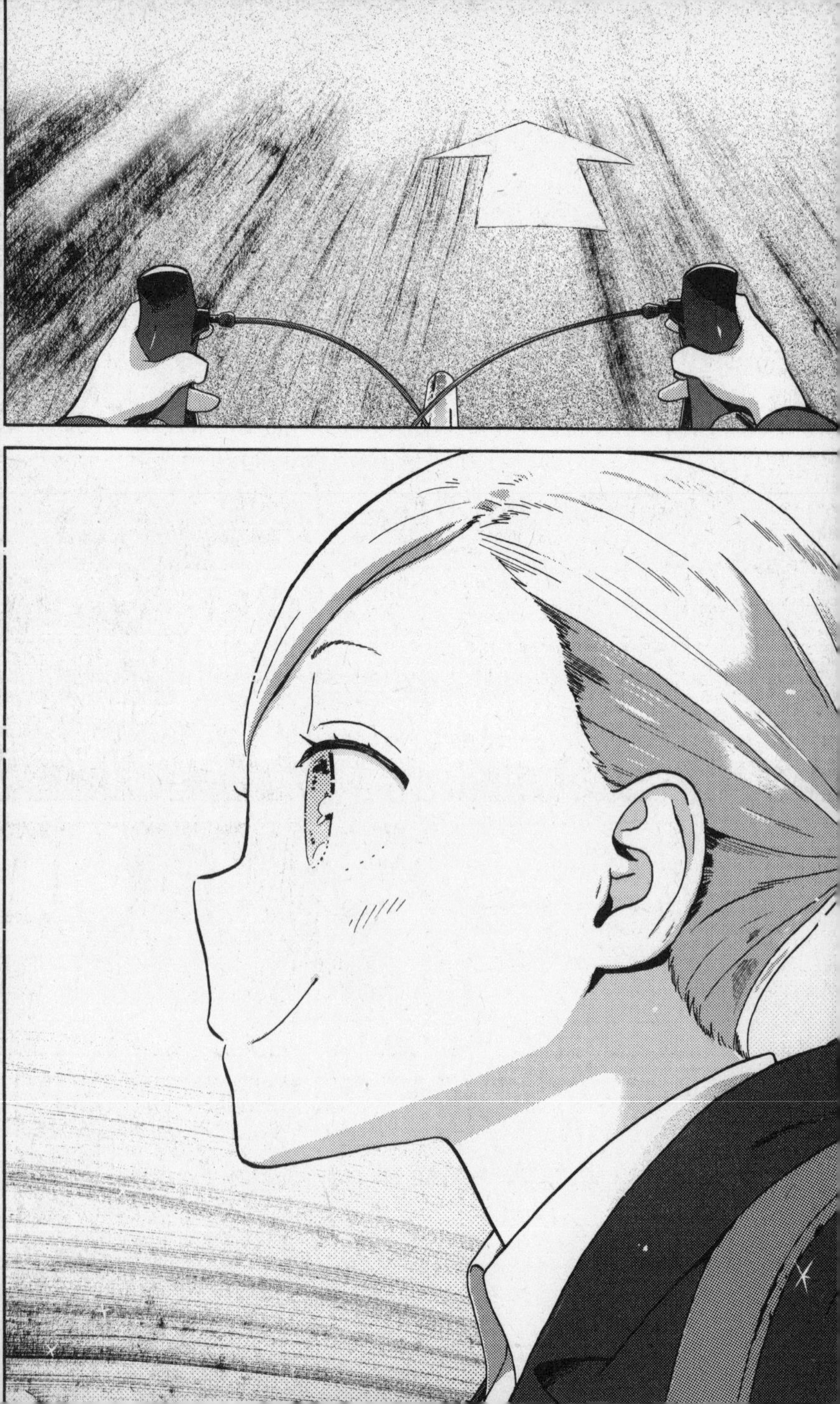

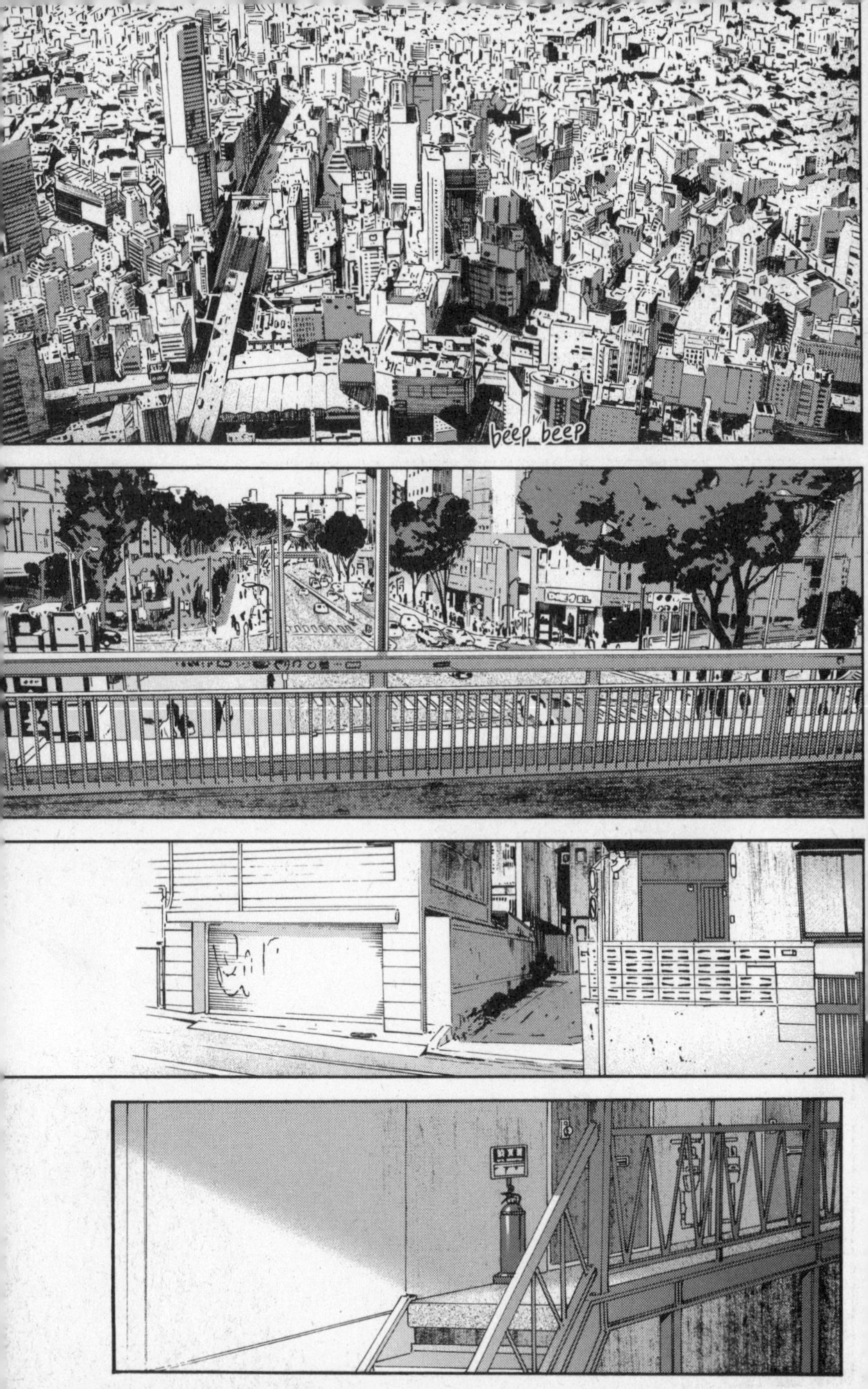
beep beep

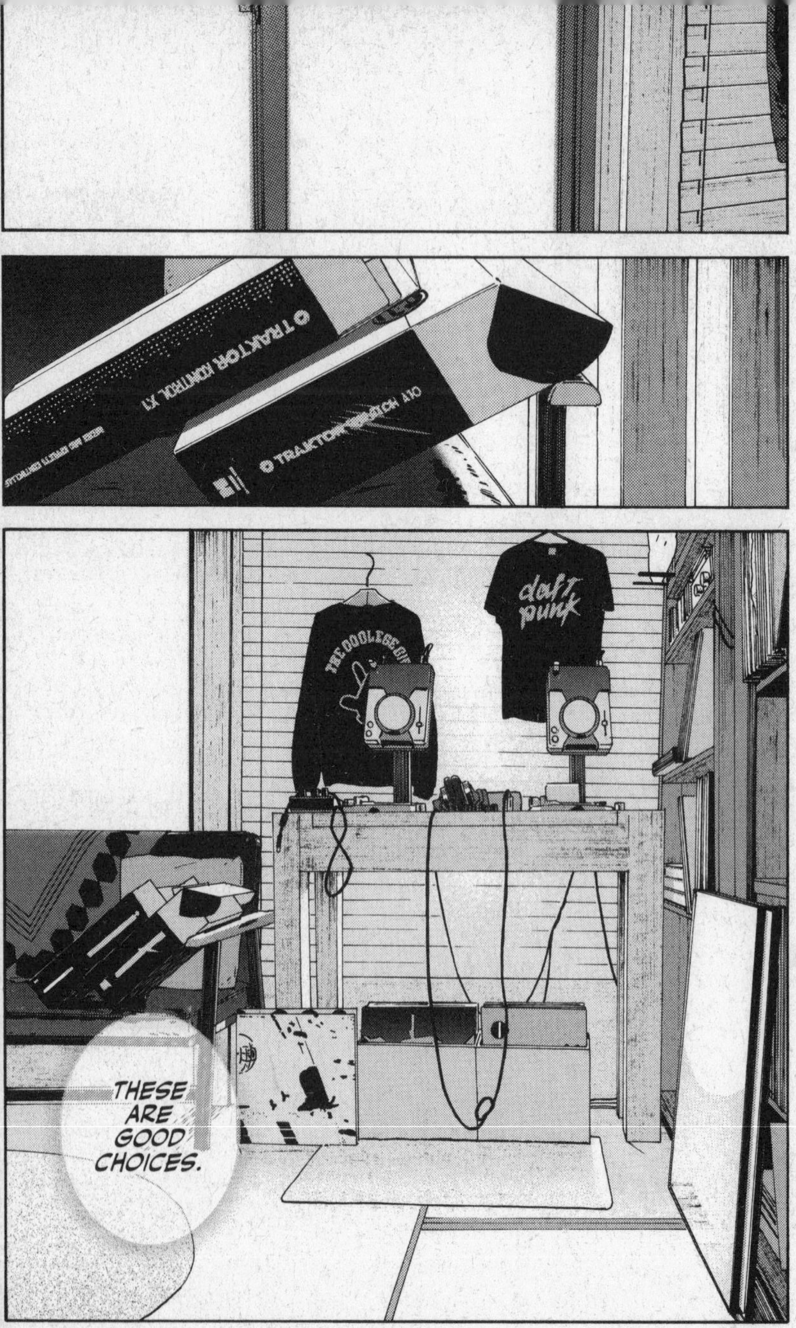
TRAKTOR KONTROL X1
daft punk
THESE ARE GOOD CHOICES.

AFTER · HOURS *end*

AFTER HOURS #1 (reprised)

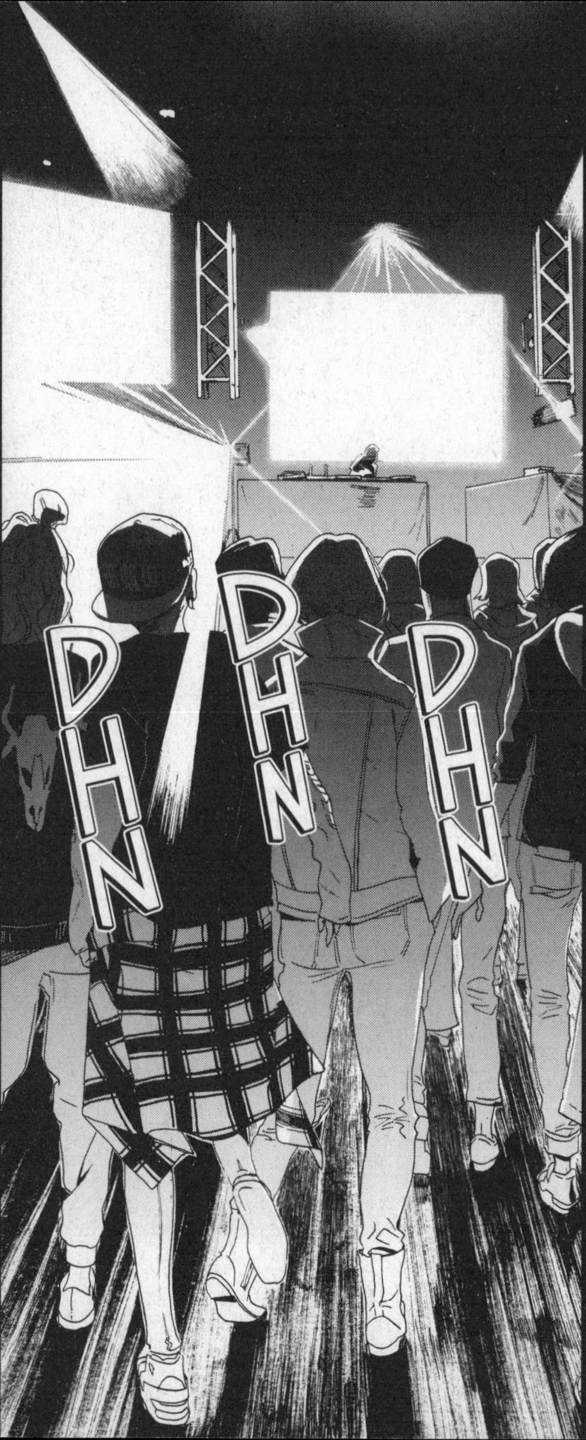
DHN
DHN
DHN

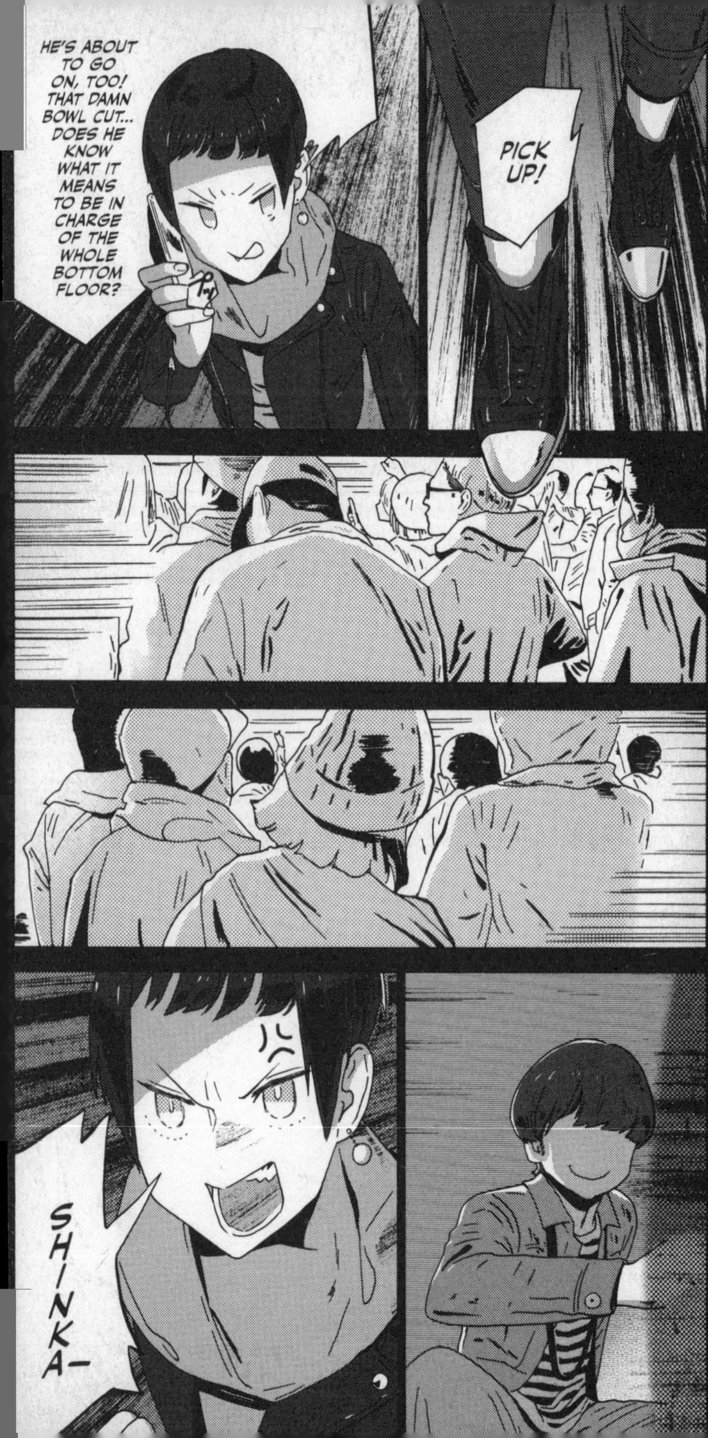
PICK UP!
HE'S ABOUT TO GO ON, TOO! THAT DAMN BOWL CUT... DOES HE KNOW WHAT IT MEANS TO BE IN CHARGE OF THE WHOLE BOTTOM FLOOR?
SHINKA—

incorporated association and their associated nonprofit arts activities organization Command N / I-Regular (ind_fris, madmaid, uchinari empire) / KAI-YOU inc. (Nao Niimi, Tomomi Yonemura) / Yuki Kawamura (Shibuya Oiran) / Souyou Kamdagawa / lapin / mikeneko homeless (mochilon, hironica) / Keita Mori (Diorama Books)

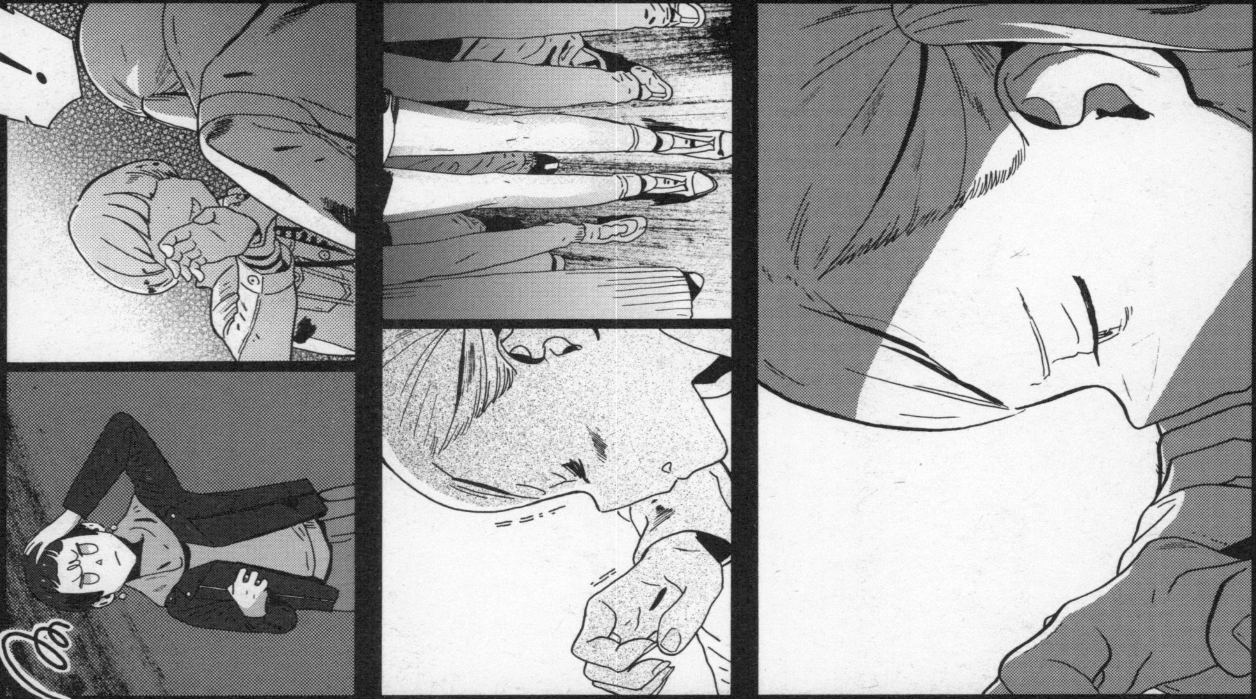
!

Thank You: Wataru Sawabe (Skirt) / Sumitomo Corporation / Sho Suzuki (LOUNGE NEO) / VenessaMichaels / VIZ Media / WISH LESS (Rob Kidney, Yoko Nagai) / Yasuhiro Yagi (Anthem) / Diorama Crew / DOMMUNE manga artists

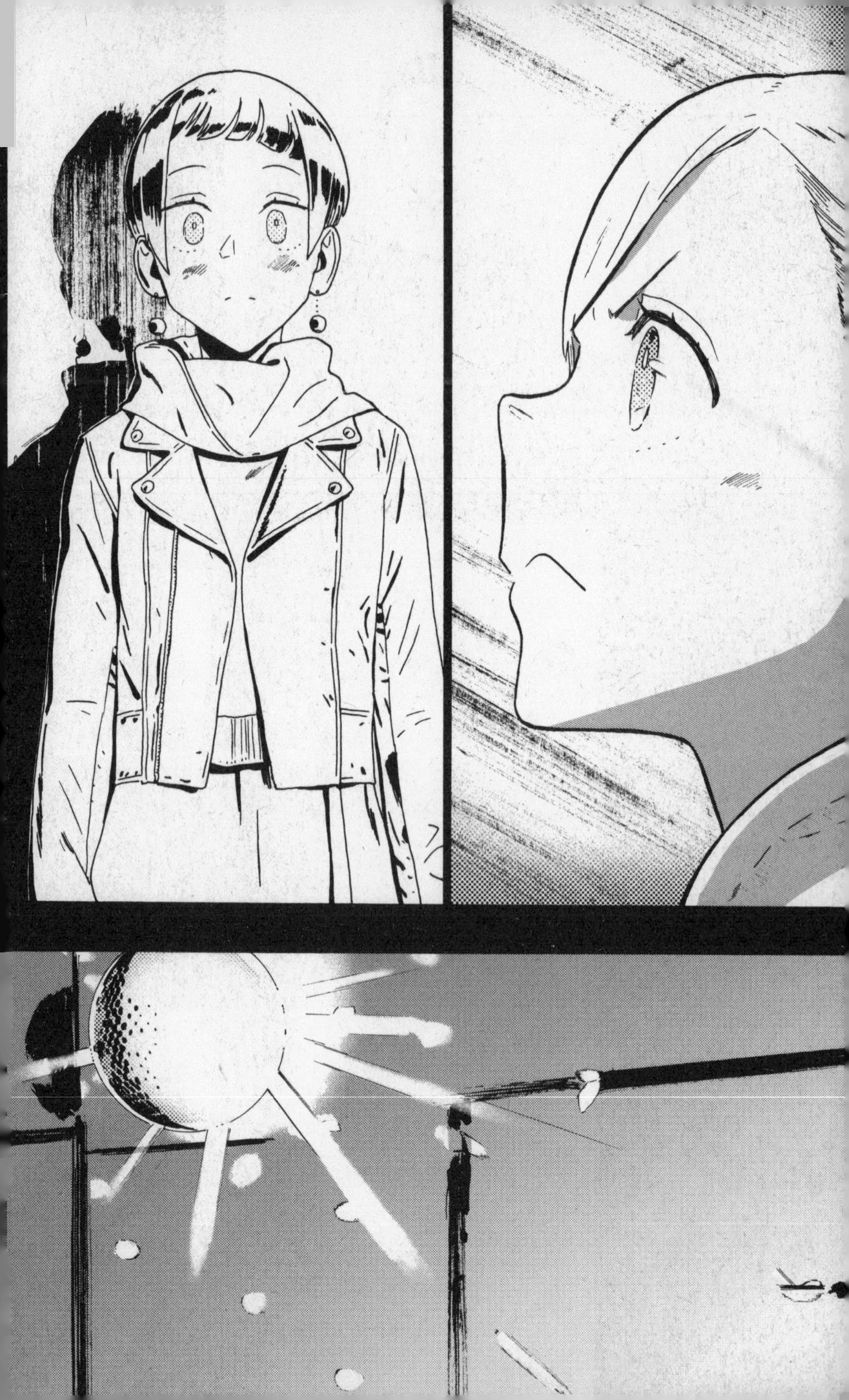

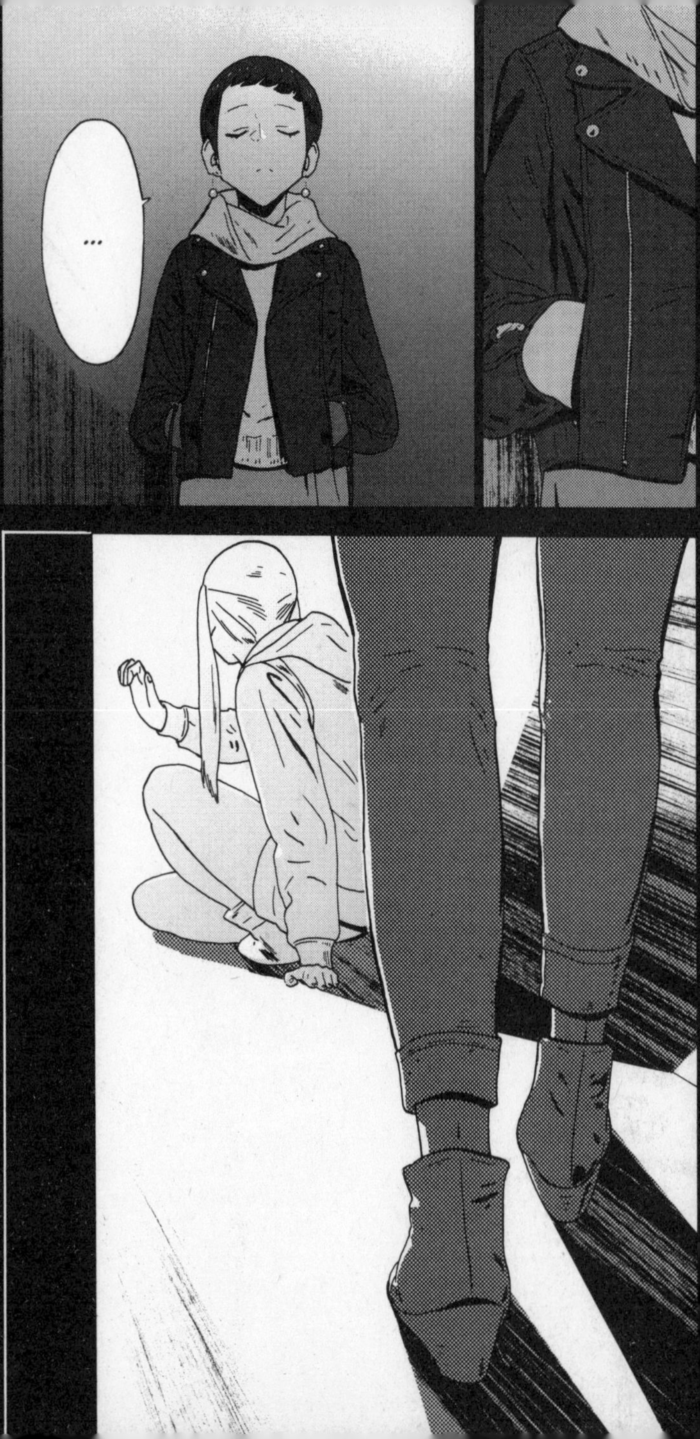
...

And to all those out there at parties: tonight is the night.

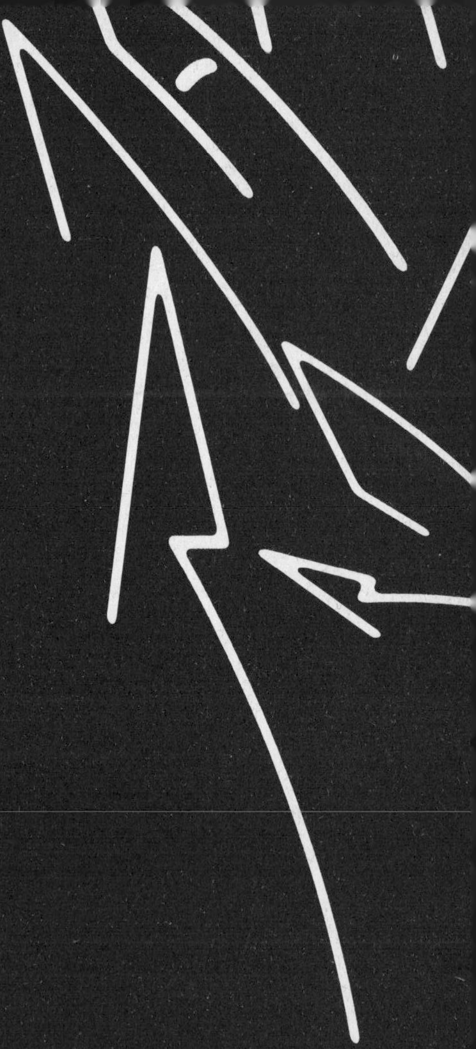

Yuhta Nishio is a manga creator, illustrator and sometime painter. He has also been a bookseller and has joined Takashi Murakami in a group exhibit as an artist. His debut manga, *Irigachi*, started serialization in *IKKI* magazine in 2014.

AFTER HOURS
VOLUME 3 • VIZ Media Edition

STORY AND ART BY YUHTA NISHIO

English Translation + Adaptation **Abby Lehrke**
Touch-Up Art + Lettering **Sabrina Heep**
Design **Shawn Carrico**
Editor **Pancha Diaz**

AFTER HOURS Vol. 3
by Yuhta NISHIO
© 2015 Yuhta NISHIO
All rights reserved.
Original Japanese edition published by SHOGAKUKAN.
English translation rights in the United States of America,
Canada, the United Kingdom, Ireland, Australia and
New Zealand arranged with SHOGAKUKAN.

Original Design **Keita MORI** (Sekine Shinichi Seisaku Shitsu)

The stories, characters and incidents mentioned in this
publication are entirely fictional.

Printed in Canada

Published by VIZ Media, LLC
P.O. Box 77010
San Francisco, CA 94107

10 9 8 7 6 5 4 3 2 1
First printing, December 2018

viz.com

PARENTAL ADVISORY
RATED **T+** FOR OLDER TEEN
AFTER HOURS is rated T+ for Older Teen and
is recommended for ages 16 and up. This
volume contains nudity and sexual situations.
ratings.viz.com

THIS IS THE LAST PAGE. *AFTER HOURS* has been printed in the original Japanese format to preserve the orientation of the original artwork.

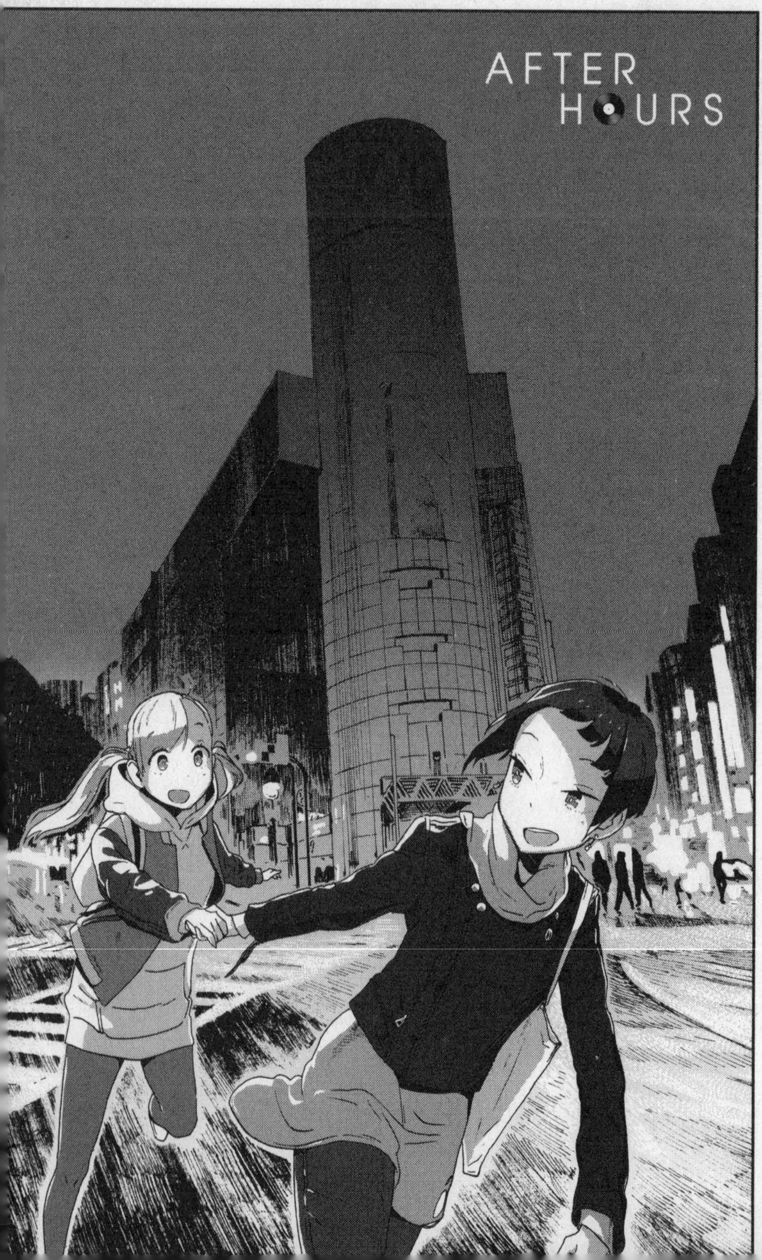
AFTER
HOURS